DAVID & GOLIATH

"If you don't read the newspaper, you are uninformed. If you do read the newspaper, you are misinformed."

–Mark Twain (attributed)

DAVID & GOLIATH

The explosive inside story of media bias
in the Israeli-Palestinian conflict

SHRAGA SIMMONS

Copyright © 2012 by Shraga Simmons

All rights reserved. No part of this book may be used or reproduced in any manner whatsoever without written permission of the author.

Printed in the United States of America.

ISBN: 978-0-9840398-0-7

Published by
Emesphere Productions
www.emesphere.com

To my parents,

for instilling, by example,

the ideals of truth and education.

To Rabbi Noah Weinberg, o.b.m.,

for leading the way forward.

In memory of the Katz and Ausch families

who perished in the Holocaust

May their greatness be an inspiration

to all people of good will.

Evelyn and Dr. Shmuel Katz

Bal Harbour, Florida

CONTENTS

Introduction 1

1. The Photo That Started It All 11
2. David & Goliath 33
3. One Man's Terrorist 73
4. "Massacre" in Jenin 107
5. The CNN Shift 131
6. Intimidation? What Intimidation?! 151
7. Fauxtography: Lebanon and Beyond 195
8. Driving the Wedge 231
9. Gaza War & "Excessive Force" 269
10. The Right to Security 305
11. The Right to Exist 355

Epilogue: The Peace Process 419

Photos 433

Acknowledgments 457

Disclaimers 461

Index 463

INTRODUCTION

Imagine an alien landing on Planet Earth.¹ Curious to find out what preoccupies the human race, he flicks on the news. Three million dead or displaced in Darfur? The Mexican drug war? Rampant Third World hunger? Barely a mention. From the pages of the *New York Times* to the airwaves of CNN, one country – Israel – is the hot topic of the day, generating more news coverage than anywhere else in the world.²

Our intergalactic visitor would wonder: What is this country all about? He opens *Time* magazine to see Israel's government described as "reminiscent of the dark ages of different places in the world in the 1930s."³ He reads *Toronto Sun* columnist Eric Margolis' depiction of Israel's "final solution campaign" against Palestinians⁴ and, on CBS's *The Early Show*, is told that Israel's prime minister is "a racist, a terrorist, a murderous war criminal."⁵

When it comes to the Middle East peace process, our visitor would hear on CNN how Israel "still occupies" the Gaza Strip,⁶ only to discover that Israel had completely withdrawn from Gaza six years earlier. At the newsstand he sees the *Time* magazine cover story, "Why Israel Doesn't Care About Peace,"⁷ and reads in *Harper's Magazine* how Israel practices "ethnic cleansing."⁸

With Israel as the focus of such widespread coverage, our space voyageur would imagine this to be a massive goliath nation whose imperialistic tentacles reach across vast continents. Yet he'd be surprised to learn that Israel is but a dot on the map – a mere nine miles wide at its narrowest point, with less strategic depth than the island of Manhattan.

The alien visitor would wonder: What kind of bizarre planet has he landed on? Why the media obsession with this tiny nation?

We, too, must wonder: How did it happen that Israel – once the object of international admiration, respect and even awe – is now the target of mass protests, boycotts and U.N. condemnations? Why is Israel – alone among the nations – demonized as the intransigent party, the trampler of human rights, the international pariah?

How did it happen that Israel's Arab neighbors – widely corrupt,[9] oppressive,[10] misogynistic[11] and homophobic[12] – have become the darlings of the Western media? Why do American newspapers extol the Hamas terror organization as "well-educated technocrats"[13] founded on a "pillar" of charity?[14] Why does *Vogue* magazine describe Bashar Assad's Syrian dictatorship as exemplifying "tolerance," "wildly democratic principles" and a "spirit of openness"?[15] Why is Agence France-Presse – the world's third-largest news agency – fawning over Iran's Mahmoud Ahmadinejad "as a simple peace-loving man"?[16]

How did Israel – a beacon of Western-style freedom and democracy – become vilified to the extent that public opinion polls conclude that the singular nation threatening world peace is not North Korea, Iran, Syria or Sudan, but rather Israel?[17]

What are the dynamics that have created these myths? What does it tell us about Israel's significance? And what does it tell us about us?

This book intends to answer these vexing questions.

By examining events of the past decade – beginning with the outbreak of the Intifada in September 2000 and continuing through to the current peace process – this book will expose the techniques used by the media to create negative perceptions of Israel. No, this book does not propose the existence of some vast anti-Israel media conspiracy. But it does document a pervasive bias against Israel, and a spurious "David and Goliath narrative" used by the Western media to keep its readers curious and connected to a conflict taking place halfway around the world.

This book will explore how Israel's alleged "massacre" in Jenin 2002 – later exposed as a sham – nonetheless laid the foundation for more evil accusations: Israel wantonly employing excessive force (Lebanon 2006); Israel intentionally targeting Palestinian civilians (Goldstone Report 2009); Israel stealing Palestinian body parts; and Israel conducting a murderous rampage aboard the Gaza flotilla in 2010.

Though these claims, too, were proven false, the perception of Israel as some kind of "cosmic demonic force" has been drilled into the public consciousness. Toronto's *Globe and Mail* labeled the Israeli government as "ethnic cleansers" and "Taliban-like religious fundamentalists,"[18] while a headline in Xinhua, the gigantic Chinese news agency, declared that "Israel Carries Out Genocide and Humanitarian Catastrophe."[19]

These media assaults are not merely an academic matter of fairness and accuracy. Israel is a small country, surrounded by enemies, the only country in the world threatened with extinction. For Israel, many of the questions spun by the media are ultimately matters of life and death: whether to call suicide bombers "terrorists" or the more mild "militants," whether Israel's response to Hamas rocket-fire is "self defense" or "military aggression," and to what extent Iran's nuclear ambitions are targeting Israel. The media plays an enormous role in shaping public perceptions, which affects Israeli security policy, and which – for me, living in Israel – impacts the safety of my own family.

The issues are complex, born out of an Arab-Israeli conflict that has been raging for nearly a century. In the wake of World War I – as new Arab states were being created in Jordan, Lebanon, Egypt and Iraq – Britain's Lord Balfour promised the Jews a fulfillment of their millennia-old yearning for a return to the Land of Israel. Arab neighbors violently opposed the idea, thus setting into motion a conflict that has, for decades, been waged on the battlefield with guns and tanks.

Today, however, with the advent of satellite phones, Internet, and a

24-hour news cycle, the prime focus has shifted to the court of world opinion. Diana Buttu, former legal advisor to the PLO and now contributor to Fox News, CNN and MSNBC, remarked that the Israeli-Palestinian conflict is "a battle over language sometimes more than over anything else."[20]

Journalism as Public Service

My interest in this topic goes back as far as I can remember. At age 16, as a high school student in suburban Buffalo, New York, I began working as a sports reporter for the *Tonawanda News*, a local daily newspaper. It started as a fun part-time job, but I soon realized that journalism would become a career. And in thinking about what kind of journalist I wanted to be, my sights kept setting on CBS News anchorman Walter Cronkite, the narrator of my vivid childhood memories: Kent State, the Apollo missions, Watergate. Cronkite was fair and balanced, with the unique ability to channel information without allowing ego and prejudice to enter the equation. Cronkite told it like "it is" – persuasively, but free of agenda. He didn't talk down to people, nor over their heads in a way that left them more confused than before. He was a real weapon of mass education.

Cronkite had learned his craft at the University of Texas at Austin, working for the *Daily Texan* – so I decided to pursue that same path.[21] In Austin, I was schooled in the fundamentals of good journalism: objectivity, integrity, and pursuit of truth with no predisposition. Just as doctors and firefighters perform a public service, my professors taught, the same is true with journalists. And bad journalism is a disservice.

The *Daily Texan* was no ad-hoc college paper. We had our own printing press, a circulation larger than most American dailies, and an alumni list studded with Pulitzer Prize winners. I relished working alongside fellow students like John Schwartz, now the national legal correspondent for the *New York Times*, and Lisa Beyer, later to become a managing editor at *Time* magazine. We were buoyed by youthful idealism and a firm belief in the power and veracity of journalism as a force for positive change.

Along the way, something happened to shake that confidence.

Freedom of the press, while a constitutional right, comes with

INTRODUCTION 5

concurrent obligations – in the words of Edward R. Murrow, to report the news "without fear or favor." But more and more, I saw that principle giving way to "advocacy journalism," where parochial positions are hidden behind a veneer of objectivity. Readers were being fed totally different spins on the same piece of news – whether in the realm of politics, ethics or the economy. Consider, as one example, these contradictory headlines published on the same day:

"Abortion Pill Sales Rising" – *Washington Post*[22]

"Abortion Pill Slow to Win Users"– *New York Times*[23]

In the ensuing years, I watched in despair as the legend of Cronkite – "the most trusted man in America" – gave way to Dan Rather (alas, another Texan), whose ego loomed larger than the news itself. Rather would flounce off the set in anger after being preempted by a tennis match,[24] then fret endlessly about whether or not to wear a trench coat (and whether to put the collar up or down).[25] As for journalistic standards, Rather described his philosophy as: "You can be an honest person and lie about any number of things."[26] Hence the pun, "rather biased."

As the 2004 U.S. presidential race heated up, Rather appeared on national TV with "authentic" memos – ostensibly written in 1973 – regarding George W. Bush's service in the Texas Air National Guard.[27] The scandal broke when the weblog *Little Green Footballs* typed out Rather's memo on Microsoft Word. By using all the default settings – font, type size, letter spacing, margins, tab stops, even the automatic word hyphenation – the result was 100 percent identical to the document that Rather claimed was produced in the days when typewriters were the norm and Microsoft was not yet a twinkle in Bill Gates' eye.[28]

Rather had been caught red-handed fabricating the news. So his defenders tried a more creative explanation: The memos were forged, but substantively true – in the nouveau realm of "fake but accurate."[29]

This supercilious approach has led some media executives to go so far as to deify their own cause. Jill Abramson, who became the *New York Times'* top editor in 2011, describes: "In my house growing up, the *Times* substituted for religion. If the *Times* said it, it was the absolute truth."[30] Hendrik Hertzberg, senior editor at *The New Yorker,* joined the chorus in saying that "the nonexistence of the *New York Times*" is "as horrifying" a prospect as the "nonexistence of the United States of America. Maybe more so..."[31]

How can the media possibly be objective if it places a newspaper above the importance of the United States and God Almighty Himself?

Unfortunately, matters keep getting worse, and public confidence in the media is now at its lowest in decades. Polls reveal that just 29 percent of Americans believe that reporters get the facts straight.[32] A British survey measuring the trustworthiness of various professions found that journalists ranked dead last.[33] Respect for journalists is so low that one reporter remarked: "When I am asked in social situations what my job is, I am sometimes tempted to pretend I am part of a more respected profession – like drug trafficking."[34]

If this was the state of journalism, I knew we were in big trouble. Or as Dan Rather himself might say: Things were shoddier than a tornado in a trailer park.[35]

About this Book

David & Goliath is designed as a historical retrospective of the years 2000-2011. The chapters, organized in a loose chronology according to the main diplomatic and military events, provide a launching pad for a broader discussion of the key issues affecting the conflict – borders, security, refugees, Jerusalem – and of the media's role in shaping this dramatic story.

This book is not a dry recounting of "myths and facts." It is a first-person account from the trenches of the media battlefield, based on my 11 years of monitoring, researching and exposing media bias. It reveals my perceptions of how information and events have been distorted by journalists who cannot – or choose not to – distinguish the objective truth from rhetorical posturing.

In recounting my private conversations with journalists, I have intentionally omitted many of the names. These conversations were usually "on background," either by specific request or with a presumption of anonymity. I am grateful to those reporters who shared their time and thoughts with me, often in a cooperative spirit of improving media coverage of the conflict.

My mentor, the late Rabbi Noah Weinberg, closely guided me in this work. Besides being an outstanding defender of Israel, Rabbi Weinberg dedicated his life to the pursuit of truth. He knew that given the human propensity to act out of subjective desire, the only way to remain grounded in reality is to be passionately devoted to *objectivity*. Rabbi Weinberg saw media monitoring as a way to educate people in the methods of objective analysis and critical thinking. This, he believed, would provide important tools to discern the truth – regarding the Israeli-Palestinian conflict in particular, and ethical issues in general.

This book focuses solely on the foreign media's reporting of the conflict. The Israeli media has its own unique set of dynamics. Given that Israeli journalists are voting citizens, personal politics invariably color their view of the conflict. This is a different field of research that could fill a book of its own, but it is not my focus.

As this book goes to print, we find ourselves at a critical juncture. The Arab Spring of 2011 has forced dictatorial Muslim regimes to confront mass uprisings for progress and reform. Iran is moving full steam ahead with its plans to build the Bomb. The Israeli-Palestinian peace process has stalled with its future in doubt. In the meantime, the Western media – the all-knowing and all-powerful modern Wizard of Oz – is busy 24/7, competing for consumer attention on everything from the popularity of Justin Bieber to the future of a Palestinian state.[36]

My hope is that *David & Goliath* will raise awareness on the topic of media bias, activate discussion, and encourage more careful consumption of the news. In this way, the Israeli-Arab conflict is bound to be the beneficiary of more honest reporting. For as the conflict moves to its next dramatic stage, the proper use of language becomes ever-more crucial to the possibility of a just and lasting solution.

Notes

1. See Alan M. Dershowitz, "Treatment of Israel Strikes an Alien Note," *National Post* (Canada), November 4, 2002.
2. NewsMap illustrates the "over-reporting of Israel" phenomenon by showing the content of the GoogleNews aggregator in graphic format; Israel consistently occupies a large block in the "World News" section. (www.newsmap.jp).
3. Karl Vick, "Israel's Rightward Lurch Scares Some Conservatives," *Time*, January 11, 2011.
4. Eric Margolis, "Eradicating Hamas," Ericmargolis.com, January 12, 2009.
5. Bryant Gumbel, "Former Middle East Envoy Dennis Ross Talks," *The Early Show*, CBS, February 7, 2001.
6. "Deadly Clashes at Syrian Border on Mideast War Anniversary," CNN.com, June 6, 2011.
7. Karl Vick, "Why Israel Doesn't Care About Peace," *Time*, September 2, 2010.
8. Stephen R. Shalom, "The Palestinian Question," *Harper's Magazine*, January 2001.
9. Fabio Forgione, "The Chaos of the Corruption: Challenges for the Improvement of the Palestinian Society," Palestinian Human Rights Monitoring Group, October 2004.
10. Khaled Abu Toameh, "PA Bans Journalists from Reporting Human Rights Abuses," *Jerusalem Post*, June 8, 2011.
11. "A Question of Security: Violence against Palestinian Women and Girls," Human Rights Watch, November 6, 2006.
12. "'Death Threat' to Palestinian Gays," BBC News Online, March 6, 2003.
13. Susan Taylor Martin, "Hamas is Building Strength in Gaza by Helping to Build an Economy," *St. Petersburg Times*, November 14, 2010; cited in Simon Plosker, "Apologist for Hamas: See No Evil, Hear No Evil," HonestReporting.com, November 15, 2010. Taylor Martin also quoted Hamas cabinet minister Ziad Shokry El Zaza: "Our hands are white and clean."
14. Ian Fisher, "Defining Hamas: Roots in Charity and Branches of Violence," *New York Times*, June 16, 2003.
15. Joan Juliet Buck, "Asma al-Assad: A Rose in the Desert," *Vogue*, March 2011.
16. "Iran's Ahmadinejad Defiant... Over His Culinary Skills," Agence France Presse, August 28, 2007.
17. Robin Shepherd, "In Europe, an Unhealthy Fixation on Israel," *Washington Post*, January 30, 2005.
18. Gerald Caplan, "With Friends Like This, Israel Needs No Enemies," *Globe and Mail* (Canada), September 30, 2011.
19. "Israel Carries Out Genocide and Humanitarian Catastrophe," Xinhua News Agency (China), May 18, 2004. See also the description of Gaza as a "slow genocide": "Maguire: Gaza Situation a 'Slow Genocide,'" *Breaking News* (Ireland), July 6, 2010.
20. Nicole Gaouette, "The Mideast Wars Over Words," *Christian Science Monitor*, June 18, 2003.
21. As a bonus, the Southwest climate offered relief from years of trekking through the snow in Buffalo.
22. Marc Kaufman, "Abortion Pill Sales Rising, Firm Says," *Washington Post*, September 25, 2002.
23. Gina Kolata, "Abortion Pill Slow to Win Users Among Women and Their Doctors," *New York Times*, September 25, 2002.
24. Peter J. Boyer, "Rather Walked Off Set of CBS News," *New York Times*, September 13, 1987.
25. Harry Shearer, Mydamnchannel.com, October 2, 2007. Rather is quoted as saying that television is "an egomaniac business, filled with prima donnas – including this one." (Famoustexans.com)
26. "Personal Stories: Dan Rather," *The O'Reilly Factor*, Fox News Network, May 15, 2001.
27. Jarrett Murphy, "CBS Stands by Bush-Guard Memos," CBS News, September 10, 2004.
28. "Bush Guard Documents: Forged," *Little Green Footballs*, September 9, 2004. After Rather was forced to resign, Walter Cronkite observed: "It surprised quite a few people at CBS and

elsewhere that, without being able to pull up the ratings beyond third in a three-man field, that they tolerated his being there for so long." (*Wolf Blitzer Reports,* CNN, March 7, 2005.)

29. Maureen Balleza and Kate Zernike, "Memos on Bush Are Fake But Accurate, Typist Says," *New York Times*, September 15, 2004.
30. Jeremy W. Peters, "Abramson to Replace Keller as The Times's Executive Editor," *New York Times*, June 2, 2011. After an outcry, the *Times* removed the quote from its website the next day. So much for "absolute truths."
31. Hendrik Hertzberg, "From Ochs and Abe to Bill and Jill," *The New Yorker,* June 3, 2011.
32. "Press Accuracy Rating Hits Two Decade Low," Pew Research Center for the People & the Press, September 13, 2009. A 2008 study by Pew Research Center found that a majority of Americans believe journalists are inaccurate (55%), biased (55%), one-sided (66%), and try to cover up their mistakes (63%). (Robert Ruby, "The State of the News Media 2008: Public Attitudes," Project for Excellence in Journalism, 2008.)
33. Jeff Jacoby, "Musings, Random and Otherwise," *Boston Globe*, July 15, 2007.
34. Chas Newkey Burden, "Not in My Name," *Ynetnews* (Israel), April 19, 2007.
35. "Dan Rather," Famoustexans.com.
36. See Clyde Haberman, "What They Don't Teach at J-School," *New York Times*, August 27, 2002.

—1—

THE PHOTO THAT STARTED IT ALL

For Tuvia Grossman, a 20-year-old Chicago native studying in Jerusalem, September 29, 2000, began like any other day. He had no idea that Sheikh Hian al-Adrisi had spent the morning preaching on Jerusalem's Temple Mount: "The Muslims are ready to sacrifice their lives and blood to protect Islamic Jerusalem and al-Aqsa!"[1]

Nor did Tuvia know that the official Voice of Palestine radio was instructing "all Palestinians to come and defend the al-Aqsa mosque." Or that the Palestinian Authority had closed schools and bused students to the Temple Mount, to join the thousands of Arabs throwing rocks at Jewish worshippers and Israeli police.[2] Or that within hours – with riots erupting throughout Israel, the West Bank and Gaza Strip – the so-called "al-Aqsa Intifada" had begun.

No, for Tuvia Grossman, it was simply the eve of Rosh Hashana, the Jewish New Year, and an opportune time to visit the Western Wall. So he gathered a few friends and hopped into a taxi. En route through the Arab neighborhood of Wadi Joz, their taxi was suddenly surrounded by a throng of Palestinians hurling rocks. They smashed the windows and pulled Tuvia out – beating, kicking, stabbing and bashing rocks on his head.

Tuvia lost a liter of blood and pronounced the words of *Shema Yisrael*, the declaration of faith a Jew utters before death. Then, on this eve of Rosh Hashana, the image of a ram's horn (shofar) suddenly flashed through his mind. In that panicked stream-of-consciousness moment, he recalled the biblical story of the prophet Gideon whose brigade of 300 men – heavily outnumbered by the Midianite army of 130,000 – blew shofars in the hope that the noise would scare the enemy. Incredibly, the ploy worked and Gideon won the battle.[3]

Now in his own moment of desperation, Tuvia Grossman yelled at the top of his lungs. His assailants were momentarily startled, and Tuvia, at the cusp of consciousness, managed to break away, run up a hill, and reach a gas station where Israeli soldiers were posted. As he collapsed on the ground with blood pouring down his face, a baton-wielding Israeli policeman (providentially, also named Gideon)[4] fended off the ferocious Palestinian mob.

At that moment, a group of photojournalists snapped pictures of the angry Israeli policeman hovering over the bloody young man.

One photographer – working for the Zoom 77 agency – rushed his photos to the Jerusalem bureau of Associated Press. Within minutes AP had transmitted that dramatic image to its 15,000 subscribing publications around the world – to be published hours later in the *New York Times*, *Boston Globe* (splashed in full color across four columns on the front page), and in scores of other papers from Los Angeles to Baltimore, Paris to Melbourne.

The photo carried this caption:

An Israeli policeman and a Palestinian on the Temple Mount.

The implication was clear: A vicious Israeli policeman had just beaten a defenseless young Arab. In reality, however, the policeman was defending an innocent Jewish victim against Palestinian attackers. The photographer never bothered to verify the victim's identity. And with that stroke of negligence, the truth had been turned on its head.

This photo caption not only misidentified the victim, but even the location. Did AP really think that the Temple Mount – the eminent holy site, totally inaccessible to motor vehicles – has a gas station? I didn't know whether to be amused or appalled.

Imagine the shock of Tuvia's father back in America, knowing that his son was lying in a Jerusalem hospital, and then opening the *New York Times* to see this inversion of reality. Why did the "newspaper of record" automatically assume that the victim was Palestinian and Israel was the aggressor? Is it because Israel has more tanks and planes? My journalism background told me that something just didn't add up.

Damage Control

From my home in central Israel, I had been looking forward to a relaxing High Holiday season with my family. But all that changed when I saw that *New York Times* photo caption. I've sat through enough editorial board meetings to know that a caption this badly botched was more than an innocent mistake.

My investigative instincts kicked in, and I tracked Tuvia down the next day. He was badly bruised, shaken and feeling doubly-victimized. Not only had he been beaten bloody – with a broken nose, multiple gashes to his head, and a severely wounded leg that would require reconstructive surgery, months in a wheelchair and physical therapy – but he had also become a victim of the media war, used to gain international sympathy for Palestinians. That, Tuvia told me, hurt even more.[5]

I offered to help however I could, and we agreed to write an article together for the Internet, explaining Tuvia's side of the story. So the night before Yom Kippur, when I should have been preparing spiritually for the most portentous day of the year, I stayed up till 4 a.m. putting the finishing touches on the article. "I hope this works out for the best," I muttered over my laptop.

Meanwhile, back at the *New York Times*, heads were rolling. The "Gray Lady" had committed what Columbia journalism professor Ari Goldman would later call "an embarrassment to journalism."[6] Would the *Times* respond by skirting the issue or by facing it head-on?

After hemming and hawing for days, the *Times* finally published a brief correction which identified Tuvia merely as an "American" – omitting the key points that he was Jewish and was beaten by Arabs.[7] This was a sham correction, and I was not going to let it pass.

I immediately organized a protest campaign: letters, phone calls, email blasts. The little voice had to be heard. I posted Tuvia's first-person account online – "Victim of the Media War" – and it quickly went viral, generating universal outrage at this media gaffe.[8] The *New York Times'* switchboard was jammed with complaints. And lo and behold, one week later, the *Times* published a rare admission of guilt: a 700-word article with a reprint of the original photo – this time with the proper caption, telling the full story of Tuvia's near-lynching at the hands of a Palestinian mob.[9] The media blunder itself had become so newsworthy that the *Times* was unable to ignore it.

But the victory was bittersweet. In the court of public opinion, the damage had already been done. From those first moments of the Intifada, the media was framing this as a battle between the so-called "Israeli aggressors and Palestinian victims."

Protestors Rage

The attack against Tuvia Grossman was just the tip of the iceberg. In the ensuing days and weeks, the territories had shot into flames, with Israeli property and civilians coming under mounting attack from Palestinian guns, rocks and bombs. For Israel, a country with a population less than that of metropolitan Chicago, the toll was up-close and personal. My friends were thrown into mourning when their son was shot dead at point-blank range in Jerusalem.[10] In my own community, a suburb of Modiin which straddles the Green Line (the 1949 armistice line) in central Israel, a patrol guard was shot dead.[11] And then things got really close, with Arab bullets literally flying past my bedroom window – a threat pooh-poohed by *Time* magazine's description of how Palestinian "bullets whizzed harmlessly through the night... fired by inexpert marksmen, they were no great threat."[12]

In the first days of the Intifada, Joseph's Tomb in Nablus, which I had visited just weeks before, was overrun by an Arab mob. Though the Palestinian Authority was obligated by agreement to protect the site, Palestinian policemen stood by as the synagogue was demolished and its library of holy books set ablaze. In reporting on this violent aggression, CNN claimed that "at least 77 people, mostly Palestinians" were killed in one week of clashes at Joseph's Tomb.[13] In truth, however, a total of *six* Palestinians had died in the fighting. In the rush to portray Palestinians as victims, the most basic facts were getting trampled.

Even worse: The Intifada had started when Arabs fabricated the idea of a Jewish takeover of their al-Aqsa holy site (the Temple Mount), and now Arabs were *in fact* destroying a Jewish holy site. The awful irony was lost on the media.

Then the horror hit a climax. On October 12, 2000, two Israeli reserve soldiers took a wrong turn into Ramallah, where they were taken in custody to a Palestinian police station. Again, under the eyes of Palestinian police, they were brutally lynched by an Arab mob – bludgeoned with metal bars, thrown from a second-story window, burned, disemboweled, and dragged through the streets of Ramallah. From the police station window, one Palestinian proudly raised his blood-soaked hands to the cheering mob below.

It was all captured on video, laid bare for the world to see. Yet even this could not crack the media refrain of Palestinian victimhood. On ABC's *World News Tonight*, Peter Jennings opened his report on the Ramallah lynchings by saying that "this week [Palestinians] are all angry at the Israelis..."[14] Here was the most barbaric act ever filmed, yet Jennings outrageously suggested some justification, some Israeli fault for the "Arab anger."

Teen Newsweek, a magazine distributed to middle school students across America, followed the same "blame Israel" act. The caption on a photo of three Palestinians – fresh from the lynching, in an angry war dance, with blood-drenched hands – read:

In the West Bank city of Ramallah, bloodied Palestinian protestors express their rage.[15]

"Protestors express their rage"? Aren't "protestors" those who carry picket signs outside a government office? Isn't a "protestor" a teenager complaining he's got too much homework? And why were these men in a "bloodied rage?" The caption didn't say. Imagine how many editors had seen and approved this text.

In response to the Ramallah lynchings, Israel issued a warning that certain Palestinian buildings would be attacked.[16] Three hours later, Israeli helicopters fired warning shots and then struck the buildings that Palestinians had been warned to evacuate. The attacks resulted in no deaths and few injuries.[17] So how did reporters refer to the Israeli strike? "Wave after wave of missiles rained down on Ramallah," declared BBC.[18] "Again and again the Israelis fired," added ABC's *World News Tonight*.[19] CNN simply called it "a very extreme abuse of power."[20]

I thought of how this compared to Panama 1989, when four unarmed American Marines encountered a military roadblock after taking a wrong turn. Panamanian soldiers opened fire, killing one Marine and wounding another. The United States regarded the attack as "an enormous outrage"[21] and responded by invading Panama with 20,000 soldiers. Upwards of 4,000 Panamanians were killed, mostly civilians.[22] Yet when Israel shelled a few empty buildings, the media deplored it as an "extreme abuse of power."

Why the double standard?

Though Israel had not yet buried the two lynched bodies, the *Washington Post* was already disregarding the horror with this front-page banner headline: "Israel Strikes Palestinian Sites."[23] The *New York Times*, meanwhile, drew a warped equation between the barbaric murders and the mild Israeli retaliation – calling the two events a "collision of what each side sees as the other's core ugliness."[24]

Something was terribly wrong and a solution urgently needed to be found. I immediately organized an email response team, and a group of friends in London did the same. It was very ad-hoc, with no budget, loose organizational structure, and little more than an intuitive sense that we were on the right track. We leveraged the speed and ease of Internet communications, and when spotting a piece of biased news, we'd send an email alert to the entire list – who would in turn complain directly to the media outlet involved.

The idea grew like wildfire. We had struck a nerve. People were furious and needed to vent. Thousands signed up to receive our critiques of Middle East media coverage. With all that energy being harnessed and directed toward the goal of positive change, it was grassroots activism at its best.

Balances Out

From the outset, CNN's coverage proved particularly flawed. To compound the problem, CNN – then the gold standard of TV news – was having an exponential effect. Hundreds of correspondents based in Israel would turn to CNN throughout the day for news updates. As a result, CNN's coverage was trickling down throughout the media.

The most basic problem was that CNN refused to acknowledge Palestinian culpability for the violence. In the first weeks of the Intifada, when Palestinian gunmen took over the Arab village of Beit Jalla and directed nightly gunfire at the adjacent Jerusalem neighborhood of Gilo, CNN wrote: "Israeli forces opened fire on the Palestinian town of Beit Jallah after *they said* Palestinians were firing into the nearby Israeli town of Gilo."[25] CNN was certain that "Israeli forces opened fire," though the Palestinians firing at Gilo was reported only as hearsay.[26]

This cause-and-effect was completely obscured by CNN, whose report, "Israel Steps Up Military Action," opened with the dramatic assertion that "Israel has launched air, land and sea strikes on Gaza in the most intensive raids of the seven months of violence." Only in the 16th paragraph – 400 words into the story – did CNN finally mention that the Israeli action was in response to Palestinian mortar attacks on the southern Israeli city of Sderot.[27]

I sent out an email alert[28] and contacted Ben Wedeman, CNN's Cairo bureau chief who had been shipped into Jerusalem for added Intifada coverage. Wedeman was feeling a bit grumpy, having recently been shot in the back while covering a clash in Gaza.[29]

"Everyone knows the Israelis didn't wake up one morning and decide to start shooting Palestinians," I told Wedeman. "For crying out loud, this is a *Palestinian* Intifada!"

Wedeman's response was a complete rebuff: "We can't say who fired first. For every Israeli who claims to be under attack, I can find you a Palestinian who says the same thing."

"Of course the Palestinians are saying that," I told him. "That's the propaganda campaign that augments the violence."

Wedeman mumbled something about "journalistic balance" and hung up. I kept my eyes on CNN, however, and a few months later saw this report on an incident in northern Israel:

Israeli police shot and killed a Palestinian in a gun battle…[30]

CNN was giving the clear impression that Israeli police simply shot and killed a Palestinian. Yet in fact, the Palestinian had fired shots at the police, thrown pipe bombs, and was strapped with an explosive belt for an imminent suicide bombing.[31] But you'd have never known any of that from CNN, which omitted these essential facts – making Israel out to be the aggressor in a nondescript "gun battle."

Wedeman's response to me this time?

"Our reporters and editors are under extreme deadline pressure. Occasionally there will be an error in judgment. But it all balances out."[32]

I shook my head and was reminded of the words of Mark Twain: While there are laws to protect the freedom of the press, there are unfortunately none to protect people from the press.

Who Started It?

On top of it all, the media was blaming Israel for starting the whole thing. The culprit was Ariel Sharon, the Israeli politician whose "provocative"[33] walk on the Temple Mount one day earlier had allegedly "sparked the violence."[34] Did he really? On the Mount, Sharon did not pray, made no public statement, and had announced his intentions far in advance, giving security officials on both sides time to confer.[35] He came during normal tourist visiting hours, got nowhere close to the mosques, and was in fact visiting the single holiest Jewish site.

Some background is instructive: In the summer of 2000, hoping for a final peace deal, U.S. President Bill Clinton convened a summit at Camp David between Palestinian leader Yasser Arafat and Israeli Prime Minister Ehud Barak. In a demonstration of Israel's unmistakable desire for peace, Barak offered more concessions than any Israeli had before – 95 percent of the West Bank and the entire Gaza Strip, plus Palestinian sovereignty over parts of Jerusalem.[36] A.B. Yehoshua, Israel's best-known literary figure and a longtime peace activist, said that Barak offered "things that even I as a permanent dove, even a zealous dove, couldn't imagine an Israeli leader would offer."[37] And Leah Rabin, the widow of peace architect Yitzhak Rabin, said he'd be "turning in his grave" from Barak's concessions.[38]

But for Palestinians, it wasn't enough. Palestinian negotiators pressed for untenable demands like the forfeit of Israeli control over the Western Wall, and for millions of Palestinian refugees to flood Israel in a wave of demographic destruction.[39]

And so, having engineered a stalemate, Palestinian negotiators simply walked away – in what Clinton later called a "colossal historical blunder."[40]

So where did that leave things? In the words of America's chief negotiator, Dennis Ross, if Arafat was going to survive politically, he "needed to re-establish the Palestinians as a victim."[41]

That's when Palestinians began beating the drums of war. Throughout the summer of 2000, Palestinian TV aired archival footage from the first Intifada, showing young people on the streets throwing stones.[42] Twenty-five thousand Palestinian boys attended Fatah-run camps where they learned to handle weapons and stage commando raids, and where favorite camper activities were mock kidnappings and "slitting the throats of

Israelis."[43] In August 2000, PA Justice Minister Freih Abu Middein warned that: "Violence is near and the Palestinian people are willing to sacrifice even 5,000 casualties."[44] And a few weeks before the outbreak, the official PA publication, *Al-Sabah*, declared: "The time for the Intifada has arrived... the time for jihad has arrived."[45]

As Palestinian leader Marwan Barghouti would later admit, the Intifada was planned and Sharon merely "provided a good excuse" for the violence.[46] Indeed, Sharon's walk was the perfect set-up and the media fell right into the trap. "Visit to Temple Mount by Prominent Israeli Sparks Violence Between Israelis and Palestinians," declared CBS News.[47]

Never mind that one day before the violence began, the Palestinian Authority designated this as "the most appropriate moment for the outbreak."[48]

Never mind that Palestinian Information Minister Imad Haluji was quoted in Arab newspapers saying that the violence was "at the request of Yasser Arafat, who envisaged the Intifada as a complementary measure... and not as a protest over Sharon's" walk on the Mount.[49]

Never mind that Issam Abu Issa, former chairman of the Palestine International Bank, explained: "When growing pressure in the Palestinian territories forced Arafat to find a scapegoat for his political failure, mismanagement and economic plunder, he turned his guns toward the Israelis."[50]

Never mind all that. The media was more interested in blaming Israel. "Temple Mount Visit Sparks Violence" blared a headline in the *Toronto Star*.[51] BBC conjured images of a military invasion of the Temple Mount, reporting that "Ariel Sharon launched his ill-fated bid to assert Israeli sovereignty over holy sites shared between Israelis and Arabs in east Jerusalem."[52]

And before you know it, the whole thing was derisively spun as "Sharon's War," in headlines everywhere from the *New York Times*[53] to *The Economist*[54] to the *Washington Post*.[55] Yet as William Safire observed, Sharon's pointed but peaceful visit was no more the "cause" of the bloody violence than the assassination of Archduke Ferdinand was the cause of World War I.[56]

Parachute Journalism

For a foreign correspondent, Israel is considered a plum assignment: It has the drama of a war zone, coupled with the comforts of Western culture. Most importantly, perennial interest in the story promises that reporters' bylines will frequently appear above the fold in newspapers and as the lead story on nightly newscasts. Yet because media outlets change their correspondents every few years, reporters don't have much opportunity to study up on all the issues. As Dr. Jorg Bremer of the respected German daily, *Frankfurter Allgemeiner*, acknowledged: "We are very superficial. If we cover the news every day, when do we have time to read a book?"[57]

This situation is exacerbated at times of crisis, when the media corps in Israel can swell to 6,000.[58] Fewer full-time journalists cover foreign news than once did, and those who remain have to hopscotch from one hot spot to another.[59] Reporters who "parachute" into the region for a few weeks are still expected to write in-depth analyses. As one correspondent told me, "When I get a new assignment, I have to hit the ground running. Most regions of the world don't have the same depth of geopolitical issues that exist in Israel. Unfortunately, I don't have time to read a lot of historical backgrounders."

This lack of preparation means that newly arriving correspondents view the Mideast conflict through the lens of their previous postings in regions with very different history and particulars. For example, Mike Hanna, CNN's former Jerusalem bureau chief (now with Al Jazeera), was hard-wired by his 20 years as a correspondent in South Africa to see Israel's situation in "black and white" apartheid terms.[60]

How do journalists compensate for the lack of time and resources to properly study the conflict? By resorting to what veteran correspondent Marvin Kalb calls the "meager one-dimensional news product" of "pack journalism."[61] This is a phenomenon where reporters band together to cover the same story – sharing the research, sources, cab fare, information and, in some cases, the same ignorance. As Russ Braley, a correspondent for the New York *Daily News*, once explained, his editors got advance notice of the *New York Times'* front-page headlines and then matched each story in the *Daily News*.[62]

So whether the initiative came from the editors or from the reporters themselves, it was undoubtedly groupthink that led both Deborah Sontag of the *New York Times* and Suzanne Goldenberg of the London *Guardian* to file stories on consecutive days from a Ramallah shrine in memory of Palestinian "martyrs":

> Sontag: "Israeli critics would say that the exhibit, '100 Martyrs – 100 Lives,' glorifies death and encourages the cult of the shaheed, or martyr."[63]

> Goldenberg: "Israeli critics would argue that the exhibit glorifies violent death, and promotes a cult of martyrdom."[64]

Beyond the nearly identical language, the real tip-off to this pack journalism was their shared use of the uncommon word "totem" to describe objects at the shrine.

As budgets and news cycles shrink, journalists wind up piggybacking more and more on each others' reporting. Unfortunately, parroting what others say does not create knowledge; it just remixes it. When done without verification, errors become increasingly frequent and amplified.[65] It reminds me of Edward R. Murrow's admonition to journalists: "Just because your voice reaches halfway around the world doesn't mean you are wiser than when it reached only to the end of the bar."[66]

This dynamic was at play in June 2011 when news outlets worldwide reported that a dog walked into a Jerusalem rabbinical court, and was identified as the reincarnation of a lawyer whom the court had cursed some two decades earlier. The court allegedly pronounced the dog liable to death by stoning, and ordered that the sentence be carried out by (presumably blood-thirsty) Jewish children.

In this gossip-hungry Internet age, this story has all the right ingredients: Religious zealotry! Violation of animal rights! Blood libel! Violent children! And best of all, it runs under 200 words and stars a dog.[67]

The only problem is that it wasn't remotely true. What started out as a rumor posted on a local blog, got picked up by an Israeli paper, *Ma'ariv*, which then promptly issued an apology explaining what really happened: A dog walked into a courtroom and someone called the dogcatcher. But even after the retraction was on record, "credible" news organizations such as BBC,[68] *Time* magazine[69] and Agence France Presse[70] plowed straight ahead in reporting the story as fact. This is not merely an "honest" mistake; this is sloppy anti-Israel sensationalism.

Every media outlet has its own stylebook, yet due to the pack mentality, foreign correspondents in Israel seem to have informally adopted language rules that follow a standard, monolithic line.

Consider the question of whether to describe political leaders as "hard-line" or "moderate." One would think that Israeli Prime Minister Bibi Netanyahu is considered at least as "moderate" as Palestinian President Mahmoud Abbas, who boasts of having "fired the first shot" that launched the PLO in 1965;[71] who financed the Munich Olympic massacre;[72] who taught terror tactics around the world to groups such as Hezbollah;[73] whose doctoral thesis was a volume of Holocaust denial;[74] and who regularly confers honor upon convicted terrorists.[75]

One would think. Yet it is Abbas who the media consistently calls "moderate," with Israel's Netanyahu cast as the "hardliner" whose governing coalition is "proto-fascist" and "racist,"[76] full of "lunatic extremes" and "poisonous ideas,"[77] "to be as feared as the prospect of Armageddon," and "a recipe for the most extreme political force ever to emerge" in the Middle East.[78] In other words, Netanyahu is worse than Qaddafi, Saddam and the Ayatollah combined.

So while a search of the LexisNexis news database returns thousands of results for "Abbas" and "moderate,"[79] a parallel search for "Netanyahu" and "hard-line" also returns thousands of results.[80]

Tellingly, LexisNexis searches for the opposite terms – "moderate Netanyahu" and "hard-line Abbas" – yield zero results from mainstream news sources.

Perhaps the argument could be made that Abbas is indeed "moderate," relative to the rival Palestinian terror organization Hamas. Yet the argument falls apart when considering that media outlets including the *New York Times*,[81] *Los Angeles Times*[82] and Agence France Presse[83] liberally apply the term "moderate" even to Hamas.

So after years of being targeted by rockets, shootings and suicide bombings, Israelis had naively begun to think that Hamas was in fact a terror organization out to spill Jewish blood. Thank goodness, then, for those intrepid journalists who've set the record straight by informing us that Hamas terror mastermind Ismail Abu Shanab – who insists that "all Israeli targets are legitimate"[84] and that Israel must be destroyed[85] – is actually "a moderate" (CNN),[86] "one of the group's more sober minds" (Associated Press),[87] and a "political leader" who is "rather moderate at that" (*Time* magazine).[88]

BBC observed that Hamas leaders "espouse a more moderate brand of Islamist politics."[89] I suppose that strictly speaking, it is accurate to say Hamas is "more moderate" than other Islamist groups like al-Qaeda. After all, Hamas has taken some responsibility for governance, whereas al-Qaeda just blows things up. But relative moderation is hardly the same as true moderation. By applying the "governance" standard, one could describe the Nazi regime as "extremely moderate."[90]

Other Arab leaders get the soft-treatment, too. *Vogue*, the high-profile fashion magazine, published a glowing profile of Asma al-Assad, wife of Syrian dictator Bashar al-Assad, describing her as "glamorous, young, and very chic – the freshest and most magnetic of first ladies." As for the brutal dictator Bashar Assad (pictured kneeling gently to help with his son's toy), *Vogue* credits him as exemplifying "tolerance," "wildly democratic principles" and a "spirit of openness." With no whiff of cynicism, *Vogue* presents the Syrian ruler as a paradigm of goodness, having studied ophthalmology because "it's almost never an emergency, and there is very little blood."[91]

In this cloud of jargon monoxide, *Vogue* neglected to mention a few relevant details: Syria has operated under emergency law since 1963, and the regime shed the blood of 20,000 of its citizens in the town of Hama alone. Poetic justice prevailed, however: *Vogue's* article hit the newsstands just as Bashar was spearheading a brutal and deadly crackdown on protesters. Sometimes he who writes the words has to eat them.

Given that journalism is a game of words, the choice of terminology means everything. And although there are probably no conspiratorial hands behind the emergence of this de facto stylebook, invariably, pack journalism rules carry a one-sided bias against Israel.[92] For in the final tally, all Palestinians and Arabs are "moderates," while even left-wing Israeli politicians like Ehud Barak and Tzipi Livni are "warmongers,"[93] the sole obstacle to peace.

CNN's Pattern of Bias

When I challenged reporters and editors about this bias, they kept coming back with the same refrain: Mistakes are sometimes made, but it all balances out. I was engaging in serious media analysis, and journalists were discounting me as some kind of nudnik.

After repeatedly getting the same reaction, I began to wonder if maybe it's true. In the words of the Talmud: "If people keep calling you a donkey, maybe it's time to buy a saddle."[94] So I started to question: *Perhaps the media is not biased. Maybe because a Jewish citizen of Israel – and an ordained rabbi, at that – I tend to look at everything from a parochial perspective. Sure, I have a mountain of anecdotal evidence pointing to bias against Israel, but that doesn't prove anything.*

I had to honestly ask myself: *Maybe it's true, as the media claims, that things really do balance out over time. Maybe I'm the one who's biased!*

I concluded there's only one way to objectively determine who's crazy and who's sane: conduct a statistical study of a large amount of data to reveal any global patterns in the coverage.

CNN – at the top of the media food chain – was the ideal subject for my study. So I printed out every article that appeared in the Mideast section of CNN.com during October 2000 – the first month of the Intifada – and then set about analyzing the articles. All 133 of them.

First, I focused on CNN's choice of photos, since images are important in creating emotional identification with the people in this conflict. For example, a photo of a funeral will arouse sympathy; the beneficiary of that sympathy depends whether it's a photo of a Palestinian or an Israeli funeral.

So using highlighting markers, tabular charts and lots of coffee, I reviewed these 133 articles to determine whether CNN favored one side or the other.

The results were statistically staggering: Arabs were depicted in 128 photos on CNN.com, and Israelis in 60 photos. More than twice as often, CNN's photos were creating sympathy for the Palestinian side.

I then focused on a second question: In these 133 articles, did CNN give both sides equal opportunity to state their position? In other words, how many times was an Israeli spokesperson quoted, versus an Arab spokesperson?

The results: Arabs were quoted 92 times, and Israelis were quoted 61 times. This is a frequency of occurrence 50.8 percent greater in favor of the Palestinian side.

Then I asked an important follow-up question: When one side was quoted, was the statement allowed to stand unchallenged, or was the other side given an opportunity to rebut?

In this regard, the results were even more skewed: 68 Arab quotes were allowed to stand unchallenged, while only 28 Israeli quotes were unchallenged. For example, when Israeli Prime Minister Ehud Barak called a timeout to reassess the peace process, CNN published a litany of harsh Arab reactions, describing Israel's "unjustified aggression" and "calling for a United Nations-led 'war crimes tribunal'" against Israelis.[95]

Readers of CNN had to wade through 13 paragraphs of one-sided reporting before Barak was finally quoted as presenting the Israeli side. Immediately, CNN then dismissed the Israeli position with a long list of condemnations:

The Palestinian chief of security, Muhammed Dahlan, said, "From the beginning, we believed Barak doesn't want peace..."

Palestinian Cabinet Minister Hanan Ashwari (sic) said, "It's clear Israel has suspended the peace process... because it has no interest in peace."

Palestinian Cabinet Minister Yasser Abed Rabbu said, "this will only add more fuel to the situation..."

[Hamas co-founder] Mahmoud Al-zahar said, "Hamas said from the beginning Israelis are not willing to make real peace..."

Intuitively I had long sensed that CNN coverage was tilted in favor of the Palestinians. Now this pattern was statistically confirmed. This was a huge epiphany, because it removed any self-doubt and put me squarely on track. Israel was in genuine danger from Intifada violence, and the media was fueling the fire. Inspired by the words of George Orwell – "During times of universal deceit, telling the truth becomes a revolutionary act" – I committed all my energies to fighting against media bias.

I recalled something drilled into us at journalism school: In Western democracies the media is the largest single factor in shaping public opinion. And because politicians are constantly courting the vote, public opinion in large part determines public policy. Politicians have been known to formulate "sound bites of the day" in response to overnight opinion polling. So in a very practical sense, what middle America sees on the evening news today, becomes reconstituted as U.S. foreign policy tomorrow.

Perhaps more than any other country, Israel – surrounded by Arab nations with 640 times the amount of land, 350 million more people, and a long history of attacking and vilifying the Jewish state – relies on Western support for its ongoing survival. Israel is forced to constantly walk a thin diplomatic line, attempting to placate a world community under pressure from oil-rich Arab states. How the media reports events will largely determine whether the White House, the United Nations and the European

Union grant Israel the necessary latitude to defend its citizens. That is why the labels of "aggressor" and "victim" are so crucial, and why media bias is ultimately so lethal.

Yet one big question remained: Why? What motive did the media have for unfairly casting Israelis as the aggressors and Palestinians as their victims?

I didn't know. But I'd read enough mystery novels to know that if you can uncover the motive, you can solve the crime. For the sake of tiny Israel, I had to find out.

Notes

1. Sharm el-Sheikh Fact-Finding Committee, "First Statement of the Government of Israel," 2000, p. 38.
2. Mitchell G. Bard, "Myths & Facts Online: The Peace Process," Jewish Virtual Library.
3. Book of Judges, chapter 7.
4. Gideon Tzefadi, former Chief Superintendent, East Jerusalem Israeli Border Police. See "Dramatic Reunion Ten Years After the Photo that Started It All," HonestReporting.com, August 31, 2010.
5. A number of Arab websites, including the Palestinian Information Center and the official Egypt State Information Service (sis.gov.eg), would later exploit Tuvia Grossman's photo even further, recasting the battered Jew as a "Palestinian martyr."
6. Email correspondence with the author.
7. *New York Times,* October 4, 2000. Other papers also ran botched "corrections," including Australia's *Melbourne Herald Sun*: "Bashed: An American student is beaten by an Israeli police officer in Jerusalem."
8. Tuvia Grossman, "Victim of the Media War," Aish.com, November 5, 2000.
9. Robert D. McFadden, "Abruptly, a U.S. Student in Mideast Turmoil's Grip," *New York Times,* October 7, 2000. Associated Press issued its own full-length "correction" article. (Tanalee Smith, "American Jewish Students Carry Grim Reminders of Arab Attack," Associated Press, October 5, 2000.) Other newspapers ran op-eds about the misidentified photo, including: Robert L. Pollock, "Carnage for the Cameras," *Wall Street Journal,* October 6, 2000; Eric Fettmann, "Impact Obvious – & Wrong – The 'Palestinian' Victim in this Photo was Really a Jew," *New York Post,* October 5, 2000. In 2002, a District Court in Paris acknowledged the damage caused by the miscaption, ordering Associated Press and the French newspaper *Liberation* to pay Grossman damages of 4,500 Euro. (See Richard B. Woodward, "Looking Through a Lens," *Wall Street Journal*, September 19, 2006.)
10. Jennifer Golson, "A Death in Israel Mourned in Jersey," *Star-Ledger* (New Jersey), November 1, 2000.
11. "14 Days – Intifada Watch," *Jerusalem Report,* April 8, 2002.
12. Matt Rees, "Fields of Fire," *Time,* December 10, 2000.
13. "Israel Evacuates Holy Site, Temporarily Surrenders Control," CNN.com, October 7, 2000.
14. Peter Jennings, "Two Israeli Army Reservists Killed in Ramallah Today by Palestinian Mob; Many Palestinians Blame America," *World News Tonight,* ABC, October 12, 2000.
15. "Peace Under Fire: Palestinians and Israelis on the Brink of War," *Teen Newsweek,* October 23, 2000.

THE PHOTO THAT STARTED IT ALL 29

16. Lisa Beyer, "Breaking Point," *Time*, October 23, 2000.
17. "Barak Calls for Unity Government after New Violence," CNN.com, October 12, 2000.
18. Martin Asser, "Lynch Mob's Brutal Attack," BBC News Online, October 13, 2000.
19. Gillian Findlay, "Two Israeli Army Reservists Killed in Ramallah Today by Palestinian Mob; Many Palestinians Blame America," *World News Tonight*, ABC, October 12, 2000.
20. "Israel Launches More Airstrikes; Peres Says Saturday Summit in Egypt Possible," CNN.com, October 13, 2000.
21. President George H.W. Bush; cited in Andrew Rosenthal, "President Calls Panama Slaying a Great Outrage," *New York Times*, December 19, 1989.
22. "U.S. Forces Invade Panama, Seize Wide Control; Noriega Eludes Capture," *Facts on File World News Digest*, December 22, 1989; Alexander Safian, PhD, "Is Israel Using 'Excessive Force' Against Palestinians?", Committee for Accuracy in Middle East Reporting in America, November 9, 2000.
23. Lee Hockstader and Keith B. Richburg, "Israel Strikes Palestinian Sites," *Washington Post*, October 13, 2000.
24. Deborah Sontag, "2 Israeli Soldiers Slain by a Mob; Helicopters Hit Back," *New York Times*, October 13, 2000.
25. "Barak Warns of 'Difficult Consequences' If Arafat Fails to Curb Violence," CNN.com, November 1, 2000. Emphasis added.
26. By contrast, some media outlets made clear that Israel was responding to unprovoked Palestinian attacks. Fox News asked an Arab resident of Beit Jalla the questions that CNN dared not: "Do these Israelis ever shoot first?" Arab in Beit Jalla: "I don't think so." Fox News: "So if there were no Palestinian gunmen shooting from here, you probably would have quiet, wouldn't you?" Arab in Beit Jalla: "Sure." (*Fox Special Report with Brit Hume*, Fox News, August 16, 2001)
27. "Israel Steps Up Military Action," CNN.com, April 17, 2001.
28. "Who Hit First?," HonestReporting.com, April 18, 2001.
29. "CNN Correspondent Ben Wedeman Wounded in Gaza," CNN.com, October 31, 2000.
30. "Israeli Police Kill Palestinian Near Army Base, Another Dies in Blast," CNN.com, February 18, 2002.
31. *Jerusalem Post*, February 18, 2002.
32. As Eason Jordan, the chief news executive of CNN, said: "One of the only things that Yasir Arafat and Ariel Sharon have in common is they both think CNN is biased toward the opposite side." (Felicity Barringer, "Mideast Turmoil: The News Outlets," *New York Times*, May 23, 2002.) Other media outlets adopted a similar refrain. After one obvious incident of bias against Israel, *Washington Post* editors acknowledged that despite "errors or lapses or imperfections," there endures "fairness over a long period of time." (Michael Getler, "Readers and Reporters – Who's Biased?", *Washington Post*, March 24, 2002.)
33. See, for example, John Kifner, "Arafat Always Seems to Survive. Peace May Not," *New York Times*, October 8, 2000; Editorial, "Conflagration in the Middle East," *New York Times*, October 3, 2000.
34. See, for example, Edith M. Lederer, "U.N. Condemns Excessive Force Against Palestinians; U.S. Abstains," Associated Press, October 7, 2000; Matthew McAllester, "A 'Day of Rage': Palestinian Muslims Seize Holy Site Temporarily," *Newsday* (New York), October 7, 2000; "Security Council Meets on Mideast Violence," Agence France Presse, October 3, 2000; Bob Edwards and Linda Gradstein, "Israelis and Palestinians Asking Each Other to Stop the Violent Clashes that Have Resulted in 31 Deaths in Four Days," *Morning Edition*, National Public Radio, October 2, 2000.
35. Israeli Foreign Minister Shlomo Ben Ami consulted with Palestinian security chief Jabril Rajoub who gave an assurance of calm, provided that Sharon did not enter any of the

mosques or pray publicly. (Ray Suarez, "Interview with Acting Foreign Minister Shlomo Ben-Ami," *Newshour with Jim Lehrer*, PBS, November 1, 2000.)
36. Dennis Ross, *The Missing Peace: The Inside Story of the Fight for Middle East Peace*, Farrar, Straus and Giroux, 2004; Gilead Sher, *The Israeli-Palestinian Peace Negotiations, 1999-2001*, Routledge, 2006.
37. "CNN: Peace Process in Limbo after Barak Calls 'Timeout,'" Aish.com, October 22, 2000.
38. "Leah Rabin Slams Barak," BBC News Online, September 8, 2000.
39. Mahmoud Abbas, *Reports of the Camp David Summit, 9 September 2000*; excerpted in the *Journal of Palestine Studies*, Winter 2001, pp. 168-170.
40. Jonathan Lis, "Clinton: Arafat Made 'Colossal Blunder' Over Camp David Offer," *Haaretz* (Israel), November 13, 2005.
41. Brit Hume, *Fox News Sunday*, Fox News, April 21, 2002. Already in the spring of 2000, six months before the Intifada, Arafat told a group in Ramallah "that the Palestinian people are likely to turn to the Intifada option." (*Al-Mujahid*, April 3, 2000.)
42. Itamar Marcus, "Rape, Murder, Violence and War for Allah Against the Jews: Summer 2000 on Palestinian Television," Palestinian Media Watch, September 11, 2000.
43. John F. Burns, "Palestinian Summer Camp Offers the Games of War," *New York Times*, August 3, 2000.
44. *Al-Hayat Al-Jadida* (Palestinian Authority), August 24, 2000.
45. *Al-Sabah* (Palestinian Authority), September 11, 2000.
46. Jeffrey Goldberg, "Arafat's Gift," *The New Yorker*, January 29, 2001.
47. Anthony Mason, "Visit to Temple Mount by Prominent Israeli Sparks Violence Between Israelis and Palestinians," CBS News, September 28, 2000.
48. *Al-Hayat Al-Jadida* (Palestinian Authority), September 29, 2001.
49. Cited in Efraim Karsh, *Arafat's War*, Grove Press, 2004, p. 193. Palestinian military commander Mamduh Nufal recounted that on the day of Sharon's walk, Arafat issued direct orders to field commanders to begin violent confrontations with Israel. (*Al-Ayyam* [Palestinian Authority], September 30, 2001; see David Samuels, "In a Ruined Country," *Atlantic Monthly*, September 2005.)
50. Issam Abu Issa, "Arafat's Swiss Bank Account," *Middle East Quarterly*, Fall 2004.
51. Sandro Contenta, "Temple Mount Visit Sparks Violence," *Toronto Star*, September 29, 2000.
52. "Q&A: What Hope for Peace?", BBC News Online, January 22, 2001.
53. James Bennet, "Sharon's Wars," *New York Times*, August 15, 2004.
54. Editorial, "Sharon's War," *The Economist*, April 6, 2002.
55. Editorial, "Mr. Sharon's War," *Washington Post*, February 22, 2002.
56. William Safire, "Israel Needs an Ally," *New York Times*, October 12, 2000.
57. Cited in David Margolis, "Bad News," June 2001.
58. Israel's withdrawal from Gaza in August 2005 was covered by more than 6,000 foreign correspondents. (Israel Harel, "Bad Guys, Fall Guys," *Haaretz* [Israel], August 17, 2005.)
59. Brian Stelter, "Rush of Events Gives Foreign News a Top Priority," *New York Times*, March 20, 2011.
60. Margolis, "Bad News."
61. Marvin Kalb, *The Nixon Memo*, University of Chicago Press, 1994, p. 190.
62. Russ Braley, *Bad News: The Foreign Policy of the New York Times*, Regnery Gateway, 1984.
63. Deborah Sontag, "Ramallah Journal; Bitter, Stark Souvenirs: Sneakers and Slingshots," *New York Times*, February 21, 2001.
64. Suzanne Goldenberg, "A Museum Fit for Martyrs," *The Guardian* (UK), February 23, 2001.
65. Eoin O'Carroll, "Did a Jerusalem Court Really Sentence a Dog to Death by Stoning?", *Christian Science Monitor*, June 21, 2011.
66. Speech to the Radio and Television News Directors Association, Chicago, October 15, 1958.

67. O'Carroll, "Did a Jerusalem Court Really Sentence a Dog to Death by Stoning?"
68. "Jerusalem Rabbis 'Condemn Dog to Death by Stoning,'" BBC News Online, June 18, 2011. The story was #1 on BBC's "Most Shared" list. BBC eventually issued a follow-up story – not a "correction," but rather disparaging the rabbinical court as "denying" the allegations. ("Jerusalem Court Denies Dog Condemned to Stoning," BBC, June 20, 2011.)
69. Nick Carbone, "Shocking Sentence: Jewish Court Condemns Dog To Death by Stoning," *Time*, June 18, 2011.
70. "Jewish Court Sentences Dog to Death by Stoning," Agence France Presse, June 17, 2011.
71. *Al-Dustur* (Jordan), February 28, 2008; cited in "Abbas: 'Armed Resistance Not Ruled Out,'" *Jerusalem Post*, February 28, 2008; Jeff Jacoby, "Slaughter and Jubilation," *Boston Globe*, March 12, 2008.
72. Alexander Wolff, "The Mastermind," *Sports Illustrated*, August 26, 2002. When Amin Al-Hindi, one of the senior planners of the Munich massacre, died in August 2010, Abbas led the dignitaries at the PA-sponsored funeral, complete with red carpet and military band. The official PA daily described Al-Hindi as "one of the stars who sparkled... at the sports stadium in Munich." (*Al-Hayat Al-Jadida*, August 20, 2010; cited in Itamar Marcus and Barbara Crook, "PA and Abbas Honor Terrorist Planner of Olympics Massacre," Palestinian Media Watch, August 25, 2010.)
73. *Al-Dustur* (Jordan), February 28, 2008.
74. Written at Moscow's Oriental College, later published as *The Other Side: The Secret Relationship Between Nazism and Zionism*. See Charles A. Morse, "The Nazism of Abu Mazen," April 14, 2003.
75. In one high-profile event, Abbas chose Latifa Abu Hmeid – the mother of four terrorist murderers, each serving multiple life sentences – to lead the procession to U.N. offices in Ramallah and officially launch the Palestinian statehood campaign. (*Al-Hayat Al-Jadida* [Palestinian Authority], September 9, 2011; cited in Itamar Marcus and Nan Jacques Zilberdik, "Mother of Four Terrorist Murderers Chosen by PA to Launch Statehood Campaign," Palestinian Media Watch, September 18, 2011.)
76. Ali Abunimah, "No Peace for Israel," *The Guardian* (UK), February 12, 2009.
77. Jonathan Freedland, "A Toxic Force Rises in Israel," *The Guardian* (UK), February 11, 2009.
78. Elizabeth Jay, "Taking Exception to Making Exceptions," *The Guardian* (UK), March 1, 2009.
79. For example, Karin Laub, "Obama Envoy: Two-State Solution is Only Solution," Associated Press, April 17, 2009; "Israeli Raids Kill Gaza Militants after Clinton Visit," Agence France Presse, March 5, 2009; Ed O'Loughlin, "Road Map to Peace Still Leads Nowhere," *Sydney Morning Herald* (Australia), November 29, 2007; Michael Matza, "A New Sense of Urgency," *Philadelphia Inquirer*, November 28, 2007; Tom Raum, "Mideast Peace Summit Holds Opportunities for Bush, But Odds of Success Seem Low," *Detroit News*, November 25, 2007; Jeffrey Fleishman, "Arab Allies Skeptical of U.S. Peace Effort," *Los Angeles Times*, October 14, 2007; Joshua Brilliant, "Analysis: Tallying Olmert's Promises," United Press International, July 9, 2007; Maggie Michel, "Palestinian Moderate Leader Abbas, Hamas Chief Mashaal Hold Rare Meeting," Associated Press, April 28, 2007; Jackson Diehl, "Israel's Diplomatic Invasion; Olmert's Forced Retreat from Unilateralism," *Washington Post*, July 3, 2006.
80. For example, Mohammed Daraghmeh, "Abbas Urges Israel to Accept '67 Border," *Boston Globe* / Associated Press, July 18, 2010; Steven R. Hurst, "Analysis: Mideast Setbacks Weigh on Obama," Associated Press, June 15, 2009; "Israel: Livni, Netanyahu Both Claim Victory," Associated Press, February 10, 2009; Tim McGirk, "Israel's Elections: Making a Hard Right," *Time*, February 8, 2009; Charles Hurt, "Barack Gives Hearty Shalom – Prays at Western Wall in Israel," *New York Post*, July 24, 2008; Matthew McAllester, "Ariel Sharon a Leader Incapacitated," *Newsday* (New York), January 6, 2006.
81. Isabel Kershner, "Attack by Hamas Casts Doubt on Future of Cease-Fire in Gaza," *New York*

Times, April 25, 2007.
82. Edmund Sanders, "Hamas is Accused of Being Moderate," *Los Angeles Times*, April 22, 2010.
83. "Israel Warns against Hamas Talks after British, Prodi Comments," Agence France Presse, August 14, 2007. See also "Hamas, Fatah Trade Accusations Over Gaza Clashes," Xinhua (China), August 15, 2009; "Hamas Nominates 'Moderate' as Leader," ABC Premium News (Australia), February 17, 2006.
84. Julie Stahl, "'This is War' Says Israeli Minister," CNSNews.com, July 7, 2008.
85. Ibrahim Barzak, "Slain Hamas Leader Had Pushed for Cease-Fire, But Israel Says He Still Plotted Attacks," Associated Press, August 22, 2003.
86. "Hamas Militant Killed in Israeli Helicopter Attack in Gaza," CNN.com, August 29, 2003.
87. Barzak, "Slain Hamas Leader Had Pushed for Cease-Fire, But Israel Says He Still Plotted Attacks."
88. Johanna McGeary, Massimo Calabresi, Jamil Hamad and Aharon Klein, "Road Map to Hell," *Time*, September 1, 2003. See Michael Freund, "The Foreign Media's Failure," *Jerusalem Post*, August 27, 2003.
89. "Al-Qaeda Seeks Unity with Hamas," BBC News Online, June 25, 2007.
90. James Taranto, "Best of the Web Today," *Wall Street Journal Online*, June 26, 2007.
91. Joan Juliet Buck, "Asma al-Assad: A Rose in the Desert," *Vogue*, March 2011. The Syrian government paid tens of thousands of dollars to an international PR firm to help coordinate the *Vogue* profile. (Kevin Bogardus, "PR Firm Worked with Syria on Controversial Photo Shoot," TheHill.com, August 3, 2011.)
92. See Lenny Ben-David, speech to the American Jewish Committee; published as "New Rules for Mideast Reporting," Aish.com, May 26, 2001.
93. Ed Harris, "Israelis Go to Polls to Choose Between Three Warmongers," *Evening Standard* (UK), February 10, 2009. (Later changed to: "Israelis Go to the Polls in Tight Election Race.")
94. Baba Kama 92b.
95. "Peace Process in Limbo after Barak Calls 'Timeout,'" CNN.com, October 22, 2000.

2

DAVID & GOLIATH

Late one night in October 2000, I was jolted awake by the ringing phone. It was a friend calling from Texas to check up on me. He'd heard about the spate of drive-by shootings on the 443 highway to Jerusalem,[1] and wanted to know, "Isn't that the road you take to work?"

I tried to sound reassuring. "Yah, but things always seem worse when you hear about them on the news. Anyway, I've stopped driving that road after dark." Then, trying to change the subject, I asked, "So what are you up to?"

"Oh, nothing much. I just watched the first half of *Monday Night Football*. The Dolphins are clobbering the New York Jets."

"No reason to watch the second half," I said.

"Well, actually, the announcers are working real hard to make this game interesting. Right now they've got Arnold Schwarzenegger in the broadcast booth, giving a whole list of reasons why the Jets are poised for a comeback. It seems like the underdog really has a chance to win this thing."

The underdog? My antenna perked up. Doesn't the media always try to increase the drama and excitement by propping up the underdog? Americans, in particular, love to root for the underdog: America itself was born as an underdog, and underdog stories – think Rocky Balboa – have been popular ever since the biblical David first aimed a slingshot at Goliath.[2]

Rooting for the underdog is more than just good drama; it's also good marketing. Corporations offer cash prices for "picking the underdog" in the NCAA basketball tournament,[3] and in the 2012 presidential race, Barack Obama declared that even as the incumbent, he is "absolutely" the underdog.[4]

Propping up the underdog is also good business. In a one-sided rout like a football game, millions of viewers will click off – unless you can keep things interesting by creating momentum for the underdog. The media, after all, needs to keep their customers rapt and engaged.

Which begs a basic question: Exactly who are the media's customers? On one level, it's the general public. But on a deeper level, the media's customers are commercial advertisers, who are sold a product called "eyeballs." (That's you and me.) The more eyeballs the media provides, the more they can charge advertisers, and the greater profit they reap.

That's why the media is constantly trying to level the playing field and make it a fair fight. In the words of Dick Ebersol, chairman of NBC Sports, "You always like a strong, scrappy underdog."[5] The more compelling the show, the more ad dollars pour in.

The unfortunate truth is that the news media operates in much the same way. That's exactly what Bernard Goldberg wrote in his best-selling book, *Bias*.[6] For decades, television news was a money-loser. The networks only funded news divisions because it was good for credibility and image. In those early days, the primary consideration was just-the-facts-journalism. As Edward R. Murrow put it: "To be persuasive, we must be believable; to be believable, we must be credible; to be credible, we must be truthful. It is as simple as that."[7]

But all that changed in the 1970s when *60 Minutes* became a ratings sensation. The CBS news division was making money for the first time ever. At that moment, network executives changed the rules: "Journalism" was no longer the goal; it was now about making money. In Goldberg's words, "The deal with the devil had been struck." And with it, the world of journalism became irrevocably altered.

That's when strange things started happening. When Janet Cooke wrote a *Washington Post* series about an 8-year-old heroin addict – the "needle marks freckling the baby-smooth skin of his thin, brown arms" – she simply fabricated the whole story (and won a Pulitzer Prize).[8] When *Dateline NBC* filmed a segment about General Motors pickup trucks exploding due to poor fuel tank design, producers planted explosive devices beneath the truck and "forgot" to tell viewers it was only a dramatization.[9] It once again proved the adage that "television is a medium because it is neither rare nor well done."[10]

This pursuit of profit creates tremendous pressure to make the news "entertaining." In the top-down chain of news production, publishers demand from editors an increased market share; editors, in turn, pressure reporters to make the storyline interesting. Along the way, journalistic ethics may fall by the wayside. This explains how Jayson Blair was able to systematically fabricate dozens of stories in the *New York Times* – inventing places, events and people who didn't exist – before anyone caught on.[11]

Today, vast competition on the Internet has strewn the turf with mine fields. *USA Today* has even introduced a plan to pay bonuses to writers based on page views.[12] Once writers realize that rumors, sensationalism and total fabrications boost web traffic, is there any limit to what fiction they might create?

Of course not every reporter is inventing stories out of thin air. But I've confronted dozens of journalists with this theory, and they all agree that business pressures affect news coverage. As one correspondent told me: "I would like to be practicing more pure journalism. But we're in the news business – emphasis on *business* – and that means ratings and advertisers are a constant factor in what and how we're reporting."[13]

Gene Weingarten, a Pulitzer Prize-winning journalist for the *Washington Post,* recounts that as a "hungry young reporter in the 1970s," he thought of himself as "an invincible crusader for truth and justice." Now, he says, the media is in a "frantic, undignified campaign… [for]

attracting more 'eyeballs.'"[14]

My mind was racing with all these thoughts, when suddenly my friend's voice crackled through the phone: "Gotta go now. The Dolphins are kicking off to start the second half." I hung up the phone and snapped back into the reality around me: relentless Intifada violence, and the looming question of why the media was stuck on the theme of "Israeli aggressor and Palestinian victim."

Then it hit me. The Palestinians are the classic underdog. Slingshots! Holy Land! It's the perfect metaphor for the archetypal biblical confrontation: Palestinians as the tiny stone-throwing "David" against the mighty tanks of the Israeli "Goliath." It's precisely how NPR's Jennifer Ludden described it: "You've got this Goliath of an Israeli army with guns... armored tanks... helicopters... directed at young kids with stones."[15] And Hilary Andersson of BBC enthused: "Each boy's slingshot is his pride... It is a modern day version of David and Goliath."[16]

The pieces were fitting together. Tuvia Grossman's misidentified photo got such wide distribution because the Israeli policeman hovering over the bloodied boy invoked the imagery of Goliath menacing the tiny David. The mass media machine – big, unified, and powerful in swaying world opinion – had latched onto its dramatic and attention-grabbing storyline. And in the process, Israel's image was being clobbered.

Impossible Standard

Of course, simple underdog status is not the only piece of this puzzle. Westerners are deeply concerned with human rights, viewing any conflict in terms of cops and robbers, good guys versus bad. So in order to rally the public – as Nelson Mandela so eloquently proved – it is crucial to stake the moral high ground.

In the Mideast conflict, Palestinian PR experts have latched onto this strategy, carefully choosing buzz-words that vilify Israel: Checkpoints! Occupation! Humanitarian crisis! Apartheid! How often have we heard Palestinian spokeswoman Hanan Ashrawi on the evening news decrying that Palestinians are "subjected to the systematic oppression and brutality of an inhuman occupation that robbed them of all their rights and liberties."[17]

Indeed, media outlets will ascribe the worst human rights violations to Israel – far out of proportion to reality. When an Israeli soldier posted on Facebook some photos of herself alongside blindfolded Palestinian prisoners, Associated Press declared that "the photographs were a reminder of snapshots taken in 2003 by American soldiers at Abu Ghraib prison in Iraq that showed Iraqi detainees naked, humiliated and terrified."[18] Newspapers across the globe accompanied this story with file photos of naked Iraqi prisoners being tortured at Abu Ghraib.[19] Did the Israeli soldier act in poor taste? Yes. But in no way comparable to the inhumanity at Abu Ghraib.

I discovered the media fueling this narrative the day a Palestinian suicide bomber killed five people in Tel Aviv. Two other Palestinians were caught assisting the bombing, and in response, the Israeli government decided to relocate them to Gaza. Yet even as Israeli rescue squads were still wiping up the splattered body parts, Reuters was recasting this event as one of "Palestinian victimhood." Reporter Nidal al-Mughrabi portrayed the relocation of the two Palestinian co-conspirators as a "crime against humanity," and then described them as being "uprooted" in "fear," "threatened" and "dumped… to fend for themselves."[20] Reuters made no mention of the pains the Israeli Supreme Court took to ensure that the relocations were in line with democratic principles. Reuters omitted the fact that Israel arranged a family reunion prior to the relocation. Reuters failed to note that Israel generously gave the men food, bottled water and 1,000 shekels each in assistance, and that the men spent the night comfortably at a Red Cross facility in Gaza.[21]

A far cry from "dumped to fend for themselves."

This episode was testament to Israel's commitment to human rights, even when dealing with terrorists. Yet Reuters manipulated the facts and turned it around as a human rights tirade *against* Israel.

Then there's the time that Israel made a voluntary goodwill gesture by reinstating 15,000 Palestinian work permits – 10 percent of the pre-Intifada number. Reuters cynically called it a "drop in the ocean." Let's see: The ocean contains approximately 300 quintillion gallons of water, and each gallon has about 20,000 drops. Granted that Reuters' reference to "drop in the ocean" was just a figure of speech, but why disparage Israel's humanitarian granting of 15,000 permits – which even Palestinian officials deemed "an important step"?[22]

A particularly insidious method of vilifying Israel is to set some standard of "perfection," and note where Israel falls short. This is criticism without context, calumnies without comparisons, arguments without considering the alternative.

Consider NPR's report on the problem of illegal African immigrants sneaking into Israel. NPR emphasized how "Israel is sending a very clear message to all asylum seekers: Beware. We are not interested in your presence here. We will do whatever is in our power to prevent you from being here."[23]

While Israel in the past has welcomed small numbers of refugees in need (Vietnamese boat people[24] and even Bosnian Muslims),[25] it simply cannot have the open door policy that NPR seems to demand. Even the United States, 450 times the size of Israel, cannot survive with such a policy. Is there any country in the world that actively seeks or welcomes migrants from Africa? (Egyptian policies are to shoot them on sight.) But to NPR, Israel is to be castigated for supposedly falling short of some absurd idealized standard.[26]

What time is it, folks? It's Israeli Double Standard Time!

Turning the Tables

During one of my visits to the foreign correspondents' favorite hangout, the American Colony Hotel in Jerusalem, I headed down to the Cellar Bar, a cave-like retreat with 130-year-old pink stone and candlelit ambiance. A group of reporters were sipping whiskey and talking shop, so I sat at an adjacent table and patiently waited for my cue. Sure enough, within a few minutes the conversation turned to the topic of Israeli aggression, and my ears caught mention of David and Goliath.

"Pardon me," I said, leaning over to their table. "I don't understand something. If we're casting roles here, shouldn't Israel be the David? After all, Israel is a tiny country of 6 million Jews surrounded by hundreds of millions of Arabs."

The journalists looked befuddled, but without missing a beat one of them said, sarcastically, "And of course, King David was a Jew!"

Actually, the State of Israel once *was* David. That was back in 1948, when the fledgling Jewish state accepted a U.N. vote to partition the land. The Arabs rejected it and sent five Arab armies on what the Arab League Secretary called "a war of extermination and a momentous massacre."[27] Yet with no planes and only three tanks, the rag-tag Israeli militia miraculously staved off annihilation.[28]

The Jewish people – after nearly two millennia of exile from their historic homeland – went on to achieve the unimaginable by ingathering the exiles, reviving an ancient language, and making the desert bloom. This was all done in the face of economic embargo, diplomatic isolation, and relentless war and terror attacks. And the world rallied behind this amazing Israeli underdog story.

So how did the Palestinians manage to turn the tables, usurp the underdog label, and gain the moral high ground?

By exploiting the fact that the collective public consciousness typically spans just one generation. A lie told often enough becomes "the truth," Lenin said, but only after a full generation can it become the benchmark of history. So although Israel was the Jewish homeland 1,900 years before Islam ever came into existence,[29] this fact is way off most people's radar screen.

In the public eye, the starting point of history is 1967. That's when something catastrophic happened from the standpoint of PR. Israel – again on the verge of annihilation by the three-front aggression of Egypt, Syria and Jordan – won the Six Day War.[30] The images of triumphant tanks, planes and paratroopers adorned with a blue Star of David were flashed around the world. Suddenly, Israel had the best army in the Middle East. And with time and effort, the Palestinians – held in refugee camps as political pawns while their Arab host countries refused to resettle them – became cast as the innocent, weak and downtrodden.[31]

That's when Palestinians began repeating the "occupation" mantra over and over and over again. Palestinian violence was transformed into a heroic liberation movement, what the *New York Times* called a "Palestinian uprising for independence,"[32] and what Max Rodenbeck of *The Economist* termed "an epic struggle of the weak against the strong."[33] Who wouldn't identify with that noble goal?

The only problem is it's not true. The Palestinian "uprising for independence" was launched long before the Six Day War – before there were any roadblocks, checkpoints or Israeli settlements in the territories. From 1948-1967, when the West Bank was occupied by Jordan, and Gaza by Egypt, Arabs perpetrated literally tens of thousands of cross-border attacks – murdering Israeli bus passengers[34] and opening fire on children in synagogue.[35] During the period of 1951-55 alone, Arabs waged more than 3,000 armed attacks, resulting in the deaths of 922 Israelis and tourists.[36] On January 1, 1965, Palestinians attempted to bomb Israel's National Water Carrier; the date became immortalized as annual "Fatah Day," celebrated until today.[37]

Yet curiously, during the entire pre-1967 era – with the "Israeli occupation" yet nonexistent – there were no calls for an "independent Palestinian state" in the West Bank and Gaza.[38] The focus of Palestinian aspirations – as codified in the original charters of both the PLO[39] and Hamas – was clearly the extermination of Israel. Fatah was founded back in 1954[40] and the PLO in 1964,[41] so what exactly did they seek to liberate?

Even as Hamas was declaring, "We do not distinguish between what was occupied in the 1940s and what was occupied in the 1960s,"[42] the *Washington Post* wrote that Hamas seeks "an independent homeland in at least the West Bank and Gaza Strip – and, Israelis fear, on the territory of the Jewish state."[43] According to the *Post*, Hamas' clearly-stated goal of annihilating Israel is merely something the Israelis "fear."

Associated Press reported with no hint of sarcasm that "Hamas officials won't say whether they see a two-state deal as a final arrangement or a step toward eliminating Israel."[44] In truth, Islamists consider it an immutable religious obligation to eradicate the Zionist presence and create an Islamic Republic in its place. As Palestinian leader Nizar Rayan explained: "True Islam would never allow a Jewish state to survive in the Muslim Middle East. Israel is an impossibility. It is an offense against God."[45]

Reporters have a method of dealing with jihadist extremism: they trot their paintbrushes and perform a whitewash. When Mahmoud Zahar, the Palestinian foreign minister, wrote, "We look forward to live in peace and security... side by side with our neighbors in this sacred part of the world," media outlets immediately jumped on this as proof of a softening stance – posting headlines like "Palestinian Tells UN His People Want Peace" (Associated Press)[46] and "Hamas Official Suggests 'Two-State' Solution" (CNN).[47]

When somebody actually bothered to ask Zahar for a clarification of his words, however, he explained: "I dream of hanging a huge map of the world on the wall at my Gaza home which does not show Israel on it... I'm certain of this [happening] because there is no place for the state of Israel on this land."[48] In other words, Zahar's dream of living "side by side with our neighbors" was an oblique reference to his *Arab* neighbors.

Even when giving an accurate description of Hamas' genocidal goals, the media will throw in some backhanded dig at Israel. The *New York Times* wrote of "Hamas, the militant Palestinian group *regarded by Israel* as a terrorist organization"[49] – elegantly avoiding mentioning that most of the free world (the United States, European Union, Australia, Japan, etc.) likewise incriminates Hamas as a terror organization. As media watchdogs wryly noted, Israel also "regards" the sun hot and the Pope Catholic.[50]

And is it my imagination, or is there something spooky about Associated Press describing Hamas as "committed to destroying the *Jewish entity*."[51]

It all starts right there at the American Colony Hotel, where the bookshop prominently displays *The Founding Myths of Modern Israel*, Roger Garaudy's tome which combines Holocaust denial with calls for Israel's destruction.[52] And it's where nine separate Palestinian groups – count 'em:

nine – work day and night to provide foreign journalists with carefully selected translators, field trips and interview subjects. All with the goal of revising Mideast history, vilifying Israel, and creating sympathy for the Palestinian victim.

So never mind the facts. You can fool all the people all the time… if the spin is right and the budget big enough.[53]

Feed the Beast

One of the biggest challenges faced by correspondents is the need to keep things fresh and interesting day after day. That's where the David and Goliath storyline fits so beautifully – a simple, ongoing narrative, with clearly defined good guys and bad guys. That's how Hollywood screenwriters work, and to some extent that's how news departments work, too. As media analyst Eric Burns observed, news executives "like the idea of creating continuing characters – as in a soap opera – because [they] feel it might be easier for the audience to understand than if they did different stories all the time."[54]

Of course, the Mideast conflict is not a soap opera that can be scripted in a vacuum. Journalists need to work within the basic milieu of characters, and from there it's all however you spin it. That explains why Yasser Arafat, quarterback of the Palestinian team, was such a media favorite all those years – described variously as "triumphant," a "hero," an "icon," a "revolutionary romantic figure"; who embodied the qualities of "charisma," "style" and "extraordinary courage"; whose life was a glorious "odyssey," "the stuff of legends."[55]

For the sake of plot and narrative, the media was willing to confer Hall of Fame mystique on even the Godfather of Terror.[56]

Toward the end of his life, the adulation reached absurd proportions. When a sickly Yasser Arafat was airlifted from Ramallah to a Paris hospital, BBC correspondent Barbara Plett was so personally affected that openly wept in identification with the terror chieftain:

When the helicopter carrying the frail old man rose above his ruined compound, I started to cry... Palestinians admired his refusal to flee under fire. They told me: "Our leader is sharing our pain, we are all under the same siege." And so was I.[57]

Rather than rebuking Plett's striking lack of objectivity, BBC defended her as meeting BBC's "high standards" of "fairness, accuracy and balance."[58] As if competing in some Palestinian marketing contest, the London *Guardian* broke new ground with a bizarre front-page article idolizing Arafat as "cuddly" and "erotic... The stubble on his cheeks was silky not prickly. It smelt of Johnson's Baby Powder."[59]

The same glowing terms were trotted out for Sheikh Ahmed Yassin, the Hamas co-founder who directly ordered dozens of suicide bombings against Israeli civilians. Knight Ridder – at the time the second-largest newspaper publisher in the U.S. with 32 dailies – gushed that "the elderly, partially blind quadriplegic was the beloved leader of a popular movement,"[60] while the *Los Angeles Times* fawned over Yassin's "passion for glory of martyrdom" and – in a true perversion of reality – praised his "moral authority."[61]

Mideast correspondents seemed to be operating in some kind of alternate universe, a phenomenon I encountered first-hand during my years as a reporter. A journalist can get into a groove, creating characters and storylines, and become so immersed that before long, he starts to believe his own narrative is true. He begins living that reality, viewing events through the lens he has crafted. This impacts how he presents facts, context and chronology.

And the process self-generates: The greater a journalist's passion and commitment to the narrative, the more excitement it imparts to readers. This feedback fuels the journalist's ego – as well as the publisher's profits – and raises the bar of how far everyone is willing to go to devise or distort the story.

It's a blurring of Hollywood and reality. Much of it is subtle, but pro-Palestinian bias is a constant undercurrent. In an article about Hamas terrorist Nasser Jarrar, the *Washington Post* played all the sympathy cards with the headline, "Disabled Militant's Defiant Last Battle: Legless, 1-Armed Palestinian Dies Shooting," glorifying Jarrar as some type of folk hero with a "resilient career." Only in the final paragraph did the article inform readers why Jarrar lost both his legs and an arm: The bomb he was making in order to kill Israelis exploded on him instead. Despite these "work accident" injuries, he continued to organize and direct terror activities – recruiting suicide bombers and planning a major attack to destroy a multi-story building in Israel.[62] But any reader who didn't make it to the last paragraph came away with an image of Jarrar as a glorious hero.[63]

When Israel knocked off Nizar Rayan – the radical Hamas leader who directed the 2004 Ashdod Port attack which killed 10 people,[64] advocated for suicide bombings against Israel (sending his 22-year-old son on such a mission in 2001),[65] and called the Jews a "cursed people" whom Allah changed into "apes and pigs"[66] – the London *Guardian* eulogized him as "highly regarded as an Islamic academic... considered a hero."[67] In the *Guardian's* warped view, today's heroes are not sports stars, firefighters or Nobel Prize winners – but Palestinian terrorists.

This scripting method is tremendously alluring. With cable and the Internet having shrunk the news cycle to 24/7, there is constant pressure to "feed the beast." The *Columbia Journalism Review* calls this "Hamsterization": running on the hamster wheel in a news panic, cranking out volumes of content.[68] And so, these "reality TV" characters become the journalist's lifeline. Is the bias conscious and calculated? Sometimes yes, and sometimes no. But whatever the case, as long as readers are happy, then editors are happy, advertisers are happy, publishers are happy – and the whole machine chugs merrily along.

Cycle of Violence

"Palestinian victimhood" is a nice theory, but promoting this narrative becomes tricky when Palestinian terror gets thrown into the mix. No matter how oppressed people may be, or how noble their goal, the deliberate targeting of innocent civilians does not resonate well with the civilized world. Such attacks are illegal under the Fourth Geneva Convention, and even the United Nations – that bastion of pro-Palestinian support – concurs "there is nothing in the fact of occupation that justifies the targeting and killing of civilians."[69] In other words, it is difficult to hold the moral high ground when you're blowing up women and children at shopping malls. The ends simply do not justify the means.

So with hundreds of Palestinian suicide bombings on record (and thousands more attempts), how does the media manage to uphold the perception of Palestinian victimhood?

With one pithy phrase: "cycle of violence."

In this way, a Palestinian blowing up a commuter bus and an Israeli trying to stop him become morally equivalent acts. Neither side is to blame for this "cycle of violence"; neither more or less justified.[70] And with this delightful turn of phrase, the raw evil of Palestinian terror is cleansed away.

Here's an example of how the media applies this amoral idiom: When two separate incidents occurred on the same day – a Palestinian terrorist sprayed machine-gun fire on shoppers in downtown Jerusalem, and Israeli soldiers killed Hamas terrorists operating a bomb factory in the West Bank – Associated Press summed up the events with this headline: "Israel Kills 4, Palestinian Wounds 8."[71] With no moral distinction, both the Israeli shoppers and the Palestinian bomb-makers get thrown together into one big pot of tit-for-tat violence.

Or how about this Reuters' headline: "Two Israelis and Two Palestinians Killed in West Bank." Sounds fair and balanced, right? Those who bothered to read the article discovered that a group of Israelis on a recreational hike had been ambushed and shot by Palestinians – and only then did the Israelis fire back, killing two of the Palestinian attackers.[72] To equate an act of self-defense with premeditated murder is not "media objectivity," but moral idiocy akin to equating a surgeon and a knife-wielding mugger because both "cut with edged weapons."[73] But in Reuterville, the scoreboard was an even 2-2.

Then there was the time a Palestinian terrorist tried to ram a car full of explosives into a crowded Tel Aviv nightclub. Fortunately, a quick-thinking

Israeli security guard was able to prevent the attack by firing at the car. Would anyone in their right mind call this "tit-for-tat violence"?

Reuters did.[74]

A genuine "tit-for-tat" would mean this exploding car was payback for the time that Israelis smashed an exploding car into a nightclub filled with Palestinian civilians. Of course, nothing of the sort has ever happened. But no matter how heinous the crime, the media refuses to hold Palestinians accountable. Indeed, Stephen Jukes, Reuters' global head of news, said it straight out: "We're trying to treat everyone on a level playing field, however tragic it's been and however awful and cataclysmic…"[75]

So when a Palestinian terrorist broke into the home of an Israeli family enjoying a holiday meal – murdering two people, including a 7-month-old baby – Reuters described the subsequent killing of the terrorist as another case of "tit-for-tat bloodshed."[76]

And when five members of the Fogel family were murdered by Palestinians – including three small children whose throats were slit – the *Los Angeles Times* had the gall to question: "Which is worse – stabbing children to death or building new houses in West Bank settlements?" *The Times* concludes that it is "impossible to say," and that the brutal murders are merely "part of a continuing cycle of violence,"[77] "the self-destructive tit-for-tat mentality."[78]

Meanwhile, as pundits debated whether to call Palestinian attacks "suicide bombing" or "homicide bombing," Associated Press reporter Ibrahim Barzak found an inventive way to level the playing field: "An Islamic Jihad revenge bombing Wednesday killed five Israelis."[79] That's right, "revenge bombing." This turns the tables and justifies the blowing up of innocent women and children in response to some generic "Israeli injustice" – as if Israelis casually shopping at a market are deserving of a gruesome death sentence.

When I complained, AP stopped its use of this misleading term. But leave it to Reuters to pick up the slack and begin referring to Palestinian mortar attacks as "revenge rockets."[80] And when a Palestinian bus bombing in Jerusalem killed 11 people including four children, BBC correspondent

Orla Guerin (described by one columnist as "doing the work of Goebbels without bothering to wear the brown uniform")[81] tried to justify the act as "revenge for Palestinians killed by Israel, including children."[82]

So there you have it: Israel responds to Palestinian violence, Palestinians respond to Israeli aggression, and round and round the cycle goes... two peoples locked in a dog fight, neither side right or wrong – but both leaving behind a pile of body bags. In the words of the *LA Times:* "You can argue forever about who is right and who is wrong. Or how far back to go to determine who started the hostilities... Those are questions for philosophers to wrestle with."[83]

This circular model, however, clearly belies the reality on the ground. The Mideast conflict is not between two morally equivalent forces, and there's a simple way to prove it: If you took away all the weapons from the Arabs, the violence would stop. If you took away all of Israel's weapons, Israel would almost certainly cease to exist.

That sounds less like a "cycle" and more like a one-sided annihilationist barrage.

Crucial Chronology

In its drive to downplay Palestinian violence, the media repeatedly obscures the chronology of events. When Hezbollah terrorists fired mortars across the Lebanese border onto northern Israel, killing a 16-year-old Israeli, the IDF responded by targeting Hezbollah launching pads in southern Lebanon. So which action made the headlines?

"Israeli Warplanes Blast Hezbollah Areas" – Associated Press[84]
"Israel Bombs Hizballah in Lebanon" – MSNBC.com[85]
"Israeli Warplanes Raid South Lebanon" – Reuters[86]

Although Israel was responding to a deadly cross-border provocation, these headlines – with sole focus on the Israeli action – subtly reinforced the narrative of "Israeli aggression." Given that these two events were inextricably linked, having occurred hours apart, and news outlets issued one report to cover both, a more balanced headline might have looked something like this:

> Israeli Boy Killed in Hezbollah Shelling;
> Israel Responds by Attacking Targets in Lebanon

Lo and behold, this exact headline *did* appear – but you'd have seen it only if you were among the few who read that morning's Casper, Wyoming *Star-Tribune*.[87]

This obscuring of chronology has become an epidemic, with the media getting caught up in the back-and-forth action and forgetting who was attacking whom. Yet whenever I complained to bureau chiefs in Jerusalem or to editors stateside, they simply dismissed me with the assertion that I had no way to prove who was initiating the violence. In classic form, the *Los Angeles Times* asserted it is "completely impossible to say with any authority who began the hostilities or to distinguish actions from reactions."[88]

Maybe I couldn't prove it. But expert statisticians could.

Two economics professors, M. Daniele Paserman and David A. Jaeger, analyzed all the incidents of Palestinian-Israeli violence over a 52-month period. They applied complex formulas like "level of time aggregation," "impulse response function," "vector moving average," and numerous other statistical tools.

After crunching the numbers, these professors reported in the scholarly *American Economic Review* that while Israelis "react in a predictable and statistically significant way to attacks against them," Palestinian violence shows no correlation to prior Israeli actions. In fact, the authors note, the precise opposite appears to be true: The effectiveness of Palestinian terror attacks "in disrupting day-to-day Israeli life is greater if they are, to some extent, unpredictable." The authors conclude that "despite the popular perception that Palestinians and Israelis are engaged in 'tit-for-tat' violence, there is no evidence to support that notion."[89]

In other words, the so-called "cycle of violence" – what the London

Economist called "cause and effect merged into a seamless continuum"⁹⁰ – simply does not exist.

Moral Equivalence

A corollary of the cycle of violence narrative is the idea of "moral equivalence," the theory that – in the name of "fairness" – both sides must be, by definition, equally perpetrators and victims of the violence.

One Associated Press report noted that "extremists on both the Israeli and Palestinian sides pose a significant threat." On one side, AP referred to Palestinian groups responsible for deadly attacks against Israelis, including the point-blank murder of a pregnant mother and her four young daughters. On the other side, AP identified "Jewish extremists" who might "make good on threats to stage provocative demonstrations."⁹¹ So let's get this straight: Jewish extremists *might* engage in demonstrations, while Palestinian extremists *actually* murder innocent people. In the eyes of Associated Press reporter Mohammed Daraghmeh (who happens to moonlight for the official Palestinian Authority daily, *Al-Ayyam*), these two actions are morally equivalent.⁹²

In the search for moral equivalence, *Time* magazine's Tim McGirk came up with this invention: "Palestinians speak of pushing the Israelis into the sea. Israelis speak of driving the Arabs into the desert sands."⁹³ While it is true that Arab leaders have long vowed to destroy Israel and "push the Jews into the sea,"⁹⁴ the Israeli promise to "drive the Arabs into the desert sands" is but a fabrication of McGirk's overactive imagination.⁹⁵

It's as if Israel's victimization simply cannot be the story. A *Washington Post* article, "In Middle East, Heaviest Toll Exacted on Civilians," purported to discuss hardships on both sides, yet dedicated 1,202 words to the plight of Palestinians, versus just 19 words to that of Israelis.⁹⁶

One especially grotesque application of "moral equivalence" arose when a Palestinian teenage girl, Ayat al-Akhras, blew herself up at a Jerusalem supermarket – killing Rachel Levy, an Israeli teenage girl. The *New York Times* drew a parallel of "two high school seniors in jeans with flowing black hair,"⁹⁷ adding wistfully that "the two looked as if they could have been sisters."[98] *Newsweek's* cover story on the bombing depicted side-by-side photos of the girls with the headline, "How Two Lives Met in Death." No positioning of one as murderer and the other as victim. Just a poetic image of destiny and fate, these two young lives with "almost-twin faces," brought together in a blaze of fire, both equal "victims of the madness of martyrdom."[99]

Imagine if *Newsweek* would have run a story on September 12, 2001, exploring the commonalities of Mohammed Atta, the 33-year-old suicide bomber who crashed a Boeing 767 into the World Trade Center, with a 33-year-old bond trader at Cantor Fitzgerald. They'd have been excoriated for media malpractice.

Absent from these media accounts was any discussion of how this young Palestinian woman had been raised, educated and eventually recruited to become a suicide bomber. On what diet of hate literature was she schooled? Who trained and funded her suicide squad operation? What kind of society makes a murderer out of a future mother?[100]

This false equivalence took another nasty turn when a Hamas terrorist placed a bomb in the Hebrew University cafeteria and murdered nine students, including 24-year old Marla Bennett of San Diego, in Jerusalem to pursue her Masters' degree. Bennett's hometown paper, the *San Diego Union-Tribune*, came up with a creative parallel – equating Bennett's victimhood with the death of Rachel Corrie, a 23-year-old from Washington State who was killed while trying to protect weapons-smuggling tunnels in Gaza. The *Union-Tribune* published a lengthy profile of the deceased young women, two "college students who... collected food for the needy" and ventured to the Mideast because they "believed in their struggle."[101]

Comparable deaths? Conspicuously absent from the *Union-Tribune* article was the fact that Corrie's time in Gaza was spent wielding automatic weapons and training Palestinian children in the art of burning American flags.[102] The *Union-Tribune* described Corrie's sponsoring organization, the International Solidarity Movement (ISM), as a "pro-Palestinian activist group" that is part of the "peace movement" – ignoring their open support of Palestinian terror groups similar to the one that murdered

Marla Bennett.[103]

Granted, good journalism requires seeking out all aspects of an issue. But blindly giving equal weight to all sides is what prompted Churchill to declare: I refuse to be impartial between the fire brigade and the fire.[104]

Over-Reporting of Israel

Back in the 1980s, a friend of mine had a young Chinese artist staying at his house. This was a very bright fellow who was eager to learn English, so every day he read the entire front page of the *New York Times*. After a while, he began to notice that three particular countries almost always made the headlines: the United States, the Soviet Union and Israel.[105]

Not being familiar with Israel, he asked my friend to point out Israel on a map.

"You see this brown section? That's Egypt. And the green, that's Syria. Now come a little closer. You see this little dot on the map? The one so small that its name is written on the Mediterranean? That's Israel."

"I can't believe it!" he said. "That tiny dot is on the front page every day? How many people live there? 200 million? 500 million?"

"No, about 6 million."

"Six million?" he said in disbelief. "The latest Chinese census shows a population of 1.1 billion, with a statistical error of 60 million. That means there are 10 times as many people lost in China as there are people living in Israel!"

The significance of this over-reporting is that Israel's security efforts are scrutinized under a magnifying glass in a manner that no other nation is forced to confront. Zimbabwe barely gets any news coverage – even though millions are underfed, 25 percent of people aged 15-49 are HIV-positive,[106] and the annual rate of inflation has hit 516 quintillion percent.[107] A search of the prestigious *British Medical Journal* reveals that Palestinian deaths receive hundreds of times more coverage than other major conflicts in Bosnia, Rwanda and Darfur.[108]

In 2002, the Arab-Israeli conflict accounted for 58 percent of all foreign coverage on American nightly news. By contrast, the heavy fighting of

U.S. troops in Afghanistan made up just 4 percent of coverage.[109] Per capita, Israel has the largest foreign press corps in the world – churning out an average of 900 English-language reports every day – in what NBC's Martin Fletcher calls "the most intensively scrutinized story in the world."[110] As one Jerusalem correspondent told me, "My editor wants a story from Israel every day – even on slow news days – whether there's anything to report or not."

This massive coverage gives the impression of Israel as a large physical presence in the Mideast – distorting the reality of a nation smaller than New Hampshire, surrounded by 25 Arab states that, at best, coldly tolerate Israel's existence.[111] Studies confirm a direct correlation between Israel's perceived size and the amount of support it receives. When Israel is portrayed as large on the map, 70 percent identify the Palestinians as the underdog. When Israel is portrayed as small on the map, the opposite effect occurs: 62 percent identify Israel as the underdog.[112]

A more accurate media would zoom back from extreme close-ups and present a picture of the region as a whole, where the Jewish speck along the Mediterranean covers less than one percent the size of Saudi Arabia alone. Yet the media does its best to hide the reality of a tiny Israel. The *Washington Post's* foreign news service has never described Israel as "tiny"[113] – yet applied the "tiny" diminutive to countries such as Azerbaijan,[114] Jordan and Eritrea[115] – each encompassing an area more than *four times* the size of Israel.[116] Apparently putting Israel's size into perspective would compromise the paradigm of the Israeli aggressor, and nothing, it seems, shall stand in the way of The Narrative.

Underdog Ethics

Unquestionably what is driving so much of the media's "underdog bias" is a sense of compassion for the downtrodden. Studies show that people tend to favor disadvantaged groups as a way to rectify perceived inequalities and reaffirm a sense of fairness and justness in the world.[117] One study asked participants to consider a hypothetical sporting event in which one team was "highly favored" to win; 81 percent preferred the underdog.[118]

In global news coverage, "oppressed" Third World peoples are widely portrayed as more virtuous than the wealthier and more powerful Western world. In reality, of course, the weaker side in a conflict is not necessarily the more worthy or moral claimant. In fact, the opposite is often true: Successful countries achieve their status through well-functioning economic institutions, democracy and a respectable legal system. Poor countries, by contrast, are often led by corrupt regimes that pilfer funds rather than invest in their citizens.[119]

In the Mideast conflict this disparity is unmistakable: In just six decades, the State of Israel has built a society with the highest standards of education, health services, communications, trade, transportation and – out of necessity due to hostile neighbors – strategic defense. What began as a subsistence agricultural economy has today transformed into a technological powerhouse. By contrast, the Palestinian Authority has taken billions of international aid dollars and squandered it on an array of guns, bombs and missiles, while lining the pockets of a successive stream of corrupt officials. (Yasser Arafat achieved the ignoble distinction of appearing on the *Forbes* list of wealthiest "Kings, Queens and Despots" – having embezzled hundreds of millions of international aid dollars from Palestinian coffers.)[120]

And so, from an ontological point of view, Jews simply cannot be the underdog. This is owing to the fact that by every conceivable account Jews have magnificently beaten the odds. Never have so few survived so much horrendous wrongdoing. So by definition Jews cannot be the underdog. What the Palestinians have done ever so brilliantly is exploit to their advantage the media's conceptual view of tolerance, which means accepting whatever the underdog says.[121]

That explains why reporters, eager to promote the underdog theory of "Israeli aggressors and Palestinian victims," justify Palestinian violence as having some kind of higher, noble purpose. Sky News reported with a note of admiration that "the tactic of suicide bombing is highly successful, and is perhaps the only tool the Palestinians have to fight the heavily-equipped

Israelis."[122] BBC featured a photo of a child wearing a fake suicide bomb belt, with the caption: "Palestinian children learn at a young age about the struggle for freedom."[123] Yes, the joys of suicide bombing for freedom.

Writing in the *International Herald Tribune*, Jonathan Cook claimed that "nonviolence is unlikely to be effective as a strategy," and that Palestinian violence is the surest way to achieve their aims.[124] In other words, this influential and respected newspaper, owned by the *New York Times* and printed in more than 180 countries worldwide, gives hope to terrorists the world over that the success of their cause will be in direct proportion to the magnitude of their attack.

Indeed, one reason why the Middle East conflict has endured so long is because Palestinian extremists believe they can destroy Israel – while counting on the media to blame Israel for its own demise.[125]

Following a double suicide bombing in Tel Aviv which killed 22 people, BBC News correspondent Orla Guerin insinuated that Israelis were getting their just desserts: "But for the Palestinians it never stops; 50 of them killed by the army each week."[126] When I alerted my email list, Guerin fired back this angry response: "If you persist in making these allegations, I will treat it as harassment (sic). If you attempt to contact me again this bureau will pass you (sic) emails on to the police..."[127]

So much for journalists welcoming an open discussion of the issues.

Selective Omission

In propping up the Palestinian underdog, the challenge for journalists is how to insert the recurring themes of "moral equivalence" and "cycle of violence" without being too obvious. I dusted off my old journalism textbooks and identified some subtle techniques that reporters use.

One method is known as "selective omission," where a reporter chooses certain key facts as a way of emphasizing one point over another. This technique lends itself especially to headlines, which – as the first and often the only item seen by readers – has a disproportionately powerful impact on any news story. (According to web marketing experts, 10 times more people read headlines than read the body copy.)[128]

Imagine a Palestinian rampaging in stolen cars for three hours – smashing into police, soldiers and pedestrians, before finally being killed by security forces. What headline would you give this story? BBC's choice – "Palestinian Driver Shot"[129] – omits the crucial context that the Palestinian driver was the aggressor, leaving readers with the impression that he was shot in cold blood. On another occasion, when a Palestinian driver attempted to run over three Israeli police officers, the *New York Times* posted this shocker of a headline: "Israeli Police Kill Palestinian Motorist in East Jerusalem."[130]

A headline from the Australian Broadcasting Corporation – "Israelis Gun Down Two Palestinians" – clearly tags Israel as the aggressor.[131] Yet as the article went on to clarify, one of the Palestinians had thrown grenades as he tried to storm a border crossing, and the other tried to infiltrate a Jewish village. The headline, however, conveys a sense of Israeli aggression, balancing out all that bad news about Palestinians slaughtering innocent civilians.[132]

In another incident, Agence France Presse posted this headline: "Three More Palestinians Shot Dead in West Bank."[133] What were these Palestinians doing when they were "shot dead?" Quietly smoking a hookah? Enjoying a post-Ramadan feast? No, they were wanted terrorists who opened fire on Israeli troops while hiding in a house filled with bombs. But for AFP readers, it's just "three more Palestinians shot dead."

Do we detect a pattern here?

Even when Palestinians attack other Palestinians, the media suggests Israeli culpability. Consider this headline from BBC: "West Bank Fighting Kills Six Palestinians."[134] Why, pray tell, might BBC have used the passive voice to describe the attacks? Because it was Palestinians who killed six Palestinians in intra-fighting. But readers scanning the headlines were left with a far different impression.

Particularly in online news where users often get their fix by scanning a list of links, it is imperative that headlines be clear and direct, leaving no confusion over "who did what." So given this headline from Associated Press – "Rockets Hit Lebanon Despite Cease-Fire"[135] – readers would presume that Israelis had broken a cease-fire and ratcheted up the "cycle of violence" again. Only those bothering to read the article, however, discovered that the Lebanese terror group Hezbollah had fired 10 Katyusha rockets that accidentally fell short, landing in southern Lebanon – hence, "Rockets Hit Lebanon Despite Cease-Fire."

Similarly, a headline from Australian Broadcast Corp. – "Israel Continues Air Raids Despite New Gaza Truce"[136] – led readers to believe that Israel was violating a truce. As it turns out, Israel wasn't a party to this truce at all. Rival Palestinian factions had struck a cease-fire deal to stop bloody *intra*-Palestinian fighting. So let's get this straight: Palestinians agree to stop attacking each other, while continuing to attack Israel – and Israel gets the blame.[137]

Here's an Associated Press headline so biased it will make your jaw drop:

Arab Man Killed in Stabbing in Northern Israel[138]

The headline clearly indicates that an Arab was stabbed. You have to read the article, however, to find out it was the Arab who did the stabbing, and was then "killed" in order to save the life of the Israeli he was stabbing!

A similar form of selective omission is to erase the word "Palestinian" from headlines whenever Palestinians attack Israelis. When readers complained about the *Boston Globe's* frequent use of this technique, *Globe* editor Martin Baron offered this excuse: "The word 'Palestinian' is nearly twice as long as the word 'Israel,' which is one very obvious limitation on headline writers." He added that when Israel is attacked, "I doubt that anyone is seriously wondering 'who did such a horrific thing?'"

Putting aside for a moment Baron's spurious contention that readers – long trained to blame Israel for every act of violence – would assume that unidentified Palestinians are responsible, the idea that "the word 'Palestinian' is too long to fit into a headline" was exposed as a lie a few days later when the *Globe* ran this headline:

Two Palestinians are Killed by Israelis in Gaza Bus Attack[139]

When Palestinians were being killed, the *Globe* suddenly found enough space to include that five-syllable word. But the real shocker of this headline is its blatant deception: The "Gaza Bus Attack" was actually an *Israeli* bus attacked by grenade-throwing *Palestinians*, who were then shot by Israeli troops.

It's this kind of double standard that should be outlawed as RWUII: "Reporting While Under the Influence of Ideology."[140]

Killer Bulldozers

Another media technique to diminish Palestinian violence is to use the passive tense or – even worse – to focus on the death of the terrorist himself. Here's an Associated Press headline from the suicide bombing at a Tel Aviv beachfront disco that killed 21 young people:

Explosion Kills Bomber in Tel Aviv[141]

AP makes it sound like the explosion just happened, as if a gas canister was left in a corner and exploded. And although dozens of Israeli casualties had already been reported, the headline's phrase "Kills Bomber" misplaces the focus of sympathy on the terrorist rather than the victims.

Another example: Shalhevet Pass, a 10-month-old Jewish baby, was sitting in her stroller at a playground, when a Palestinian sniper sadistically placed her in the crosshairs of his scope and shot her in the head. Here's how Associated Press headlined this heinous crime:

Jewish Toddler Dies in West Bank[142]

No mention of who perpetrated the murder, and no indication of the gruesome nature of the killing. According to AP, the baby just passively "died" – as if she contracted some disease, or perhaps suffered a playground accident.

When a Jewish teenager was brutally killed by an ax-wielding Palestinian, the New York Times posted this anthropomorphic headline: "Ax Attack Kills Teen in West Bank."[143] Memo to the Times: Axes don't kill people; people do.[144]

In 2008, a Palestinian driving a huge bulldozer-like construction vehicle went on a rampage in Jerusalem – ramming several cars and buses, and killing three civilians before being shot dead. The New York Times' headline, "Construction Vehicle Kills 3 in Israel Attack," again blamed the murders – not on the Palestinian perpetrator, but on an inanimate machine.[145] Someone ought to call customer service at the Caterpillar company and complain about those violent out-of-control construction vehicles.

The International Herald Tribune, a subsidiary of the New York Times aimed at a European audience, watered down the headline even more: "At Least 3 Die as Man Uses Earthmover in Jerusalem Attack." Not a Palestinian; just an unidentified "man." The three victims were not brutally murdered; they just passively "died." And even the term "bulldozer" is replaced by the gentler, innocent-sounding "earthmover."[146]

Any hope that the Times learned from their mistake was laid to rest a few weeks later, when a Palestinian copycat terrorist plowed a huge tractor into traffic on a busy Jerusalem street, injuring 24 people and destroying a bus and five cars. The Times' benign headline once again? "Construction Vehicle Attack in Israel."[147]

And when yet a third Palestinian ran amok with a construction vehicle in Jerusalem – attempting mass murder but succeeding in getting only himself killed – BBC rushed out with a headline that portrayed the terrorist as victim: "Tractor Driver Shot Dead in Jerusalem."[148]

It was yet another bullet in the media arsenal against Israel.

Hidden Captions

This "hide the facts" technique is equally effective in photo captions, where a purposely vague caption can let a provocative photo speak its "thousand words." When a Palestinian suicide bomber blew himself up in northern Israel, police sent a robot to examine the body, suspecting it was strapped with additional explosives. (The bomber was seriously injured, but not dead.) Reuters sent this photo caption around the world: "An Israeli bomb squad robot dragged a wounded Palestinian man on a road in northern Israel yesterday."[149] Reuters hid the basic fact that this "wounded Palestinian" had just blown himself up and was wired for more – leaving readers with the image of cruel Israelis, dragging around another wounded Arab man.

Another Reuters' photo, accompanying the article, "Israel Rejects U.N. Jenin Probe," showed a body being dragged through the street. There was no caption, so readers would naturally assume that the photo depicted Israelis abusing Arabs in Jenin. In reality, however, the "conveniently unidentified" photo was of a Palestinian who had been lynched by fellow Palestinians in Hebron.[150]

Or how about the photo from BBC that showed two Palestinians, hands tied behind their backs, and kneeling on the ground. Standing over them is an Israeli soldier with a rifle pointed directly at them. In assigning a caption, a responsible editor in the BBC newsroom would first need to explain who the Arabs are in this photo: Did they just commit an attack against Israeli civilians, or were they innocently buying bread at the local market? And why is the soldier pointing the gun: Is he guarding dangerous prisoners until reinforcements arrive, or perhaps he is about to execute them at point-blank range.

BBC didn't provide any of this crucial context, instead issuing a nondescript caption – "Tension has been high around the Jewish settlements."[151] Readers were thus left with a provocative image of two Palestinians, hands tied behind their backs, kneeling on the ground, and an armed Israeli soldier looming over them. Is it David and Goliath? BBC let the implication stand for itself.[152]

Agence France-Presse (AFP) portrayed an image of Palestinian victimhood with this photo caption: "A Palestinian woman expresses her anger after Israeli Defence Forces detonated an explosive belt they found in her house, destroying the ground and first floor of the building."[153] From the caption, one would not imagine this woman had any personal connection to the explosive belt – it was merely "found in her house," which the Israelis then brutally destroyed. In truth, however, this woman's husband had planned to carry out a suicide bombing, and shrewdly hid the explosive belt hidden under his daughter's crib. After being tipped off, Israeli soldiers rushed to the house, evacuated its inhabitants, and safely detonated the explosives. The blast caused the first story of the house to fall – testimony to the explosive force that was intended to massacre Israeli civilians. Yet the AFP caption omitted this essential context, leaving readers with the image of an "angry" Palestinian woman (angry perhaps at the Israelis for not allowing her husband to detonate the bomb on a bus full of civilians as originally planned).[154]

One spring day, *Globe and Mail* readers in Toronto opened their morning paper to see a large photo (five column inches, above the fold) of an Israeli soldier cruelly aiming his rifle at a Palestinian toddler in a stroller. A closer examination of the photo, however, reveals that it is all a function of clever positioning by Associated Press photographer Nasser Shiyoukhi – and the soldier was not pointing any weapon at the baby. Nor was there any relation between the photo and the story that appeared alongside it, about U.S. efforts to renew Mideast peace talks.[155]

Just in case readers failed to get the message, the *Globe and Mail* published another photo from the same AP photographer, showing an Israeli soldier apparently aiming his weapon at Palestinian schoolgirls. Again, the angle and context were distorted, and again there was no relation between the photo and the accompanying article about a hang-glider that drifted from Israel into Lebanon.[156]

With such an extreme lack of context, getting the truth by reading the news is about as effective as telling the time by watching the second hand of a clock.[157]

Headline Study

Whatever the method – selective omission, employing the passive voice, or lack of context – anti-Israel bias was rampant. But as usual, editors brushed off each of my complaints as an "isolated occurrence." So I decided once again to prove things the only way I knew how – by conducting a broad study, this time of Reuters' headlines.[158] Reuters files stories from over 200 countries in 18 languages, and given that 50 percent of all reporting and 90 percent of the attitude comes from the news agencies, Reuters carries a lot of clout.

Over a one-month period, I examined all Reuters' headlines that described either Palestinian or Israeli military actions,[159] and asked a number of key questions:

1) Is the perpetrator of the act identified either as Palestinian or Israeli?
2) Is the "victim" identified either as Palestinian or Israeli?
3) Is the act reported in active or in passive terms?

The results were astounding.

Regarding the first question – "Was the perpetrator of the act identified?" – Reuters named the Palestinian perpetrator in only 33 percent of the relevant headlines, whereas the Israeli perpetrator was named in 100 percent of the time. Moreover, Israel was always emphasized by appearing as the *first word* in the headline.

The second question – "Is the victim of the act identified?" – revealed that Palestinian casualties were labeled "Palestinian" or "Hamas" in 50 percent of the relevant headlines. (Considering "militant" as a Palestinian-specific term raised this figure to 71 percent.) By contrast, when the victim was Israeli, casualties were so labeled only 11 percent of the time.

And finally, "Was the act reported in active or in passive terms?" Reuters' headlines described Palestinian violence using "active" terms only 33 percent of the time, whereas Israeli actions used "active" terms in 100 percent of the relevant headlines, often with ferocious overtones such as "Israeli Army Swoops in..."[160] and "Israel Threatens New Raids..."[161]

Here are more examples of Reuters' double standard from this one-month study:

	Headline	Perpetrator Identified?	Victim Identified?	Passive or Active?
Israelis Killing Palestinians	Israeli Troops Shoot Dead Palestinian in W. Bank[162]	Yes	Yes	Active
	Israel Kills Three Militants; Gaza Deal Seen Close[163]	Yes	Yes	Active
	Israeli Tank Kills 3 Militants in Gaza[164]	Yes	Yes	Active
Palestinians Killing Israelis	New West Bank Shooting Mars Truce[165]	No	No	Passive
	Bus Blows Up in Central Jerusalem[166]	No	No	Passive

Reuters' insidiously subtle (or perhaps not-so-subtle) message: Israel is the aggressor and Palestinians are the victims. Given that most newspaper editors – under intense deadline pressure – rely on wire reports without giving second thought to their accuracy, this Reuters' bias has an exponential effect in leveling the playing field, fueling the David and Goliath narrative, and keeping the media's Mideast reality show fresh and exciting. Which is, after all, the bottom line.

The Real Goliath

The next day I checked my email and found a message from my friend in Texas. "You'll never believe what happened," he wrote. "That Monday Night Football game turned out to be one of the biggest comebacks in sports history. After trailing 30-7 in the fourth quarter, the Jets came back to beat Miami in overtime!"[167]

I realized that in a very real way, the media can affect the outcome. When the underdog feels a groundswell of support, he is inspired to hang in there and fight. It's like the sociology experiment where a schoolteacher is given a class of "under-achievers" and is told they're the honors group. By treating them as "winners," they actually become so.

In this way, the media has gone from being mere observers in the broadcast booth to players on the field. The vast over-reporting of Israel, combined with the psychological support given to Palestinian rioters and bombers, actually encourages further acts of violence. Just as an NFL underdog gets pumped up for a nationally-televised game, when the news cameras are rolling, Palestinian attacks will be that much more intense.

Italian photojournalist Ruben Salvadori, who covered Palestinian riots in Jerusalem, likened it to the "observer effect" in physics, according to which a situation cannot be witnessed without changing it to some extent:

> If you point a tiny [pocket] camera toward somebody, what does he do? Most likely he is going to smile or do something. Now extrapolate this with a group of photographers that shows up with helmets, gas masks, at least two big cameras each... You are not going to sit there twiddling your thumbs. We might not throw rocks or shoot tear gas, but this does not mean we are invisible entities that do not alter the scene."[168]

Beyond the realm of psychology, the media sometimes exerts influence in a more direct way. "We know from experience," one Israeli soldier told me, "that when cameramen turn up, something is going to happen." One photojournalist told me of the time he was among a group of photographers in Ramallah, "waiting for some clashes to start." When word got out that the media was in position, a bunch of Palestinian youths (pre-Twitter days) showed up with their slingshots and performed a riot. A BBC reporter immediately went live on the air, saying that the clashes had been going all day, with several casualties.

With 24 hours of news coverage to fill every day, reporters sometimes have to manufacture it themselves. Martin Fletcher of NBC candidly described it like this: "TV needs to simplify things. And anything that can be presented in a simplified manner thrives on TV. So of course, Arabs and Jews, kids and soldiers, stones and guns. These are also David and Goliath... Ultimately maybe it didn't serve the real purpose of telling the whole truth, but it was great TV."[169]

And that's when I realized: Israel was not only fighting a battle against gunmen and bombers. There was another front, a new ethereal force, for tiny Israel to contend with: the mass media machine. By promoting moral equivalence and the cycle of violence, the media was hampering Israel's ability to defend its civilians from a violent and mortal threat.

Ironically, Israel was being thrust back into the role of *David* – this time fighting against the *Media Goliath*.

It was then that I stepped up my commitment to stopping the real Goliath in his tracks. For I knew that if left unmonitored, the media would repeat the myth – again and again – of an angry, club-wielding Israeli policeman, brutally beating yet another "Palestinian victim."

Notes

1. In the ensuing months, shootings on the 443 resulted in a number of Israeli fatalities; see Margot Dudkevitch, "Israeli Driver Killed in Ambush Near Givat Ze'ev," *Jerusalem Post*, December 22, 2000; Margot Dudkevitch, "Couple Shot Dead in Ambush, Children Lightly Hurt," *Jerusalem Post*, August 26, 2001; "Two Murdered in Terror Attacks," *Jerusalem Post*, January 16, 2002.
2. 1-Samuel, chapters 16-18.
3. www.underdogbracket.com.
4. George Stephanopoulos, "President Obama One-on-One," *Newsmakers*, ABC News and Yahoo.com, October 3, 2011.
5. Phil Mushnick, "NBC Sells Buffalo Fans False Bill of Goods," *New York Post*, November 18, 2007.
6. Bernard Goldberg, *Bias: A CBS Insider Exposes How the Media Distort the News*, Regnery Publishing, 2001.
7. Testimony before Congressional subcommittee, 1963; cited in Alexander Kendrick, *Prime Time: The Life of Edward R. Murrow*, Little, Brown and Company, 1969, p. 466.
8. Ellie McGrath, "A Fraud in the Pulitzers," *Time*, April 27, 1981.
9. William A. Henry III, "Where NBC Went Wrong," *Time*, February 22, 1993. The tip-off was that the film showed smoke coming out of the fuel tank prior to impact. Fifteen years earlier, ABC's *20/20* pulled the same stunt with a story about "exploding Fords."
10. Ernie Kovacs, cited in Asa Briggs and Peter Burke, *A Social History of the Media*, Polity, 2005,

p. 197.
11. Dan Barry, et al, "Times Reporter Who Resigned Leaves Long Trail of Deception," *New York Times*, May 11, 2003.
12. "USA Today Takes the Plunge: Paper to Pay Bonuses to Writers Based on Page Views," Thebiglead.com, April 7, 2011.
13. Blurring the lines between journalism and public relations, the Reuters news feed delivered to Yahoo! Finance (the world's most popular investing website) now includes complete, unedited press releases from Thomson Reuters' commercial interests mixed in with Reuters news articles. The press release headlines are virtually indistinguishable from the newswire's editorial content. (Dominic Jones, "Reuters Distributes Press Releases in Editorial Feed," *IR Web Report*, December 29, 2010.)
14. Gene Weingarten, "How 'Branding' is Ruining Journalism," *Washington Post*, June 24, 2011.
15. Jennifer Ludden, "Violence in Jerusalem Continues Between Palestinians and Israelis Over the Temple Mount," *Weekend Edition Sunday*, National Public Radio, October 1, 2000.
16. Hilary Andersson, "Why are So Many Palestinian Children Being Killed?", *BBC Newsnight*, BBC News, 2001.
17. Hanan Ashrawi, speaking at World Conference Against Racism, Racial Discrimination, Xenophobia and Related Intolerances, Durban, South Africa, August 28, 2001.
18. Diaa Hadid, "On Facebook: Israeli Soldier Posed with Bound Arab," Associated Press, August 16, 2010.
19. See, for example, David Williams, "Smiling for the Camera, Israeli Soldier Poses with Blindfolded Palestinians...", *Daily Mail* (UK), August 18, 2010; Jason Koutsoukis, "Facebook Photos Innocent, Says Israeli Soldier," *Sydney Morning Herald* (Australia), August 18, 2010. Se also Karl Vick, "Out of Israel, an Embarrassing Facebook Post," *Time*, August 19, 2010.
20. Nidal al-Mughrabi, "Two West Bank Deportees in Limbo in Gaza Strip," Reuters, September 5, 2002.
21. See "Dishonest Reporting 'Award' for 2002," HonestReporting.com, December 30, 2002.
22. Timothy Heritage, "Sharon Seeks Putin's Help Deflecting Road Map Vote: Visits Russia," Reuters / *National Post* (Canada), November 3, 2003.
23. Sheera Frenkel, "In Israel, No Welcome Mat for African Migrants," National Public Radio, December 30, 2010.
24. In 1977, an Israeli cargo ship near Japan spotted a leaking boat crammed with 66 Vietnamese men, women and children, fleeing their war-ravaged country following the end of the Vietnam War. The Israeli ship picked up the refugees, who were out of food and water, and brought them to Israel where Prime Minister Menachem Begin authorized their permanent residency. (Tom Tugend, "Vietnamese 'Boat People' Become Israeli," Jewish Telegraphic Agency, October 3, 2006.)
25. Stephen Kinzer, "Israel Accepts 84 of Bosnia's Muslim Refugees," *New York Times*, February 18, 1993.
26. "How to Defame Israel – NPR Edition," *Elder of Ziyon* blog, December 30, 2010.
27. Azzam Pasha, Arab League Secretary, speaking on Cairo radio; cited in Benny Morris, *Righteous Victims*, Alfred A. Knopf, 1999, p. 219.
28. Invading Arab armies boasted 270 tanks, 150 field guns and 300 aircraft; see A.J. Barker, *The Arab Israeli Wars*, Hippocrene Books, 1981. Initially, the Jewish forces had no heavy machine guns, artillery, armored vehicles, anti-tank or anti-aircraft weapons, nor military aircraft or tanks. (See Efraim Karsh, *The Arab-Israeli Conflict: The Palestine War 1948*, Osprey Publishing, 2002, p. 25; Benny Morris, *1948*, Yale University Press, 2008, p. 16.)
29. Joshua and the Israelites conquered Canaan circa 1270 BCE; Mohammed founded Islam 19 centuries later in 610 CE.
30. As former Israeli Foreign Minister Abba Eban observed: "[We first] had the advantages of

the underdog. Now we have the disadvantages of the overdog."
31. In the words of Ralph Galloway, former director of U.N. aid to the Palestinians: "The Arab states do not want to solve the refugee problem. They want to keep it as an open sore, as a weapon against Israel. Arab leaders do not give a damn whether Arab refugees live or die." (Cited in Maurice Roumani, *The Case of the Jews from Arab Countries: A Neglected Issue*, World Organization of Jews from Arab Countries, 1983.)
32. Joel Greenberg, "10 Die as Violence Surges on Palestinian 'Day of Rage,'" *New York Times*, December 9, 2000.
33. Max Rodenbeck, "Broadcasting the War," *New York Times*, April 17, 2002.
34. On March 17, 1954, Arab terrorists ambushed a bus traveling from Eilat to Tel Aviv, killing 11. See "Massacre at Scorpion's Pass," *Time*, March 29, 1954.
35. Homer Bigart, "Arab Guerrillas Raid Israel Again, Kill 4 at Prayer," *New York Times*, April 12, 1956.
36. Herb Keinon, "Foreign Ministry Arms Israelis Traveling Abroad with Terror Statistics," *Jerusalem Post*, March 27, 2002.
37. Joel Greenberg, "Founding of Fatah Is Celebrated in a Militant Mood," *New York Times*, January 2, 2001.
38. The text of the 1964 PLO Covenant states that the Palestinian movement "does not exercise any regional sovereignty" over the West Bank and Gaza Strip. The Palestinian movement first seriously considered the option of statehood at the Palestine National Council summit in Algiers in 1988.
39. Resolutions of the Palestine National Council, July 1-17, 1968; Steven Erlanger, "Hamas Leader Sees No Change Toward Israelis," *New York Times*, January 29, 2006.
40. Said K. Aburish, *Arafat: From Defender to Dictator*, Bloomsbury, 1999.
41. "Statement of Proclamation of the Organization," Palestine Liberation Organization, Jerusalem, May 28, 1964. Egyptian dictator Gamal Abdel Nasser envisioned the PLO as a "tame" alternative to Fatah.
42. Sheik Nizar Rayan, Al Jazeera, September 16, 2005; translation by Middle East Media Research Institute.
43. Lee Hockstader, "Palestinians Find Heroes in Hamas," *Washington Post*, August 10, 2001.
44. "Hamas PM: We're Ready for Referendum on Peace Deal," Associated Press, December 1, 2010.
45. Jeffrey Goldberg, "Nizar Rayyan of Hamas on God's Hatred of Jews," *The Atlantic*, January 2, 2009.
46. Edith M. Lederer, "Palestinian Tells UN His People Want Peace," Associated Press, April 5, 2006.
47. "Hamas Official Suggests 'Two-State' Solution," CNN.com, April 5, 2006.
48. "Hamas Leader Urges Int'l Community to Respect Palestinian People's Choice," Xinhua News Agency (China), April 2, 2006.
49. Ethan Bronner, "Netanyahu Announces Deal to Free Shalit," *New York Times*, October 11, 2011. Emphasis added.
50. Avi Shafran, "Pray for the Gazan Boy," Am Echad Resources, January 1, 2009.
51. Ali Daraghmeh, "Hamas to Participate in Palestinian Parliamentary Elections," Associated Press, March 12, 2005. Emphasis added.
52. Jonathan Spyer, "In the Heart of Israel, Jew Hatred is on Full Display," *Pajamas Media*, July 5, 2011.
53. Paraphrase of Joseph E. Levine (1905-1987).
54. Eric Burns, Fox News, 2004; cited in Stephanie Gutmann, *The Other War*, Encounter Books, 2005.
55. BBC, *Guardian*, et al, cited in Tom Gross, "Arafat Gets the Di Treatment," *National Review*

Online, November 11, 2004. See also Mohammed Daraghmeh, "Fatah Convention Draws Palestinian Exiles," Associated Press, August 2, 2009.
56. Five years after Arafat's death, BBC was still hanging onto the illusion that "he abandoned armed struggle in the 1990s." ("Palestinians Mark Arafat's Death," BBC News Online, November 11, 2009.)
57. Barbara Plett, "Yasser Arafat's Unrelenting Journey," BBC News Online, October 30, 2004.
58. Jason Deans, "BBC's Arafat Report Sparks Protests," *The Guardian* (UK), November 5, 2004. BBC's Board of Governors later ruled that Plett "did breach the requirements of due impartiality," and BBC's director of news, Helen Boaden said that Plett "unintentionally gave the impression of over-identifying with Yasser Arafat and his cause." ("Arafat Report 'Broke BBC Rules'," BBC News Online, November 25, 2005; Tara Conlan, "BBC Governors Overturn Ruling on Arafat Report," *The Guardian* [UK], November 25, 2005.)
59. David Cornwell, "He Pressed My Hand to His Breast. The Palestinian Heart is Here!", *The Guardian* (UK), November 12, 2004.
60. Soraya Sarhaddi Nelson, "Hamas Leader Yassin Revered by Palestinians," Knight Ridder, March 23, 2004; published in the *Miami Herald, Pittsburgh Post-Gazette, Milwaukee Journal Sentinel, Akron Beacon Journal,* et al.
61. Laura King, "Hamas Leader Slain; Yassin Instilled Passion for Glory of 'Martyrdom,'" *Los Angeles Times*, March 22, 2004.
62. Molly Moore, "Disabled Militant's Defiant Last Battle; Legless, 1-Armed Palestinian Dies Shooting," *Washington Post*, August 15, 2002.
63. See "Dishonest Reporting 'Award' for 2002," HonestReporting.com, December 30, 2002.
64. "Profile: Nizar Rayyan," Aljazeera.net/english, January 3, 2009.
65. "Obituary: Nizar Rayyan," BBC News Online, January 1, 2009.
66. Jeffrey Goldberg, "Nizar Rayyan of Hamas on God's Hatred of Jews," *The Atlantic*, January 2, 2009.
67. Trevor Mostyn, "Obituary: Nizar Rayan," *The Guardian* (UK), January 3, 2009.
68. Dean Starkman, "The Hamster Wheel," *Columbia Journalism Review*, September/October 2010. Demand Media, the world's leading hamster-powered content farm, employs 20,000 freelancers, uses algorithms to figure out what to write – and has surpassed the *New York Times* in traffic.
69. Cited in Lee Feinstein, "The UN Panel Report and Conditional Sovereignty," *American Society of International Law Newsletter*, January-February 2005.
70. See former HonestReporting editor Michael Weinstein, cited in Barbara Matusow, "Caught in the Crossfire," *American Journalism Review*, June/July 2004.
71. "Israel Kills 4, Palestinian Wounds 8," Associated Press, January 22, 2002.
72. "Two Israelis and Two Palestinians Killed in West Bank," Reuters, December 28, 2007.
73. Bruce Thornton, "The Distorted View of Israel," *Private Papers*, February 6, 2005.
74. The Reuters' report by Matt Spetalnick was published by news outlets worldwide as "Suicide Bomber Killed in Tel Aviv," *Globe and Mail* (Canada), May 23, 2002, "Guard Foils Suicide Car Blast," *Courier Mail* (Australia), May 25, 2002, et al.
75. Howard Kurtz, "Peter Jennings, in the News for What He Didn't Say," *Washington Post*, September 24, 2001.
76. Atef Sa'ad, "Palestinians Mark Anniversary with Vow to Fight On," Reuters, September 29, 2003.
77. Editorial, "A Fatal Israeli-Palestinian Flaw," *Los Angeles Times*, March 14, 2011.
78. "LA Times Defends 'Tit-for-Tat Mentality,'" *Snapshots* blog, March 27, 2011.
79. Ibrahim Barzak, "Israeli Aircraft, Artillery Bombard Northern Gaza," Associated Press, October 29, 2005. See also Ibrahim Barzak, "Slain Hamas Leader Had Pushed for Cease-Fire, But Israel Says He Still Plotted Attacks," Associated Press, August 21, 2003; Dan

Perry, "Israelis Rebuff Palestinian Offer of Comprehensive Cease-Fire," Associated Press, September 17, 2003.
80. "Revenge Rocket Kills Israeli Woman," Reuters, November 15, 2006.
81. Barbara Amiel, "Truth About Israeli Casualties is Being Ignored in this War," *Daily Telegraph* (UK), April 15, 2002.
82. Orla Guerin, *10 O'clock News*, BBC1, November 21, 2002.
83. "Israel-Palestine: Tit-for-tat?", *Los Angeles Times*, March 24, 2011.
84. Peter Enav, "Israeli Warplanes Blast Hezbollah Areas," Associated Press, August 10, 2003.
85. "Israel Bombs Hizballah in Lebanon," MSNBC.com, August 10, 2003.
86. "Israeli Warplanes Raid South Lebanon," Reuters, August 10, 2003.
87. The headline was rewritten for an article by Gavin Rabinowitz of Associated Press, August 11, 2003. See "Shlomi Shelling," HonestReporting.com, August 11, 2003.
88. Editorial, "A Fatal Israeli-Palestinian Flaw," *Los Angeles Times*, March 14, 2011.
89. M. Daniele Paserman and David A. Jaeger, "The Cycle of Violence? An Empirical Analysis of Fatalities in the Palestinian-Israeli Conflict," *American Economic Review*, Vol. 98 Issue 4, September 2008.
90. "The Bloody Conundrum of Gaza," *The Economist*, March 6, 2008.
91. Mohammed Daraghmeh, "Palestinian and Israeli Extremists Pose Threat to Truce," Associated Press, March 18, 2004.
92. "One of These Things is Not Like the Other," *Little Green Footballs*, March 19, 2005.
93. Tim McGirk, "Israel at 60: The Long View," *Time*, May 19, 2008.
94. See, for example, Hafez Assad of Syria, May 24, 1966: "We shall never call for nor accept peace. We shall only accept war. We have resolved to drench this land with your [Israel's] blood, to oust you as aggressor, to throw you into the sea."
95. "Time Magazine's McGirk Invents False Balance in Palestinian-Israeli Conflict," *Snapshots* blog, May 12, 2008.
96. Molly Moore, "In Middle East, Heaviest Toll Exacted on Civilians," *Washington Post*, October 19, 2002. The *Post's* ombudsman later wrote that he found it "hard to understand" why the newspaper ignored the thousands of Israelis killed and injured by Palestinian terrorists. (Michael Getler, "Plugging the Holes," *Washington Post*, July 6, 2003.)
97. Joel Greenberg, "2 Girls, Divided by War, Joined in Carnage," *New York Times*, April 5, 2002.
98. Elizabeth Jensen, "Grieving Mothers on 2 Sides of a Suicide Bombing," *New York Times*, October 24, 2007.
99. Joshua Hammer, "How Two Lives Met in Death," *Newsweek*, April 15, 2002.
100. Bret Stephens, "Eye on the Media: Depending on Your Point of View," *Jerusalem Post*, April 14, 2002.
101. Sandi Dolbee, "Worlds Apart: the Fate of Two Young American Women," *San Diego Union-Tribune*, July 20, 2003. The *Union-Tribune* compounded its imprudence with insensitive timing – publishing the article to coincide with the one-year memorial service for Marla Bennett. See "Tactless in San Diego," HonestReporting.com, July 21, 2003.
102. Photo by Khalil Hamra, Associated Press; see "Teaching the Children," *Little Green Footballs*, March 16, 2003. Corrie later received the dubious honor of having a street named for her in Tehran, the first time an Iranian street was named for an American since the 1979 Islamic Revolution. ("Iran Names Street After U.S. Activist Rachel Corrie," Associated Press, August 11, 2011.)
103. In the words of ISM founders Adam Shapiro and Huwaida Arraf: "The Palestinian resistance must take on a variety of characteristics, both nonviolent and violent... No other successful nonviolent movement was able to achieve what it did without a concurrent violent movement..." (Adam Shapiro and Huwaida Arraf, "Why Nonviolent Resistance is Important for the Palestinian Intifada: A Response to Ramzy Baroud," *Palestine Chronicle*,

January 29, 2002.)
104. House of Commons, July 7, 1927.
105. A comprehensive study of foreign news coverage in the American media from 1950-2006 found that Russia (USSR) and Israel were covered most consistently. See Timothy M. Jones, Peter Van Aelst and Rens Vliegenthart, "Foreign Nation Visibility in U.S. News Coverage: A Longitudinal Analysis (1950-2006)," *Communication Research*, July 19, 2011.
106. Alex Whiting, "Crisis Profile: Zimbabwe's Humanitarian Situation," Reuters AlertNet, July 26, 2005.
107. At this rate, prices double every 1.3 days. (Sebastien Berger, "Zimbabwe Hyperinflation 'Will Set World Record Within Six Weeks,'" *Daily Telegraph* [UK], November 13, 2008.) In 2009, Zimbabwe introduced a 100 trillion dollar banknote. (Paul Lewis, "Zimbabwe Unveils 100 Trillion Dollar Banknote," *The Guardian* [UK], January 16, 2009.)
108. Search entered into PubMed, the medical version of Google that includes over 18 million citations from life science journals. See "BMJ's Bad Medicine," HonestReporting.com, March 3, 2009.
109. "The Not-So-New Television News Landscape: The Face of Evening News," Pew Research Center's Project for Excellence in Journalism, May 23, 2002.
110. Andrew Gold, "NBC Exposed," *Near East Report*, August 5, 1991. A study of Associated Press showed that the coverage-to-population ratio of Israel far outweighed anywhere else in the world, with the occasional exception of Iraq. (Ethan Zuckerman, "Global Attention Profiles," Berkman Center for Internet and Technology, Harvard University.)
111. Roxanne Roberts, "The Tense Vigil of the Israeli Ambassador," *Washington Post*, January 18, 1991; "Skewed News? 25 Years of CNN's Israel Coverage," *Jewish News Weekly of Northern California*, June 24, 2005.
112. Joseph A. Vandello, Nadav P. Goldschmied, and David A. R. Richards, "The Appeal of the Underdog," *Personality and Social Psychology Bulletin*, December 2007. See also David Horovitz, "The Word According to Frank," *Jerusalem Post*, July 16, 2010.
113. "'Tiny Eritrea,' Un-Tiny Israel, *Snapshots* blog, November 6, 2007.
114. "U.S. Turns to Other Routes to Supply Afghan War as Relations with Pakistan Fray," *Washington Post*, July 3, 2001.
115. "Ethiopia, Eritrea on Verge of Border War, Report Says," *Washington Post*, November 6, 2007.
116. Sophie Linshitz, "Washington Post versus 'Tiny' Israel. Again," *Snapshots* blog, July 12, 2011. Azerbaijan encompasses 33,436 square miles; Jordan is 35,637; Eritrea is 45,405. By contrast, Israel is 8,019 square miles.
117. Joseph A. Vandello, Nadav P. Goldschmied, and David A. R. Richards, "The Appeal of the Underdog," *Personality and Social Psychology Bulletin*, December 2007.
118. J.A. Frazier and E.E. Snyder, "The Underdog Concept in Sport," *Sociology of Sport Journal*, 1991.
119. Bradley Ruffle, "Five Bogus Criticisms of Israel," Onejerusalem.org, January 22, 2009.
120. "The World's Billionaires: Kings, Queens & Despots," *Forbes*, March 17, 2003. The International Monetary Fund (IMF) claimed that Arafat had $900 million in an undisclosed bank account, and Rawya Shawa of the Palestinian Legislative Council pegged Arafat's wealth at a staggering $4 billion. (Cited in Yaacov Bash, "Palestinian Corruption and Poverty," Aish.com, November 23, 2003.) Arafat maintained secret investments in a Ramallah-based Coca Cola plant, a Tunisian cell phone company, and venture capital funds in the Cayman Islands. Meanwhile, his wife Suha – living lavishly in Paris – received an annual allowance in excess of one million dollars. (Leslie Stahl, "Arafat's Billions," *60 Minutes*, CBS News, November 9, 2003.)
121. Laurence Thomas, "The Middle East Conflict and the Left's Conception of Tolerance," Scholars for Peace in the Middle East, January 7, 2009.

122. July 2002. Following complaints, SkyNews agreed that the report was "badly phrased and ill-judged."
123. "In Pictures: Shooting Paradise Now," BBC News Online, November 18, 2005. Later amended.
124. Jonathan Cook, "Nonviolent Protest Offers Little Hope for Palestinians," *International Herald Tribune*, August 31, 2004.
125. Thomas, "The Middle East Conflict and the Left's Conception of Tolerance."
126. Cited in "Tel Aviv Fallout," HonestReporting.com, January 8, 2003.
127. See "Time's Photo Flop," HonestReporting.com, January 9, 2003.
128. Gary Witt, "What to Say After You've Got Their Attention," Marketingpsychology.com, 1999.
129. "Palestinian Driver Shot," BBC News Online, January 28, 2002. After reader complaints, BBC changed the headline to "Hit-and-Run Palestinian Shot Dead."
130. Isabel Kirshner, "Israeli Police Kill Palestinian Motorist in East Jerusalem," *New York Times*, April 7, 2009. Later amended.
131. "Israelis Gun Down Two Palestinians," ABC News Online (Australia), February 22, 2003.
132. See "AP's Snow Job," HonestReporting.com, February 27, 2003.
133. "Three More Palestinians Shot Dead in West Bank," Agence France Presse, February 23, 2006.
134. "West Bank Fighting Kills Six Palestinians," BBC News Online, May 31, 2009.
135. Steven R. Hurst, "Rockets Hit Lebanon Despite Cease-Fire," Associated Press, August 15, 2006.
136. "Israel Continues Air Raids Despite New Gaza Truce," Australian Broadcast Corp. / Agence France-Presse, May 20, 2007.
137. James Taranto, "Best of the Web Today," *Wall Street Journal Online*, May 21, 2007.
138. "Arab Man Killed in Stabbing in Northern Israel," Associated Press, February 6, 2003.
139. "Two Palestinians are Killed by Israelis in Gaza Bus Attack," *Boston Globe*, January 14, 2003.
140. Richard Landes, "Reutersgate 2.0: Honor-Shame vs. Liberal MSNM," *Augean Stables*, June 7, 2010.
141. Dan Perry, "Explosion Kills Bomber in Tel Aviv," Associated Press, June 1, 2001.
142. "Jewish Toddler Dies in West Bank," Associated Press, March 26, 2001.
143. Myra Noveck and Alan Cowell, "Ax Attack Kills Teen in West Bank," *New York Times*, April 2, 2009.
144. "NY Times and the Anthropomorphic Ax," Mediabackspin.com, April 2, 2009.
145. Isabel Kershner, "Construction Vehicle Kills 3 in Israel Attack," *New York Times*, July 2, 2008. Following complaints, the *Times* amended the headline to, "Palestinian Kills 3 with Construction Vehicle."
146. Ricki Hollander, "Terrorist Attack in Jerusalem: Bias in Euro Headlines," Committee for Accuracy in Middle East Reporting in America, July 2, 2008.
147. Isabel Kershner, "Construction Vehicle Attack in Israel," *New York Times*, July 23, 2008.
148. "Tractor Driver Shot Dead in Jerusalem," BBC News Online, March 5, 2009.
149. Reuters, May 9, 2002; see Christine Chinlund, "Mideast News Touchy for Both Sides," *Boston Globe*, May 27, 2002.
150. James Taranto, "Best of the Web Today," *Wall Street Journal Online*, April 24, 2002.
151. "Israel Accused Over Commando Deaths," BBC News Online, November 27, 2000. Later amended.
152. In another article, exploring internal Israeli politics, BBC threw in a completely unrelated photo of an Israeli soldier alongside a Palestinian in handcuffs, with this loaded caption: "The situation in the West Bank and Gaza will not be solved by this." (Martin Asser, "Analysis: Sharon Government's Collapse," BBC News Online, November 5, 2002.)

Following complaints, the caption was later changed to the equally inane, "Can elections solve the situation in the West Bank and Gaza?"
153. Photo by Atta Hussein, Agence France-Presse, November 1, 2003.
154. "How Palestinians 'Think,'" *Powerline* blog, November 1, 2003.
155. Mike Fegelman, "Globe and Mail Must Apologize," HonestReporting Canada, March 6, 2008.
156. Ibid.
157. Paraphrase of Ben Hecht.
158. "Study: Reuters Headlines," HonestReporting.com, July 14, 2003.
159. Over the 30-day trial period, six Reuters' articles described militaristic acts by Palestinians against Israelis; 12 articles described acts by the Israeli army against Palestinians.
160. "Israeli Army Swoops in Nablus After Security Talks," Reuters, June 23, 2003.
161. "Israel Threatens New Raids After Anti-Hamas Strike," Reuters, June 22, 2003.
162. "Israeli Troops Shoot Dead Palestinian in W. Bank," Reuters, July 3, 2003.
163. Nidal al-Mughrabi, "Israel Kills Three Militants; Gaza Deal Seen Close," Reuters, June 27, 2003.
164. "Israeli Tank Kills 3 Militants in Gaza," Reuters, June 22, 2003.
165. "New West Bank Shooting Mars Truce," Reuters, July 1, 2003.
166. "Bus Blows Up in Central Jerusalem," Reuters, June 11, 2003.
167. Judy Battista, "Another Jets Comeback Is Just Like Another Day at the Office," *New York Times*, October 25, 2000.
168. Ruben Salvadori, "Photojournalism Behind the Scenes," September 2011; Simon Plosker, "Exposed: Photographer Reveals Market, Not Truth, Behind Conflict Images," HonestReporting.com, October 10, 2011.
169. Cited in William J. Drummond, "From Hasbara to Intifada," *The Big Story*, University of California, Berkeley, Graduate School of Journalism, June 1, 2002.

— 3 —

ONE MAN'S TERRORIST

Let's start with a little quiz. Which of the following is an act of terror?

1) blowing up 21 people outside a discotheque in Tel Aviv[1]
2) stoning to death two teenagers hiking near their home south of Jerusalem[2]
3) machine-gunning guests at a Bat Mitzvah celebration in northern Israel[3]

Answer: none of the above.

Amazingly, if you'd been getting your news from MSNBC, Associated Press, the *New York Times* or most other mainstream media, none of these ghastly acts were labeled as "terror." Instead, journalists were digging deep into the thesaurus to describe the perpetrators as Palestinian "militants" or "activists" – but not "terrorists."

Isn't the term "militant" more appropriate for those who aggressively work in support of a cause, within the bounds of law, humanity and civil disobedience – such as militant reformers, militant feminists and militant animal rights advocates?

But bombing commuter buses and blowing up kids in pizza shops? If that's not the know-it-when-I-see-it definition of "terrorism," then what is?

I put the question straight to Richard Carleton of *60 Minutes* in Australia.

His response: "It's really not possible to define 'terrorism.'"

"That would be true," I said, "except for the widely accepted United Nations definition of terrorism as 'a violent attack against civilians.'[4] Or in the legalese of the U.S. State Department – Title 22 of the U.S. Code, Section 2656f-d, if you want to look it up – terrorism is 'premeditated, politically motivated violence perpetrated against noncombatant targets.'"

"We don't have to follow definitions set by the Americans or any other government," Carleton replied. "We have our own rules of style."

Okay, maybe. But how about Merriam-Webster. Is that good enough?

> **ter·ror** (noun): Violent or destructive acts committed by groups in order to intimidate a population or government into granting their demands.

No, not good enough. Carleton's pithy response: "It's all subjective. You know, one man's terrorist is another man's freedom fighter."

Again I tried logic: "A freedom fighter would only attack military and government institutions, while a terrorist attacks innocent civilians. Isn't the difference clear?"

"Not really," he said. "Suicide bombing is the only means the Palestinians have to defend themselves. They're only doing this because they want freedom."

He'd given me the old "freedom" fall-back line, one of the media's biggest "leveling" tricks to preserve the semblance of a Palestinian moral high ground. Where did Carleton get this idea? Probably from his colleagues at ABC Australia, whose official style guide says in black and white: "Remember, one person's 'terrorist' is usually someone else's 'freedom fighter.'"[5]

I made one last attempt: "A freedom fighter supports the cause of freedom – both mine and yours. But a terrorist wants to wipe out the other side completely. Hamas, Islamic Jihad and Hezbollah proclaim from their mosques, rooftops and websites a desire to kill every Jewish man, woman and child. By any rational standard, they're terrorists."

But Carleton refused to budge. So I took care of things the democratic way: I launched an online petition, calling on the media to label Palestinian suicide bombers as "terrorists."[6] If it was "consumer eyeballs" that would get the media's attention, then I was ready to play that game. And apparently there were enough disgruntled consumers who felt the same way. Within a few weeks, the petition had collected 100,000 signatures.

It was a classic case of consumer activism. No yelling, no threats. Just voting with the click of a mouse.

MSNBC's Moran

Bringing this issue to the fore unleashed an intense philosophical battle, and soon journalists were rushing to defend their non-use of the term "Palestinian terror." MSNBC reporter Michael Moran wrote a blog post about my petition campaign, which – as evidenced by the sarcastic title, "The Terrorism Thing" – was a cavalier look at a very serious topic. Moran laid out his thesis like this:

> MSNBC.com does use the word "terrorist" to describe someone who has been convicted of a terrorist act, or someone who has admitted the act, or been caught in the act.[7]

Follow Moran's words carefully: MSNBC will use the word "terrorist" only to describe someone who was *convicted* of a terrorist act, *admitted* to the act, or was *caught* in the act. According to this definition, no suicide bomber could ever be called a terrorist: Since the bomber's goal is mass murder, there are often no surviving witnesses to have "caught him in the act." And since the bomber commits suicide, by definition he never has a chance to "admit" involvement or be "convicted." Must Israel conduct posthumous trials (Is there such a thing?) of suicide bombers before

MSNBC will concede these are "terrorists"?

I knew Moran was not making sense, but I always try to give people the benefit of the doubt. So at the time he made this claim, I ran a test using MSNBC.com's own search engine to find out how many times the word "terrorist" had been applied to Palestinian suicide bombers.

The number of occurrences? A big fat zero.

The good news, however, is that Moran's post was linked on the MSNBC.com homepage, producing thousands of new signatures for my petition campaign.

Moran must have sensed he was losing the argument, because he slipped into a desperate name-calling attack to discredit the critic. He said that I was "aimed at muzzling free speech" and accused me of having "urged subscribers to vent their collective spleen by pelting the accused with angry e-mails demanding that we fall into line, or else."

Well, calling for journalistic accountability can hardly be equated with muzzling free speech. And last time I checked, the majority of my email subscribers had non-vented spleens.

Did you ever get into an argument where the other guy was just setting up a smokescreen? In such a case, it's best to give him just enough rope to hang himself. So I wasn't surprised to see Moran's policy contradicted from within his own ranks, by MSNBC ombudsman Dan Fischer:

> Suicide bombings at night clubs, pizza parlors, or wedding celebrations are "terrorist" attacks in my book. So is the ambush of a civilian bus, nationalist-inspired kidnapping and murder, or the placement of a bomb in a schoolyard. I think it's inherently inconsistent to refer... [in such cases] to "militants killing civilians."[8]

Things were shaking up at MSNBC. But the problem was widespread and the media was twisting itself into a pretzel to find some way – any way – to avoid the, ahem, T-word. In reporting on a Palestinian missile attack, the *Washington Post* wrote that "gunmen fired three rockets at the Israeli town of Sderot."[9] Gunmen? A rocket is hardly a gun, but if the *Post* can't bring itself to call them terrorists, then what's left? Perhaps "militants" is becoming hackneyed. How about "rocketeers"?[10]

Then there's the headline from Agence France Presse referring to a "Palestinian Rocket Militant"[11] – leaving readers to wonder if that requires a degree in rocket science.

When Palestinians rioted on the Temple Mount, AP referred to "thousands of Muslim worshippers who hurled stones, bottles and trash."[12] I am familiar with the Islamic custom of throwing stones at the Kaaba in Mecca. But does Associated Press really believe that hurling stones at Israelis in Jerusalem also qualifies as a method of "Muslim worship"?

One rainy day, I decided to play the "media thesaurus game." A perusal of mainstream news outlets turned up dozens of euphemisms for "Palestinian terrorists":[13]

Activists	BBC[14]
Assailants	Associated Press[15]
Assassins	*Washington Post*[16]
Attackers	CNN[17]
Bombers	*Washington Post*[18]
Captors	*Los Angeles Times*[19]
Combatants	*Orlando Sentinel* (Florida)[20]
Commandos	*Philadelphia Inquirer*[21]
Criminals	United Press International[22]
Dissidents	*Orange County Register* (California)[23]
Extremists	Associated Press[24]
Fighters	*New York Times*[25]
Freedom Fighters	*The Guardian* (UK)[26]

Fugitives	*The Sunday Times* (UK)[27]
Guerrillas	*Christian Science Monitor*[28]
Gunmen	*Houston Chronicle*[29]
Hostage-takers	Agence France Presse[30]
Insurgents	*Newsweek*[31]
Kidnappers	CBS News[32]
Martyrs	*USA Today*[33]
Militants	*Time* magazine[34]
Miscreants	*Orlando Sentinel* (Florida)[35]
Nationalists	*Chicago Tribune*[36]
Perpetrators	*Pittsburgh Post-Gazette*[37]
Protesters	Fox News[38]
Radicals	*Newsweek*[39]
Rebels	*Seattle Times*[40]
Resistance Fighters	*San Diego Union-Tribune*[41]
Revolutionaries	*Publishers Weekly*[42]
Ultras	*The New Republic*[43]
Underground	Associated Press[44]
Vigilantes	*Newsday* (New York)[45]
Warriors	*The New Yorker*[46]

These are only the runners-up. The prize for the most mendacious euphemism goes to the *Philadelphia Inquirer* for its report on a Palestinian who burst into the home of a Jewish family and sprayed machine gun fire in all directions – killing the mother and her three children, plus a neighbor who had come to their aid. Under the headline, "Home Invaders Kill

5 Israelis, Hurt 8," the *Inquirer* article opened with the words, "Suspected Palestinian infiltrators..."⁴⁷

Home invaders? Suspected? Infiltrators? Someone who breaks into a house and steals the silverware can be called a "home invader." Someone who enters surreptitiously is an "infiltrator." But someone who unloads his machine gun at point-blank range on a helpless mother and children? What would the *Inquirer* have called those who crashed jet planes into the World Trade Center – "skyscraper invaders"?

Israel was awash in blood, but for the media, "Palestinian terrorists" were like Santa Claus; they simply did not exist.

Every time another Palestinian suicide bomber struck, I thought *for sure* this time the media would be unable to deny the obvious. But no matter how gruesome it got, they still refused to use the T-word:

> *One summer afternoon, Israeli shoppers stopped into Sbarro in downtown Jerusalem for a slice of pizza. They didn't notice the Palestinian man with a guitar case strapped on his back, and they didn't know it contained a large bomb, packed with screws and rat poison to magnify the devastation.*
>
> *The ensuing explosion put 130 people in the hospital. Five members of the Schijveschuurder family – mother, father and three children – were murdered. My friends from Los Angeles saw their only child – pregnant with their only grandchild – murdered. And my friend Arnold Roth buried his 15-year-old daughter Malki the next day, side by side with her best friend.*

In reporting on the horrific attack, major media made no reference to "terror," except when citing direct quotes from Israeli leaders. CNN even claimed that "Israeli and Palestinian officials each blamed the other for the attack" – an obscenely insensitive and warped equivalence.⁴⁸ And London's *Guardian*, while calling the bomber a "militant," actually used the T-word twice – in describing *Israeli* military actions.⁴⁹

These verbal contortions bring to mind the George Orwell quote: "When there is a gap between one's real and one's declared aims, one turns as it were instinctively to long words and exhausted idioms, like a cuttlefish squirting out ink."[50]

In the case of Palestinian terrorists, the cuttlefish was squirting ink all over America's newspapers.

Freedom Fighters

Then, on September 11, 2001, everything changed. Al-Qaeda had carried out the biggest suicide bombing in history. Now it was certain that the media would unambiguously – and correctly – label suicide bombers as "terrorists." For years, the media's policy on the T-word had been crafted vis-à-vis Palestinian attacks, which were exculpated as a supposed reaction to Israeli policies. But now everyone would understand that Israel's struggle against terror was part of the larger battle against radical Islam. The calculated murder of 3,000 innocent civilians was so clearly evil that nobody in their right mind would hesitate to call 9-11 an act of terror.

Nobody, that is, except for Reuters.

Stephen Jukes, Reuters' global head of news, declared in an internal memo:

> We all know that one man's terrorist is another man's freedom fighter, and that Reuters upholds the principle that we do not use the word terrorist... To be frank, it adds little to call the attack on the World Trade Center a terrorist attack.[51]

To be frank, Jukes, it adds little to call what Reuters does "journalism."

Under the guise of objectivity, Reuters was committing an outrageous double-error: Not only refusing to call the mass murder of civilians "terror," but audaciously elevating it to the realm of "freedom."[52]

Let's follow Reuters' theory to its logical conclusion. If one man's terrorist is truly another man's freedom fighter, then how could the media have forfeited their objectivity by calling Adolf Hitler a dictator? After all, one man's dictator is another man's "decisive perennial leader." And what about those rooms filled with sadistic contraptions found all over Iraq after the downfall of Saddam? The media called them "torture chambers," but isn't one man's torture chamber just another man's "re-education room"?

To claim that the terrorists who perpetrated 9-11 were "freedom fighters" is an insult to true freedom fighters throughout history like George Washington, Mahatma Gandhi and Martin Luther King, Jr. Was Reuters really prepared to include Osama bin Laden on this list?

Defenders of Reuters argued that from the perspective of al-Qaeda, American military bases in Saudi Arabia and the expansion of secular Western values constitute legitimate grievances. Mohammed Atta is their Thomas Jefferson. So who are we to judge?

This blinding lack of moral clarity plays right into the terrorists' hands. In 1974, when Yasser Arafat spoke at the U.N. General Assembly with a gun holster strapped to his hip, he compared himself to George Washington and Abraham Lincoln bearing a "freedom fighter's gun."[53] And decades later as the Intifada raged, pro-Palestinian activists bought a full-page ad in the *New York Times*, invoking the U.S. Declaration of Independence in support of their cause, with the proclamation that Palestinian militants act in "pursuit of liberty and independence."[54]

Jeff Jacoby of the *Boston Globe* spelled out the travesty of comparing Muslim terrorists to the American Revolution:

> Thomas Jefferson and his colleagues did not urge Americans to massacre civilians or destroy places of worship. Nor did their children's schools and textbooks promote blind hatred of all Englishmen... or depict Great Britain as a fascist horror that God wanted them to destroy... nor did their maps show a Europe wiped clean of England.[55]

But Reuters would have you believe that 9-11 was just a modern version of the Boston Tea Party.

Poverty and Despair

Why is the media so adamantly opposed to using the word "terror"?

A deep cultural chasm divides Western and Islamist society. The Western mind comes equipped with a certain set of moral furniture: peace on earth, sanctity of life, the protection of children. These values are so essential to our concept of humanity that we cannot fathom any society operating outside that system.

So when a suicide bomber blows up a commuter bus – killing women and children, and taking his own life, too – Western journalists try to make sense of the whole thing by projecting their personal values upon the terrorist. They shake their heads and ask, "What would lead me to take *my own life* in such a way?"[56] And because Westerners tend to think in socio-economic terms, the conclusion is: These must be people who have nothing to live for.[57]

In applying this paradigm, the media tries to excuse these heinous acts by attributing them to the lowest elements of society – oppressed, depressed, impoverished Palestinians with low self-esteem. In the words of Palestinian propagandist Hanan Ashrawi, it's all rooted in the despair born of occupation: "If you push the Palestinians into a corner, if you drive them to desperation, there will be desperate acts."[58]

That's exactly what the media parrots. Writing in the *New York Times*, Pulitzer Prize-winning journalist John F. Burns claimed that suicide recruits are "commonly young men raised in poverty."[59] The *Christian Science Monitor* referred to "the poverty and anger that turn ordinary men and women into militants."[60] After one suicide bombing at a shopping mall in Netanya, Associated Press said that "grinding poverty could breed more such attackers."[61] As if bombarding Gaza with food and cash will solve the problem.

Although the "poverty breeds terrorism" argument might sound logical, it is simply not true. Kolkata, Nairobi and Rio de Janeiro are all teeming with poverty and despair, yet have produced no waves of suicide bombers.

Nor does this argument apply to Palestinian terrorists. The *New York Times* cited a research study of 250 aspiring Palestinian suicide bombers and their recruiters. The findings? "None were uneducated, desperately poor, simple-minded or depressed."[62] None.

Far from being poor and downtrodden, the opposite may in fact be true. Many of these bombers come from the most intelligent, accomplished, idealistic and motivated strata of society.[63] The London-based Arab daily, *Asharq Alawsat*, studied Palestinian suicide bombers and concluded that "economic hardship was not the motive... as the majority of the bombers belonged to relatively affluent families... were pursuing higher education and came from stable families."[64] Another Palestinian-led study rejected the widely-held view of suicide bombers as motivated by personal pain, describing it as an insult to terrorists: "It is wrong to associate Palestinian martyrs with these factors," said Bassam Yousef Banat of Al-Quds University in Jerusalem, "since this underestimates the real value of a martyr."[65]

Zainab Ali Issa Abu Salem, an 18-year-old female suicide bomber who killed two Israelis and wounded 17 more, came from a wealthy family and was a local Palestinian television celebrity.[66] Raed Abdel-Hamed Mesk, who blew up a busload of Jews returning from the Western Wall – killing 20 and injuring 100 – was married, the father of two young children, and studying for his master's degree.[67] As Sheikh Bassam Jarrar, a Palestinian religious leader in Ramallah, confirmed: "The idea is not despair. Most of those who carry out [suicide] operations were university graduates."[68]

This is not solely a Palestinian phenomenon. A study conducted by the United States Military Academy found that most al-Qaeda members had a college education.[69] Mohamed Atta, who crashed a jet into the World Trade Center, was an architecture student. Ahmed Omar Saeed Sheikh, who planned the beheading of Daniel Pearl, studied at the prestigious London School of Economics.[70] The world's most reviled terrorist, Osama bin Laden, came from a billionaire family.[71] Al-Qaeda mastermind Ayman Al-Zawahiri, who appeared at Bin Laden's side in televised messages from the caves of Afghanistan, is an eye surgeon.[72] Umar Farouk Abdulmutallab, the Nigerian who attempted to detonate plastic explosives in his underwear en route to Detroit, is the son of one of the richest men in Africa, and studied engineering at one of Britain's top universities.[73] When car bombs packed with gas cylinders and nails were discovered in London's West End, and a fiery SUV rammed into the main terminal at Glasgow International Airport, all seven Muslim men arrested were physicians.[74] Faisal Shahzad, arrested for the attempted 2010 Times Square car bombing, holds a Masters of Business Administration,[75] and comes from a wealthy, well-educated family which afforded him a cadre of personal servants, chauffeurs and body guards.[76]

No, the common denominator of these terrorists is not poverty or lack of education. Far from being depressed, suicide bombers are the smartest of smart bombs, militant idealists who want to change the world. Their blind hatred stems from aspiration, not desperation.

For the Western mind, committed to the sanctity of life, this demands an enormous paradigm shift. Westerners see suicide bombing as a tragic lose-lose – the bomber dies, and many innocent people die, too. But for Islamists, suicide bombing is a win-win: The infidels are dead, and the bomber achieves an "eternal reward of 80,000 servants and 72 wives."[77]

As Jeffrey Goldberg of *The Atlantic* observed, Americans are hard-pressed to understand how Islamic terrorists think. "It's alien to us. The feverish racism and conspiracy mongering, the obscurantism, the apocalyptic thinking – we can't relate to that. Every so often, there's an eruption of that in a place like Waco, Texas, but we're not talking about 90 people in a compound. We're talking about whole societies that are captive to this kind of absurdity." Goldberg concludes with a warning against denial: "Just because a belief sounds ridiculous to you doesn't mean it's not sincerely held."[78]

Yet the media ignores the reality. Hanadi Tayseer Jaradat, a 29-year-old Palestinian woman who murdered 20 people at a restaurant in Haifa, had recently received her law degree."[79] To ABC's *Nightline* reporter John Yang, however, she could only be a victim. He asked a group of Palestinians: "Was she another victim? Was she a victim, as well as the other people who were in that restaurant?" The interviewees readily picked up Yang's cue, proffering: "I think she is, actually. Every Palestinian considers himself a victim," adding that the Haifa bomber was even "more of a victim" than those she killed.[80]

Continuing the charade, the *Los Angeles Times* wrote of Palestinian suicide bombers: "Their anguish seems palpable – born of some mixture of poverty, hopelessness, fatherlessness and disenfranchisement."[81] And when Sheikh Abdullah Shami of Islamic Jihad said on CNN that the cause of suicide bombing is "despair," CNN correspondent Mike Hanna added his own two cents that "poverty" brought new suicide recruits.[82]

It all goes back to what one pundit calls "underdogma" – a knee-jerk championing of the underdog, and the erroneous belief that the downtrodden have an inherent moral superiority. If Israel has jetfighters and the Palestinians have slingshots, Israel must be the guilty party.[83] That's the Palestinian rhetoric amplified through the media megaphone.

Moral Confusion

The media claims to avoid the term "terrorist" because it has a negative connotation. They're right, it does. But so do other nasty labels. When Seung-Hui Cho gunned down 32 people at Virginia Tech,[84] should the press have avoided that oh-so-charged word, "murderer"? Perhaps a more neutral choice would have been "student activist." And when paraplegic Ray Mason rolled his wheelchair up to a drive-thru window and robbed a Nebraska bank,[85] why label him with the pejorative term "bank robber," especially since that might typecast all handicapped people? Why not simply call him a "mobile expropriator"?

No, only the T-word seems to leave journalists feeling uneasy. In Florida, Manning Pynn of the *Orlando Sentinel* explained that he avoids the term "terrorist" because it imputes the motive "of trying to instill fear."[86]

"Foolish me," wrote editor Philip Gailey of the *St. Petersburg Times* in a rebuttal. "I thought instilling fear is exactly what Hamas and Islamic Jihad mean to do when they send their suicide bombers into markets, restaurants and buses to kill and terrorize Israeli civilians."[87]

Why is the media so militantly opposed to the T-word? Here's how Reuters' news chief Stephen Jukes explained it: "We're there to tell the story. We're not there to evaluate the moral case."[88] So when Iraqi terrorists drove a carload of children into a crowded Baghdad market and detonated it with the children still inside (the children had lowered the suspicion of guards at a nearby checkpoint), Reuters called it a "militant" attack by "insurgents" – but nowhere did the word "terrorist" appear.[89]

Jukes claims that by using the word "terrorist," journalists are making a moral judgment, which would be incompatible with the rules of journalistic objectivity. But is it really? Although suicide bombing fits the *objective* definition of terror, Reuters doesn't want to sound judgmental. So they pick another word, like militant. The problem is that "militant" is not neutral, either. It has its own objective definition: someone working aggressively in support of a cause. So substituting "militant" for "terrorist" is in itself making a judgment – presenting suicide bombings of buses and skyscrapers as legitimate, legal and perhaps even moral.

If readers open their morning paper to find that a "militant union" of unhappy mechanics went on strike at Northwest Airlines,[90] and that Hamas "militants" blew up 20 Israelis at a shopping mall, the net effect is to melt away the revulsion that Westerners would otherwise feel for Palestinian terror attacks. So while Reuters may aspire to impartiality, by using inaccurate words, they actually *sacrifice* objectivity – the very thing they claim to be trying to avoid. In other words, Reuters also appears to be taking sides. The terrorists' side.

Despite the media's strong aversion to the T-word, correspondents in Israel occasionally did turn on the Acme T-Word Generator and flash the word "terror" – but only when Jews were doing it. When suicide bombers killed 26 Israeli civilians in Jerusalem and Haifa, the word "terror" was – incredibly – used by BBC only to describe Israel's retaliatory attacks: "Terror overhead in Gaza today and panic below... Israel is pounding Gaza for a second day."[91]

When an Israeli admitted to having killed two Arabs a decade ago, even the T-word-allergic Reuters trotted out "terror" in the headline, the article's lead sentence, and the bulleted summary points.[92] Granted, an Israeli attacking civilians is reprehensible and fits the definition of terror. But for a news outlet refusing to acknowledge "Palestinian terror," this is a blatant double standard.

Ironically, Palestinians themselves occasionally show more clarity than the Western media. Writing in the Egyptian weekly *Al-Ahram*, the late Columbia professor and Palestinian spokesman Edward Said declared: "[I]t is this calamitous policy of killing Israeli civilians, which further proves to the world that we are indeed terrorists and an immoral movement."[93] Even Yasser Arafat had his moment in a *New York Times* op-ed, labeling Palestinians who attack Israeli civilians as "terrorists."[94]

As media outlets refused to print the T-word, many good journalists concluded that their own policies promoted biased reporting. James Bennet, the *New York Times'* Jerusalem bureau chief during the Intifada, wrote in an internal memo that he avoided the word terrorism "so that readers could decide their own labels" – but then later concluded that never using the word "felt so morally neutral as to be a little sickening."[95] Bennet observed:

> The calculated bombing of students in a university cafeteria, or of families gathered in an ice cream parlor, cries out to be called what it is. I wanted to avoid the political meaning that comes with "terrorism," but I couldn't pretend that the word had no usage at all in plain English… *[And] not to use the term began to seem like a political act in itself.*[96]

Faced with this predicament, journalists turned to a new way of minimizing Arab terror – by describing Israeli victims as "bystanders." Associated Press noted that "357 bystanders have been killed" by Palestinian suicide bombings;[97] Florida's *Sun-Sentinel* reported that a Palestinian suicide bomber had killed a "security guard and two bystanders;"[98] and the *New York Times* wrote that "a barrage of four Palestinian attacks killed nine bystanders."[99] In common usage, a "bystander" is peripheral to the central event – e.g. a bystander injured in a bank robbery. By describing Israeli terror victims as "bystanders," the media obscures the basic fact that Israeli civilians are the *intentional* target of these bombers.

From here it was a short – but predictable – step to the media equating Palestinian terror attacks that *intentionally* kill "bystanders" with Israeli strikes that *collaterally* kill "bystanders."[100]

Then there's Michael Slackman of the *New York Times* who claimed to have finally figured out the key to lasting peace in the Middle East: Stop saying the T-word. Slackman argued that the Arab world sees "little distinction between Hamas's shooting rockets into civilian areas of Israel, and Israel's shooting rockets into civilian areas of Gaza." He then quoted one Arab as saying that if the United States thinks that Hamas and Hezbollah "are terrorists, there will never be peace."[101]

The *Times'* warped argument boils down to this: In order to achieve peace with people who randomly fire missiles into a civilian population, it is necessary for us to assume the ultimate relativist position – that murderers exist on the same moral plane as their victims.[102]

If we erased the dreaded T-word from our lexicon, does anyone believe that Hamas and Hezbollah would stop firing their (morally relative) missiles? Hamas didn't start firing rockets into Israel because some columnist called it a terrorist organization.[103] Yet in the view of the *New York Times*, the Israeli-Arab impasse is based more on a semantic misunderstanding, rather than the concrete fact of jihadists wanting to drive Israel into the sea.

Media Suicide

At a certain point, with journalists hiding behind that singular value of "neutrality," one has to wonder if they perhaps identify with the attackers. When Robert Fisk, the London *Independent's* Mideast correspondent for 30 years, was beaten to a pulp by Taliban supporters in Afghanistan, he wrote: "I couldn't blame them for what they were doing. I would have done just the same to Robert Fisk. Or any other Westerner I could find."[104]

This warped affinity for terrorists was quite revealing. So when Reuters came out with its flawed policy of refusing to call 9-11 "terror," I suspected that something deeper must be driving it. I phoned a Reuters correspondent and invited him to dinner. As we sat in a restaurant eating shwarma, I asked him point-blank: "What's the deal with not calling 9-11 'terror'?"

"At Reuters," he said, "the single highest ideal is neutrality. We cannot impose any semblance of moral judgment."

"I appreciate your commitment to moral neutrality," I said. "But tell me something: Who do you think al-Qaeda is targeting? Who are they out to destroy?"

"Well," he said, "al-Qaeda is mainly fighting against Western values: freedom of expression, gender equality, freedom of religion..."

"And freedom of the press!" I exclaimed. "I absolutely agree that journalists need to maintain critically distanced reporting. But there's one value that's not negotiable: democracy. That's the 'macro-value,' the institution that protects all the other values. It's what enables the media to function objectively, and it's what gives us the very freedom to be sitting here now discussing all this."

He got quiet and poured some more tehina sauce on his shwarma, while I stayed on my soap-box.

"Did it ever occur to you that as a journalist, *you* are the target? These terrorists are hijacking our principles in order to destroy us, using the classic judo technique of turning your opponent's strength against him. Don't you realize that by sanitizing this terror, you are actually strengthening the terrorists in their war against... you!"

He deadpanned: "That doesn't bother me. I cannot compromise my journalistic integrity just because there's a war going on."[105]

I shook my head in disbelief, and then offered a little history lesson: "During World War II – when a dictatorial madman set out to conquer the world – every American was part of the cause. Whether you were manufacturing automobile tires or sewing uniforms, every resource was harnessed. Everyone knew that life and liberty was on the line. Even the activities of journalists – who General Eisenhower viewed as de facto staff officers – were integrated into the war effort.[106] Like it or not, we were all under attack. The threat was so clear that no one had to analyze it or philosophize. Our basic freedoms and our very lives were being threatened, and democracy needed to defend itself.

"It's the same thing today. With radical Islam, the entire basis of our free society is being threatened. My freedom, your freedom, everyone's freedom. The problem is that too many journalists do not fathom what losing this war means. They may imagine that losing means hanging our heads, bringing troops home, and going on about our business, like post-Vietnam. Far from it. Radical Islam wants the West neutered and submissive.[107]

"Nobody is expecting you to toss away your objectivity and blindly join the battle. Don't forget, *I'm* the one crusading for media objectivity! But the bottom line is that the media has the power and the position to either make or break this threat. By pussyfooting around, the media unwittingly supports the goals of radical Islam – emasculating the free press and co-opting it into the service of jihad. If the world goes down because you're uncomfortable with calling it terror, you're going down with it."

His response? "I'm fine with that."

Maybe he was just trying to save face in the conversation. But I do know that my arguments got mainstream journalists to think about their role in all this. In a moment of refreshing clarity, Daniel Okrent, Public Editor of the *New York Times*, wrote regarding the T-word that there is "something uncomfortably fearful, and *inevitably self-defeating*, about struggling so hard to avoid it."[108]

Yes, inevitably self-defeating – what one observer calls "being shot with our own arrow."[109]

Curly Chestnut Hair

Lately, America's "most revered" newspapers have begun using their op-ed pages to raise Arab extremism to a new level of respectability. Hamas terrorist Mousa Abu Marzook – indicted in the U.S. as a co-conspirator on racketeering and money-laundering charges,[110] and listed as a "Specially Designated Terrorist" by the U.S. government – was given free space in the *Los Angeles Times* to invoke Western feel-good words like "dignity" and "justice," claiming that Gaza is "calm under the rule of law – a place where all journalists, foreigners and guests of the Palestinian people will be treated with dignity." Given the reality – the Talibanization of Gaza under Hamas[111] – the *Times* should receive an Academy Award for letting Marzook say all that with a straight face.

The *Times* loved Marzook's creative writing so much that a few months later he gave a repeat performance of another 1,200 words.[112] The *New York Times*, too, joined the pack in giving Hamas op-ed space,[113] while the *Washington Post* – never to be outdone – printed three Hamas op-eds within a matter of months.[114]

I'm all for free speech and everything, but these publications are directly aiding a terrorist organization that speaks in two voices – a "moderate" one for the West and its true, extremist voice heard only in the Arab media. Surely the proclamations of terrorists deserve real-time coverage, the same way that Hitler and Stalin received coverage in their day. But by offering Hamas a sagely byline, the media erases the distinction between those bound by the ideals of freedom, and the terrorists eager to destroy them.[115]

Given that these op-eds have real cash value, and the U.S. Supreme Court has barred "peaceful aid" to terror organizations,[116] some have suggested that the *LA Times* and other newspapers have broken U.S. federal law by providing Hamas with a propaganda platform to facilitate their terror agenda.[117]

Even the pro-Palestinian news agency Reuters was shocked that Hamas – "shunned by the U.S. government as a terrorist organization" – was able to score the "unprecedented" "publicity coup" of being featured in America's top newspapers to "express their views unfiltered."[118]

On this slippery slope, the next step is to portray these terrorists as upstanding members of society. When Wafa Idris "made history"[119] as the first Palestinian female suicide bomber, blowing herself up in downtown Jerusalem, the media positioned her as a folk hero – offering details of her love life, education, hobbies and volunteer work. She was hailed as a "charitable" (Agence France Presse),[120] "sweet-natured" woman (Knight Ridder News Service)[121] who "joked with the neighborhood children" (*Philadelphia Inquirer*).[122] The *New York Times* spoke forlornly of Idris' "chestnut hair curling past her shoulders" and romanticized how she "raised doves and adored children."[123]

It is beyond absurd to say that a woman who attempted to murder children in baby carriages and who put 150 innocent people in the hospital "adored children." Yet if it enhances the narrative of the Palestinian David, the *New York Times* considers it fit to print.

How about Aziz Salha, the Palestinian best known for waving his bloody hands out the window of the Ramallah police station during the brutal lynching of two Israeli reservists. The *Washington Post* ran a 1,300-word defense of Salha, sympathizing that "the young man... stuttered, he was shy... he was a calm, good-natured and athletic kid..."[124] In this obscene inversion of reality, the barbarian had become a human interest story.

Can you imagine the outcry if the *Washington Post* had profiled Timothy McVeigh as "the strawberry blond with delicate freckles and a dimple"? (In fact, when a character witness testified at McVeigh's murder trial: "If you don't consider what happened in Oklahoma, Tim was a good person," *Time* magazine called it "absurd" and "morally obtuse.")[125]

Then there's the time a Palestinian bus driver rammed his vehicle into a crowd, killing eight Israelis. The *Los Angeles Times* published a photo on the front page, showing the destroyed bus and the injured Palestinian still slumped in the driver's seat, with this photo caption:[126]

> Palestinian bus driver Khalil abu Olbeh, 35, sits wounded after leading police on a 19-mile chase.

Those nasty Israelis chased him for 19 miles! No word yet about his killing of eight innocent people. The photo caption continues:

> Family members said he was distraught over financial problems

and upset by current unrest.

Look at this poor man: He's sad and injured. He has a family. He's distraught. He's got financial problems. He's upset by the current unrest. And on top of it all, his bus has been ruined! This man isn't a cold-blooded murderer – he's a bona fide victim!

For its part, the *New York Times*, in a review of the HBO film *Hot House*, featured a large, color photograph of a smiling young woman with straight white teeth and smooth, youthful skin beaming beneath a hijab framing her face. The woman is Ahlam Tamimi, sentenced to 320 years in Israeli jail for her role in the gruesome Sbarro Pizzeria bombing that killed 15 Israelis. Yet the *Times'* photo presents her as a glamorous young woman, radiating with contentment and pride.[127]

On page one, the *Washington Post* poetically described Palestinian arch-terrorist Zakaria Zbeida as having eyes "the color of rich toffee,"[128] and – one month later, also on page one – described another Palestinian terrorist as having skin "the color of roasted pecans."[129] What creative and colorful metaphors will the *Post* think up next?

Then there's Katharine Viner of London's *Guardian* – twice named as British Newspaper Magazine Editor of the Year – whose description of Palestinian terrorist Leila Khaled suggested pure adoration:

> ...[T]he gun held in fragile hands, the shiny hair wrapped in a keffiah, the delicate Audrey Hepburn face refusing to meet your eye. But it's the ring, resting delicately on her third finger. To fuse an object of feminine adornment, of frivolity, with a bullet: that is Khaled's story, the reason behind her image's enduring power.[130]

This delicate Audrey Hepburn look-alike hijacked and then blew up TWA Flight 840. This is what passes for objective journalism?

As for Abdel Aziz Rantisi, mastermind of the bloody Hebrew University cafeteria bombing, who also called on Iraqis to carry out suicide bombings against American forces, Associated Press painted him as a "pediatrician and poet" who "wears gold-framed tinted glasses." AP then quoted effusively from Rantisi's love poems: "The mockingbird burst into song..."[131]

Hamas is one of the world's most vicious terror groups, yet the *New York Times* painted a portrait of Hamas fostering love not war: "Hamas leaders have turned to matchmaking, bringing together single fighters and widows, and providing dowries and wedding parties..."[132] How touching. The next *Times* installment could feature al-Qaeda's mixers for Gen-Y terrorists too shy to walk up to a female mujahid and ask if she likes his AK-47.[133]

NBC's Tel Aviv bureau chief Martin Fletcher – under the predictably lame headline, "One Man's Terrorist, Another's Freedom Fighter" – visited the home of 20-year-old Ahmed Sanakreh, best known for murdering Israelis and constructing bomb belts for suicide terrorists. Fletcher adoringly describes Sanakreh as "baby-faced with black hair sticking up in gelled spikes, and a passion for his Nokia 90 cell phone." The report included a photo of the terrorist and his brother, hanging out with Fletcher looking like some starry-eyed school kid meeting up with Lebron James.[134]

And who could forget the 7,700-word paean in the *New York Times* Sunday magazine, showing the warm, fuzzy side of Palestinian terrorist Abed al-Raouf Barbakh, a gunman so violent that even Arafat sought his arrest. The *Times* described Barbakh as "polite," "a kind of youth counselor," who "talked of planning a garden among the weeds." The *Times* then turned its attention to Sayeed Siyam of Hamas, "an elementary school teacher" who "spoke as softly as if he were in a library explaining the Dewey Decimal System."[135] Ignoring for a moment his support of suicide bombings and the total annihilation of Israel, the man almost sounds like the Hamas version of Mr. Rogers.

Actually, the *Times* article *did* describe Siyam as "the Mr. Rogers of Hamas."[136] In the newspaper of record.

Then there's Dion Nissenbaum, Jerusalem bureau chief for McClatchy Newspapers, who paid a visit with Samir Kuntar, the unrepentant Palestinian terrorist who crushed a 4-year-old girl's head with his rifle butt in front of her father before killing him, too. No, it wasn't a fearful, skeptical interview session; it was a laid-back, buddy-buddy visit, with Nissenbaum calling Kuntar "a hero," "humble," "patriotic," and a "symbol of ascendant power."[137]

In case readers didn't get the message, Nissenbaum – the prime source of Mideast news for McClatchy's 32 daily newspapers including the *Miami Herald, Charlotte Observer, Kansas City Star* and *Fort Worth Star-Telegram* – proudly posted a photo of himself cavorting on a couch with the terrorist Kuntar, smiling broadly and waving a cigarette. It's all under the headline, "Kickin' it with Samir Kuntar."

What's next, Dion – heading down to Guantánamo Bay to party with 9-11 architect Khalid Sheikh Mohammed?

Double Standard

While the media was busy glorifying Palestinian suicide bombers, news coverage in the rest of the world was quite different. With al-Qaeda and other Islamic groups setting off deadly bombs in Madrid, London, Bali and Istanbul, major media did not hesitate to call these acts of "terror." Further, as Associated Press[138] and the *New York Times*[139] published comprehensive lists of "Terror Attacks Around the World," these lists inexplicably omitted the dozens of suicide bombings committed by Palestinians.

After complaints about one such compilation in London's *Sun* newspaper, editors offered this upside-down explanation: "We have not included the unforgivable Palestinian terror attacks and suicide bombings in Israel due to their sheer number."[140] In other words, Israel is the world hot-spot of terror, so that's why we ignore it. It's like George Burns would say: You've got to be honest. If you can fake that, you've got it made.

This double standard was confirmed by media monitors in California who analyzed hundreds of articles in the *San Jose Mercury News* over a five-month period. They found that the *Mercury News* regularly applied the term "terror" to acts of violence in countries such as China, Indonesia, Iraq, Russia and Turkey – but in reporting on nine major terrorist attacks in Israel during the five months of the study, the *Mercury News* never used the word "terror" in a headline, and used it only once in a news article.[141]

In other words, the T-word had become as untouchable as an abandoned backpack at an Israeli bus stop.

Major media outlets like CNN were caught employing a similar double standard. When two separate acts of terror occurred in succession on March 4, 2001 – a bombing outside of BBC's offices in London, and a bombing in the Israeli city of Netanya – CNN reported:

> A dissident Irish Republican **terror** group is suspected of planting a bomb that exploded outside the British Broadcasting Corporation's main office.[142]

> In addition, one Israeli was killed Thursday and nine people were wounded when a Palestinian **militant** set off a bomb inside a taxi in northern Israel.[143]

Same date, same CNN, same explosive material, same targeting of civilians on a busy street. Yet the Irish bomber in England was a "terrorist," while the Palestinian bomber in Israel was a "militant." At journalism school, my professors would "invent" articles like this to illustrate what constitutes biased journalism.

When an Iraqi killed five American soldiers by blowing himself up in a taxi, Associated Press called it a "terror attack." Concurrently, when a Palestinian ignited his explosive belt at a café in Netanya, causing 50 Israeli casualties, AP called that attack the work of a "Palestinian militant."[144] Note the counter-intuitive disparity: Although the widely accepted definition of terrorism is "an attack against civilians," Associated Press regarded the attack against an American *military* target more as "terror" than the attack against Israeli *civilians*.

BBC – the largest broadcast organization in the world – has always tried to play both sides of the fence. BBC's editorial guidelines infamously state: "The word 'terrorist' itself can be a barrier rather than an aid to understanding. We should try to avoid the term, without attribution. We should let other people characterise while we report the facts as we know them."[145]

In keeping with that policy, BBC's list of Palestinian bombings against Israelis does not refer to these acts as "terror."[146] Yet BBC violated their guidelines when reporting on the 2005 bombing of London's Underground and a double-decker bus barely half a mile from BBC's central headquarters – posting headlines such as: "Terror of Passengers Stuck on Tube" and "London Rocked by Terror Attacks."[147]

When previously challenged about this inequity, BBC came up with some very creative answers. BBC editor Maya Fish told me that the T-word is used only in reference to bombings within the UK itself, while "in BBC World Service reporting, the word 'terrorist' is not used, no matter who plants bombs, kills or murders."[148]

In other words, it's only terrorism when my ox is being gored.

This biased policy ultimately proved even too much for BBC. After alert readers spotted this double standard, BBC quietly altered their online reports: "Responsible for the terrorist bomb attacks in London" suddenly became "responsible for the bomb attacks in London," and "the worst terrorist atrocity Britain has seen" was replaced by "the worst peacetime bomb attacks Britain has seen."[149]

Media policies regarding the T-word are so convoluted and inconsistent that many journalists are left struggling to produce a rational explanation. When *Philadelphia Inquirer* ombudsman Lillian Swanson was asked why her paper uses the T-word when violence is committed against Americans, but not when directed against Israelis, here was her candid response:

"I can't explain that."[150]

Minnesota Mutations

Which brings us to the Minneapolis *Star Tribune*, a newspaper whose editors vowed to never use the T-word, no matter how monstrous the attack:

In the case of the term "terrorist," other words – "gunman," "separatist" and "rebel," for example – may be more precise and less likely to be viewed as judgmental. We also take extra care to avoid the term "terrorist" in articles about the Israeli-Palestinian conflict because of the emotional and heated nature of that dispute.[151]

The *Star Tribune's* policy lasted only until they were caught breaking their own rules. No, they didn't use "terror" to describe the horrific murder of my friend Chezi Goldberg, a social worker and devoted father of seven children, along with 10 other people on a Jerusalem bus. That, the *Star Tribune* said, was the work of a '"militant group."[152]

So where did the *Star Tribune* find terror? In the same article describing Hezbollah (a U.S.-designated terror organization) as "guerrillas," the *Star Tribune* referred to Israelis involved in "terror organizations."[153] Apparently, all that sophisticated talk about "extra care to avoid the term 'terrorist' in articles about the Israeli-Palestinian conflict" was just a lot of hot air – masking an anti-Israel double standard.

I teamed up with a local group called Minnesotans Against Terrorism[154] and issued a double-barreled protest against the *Star Tribune:* Not only were they refusing to apply the T-word to Palestinian suicide bombings, but they were contradicting their own policy and calling it "terror" only when Jews were involved. Email notices went out, readers complained, and after a wave of negative publicity the *Star Tribune* fessed up to what deputy managing editor Roger Buoen called a "mistake" that "gave readers an unfair and unbalanced description."[155]

That was a step in the right direction, but then another bogus policy was discovered: When printing wire stories which referred to "Palestinian terror," the *Star Tribune* was editing out the T-word – even when it appeared in a quote. This policy of altering quotes was so grossly unethical that – following a heated closed-door meeting with local activists – *Star Tribune* managing editor Pam Fine broke down and promised to "publish the word terrorist when... it appears in wire stories."[156] Media activists could celebrate the fact that America's favorite "terror-free" newspaper was finally taking steps to redress its endemic anti-Israel bias.

It turned out to be a short-lived celebration. The same day that Fine made her promise, the *Star Tribune* cleansed the word "terror" from stories – not once, but *five times*. Phrases such as "the Israelis will not begin political talks until the *terrorism* ceases"[157] were magically transformed into "the Israelis will not begin political talks until the *attacks* cease."[158]

When readers complained, a *Star Tribune* columnist called the protests a "bullying effort."[159] One wonders how the folks who own the ink are bullied.

That's when someone decided that two can play this game. The late Izzy Asper, head of CanWest, the largest newspaper chain in Canada, created a little "what if" scenario: What if we turned the whole thing on its head, and instead of editing the T-word *out* of wire reports, we would actually *insert* the T-word to describe Palestinian attacks.

Asper ran with the idea. And so, when Reuters referred to the al-Aqsa Martyrs Brigades as "involved in a four-year-old revolt against Israeli occupation,"[160] CanWest changed it to "a *terrorist* group that has been involved in a four-year-old campaign" against Israel.[161]

As expected, Reuters went ballistic. David Schlesinger, the global managing editor of Reuters, exclaimed: "If they [CanWest] want to put their own judgment into it, they're free to do that, but then they shouldn't say that it's by a Reuters' reporter."[162]

Something strange was going on. It's one thing if Reuters didn't want to initiate use of the word "terror," but why should Reuters object to their byline appearing on *any* report that uses the word terror? What exactly was Reuters afraid of?

A few months later, Schlesinger spilled the beans and revealed exactly what Reuters was afraid of: He described the "serious consequences" if certain "people in the Mideast" were to believe that Reuters called such men "terrorists."[163]

This was a stunning admission. A top Reuters executive openly confessed that the refusal to call terrorists "terrorists" had nothing to do with standards of objectivity – but was aimed at protecting their own position in the face of intimidation from Arab thugs. Reuters' news chief Stephen Jukes reiterated that certain words are never used when reporting on Palestinian areas because "we don't want to jeopardize the safety of our staff."[164]

In every other arena, journalists pride themselves for bravely "telling it as it is," regardless of hostile reaction. But in this case, Reuters – and presumably other news outlets – are bending over backward to use "safe" language to appease the terrorists. As William Safire said, the T-word "terrifies many fair-minded editors."[165] And that makes the Media Goliath look pretty timid after all.

Notes

1. Inigo Gilmore, "Israeli Mourners Cry Out for Vengeance," *Sunday Telegraph* (UK), June 3, 2001.
2. Yoav Appel, "Two Israeli Teenagers Killed; Palestinian Militants Suspected." Associated Press, May 9, 2001.
3. James Bennet, "Six Israelis Slain by Arab Gunman," *New York Times*, January 18, 2002.
4. United Nations Secretary-General Ban Ki-moon, "Efforts by the Secretary-General to Counter Terrorism," February 16, 2007.
5. Fran Feldman, "'T' is for 'Freedom Fighter' at the ABC," *National Forum*, June 29, 2005.
6. "Petition Drive Calls on News Agencies to Label Palestinian Suicide Bombers as 'Terrorists,'" HonestReporting.com, June 1, 2002.
7. Michael Moran, "The Terrorism Thing," MSNBC.com, June 10, 2002.
8. Dan Fischer, "Ombudsman's Column," MSNBC.com, March 11, 2002.
9. "World in Brief," *Washington Post*, August 3, 2005.
10. "Post Buries Story of Palestinian Terrorists Misfiring Rockets," *Eye on the Post*, August 3, 2005.
11. "Israeli Drone Targets Palestinian Rocket Militant," Agence France Presse, September 28, 2009.
12. Dalia Nammari, "Police, Muslim Worshippers Clash at Disputed Jerusalem Holy Site," Associated Press, February 9, 2007.
13. Based on an idea by Daniel Pipes.
14. "Fatah Commander Escapes Attack," BBC News Online, August 18, 2001.
15. Steve Weizman, "Palestinian Assailant Fatally Stabs Israeli Man," Associated Press, October 23, 2008.
16. Samuel Sockol, "From Prison, Rabin Assassin Cites Influences," *Washington Post*, November 1, 2008.
17. Wolf Blitzer, *The Situation Room*, CNN, July 22, 2008.
18. Craig Whitlock, "Homemade, Cheap and Dangerous; Terror Cells Favor Simple Ingredients in Building Bombs," *Washington Post*, July 5, 2007.
19. "Palestinian Captors Free Photographer," *Los Angeles Times*, October 25, 2006.
20. "Ambush Kills 12 Israelis," *Orlando Sentinel* (Florida), November 16, 2002.
21. Michael Matza, "Both Sides in Mideast Have Their Mental Artillery," *Philadelphia Inquirer*,

June 30, 2006.
22. "Egyptian Hostage Released in Gaza," United Press International, February 11, 2006.
23. Craig Outhier, "Riding the Cycle of Death," *Orange County Register* (California), December 23, 2005.
24. Albert Aji and Bassem Mroue, "Car Bomb Kills 17 in Tightly Controlled Syria," Associated Press, September 27, 2008.
25. Steven Erlanger, "Israeli Forces in Gaza Kill 9 and Destroy Homes," *New York Times*, January 4, 2008.
26. Will Hodgkinson, "The Guide: Television Friday 13: Pick of the Day," *The Guardian* (UK), April 7, 2007.
27. Uzi Mahnaimi, "After Hamas's Bloody Triumph, Show Down with Israel Looms," *The Sunday Times* (UK), June 17, 2007.
28. Nicholas Blanford, "Despite Delays, Prisoner Swap Leaves Hezbollah Emboldened," *Christian Science Monitor*, July 17, 2008.
29. "Around the World," *Houston Chronicle*, April 12, 2008.
30. "Egypt and Cyprus Sign Five Cooperation Deals," Agence France Presse, May 4, 2006.
31. Malcolm Jones, "Their Right Arms," *Newsweek*, June 9, 2008.
32. Charles Osgood, "Kidnapped British Journalist Alan Johnston Released," *The Osgood File*, CBS News, July 5, 2007.
33. Elliot Blair Smith, "Arab Bank Agrees to $24M Fine," *USA Today*, August 18, 2005.
34. Tim McGirk, "Gaza Rocket Rocks Bush's Israel Trip," *Time*, May 14, 2008.
35. "Relentlessly Pursue Peace," *Orlando Sentinel* (Florida), June 4, 1994.
36. Richard Boudreaux, "Israeli Police Shot Dead," *Chicago Tribune*, March 16, 2009.
37. Barry Paris, "The Lessons of Munich," *Pittsburgh Post-Gazette*, December 23, 2005.
38. Rick Leventhal, "Political Headlines," Fox News, October 5, 2002.
39. Christopher Dickey, Kevin Peraino and Babak Dehghanpisheh, "The Hand that Feeds the Fire," *Newsweek*, July 24, 2006.
40. "Around the Globe," *Seattle Times*, January 8, 2007.
41. Jane Clifford, "Religion & Ethics; Weekly Offerings," *San Diego Union-Tribune*, June 14, 2008.
42. "Terror in Black September," *Publishers Weekly*, June 4, 2007.
43. "Crunch Time," *The New Republic*, March 14, 2005.
44. Steven Gutkin, "A Pragmatist Who Opposes Violence, Abbas Can be Expected to Drive Hard Bargains," Associated Press, January 9, 2005.
45. Sonia Verma, "Enemy Lines Blurred for Collaborators," *Newsday* (New York), June 25, 2007.
46. David Denby, "Bulges; the Incredible Hulk and You Don't Mess with the Zohan," *The New Yorker*, June 23, 2008.
47. Mark Lavie, "Home Invaders Kill 5 Israelis, Hurt 8," *Philadelphia Inquirer* / Associated Press, June 21, 2002.
48. "Israel Hits Back after Deadly Bombing," CNN.com, August 10, 2001.
49. Suzanne Goldenberg, "The Street was Covered with Blood and Bodies: the Dead and the Dying," *The Guardian* (UK), August 10, 2001.
50. George Orwell, "Politics and the English Language," 1946.
51. Howard Kurtz, "Media Notes," *Washington Post*, September 24, 2001; Gloria Cooper, "Darts & Laurels," *Columbia Journalism Review*, May-June 2003.
52. The refrain of "one man's terrorist is another man's freedom fighter" was picked up by a number of media outlets, including CNN Senior Editor Octavia Nasr ("Quick Guide & Transcript: Inside al Qaeda," *CNN Student News*, June 14, 2006), and *Boston Globe* ombudsman, Christine Chinlund ("Who Should Wear the 'Terrorist' Label?", *Boston Globe*, September 7, 2003).
53. "Agenda Item 108: Question of Palestine," United Nations General Assembly, 2282nd

Plenary Meeting, November 13, 1974. Decades later, Arafat was still comparing himself to George Washington; see "Bush's Scolding Prompts Plea from Arafat," CBC News (Canada), January 26, 2002.

54. Ad by American-Arab Anti-Discrimination Committee; cited in Jeff Jacoby, "'Peace Process' in Middle East Brings Only War," *Boston Globe*, November 20, 2000.
55. Jacoby, "'Peace Process' in Middle East Brings Only War."
56. When Wafa Idris became the first Palestinian female suicide bomber, Saddam Hussein said he would build a monument to her in one of Baghdad's main squares, saying that her death would cause Western society to wonder, "What kind of injustice has been done to Arabs in general and Palestinians in particular that makes women carry out a suicide operation?" (Uri Dan, "The Angel Paramedic Who Turned Herself into a Suicide Bomber," *New York Post*, January 31, 2002.)
57. Alan Krueger of Princeton University, in Bob Edwards and Christopher Joyce, "Look at the Mind of a Suicide Bomber," *Morning Edition*, National Public Radio, March 7, 2003.
58. Jerrold Kessel and Mike Hanna, "Israel Attacks Palestinian Targets," CNN.com, March 28, 2001.
59. John F. Burns, "The Promise of Paradise that Slays Peace," *New York Times*, April 1, 2001.
60. Michael B. Farrell, "A Look 'Inside Hamas,'" *Christian Science Monitor*, July 2, 2007.
61. Ali Daraghmeh, "Netanya Suicide Bomber Too Poor to Care About Politics, His Family Says," Associated Press, December 5, 2005.
62. Scott Atran, "Who Wants to Be a Martyr?", *New York Times*, May 5, 2003. See also Nasra Hassan, "An Arsenal of Believers; Talking to the 'Human Bombs,'" *The New Yorker*, November 19, 2001.
63. Fareed Zakaria, "Report: Poverty Does Not Breed Extremism," CNN.com, June 7, 2011.
64. Osama Al-Essa, "Portrait of a Suicide Bomber," *Asharq Al-Awsat* (UK), April 26, 2006. A poll by the nonprofit Palestinian Center for Policy and Survey Research indicated that Palestinian adults with higher levels of education are far more likely to support bomb attacks than those who cannot read. And Brian Barber, a psychologist at the University of Tennessee who interviewed 900 Muslims in Gaza, found that those with higher self-esteem and more hope for the future had a greater inclination toward suicide bombing. (Cited in Atran, "Who Wants to Be a Martyr?")
65. Maayana Miskin, "PA Study: Terrorists Motivated by Ideology, Not Suffering," *Israel National News*, November 25, 2010.
66. Cited in Tom Gross, "On Bus Bombs and Bystanders," Tomgrossmedia.com, September 24, 2004.
67. James Bennet, "Bombing Kills 18 and Hurts Scores on Jerusalem Bus," *New York Times*, August 20, 2003.
68. Lori Allen, "There Are Many Reasons Why: Suicide Bombers and Martyrs in Palestine," *Middle East Report*, Summer 2002.
69. Maayana Miskin, "PA Study: Terrorists Motivated by Ideology, Not Suffering," *Israel National News*, November 25, 2010.
70. "Profile: Omar Saeed Sheikh," BBC News Online, July 16, 2002.
71. David Johnson, "Osama bin Laden," Infoplease.com.
72. "Profile: Ayman al-Zawahiri," BBC News Online, September 27, 2004. His father, Dr. Mohammad Rabi al-Zawahiri, is a professor of pharmacology at Ain Shams Medical School in Cairo.
73. Karen DeYoung and Michael Leahy, "Uninvestigated Terrorism Warning About Detroit Suspect Called Not Unusual," *Washington Post*, December 28, 2009.
74. Shawn Pogatchnik, "UK: 2 Doctors Face Car-Bomb Terror Trial in London," Associated Press, October 8, 2008.

75. "Faisal Shahzad's Life in America and Path to Citizenship," *Wall Street Journal*, May 4, 2010.
76. Andrea Elliott, Sabrina Tavernise and Anne Barnard, "For Times Sq. Suspect, Long Roots of Discontent," *New York Times*, May 15, 2010.
77. A prominent Palestinian mufti, Sheikh Abd Al-Salam Abu Shukheydem, enumerates the benefits accrued to suicide bombers: "From the moment the first drop of his blood is spilled, he does not feel the pain of his wounds and he is forgiven for all his sins. He sees his seat in Paradise; he is saved from the torment of the grave; he is saved from the great horror of Judgment Day; he marries 'the black-eyed' [virgins]; he vouches for 70 of his family members; he gains the crown of honor, the precious stone of which is better than this entire world and everything in it." (*Al-Hayat Al-Jadida* [Palestinian Authority], September 17, 1999; cited in "'72 Black Eyed Virgins': A Muslim Debate on the Rewards of Martyrs," Middle East Media Research Institute, October 31, 2001.)
78. Michael Totten, "The Real Quagmire in the Middle East," Michaeltotten.com, July 7, 2009.
79. John Ward Anderson and Molly Moore, "Bomb Kills at Least 19 in Israel," *Washington Post*, October 5, 2003.
80. *Nightline*, ABC, October 9, 2003; cited in Tamar Sternthal, "Nightline: Suicide Bombers as Victims," Committee for Accuracy in Middle East Reporting in America, November 3, 2003.
81. Rachel Abramowitz, "Killers Rendered in Shades of Gray," *Los Angeles Times*, October 30, 2005.
82. *Live This Morning*, CNN, August 8, 2001.
83. Michael Prell, *Underdogma*, BenBella Books, 2011; see Shmuley Boteach, "No Holds Barred: Jimmy Carter? Priceless!", *Jerusalem Post*, September 30, 2009.
84. "Deadly Rampage at Virginia Tech," *New York Times*, April 19, 2007.
85. "2007 Annual Report," United States Attorney's Office, District of Nebraska.
86. Manning Pynn, "Militant or Terrorist: Judging the News," *Orlando Sentinel* (Florida), August 24, 2003.
87. Philip Gailey, "Word Choice Matters in Mideast Reporting," *St. Petersburg Times* (Florida), August 31, 2003.
88. Howard Kurtz, "Media Notes," *Washington Post*, September 24, 2001.
89. Kristin Roberts, "Children Used in Iraqi Militant Attack – US General," Reuters, March 20, 2007; cited in "Deliberately Blowing up Children in Cars 'Is Not Terrorism,'" Tomgrossmedia.com, March 27, 2007.
90. Joshua Freed, "Northwest Strike Offers Lessons for Both Management and Labor," Associated Press, August 23, 2005.
91. *10 O'clock News*, BBC Radio 1, December 4, 2001; cited in Trevor Asserson, "The BBC and the Middle East: A Critical Study," BBC Watch, March 2002.
92. Ori Lewis and Alastair Macdonald, "'Jewish Terrorist' Stirs Fear of Israeli Radicals," Reuters, November 3, 2009.
93. Edward Said, "Palestinian Elections Now," *Al-Ahram* (Egypt), June 13-19, 2002.
94. Yasser Arafat, "The Palestinian Vision of Peace," *New York Times*, February 3, 2002.
95. Clark Hoyt, "Separating the Terror and the Terrorists," *New York Times*, December 14, 2008.
96. Daniel Okrent, "The War of the Words: A Dispatch from the Front Lines," *New York Times*, March 6, 2005. Emphasis added.
97. Jason Keyser, "Suicide Bombing on Jerusalem Bus, Seven Killed," Associated Press, May 18, 2003.
98. Cited in "Bystander Bias," *Sun-Sentinel* (Fort Lauderdale, Florida), May 27, 2003.
99. James Bennet, "Israel Pulls Back From Peace Plan After 4 Attacks," *New York Times*, May 19, 2003.
100. Manning Pynn, "Militant or Terrorist: Judging the News," *Orlando Sentinel* (Florida), August 24, 2003.

101. Michael Slackman, "Disentangling Layers of a Loaded Term in Search of a Thread of Peace," *New York Times*, February 25, 2009.
102. "That Dreaded T Word," *Little Green Footballs*, February 26, 2009.
103. Eric Trager, "That 'Loaded Word,'" *Commentary Magazine Online*, February 26, 2009.
104. Robert Fisk, "My Beating by Refugees is a Symbol of the Hatred and Fury of this Filthy War," *The Independent* (UK), December 10, 2001.
105. This is reminiscent of ABC News President David Westin's speech at Columbia University's Graduate School of Journalism. When asked if the Pentagon was a legitimate target for attack by America's enemies, Westin said, "I actually don't have an opinion on that... as a journalist I feel strongly that's something I should not be taking a position on." Westin later apologized. (Donald A. Ritchie, *Reporting from Washington: The History of the Washington Press Corps*, Oxford University Press, 2005, p. 300.)
106. Alexander S. Neu, *Media and War*, Wissenschaft und Frieden (German), 2007. One week after the 9-11 attacks, Dan Rather declared: "[I'm] just one American, wherever [the president] wants me to line up, just tell me where. And he'll make the call." (*Late Show with David Letterman*, NBC, September 17, 2001.) Rather later expounded: "No journalist should try to be a robot and say, 'They've attacked my country, they've killed thousands of people, but I don't feel it.'" ("Buying the War," *Bill Moyers' Journal*, PBS, April 25, 2007.) In announcing his decicison to cover America's attack on the Taliban in Afghanistan, Geraldo Rivera said: "I'm itching for justice or maybe just revenge... Edward R. Murrow said [that] on some stories, there is no other side, and this is one of them." (*War on Terror: The Hunt for the Killers*, Fox News, November 9, 2001.)
107. See Dr. Vernon Chong, "This War Is Real."
108. Daniel Okrent, "The War of the Words," *New York Times*, March 6, 2005. Emphasis added.
109. Noah Simmons, "Shot with Our Own Arrow," Pennsylvania State University, April 30, 2010.
110. Mousa Abu Marzook, "What Hamas Is Seeking," *Washington Post*, January 31, 2006.
111. Hamas has "imposed strict rules on women; discouraged activities commonly associated with Western or Christian culture; oppressed non-Muslim minorities; imposed sharia law; and deployed religious police to enforce these laws." (Jonathan Schanzer, "The Talibanization of Gaza," August 19, 2009.) Hamas forces have stopped women for wearing Western clothes, detained singers for performing immoral songs, attacked mixed bathing at Gaza beaches, and seized alcohol throughout the Gaza Strip. (Reuven Ehrlich, "Hamas Imposes an Islamic Social Code in Gaza," Israel Intelligence Heritage & Commemoration Center, August 31, 2007.)
112. Mousa Abu Marzook, "Hamas Speaks," *Los Angeles Times*, January 6, 2009.
113. Ahmed Yousef, "What Hamas Wants," *New York Times*, June 20, 2007.
114. Marzook, "What Hamas Is Seeking"; Ahmed Yousef, "Engage With Hamas; We Earned Our Support," *Washington Post*, June 20, 2007; Muhammad Hussein Fadlallah, "The Many Meanings of Jihad to 2 Prominent Muslims," *Washington Post*, July 28, 2007.
115. Marvin Hier and Abraham Cooper, "A Byline for Hamas?", *Los Angeles Times*, July 22, 2007.
116. Adam Liptak, "Court Affirms Ban on Aiding Groups Tied to Terror," *New York Times*, June 21, 2010.
117. "Op-Ed Soapbox for Terror Is Illegal Too," Mediabackspin.com, June 23, 2010.
118. Bernd Debusmann, "Hamas Scores Publicity Coup in U.S.," Reuters, June 22, 2007.
119. Michael Matza, "A Woman's Double Life: Volunteer, Suicide Bomber," *Philadelphia Inquirer*, January 31, 2002.
120. Hossam Ezzedine, "Family of First Female Kamikaze Shocked, But Not Wholly Surprised," Agence France Presse, January 31, 2002.
121. Tim Johnson, "Identity of Suicide Bomber a Surprise," Knight Ridder News Service, February 3, 2002; published in the *Miami Herald, Detroit Free Press, Charleston Gazette* (West Virginia),

Milwaukee Journal Sentinel, *The Record* (New Jersey), and *Charlotte Observer* (North Carolina).
122. Matza, "A Woman's Double Life: Volunteer, Suicide Bomber."
123. James Bennet, "Arab Woman's Path to Unlikely 'Martyrdom,'" *New York Times*, January 31, 2002.
124. Lee Hockstader, "Infamous Killer or Mistaken ID?", *Washington Post*, July 7, 2001.
125. James Collins, "Crime and Punishment: Day of Reckoning," *Time*, June 16, 1997.
126. Tracy Wilkinson and Davan Maharaj, "Israel Tightens Blockade After Bus Stop Attack," *Los Angeles Times*, February 15, 2001.
127. Neil Genzlinger, "An Odd Understanding Reached in Israeli Prisons," *New York Times*, June 27, 2007. See Noah Pollak, "The Real Ahlam Tamimi You Didn't Read About in the *Times*," August 3, 2007. In October 2011, Tamimi was released from jail in the deal for kidnapped Israeli soldier Gilad Shalit.
128. Molly Moore, "In Jenin, Seven Shattered Dreams," *Washington Post*, July 19, 2004.
129. Molly Moore, "Refuge Is Prison for Hunted Palestinian," *Washington Post*, August 23, 2004.
130. Katharine Viner, "I Made the Ring from a Bullet and the Pin of a Hand Grenade," *The Guardian* (UK), January 26, 2001.
131. Jason Keyser, "Rantisi, 55-year-old Pediatrician and Occasional Poet, Is Voice of Hamas," Associated Press, June 10, 2003.
132. Taghreed El-Khodary, "For Conflict's Widows, Hamas Recruits an Army of Husbands," *New York Times*, October 31, 2008.
133. Steve Emerson, "Why Does the New York Times Love Hamas?", *The Daily Beast*, January 6, 2009. See also Diaa Hadid, "Love Connection: Hamas Gets Into Matchmaking Biz," Associated Press, June 7, 2009.
134. Martin Fletcher, "One Man's Terrorist, Another's Freedom Fighter," *NBC News World Blog*, January 23, 2008.
135. Deborah Sontag, "The Palestinian Conversation," *New York Times*, February 3, 2002.
136. Ibid.
137. Dion Nissenbaum, "Kickin' it with Samir Kuntar," *Checkpoint Jerusalem*, July 20, 2008.
138. "Recent Terror Attacks Around the World," Associated Press, November 8, 2003; "The War on Terror: Attacks Since 9/11," Associated Press, September 2006.
139. "Threats and Responses: Targeting Terror," *New York Times*, May 15, 2003.
140. "Evil Across Our Planet," *Sun* (UK), July 8, 2005.
141. Andrew Gross and Michelle A. Gross, "San Jose Mercury News Terror Study," HonestReporting.com, March 15, 2004.
142. "Real IRA Blamed for BBC Blast," CNN.com, March 4, 2001.
143. "Bomb Kills 4 in Israeli Resort," CNN.com, March 4, 2001. Emphasis added.
144. Cited in "Two Bombs, Two Standards," HonestReporting.com, April 1, 2003.
145. "Editorial Guidelines: War, Terror & Emergencies," bbc.co.uk.
146. "Israel's History of Bomb Blasts," BBC News Online, February 25, 2005.
147. "London Rocked by Terror Attacks," BBC News Online, July 7, 2005.
148. Email correspondence, cited in "BBC's Double Standard," HonestReporting.com, March 11, 2001.
149. Brian Wheeler, "Testing the Underground Mood," BBC News Online, July 8, 2005.
150. Jonathan Valania, "War on Words," *Philadelphia Weekly*, August 28, 2002.
151. Assistant managing editor Roger Buoen, quoted by *Star Tribune* ombudsman Lou Gelfand, February 4, 2002.
152. "Israeli Forces Raid, Then Blow Up House of Suicide Bomber," *Star Tribune* (Minneapolis), January 31, 2004.
153. *Star Tribune*, January 21, 2004. Another article referred to the pre-State activities of Menachem Begin as "Zionist terror" (Kay Miller, *Star Tribune*, January 31, 2004).

154. Matmn.org, a project of Mark Rotenberg and Marc Grossfield.
155. Email from Roger Buoen to the Minnesota JCRC; cited in "Star Trib Apologizes," Mediabackspin.com, February 4, 2004.
156. "Minn Star Tribune Admits Errors in Coverage of Alleged Massacre in Jenin," Minnesotans Against Terrorism, June 15, 2002.
157. Michael R. Gordon and Todd S. Purdum, "White House Feels Its Way as Crisis Deepens," *New York Times*, April 3, 2002.
158. "Bush Faces New Mideast Policy Choices," *Star Tribune* (Minneapolis), April 3, 2002. Emphasis added.
159. Jim Boyd, "Using Word 'Terrorist,' Or Not," *Star Tribune* (Minneapolis), April 5, 2002.
160. Jeffrey Heller, "Sharon Faces Netanyahu Challenge," Reuters, September 13, 2004.
161. September 14, 2004. CanWest's Kelly McParland said he doctored the Reuters copy in order to convey the real nature of Palestinian groups "dedicated to destroying Israel" who "aim to achieve that goal through a campaign of violence" and "killing civilians." (Kelly McParland, "Call Them the Terrorists They Are," *National Post* [Canada], September 25, 2004.)
162. "Reuters Upset by CanWest's Misuse of 'Terrorist,'" CBC News (Canada), September 17, 2004.
163. Ibid. See also Ian Austen, "Reuters Asks a Chain to Remove Its Bylines," *New York Times*, September 20, 2004.
164. Howard Kurtz, "Peter Jennings, in the News for What He Didn't Say," *Washington Post*, September 24, 2001.
165. William Safire, "On Language; Forward, Lean!", *New York Times*, August 5, 2001.

— 4 —

"MASSACRE" IN JENIN

By March 2002, deadly Palestinian terror attacks had become a near-daily occurrence: 11 murdered at a bar mitzvah in Jerusalem on March 2;[1] deadly shootings near Ofra and the Kissufim crossing a day later;[2] fatal attacks in Tel Aviv,[3] Jerusalem and Afula on March 5;[4] the slaughter of five teenagers in Atzmona on March 7,[5] followed the next day with a bombing in Ariel,[6] and the next day with a fatal shooting in Netanya[7] and the horrific suicide bombing at the Moment Café in Jerusalem;[8] deadly roadside ambushes near Kiryat Sefer and Kibbutz Metzuba on March 12;[9] attacks in Kvar Sava and Jerusalem on March 17;[10] suicide bombings on a bus near Afula on March 20[11] and in Jerusalem the next day;[12] followed by two deadly shooting attacks on March 24.[13]

The violence had reached the point of unbearable. I wanted to take my family out for some fresh air, but we couldn't think of anywhere safe to go. A picnic in the park? The shopping mall? A restaurant? An afternoon drive? All too dangerous. The bombs were hitting with such frequency and intensity that one literally had to think twice before stepping outside the house.

The terror hit horrific heights on March 27 with the Passover Seder massacre at a hotel in Netanya.[14] This attack shocked Israelis not only for its sheer numbers – 30 dead, 140 wounded – but because it occurred at a religious event, celebrating the Jewish people's escape from oppression. And worse, many of the victims were Holocaust survivors who thought they had left the genocidal murderers behind.

Three more deadly suicide bombings immediately followed the Passover massacre,[15] while the weapons continued to flow. Just a few months earlier, Israeli troops had intercepted the *Karine-A*, a freight ship carrying 50 tons of rifles, ammunition, rockets, missiles and C-4 – the powerful plastic explosive used in the bombing of the USS Cole and by shoe-bomber Richard Reid.[16] It was a $10 million weapons shipment from Iran – but who had arranged it?

In a television interview, the captain of the *Karine-A* said he was an employee of the Palestinian Authority, had received his orders from the Palestinian Authority, and that the weapons were destined for the Palestinian Authority.[17] The shipment was organized by Fuad Shubaki, the Palestinian Authority's top financial advisor.[18] Though the evidence was incontrovertible, Yasser Arafat flatly denied it. I almost expected to see him on TV saying: "It's all a simple ordering error. We'd requested a shipload of *art* supplies. But our friends in Iran read it wrong and sent us *arms* supplies."

Unless Israel took action to stop the terror, there would be much more coming. So in April 2002, the Israeli army launched Operation Defensive Shield – aimed at uprooting the problem by destroying the terrorist infrastructure. The principle target: Jenin, the infamous "martyrs' capital," from where dozens of suicide bombers had already come, and where bomb-making factories were working overtime to ensure more were on the way.

Israel – by now acutely sensitive to the media's propensity to invert victim and aggressor – launched its operation in Jenin with a strategic two-point plan:

First, Israeli soldiers would target only one concentrated area of Jenin: a refugee camp, comprising less than one percent of the city limits. Within the camp, Israel further limited the operation to one small area, the

Hawashin district, where the terror cells and bomb factories were most highly concentrated.

The second strategy was that no war planes would be involved in any way. Instead, Israeli soldiers would engage in house-to-house combat, in order to minimize Palestinian casualties. Although this posed a far greater risk to its soldiers, Israel wanted to be certain there would be no possible way for the media to spin this as an immoral or unrestrained assault.

Israel adopted this approach despite international rules of engagement that affirm a moral right to bomb from the air. In 1999, NATO planes bombed Serbia's infrastructure from safe altitudes, despite causing over 500 Serbian civilian deaths and billions of dollars of infrastructure damage,[19] and concurrent with the Israeli operation in Jenin, American and British pilots were bombing Afghanistan at a high cost to civilian life.[20]

The import of Israel's decision to use troops, not planes, was not lost on Palestinian fighters. One Fatah leader told *Time* magazine that it was only when his forces saw the Israelis advancing on foot that they decided to stay and fight.[21] Islamic Jihad leader Thabet Mardawi enthusiastically told CNN that the Israeli plan was like giving the Palestinians "a prize." Palestinians had planted "between 1,000 and 2,000 bombs and booby traps" throughout the camp, Mardawi said. "Any soldier who went into the camp like that was going to get killed. I've been waiting for a moment like that for years."[22]

Israel's supra-moral strategy, it turns out, was a very costly decision. Israel lost 23 soldiers in the fighting, mostly due to Palestinian booby traps and ambushes in the densely packed buildings and labyrinthine alleys. Indeed, the infrastructure damage that would later dominate news reports from Jenin was caused in large part by Palestinians blowing up buildings in an attempt to kill IDF soldiers[23] – a unique Palestinian predilection for both destruction and self-destruction.

Beyond this, the battle of Jenin would prove to be a seminal event, a touchstone to be revisited in news analyses and documentary films for years to come. As well, Jenin lowered the bar for outrageously irresponsible media coverage, opening the floodgates to new false charges of "massacre" in the confrontations of Lebanon 2006, Gaza 2008/9, and the flotilla raid of 2010.

Grisly Evidence

Given the delicate nature of the operation and the concern for journalists getting caught in dangerous positions, the battle of Jenin was off-limits to media coverage. So when the fighting ended after 10 days, journalists began filtering into the camp to gather their facts. Suddenly – as if emerging from an information vacuum – the media began reporting that hundreds or thousands of Palestinians were killed in a "Jenin Massacre." The British media, in particular, conjured up the most heinous accusations:

- "The monstrous war crime... extraordinary, sinister events... the camp that became a slaughterhouse." – *The Independent*[24]
- "Hundreds of victims 'were buried by bulldozer in mass grave.'" – *Daily Telegraph*[25]
- "We are talking here of massacre, and a cover-up, of genocide..." – *Evening Standard*[26]

London's *Guardian* let loose with a barrage of allegations so intense that readers could be forgiven for thinking that 9-11 was happening all over again:

[Jenin's] concrete rubble and tortured metal evokes another horror half a world away in New York, smaller in scale but every bit as repellent in its particulars, no less distressing, and every bit as man-made. Jenin smells like a crime. The stench of decaying flesh, of dead bodies left to rot or buried unabsolved under collapsed buildings... Jenin already has that aura of infamy that attaches to a crime of especial notoriety...[27]

Reports of "genocidal destruction" quickly spread. On CNN, reporter Rula Amin – who grew up in Ramallah and moonlights for the Arabic news station Al Jazeera – paraded a naked, emaciated Palestinian man, wrapped in an army blanket, in a not-too-subtle insinuation that Israel was imposing a Holocaust on Palestinians.[28] Picking up on the genocidal imagery, the *New York Times* cited Palestinian reports of "bodies cut in pieces, bodies scooped up by bulldozers and buried in mass graves..."[29]

Mass graves! Slaughterhouse! Genocide! Israel was accused of such terrible atrocities that the battle was dubbed "Jeningrad"[30] – evoking comparisons to the 800,000 Russians killed during the 900-day siege of Leningrad, and the 1.3 million who died in the bloody Nazi attack on Stalingrad.

The "massacre" canard had gained traction and was being reported as fact. To get the story first-hand, I jumped in my car and headed to Jenin – only to discover there was no entry; access to the area was highly restricted. This made things even more mysterious: Where was all this (mis)information coming from?

It all came down to a handful of Palestinian spokesmen. Ahmed Abdel Rahman, a Palestinian official, had told reporters that "thousands of Palestinians were either killed and buried in massive graves or smashed under houses..."[31] Yasser Abed Rabbo, the Palestinian Minister of Information, accused Israel of digging mass graves for 500 Palestinians, half of them women and children.[32] And Palestinian spokesman Saeb Erekat spared the details, declaring on CNN that "the Jenin refugee camp is no longer in existence."[33]

I called a friend who was serving on army reserve duty in Jenin. Had there in fact been a massacre?

"Nothing remotely resembling that happened here," he told me. "And if it did, you'd be sure to know about it. We've got thousands of Israeli reservists down here from all walks of life and all political shades. If there was any massacre, soldiers would have picked up their cell phones to report it to the media, and right now there'd be thousands protesting in front of the Knesset."

For its part, Israeli spokesmen estimated the number of Palestinian deaths at 65.[34] Yet the media gave sole credence to the Palestinian version, with BBC's headline declaring: "Jenin 'Massacre Evidence Growing.'"[35] In the London *Independent,* under the headline "Amid the Ruins of Jenin, the Grisly Evidence of a War Crime," Phil Reeves described "hundreds of corpses, entombed beneath the dust... the sweet and ghastly reek of rotting human bodies is everywhere, evidence that it is a human tomb."[36]

The calumny went beyond the media. United Nations envoy Terje Roed-Larsen described Jenin as "horrifying beyond belief" and concluded that "Israel has lost all moral ground in this conflict."[37] Peter Hansen, director of U.N. relief efforts, testified to "wholesale obliteration," "a human catastrophe that has few parallels in recent history... with bodies piled up in mass graves"[38] – some of which he claimed to have seen "with my own eyes."[39] And despite Israel's attempt to rebut the massacre claim, U.N. Secretary General Kofi Annan scoffed: "I don't think the whole world... can be wrong."[40]

Bitter Irony

The "massacre" story, it turns out, was a huge pack of lies. An extensive, independent investigation by Human Rights Watch – a notoriously pro-Palestinian NGO – concluded that 52 Palestinians were killed, the majority being armed combatants.[41] The casualty count, it turns out, was even *lower* than the original Israeli estimate.

And why were the numbers so low? Because Israel had taken every precaution to protect Palestinian civilians, to eliminate any possible accusation of human rights violations. This policy was so extraordinary that the families of the 23 Israeli soldiers killed in Jenin later sued the Israeli army for prioritizing the lives of Palestinians over the lives of its own soldiers.[42]

Imagine being an Israeli soldier and risking your life to minimize any harm to Palestinians. You come home from a comrade's funeral and open the newspaper to find that instead of being praised, you are compared to the terrorists of 9-11. Natan Sharansky, the icon of Soviet human rights activism, articulated the bitter irony: "One of the finest examples in history of a democracy protecting human rights in wartime became infamous as a horrific assault on human rights."[43]

The media – without bothering to check the facts – had lapped up the Palestinian lies. "All my nine children are buried under the ruins," a Jenin resident named Abu Ali told the influential French magazine, *Le Nouvel Observateur*, across a double-page spread. In the end, it was proven to be a bluff: the final U.N. investigation found that a total of three children had died in Jenin; all of Abu Ali's nine children were alive and well.[44]

Not only was there no massacre, but the opposite was true. In a candid moment, a senior Palestinian military officer told *Time* magazine that it was probably the Palestinians' own booby traps that buried some Palestinians alive.[45] And the *Boston Globe* quoted a 14-year-old "Islamic Jihad grenade-thrower" saying that Jenin "was a massacre of the Jews, not of us."[46]

The media, meanwhile, was stuck on the flip-side of reality. Ben Wedeman of CNN reported "stories of mass graves, of bodies being loaded into trucks and driven away, of bodies being left in the sewers and bulldozed."[47] This libelous reporting proved Winston Churchill's adage: "Men occasionally stumble over the truth, but most of them pick themselves up and hurry off as if nothing ever happened."

Palestinian "Eyewitness"

I shook my head at the journalistic anarchy that operated in Jenin. The media code of ethics, as defined by the Society of Professional Journalists, demands that reporters "test the accuracy of information from all sources" and "always question sources' motives."[48] Particularly when throwing around inflammatory words like "mass graves" and "genocide," journalistic ethics demand rigor in assessing the credibility of witnesses and circumstantial evidence.

Yet this protocol completely broke down in Jenin. What went wrong?

The answer, I'm afraid, is that reporters are living in the bubble of "Israeli aggressors and Palestinian victims." Journalists are so wedded to this narrative that they cannot depart from it, regardless of reality. So when a big story breaks, they latch onto this preconceived script, and in order to preserve some semblance of factual reporting, go looking for sources to "confirm" it all.

That's how the British media became acquainted with a Palestinian named Kamal Anis, a lone individual whose "eyewitness testimony" gave a veneer of credibility to this 21st century blood libel:[49]

- *The Independent*: "**Kamal Anis** saw the Israeli soldiers pile 30 bodies beneath a half-wrecked house. When the pile was complete, they bulldozed the building, bringing its ruins down on the corpses. Then they flattened the area with a tank."[50]

- *The Times* of London: "**Kamal Anis** says the Israelis leveled the place; he saw them pile bodies into a mass grave, dump earth on top, then ran over it to flatten it."[51]

- *Daily Telegraph*: "**Kamal Anis**, 28, said he saw an Israeli bulldozer scooping up 30 bodies and dumping them beside a ruined house. It knocked down the building, covering the corpses with rubble. It then drove over the pile, leveling it into a crude mass grave."[52]

If the massacre were true, wouldn't there have been *hundreds* of eyewitnesses? Reporters apparently didn't care, as long as someone – anyone – could be quoted. One journalist explained it to me like this: "We're not particular. Our main priority is to find someone who can speak English properly." And so, in the best tradition of "pack journalism," this major international story with far-reaching implications all came down to the gospel of 28-year-old Kamal Anis.

It was as if the media had compiled their news reports in reverse – first composing the narrative, then finding the "facts" to fit. This reminds me of a story told by the Dubno Maggid, a great 18th century rabbi:

A man was walking through the forest when he saw a tree painted with a target. An arrow had hit the target dead-on. The man continued walking and saw another tree with a target; amazingly, this too was hit with a bullseye. And another, and another.

The man walked a bit further and saw a young boy with a bow and arrow. "Do you know who shot these arrows at the trees?" the man asked.

"Yes," the boy replied. "I did."

"That's amazing!" the man said. "How are you able to hit each arrow dead-center?"

"It's easy," said the boy. "First I shoot the arrow, then I paint the target."[53]

Journalists in Jenin were shooting the arrow, then painting the target.

Stench and Bones

With two parts of the package in place – Palestinian spokesmen who brazenly lied and Kamal Anis the "eyewitness" – all that remained for journalists was to find some circumstantial evidence. But there was one obvious problem: Where were the thousands of dead bodies?

Palestinian spokesman Nabil Sha'ath gave this creative excuse to CNN's Wolf Blitzer: "There has been a cover-up, and bodies have been taken away... already a lot of the bodies have been snatched and buried elsewhere in unidentified graves."[54] Under the headline, "Palestinians: Thousands in Mass Graves," UPI quoted Palestinian official Ahmed Abdel Rahman that Israeli solders "took hundreds of bodies to northern Israel to hide their massacre they committed against our people."[55] And one Palestinian woman told TV cameras that the IDF "threw bodies into the sewage so your journalists wouldn't see them."[56]

Other Palestinians tried a different solution: creating a noxious stench in Jenin by placing the bodies of dead dogs under the rubble. Even more macabre, human bodies were dug up from local cemeteries and transplanted to Jenin.[57] The dogs provided the smell of rotting flesh, and the bones were positioned ready to be unearthed.[58]

So in the end, the media had their complete package: spokespeople, eyewitnesses, and even circumstantial evidence. This became their fig leaf to give the appearance of a legitimate news story. And by sticking with pack reporting, each journalist gave cover to the other.

That's how CBS News came to refer to the "largely demolished Jenin refugee camp,"[59] even though – as confirmed by "before-and-after" satellite photos – the fighting took place in only *one-tenth of one percent* of the city of Jenin.[60] And that's how London's *Evening Standard* could get away with evoking a reference to Jenin as "Ground Zero... eerily reminiscent of the wreckage of New York's World Trade Center after Sept. 11."[61]

Was the "Massacre at Jenin" a malicious media conspiracy? On one hand, the reporting was so contrary to journalistic protocol that it had the "stench" of deliberate bias. More likely, however, reporters were subconsciously swept up in the frenzy, and the storyline was just too good to pass up. Journalists are in tune with their audience and know that sensational headlines blaring "Slaughterhouse" and "Massacre" are far juicier than some droll tale of Israel's "moral restraint." As Ethan Bronner observed in the *New York Times*: "If journalists are given a choice between covering death and covering context, death wins."[62] In other words, Hannah Montana is no match for The Terminator.

For its part, the consumer public had indication it was all a hoax. As Mark Twain said: "A lie can travel halfway around the world while the truth is putting on its shoes."[63] And Twain never saw the Internet.

Spokesliars

Shortly after the battle of Jenin, I was giving a talk in Jerusalem to a group of Jewish community leaders on the topic of media bias. I noted that although Israel did not use a single fighter plane in Jenin, Dr. Mustafa Abu Gali, manager of the Jenin hospital, still claimed that "Fighter planes launched their missiles every three minutes"[64] and PA spokesman Abdel Rahman told CNN that Jenin was hit with "blanket bombing... I'm not lying."[65]

One young woman in the group raised her hand and said, "Why do you blame the media? They're not stating a fact; they're simply quoting accusations."

"Actually," I said, "just because somebody makes a statement doesn't mean it deserves to be printed. Otherwise there would be no limit to outlandish claims. Even if something is labeled 'allegation,' the mere fact that an editor considered it serious enough to print confers a degree of legitimacy."

Relishing her role as devil's advocate, she shot back: "How could journalists have possibly known that the Palestinians were lying?"

By simply following the ABCs of investigative journalism. Imagine you're a reporter on the scene in Jenin. Israelis say there were a few dozen casualties; Palestinians say there were thousands. How should a journalist handle these disparate claims? Does the mandate to be fair and impartial mean that both sides are always presented with equal credibility? Or is there some basis to weigh one side's claim over the other?

While the "fully equal" approach appears sensible on one level, it is ultimately superficial and flawed. A journalist needs to look deeper and consider the information in context: What is the track record of the spokespeople, and how credible have they proven over time? If one side has shown a consistent disregard for the truth, that must be taken into account.

That's why, in the case of Jenin, the media cannot claim they never saw the hoax coming. In the years before and since, Palestinian efforts to demonize Israel have produced every sort of fabrication imaginable. Who can forget Yasser Arafat's wife, Suha, kissing Hillary Clinton at a press conference while claiming that Israel is poisoning Palestinian women and children on a daily basis with carcinogens.[66] Or how about Yusuf Abu Safia, chairman of the Palestinian Environmental Authority, charging Israel with a "disguised war" – by flooding the Palestinians market with cancer-causing food and with sports shoes that cause paralysis.[67] And that "Israelis welcome and encourage" drug addiction by offering payments of 4,500 shekels to any Palestinian who can prove he's addicted to drugs.[68]

Then there's the claim that Israel foists games on Palestinian children that beam radioactive rays,[69] that Israel drops bombs disguised as children's toys into Palestinian areas,[70] and that Israel handed out 200 tons – yes, tons – of drug-laced bubble gum to Palestinian children, which Palestinian Supply Minister Abdel Aziz Shaheen said was capable of "completely destroying the genetic system of young boys."[71] And what smear campaign would be complete without the accusation that Israel sends "pretty HIV-positive Jewish prostitutes" to spread AIDS among Arab youth.[72]

In the words of Stephen Colbert, is there no paranoid delusion that Israel won't stoop to being accused of?

These crazy accusations find their way into the mainstream media. Agence France Presse, under the headline, "Hamas Says Israel Dumping Aphrodisiac Gum on Gaza," reported this astonishing libel without a note of skepticism; only in the final sentence did the article offer an Israeli response.[73] CNN crossed the line as well, reporting the fiction that Israel uses poisonous nerve gas against Palestinians.[74] And Xinhua, the gigantic Chinese news agency that reaches over a billion people worldwide in eight languages, ran the headline: "Israel Accused of Selling Carcinogenic Juices to Palestinians" – and proffered no rejoinder.[75]

This reminds me of 19th century writer Elbert Hubbard's definition of "newspaper editor": someone whose job it is to separate the wheat from the chaff, and to see that the chaff is printed.[76]

More recently, Arabs have accused Israel of a whole zoo-full of schemes:

In 2010, following a string of deadly shark attacks near the Egyptian resort of Sharm el-Sheikh, Egyptian officials suggested this was part of a sinister Zionist plot: "We must not discount the possibility that Israel's intelligence agency, the Mossad, threw the shark into the sea, in order to attack tourists," said Southern Sinai Governor Abed Al-Fadij. "The Mossad is trying to hurt Egyptian tourism in any way possible, and the shark is one way for it to realize its plan."[77]

The story spread quickly, with headlines such as "Shark 'Sent to Egypt by Mossad'"[78] and "Egypt Refuses to Rule out Mossad Plot Link to Deadly Shark Attacks."[79] Perhaps the theory is not so far-fetched; after all, Jewish film director Steven Spielberg has been known to control large, mechanical sharks.

A few weeks later, when a vulture landed in the Saudi Arabian city of Hyaal, law enforcement agents "arrested" the bird as a suspected Israeli spy. The vulture was carrying a GPS transmitter bearing the name of Tel Aviv University – as part of an academic study on the migratory habits of birds – which Saudi officials claimed to be "sophisticated espionage equipment."[80] Thankfully, the bird was later released, producing the farcical headline, "Israeli Vulture Spy Declared Innocent by Saudi Arabia,"[81] while leaving pundits to wonder: Under interrogation, did the bird sing?

On another occasion, Iranian intelligence agents arrested 14 squirrels for allegedly carrying advanced Western spy gear.[82] Meanwhile, Palestinian officials (including PA Chairman Mahmoud Abbas) concoct the idea that Israel uses wild pigs to drive Palestinians off their land,[83] infects mosquitoes with HIV,[84] and floods Arab neighborhoods with rats.[85]

Such widespread use of animals to carry out spectacular feats of harassment and espionage gives new meaning to the idea of Israel attacking "land, sea and air."

Which raises the question: How have the Jews managed to so successfully control the animal kingdom? Perhaps the answer can be found in the Koran, which claims that the evil Jews were "turned into apes and pigs" – enabling Jews to communicate with other animals and instruct them to do their bidding.[86]

Duplicity

Another technique that Palestinians use to manipulate the media – and deceive the world – is to say one thing in English to a Western audience, while declaring their true intent in Arabic. Palestinian leader Marwan Barghouti, as he was marched into court on indictment for murder, delivered two very different messages. Raising his handcuffed hands, Barghouti defiantly declared, "The uprising will be victorious."

Continuing in English, he said, "I am a peaceful man. I was trying to do everything for peace between the two peoples."[87]

In 2011, when a family of five Israelis were brutally murdered in their home, CNN dutifully reported that "Palestinian Authority Prime Minister Salam Fayyad denounced the killings."[88] What CNN never told readers is that days later, the compassionate Fayyad heaped praise on Palestinian terrorists, noting "with honor and admiration the resolve" of those who perpetrate suicide bombings.[89]

The master of this technique was Yasser Arafat, who would famously say something conciliatory while speaking to the international press, then turn around and deliver a fiery speech in Arabic calling for the extermination of Israelis. Thus, he pleased both sides well enough to earn a Nobel Peace Prize from his naive Western audience, while simultaneously being hailed as a jihad leader by his Arab audience.[90]

In 1993, Arafat stood on the White House lawn, shook Yitzhak Rabin's hand, and signed the Oslo Accords calling for an end to "decades of confrontation and conflict." While this was reported on the front page of every major newspaper in the world, no one reported the radical statement that Arafat made on Jordanian TV the very next day:

"Since we cannot defeat Israel in war; we do this in stages. We take any and every territory that we can of Palestine, and establish sovereignty there, and we use it as a springboard to take more. When the time comes, we can get the Arab nations to join us for the final blow against Israel."[91]

And yet, having been duped time and time again, the media continues to give credibility to Palestinian spokespeople. When Palestinians claimed that the Israeli Mossad set up a fake al-Qaeda cell in Gaza, Israeli spokesmen dismissed it as sheer nonsense, but BBC's headline trumpeted the Palestinian accusation as if it were undisputed fact: "Israel 'Faked al-Qaeda Presence.'"[92]

Confronted with irrefutable facts, Palestinians will often simply invent a new set of lies. When Israeli soldiers searched Palestinian homes and found disturbing photos of children wielding machine guns and babies strapped with explosive belts, BBC quoted Palestinian spokesliar

Yasser Abed Rabbo dismissing it as "cheap Israeli propaganda."[93] In case viewers missed it, BBC then put this question to an Israeli spokesman: "The Mossad has the most amazing forgery capabilities in the world. Why should we believe this is real?"[94]

Then there's the time that Israeli troops raided Palestinian Authority headquarters and discovered invoices proving that top Palestinian officials were using "humanitarian aid funds" from the U.S. and European Union to supply terrorists with assault rifles and explosives. Caught red-handed? Speaking on CNN, Palestinian spokesliar Abdel Rahman shrugged it all off as "a fraud by the Israeli intelligence." The Israelis, he said, "have a department that specializes in putting out lies."[95] Also on CNN, Palestinian U.N. representative Nasser Al-Kidwa dismissed the incriminating evidence as "some kind of James Bond activities... bits and pieces of rumors and unsubstantiated claims."[96]

How do these spokesmen get away with such blatant lies? Nobel Prize-winning author Gabriel García Márquez explained the psychology of it all: If you say there are elephants flying in the sky, people will not believe you. But if you say there are 425 elephants in the sky, people are far more likely to believe you.[97] To wit: When a Jewish baby sitting in her stroller at a playground was shot dead by Palestinians, the official Voice of Palestine radio assured listeners that the baby was retarded and had been smothered by her own mother.[98]

Here's the most perplexing question: If Palestinians repeatedly use the media to promote outright lies, why do journalists continue to take them seriously? In dealing with totalitarian regimes, journalists are trained to treat officially-released information with due skepticism. (Think the Iraqi Minister of Information, whom the media dubbed Comical Ali, announcing from Baghdad that hundreds of American troops were committing suicide at the city's gates.)[99] So why are Palestinian groups – dictatorial, corrupt, terror organizations – not held to those same standards? Even more, shouldn't there be a policy to blacklist Palestinian spokesmen who are caught lying?

I confronted a Jerusalem bureau chief with these very questions.

"Journalists have to be impartial," he told me. "When two sides are locked in battle, we are obligated to equally report both sides' claims."

"Wait a second," I said. "Objectivity doesn't mean that you mindlessly repeat everything in a computerized 'he said, she said' way. It's basic due diligence to skillfully filter the information, and qualify it with background and context. That's the role of a journalist."

"It's difficult," he said, "to discern between a solid source providing an accurate account, and someone lying through his teeth in an elaborate conspiracy theory."

I couldn't believe his naiveté. "You're dealing here with Palestinians who have repeatedly used deceit, exaggeration and disinformation as propaganda against Israel," I said. "When Palestinians claimed thousands of dead in Jenin, did you verify the credibility of those you quoted? Did you use outside sources to substantiate this claim? That would have been *true* objectivity!"

On rare occasions, the media does confront Palestinian lies. During the battle of Jenin, CNN's Bill Hemmer challenged Saeb Erekat to provide evidence that 500 Palestinians had been killed. "If your numbers are wrong," Hemmer said, "will you come back here on our network and retract what you said?"

"Absolutely," Erekat deadpanned. "Absolutely."[100]

Since then, I have repeatedly reminded CNN of their promise to have Erekat set the record straight. CNN's response? "We're dealing with it." Erekat, the confirmed spokesliar, has subsequently appeared dozens of times on CNN. As for the long-promised retraction, we're still waiting.[101]

Aftermath of Jenin

After all the dust had settled in Jenin – after Human Rights Watch and a United Nations inquiry had confirmed a total of 52 Palestinian casualties – one would have expected the media to clean up its mess. On balance, if you put a lie on page one, then you should put the truth on page one, too.

To his credit, Phil Reeves of the London *Independent* – who'd sounded alarms of a "monstrous war crime" – retrospectively admitted that his reporting had been "highly personalized." "Even journalists have to admit they're wrong sometimes..." he wrote. "Palestinian officials must bear much blame for this. Regrettably, I also made a contribution."[102]

Reeves was an exception. Other journalists clung tenaciously to the massacre lie. Months after the Human Rights Watch report was released, Peter Cave of Australia's ABC insisted:

> I personally saw 30 Palestinian corpses at the hospital on April the 20th, and with dozens of other foreign reporters, watched them being buried at a **mass grave** just up the road from the hospital... Just as happened in Tiananmen Square, the uninformed and those with their own agenda are now claiming there was no massacre. **There was a massacre...**[103]

Other media outlets twisted the U.N. investigation in an attempt to validate their own original lies. The London *Guardian* wrote: "As we said last April, the destruction wrought in Jenin looked and smelled like a crime. On the basis of the UN's findings, it still does."[104]

One audacious distortion came from the Minneapolis *Star Tribune*, the same folks who infamously cleanse the T-word from wire stories. This time, when a *New York Times* wire story reported that Human Rights Watch found "no evidence" of a massacre in Jenin, *Star Tribune* editors altered the original *Times'* headline – "Rights Group Doubts Mass Deaths in Jenin" – and moved the "disproven massacre" statement from the first paragraph down to the 21st.[105] After media monitors caught the *Star Tribune* red-handed, the newspaper's own ombudsman was forced to admit what he called an "editorial disaster," an "egregious stumble," and an "embarrassing wart."[106]

And then there's Janine di Giovanni, correspondent for the London *Times*, who originally wrote from Jenin: "Rarely in more than a decade of war reporting from Bosnia, Chechnya, Sierra Leone, Kosovo, have I seen such deliberate destruction, such disrespect for human life."[107] Having equated Jenin to places where millions of civilians were murdered and displaced, how did Giovanni later respond to this flagrantly false comparison? "I stand by everything I wrote," she blankly said.[108]

Even worse, some journalists brazenly tried to deny their reports – on record in black and white – were ever written in the first place. When confronted about his reporting on Jenin, David Blair of the *Daily Telegraph* declared: "My articles never used the word 'massacre'... They never used the word 'atrocities' – anywhere."[109]

Well, not exactly. Blair's articles did in fact use the words "massacre" and "atrocities" – though he cleverly couched the slander by attributing it to unidentified Palestinian sources. Blair wrote: "Palestinians accuse the Israeli forces of *massacring* hundreds of civilians... Palestinians gave detailed accounts of alleged *atrocities* by Israeli soldiers." Blair then corroborated this with his own observation that "the Palestinians' estimate of hundreds [killed] may be more accurate."[110]

Yet David Blair – apparently hoping that readers would never bother to research the facts – looked straight into the camera and claim to have never written anything of the sort. As Serge Schmemann of the *New York Times* observed: "There is nothing a journalist fears more than having a correction printed about his story."[111]

Irrespective of whether journalists later issued corrections, the genie was out of the bottle and impossible to put back in. Studies show that when people are fed incorrect information – and subsequently told it's incorrect – they remember *only* the misinformation, which stays lodged in the brain.[112] In this way, when it comes to the news media, corrections can actually push readers further away from the facts. Whether health care reform, climate change, or the battle of Jenin, psychologists call these "narrative scripts" – stories that confirm pre-exiting beliefs and give permission to continue feeling as you already do. Corrections are seen as part of the conspiracy and actually strengthen previous misconceptions. In other words, corrections backfire.[113]

Indeed, when an urban legend starts it is nearly impossible to erase. Everyone knows that before Columbus sailed to the New World, scientists thought the world was flat. Not true. It was only in 1828 that novelist

Washington Irving popularized the flat-earth fable in his best-selling biography of Columbus.[114] Writers of American history then picked up the story, and since textbooks tend to be clones of each other, Irving's little hoax persists to this day.[115]

So too, "Jenin Massacre" became a permanent part of the media lexicon – the 21st century version of the Flat Earth Society. Until today, newspapers from Canada[116] to South Africa[117] to England[118] continue to describe Jenin as a "massacre." As Mark Twain said, "A lie told well is immortal."[119]

Tragically, these lies are more than just factual inaccuracies or a PR issue. These myths remain firmly engraved in Palestinian lore, fomenting an atmosphere of mistrust that will linger for decades, and ultimately undermine the possibility of peaceful coexistence. As one Palestinian woman said on camera: "We'll never forget this massacre. This is similar to the Holocaust. We will teach our generations not to forget this."[120]

Even more, by introducing this "massacre" idea, Jenin laid the foundation for future blood libels to follow. Though many dismissed the Jenin reports as off-the-wall accusations, these ideas became part of the public discourse so that the next time – think Gaza 2009 – the anti-Israel envelope could be pushed even further.

In Jenin, Palestinians and journalists duped the public, harmed Israel's interests, and further widened the Israeli-Palestinian gulf. As Richard Cohen opined in the *Washington Post*, what got massacred in Jenin "was not Palestinians, but truth itself."[121] And yes, Kofi, the whole world was wrong.

Notes

1. James Bennet, "In Jerusalem, Suicide Bomber Kills at Least 9," *New York Times*, March 3, 2002.
2. Peter Hermann, "Sixteen Israelis Killed in Two Attacks; West Bank Shooting, Jerusalem Bombing Injure More than 50," *Baltimore Sun*, March 3, 2002.
3. Corky Siemaszko, "A Slaughter in Tel Aviv: Palestinian Gunman Kills 3 in Attack at Restaurants," *Daily News* (New York), March 5, 2002.
4. Ellis Shuman, "5 Israelis Killed in Attacks on Tel Aviv Restaurant, Afula Bus and Gush Etzion Car," *Israel Insider*, March 5, 2002.
5. Tracy Wilkinson and Mary Curtius, "Mideast Conflict Kills 44 in Deadliest Day in 17 Months," *Los Angeles Times*, March 9, 2002.
6. Matthew Gutman, "Ariel Bombing Interrupts Local Terror Victim's Funeral," *Jerusalem Post*, March 8, 2002.

7. Serge Schmemann, "14 Israelis Killed in Two Terror Attacks," *New York Times,* March 10, 2002.
8. Suzanne Goldenberg, "Bombing Shatters Illusions in an Oasis of Civility," *The Guardian* (UK), March 11, 2002.
9. "Six Israelis Die in Ambush," BBC News Online, March 12, 2002.
10. "Suicide Attacks in Kfar Saba and Jerusalem Kill One Israeli," *Israel Insider,* March 17, 2002.
11. Jack Katzenell, "Bus Blast Kills Seven," Associated Press, March 20, 2002.
12. "Bomb Rips through Jerusalem Shopping Centre, *The Guardian* (UK), March 21, 2002.
13. Full listing at "Victims of Palestinian Violence and Terrorism since September 2000," mfa.gov.il.
14. Corky Siemaszko, "Passover Bombing Leaves 120 in Israel Hurt," *Daily News* (New York), March 28, 2002.
15. Uri Dan, "Latest Lady Suicide Bomber Led Two Lives," *New York Post,* March 30, 2002; Peter Hermann, "Israel Expands 'War' as Violence Escalates," *Baltimore Sun,* April 1, 2002; Etgar Lefkovits, "Hero Policeman Laid to Rest," *Jerusalem Post,* April 4, 2002.
16. James Bennet, "Seized Arms Would Have Vastly Extended Arafat Arsenal," *New York Times,* January 12, 2002.
17. "Arafat Fires Official Over Arms Ship," CNN.com, January 28, 2002.
18. Caroline B. Glick, "The Baghdad-Ramallah Axis," *Jerusalem Post*, October 11, 2002.
19. "The Crisis in Kosovo – Civilian Deaths as a Result of Attacks," Human Rights Watch, 2000; "Kosovo: the Conflict by Numbers," BBC News Online, June 11, 1999.
20. David Zucchino, "The Americans... They Just Drop Their Bombs and Leave," *Los Angeles Times,* June 2, 2002.
21. Matt Rees, "The Battle of Jenin," *Time,* May 5, 2002.
22. "Palestinian Fighter Describes 'Hard Fight' in Jenin," CNN.com, April 23, 2002.
23. Bill Saporito, "Jenin: Defiant to the Death," *Time,* April 22, 2002.
24. Phil Reeves, "Amid the Ruins of Jenin, the Grisly Evidence of a War Crime," *The Independent* (UK), April 16, 2002.
25. David Blair, "Hundreds of Victims 'Were Buried by Bulldozer in Mass Grave,'" *Daily Telegraph* (UK), April 13, 2002.
26. A.N. Wilson, "A Demo We Can't Afford to Ignore," *Evening Standard* (UK), April 15, 2002.
27. "The Battle for the Truth: What Really Happened in Jenin Camp?", *The Guardian* (UK), April 17, 2002. Six years later, *Guardian* editor Alan Rusbridger finally apologized, saying "I take full responsibility for the misjudgment." (Jonny Paul, "Guardian Editor Apologizes for Jenin Editorial," *Jerusalem Post*, March 3, 2008.)
28. CNN later edited or deleted the account. See Alyssa A. Lappen, "The Israeli Crime that Wasn't," Frontpagemag.com, December 28, 2004; Talya Halkin and Herb Keinon, "How CNN Changed Israel's World," *Jerusalem Post*, June 14, 2005.
29. James Bennet, "Jenin Refugee Camp's Dead Can't Be Counted or Claimed," *New York Times,* April 13, 2002.
30. Tom Gross, "Jeningrad: What the British Media Said," *National Review Online,* May 13, 2002.
31. "Palestinians: Thousands in Mass Graves," *United Press International,* April 12, 2002.
32. Peter Mackler, "Arafat Comes Out Against Terror, Palestinians Say Powell Meet Back On," Agence France Presse, April 13, 2002.
33. Interview with Jim Clancy, CNN, April 10, 2002; cited in "UN Report on Jenin: Media Distortions Fed Final Report on Jenin," *Arab American News,* August 16, 2002.
34. "Jenin 'Massacre Evidence Growing,'" BBC News Online, April 18, 2002.
35. Ibid.
36. Phil Reeves, "Amid the Ruins of Jenin, the Grisly Evidence of a War Crime," *The Independent* (UK), April 16, 2002.

37. "UN Envoy Stands by 'Horrific' Reaction to Israel's Destruction in Jenin," Agence France Presse, April 22, 2002.
38. Mortimer B. Zuckerman, "A Tragic Miscalculation," *U.S. News & World Report*, May 20, 2002.
39. David Tell, "The U.N.'s Israel Obsession," *Weekly Standard*, May 6, 2002.
40. Speaking in Madrid, Spain; cited in "Actually, the World is Wrong," *National Post* (Canada), April 11, 2002.
41. "Jenin: IDF Military Operations – Civilian Casualties and Unlawful Killings in Jenin," Human Rights Watch, Vol. 14, No. 3 (E), May 2002.
42. David J. Craig, "Human Rights Champion Sharansky: Palestinian Democracy Key to Peace," *Boston University Bridge*, September 19, 2003.
43. Natan Sharansky, "Jenin: Anniversary of a Battle," Frontpagemag.com, April 29, 2005.
44. Hanoch Marmari, "Truth and Consequences on the Palestinian Beat," *Los Angeles Times*, June 16, 2002; Stephanie Gutmann, "Can We Trust the Casualty Numbers?", *National Review Online*, January 14, 2009.
45. Matt Rees, "The Battle of Jenin," *Time*, May 5, 2002.
46. Charles A. Radin and Dan Ephron, "Claims of Massacre Go Unsupported by Palestinian Fighters," *Boston Globe*, April 29, 2002.
47. "Results of Fighting in Jenin Unclear," *American Morning with Paula Zahn*, CNN, April 12, 2002.
48. "Code of Ethics," Society of Professional Journalists, 1996.
49. "Atrocities of the British Press," HonestReporting.com, April 16, 2002.
50. Phil Reeves, "Amid the Ruins of Jenin, the Grisly Evidence of a War Crime," *The Independent* (UK), April 16, 2002.
51. Janine di Giovanni, "Inside the Camp of the Dead," *The Times* (UK), April 16, 2002.
52. David Blair, "Blasted to Rubble by the Israelis," *Daily Telegraph* (UK), April 16, 2002.
53. E. Shteinman, *Kitvei HaMagid M'Dubno*, Mesoret Publications, 1952.
54. "Interview with Ariel Sharon; New Osama Bin Laden Video Released," *Wolf Blitzer Reports*, CNN, April 15, 2002.
55. "Palestinians: Thousands in Mass Graves," United Press International, April 12, 2002.
56. Amnon Rubinstein, "The Massacring of the Truth," *Haaretz* (Israel), September 11, 2002.
57. These reinternments were caught on film by hidden Israeli cameras.
58. "Israeli Drone Films Palestinians Faking Funeral in Jenin," *Israel Insider*, May 5, 2002.
59. "Palestinian Leader Yasir Arafat Imposes Conditions to His New Call for Elections," *CBS Evening News*, May 17, 2002.
60. Ken Lee, "Jenin Rises from the Dirt," BBC News Online, June 24, 2003.
61. Mitch Potter, "'Ground Zero' of Jenin Still Site of Spin Battles," *Evening Standard* (UK), August 2, 2002.
62. Ethan Bronner, "Israel Puts Media Clamp on Gaza," *New York Times*, January 6, 2009.
63. This quote may have originated in a sermon by Charles Haddon Spurgeon, April 1, 1855.
64. *Jenin, Jenin*, directed by Mohammed Bakri, 2002.
65. Kyra Phillips, "Interview with Hasan Abdel Rahman, Alon Pinkas," *CNN Saturday Morning News*, April 6, 2002.
66. "Profile: Suha Arafat," BBC News Online, November 11, 2004.
67. *Al-Hayat Al-Jadida* (Palestinian Authority), June 17, 2004; cited in Itamar Marcus and Barbara Crook, "Hamas Police Official: Israel Smuggles 'Sexual Stimulants' to Destroy Palestinian Youth," Palestinian Media Watch, July 17, 2009.
68. *Al-Hayat Al-Jadida* (Palestinian Authority), May 18, 2003; cited in Khaled Amayreh, "Palestine: Horror and Shame," *Global Research*, March 2, 2008.
69. Ola Attallah, "Israel Floods Palestinians with Carcinogens: Official," *Islam Online*, June 20, 2005.

70. Palestinian Authority Television, March 3, 2003; cited in Itamar Marcus and Barbara Crook, "PA Libels and Lies Part 2: 2000-2006," Palestinian Media Watch, October 16, 2008.
71. The *Washington Post* commissioned a test of allegedly contaminated chewing gum provided by Palestinian health officials. Using a mass spectrometer capable of detecting a microgram of progesterone, none was found in the gum. (Cited in Raphael Israeli, "Poison: The Use of Blood Libel in the War Against Israel," Jerusalem Center for Public Affairs, April 15, 2004.) In 2009, Hamas police spokesman Islam Shahwan revised the libel, claiming that Israeli intelligence was smuggling sexually stimulating chewing gum into Gaza to "weaken and destroy" Palestinian youth and the social structure. (Itamar Marcus and Barbara Crook, "Hamas Police Official: Israel Smuggles 'Sexual Stimulants' to Destroy Palestinian Youth," Palestinian Media Watch, July 17, 2009.) Egyptians, too, claimed that an Israeli hair product causes infertility in both men and women, for the purpose of eliminating all childbirth in Egypt. (Mohammed Abdul Latif, "Arrest of the Jordanian Mossad Spy Promoting Drug that Causes Infertility," *Al-Ahram* [Egypt], August 17, 2011.)
72. Palestinian newspaper *Al Quds*, June 1997, quoting the head of the Criminal Division of the Palestinian Police in Nablus; cited in *Maariv* (Israel), June 27, 1997. See also statement by Nabil Ramlawi, PLO representative to the United Nations Commission on Human Rights in Geneva, March 11, 1997. Such rhetoric translates into lethal action: In 2002, an Egyptian Muslim who believed that "the Israelis tried to destroy the Egyptian nation and the Egyptian population by sending prostitutes with AIDS to Egypt" shot and killed two Jews at the El Al counter in Los Angeles International Airport. (Rick Lyman and Nick Madigan, "Officials Puzzled About Motive of Airport Gunman Who Killed 2," *New York Times*, July 5, 2002.)
73. "Hamas Says Israel Dumping Aphrodisiac Gum on Gaza," Agence France Presse, July 14, 2009.
74. "Arafat Accuses Israel of Using Poison Gas," CNN.com, February 15, 2001.
75. "Israel Accused of Selling Carcinogenic Juices to Palestinians," Xinhua News Agency (China), June 13, 2005.
76. Cited in Fred R. Shapiro and Joseph Epstein, *The Yale Book of Quotations*, Yale University Press, 2006.
77. "Egyptian Official: Israel Could Be Behind Deadly Shark Attack," *Fox News*, December 7, 2010; Mohamed Zaki, "Egypt Puzzled After String of Red Sea Shark Attacks," Reuters, December 6, 2010.
78. Nick Collins, "Shark 'Sent to Egypt by Mossad,'" *The Telegraph* (UK), December 7, 2010.
79. Mohamed Zaki, "Egypt Refuses to Rule Out Mossad Plot Link to Deadly Shark Attacks," *The Scotsman*, December 7, 2010. The paper reported without a hint of skepticism that "Shark attacks on tourists in the Red Sea have triggered a flurry of speculation as to what could have caused them, with suggestions ranging from overfishing to an Israeli plot to harm Egyptian tourism."
80. James Hider, "Vulture Held as Mossad Spy by Saudi Arabia," *The Times* (UK), January 7, 2011; "Saudi Arabia 'Detains' Israeli Vulture for Spying," BBC News Online, January 5, 2011.
81. Alexander Marquardt, "Israeli Vulture Spy Declared Innocent by Saudi Arabia," ABC News, January 10, 2011.
82. Dudi Cohen, "Iranians Arrest 14 Squirrels for Spying," *Ynetnews* (Israel), July 13, 2007.
83. "President: Going to the Security Council," Wafa News Agency, September 16, 2011. See also "Wild Boars Released by Israeli Settlers Attack Palestinian Workers," Palestinian Ma'an News Agency, April 24, 2007.
84. Charles Bremner, "Gaddafi Faces Outrage as Nurses on Mercy Mission are Sentenced to Die," *The Times* (UK), December 20, 2006.
85. Khaled Abu Toameh, "Israel Using Rats Against J'lem Arabs," *Jerusalem Post*, July 20, 2008.
86. "The Top 13 Zionist Animal Conspiracy Theories," *Elder of Ziyon* blog, February 20, 2011.

87. Zvi Harel, "Tanzim Boss Marwan Barghouti Indicted for Murder, Branded 'Arch Terrorist,'" *Haaretz* (Israel), August 13, 2002.
88. Kevin Flower, "Israeli Family of 5 Killed in Terror Attack, Military Says," CNN.com, March 13, 2011.
89. *Al-Hayat al-Jadida* (Palestinian Authority), March 24, 2011; cited in Itamar Marcus and Nan Jacques Zilberdik, "Fayyad's Duplicity: Honors Terrorist Bombers, Then Condemns Terror Bombing," Palestinian Media Watch, March 27, 2011. Fayyad made "special mention" of female Palestinian terrorists: Latifa Abu Dhiraa, who smuggled a bomb into Israel for a suicide attack in 2003; Qahira Al-Sa'adi, who drove a suicide bomber to an attack that killed three in Jerusalem in 2002; Irena Sarahneh, who drove a suicide bomber to an attack that killed two and injured dozens, in the Israeli city of Rishon Litzion in 2002; Iman Ghazawi, who placed a bomb at the central bus station in Tel Aviv in 2001.
90. "The Left's Big Blunder," *Zombietime*, October 15, 2008.
91. Jordanian Television, September 14, 1993.
92. "Israel 'Faked al-Qaeda Presence,'" BBC News Online, December 8, 2002.
93. "'Baby Bomber Photo' Shocks Israel," BBC News Online, June 28, 2002.
94. Cited in Stephanie Gutmann, *The Other War*, Encounter Books, 2005.
95. "Israel: Documents Link Al Aqsa to Palestinian Finance Official," CNN.com, April 3, 2002.
96. "Ambassadors Debate Arafat Presence in Israel," *American Morning with Paula Zahn*, CNN, April 3, 2002.
97. Cited in Naomi Epel, *The Observation Deck*, Chronicle Books, 1998.
98. "News at a Glance," Jewish Telegraphic Agency, April 4, 2001.
99. John Crowley, "Son Defends Iraqi Spin Doctor," *The Telegraph* (UK), April 14, 2003.
100. "Jerusalem: Could Mideast Conflict Widen?", *Live on Location*, CNN, April 14, 2002.
101. Erekat later attempted to vindicate himself by saying: "In 25 years, this is the only time I made a mistake." (*Jenin: Massacring Truth*, directed by Martin Himel, produced by CanWest MediaWorks, 2004.)
102. Phil Reeves, "Even Journalists Have to Admit They're Wrong Sometimes," *The Independent* (UK), August 3, 2002.
103. Peter Cave, "UN Report on Jenin Massacre Flawed," *Correspondents Report*, ABC Radio National, August 4, 2002. Emphasis added.
104. "Truth-seeking in Jenin," *The Guardian* (UK), August 2, 2002.
105. *Star Tribune* (Minneapolis), May 3, 2002.
106. Lou Gelfand, "Star Tribune Reader Representative Column," *Star Tribune* (Minneapolis), May 12, 2002.
107. Janine di Giovanni, "Inside the Camp of the Dead," *The Times* (UK), April 16, 2002.
108. *Jenin: Massacring Truth*. The film won top documentary prize at the 38th Annual WorldFest-Houston International Independent Film Festival.
109. Ibid.
110. David Blair, "Jenin Siege Victims Tell Tales of Terror; Palestinians Say Hundreds of Civilians have been Massacred in Two Weeks," *Daily Telegraph* (UK), April 15, 2002.
111. Cited in Jeff Helmreich, "Journalistic License: Professional Standards in the Print Media's Coverage of Israel," Jerusalem Center for Public Affairs, August 15, 2001.
112. "Photography as a Weapon," *Opinionator* blog / *New York Times*, August 11, 2008.
113. Brendan Nyhan and Jason Reifler, "When Corrections Fail: The Persistence of Political Misperceptions," 2006; David McRaney, "The Backfire Effect," Youarenotsosmart.com, June 10, 2011.
114. Washington Irving, *The Life and Voyages of Christopher Columbus*, 1828.
115. James Loewen, "Top 10 Worst Historical Sites in the United States," History News Network, July 2, 2002. In 1945, the Flat Earth Myth was listed by the British Historical Association as

the "second most common error" in history.
116. Oakland Ross, "West Bank Project Unites Former Foes," *Toronto Star*, December 4, 2008.
117. Ronnie Kasrils, "Remembering the Massacre – A Call to Confront the Past," The Star (South Africa), April 7, 2008. In investigating the libelous error, the South Africa Press Council invoked the "fake but accurate" excuse: "Whether one agrees or disagrees with [Star reporter] Kasrils on the source of the violence, it is true that Israel has been on a bloody path. The intention of the newspaper in using these pictures was to illustrate that path." (Joe Thloloe, "The South African Zionist Federation vs The Star and the Cape Argus: Ruling by Press Ombudsman," Press Council of South Africa, October 14, 2008.)
118. Robin Yassin-Kassab, "Book Review: Mornings in Jenin by Susan Abulhawa," *The Times* (UK), February 6, 2010.
119. Mark Twain, "Advice to Youth," 1882.
120. *Jenin: Massacring Truth*.
121. Richard Cohen, "Truth Massacred," *Washington Post*, August 6, 2002.

—5—

THE CNN SHIFT

As the conflict raged, there was an ever-growing mountain of evidence that the media was biased against Israel, yet I kept bumping into the same problem. Every time I'd find a new violation of objectivity – selective omission, lack of context, or distortion of facts – journalists would simply shrug and say, "Sure, that particular phrase or headline may be skewed against Israel. But it doesn't matter how many examples you give. We get complaints from both sides, which proves that overall, our reporting is 100 percent fair and impartial."

Arthur Brisbane of the *New York Times* asserts: "Coverage of the Israeli-Palestinian conflict brought out passionate reader complaints, on both sides of the issue – as usual,"[1] and says BBC, "For every Jew who thinks the BBC is violently anti-Semitic, there is an Arab who fervently believes that we are pro-Israel."[2] In other words: Both sides complain, so our coverage must be fair.

Yet things definitely did *not* balance out. At the outset of the Intifada, my comprehensive study of CNN set up a standard model that other media monitors would use to measure long-term patterns at the *Philadelphia Inquirer*[3] (better than the *National Enquirer*, but only slightly), the *San Jose*

Mercury News[4] and other major dailies. Time and again, the results showed an ingrained institutional bias against Israel – confirming my suspicions and increasing my confidence that I was on the right track.

One study, conducted by media activists in Australia, analyzed two months of Middle East coverage in Melbourne's major daily, *The Age*. Researchers identified 210 violations of media objectivity, and the results were staggering: 205 instances (97.6%) of biased reporting were anti-Israel in nature, while just five occurrences (2.4%) were anti-Arab.[5]

Although the Media Goliath was spreading its bias across the globe, I determined that the most effective way to counteract it would be to focus my energies on CNN. Not only was CNN reaching over a billion viewers worldwide, but its coverage was having a ripple effect: Foreign correspondents in Jerusalem would typically wake up in the morning, flick on CNN to catch the headlines, and plan their news day. As a result, CNN's spin was filtering down to other media outlets, giving rise to what industry insiders called "the CNN effect."

At first, I tried the direct approach – contacting CNN editors and stating my case. But I was stonewalled by what seemed to be corporate arrogance. So I devised an end-around strategy: Raise the public's perception that CNN was biased, with the ultimate goal of affecting their bottom line.

Just as Ford sells automobiles, the media sells a product called "objectivity." As one editor explained: "Credibility is the lifeblood of our profession as journalists. Credibility is to us what oxygen is to the human body. Without it, we are nothing."[6]

If Ford sells you a lemon, the quality of their product is called into question and the next time you'll go elsewhere (and tell your friends to do so, too). I figured if I could simulate that effect in the news business, CNN could ignore the backlash for only so long. In the end, they'd do whatever it takes to clean up their act.

CNN made my job easier by continuing their outrageous coverage. In reporting on a Jewish rally near the Old City of Jerusalem, CNN identified the location as "Jaffa Gate, or Bab al-Khalil, the main western entrance to the walled city."[7] Everyone knows that "Jaffa Gate" is the standard reference in every encyclopedia, university textbook, diplomatic document, media style guide, or any other acceptable Western source. So why did CNN go out of its way – especially in the context of reporting on a *Jewish* rally – to dredge up the obscure Arabic reference, "Bab al-Khalil"? Would CNN likewise refer to Manhattan as *Man-a-hat-ta*, or "Island of Hills," the name given by the Algonquin Indians?

On top of that, CNN's follow-up article, published after the Jerusalem rally had concluded, offered no quotes from any of the distinguished Israeli speakers, nor from any of the quarter-million attendees. CNN's lone quote was from a Muslim religious leader who called the rally "provocative"[8] – a description directly contradicted by other media reports which described the Israeli demonstrators as peaceful, "unlike the Palestinian 'demonstrators' that have sparked much of the violence."[9] So why did CNN characterize this peaceful rally as "provocative"? And were there no Jews available for comment?[10]

At times, it seemed like CNN was simply reprinting press releases from the Palestinian propaganda office. Here's how Hamas – on the U.S. State Department's list of terror organizations for its incessant suicide bombings, rocket attacks, arms smuggling and abductions – was described by CNN in an article about Palestinian bomb-makers: Hamas is an organization known "for actions such as building schools, hospitals and helping the community in social and religious ways..."[11] Readers of CNN would think that Hamas is the Palestinian version of Mother Theresa.

Not only was CNN exonerating the Hamas connection to terror, but in an article entitled "Terrorism Q&A," CNN flipped reality on its head and credited the *Jews* with inventing terror: "The oldest terrorists were holy warriors who killed civilians. For instance, in first-century Palestine, Jewish Zealots would publicly slit the throats of Romans and their collaborators..."[12]

At least CNN wasn't giving credence to the canard that Israel was responsible for 9-11.

Well, actually, CNN's special report on "Roots of Terror" did cite the libelous claim that "some Arabs believe Israel [is] behind Sept. 11."[13]

Then, with the demonization of Israel in full swing, CNN cut to the chase and blamed Israel for all the world's problems:

> It is impossible now to separate the taking of hostages in Iran, the bombing of barracks in Lebanon, the war with Iraq or even the current conflict in Afghanistan, from the question of Israel.[14]

CNN was demonstrating such antagonism toward Israel that some theory had to explain it. When Watergate was at its height, Deep Throat told Bob Woodward: "Follow the money."[15] So I followed the money and discovered that Alwaleed bin Talal – the same Saudi Prince who unsuccessfully tried to give Rudy Giuliani a $10 million check after September 11[16] – has long-term stock investments worth billions in CNN's parent company, Time-Warner.[17]

Does that financial stake necessarily translate into influence? In this case, apparently yes. In describing his vast media holdings, bin Talal told *The Times* of London: "If I feel very strongly about something, I convey a message directly to the chairman or the chief executive."[18]

Was CNN kowtowing to petro dollars? According to Reese Schonfeld, the first President and Chief Executive of CNN, the network maintains a "very cozy relationship" with Arab regimes in which CNN has "economic presence and they make a certain amount of money... from marketing their product in the Arab worlds." Schonfeld explained that CNN bigwigs "want access to those [Arab] guys, so they bend over backwards."[19]

When I raised this issue with one CNN editor, he shot me back an earful: "Why are you picking on one Arab billionaire? Everyone knows that Jews dominate the media. Hollywood is run by Jews, and the publishing industry, too."[20]

"Unfortunately," I explained, "it often works in the opposite. Jews will sometimes bend over backwards to avoid the perception of being 'too Jewish.' In the process, Jewish concerns suffer."

"Sounds like an interesting sociological theory," he said. "But the bottom line is that Jews have disproportionate representation in the media."

So I gave him a history lesson. Back in the 1930s, Arthur Hays Sulzberger, publisher of the *New York Times,* was a committed *anti-*Zionist; when the British issued the White Paper of 1939 restricting Jewish immigration to Palestine, a *Times* editorial praised the move as necessary "to save the homeland itself from overpopulation as well as from an increasingly violent resistance on the part of the Arabs."[21] No pro-Jewish positioning there.

And then there's the issue of the Holocaust. As early as 1942, leading newspapers like the *Manchester Guardian* – under headlines like "How the Jews in France were Rounded Up"[22] and "The German Massacres of Jews in Poland"[23] – wrote extensively of "the German scheme for total extermination" of the Jews. So how is it possible that the average American was unaware of Nazi atrocities until after the war, blind to the gruesome facts of the Holocaust as they were happening?

The tragic answer is that America's premier source of wartime news, the *New York Times* – in the repentant words of former *Times'* executive editor Max Frankel – buried the Holocaust "inside its gray and stolid pages, never featured, analyzed or rendered truly comprehensible."[24] Typical of the *Times'* coverage was a November 25, 1942 report – relegated to page 10 – of roundups, cattle cars, gassings, and the disappearance of 90 percent of the Warsaw Ghetto population.[25] As the genocide of Hungarian Jewry hit full stride, with 400,000 Jews murdered and another 350,000 to be exterminated within weeks, the *Times* posted the news as a small item on page 12.[26]

The *Times'* influential columnist and Washington bureau chief, Arthur Krock (a Jew), published nearly 1,200 columns during World War II – without one mention of Jewish persecution.[27] When the *Times'* publisher wrote a front page story about the Buchenwald concentration camp, he made no mention that Jews had been killed there.[28] Nor would readers of the *Times* know that the Warsaw Ghetto Uprising involved Jews; the *Times* referred obliquely to "Poles" and "Warsaw patriots."[29]

The cover-up extended to the editorial pages, too. Of more than 17,000 *Times* editorials during the war, only five mentioned Europe's Jews. Typical was the editorial of December 2, 1942, after the State Department had unofficially confirmed that 2 million Jews had been slain and 5 million more were "in danger of extermination." The *Times* retreated from any show of special concern, insisting that Jews were merely "the first to suffer."[30]

Years later, the *Times* admitted that this policy was directed by publisher Arthur Hays Sulzberger, for both political and personal reasons: He didn't want his paper criticized as Jewish, and he didn't approve of Jews helping fellow Jews. By defining the Holocaust as a non-story for the national media, the *Times* – as the newspaper of record – made it impossible to galvanize the public or politicians to save Hitler's Jewish victims.[31] Other media took the cue; BBC records show explicit orders not to report on the Holocaust.[32]

All told, it was what Frankel called "the century's bitterest journalistic failure."[33]

At that point, having completed my little homily, I asked the CNN editor: "Some of this mentality continues today, with some Jewish journalists propagating the most virulent anti-Israel coverage. Is this what you mean by 'disproportionate Jewish influence' in the media?"[34]

The Bottom Line

To keep the pressure on CNN, I sent out email alerts – week after week, to tens of thousands of subscribers – detailing CNN's latest transgressions.[35] These people were in turn bombarding CNN with emails, creating a tidal wave of protest. Websites sprung up with names like CNN-Watch, and a bumper sticker – "CNN Lies" – became popular on America's roads.

CNN was getting flack from all angles, even mocked in an email parody entitled, "If the Passover Exodus Story were Reported by CNN":

> The cycle of violence between the Jews and Egyptians continues with no end in sight. Following eight previous plagues that destroyed the Egyptian infrastructure and disrupted the lives of Egyptian civilians, the Jews have now launched their latest offensive, code-named Plague of Darkness.

Western journalists are particularly enraged by this plague. "It is simply impossible to report when you can't see an inch in front of you," complained a frustrated Wafa Menkaura of CNN. "I have heard from my reliable Egyptian contacts that under the cover of darkness, the Jews are annihilating thousands of Egyptians. Their word is solid enough evidence for me."

The hard-line Jewish leader Moses contends that the plagues are justified, given the harsh slavery imposed by the Egyptians. Pharaoh issued a swift and harsh rebuttal: "If only the plagues would let up, there would be no slavery. We just want to live plague-free. It is the right of every society."

Saeb Amenemhat, an Egyptian spokesperson, justified the slavery as "the only means to fight the Jews' superior weaponry supplied by the superpower God." He called for an international inquiry into the plagues, which have caused a humanitarian crisis and are being labeled as "war crimes."

The United Nations held an emergency session to condemn the latest Jewish offensive. "Moses is sabotaging peace talks with these plagues and must return to the negotiating table," a U.N. spokesman said. "Better yet, the Jews should go back to slavery, for the good of the rest of the world."[36]

This parody of CNN coverage went viral, forwarded from friend to friend around the Internet. Like every successful joke, it touched on deep truths – of the media's often-ridiculous apologetics for Arab aggression, and of journalists' unique ability to compress the largest number of words into the most useless idea.

The Turner Bomb

Any doubts about CNN's pro-Palestinian bias were laid to rest on

May 27, 2002, when a Palestinian suicide bomber blew himself up at an ice cream stand in the Israeli town of Petach Tikva, killing a grandmother and her one-year-old granddaughter. CNN sent a news team to conduct a lengthy interview with Chen Keinan, the Jewish woman grieving simultaneously for both her mother and daughter. Yet to the Keinan family's shock, CNN aired a 30-minute report which focused not on the Israeli victims, but rather on the Palestinian bomber's family and their various "grievances."[37]

This was blatant empathy for Palestinian terror, and an outraged public had no patience for nuanced explanations. Faced with a barrage of complaints and withering credibility, CNN quickly re-broadcast the full Chen Keinan interview and issued a statement regretting "any extra anguish the Keinan family has suffered as a result of CNN's broadcast."[38]

CNN was up against the ropes. But with no corrective measures in place, the network slipped deeper and deeper into self-destruction. In June 2002, when two Palestinian suicide bombings on consecutive days killed 26 Israelis in Jerusalem, CNN founder Ted Turner was quoted in the London *Guardian* as supporting the bombings. Turner said:

> "Aren't the Israelis and the Palestinians both terrorising each other?... The Palestinians are fighting with human suicide bombers, that's all they have. The Israelis... they've got one of the most powerful military machines in the world. The Palestinians have nothing. So who are the terrorists? I would make a case that both sides are involved in terrorism."[39]

CNN executives quickly went into damage control mode, disavowing Turner's remarks on the grounds that he "no longer runs CNN."[40] But as Jonah said after being swallowed by the whale, something sure smelled fishy. Turner didn't need any official editorial position, because at the time he was serving as the influential vice-chairman of CNN's parent company, AOL-Time Warner.

For media monitors, this scandal was more fuel for the fire. My email alerts hit a peak of effectiveness and the inbox of Eason Jordan, CNN's news chief, was being flooded with thousands of emails each day. This was not computer-generated spam; these were genuine, personal complaints from masses of outraged individuals.

And then the final hammer blow: Fox News overtook CNN in the ratings.[41] CNN had been number one ever since Turner invented the cable news market in 1980. But CNN's product was now seen as defective: "America's most trusted news source" had, quite simply, lost the public's trust.

As CNN's American ratings dropped, foreign news markets quickly followed suit. Days after Turner's outrageous comments, some cable and satellite TV companies threatened to pull the plug on CNN, replacing it with competitor Fox News instead.[42]

For a time, CNN may have been able to dismiss me as a pesky media activist with a high-speed Internet line, but they could not ignore the financial bottom line. With an earthquake of bad energy directed at CNN, the mighty fortress in Atlanta was crumbling.

CNN executives held emergency meetings to identify the factors causing their decline. The board of directors was losing patience and the pressure to make changes was immense. That's when CNN in effect threw up their hands and effectively said: We can't handle this anymore. The bad publicity and the email campaigns have to stop.

In the face of this public relations meltdown, CNN news chief Eason Jordan and other top CNN officials flew to Israel, where they made the rounds to apologize and basically beg everyone to lay off. Jordan ate a big piece of Mideast humble pie, admitting that CNN had made "inexcusable mistakes" by presenting "incorrect perceptions" of the Arab-Israeli conflict.[43]

But for me, apologies were not enough. A mechanism had to be put in place to ensure that the bias did not recur. That's when CNN agreed to assign a senior executive as my private liaison. This executive told me up front: "If you have a problem, come to me directly. Assuming that it's reasonable, we'll cooperate and make appropriate changes. But please – stop sending alerts to your email list!"

The dreaded power of consumerism had sent CNN execs into a tizzy.

CNN also agreed to address specific core issues, like ceasing to sympathize with terrorists and eliminating the "cycle of violence" narrative from its coverage. Eason Jordan ordered his staff to "go to extremes" to avoid any impression of moral equivalence between terror victims and their attackers. CNN also announced that, barring an "extraordinarily compelling situation," it would refuse to air any statements from suicide bombers or their families.[44]

CNN took further steps to repair the damage. Wolf Blitzer flew to Israel to file a series of special reports on Israeli victims of terror, and CNN.com launched a special online section devoted to Israeli victims – including personal biographies, descriptions of the attacks, and interviews with victims' families.[45]

For me, these CNN concessions marked a huge triumph. Day after day, month after month, it's as if I had been chiseling away at a colossal chunk of granite, banging the hammer again and again, never sure if the big breakthrough would ever really occur. But I kept banging – another critique and another email alert. And then suddenly the whole thing cracked open.

The story was so big that the *New York Times* devoted a 1,300-word news article to the shift at CNN – citing my work with HonestReporting for contributing to the change.[46]

In the end, it was the public groundswell that pushed CNN over the edge. The *Jerusalem Post* reported that readers of my communiqués "sent up to 6,000 e-mails a day to CNN executives, effectively paralyzing their internal e-mail system."[47]

The voiceless consumer had united to bring the mighty CNN to its knees.

Best of all, the "ripple effect" was now happening in reverse: News outlets worldwide saw one Media Goliath fall and feared they could be next. As one foreign correspondent told me: "Many of us were operating under a sense of unbridled affinity for the Palestinians. Those days are now over."

In this corner of the world, sanity was restored. Justice had prevailed.

Process of Change

But sometimes, the more things change, the more they remain insane. Although CNN had taken steps to become more balanced, bias against Israel would prove to be an ingrained culture, seeping out of CNN's fissures.

One day I was browsing the special "Victims of Terror" section on CNN.com, which included a week-by-week summary of all terror attacks in Israel. One listing, for the last week of July 2002, included the following three attacks:

1) A Palestinian terrorist detonated a large bomb at the cafeteria of Hebrew University in Jerusalem, killing seven and wounding 80 more.
2) A Palestinian suicide bomber blew himself up near a falafel stand in Jerusalem.
3) Salah Shehadeh, head of military operations for Hamas, was killed by an Israeli targeted strike in Gaza.

I read this and did a double-take. According to CNN, Israel's strike on a terrorist mastermind was a "terror attack" equivalent to Palestinians blowing up civilians at a cafeteria and falafel stand.

Surely CNN was aware that Israel had scheduled the attack on Shehadeh three times prior, each time postponing it because of fears of civilian casualties.[48] And surely CNN was not decrying the loss of Shehadeh's wife as some kind of "innocent civilian victim" – given the widely-available photos of her in full military gear, holding an assault rifle.[49]

No, this was simply the ugly ghost of Ted Turner roaming the halls of CNN all over again.

I immediately got on the phone to my contact at CNN. "What kind of warped moral equivalence are you promoting over there?" I asked him.

"What are you talking about?" he said.

"The Shehadeh strike – CNN is calling that a *terror* attack!"

"What are you talking about?" he repeated.

I shook my head. CNN's top news executives were apparently oblivious to the contents of their own website. So I walked him through it. "Go to CNN.com's special report on terror in Israel."

"Okay," he said, "I'm there."

"Now click on the section that lists all the attacks."

"Okay, I'm there."

"Now go to July 2002 and scroll down."

"Oh... my... gosh..."

Then he dropped the phone.

A few seconds later, I heard a low, moaning voice.

"Shraga, that is not our policy."

"I know it's not your *official* policy," I said. "But policy doesn't count for much if it's not being implemented by your staff."

"I'm walking down to the newsroom right now," he said. "We're going to change this on the spot."

"That's fine," I said. "I expect you to change it. But let's move past the cosmetic stuff. There's a deeper problem here: You've got writers on the CNN staff who actually believe that the killing of Shehadeh was terrorism."

"We'll fix that, too," he said with urgency in his voice. "We'll add another layer of oversight to the editorial process."

And then his tone turned somber:

"But we can't handle any more bad publicity. Promise me that you won't send out an alert to your email list."

I promised – this time.

Bulldozers in Gaza

The relationship see-sawed back and forth, with CNN making mistakes and me needing to step in to correct them.

One such exchange occurred in March 2003, just as American troops were invading Iraq. A young American woman named Rachel Corrie had been hanging out in Gaza, chumming with terrorists and burning

American flags. One day, as an Israeli bulldozer was dismantling tunnels used by Gazans to smuggle weapons, Corrie decided to protest. She positioned herself in a trench, in a spot invisible to the Israeli bulldozer driver, and was accidentally crushed to death.[50]

This was the moment that pro-Palestinian activists were so cynically waiting for. They seized the opportunity to promote Corrie's death as a blood libel, accusing Israel of intentional murder. As George Rishmawi, director of the group that sponsored Corrie's stay in Gaza, told the *San Francisco Chronicle*: Placing American students in dangerous positions is good for the Palestinian cause because "if some of these foreign volunteers get shot or even killed, then the international media will sit up and take notice."[51]

CNN got hooked by the "intentional murder" bait and posted an online report that juxtaposed before-and-after photos: The first photo showed Corrie standing in plain view of an Israeli bulldozer, with a megaphone in hand. The second photo showed Corrie bleeding on the ground. Here's the photo caption from CNN:

> Photos released by the International Solidarity Movement show Rachel Corrie **before and after** she was hit by an Israeli bulldozer in Gaza on Sunday.[52]

This distinct "before and after" chronology implies the libelous version of the story – that at the moment she was crushed, Corrie was clearly visible, standing with a megaphone. In truth, the two photos were taken hours apart. At the time of the accident, Corrie was *without* the megaphone and in a hidden position. In fact, any alert editor could see that the second photo shows a *different* bulldozer – with narrow, double-glazed, bulletproof windows and an 8-foot-tall bulldozer blade that greatly obscures driver visibility.[53]

I got on the hotline to CNN.

"Oops," my contact said, after I explained. "I see the problem. But we're busy with a war right now. U.S. troops are on the outskirts of

Baghdad, ready to invade. Can this wait till next week?"

"No, it can't wait," I told him. "Israel is being accused of murdering a young American girl in cold blood. CNN is fueling that misperception. You're free to decide not to deal with this, but my job is to make sure this libel does not go unanswered."

"We'll issue a 'caption clarification' right away," he told me, "to emphasize the chronological difference between the two photos. Just please don't send out an alert."

I wasn't going to let him off the hook that easily. "I appreciate your changing it," I said, "but I'm not happy with this pattern of CNN making mistakes and then glibly agreeing to issue a correction. I don't receive a salary from CNN, and I'm getting tired of having to edit your reports for accuracy."

"Whatever you say – just no alert, right?"

"I'm afraid that won't do this time," I replied. "Too many people have already seen the false CNN report. I'm going to send out an email alert, and maybe that will stir things up down there.[54] Now I won't keep you any longer from the war in Baghdad."

Jewish Jihad

Since then, things have gotten noticeably better, but the self-proclaimed "most trusted name in news" still has a long way to go. I was abruptly reminded of this in 2007 with CNN's three-part documentary on religious fundamentalism, *God's Warriors*.[55] Under the guise of even-handedness, CNN gave equal air-time to the three major religions, equating Jewish and Christian "extremism" with the worldwide jihadist phenomenon of radical Islam.

This blatantly false moral equivalence (when was the last time you saw someone hijack a plane, blow up a commuter train, bomb a nightclub, or destroy a skyscraper in the name of Judaism or Christianity?) came not from a two-bit reporter, but from CNN's 27-year veteran and chief international correspondent at the time, Christiane Amanpour. It was a textbook case of agenda-driven journalism, with Amanpour comparing Islamic terror – which has spawned over a thousand suicide attacks since 9-11 – to benign activities like fundraising for Israel. It's what Dan Abrams of MSNBC later called "a defense of Islamic fundamentalism and the worst type of moral relativism."[56]

The problem was not limited to Amanpour alone. One of the producers of *God's Warriors* was Nidal Rafa, a pro-Palestinian activist who for many years served as a CNN senior producer in Jerusalem.[57] To get a sense of how Rafa combines her journalistic pursuits with pro-Palestinian advocacy, consider the time she served as interpreter for Fox News correspondent Jennifer Griffin on a trip to Israel's Wadi Ara region. According to one journalist who accompanied the group, Griffin was "totally dependent" on Nidal Rafa, who decided what to translate from Arabic "and what to leave untranslated." When Griffin asked an Israeli spokesman to describe the Wadi Ara region, here's what happened:

> I don't manage to get out even one whole sentence before Rafa interjects herself, in English, with an obvious edge to her voice: "I will give you the background," she says. "This whole area was expropriated by Israel from the Arabs. Everything here belonged to the Arabs. There are Jewish settlements such as Katzir and Harish above: villas, beautiful homes. And all of it on our land."[58]

This from Nidal Rafa, the same "objective journalist" who filled a senior position at CNN's Jerusalem bureau.

Fast-forward to a spring day in 2009, when a group of respected Western reporters gathered in downtown Jerusalem to hear a talk by Knesset member Danny Ayalon. In attendance that day was our old friend Nidal Rafa, who asserted her "journalistic objectivity" by repeatedly interrupting the debate, heckling Ayalon, calling him a "fascist" and lashing out:

> "Do you not recognize that there is an occupation? Yes or no? Yes or no? Do you agree that there is an occupation? Do you recognize

the occupation? Yes or no? Give me an answer... It's Palestinian land."[59]

For media monitors who had long accused CNN of institutional pro-Palestinian bias (going back to the 1980s when Robert Wiener, CNN's Jerusalem bureau chief, is said to have changed the sign under the office clock from "Jerusalem" to "Palestine"),[60] Rafa's outburst was pure corroborating evidence. CNN immediately tried to staunch the damage by claiming that Rafa no longer worked for the network, but a bit of investigative work showed that Rafa was reporting on Israel events for CNN as recently as December 2008,[61] and at the event that day in March 2009, she handed out her CNN business card to several people.[62]

In the wake of this biased reporting, CNN's credibility has taken a huge hit, from which it may never recover. CNN's prime-time ratings have dropped dismally behind cable news competitors Fox News, MSNBC, and at times even behind its sister network HLN (formerly Headline News).[63]

CNN is trying to improve, but I still catch some wacky perspectives. When Ayatollah Mohammed Hussein Fadlallah – the spiritual leader and mentor of Hezbollah – died in July 2010, CNN's Senior Editor of Mideast Affairs, Octavia Nasr, posted on Twitter her sadness over the passing of "one of Hezbollah's giants I respect a lot."[64]

Exactly which of Fadlallah's views did this CNN senior editor admire? Was it his support for the seizure and hostage-taking at the U.S. Embassy in Tehran in 1979?[65] His call for an Iranian-style Islamic Revolution in Lebanon? His providing the fatwa (religious permission) for the suicide bomber who killed 241 American servicemen at the Marine barracks in Beirut in 1983?[66] His fatwa calling for the boycott of all American products?[67] Or perhaps it was his praise for the massacre of eight Israeli students in Jerusalem[68] and his deathbed wish "for the Zionist entity to cease to exist."[69]

Following a firestorm of criticism over her 140-character tweet, Nasr later issued a 4,000-character apology. Alas, even that was not enough for CNN, who fired Nasr.[70]

And so it goes at CNN. When media monitors spot something awry, they sound the alarm bells directly to CNN's Atlanta headquarters. The messages are distributed to CNN executives and their team of assistants – and invariably a Blackberry reply arrives within minutes. Anything to be spared the dreaded email alert.

Notes

1. Arthur S. Brisbane, "Where Words Can Never Do Justice," *New York Times*, June 11, 2011.
2. Paul Adams, "Journalists Caught in the Middle," BBC News Online, November 13, 2000.
3. "100-day Study of Philadelphia Inquirer," HonestReporting.com, August 28, 2003.
4. Andrew Gross and Michelle A. Gross, "San Jose Mercury News Terror Study," HonestReporting.com, March 15, 2004.
5. "The Age Newspaper Study," Media Study Group, November 5, 2003.
6. Jovial Rantao of South Africa's *Sunday Independent*, cited in Franz Kruger, *Black, White and Grey: Ethics in South African Journalism*, Double Store, 2004. As another media executive put it: "Every news organization has only its credibility and reputation to rely on." (Tony Burman, ex-editor of CBC News, cited in Gayle MacDonald, "Media Can't Sate News Hunger," *Globe & Mail* [Canada], October 17, 2001.)
7. "Tens of Thousands of Israelis Protest U.S.-Proposed Peace Plan," CNN.com, January 8, 2001.
8. CNN.com, January 8, 2001; also cited in Ellen Knickmeyer, "Palestinians Promise to Resist Efforts Prodding Them Toward Framework Deal," Associated Press, January 8, 2001.
9. *Wall Street Journal Europe*, January 8, 2002.
10. See "Dishonest Reporting 'Award' for 2001," HonestReporting.com, January 7, 2002.
11. "Al Aqsa Claims Responsibility for Jerusalem Shooting," CNN.com, January 22, 2002.
12. Cited in Toby Klein Greenwald, "CNN's Chain of Bias," *Jerusalem Post*, June 21, 2002.
13. "Behind the Headlines: Roots of Terror," CNN, October 15, 2001.
14. Ibid.
15. See "Ex-FBI Official: I'm 'Deep Throat,'" Associated Press, June 1, 2005.
16. Jennifer Steinhauer, "Citing Comments on Attack, Giuliani Rejects Saudi's Gift," *New York Times*, October 12, 2001.
17. Andy Serwer, "Alwaleed: The Prince of All Media," *Fortune*, October 3, 2005.
18. Garth Alexander, "Prince Loses Crown in Internet Bubble," *The Sunday Times* (UK), November 5, 2000.
19. "Unresolved Problem Calling Terrorists Terrorists," *The O'Reilly Factor*, Fox News, September 28, 2001.
20. None of the top 20 people on the Forbes Celebrity 100 is Jewish, and none of the major television news operations – Fox News, CNN, MSNBC, ABC News, CBS News, or NBC News – is headed by a Jewish executive. (Brian Palmer, "Do Jews Really Control the Media?", Slate.com, October 5, 2010.)
21. Ira Stoll, "The Legacy of Arthur Hays Sulzberger," *The Sun* (New York), April 13, 2005.
22. "How the Jews in France were Rounded Up," *Manchester Guardian*, September 3, 1942.
23. "The German Massacres of Jews in Poland," *Manchester Guardian*, December 11, 1942.
24. Max Frankel, "Turning Away From the Holocaust," *New York Times*, November 14, 2001.
25. Cited in Bret Stephens, "Sympathy for the Devil," *Jerusalem Post*, July 19, 2002. During the six years of the war in Europe, out of 24,000 front-page stories, the story of the Holocaust made the *Times* front page only 26 times. See Laurel Leff, "How the NYT Missed the Story of the

Holocaust While It Was Happening," History News Network, April 4, 2005. See also Laurel Leff, *Buried by The Times: The Holocaust and America's Most Important Newspaper*, Cambridge University Press, 2006.
26. Stephens, "Sympathy for the Devil."
27. Stoll, "The Legacy of Arthur Hays Sulzberger."
28. See *Holocaust: The Untold Story*, Newseum.org/holocaust.
29. Susan Tifft and Alex Jones, *The Trust: The Private and Powerful Family Behind The New York Times*, Little Brown, 1999.
30. Frankel, "Turning Away From the Holocaust."
31. Karin McQuillan, "Wikipedia's Jewish Problem," Frontpagemag.com, July 13, 2010.
32. *Holocaust: The Untold Story*.
33. Frankel, "Turning Away From the Holocaust."
34. William J. Drummond, former Jerusalem bureau chief for the *Los Angeles Times* and now a journalism professor at UC-Berkley, wrote: "Pro-Palestinian partisans might decry Jewish reporters as biased, but in fact reporting by Jews in foreign publications about Israeli actions and policy has frequently been mercilessly critical." (William J. Drummond, "From Hasbara to Intifada," *The Big Story*, University of California, Berkeley, Graduate School of Journalism, June 1, 2002.)
35. See, for example, HonestReporting.com: "The Warp, Botch and Skew," January 24, 2002; "Classic CNN Bias," February 18, 2002; "Terror Continues, Media Responds," March 5, 2002.
36. Attributed to Daniel P. Waxman, April 2002.
37. Steve Weizman, "CNN Cites Error in Israel Coverage," Associated Press, June 23, 2002; "CNN Statement Concerning the Interview with the Keinan Family," June 4, 2002, posted on Imra.org.il.
38. Zain Verjee, "European Views of Middle East Conflict," CNN, June 6, 2002; "Mother of Baby Killed by Bomb: 'Please Help,'" *CNN Access with Paula Zahn*, CNN, May 31, 2002.
39. Oliver Burkeman and Peter Beaumont, "CNN Founder Accuses Israel of Terror," *The Guardian* (UK), June 18, 2002. Turner also famously called the September 11 hijackers "brave." (John F. Morrison, "Ted Turner has 'Nutty' Perception of 9-11," *Philadelphia Daily News*, February 13, 2002.)
40. "Suicide Bombers Strike Israel Again," *CNN's Insight with Jonathan Mann*, CNN, June 19, 2002.
41. Jon Fine, "How Fox Was Outfoxed," *Business Week*, February 13, 2006.
42. Phyllis Furman, "Israeli Cable Networks Threatening to Drop CNN Over Coverage," *Daily News* (New York), June 21, 2002.
43. Ellis Shuman, "Amid Allegations of Biased Coverage, CNN Highlights Israeli Victims of Terror," *Israel Insider*, June 24, 2002.
44. David Bauder, "CNN Executive on Visit to Israel Issues New Policy on Airing Terrorist Tapes," Associated Press, June 21, 2002.
45. Matt Wells, "Media: Back from the Blink," *The Guardian* (UK), July 1, 2002.
46. Jim Rutenberg, "CNN Navigates Raw Emotions in Its Coverage from Israel," *New York Times*, July 1, 2002.
47. Miriam Shaviv, "When CNN is the Story; The Biased Beeb," *Jerusalem Post*, June 28, 2002.
48. "Hamas to Blame for Civilian Deaths," *Chicago Sun-Times*, July 24, 2002. (Israeli Defense Minister Binyamin Ben-Eliezer said that this time, "the information we had was that there were no civilians near him.")
49. Photo Essay: "Attack in Gaza," Time.com, July 23, 2002.
50. Testifying under oath, the bulldozer driver said he did not realize he had run over Corrie until he heard what had happened over the radio network. (Ahiya Raved, "Bulldozer Driver: I Didn't Realize I Crushed Rachel Corrie," *Ynetnews* (Israel), October 21, 2010.)

51. Matthew Kalman and Teresa Castle, "S.F. Jewish Activist Held as Security Threat in Israel," *San Francisco Chronicle*, July 14, 2004. With extreme irony, Rachel's parents, Craig and Cindy Corrie, were the targets of an attempted kidnapping at the hands of five Palestinian gunmen in the Gaza Strip – on the same day that Palestinians were using stolen bulldozers to smash through the border wall between Egypt and Gaza. (See Steven Erlanger, "Rockets and Border Attacks Add to the Strife in Gaza," *New York Times*, January 5, 2006.)
52. "Israeli Bulldozer Kills American Protester," CNN.com, March 25, 2003. Emphasis added.
53. The *Christian Science Monitor* took the false chronology one step further by distributing the earlier photo of Corrie with the megaphone, and adding the words "moments before" into the caption: "Death of a protester: Rachel Corrie, wearing a reflective Day-Glo jacket, shouts through a bullhorn at an oncoming Israeli army bulldozer in southern Gaza Sunday moments before it ran her over." The group that sponsored Corrie, the International Solidarity Movement, further tried to capitalize on her death by releasing a crude image – heavily doctored in Photoshop – purporting to depict Corrie standing in full view of an Israeli bulldozer. (See Nigel Parry and Arjan El Fassed, "Photostory: Israeli Bulldozer Driver Murders American Peace Activist," Electronic Intifada, March 16, 2003.)
54. See "Rachel Corrie, Continued," HonestReporting.com, March 25, 2003.
55. "God's Warriors," CNN, August 22-24, 2007.
56. Dan Abrams, *Live with Dan Abrams*, MSNBC, August 27, 2008.
57. "Program Descriptions of duPont-Columbia Awards Winners," Columbia University Graduate School of Journalism, 2009. On various occasions Rafa publicly called for Israel to cease to exist as a Jewish state; she also worked on the noxious anti-Israel documentary, *Palestine Is Still the Issue*. Rafa's "loyalty to Fatah" led to suspicious activities in Ramallah such as "handing off unmarked packages to men who dart out of storefronts and alleyways." (David Samuels, "In a Ruined Country," *The Atlantic*, September 2005.)
58. Vered Levy-Barzilai, "Out-foxing CNN," *Haaretz* (Israel), March 7, 2002.
59. "Nidal Rafa's Verbal Assault on Danny Ayalon," YouTube.com, March 16, 2009; "More Shocking Evidence of CNN's Faulty Hiring Policy," HonestReporting.com, April 6, 2009.
60. Talya Halkin and Herb Keinon, "How CNN Changed Israel's World," *Jerusalem Post*, June 14, 2005.
61. See Nidal Rafa, Michal Zippori and Jordana Miller, "Hebron Mayor: Jewish Settlers on 'Terror' Rampage," CNN.com, December 4, 2008.
62. "Exclusive: This is CNN (& BBC-UNRWA Connection Revealed)," Tomgrossmedia.com, March 18, 2009.
63. Bill Carter, "MSNBC Is Close to Falling to Third Place in Cable News Ratings," *New York Times*, September 26, 2011; Bill Carter, "With Rivals Ahead, Doubts for CNN's Middle Road," *New York Times*, April 26, 2009.
64. octavianasrCNN, Twitter, July 4, 2010.
65. Martin Kramer, "The Oracle of Hizbullah: Sayyid Muhammad Husayn Fadlallah (Part 1)," *Spokesmen for the Despised: Fundamentalist Leaders of the Middle East*.
66. Cited in Dr. Shimon Shapira, "Lebanon's Ayatollah Fadlallah and the Mercaz Ha-Rav Yeshiva Attack in Jerusalem," Jerusalem Center for Public Affairs, March 10, 2008.
67. Sayyed Fadlullah, "Boycott Israeli and American Good and Products," english.bayynat.org. Ib.
68. Al-Manar TV (Hezbollah), March 8, 2008.
69. Laila Bassam, "Senior Lebanese Shi'ite Cleric Fadlallah Dies," Reuters, July 4, 2010.
70. Octavia Nasr, "Nasr Explains Controversial Tweet on Lebanese Cleric," *This Just In* blog, CNN, July 6, 2010; Brian Stelter, "CNN Drops Editor after Hezbollah Comments," *Media Decoder / New York Times*, July 7, 2010. Six months later, in its prominent "Person of the Year" Issue, *Time* magazine offered a "fond farewell" tribute to Fadlallah, calling him a "brilliant"

"pioneer," "soft-spoken and gracious." (Thanassis Cambanis, "Fond Farewells: Ayatollah Fadlalah," *Time*, December 27, 2010.)

— 6 —

INTIMIDATION? WHAT INTIMIDATION?!

Toward the beginning of the Intifada, *Newsweek's* Jerusalem bureau chief, Joshua Hammer, was interviewing some Palestinian leaders in Gaza. When the interview ended, the Palestinians announced: "Now we're kidnapping you." They held Hammer and a photographer captive for four hours before releasing them.

How would we expect Hammer to describe being kidnapped? "A harrowing experience… I felt anger toward my captors… a grave violation of freedom of the press… I had no idea if I'd get out dead or alive…"

No, Hammer didn't say anything remotely like this. Here's how he described the experience in *Newsweek*:

> …Hammer says he never feared his captors would hurt him… "They never threatened us or pointed their guns at us," Hammer says. "They actually fed us one of the best meals I've eaten in Gaza."[1]

For Hammer it may have been a delicious meal, but for me it set off some serious alarm bells. Why had Hammer been kidnapped? And why did he report the episode in such glowing terms?

First things first: Hammer was kidnapped because that's the way things often work in the Arab Middle East. For Americans, freedom of the press is a core value, guaranteed by the Constitution and ingrained in our mother's milk. But for Arab regimes the media is just another propaganda tool, tightly controlled with government-appointed editors who have zero tolerance for criticism. That's one of the primary ways these dictators survive. So if a writer is not careful, things can get pretty rough. (Think Salman Rushdie.)

In Palestinian areas, journalists are consistently being threatened if they don't toe the line. The quasi-governmental Palestinian Journalists Syndicate in the Gaza Strip constantly harangues local reporters and photographers for coverage that fails to "benefit the struggle of the Palestinian people for liberation and independence" – warning that anyone who violates its guidelines will bear the personal and legal consequences.[2] Translation: Independent-minded reporting may result in being shot in the town square, dragged through the streets, and hung upside down from a lamp post.[3]

When journalists tried to cover an anti-Hamas protest in Gaza, Hamas security men seized reporters' cameras and raided media offices to prevent any news footage from getting out.[4] On another occasion in Gaza, a reporter for a Saudi-owned news channel was shot, dragged from his car, and beaten – because his station had allowed criticism of Palestinian officials.[5]

In the days of the Wild West, the code of honor considered it crass to shoot somebody in the back; instead you fought a duel. But in Palestinian areas today, things are somewhat more chaotic and lawless. Dozens of renegade groups – not to mention the "mainstream" Hamas and Fatah – are jockeying for power and wielding their weapons against journalists who dare to defy them.

This dark phenomenon is highlighted in the "Press Freedom Index" published by the respected media rights agency Reporters Without

Borders. In terms of "press freedom," Israel ranks comparably to the United States, whereas the Palestinian Authority ranks 163rd out of 173 – even worse than Iraq, where over 150 media workers have died since the 2003 American invasion.[6] Here's how Reporters Without Borders described life as a journalist in Palestinian areas:

> Both Hamas and Fatah ride roughshod over press freedom and arrest journalists without any justification... Hamas has become a real press freedom predator. This latest violation of journalists' rights is all the more unacceptable as senior Hamas officials were party to it.[7]

To wit: *Chicago Tribune* reporter Hugh Dellios was severely beaten by Palestinians.[8] In Ramallah, three masked gunmen attacked and broke the arms of Jamal Arouri, who works for Agence France Press.[9] And when Associated Press ran a series of stories critical of the PA, the Palestinian Journalists' Union threatened that if AP did not change its coverage, "all necessary measures would be adopted against AP staffers."[10]

Tellingly, none of these incidents were reported by the journalists who were attacked.

Here's the dilemma: Since reporting negatively about Palestinians can get you killed, journalists constantly need to prove their loyalty to the Palestinian side. When the brutal lynching of two Israelis in Ramallah was filmed by an Italian television crew, a different Italian TV station – fearing reprisals – printed a craven apology in Arabic in the Palestinian daily newspaper, promising to "respect the journalistic rules of the Palestinian Authority."[11]

What unstated "rules" of reporting was the Italian crew referring to? The rule is that anything harmful to the Palestinian cause is off-limits – and woe to the journalist who crosses that line. British photojournalist Mark Seager described his experience at the lynchings in Ramallah:

> [The lynchings] were just a few feet in front of me and I could see

everything. Instinctively, I reached for my camera. I was composing the picture when I was punched in the face by a Palestinian. Another Palestinian pointed right at me shouting "no picture, no picture!" while another guy hit me in the face and said "give me your film!" I tried to get the film out but they were all grabbing me, and one guy just pulled the camera off me and smashed it to the floor... I'll have nightmares for the rest of my life.[12]

How can a journalist report honestly if his life is being threatened?

Complicating the problem is that journalists who suffer this abuse have no recourse. You can't just wander into a Palestinian police station to report an incident, because it's frequently the Palestinian police themselves causing the trouble. Aguirre Bertrand of France's TF1 found this out the hard way when he shot a video that portrayed Palestinians unfavorably; Palestinian police confiscated the tape at gunpoint.[13] (Imagine the outcry if Israel had tried that.)

This policy of threat and intimidation is actually written into the legal code. Freedom House, the well-known human rights group, reports that under Palestinian Authority law, journalists may be fined and jailed, and newspapers closed, for publishing "news that might harm national unity."[14]

Here's how this works: When Seif al-Din Shahin, senior Gaza correspondent for the Al Jazeera network, reported on Fatah's claim of responsibility for a double suicide bombing in Tel Aviv, he was arrested by Palestinian General Intelligence on charges of "inflicting damage to the interests and reputation of the Palestinian people and their struggle."[15] (Palestinian officials later averred that the Israeli Mossad had fabricated the statements of Palestinian responsibility, and threatened that any journalist who blames Fatah for the bombing "will be severely punished.")[16]

When journalist Fayeq Jarada stepped on some toes, he found out about "Palestinian rules for journalists" the hard way. PA officials searched his home and seized his computer, a camera and several videotapes. Jarada was then taken to Gaza City's main prison where he was "brutally tortured." After finally being released – unable to walk – he somehow managed to make his way to an Israeli hospital for treatment.[17]

Amnesty International describes Palestinian "torture" tactics for controlling the press:

> Since its establishment in 1994, the PA has progressively restricted the right to freedom of expression through a variety of means, including arrest and detention by various security forces... Many detainees have been held incommunicado and some have been subjected to torture... [T]he fact that their arrest took place hours or days after they delivered a controversial speech or wrote a critical article, for example, leaves little room for doubt as to the reason for their detention.[18]

This is the reality of life for journalists in Palestinian areas. When Hamas thugs roamed the streets of Gaza beating and terrorizing civilians, at least seven journalists covering the clashes were likewise beaten. In the town of Jebaliya, a Hamas security officer told reporters, "If a single shot is [broadcast] on TV, you know what will happen." He then drew his finger across his throat.[19]

The problem was most acute on September 11, 2001. Upon hearing the news of the World Trade Center attack, Palestinians in Beirut, Nablus and eastern Jerusalem exploded in street celebrations – rejoicing, dancing and handing out candies.[20] Then, to prevent the world from seeing these incriminating images, armed Palestinians – some wearing uniforms of official PA security – trapped photojournalists inside a Nablus hotel while festivities continued in the streets.[21]

One cameraman on assignment for Associated Press Television News was summoned to a Palestinian Authority security office and threatened by cabinet secretary Ahmed Abdel Rahman. If the 9-11 footage is broadcast, Rahman warned, the PA "cannot guarantee the life" of the cameraman.[22] As thugs held guns to his head, the cameraman called AP's Jerusalem bureau, which in turn contacted AP headquarters in New York.

You might expect the world's largest news agency to stand up for freedom of the press, refusing to be intimidated by Palestinian thugs. So did AP respond with righteous indignation and organize a loud public protest? No. They succumbed to the pressure and agreed not to release the footage.

When video footage of Palestinians celebrating 9-11 was eventually released by another wire service, pro-Palestinian activists claimed it was a hoax using archival footage from a decade earlier. This tactic proved untenable, however, given that the footage showed 21st century automobiles. So activists went to Plan-B: claiming that the IDF handed out candy to Palestinians in order to induce them into staging a "celebration" for the cameras.[23]

And so, under a web of lies and threat of intimidation, the true story of September 11 was cast by the wayside. When all was said and done, the most widely reported "Palestinian" angle was the cynical photo-op of Palestinian leader Yasser Arafat, laid out in a health clinic, "donating blood for U.S. victims."[24]

Self-Censorship

For me, the salient question is: How does this reign of intimidation impact new coverage?

Imagine you're on assignment in Gaza City. You witness some Palestinians committing a heinous act of violence and manage to surreptitiously snap some photos. You now have an exclusive story that will make the front page. But you hesitate. Since the information portrays Palestinians in a negative light, you consider the consequences: *Will my house be raided and my camera smashed? Will this jeopardize my access to future stories and eventually cost me my job? Will I be kidnapped and not see my family for months? Why take the chance?*

These fearful thoughts play in a journalist's head, resulting in a form of self-censorship. With stories of Palestinian corruption and violence deemed off-limits, a reporter's perspective undergoes a subconscious shift, which then plays out in everyday reporting – or more significantly, systematic "non"-reporting – of important news. As the Palestinian Human Rights Monitoring Group explained:

> Self-censorship is considered more serious than external censorship because it not only prevents the journalist from publishing what he writes, but it also hinders his writing, thinking or analyzing. He or she would not think of wasting time writing material that will surely not be published...[25]

The insidious part of self-censorship is that consumers never know it's being practiced. Did your local paper ever report on the Palestinian TV show – a children's program, no less – which claimed that Israel was burning Palestinians in ovens?[26] Or when the Swine Flu raged in 2009, did your favorite news outlet quote the Muslim leader who decreed it a religious obligation to go out and kill pigs because "pigs are the direct descendants of Jews"?[27]

The reason you never hear about these shocking stories is because no reporter is crazy enough to antagonize Palestinian leaders. According to journalist Saif el-Deen Shahin, only about 10 percent of reporters in Gaza dare to carry out their profession. "The rest have stopped working because of pressure and fears for their lives." (Shahin himself had to flee to Norway after receiving death threats.)[28]

It's obvious that when a journalist sits down to write a story, the part you'll never see is the hesitation and the "pause," given the consequences of telling the truth about Palestinians. One journalist put it this way: "The worst the Israelis can do is take away our press cards. But if we irritate... Hamas, you don't know who might be waiting in your kitchen when you come home at night."[29]

Pulitzer Prize-winner Thomas Friedman described the problem a bit more bluntly: Upon learning that Palestinian officials wanted to see him "immediately" to talk about the stories he'd been writing for the *New York Times*, he "lay awake in my bed the whole night worrying that someone was going to burst in and blow my brains all over the wall."[30]

And so, when it comes to Palestinian brutality, many stories never get reported.

Arab reporter Khaled Abu Toameh says that when he tried to alert foreign journalists that Palestinians were dying because of an internal power struggle and gross corruption, their reflex response was: "Where's the anti-Israel angle to the story? Give us an anti-occupation story... An Arab killing an Arab, that's not a story for us."[31]

Abu Toameh described an incident in Ramallah, where Palestinian police threw a man against the wall and sprayed him with bullets – right underneath the window of the Palestinian president's office. When a crowd of international reporters asked for details, a Palestinian policeman shrugged it off as a simple execution, nothing to get excited about. And no one did. In fact, none of the mainstream media reported it.[32]

Imagine if police in America or Israel were to violate human rights with such imprudence. The media outcry would be earsplitting. (Think Rodney King.)

Were journalists practicing a form of self-censorship, aware of the consequences of portraying Palestinians in an unfavorable light? Absolutely. In 2007, Associated Press reported that "several Gaza journalists received anonymous overnight phone calls warning them not to cover" events that could make Hamas look bad. (Predictably, the reporters who received these calls asked that their names be withheld "because they feared retribution from Hamas.")[33]

Palestinian officials are constantly issuing new "rules" to eliminate negative coverage. The Palestinian journalists' union declared that photographers and cameramen are "absolutely forbidden" from taking pictures of Palestinian children carrying weapons or taking part in activities by terror groups. Journalists refusing to adhere to the ban were threatened with retaliation.[34]

That's why your local media will never publish photos of Gaza kindergarteners parading in suicide belts or young Palestinian girls toting AK-47s. These scenes are all-too-common, but journalists steer clear. During the 2006 Israel-Hezbollah war in Lebanon, *Time* magazine contributor Christopher Allbritton described it like this: "Hezbollah is launching Katyushas, but I'm loathe to say too much about them. The Party of God (Hezbollah) has a copy of every journalist's passport..."[35]

So this is what media coverage of the Mideast conflict boils down to: "A copy of every journalist's passport." Time and again, through the force of intimidation, news stories that would tilt public opinion against Palestinians are being erased from the record. And media consumers are none the wiser.

The Joys of Abduction

Verbal intimidation and smashing cameras is one thing, but as Daniel Pearl could attest – if he were alive – it can go way beyond this.

In August 2005 during the Israeli withdrawal from Gaza, Mohamed Ouathi, an Algerian working for France 3 Television was forced into a car by three men with rifles in Gaza City and held for eight days. One month later, journalist Lorenzo Cremonesi of Italy's *Corriere della Serra* was abducted by masked gunmen in the town of Deir el-Balah in the central Gaza Strip. And a month after that, reporter Dion Nissenbaum and photographer Adam Pletts – working for the American news syndicate Knight Ridder – joined the long and illustrious list of journalists kidnapped in Gaza.[36]

For Palestinian security chiefs, the motive for abducting these reporters is simple: Having a bunch of foreign correspondents snooping around for stories of Palestinian violence and corruption violates the rules of the game. The kidnapping of foreign correspondents, the theory goes, takes these journalists out of commission, and more importantly, is an effective method of persuading their colleagues that Gaza is too dangerous to cover. The result is that media outlets are forced to replace foreign correspondents with Palestinian "stringers" who fill the information vacuum with their own "specialized" version of events.

After the Israeli withdrawal from Gaza, things got so bad that Western news agencies almost entirely cleared out – leaving veteran BBC correspondent Alan Johnston as the lone Western news reporter permanently based in Gaza.[37] Predictably, it didn't take long before Johnston was abducted at gunpoint by Palestinians. "I'd been in Gaza three years. I'd covered 27 kidnappings... And there I was before I knew it, on my back in the backseat with a hood over my head,"[38] Johnston later said. "Now, as I always feared it might, my turn had come."[39]

Johnston's captors forced him to lie face down on the floor, with wrists handcuffed behind his back, and a black hood pulled over his head. He was beaten, threatened to have his throat cut, and even made to wear a suicide bomber's vest.[40] The situation was so dire that at one point BBC assumed Johnston had been executed.[41]

Johnston was held hostage for 114 days, and his release did not come cheap. The Palestinian newspaper *Al-Hayat Al-Jadida* reported that Johnston's kidnappers received a ransom of $5 million, plus one million Kalashnikov rifle bullets.[42]

One can't help but imagine if the situation had been reversed and Johnston was kidnapped by Israelis. For starters, notes writer Charles Moore, this would never happen. There are no Israeli organizations – governmental or freelance – that would contemplate such a thing. That itself speaks volumes.

But suppose that some fanatical Jews had grabbed Johnston. How would the world have reacted? Wouldn't there surely have been mass protests in all the European capitals, scathing editorials, and U.N. denunciations of the extremist Zionist doctrine which had given rise to this vile act?

Absolutely. But because jihadists were the ones holding Johnston, everyone was treading on eggshells. Throughout the ordeal, BBC constantly emphasized how Johnston gave a voice to the Palestinian people, the implication being that he supported their cause and should therefore be released. BBC's Bridget Kendall described Johnston as having been "asked" to record a video denouncing the British government for "working to occupy Muslim lands."[43] In BBC's version of events, Johnston was not forced at gunpoint or threatened with torture – just politely "asked."[44]

One satirist imagined BBC spinning the kidnapping like this: "Calling it a 'hostage taking' is a misnomer. We prefer to view it as an extended 'educational retreat.' Alan's captors generously gave of their time, tutoring him on the history of the Mideast conflict, the rightfulness of their cause, and showing him how to make a roadside explosive device out of children's toys and oven cleaner."[45]

For journalists in Gaza, the reality was far from humorous. A few months earlier, Steve Centanni and Olaf Wiig – two Fox News employees – were seized in Gaza and held for two weeks. They were blindfolded, handcuffed, and made to lie face down on a concrete floor. Wiig was dressed in an Arab-style robe and coerced into making a videotaped denunciation of the West. The men were then forced to convert to Islam at gunpoint.[46]

In reporting on the kidnapping, however, Fox News correspondent Jennifer Griffin made the ordeal sound so delightful that I almost expected her to voluntarily offer herself as a captive to the Gaza thugs:

> [Centanni and Wiig described] how their captors had treated them with respect. They had given them clean clothes and water and food, and they went out of their way to talk about how they had access to bathrooms and all sorts of things and that they are being treated as guests. This is important in Palestinian society and in an Arab society. Being a guest is almost an honored value, something that you and I perhaps wouldn't necessarily pick up on being from the West. But this is a very important point...[47]

Back in the old days, the "Hanoi Hilton" derogatorily described the North Vietnamese torture of U.S. prisoners with beatings and prolonged solitary confinement. But in reporting on Palestinian kidnappings, someone forgot to tell Jennifer Griffin that prisoners are not truly "honored guests."

Someone apparently also forgot to tell the two kidnapped Fox News journalists. Upon his release, Centanni followed Griffin's lead by gushing about the joys of Arab abduction:

> The Palestinian people are very beautiful, kind-hearted, loving people who the world needs to know more about... Don't get me wrong here. I have the highest respect for Islam, and I learned a lot of good things about it...[48]

It appears that the Stockholm Syndrome – the propensity for hostages to express adulation toward their captors – has moved to the Middle East.[49]

Access Above All

Beyond the threat of physical abuse, there is another insidious reason why journalists are so loathe to criticize Palestinians: Doing so cuts off their access to sources of information and interviews.[50] Like any business, the news media needs to keep supply lines open, otherwise their product – in this case, the storyline – dries up. So in order to preserve access, journalists are willing to go along with a degree of manipulation and blackmail.

One journalist described to me the state of affairs: "Without access there is no story and you'll have to go find a new job. So the decision is essentially made for you. You keep quiet and just report the 'safe stuff.'"

This reality rots news coverage at its core. It's one thing if you're in the business of producing widgets and are involved in backroom deals; when a consumer buys a widget, the quality of the product is generally not affected by the ethics of the manufacturing process. But in the news business, the essential product depends on objective and independent reporting, free of emotional constraints. Sacrificing objectivity for the sake of access invariably dilutes and distorts the merchandise.

Even in the rare instance when a journalist chooses to (literally) stick his neck on the line, editors will likely kill the story, not wanting to jeopardize their news organization's access. As Amnesty International reports:

> [Journalists in Palestinian areas] now admit that they practice self-censorship, either by modifying the manner in which they report a story or not reporting or commenting on certain topics at all.

> Even if a journalist is prepared to take risks, his or her editor may not be willing to carry the responsibility of authorizing publication of a critical article...[51]

This is more than just theory; it plays out every day. When *60 Minutes* broadcast a report critical of the Palestinian Authority, PA officials announced that CBS News would "no longer be given unrestricted access to either our officials of government or the territories under our control."[52]

Do the math: If reporting negatively about Palestinians *costs* a reporter "unrestricted access," then the only way to *gain* that access is to report favorably about Palestinians.

At many levels, this is a massive cover-up. In fact, some news executives are now coming clean and admitting that when it comes to the Middle East, journalistic standards are sacrificed on the altar of "protecting access."

Case in point: Two days after U.S. troops entered Baghdad and toppled the statue of Saddam, Eason Jordan, the (now-former) Chief News Executive at CNN, described in a *New York Times* op-ed how CNN had been sanitizing its reports from Iraq for the past 13 years. This information was apparently tormenting Jordan's soul and he had to publicly purge the demons. He described how CNN had knowledge of brutal Iraqi murders, tortures and various unimaginable atrocities – but didn't report them because CNN wanted to protect its own Baghdad bureau.[53] It's what one writer called a "propaganda-for-profits deal with Saddam."[54]

This is a vicious cycle in which journalists, desperate for a scoop, are forced to forgo impartiality; as a result, the news winds up resembling propaganda. When Saddam "won" Iraq's presidential "election" (out of 11 million eligible voters, he received 100 percent of the vote),[55] CNN's Baghdad reporter Jane Arraf treated the sham event as meaningful: "The point is that this really is a huge show of support." On another occasion, when Saddam granted amnesty to some prisoners, Arraf reported that this "really does diffuse one of the strongest criticisms over the past decades of Iraq's human-rights records."[56] You could almost hear the CNN bigwigs snickering back in Atlanta.

According to Peter Arnett, who worked CNN's Iraq beat for a decade, "there's a quid pro quo" for reporting in Iraq. "You go in and they control what you do... So you have no option other than to report the opinion of the government of Iraq."[57]

Some of the most damning evidence comes from Peter Collins, who worked for CNN in Baghdad and attended meetings with network executives trying to negotiate an exclusive interview with Saddam Hussein:

> The day after one such meeting, I was on the roof of the [Iraqi] Ministry of Information, preparing for my first "live shot" on CNN. A producer came up and handed me a sheet of paper with handwritten notes. "[CNN President] Tom Johnson wants you to read this on camera," he said. I glanced at the paper. It was an item-by-item summary of points made by [Iraqi] Information Minister Latif Jassim in an interview that morning with Mr. Johnson...
>
> I read the information minister's points verbatim. Moments later... Mr. Johnson approached, having seen my performance on a TV monitor. "You were a bit flat there, Peter," he said. Again, I was astonished. The president of CNN was telling me I seemed less-than-enthusiastic reading Saddam Hussein's propaganda.[58]

All this raises a fundamental question of journalistic ethics: Is it better for reporters to expose the truth, but then lose access to future stories, or is it better to whitewash half the story and maintain access? From my perspective, journalism is all about getting the story straight – and if you can't stand the truth, get out of the newsroom.

But one thing is clear: In the interest of full disclosure, if a news agency decides to report only half the story, the public must be informed. This at least allows consumers to extrapolate what the full story might be like. Otherwise, the news media – in the words of Carl Bernstein, "probably the most powerful of all our institutions today" – is doing the grave disservice of "squandering our power and ignoring our obligations."[59]

Fatwa Fears

Not long ago I scheduled a meeting with a foreign correspondent in Jerusalem, but he never showed up. When I got a hold of him the next day, he explained that his editor stateside had insisted that he attend a seminar for journalists.

"What topic was so urgent?" I asked him. "Interview techniques? The use of social media? The latest satellite technology?"

"None of that," he laughed. "We were taught how to handle being taken hostage by Palestinians. Things have gotten so bad that this is now standard training for Middle East correspondents."

Here's one handy piece of advice from the seminar: "Do your best, surreptitiously, if possible, to disconnect the wires from any explosive device placed near or on you; don't worry about which wires to pull out, because it is only in the movies that bombs are designed to detonate if the hero cuts the wrong strand..."[60]

In Palestinian areas, reporters constantly have to look over their shoulders for trouble, taking precautions against kidnapping by switching cars and keeping their movements random and unpredictable. James Bennet, a *New York Times* Jerusalem bureau chief, was apparently not careful enough. One spring evening, armed Gazans grabbed Bennet and attempted to shove him "into an aging Mercedes sedan that pulled up, its rear door open. A struggle and cries for help... and after a further struggle, the men jumped in the car and disappeared."[61]

When Bennet had the audacity to defy Palestinian "rules" and publicize the incident, senior PA officials phoned Bennet and tried to convince him that the entire incident was actually the product of his wild imagination. They pressured him to revise the story, suggesting that the gunmen who had tried to force Bennet into the back seat of the car "only wanted to check his identity."[62]

So reporters are not only subject to the intimidation of Palestinian thugs, but PA officials get involved with an "Orwellian re-education" of what journalists have personally witnessed. Six journalists covering a demonstration in Gaza City were threatened with the same tactic: After being arrested and having their equipment seized and videotape destroyed, Hamas ruffians tried to force them to say publicly "that no journalist was mistreated during the demonstration."[63]

Shortly after Bennet's attempted kidnapping, I asked one of his colleagues to what degree this physical and emotional harassment impacts the coverage. "Oh, not at all," he said. "We're professionals. We go right back in there and don't really think about it."

Do you believe that? I don't. But that's the type of denial that comes from being under this degree of threat and intimidation.

These bullying tactics extend even beyond the realm of hard news. In 2003, London's *Independent* published a grotesque cartoon by Dave Brown that depicted Israel's prime minister eagerly devouring a Palestinian baby.[64] The cartoon was so vile that it was later adopted by radical Islamic groups as an icon of their anti-Israel campaign.[65] So imagine my shock when the British Political Cartoon Society awarded this *first prize* in its annual "Cartoon of the Year" competition.[66]

I contacted Dr. Tim Benson, director of the Cartoon Society, to question not only the inaccuracy of portraying "Israeli-style infanticide," but also the ethics of giving an award to such a biased cartoon. Benson responded by taking the moral high road:

> You have all taken this award completely out of perspective and context. Shame on you! We do so much good. If only you looked at our website properly you would have noticed that in fact we promote anti-fascism and educate about the dangers of extremism.[67]

I always try to take criticism seriously. So when he said, "Shame on you," I reasoned that I must have misjudged this one. Dr. Benson is apparently an honest man of great moral integrity, committed to the highest standards of journalism. *How could I have accused him of anti-Israel bias?* I chastised myself.

Well, that theory was shot to pieces a few months later when filmmaker Martin Himel interviewed Benson and asked him to explain why political cartoonists frequently portray Israelis as Nazis, devils and cannibals – while Palestinian leaders are not depicted in similarly vile ways. In a moment of candor, Benson was caught on camera saying:

> Well, if you upset an Islamic or Muslim group, as you know, fatwas can be issued by Ayatollahs and such, and maybe it's at the back of each cartoonist's mind, that they could be in trouble if they do so.[68]

Oh, now I get it. Israelis are vilified because Jews don't issue death fatwas. And Dr. Tim Benson, the supposed standard-bearer of objectivity and ethics, is kowtowing to Arab intimidation.

Epidemic in Beirut

This policy of intimidating journalists goes back to the very beginnings of the Palestinian movement. During the PLO's reign of terror in Lebanon (1976-82), journalists were so severely harassed that *The Guardian* described the atmosphere in Beirut as "censorship by terrorism."[69]

In his memoir, *From Beirut to Jerusalem*, Thomas Friedman writes that journalists in Lebanon regularly skewed their coverage in order to avoid incurring Palestinian wrath:

> There were... stories which were deliberately ignored out of fear... Instead of reporting what they knew, journalists censored themselves. The Western press coddled the PLO. For any Beirut-based correspondent, the name of the game was keeping on good terms with the PLO.[70]

For those who didn't follow the rules, there was no mercy. At least eight foreign journalists – American, French, German, Italian – were killed by the PLO in Lebanon.[71] The lucky ones simply fled.

Case in point: After ABC produced *The Unholy War*, a documentary critical of the PLO, word was spread to ABC staff to "get out of Lebanon and don't come back." The documentary's producer, Barbara Newman, was on assignment in Sudan when she met an ABC camera crew from Beirut. "They told me never to go back there, that it was dangerous... One guy said he and his wife had had to stay inside their house for ten days after *The Unholy War* aired. They were afraid they'd get killed because of the anger in Beirut over our piece."[72]

A reporter for ABC Radio, Sean Toolan, was brash enough to stick around Beirut. He met a quick end – murdered by Palestinian thugs a few weeks after the ABC documentary was broadcast.[73]

One can only imagine the degree of outrage that ABC must have expressed at having their reporters threatened and killed. Yes, "one can only imagine," because ABC's response was the precise opposite. Two weeks after Toolan's murder, ABC's *World News Tonight* called the PLO "a benevolent group dedicated to peaceful struggle and welfare programs,"[74] and ABC aired a report on *20/20* that was, in the words of *Time* magazine, "inordinately sympathetic to the Palestinians."[75]

In that fear-filled atmosphere of Lebanon, the most typical response to Palestinian intimidation was to simply cover it up. When a group of reporters from the *New York Times, Washington Post, Newsweek* and Associated Press were abducted at gunpoint by Palestinian agents and taken to a "coffin-like" cell where they were detained for 15 hours, guess how this incident was reported in the *Times, Post, Newsweek* and AP?

It wasn't. That's because the detained journalists "made an informal agreement that we would not write about the incident. The stories would have just embarrassed everyone involved."[76]

Sure enough, this intimidation translates directly into skewed coverage. When the Reuters correspondent in Beirut, Berndt Debusmann, published a story critical of Syria's president, Arab security officials issued repeated threats. Then one night as Debusmann was getting into his car in West Beirut, he was the victim of attempted murder, a drive-by shooting. How did Reuters respond? By deadpanning: "There is no known reason for the shooting."[77]

During this same period, Syrian troops were massacring hundreds of civilians in Hama – yet the incident was never mentioned in the pages of the *New York Times*, *Newsweek* or other major media. Journalists certainly knew about it, so why the hesitation to report? The *Washington Post* later revealed the secret: In the aftermath of the Berndt Debusmann shooting, journalists simply stopped publicizing stories considered "unfriendly to Syria."[78]

Till today, journalists operating in Palestinian areas are mindful of this Lebanon legacy. One foreign correspondent described the rash of abductions in Gaza as "a really bad omen for journalists who work in the territories. These sorts of things tend to be infectious, and others may surely get ideas. We have all been thinking lately of Lebanon in the 1980s, and wondering if it could happen here."[79]

Journalists like to view themselves as idealistic warriors, making forays into all corners of the world to bravely "tell it like it is." Pierre Rehov, producer of eight films about the Israeli-Palestinian conflict, observed that "a lot of journalists, in very good faith, think of themselves as intellectuals and freedom fighters at the same time. They believe that they are the last real adventurers of this world."[80]

But in Palestinian areas, the reality is sadly different, with reporters practicing self-censorship out of fear and violating their most basic duty to report the facts. Meanwhile, democratic Israel vigilantly guards its freedom of the press, where journalists, politicians and NGOs are free to eagerly air their criticisms of Israeli policy. The result is that coverage is skewed in favor of the Palestinians, and Israel is left fighting the battle for public opinion with one hand tied behind its back.

Jihad and the Infidels

Don't make the mistake, however, of thinking this is a Mideast-specific problem. Since 9-11, radical Islam has unleashed a global wave of terror, with over 10,000 recorded acts of Islamic violence in Beslan, Bangkok, Baghdad, London, Tel Aviv, Casablanca, Bali, Madrid, Moscow, etc.[81] Polls show that a sizeable group of Muslims – estimated at 100 million worldwide – support radical Islam and its goal of global jihad.[82]

Because Islamists wield the threat of mass violence, presenting Islam in a negative light can be a very hazardous pursuit. In 2005, when the Danish newspaper *Jyllands-Poste* published editorial cartoons depicting the prophet Muhammad (including one which showed him wearing a bomb as a turban with a lit fuse), mass riots broke out everywhere from Indonesia to New Zealand to Gaza City.[83] Over 150 people were killed by rioters (whom Associated Press favorably described as "human rights activists)."[84]

The most intense pressure, however, was directed at the media itself. Newspapers in England,[85] Russia,[86] Canada[87] and France[88] were shut down and editors fired for reprinting the Muhammad cartoons.[89] At the University of Illinois – that academic bastion of free speech and inquiry – two editors of the student paper were suspended for reprinting the cartoons.

Why the self-imposed censorship?

Most editors claim to have not published the Muhammad cartoons out of a so-called "sensitivity to Muslim feelings." This is a feeble and transparent attempt to cover up the true reason: cowardice. If someone had drawn cartoons offensive to Christians or Jews, would the Western press have hesitated to publish them?[90]

Indeed, newspapers such as *USA Today, Los Angeles Times, Boston Globe,* and *New York Times* – all of whom had no compunction publishing an inflammatory photograph depicting Jesus submerged in a jar of urine – refused to publish the Muhammad cartoons.[91]

When *Free Inquiry* magazine had the temerity to publish the Muhammad cartoons, the Borders bookstore chain refused to sell it.[92] When I challenged this policy, Borders acknowledged it was purely out of fear:

> In this particular case, we decided not to stock this issue in our stores because we place a priority on the safety and security of

our customers and our employees. We believe that carrying this issue presented a challenge to that priority.[93]

Meanwhile, Boston's leading "alternative" newspaper, the *Phoenix* – brash enough to print the grisly photo of a beheaded Daniel Pearl[94] – explained their refusal to print the Muhammad cartoons:

> Our primary reason is fear of retaliation from... bloodthirsty Islamists who seek to impose their will on those who do not believe as they do... Simply stated, we are being terrorized, and... could not in good conscience place the men and women who work at the *Phoenix* and its related companies in physical jeopardy. As we feel forced, literally, to bend to maniacal pressure, this may be the darkest moment in our 40-year publishing history.[95]

In other words, the First Amendment was being vetoed by a bloodthirsty Islamist mob.

The threats repeated in earnest in 2008 with the release of *Fitna*, a film that exposed Muslim acts of violence. The film was removed from the video sharing website LiveLeak – not because of any content issues, but because of "threats to our staff of a very serious nature." LiveLeak explained:

> This is a sad day for freedom of speech on the net, but we have to place the safety and well being of our staff above all else... We stood for what we believe in, the ability to be heard, but in the end the price was too high.[96]

Dutch filmmaker Theo van Gogh, whose short film *Submission* showcased the mistreatment of Muslim women, discovered for himself what a high price it was. Soon after the film aired on Dutch TV, van Gogh was bicycle riding near his home when a Muslim man shot him eight times, tried to decapitate him with a knife, and then stabbed into his body a five-page note threatening Western countries.⁹⁷

Lately, jihadists are trying out a new tactic: using the Western legal system to bankrupt anyone who disseminates material critical of Islam. Dr. Rachel Ehrenfeld, author of *Funding Evil: How Terrorism Is Financed and How to Stop It*, assumed that as an American citizen, residing in America, and publishing in America, she would be protected by the First Amendment. But shortly after the publication of *Funding Evil*, Saudi businessman Khalid bin Mahfouz sued Ehrenfeld in a UK court – on the basis of a few dozen copies that had been sold to British buyers on Amazon.com. Unwilling to travel to England or acknowledge the authority of British libel laws, Ehrenfeld lost by default and was ordered to pay heavy fines, apologize and destroy her books. With that ruling in his pocket, Mahfouz was then free to sue in a U.S. court to collect the judgment.⁹⁸

Even if these lawsuits don't succeed, Islamic "lawfare" tactics have the potential to create a chilling effect on public discourse. Already, publishers have canceled books on the subjects of Islam and terrorism, and no doubt other authors have self-censored due to the looming threat of a suit. In 2008, Random House cancelled the publication of *The Jewel of Medina*, a novel about Aisha, the "child-bride" of Muhammad, citing fears that "publication of this book might be offensive to some in the Muslim community" and "could incite acts of violence."⁹⁹ And when Mahfouz threatened to sue Cambridge Press for the publication of *Alms for Jihad*, an exposé on charity and terrorism in the Islamic world, the publisher immediately capitulated – publicly apologizing, taking the book out of print and shredding all unsold copies.¹⁰⁰

This is not freedom of the press, but silence of the press.

And this intimidation extends to all realms of entertainment. In 2008, when Paul McCartney insisted on performing in Israel despite pressure from pro-Palestinian activists, Islamist leader Omar Bakri Muhammad threatened:

> "Paul McCartney is the enemy of every Muslim... If he values his life, Mr. McCartney must not come to Israel. He will not be safe

there. The sacrifice operatives will be waiting for him."[101]

This intimidation afflicts Hollywood films, too. Roland Emmerich's disaster movie, *2012*, depicts the destruction of the White House, along with religious landmarks such as the Sistine Chapel and St. Peter's Basilica. One notable omission is the Kaaba in Mecca, Islam's holiest site. "I wanted to do that, I have to admit," Emmerich said. "But my co-writer Harald said, 'I will not have a fatwa on my head because of a movie'... So I kind of left it out."[102]

Tom Clancy's novel, *The Sum of all Fears,* revolves around a plot by Palestinian terrorists to detonate a nuclear bomb at the Super Bowl. The book is filled with radical Islamic imagery and ends with a beheading in Saudi Arabia. But when it was turned into a Hollywood action film, the villains were somehow changed from Palestinian terrorists to neo-Nazis – ostensibly to avoid offending Arabs or Muslims.

Similarly, the British television series *Casualty* – the world's longest-running emergency medical drama – wanted to feature a storyline about an explosion caused by Islamic extremists. But "to avoid offending Muslims" (code language for "afraid they will blow up our building and decapitate our staffers"), BBC changed the script to have the bomb set off by animal rights activists instead.[103]

In 2010, following threats from Islamic extremists offended at a portrayal of Muhammad, the Comedy Central TV network censored an episode of the popular *South Park* cartoon.[104] When producers capitulated and disguised Muhammad in a bear suit, outraged Muslim groups still threatened the show's creators with a fate similar to butchered Dutch filmmaker Theo van Gogh.[105]

The same folks who exhibit hyper-caution against any affront to Muslims apparently have no problem employing a double standard with Israel. The Comedy Central website featured a videogame – "I.S.R.A.E.L. Attack!" – where a robot named Israel destroys everything and everyone in its path, including children. The game's introduction begins with a character stating, "You lied to me, Jew Producer."[106]

The intimidation knows no bounds. When Wiley Miller of "Non Sequitur," a popular comic that runs daily in 800 newspapers, drew an episode reminiscent of "Where's Waldo?" entitled, "Where's Muhammad: Picture Book Title Least Likely to Ever Find a Publisher," newspapers refused to run the cartoon out of fear that Muslims might be offended – even though the cartoon did not contain any depiction of Muhammad. Miller said the cartoon was meant to satirize the "media cowering in fear of printing any cartoon that contains the word 'Muhammad.' The wonderful irony [is that] great newspapers like the *Washington Post*, that took on Nixon... run in fear of this very tame cartoon, thus validating the accuracy of the satire."[107] As further irony, suppressing speech in fear of Muslim reaction is precisely the "Islamophobia" that editors at the *Post* and other newspapers so staunchly purport to condemn.[108]

One news executive, Mark Thompson of BBC, admitted that his network treats Islam differently from other religions, but justified it with the gobbledygook that Islam has an "ethnic identity which has not been fully integrated."[109] Translation: We avoid offending Muslims so our staffers don't wind up on an Internet video, wearing a hood and surrounded by a pack of sword-wielding jihadists.[110]

Indeed. When political cartoonist Molly Norris published a cartoon entitled "Everybody Draw Mohammed Day," American-born preacher Anwar al-Awlaki issued a fatwa declaring that Norris "should be taken as a prime target of assassination."[111] These were no idle threats. The next thing you know, Norris announced the sudden discontinuation of her column. As reported by *Seattle Weekly*:

> On the insistence of top security specialists at the FBI, she is, as they put it, "going ghost": moving, changing her name, and essentially wiping away her identity. She will no longer be publishing cartoons in our paper or in *City Arts* magazine, where she has been a regular contributor. She is, in effect, being put into a witness-protection program – except, as she notes, without the government picking up the tab. It's all because of the appalling

fatwa issued against her this summer, following her infamous "Everybody Draw Mohammed Day" cartoon.[112]

All things being equal, journalists do want to report fairly. Yet in the Middle East, all is not equal.

The M-Word

This widespread fear and intimidation has given rise to a new phenomenon: Just as the media refuses to use the T-word in describing terrorists, they now dodge the M-word whenever Muslims commit heinous crimes.

When terrorists attacked the Russian city of Nalchik, striking the main airport and key government installations in a large-scale, daytime assault that left at least 85 people dead, media reports kept the ethnic identity of the attackers mysteriously hidden. The *New York Times* squelched the M-word until paragraph seven, and Agence France Presse buried it in paragraph 22. For its part, NPR's *All Things Considered* aired a bland interview with a Russian geopolitical academic who chitchatted through every conceivable aspect of the situation and then – as columnist Mark Steyn observed – finally got around to kinda sorta revealing the Muslim identity of the perpetrators in the very last word of his very last sentence.[113]

In 2006, when 17 Canadian members of an Islamic terror cell were arrested on charges of plotting to bomb targets near Toronto, the *New York Times* managed the remarkable feat of publishing an 1,843-word report without once calling them "Muslims." The only identifying information provided by the *Times* was that they are of "South Asian descent" and "represent the broad strata" of society.[114]

Let's look at the names of the suspects and try to discern what "broad strata" they might possibly represent: Fahim Ahmad, Zakaria Amara, Asad Ansari, Shareef Abdelhaleen, Qayyum Abdul Jamal, Mohammed Dirie, Yasim Abdi Mohamed, Jahmaal James, Amin Mohamed Durrani, Ahmad Mustafa Ghany, Saad Khalid. Any clue of the profile shared by these terrorists of "South Asian descent"? Perhaps they are Christians of Dutch ancestry living in the Maldives? Or maybe British citizens from the

Chagos Islands? The *Times* doesn't say.

Skirting the M-word is becoming a full-fledged media trend. In 2007, when eight people – all Muslims – were arrested in the UK for plotting car bombings, the *New York Times* again referred to them as a "disenfranchised South Asian population,"[115] while Associated Press vaguely noted that they "shared some common ideology."[116]

In 2009, when four New York men were arrested for plotting to bomb synagogues and "bring death to Jews," readers of CNN.com were left to wonder exactly what ideology drove these men. Were they General Motors shareholders upset about getting stiffed in bailout proceedings? Or New York Yankees fans furious about rumors of an A-rod trade?[117] It turns out that the suspects were Muslims, a minor detail that CNN finally revealed in the 11th paragraph.[118] (The *New York Times* fared slightly better, mentioning the M-word at the end of the ninth paragraph.)[119]

And again in 2011, when two more Muslim men were arrested for plotting to attack Manhattan synagogues – one of whom told police he was "dealing for jihad"[120] – the *New York Times* pandered to political correctness and omitted the M-word.[121]

These media apologetics are dangerous because they obscure the real issue of radical Islam waging jihad against the free world. It's important to call a Muslim terrorist a "Muslim terrorist," because unless we recognize the threat we cannot possibly confront it.

Consider as well the Islamic concept of jihad, the violent struggle for world domination where all methods of terror are fair game against the "infidel." ABC News defined jihad as a "struggle against evil inclinations within oneself" and the "struggle to improve the quality of life in society."[122] This may be true in one narrow sense, but "self-struggle" is also the meaning of *Mein Kampf*, the title of Hitler's manifesto which also promised to "improve the quality of life in society."

At times, avoidance of Arab appellations can have a decidedly biased effect. In 2010, when Elias Abuelazam – an Israeli citizen accused of serial killings in the U.S. – was arrested in Atlanta while boarding a flight bound for Tel Aviv, BBC headlined its report, "Israeli Man Held in Airport Over US

Serial Stabbings,"[123] while MSNBC's account, "Israeli Held in Investigation of Serial Stabbings," mentioned the word Israel or Israeli eight times in the article.[124] Given that most readers assume "Israeli" is equated with "Jewish," reporters would seem remiss in failing to inform viewers that this man accused of murdering Americans is actually an Israeli *Arab*. Yet this fact was mysteriously omitted from these and literally hundreds of other news reports – including America's three major networks who all furtively referred to the killer as an "Israeli national."[125]

Yet it's the M-word that gets the most convoluted treatment. In 2008, when Muslim terrorists slaughtered 200 people in Mumbai, an Australian newspaper described the perpetrators as "teenage gunmen run amok,"[126] while Jon Snow, one of Britain's most respected TV journalists, called them "practitioners."[127] As in "nurse practitioners"?

In 2009, when Nidal Malik Hasan killed 13 American soldiers at Fort Hood, Texas, *CBS Evening News* avoided the M-word, with Katie Couric describing the killer as simply "a licensed psychiatrist and drug and rehab specialist."[128] Meanwhile, on *NBC Nightly News*, Pete Williams insisted that "nothing extraordinary stands out about his background."[129]

Nothing extraordinary? Hasan was a practicing Muslim who allegedly shouted "Allah Akbar" (Arabic for "God is great") as he opened fire.[130] In 2001, he had joined two of the September 11 terrorists at the controversial Dar al-Hijrah mosque in Great Falls, Virginia,[131] and prior to his shooting attack was attempting to make contact with al-Qaeda.[132] Hasan had a long record of virulent, anti-American, pro-jihadist sentiments; the *Sunday Telegraph* reported that he "once gave a lecture to other doctors in which he said non-believers should be beheaded and have boiling oil poured down their throats."[133]

Yet the media was desperate to avoid the M-word. ABC's senior foreign affairs correspondent, Martha Raddatz, concluded her report on the Fort Hood shooting with these telling words: "I wish his name was Smith."[134]

The problem persists. When Faisal Shahzad was arrested for the failed Times Square car bombing in 2010, the *New York Times* ran a 900-word article with no mention of the M-word,[135] even as information was available that Shahzad had admitted to training at an Islamist terror camp in Pakistan.[136]

Worse than avoiding the Islamists, some media outlets go for direct surrender. *The Guardian* reported that during the French riots of 2005, a Saudi Prince – with large stock holdings in News Corp. – phoned Rupert Murdoch directly to complain about Fox News describing the chaos as "Muslim riots." Within 30 minutes, he said, "Muslim riots" had become "civil riots."[137]

This policy of pressuring journalists comes from the highest echelons of the Muslim world. At a meeting of the 57-nation Organisation of the Islamic Conference – the world's largest Islamic body – Muslim businessmen were called upon to buy stakes in global media outlets.[138] Indeed, those petro-dollars are being put to good use – intimidating journalists into covering up "M" acts of "T."

Foot Soldiers

When it comes to Muslims having a built-in media advantage, nowhere is the impact felt more than in the Arab-Israeli conflict. Israel is a Western-style democracy, granting foreign reporters free access to individuals expressing a full range of views. But the Palestinian "message" is much more tightly controlled from the top, and access to Palestinian areas is largely restricted; journalists can't just walk into Gaza and begin snapping pictures. That means that Western news agencies have to rely on Arab "stringers" – also known as "fixers" – to do the actual reporting, legwork and photography.

Zoran Bozicevic, associate photo editor at Canada's *National Post* says that the ease of digital photography – coupled with media outlets constantly eyeing cost-cutting measures – means increasing reliance on cheap, sometimes unscrupulous, local stringers who often flout professional objectivity and take sides in the conflict they cover.[139] One veteran journalist estimated that over 95 percent of the news photos and videos coming out of Palestinian areas are provided by Palestinians themselves.[140]

Palestinian translators are known to interject their bias by intentionally mistranslating, or even reprimanding Palestinian interviewees critical of the Palestinian Authority. Khaled Abu Toameh, former correspondent for the PLO newspaper *Al Fajr*, tells of a journalist interviewing a Palestinian in Ramallah through a fixer who provided the translation: "Speaking in Arabic, the Palestinian said something critical of the PA, but the fixer translated into English that he was speaking about the weather. Then the fixer turned to the interview subject and – in Arabic – rebuked him for speaking critically of the PA."[141]

Indeed, Yussef al-Qazzaz, a senior official with the Palestinian Broadcasting Corporation, lashed out at Palestinian journalists for not placing the interests of their people above everything else. Qazzaz said that Palestinian journalists should not make "harmful" remarks and – alluding to the unwritten constraints imposed upon reporters – emphasized how this is "a time when *even foreign journalists* are careful not to alienate the Palestinians."[142]

Khaled Abu Toameh described the pressure he feels as an Arab journalist to toe the Palestinian line:

Intimidation of journalists in the West Bank and Gaza Strip… becomes even more complicated and dangerous if, like myself, you are an Arab journalist working with the foreign or Israeli media. Then you are expected to be an "obedient servant" or a "soldier" in the war of propaganda. You are expected to tell the truth only if it sounds and looks convenient and appropriate. Otherwise, you could be risking your life.[143]

In many cases a reporter's connections to the Palestinian "inside track" count far more than journalistic abilities. Take the case of Wafa Amr, whose father was a close confidant of Yasser Arafat and who is a cousin of former Palestinian minister Nabil Amr. She started out as a correspondent for the Arabic media, and was then hired by Reuters so that her access to the Palestinian Authority could be exploited. "She occupies this position in spite of lacking a basic command of English grammar," one former Reuters' journalist said. "The information passed through her is controlled, orchestrated. Reuters would never allow Israeli government propaganda to be fed into its reports in this way."[144]

One example of Wafa Amr's "journalism" published by Reuters is her definition of the Islamic concept of "martyrdom":

> Martyrdom in Islam refers to when a person gets killed by accident or for the sake of a noble cause such as defending his land or religion.[145]

Killed by accident? A noble cause? Apparently we've all been mistaken in thinking that Islamic martyrdom had something to do with intentionally blowing up busloads of schoolchildren or flying airplanes into skyscrapers.[146]

And then there's Diaa Hadid, whose personal animosity for Israelis prompted her to declare: "I can't look at Israelis... I don't want to be friends with them, I don't want to talk to them." Yet she is apparently "objective" enough to write news reports about Israel for the *Los Angeles Times* and Associated Press.[147]

Other journalists are less discreet. In the summer of 2010, when Israel soldiers went to prune a tree that was blocking the view of security cameras on the Lebanese border, Arab snipers hiding in the foliage fired on the gardening crew – killing one Israeli (in what Reuters fallaciously termed "warning shots").[148] Israeli troops fired back, killing three Lebanese soldiers and a local journalist.

The strange part about this incident is that Reuters had *five* photographers – and even broadcast trucks – at the scene even before the clash occurred.[149] Why were so many photographers assigned to cover this routine border maintenance? After all, pruning foliage is hardly headline news. Who tipped them off?[150]

In many cases reporters seem more like political activists loyal to the cause. When one Associated Press article – by Ibrahim Barzak – reported as "fact" the fabrication that Israel was kidnapping Palestinian cabinet ministers,[151] I picked up the phone and called AP's Jerusalem bureau. "Is it possible that AP's consistent bias is the result of employing Palestinian reporters?" I asked.

That was apparently the most un-PC thing I could have said. The AP staffer exploded at me: "Are you questioning the objectivity of Ibrahim Barzak, Sarah El Deeb and Khalil Hamra?!"

PC or not, the reality is that many journalists have a built-in alliance with the Palestinian side. As one Palestinian stringer explained:

> This is the way the [Palestinians] were trained, to be loyal, not to air the dirty laundry... Unfortunately 100% of the fixers see themselves as foot soldiers in the revolution. They will not tell foreign journalists anything that reflects badly on the PA.[152]

The fact is that a conflict of interest exists for many Palestinians who do the legwork where foreign news crews fear to tread. Muhammad Daraghmeh was concurrently employed by Associated Press and the official Palestinian Authority daily, *Al-Ayyam*. That's akin to an Israeli government employee writing "objective news" pieces for the *New York Times* – a violation of standards that would never be tolerated. Perhaps that explains why – even as Daraghmeh's byline continued to appear in *Al-Ayyam* – AP's Jerusalem bureau chief tried to deny it was happening.[153]

In fact, many Western reporters have moonlighted on the payroll of the Palestinian Authority. Adel Zanoun reported simultaneously for the world's third-largest wire service, Agence France-Presse, and the PA's Voice of Palestine radio station.[154] Another AFP reporter, Majida al-Batsh, was concurrently on the payroll of the PA's official organ, *Al-Ayyam*. As if to dispel any doubts about her partisanship, al-Batsh later announced her candidacy for President of the Palestinian Authority, and during the campaign continued to make use of AFP's office. When questioned about this shocking breach of ethics, AFP Jerusalem bureau chief Patrick Anidjar refused to discuss the issue, saying, "I don't understand why you have to have the name of our correspondents."[155]

Could we ever imagine an AFP reporter running for a seat in the Knesset – and utilizing AFP's offices to do so?

Typical of Palestinian sympathizers is Abdul Bari Atwan, a popular foreign affairs analyst who seems quite moderate when appearing on BBC and CNN.[156] Yet in his job as editor of the Arabic daily, *Al-Quds Al-Arabi*, Bari Atwan reveals a decidedly different slant. When a Palestinian terrorist killed eight teenagers in a Jerusalem school, Bari Atwan called the attack "justified," and described the celebrations in Gaza that followed the massacre as symbolizing the "courage of the Palestinian nation."[157]

When presented with this information, Adrian Wells, head of foreign news at Sky-TV where Bari Atwan is a frequent analyst, said dryly: "It is not our policy to comment on what contributors may or may not say on other channels." A BBC spokesman brushed off Bari Atwan's anti-Israel oratory by saying that "BBC is required to explore a range of views, so that no significant strand of thought is knowingly unreflected or underrepresented."[158] It is impossible to imagine BBC being so cavalier had the shoe been on the other foot – if one of its Jewish correspondents had come out in favor of massacring Palestinians.

So Bari Atwan continues to be a guest commentator for mainstream Western media, where his anti-Israel ideology is cleverly disguised. This is the same Bari Atwan who was welcomed into the cave of Osama bin Laden for an exclusive interview.[159] The same Bari Atwan who told a Lebanese TV station: "If the Iranian missiles strike Israel, by Allah, I will go to [London's] Trafalgar Square and dance with delight."[160] The same Bari Atwan who was being paid thousands of dollars every month by Libya's Gaddafi.[161] The same Bari Atwan who expressed the hope that Palestinian violence would "mark the countdown to Israel's destruction."[162] Keep this all in mind the next time you see Bari Atwan offering one of his "expert commentaries" on CNN.

Shoulder to Shoulder

Not only Palestinians, but often Westerner reporters as well assume the role of foot soldiers for the Palestinian cause. In an interview with Palestinian human rights campaigner Bassem Eid, BBC anchor Clair Bolderson called for more violence against Israel:

> The Palestinian people are the people who are rising up against what they see as the Israeli occupation, the brutality of the Israelis. Are you saying they just shouldn't do that at all – that they should be just completely peaceful and quiet?[163]

Eid, the Palestinian, replied that violence is counterproductive, given that the Palestinians "signed an agreement with the Israelis" and committed to "peace talks and the peace process – rather than doing the shootings." Undeterred by this logic, BBC's Bolderson pressed on:

> But aren't we just seeing a spontaneous uprising of the people who are frustrated with the process, with the fact that the peace process hasn't moved forward? Are you saying that they should keep their frustrations bottled up, that they shouldn't take to the streets?

When Nisha Pillai of BBC interviewed Amr Moussa, the U.N. Ambassador from the Arab League, she took him to task for going too slowly in getting the Palestinians to unite against Israel: "At this moment you have a massive assault going on in Gaza. Don't you have to have Hamas there with Fatah sitting together trying to sort out a joint response to Israel. Isn't it a matter of urgency?"[164]

With this kind of partisan journalism, it's understandable why Palestinian Information Minister Mustafa Barghouti heaped praise on BBC reporters for having "done a lot for our cause."[165]

Indeed, a number of BBC correspondents have stopped masquerading as "objective reporters" and moved into more comfortable Muslim territory: Phil Rees, who produced nearly 40 documentaries for BBC, became a regular news analyst for Al Jazeera, *Al Arabiya* and the Islam Channel.

Tim Llewellyn, BBC's Middle East correspondent for 10 years, became an executive member of the pro-Palestinian lobby group, the Council for the Advancement of Arab British Understanding, while hosting the *Middle East Today* talk show on – you guessed it – Iranian TV.

BBC is so entrenched in its anti-Israel corporate culture that one employee described it as "like traveling to another professional planet... What strikes you most about the BBC scene is what a closed world it is. Walk into a BBC newsroom and you will hear more talk about the BBC itself than about the outside world."[166]

Sometimes the connection between Palestinians and the media is so close as to defy belief. When Reuters staffers in Israel were preparing a "farewell video" for one of their colleagues, who did they call on to play the role of the Reuters' news chief? None other than Zakaria Zubeidi, a leader of the al-Aqsa Martyrs Brigade (on the U.S. State Department's list of terror organizations) and a key figure in organizing hundreds of terror attacks.[167] Reuters' spokeswoman Susan Allsopp confirmed the video's existence and said it "was meant to be humorous." Civilized human beings, however, failed to see the humor in notorious terrorists yucking it up with Reuters' journalists.

Even when caught red-handed, the media will simply cover it up. In 2004, when BBC's senior editor Malcolm Balen compiled a 20,000-word report said to be highly critical of BBC's Israel coverage, BBC executives refused to let anyone see the Balen Report – even spending $360,000 in legal fees to block its publication.[168] How's that for a twist on the idea of journalists "fighting for the public's right to know"?

One former BBC reporter described the "pervasive mindset inside the BBC" as characterized by "a failure to give credence to Israeli sources, but to believe Palestinian ones." He recalled the time he filed a story about a certain incident which turned out to be erroneous. "I immediately called the BBC to tell them that the story wasn't true, but they decided to run it anyway, a number of times that day."[169]

Another journalist's personal experience is quite telling. After graduating from Oxford in 1990, Tom Gross applied to BBC News' prestigious training program. In the final interview, BBC senior executives asked Gross what changes he would make to improve the news coverage. Gross recalls: "This was soon after Saddam Hussein had gassed thousands of Kurds. But the BBC had only run it as the fifth story on their main evening news broadcast, buried after some inane story about Prince Charles. So in answer to their question, I suggested that an atrocity of such magnitude should have been treated by BBC as a much bigger story."

With that, the room suddenly went silent, as the cadre of senior executives cast knowing glances at each other. One then turned to Gross and said, "What exactly are your views on Israel?"

The distorted worldview of BBC is such that opposition to Saddam gassing the Kurds is viewed with suspicion as a pro-Israel policy. Suffice to say, Gross didn't get the job.

The seriousness of the problem hit me square in the eyes when Fayad Abu Shamala,[170] BBC's correspondent in Gaza for 10 years, spoke at a Hamas rally. That alone was an egregious breach of ethics. But here's what he declared at the rally:

> "Journalists and media organizations [are] waging the campaign shoulder-to-shoulder together with the Palestinian people."[171]

Read it again: BBC reporters are fighting outright for the Palestinian cause.

If anyone doubted the sincerity of Fayad's statement, confirmation came from Fathi Hamad, the Hamas media relations official who verified that Fayad is a member of Hamas who "works for the BBC, and that way he writes the story in favor of the Islam [sic] and Muslims."[172]

What was BBC's reaction to this scandalous revelation? Did they fire Fayad immediately? Did they delete all his stories from their website? Did they institute new levels of editorial safeguards? Did they at least apologize for Fayad's 10 years of biased reporting?

No, they didn't do any of that. They simply shrugged the whole thing off as irrelevant. Here's the official BBC statement:

Fayad's remarks were made in a private capacity. His reports have always matched the best standards of balance required by the BBC.[173]

At least now we know what BBC considers to be their "best standards of balance."

With this incident, I began to connect the dots: Following Israel's withdrawal from Gaza in 2005, BBC was the only Western news organization to maintain a reporter permanently based in Gaza, operating with what one commentator called "a sense of political impunity."[174] This is the same BBC that employed Fayad Abu Shamala for 10 years as a mouthpiece for the Palestinians. Is it any wonder that BBC enjoyed access that other Western media did not?

Some of this outrageous bias has become known; others we can only speculate about. But one thing is certain: Palestinians are carrying on a reign of intimidation against journalists – with threats, beatings and kidnappings. Add to this equation the Western media's heavy reliance on Palestinian reporters, and long before the first shot is ever fired, the deck is well-stacked against Israel. That, my friends, is the dirty little secret of Middle East journalism.

Notes

1. "Newsweek Reporter Detained by Palestinians," Newsweek.com, May 29, 2001.
2. Khaled Abu Toameh, "Fatah Bans Coverage of PA Clashes with Hamas," *Jerusalem Post*, July 20, 2005.
3. "Palestinian Civil War Watch," *Little Green Footballs*, July 21, 2005.
4. Yoav Stern, "Palestinian Journalists Protest Hamas Media Crackdown in Gaza," *Haaretz* (Israel), August 25, 2007.
5. Jay Bushinsky, "Arafat's Rule a Nightmare for Palestinian Journalists," *Chicago Sun-Times*, March 5, 2004.
6. "Iraq Coalition Casualty Count: Journalist Deaths," Icasualties.org.
7. "Press Freedom Index 2008," Reporters Without Borders.
8. Michael Miner, "Beaten Into Submission?", *Chicago Reader*, December 21, 2000.
9. Khaled Abu Toameh, "Aksa Martyrs Admit Attacking Journalist," *Jerusalem Post*, June 21, 2004.
10. Stephanie Gutmann, "Lights, Camera, Intifada," *Weekly Standard*, January 1-8, 2001.
11. Hillel Halkin, "Why Israel Gets Spun," *National Post* (Canada), February 17, 2006.
12. Mark Seager, "I'll Have Nightmares for the Rest of My Life," *Sunday Telegraph* (UK), October 15, 2000. Similarly, Nasser Atta, a Palestinian producer with ABC, testified how his

cameraman was beaten and his crew prevented from filming the Ramallah lynchings. (Ted Koppel, "Impact of Photographs on Public and Political Opinion," *Nightline*, ABC News, October 13, 2000.)
13. Beatrice Roberti, "'Tense' Atmosphere for Foreign Reporters in Palestinian Areas," *Jerusalem Report*, November 20, 2000.
14. "Country Report: Palestinian Authority-Administered Territories [Israel]," Freedom House, 2004.
15. Dan Diker, "The Influence of Palestinian Organizations on Foreign News Reporting," *Jerusalem Issue Brief*, Vol. 2, No. 23, Jerusalem Center for Public Affairs, March 27, 2003.
16. Khaled Abu Toameh, "PA Arrests al-Jazeera Reporter for Blaming Fatah for Attack," *Jerusalem Post*, January 7, 2003.
17. Khaled Kasem Basheer, "Press Freedom in the Palestinian Territories," Palestine Partners Center for Media Development, 2007.
18. "Annual Report 2000," Amnesty International.
19. Sarah El Deeb, "Hamas Blocks Fatah Protests in Gaza," Associated Press, September 7, 2007.
20. Beth Gardiner, "World Leaders Condemn Act; Some Palestinians Celebrate," Associated Press, September 12, 2001.
21. "Armed Palestinians Threatened Photojournalists," *Jerusalem Post*, September 12, 2001.
22. "AP Protests Threats to Freelance Cameraman Who Filmed Palestinian Joy," Associated Press, September 12, 2001. ("An AP still photographer did not take pictures of the Nablus rally after being warned at the scene not to do so.")
23. "CNN Statement About False Claim It Used Old Video," CNN.com, September 20, 2001. See "False Footaging," Snopes.com.
24. Chris Fontaine, "After Attacks, Aid Offers Flood into the United States from Around the World," Associated Press, September 14, 2001.
25. "Media in Palestine: Between the Hammer of the PNA and the Anvil of Self-Censorship," Palestinian Human Rights Monitoring Group, March 2000.
26. Palestinian Authority Television, March 25, 2004; cited in Itamar Marcus and Barbara Crook, "When Hatemongering is Common Currency," *Ottawa Citizen* (Canada), April 27, 2009.
27. Sheikh Ahmed Ali Othman, quoted in *Al-Hakika Al-Dawliya* (Jordan), May 9, 2009, and Al-Moheet Arab News Network (Egypt), May 10, 2009; cited in Itamar Marcus and Barbara Crook, "All Pigs Must Die Because They Descend from Jews: According to Egyptian Islamic Scholar," Palestinian Media Watch, May 13, 2009.
28. "Report: Gaza TV Journalist Seeks Asylum in Norway," Associated Press, July 1, 2007.
29. Tom Gross, "The Case of Reuters," *National Review*, July 26, 2004.
30. Thomas L. Friedman, *From Beirut to Jerusalem*, Anchor Books, 1990, p. 58.
31. Arsen Ostrovsky, "Abu Toameh: What the Western Media Misses," FrumForum.com, November 12, 2010.
32. Khaled Abu Toameh, "Execution in Arafat's Compound – An Eye-Witness Account," *Newsweek*, August 7, 2002.
33. Ibrahim Barzak, "Gaza Journalists Warned Away from Fatah Event," Associated Press, December 31, 2007.
34. Ibrahim Barzak, "Palestinian Group Warns Journalists," Associated Press, August 26, 2002.
35. "Tales from the South, Sort of...", posted on Back-to-iraq.com, July 26, 2006.
36. See "Foreign Kidnappings in Gaza and West Bank," Agence France Presse, June 1, 2007; see also Committee to Protect Journalists – cpj.org.
37. Bret Stephens, "A Reporter's Fate," *Wall Street Journal*, May 22, 2007.
38. Charles Osgood, "Kidnapped British Journalist Alan Johnston Released," *The Osgood File*, CBS Radio News, July 5, 2007.
39. "BBC Kidnap Victim Recounts 'Dark Education' in Gaza," Agence France Presse, October 25,

2007.
40. "BBC Captive in 'Bomb Vest' Video," BBC News Online, June 25, 2007.
41. "BBC's Concern at Gaza Man's Fate," BBC News Online, April 15, 2007.
42. *Al-Hayat Al-Jadida* (Palestinian Authority), July 6, 2007.
43. "Video Released of BBC's Johnston," BBC News Online, June 1, 2007.
44. Charles Moore, "Imagine the Outcry Had the BBC Man Been Abducted by Israelis," *Daily Telegraph* (UK), June 2, 2007.
45. Kevin Ray, "BBC Praises Hamas; Requests More Kidnappings," Jewlarious.com, July 8, 2007.
46. John M. Higgins, "Hostage Centanni Speaks," *Broadcasting and Cable* magazine, September 4, 2006.
47. "Video of Kidnapped Fox News Journalists Released," *Special Report with Brit Hume*, Fox News, August 23, 2006.
48. "Kidnapped Fox Journalists Released," CNN.com, August 27, 2006.
49. In 1973, four hostages were taken in a botched bank robbery in Stockholm, Sweden. At the end of their captivity, six days later, the hostages actively resisted rescue. They refused to testify against their captors and raised money for their legal defense. Psychologists later defined this as the "Stockholm Syndrome" – a hostage's strategy of trying to please the captor in order to stay alive. The hostage identifies so much with the captor that the hostage's psyche is warped to the point of sympathizing with the tormenter. ("Newsweek's Hammer-Blow," HonestReporting.com, June 7, 2001.)
50. Interview with Danny Seaman, *Kol Ha'Ir* (Jerusalem), October 11, 2002.
51. "Palestinian Authority: Silencing in Dissent," Amnesty International, September 5, 2000.
52. Lawrie Mifflin, "Palestinians Protest to CBS News Over a Report on the West Bank," *New York Times*, January 6, 1998.
53. Eason Jordan, "The News We Kept to Ourselves," *New York Times*, April 11, 2003. Jordan also revealed that CNN supplied gifts to Saddam's family. Jordan's credibility hit rock-bottom in 2005, when he made the outrageous accusation that American troops were intentionally targeting journalists in Iraq. Jordan was forced to resign. (Howard Kurtz, "CNN's Jordan Resigns Over Iraq Remarks," *Washington Post*, February 12, 2005.)
54. Editorial, "CNN Knew," *Washington Times*, April 14, 2003.
55. "Saddam 'Wins 100% of Vote,'" BBC News Online, October 16, 2002. ("The government insists the count was fair and accurate.")
56. Cited in Franklin Foer, "CNN's Access of Evil," *Wall Street Journal*, April 14, 2003.
57. Franklin Foer, "Air War," *The New Republic*, October 28, 2002.
58. Peter Collins, "Corruption at CNN," *Washington Times*, April 15, 2003.
59. Speech to annual convention of the Radio and Television News Directors Association, September 26, 1998.
60. See Oakland Ross, "Seminars Teach Journalists How to Behave as Hostages," *Toronto Star*, October 27, 2007.
61. James Bennet, "At a Palestinian Protest, Israeli Gunfire Leaves at Least 10 Dead, Including Children," *New York Times*, May 20, 2004.
62. Zakariya Talmas of the Palestinian Journalists' Syndicate, quoted in *Jerusalem Post*, May 23, 2004.
63. "Press Freedom Situation Continues to Deteriorate in Hamastan," Reporters Without Borders, August 28, 2007.
64. The cartoon is modeled after a painting by Spanish artist Francisco Jose de Goya (1746-1828), entitled "Saturn Devouring His Children."
65. "Evolution of an Outrage," Mediabackspin.com, November 26, 2003.
66. Politicalcartoon.co.uk.
67. "Evolution of an Outrage."

68. *Jenin: Massacring Truth*, directed by Martin Himel, produced by CanWest MediaWorks, 2004.
69. Cited in "News Gathering Under the Gun," *Time*, March 1, 1982.
70. Thomas L. Friedman, *From Beirut to Jerusalem*, Anchor Books, 1990, pp. 72-73.
71. Zev Chafets, *Double Vision: How America's Press Distorts our View of the Middle East*, Morrow, 1985.
72. Ibid.
73. "News Gathering Under the Gun."
74. Chafets, *Double Vision*.
75. "News Gathering Under the Gun."
76. Ibid.
77. *The Media's Propaganda War Against Israel*, Shapolsky, 1986, p. 175.
78. Jim Hoagland, "Is Syria Intimidating the Western Press?", *Washington Post*, March 4, 1982.
79. Arieh O'Sullivan, "Fatah Abducts 'Newsweek' Bureau Chief Photographer," *Jerusalem Post*, May 30, 2001. In 1985, Terry Anderson, Associated Press' chief Mideast correspondent, was abducted from the street in Beirut, placed in the trunk of a car, and taken to a secret location where he was held captive by Hezbollah for 2,454 days.
80. Jamie Glasov, "Suicide Killers," Frontpagemag.com, December 12, 2005.
81. Attacks listed on Thereligionofpeace.com.
82. Figure based on 1.45 billion Muslims worldwide (World Factbook 2008, Central Intelligence Agency), and a 2006 Gallup poll which found that 7 percent of Muslims hold the "radical" view that the 9-11 terror attacks were "completely justified" (Dalia Mogahed, "The Battle for Hearts and Minds: Moderate vs. Extremist Views in the Muslim World: A Gallup World Poll Special Report").
83. "Process Behind Decision Making," *The Daily Illini* (University of Illinois), February 16, 2006.
84. "Pakistani human rights activists burn a Danish flag at a protest rally to show their anger over the reproduction of Prophet Muhammad cartoons in Denmark." Caption on Associated Press photo by Aftab Rizvi, February 21, 2008. (Later revised.)
85. "Paper Withdrawn Over Cartoon Row," BBC News Online, February 13, 2006.
86. "Russian Paper Closes After Publishing Cartoons," *The Guardian* (UK), February 21, 2006.
87. "P.E.I. Student Paper Publishes Cartoons of Prophet," CBC News (Canada), February 8, 2006.
88. "French Editor Fired Over Cartoons," BBC News Online, February 2, 2006.
89. The cartoonist, Kurt Westergaard, was forced into hiding. In 2008 two Tunisian men were arrested for planning to assassinate him. In 2010, a Somali man was shot as he tried to enter Westergaard's home while wielding an ax and a knife. ("Somali Shot after Allegedly Attempting to Attack Danish Cartoonist," CNN.com, January 2, 2010.) In 2010, five men were arrested for planning to commit a deadly shooting spree at the editorial offices of *Jyllands-Posten*, the newspaper that published the cartoons. Another man was wounded when a letter bomb intended for the daily prematurely exploded.
90. Dennis Prager, "American News Media: Little Courage and Little Honesty," Townhall.com, February 14, 2006.
91. Arthur Bright, "US, British Media Tread Carefully in Cartoon Furor," *Christian Science Monitor*, February 6, 2006; Richard Chacon, "Questionable Cartoons," *Boston Globe*, February 12, 2006; Rocco DiPippo, "Piss Christ vs. Cartoon Jihad," Frontpagemag.com, February 6, 2006.
92. Carolyn Thompson, "Borders, Waldenbooks Won't Carry Magazine," Associated Press, March 29, 2006.
93. Email correspondence with Beth Bingham of the Borders Group Inc., March 29, 2006.
94. Owen Moritz, "Pearl Beheading Showing On 'Net," *Daily News* (New York), June 8, 2002.
95. "World of Pain," *The Phoenix* (Boston), February 10, 2006.

96. Cited in "Website Withdraws Dutch MP's Anti-Islam Film After Threats," ABC News (Australia), March 29, 2008.
97. "Gunman Kills Dutch Film Director," BBC News Online, November 2, 2004.
98. Adam Cohen, "'Libel Tourism': When Freedom of Speech Takes a Holiday," *New York Times*, September 14, 2008. Prior to his death in 2009, Mahfouz – listed by *Forbes* as one of the richest people in the world – used his resources to sue dozens of publishers and authors. New York State later passed a bill – nicknamed "Rachel's Law" – blocking enforcement of libel judgments from countries that provide less free-speech protection than the United States.
99. "The Jewel of Medina Statement," Random House Publishing Group, August 2008.
100. Brooke M. Goldstein, "Mark Steyn Is Not Alone," *American Spectator*, January 15, 2008.
101. Cited in Dennis Rice, "Sir Paul: Terror Target," *Sunday Express* (UK), September 14, 2008. Other rock musicians such as Elvis Costello, the Pixies, Gil Scott-Heron and Carlos Santana have cancelled tour stops in Israel. (Isabel Kershner, "Artists' Boycott Strikes a Dissonant Note Inside Israel," *New York Times*, June 9, 2010.)
102. Patrick Lee, "What Even Roland Emmerich Won't Destroy: An Islamic Landmark," SciFiWire.com, November 2, 2009.
103. BBC Drops Fictional Terror Attack to Avoid Offending Muslims," *Evening Standard* (UK), April 27, 2009.
104. Patrick Goldstein, "The Big Picture: Muslim Threats to 'South Park': Did Comedy Central Cave in to Knucklehead Extremists?", *Los Angeles Times*, April 23, 2010.
105. RevolutionMuslim.com, cited in *Anderson Cooper 360 Degrees*, CNN, April 20, 2010.
106. Following complaints, Comedy Central removed the game from its website. ("Success! Comedy Central Caves in to Pressure," HonestReporting.com, May 27, 2010.)
107. As the *Washington Post* ombudsman lamented, "[This] sets an awfully low threshold for decisions on whether to withhold words or images that might offend." (Andrew Alexander, "Where was the 'Where's Muhammad?' Cartoon?", *Washington Post*, October 10, 2010.)
108. James Taranto, Best of the Web, *Wall Street Journal*, October 14, 2010.
109. Liz Thomas, "The BBC Will Tackle Islam Differently to Christianity, Admits its Director General," *Daily Mail* (UK), October 15, 2008.
110. Mike McNally, "Fearful BBC Walks on Eggshells Around Muslims," *Pajamas Media*, October 25, 2008.
111. Brian Stelter, "Cartoonist in Hiding After Death Threats," *New York Times*, September 16, 2010. This is the same al-Awlaki that the *New York Times* described in 2001 as a moderate who "is held up as a new generation of Muslim leader capable of merging East and West." (Laurie Goodstein, "The American Muslims; Influential American Muslims Temper Their Tone," *New York Times*, October 19, 2001.)
112. Mark D. Fefer, "On the Advice of the FBI, Cartoonist Molly Norris Disappears From View," *Seattle Weekly*, September 15, 2010.
113. Mark Steyn, "Media Utters Nonsense, Won't Call Enemy Out," *Chicago Sun-Times*, October 16, 2005.
114. Ian Austen and David Johnston, "17 Held in Plot to Bomb Sites in Ontario," *New York Times*, June 4, 2006.
115. Alan Cowell and Raymond Bonner, "Britain at Top Terror Alert After Air Terminal is Struck," *New York Times*, July 1, 2007.
116. David Rising, "UK Cops Working to Unravel the Failed Car Bombing Plots, Establish Ties Between Suspects," Associated Press, July 4, 2007.
117. Max Boot, "Oh, and Incidentally...", *Contentions* blog / *Commentary*, May 21, 2009.
118. Susan Candiotti, "Suspects in Alleged Synagogue Bomb Plot Denied Bail," CNN.com, May 21, 2009.
119. Al Baker and Javier C. Hernandez, "4 Accused of Bombing Plot at Bronx Synagogues," *New*

York Times, May 20, 2009.
120. Richard Esposito, Mark Crudele and Aaron Katersky, "Two Arrested in New York City Synagogue Attack Plot Sting," ABC News, May 12, 2011.
121. William K. Rashbaum and Al Baker, "Suspects in Terror Case Wanted to Kill Jews, Officials Say," *New York Times*, May 12, 2011; cited in "NYT Political Correctness in NYC Terror Arrest," *Elder of Ziyon* blog, May 12, 2011.
122. "Common Misunderstandings about Muslims," ABC News, February 26, 2008.
123. "Israeli Man Held in Airport Over US Serial Stabbings," BBC News Online, August 12, 2010.
124. "Israeli Held in Investigation of Serial Stabbings," NBC News and News Services, August 12, 2010.
125. On ABC's *World News Now* (August 12, 2010), correspondent Steve Osunsami described the serial killer as an "Israeli national," while *Good Morning America* mentioned three times that Abuelazam was arrested while trying to fly to his native Israel. (Juju Chang and Jeremy Hubbard, *Good Morning America*, ABC, August 13, 2010.) On *CBS Evening News*, correspondent Elaine Quijano described Abuelazam as an "Israeli national," while guest anchor Erica Hill referred to his "native Israel." (*CBS Evening News with Katie Couric*, CBS, August 12 and August 13, 2010.) On NBC's *Today Show* (August 14, 2010), co-host Amy Robach tagged him as "a 33-year-old Israeli national," while correspondent Ron Mott identified him as "an Israeli citizen." Examples cited in Brad Wilmouth, "Some Media Tag Serial Stabber as 'Israeli National,' Others See 'Israeli Arab' or 'Palestinian Christian,'" Newsbusters.org, August 14, 2010; see also "Reporting the Story of an Alleged Israeli-Arab Serial Killer," *Snapshots* blog, August 12, 2010.
126. Lex Hall, "Lucky Escape for Adelaide Designer," *The Australian*, November 27, 2008.
127. Cited in Tom Gross, "If This Isn't Terrorism, What Is?", *Wall Street Journal Europe*, December 1, 2008.
128. Katie Couric, *CBS Evening News*, November 5, 2009.
129. Pete Williams, "Dr. Nadal Malik Hasan Believed to be Shooter on Fort Hood Military Base," *NBC Nightly News*, November 5, 2009.
130. Helen Pidd and Ewen MacAskill, "Fort Hood Army Officer Shouted 'Allahu Akbar' Before Shooting Rampage," *The Guardian* (UK), November 6, 2009.
131. Philip Sherwell and Alex Spillius, "Fort Hood Shooting: Texas Army Killer Linked to September 11 Terrorists," *Daily Telegraph* (UK), November 7, 2009.
132. Richard Esposito, Matthew Cole and Brian Ross, "Army Major in Fort Hood Massacre Used 'Electronic Means' to Connect with Terrorists," ABC News, November 9, 2009.
133. Nick Allen, "Fort Hood Gunman Had Told US Military Colleagues that Infidels Should Have Their Throats Cut," *Daily Telegraph* (UK), November 8, 2009.
134. "Fort Hood Tragedy," *World News with Charles Gibson*, ABC News, November 5, 2009.
135. William K. Rashbaum, Mark Mazzetti and Peter Baker, "Arrest Made in Times Square Bomb Case," *New York Times*, May 3, 2010.
136. Clifden Kennedy, "Faisal Shahzad Charged with Five Counts, Admits Training in Pakistan," *CBS News Investigates*, May 4, 2010; Eileen Sullivan and Kimberly Dozier, "AP Sources: Bomber Trained at Pakistan Terror Camp," Associated Press, May 4, 2010.
137. "Saudi Prince Changes Fox's Paris Riots Coverage," *The Guardian* (UK), December 12, 2005. In 2010, the same Saudi Prince, Alwaleed bin Talal, announced plans to launch a 24-hour Arabic-language news channel in partnership with Fox News. ("Saudi Prince, Fox to Start Arabic News Channel," CBC News [Canada], July 12, 2010.)
138. "Muslims Urged to Buy Influence in World Media," Reuters, September 13, 2006. Egyptian Information Minister Anas el-Feki specifically pointed to Israeli defense policies as an issue where Muslims need to make their views and influence felt.
139. Zoran Bozicevic, "Not-so-candid Camera," *National Post* (Canada), June 16, 2006.

140. Ehud Ya'ari, "Neighborhood Watch," *Jerusalem Report*, May 7, 2001.
141. Khaled Abu Toameh, speech in Jerusalem, June 2004.
142. Khaled Abu Toameh, "Palestinian Journalists Vow Fealty to Arafat," *Jerusalem Post*, January 14, 2004. Emphasis added.
143. Khaled Abu Toameh, "I was Threatened by a Palestinian Official for a Story in the 'Post,'" *Jerusalem Post*, September 24, 2002.
144. Tom Gross, "The Case of Reuters," *National Review*, July 26, 2004.
145. Wafa Amr, "Arafat: Willing to Die a 'Martyr,'" Reuters, September 17, 2003.
146. "Reuters Defines 'Martyrdom,'" *Little Green Footballs*, September 17, 2003.
147. Diaa Hadid, "My Israel, My Palestine," *Reportage*, Australian Centre for Independent Journalism, 2002; cited in "MSM Terror Propaganda Roundup," *Little Green Footballs*, November 25, 2006.
148. Andrew Bosson, "Five Killed in Lebanon-Israel Clash," Reuters, August 3, 2010. The *New York Times* falsely described the premeditated sniper fire as a "skirmish [that] seems to have been accidental." (Robert F. Worth, "U.S. Weighs Tough Choice Over Aid for Lebanon," *New York Times*, August 21, 2010.)
149. Smadar Peri, "IDF: Journalists Were Tipped Off," *Ynetnews* (Israel), August 4, 2010.
150. See "Border Clash: A Case Study in Reuters Photography," Mediabackspin.com, August 5, 2010. Similarly, in 2007, Pulitzer Prize-winning photographer Bilal Hussein of Associated Press aroused suspicion by appearing at the scene of Iraqi insurgent attacks before they occurred. His house was discovered to contain bomb-making materials and he was arrested as a suspected terrorist operative. ("Iraq Reporter Faces Terror Charge," BBC News Online, November 20, 2007.)
151. Ibrahim Barzak, "Palestinian PM Lashes Out at Israelis," Associated Press, June 30, 2006.
152. Alyssa A. Lappen, "The Israeli Crime That Wasn't," Frontpagemag.com, December 28, 2004.
153. "Where the Reporting Stops," *Jerusalem Post*, January 18, 2005.
154. Ibid.
155. Ibid.
156. "Abd al-Bari Atwan," Wikipedia.org.
157. Jonny Paul, "London Arabic Daily Editor: Mercaz Harav Attack was 'Justified,'" *Jerusalem Post*, March 16, 2008.
158. Jonny Paul, "London Editor Prays for Nuclear Attack on Israel," *Jerusalem Post*, August 28, 2007; Tom Gross, "BBC and Sky News Analyst Praises Jerusalem Yeshiva Massacre," Tomgrossmedia.com, March 20, 2008.
159. Abdul Bari Atwan, "Inside Osama's Mountain Lair," *The Guardian* (UK), November 12, 2001.
160. ANB-TV (Lebanon), June 27, 2007; cited in "Abd Al-Bari Atwan, Editor-in-Chief of *Al-Quds Al-Arabi*: If Iranian Missiles Hit Israel, I Will Dance in Trafalgar Square," Memritv.org.
161. "Secret Documents from Libyan Intelligence Reveal Abdel Bari Atwan Received Money from Gaddafi," Palestine Press News Agency, September 15, 2011.
162. Paul, "London Arabic Daily Editor: Mercaz Harav Attack was 'Justified.'"
163. BBC World Service, December 12, 2000; cited in Andrea Levin, "The BBC Goes to War," *Jerusalem Post*, March 30, 2001.
164. Cited in Richard Landes, "The Media Honor-Shame Game: Humiliate Israel, Spare and Taunt the Arabs," *Augean Stables*, May 13, 2010.
165. Bret Stephens, "A Reporter's Fate," *Wall Street Journal*, May 22, 2007.
166. Janet Daley, "The BBC is a World, Not a Law, Unto Itself," *The Telegraph* (UK), July 22, 2003.
167. Yaakov Lappin, "Terrorist at Journalists' Party," *Ynetnews* (Israel), July 15, 2005.
168. Paul Revoir, "BBC Pays £200,000 to 'Cover Up Report on Anti-Israel Bias'," *Daily Mail* (UK), March 22, 2007. In 2006 BBC was again forced to appoint an independent "Impartiality Review Panel, which found that BBC's reporting of the Israeli-Palestinian conflict did

"not consistently constitute a full and fair account of the conflict but rather, in important respects, presents an incomplete and in that sense misleading picture." The panel further concluded that BBC displays "gaps in coverage, analysis, context and perspective" and fails to "maintain consistently the BBC's own established editorial standards." (Owen Gibson, "BBC's Coverage of Israeli-Palestinian Conflict 'Misleading'," *The Guardian* [UK], May 3, 2006.) In 2009, a bid to force BBC to publish the Balen Report was rejected by the British High Court. ("BBC Report to Stay Confidential," BBC News Online, October 2, 2009.) See also, Kari Lipschutz, "BBC Spends Big Money Defending Israel-Palestine Coverage," *Adweek*, May 23, 2011.

169. Ori Golan, "In Poisoned English," *Jerusalem Post*, March 27, 2003.
170. Also transliterated as Faiz Abu Smala.
171. Martin Walker, "The BBC Pro-Israeli? Is the Pope Jewish?" *The Times* (UK), May 11, 2006.
172. Arnon Regular, "Leading Hamas Preacher Warns of Clash with Islamic Jihad," Haaretz (Israel), December 15, 2004.
173. Walker, "The BBC Pro-Israeli? Is the Pope Jewish?"
174. Bret Stephens, "A Reporter's Fate," *Wall Street Journal*, May 22, 2007.

7

FAUXTOGRAPHY: LEBANON AND BEYOND

I t all started in July 2006 when Hezbollah terrorists crossed the border from Lebanon, kidnapping two Israeli soldiers and killing eight more. Hostilities quickly erupted, with Hezbollah firing deadly missiles into Israeli towns, and Israel conducting retaliatory air raids.[1]

Amidst the fighting, Reuters issued a photo showing plumes of smoke rising from Beirut after an Israeli attack. The eagle eye of the weblog Little Green Footballs detected unnatural repeating patterns in the smoke over the Beirut skyline, plus a series of "duplicate" buildings.[2] It turns out that Adnan Hajj, a Lebanese photographer employed by Reuters since 1993, had used photo-editing software – the Photoshop "clone tool" – to make the damage to Beirut seem greater than it really was.

When confronted, Moira Whittle of the Reuters' crisis team (who was concurrently serving as PR contact for the Arabic network Al Jazeera) came up with this implausible excuse: The photographer, she said, was "trying to remove dust marks" and, um, "made mistakes due to the bad lighting conditions."[3]

One would expect other journalists to denounce Hajj's manipulations as beyond the bounds of acceptable journalism. Yet Phil Coomes, photo editor of BBC News Online, took the amoral position that "one man's colour balancing is another's grounds for dismissal."[4]

This was just the tip of the iceberg. Dozens of fake images were emerging from Lebanon, each one designed to exaggerate Israeli military actions and turn public opinion in favor of Hezbollah. Another Hajj photo showed an Israeli jet firing three missiles in what appeared to be a bombardment of Lebanese civilians. Not quite. The jet was actually dropping a *single defensive flare*, and Hajj had fired up his trusty clone tool so that the version Reuters distributed to thousands of media outlets gave the exaggerated effect of a massive Israeli "missile attack."[5]

As word of the hoax spread and Reuters became the butt of late-night comedy jokes, the "news agency" deleted all 920 of Hajj's "photographs" from its database.[6] It was a step in the right direction, but by erasing the complete Hajj archive, Reuters made it impossible for anyone to track how many other Hajj forgeries had been distributed over the years.[7] As for Israeli PR, no simple retraction could erase the damage caused by a decade of Hajj's "photos" appearing on the pages of the *New York Times*, *Washington Post*, and in countless other contexts.

In this age of scandal-obsessed media, what's shocking is that no investigative reporter ever followed up this story in any meaningful way. Adnan Hajj seemed to simply vanish off the face of the earth – no interviews, no photos of him, no investigations. Just one statement from Reuters that his fakery was to "remove dust." Then, poof! Adnan who?[8]

Besides the repeating patterns of smoke, the real "repeating pattern" was how Arab stringers were supplying a steady stream of propaganda against Israel – and how leading news organizations were sending those unscrutinized images right to your breakfast table. In the words of one prominent photo editor: "Digital photography has altered the landscape of photojournalism like nothing before it, placing the photographers in total control of their output."[9] Were it not for astute media monitors, Adnan Hajj might well have won a prize for wartime photography.

Staged Scenes

Hajj's transgression – digital manipulation – is only one example of the photo fraud that proliferated in Lebanon. Beyond this was a rash of staged scenes being presented as spontaneous news events.[10]

Take the case of Salam Daher, a green-helmeted Lebanese rescue worker who mysteriously seemed to appear at every battle scene. In one sequence of news photos following Israel's bombing of the town of Qana, the ubiquitous "Green Helmet Guy" is seen parading a ghoulish dead baby in front of cameramen, holding it aloft as some kind of sadistic trophy. The event in Qana was an unmistakable human tragedy, yet this photo, splashed on the front pages of newspapers around the world, was not a genuine image of a rescue operation, but rather a cynical exploitation – a staged scene to ensure maximum shock value.

Bloggers later unearthed another photo – taken from a different angle – showing a crowd of photographers, shoulder-to-shoulder and several rows deep, shooting frontal images of the corpse. Of course, this photo – which reveals the whole thing as a set-up rather than a candid shot – was never published. Like the scaffolds, lights and fake landscapes behind the scenes at a theater, this photo ruins the "suspension of disbelief" needed to convince an audience.[11]

In one sequence videotaped by German television, Green Helmet Guy is shown gesturing toward news cameras in an unmistakable circular motion with his finger, instructing them to "keep on filming." Once he has the film crew's attention, Green Helmet Guy instructs aid workers to remove a dead child's body from an ambulance – and lay it on the dusty ground. He then clears onlookers out of the way and beckons the news cameras to come closer, as he dramatically pulls away the blanket to reveal the dead child's body.[12] Rescue worker or movie director? You decide.

Whatever the case, the media lapped it up. An Associated Press memo praised its photographers in Lebanon for "a stunning series of images... that beat the competition and scored huge play overnight." AP rewarded the photographers with cash bonuses and gushed poetically over one gruesome photo of the dead: "Calm, morning light shone down on man and child, highlighting them against an almost monochrome background of pure rubble."[13]

Art, Andy Warhol said, is whatever you can get away with.

In another instance, Green Helmet Guy was caught parading around with dead bodies long after they'd been rescued. A photo by Associated Press – time-stamped 7:21 a.m. on July 30, 2006 – shows a dead girl in an ambulance. A second Associated Press photo – stamped three hours later at 10:44 a.m. – shows Green Helmet Guy displaying the *same girl* for news cameras.[14] Is it any surprise that one of the fauxtographers shooting the Green Helmet scenes was Adnan "Clone Tool" Hajj?[15]

Green Helmet Guy is a long-time veteran of these charades. News photos two decades earlier from the first Israel-Lebanon war show the same Green Helmet Guy – albeit a younger version with no glasses – in the center of the action, posing for cameras as he brandishes the headless body of a child.[16]

Bryan Denton, a photographer whose work has appeared in the *New York Times*, was on the scene in Lebanon during the 2006 war, witnessing what he called "the daily practice of directed shots." He noted one case "where a group of photojournalists were choreographing the unearthing of bodies, directing emergency workers here and there, asking them to position bodies just so, even removing bodies that had already been put in graves so that they can photograph them in people's arms." As Denton observed, "these photographers have come away with powerful shots, that require no manipulation digitally, but instead, manipulation on a human level – and this itself is a bigger ethical problem."[17]

The more I delved, the more I found photos being staged. BBC posted a photo of a young boy in southern Lebanon standing next to an unexploded bomb in his living room. BBC reporter Martin Asser noted that "the young boy [was] pushed forward to stand reluctantly next to it while we get our cameras out and record the scene for posterity."[18]

I immediately contacted BBC. "I appreciate you informing readers that this photo was staged. But the bottom line is this imagery exists only because the boy was pushed into position."

Steve Herrmann, editor of BBC News, said there was nothing to get excited about. This scene, he explained, is "repeated countless times whenever photojournalists are at work: bystanders get in the shot and pose."[19] In other words, BBC publishes lots of staged photos. The only difference is that this time they bothered to mention it; the "countless" other times, readers don't know it's happening.

In many cases, it's not clear who orchestrated the shot. If propagandists stage a scene, and then a photojournalist "buys into it" by pressing the shutter, the journalist may be a collaborator but he's not the sole perpetrator. In Lebanon, however, many journalists took the step of placing objects into a scene – doubling as both photographer and set designer.

One Reuters' photo from the Lebanese village of Qana depicts a scene of destroyed buildings, with a mannequin in a wedding dress dramatically posed in front of the wreckage.[20] Anyone willing to bet that someone – either a Hezbollah operative or Reuters' photographer Sharif Karim – found the mannequin elsewhere and then placed it for that "perfect shot"?

In *Platoon*, Oliver Stone said the first casualty of war is innocence. He was wrong. When fauxtography is at play, the first casualties of war are the *symbols* of innocence.[21] During the 2006 fighting, Associated Press distributed a photo of Mickey Mouse, lying dramatically in a battle-scarred Lebanese cityscape.[22] The giveaway it's a setup is that the toy is completely clean, while the rest of the scene is a thick layer of dust-covered rubble. Not to be outdone, Reuters released a photo of Minnie Mouse – magically clean, fresh and dust-free in the rubble.[23] The same Reuters' photographer, Sharif Karim, then issued a photo of a stuffed teddy bear in the same dust-free condition, and yet another photo of a perfectly positioned stuffed tiger. As if competing in some new Olympic sport, Reuters' colleagues Issam Kobeisi and Mohamed Azakir came up with their own photos of stuffed dolls positioned in Lebanese war scenes.[24]

The odds of these shots being genuine are miniscule. On the other hand, I couldn't prove that they were staged… until I located photos of an Arab "prop man" walking through the rubble of Beirut carrying a suitcase full of stuffed animals.

"A good picture is a dusty teddy bear placed by Hezbollah at the scene of sites bombed by Israel," explained Giulio Meotti, a reporter with Italy's *Il Foglio* newspaper. Photos of dead Israelis "just interfere with the story the European media is trying to tell."[25]

With these staged events, journalists and terrorists have forged a corrupt symbiotic relationship. Gaining media attention is actually the goal of terrorists, and reporters play along with full knowledge – because these scenes of death and destruction are their ticket to high ratings, employee bonuses and prestigious awards.[26]

Consider the Reuters' "news" photo of a bombed-out automobile following an Israeli strike on Beirut.[27] A second photo, from Associated Press, shows the same scene from the same angle – except in this case, a wall-hanging of Koranic verses is positioned atop the car.[28] How did it get there? What is the probability of a wall-hanging being thrown onto the street and landing upright on the edge of a car door? The only rational explanation is that the Islamic verses were intentionally placed in the rubble to send a symbolic message: "Israel is trying to destroy Islam."[29] And why not? It is this "quality work" that made AP fauxtographer Lefteris Pitarakis a finalist for the 2006 Pulitzer Prize.

In the midst of these revelations, Jules Crittenden, an editor at the *Boston Herald*, asked the billion-dollar question: "Why would photo editors who presumably are looking at a chronological series of photos from any given scene, fall for tricks that have been uncovered by amateurs?" Crittenden concluded: "Because people see what they want to see. Magicians and scammers have known this since the time of the pharaohs. Psychological studies have confirmed it is true."[30]

Worst of all, obscured in this maze of images was the underlying truth that Hezbollah had instigated the war by infiltrating Israel in a spate of murder and kidnapping, coupled with a barrage of 4,000 rockets on northern Israeli towns. (My family's vacation apartment in Tzfat took a direct hit.) Yet with the media's penchant for dramatic "news" photos that offered little context, the conflict became increasingly portrayed as the "powerful Israeli army" against "heroic Hezbollah defending a civilian population."[31] Israel's enemies were playing the media like a chess match, with the consumer public cast as the unwitting pawns.

Indeed, a survey by Marvin Kalb of Harvard University found that of the BBC's 117 stories during the war, 38 percent identified Israel as the aggressor, while only 4 percent cast Hezbollah in that role. Meanwhile, on the front pages of the *New York Times* and the *Washington Post*, Israel was portrayed as the aggressor nearly twice as often in headlines, and three times as often in photos.[32]

To be fair, not every journalist went along with this smoke-and-mirrors show. When journalists were taken by Hezbollah PR reps to a Beirut alley full of ambulances, CNN's Anderson Cooper told the behind-the-scenes truth:

> One by one, they've been told to turn on their sirens and zoom off so that all the photographers here can get shots of ambulances rushing off to treat civilians... These ambulances aren't responding to any new bombings. The sirens are strictly for effect.[33]

Other networks, meanwhile, dutifully videotaped the ambulances going by, neglecting to inform their viewers that it was all a set-up. To paraphrase Art Buchwald: Every time you think television news has hit its lowest ebb, something else comes along to make you wonder where the ebb was.

Professional Weeping Grandmothers

Photos "that purport to depict reality must be genuine in every way," states the *New York Times'* code of ethics.[34] So imagine my skepticism at the "picture perfect" news photo of a Palestinian woman weeping in front of the Israeli security barrier. In one respect, the photo appeared to be a candid expression of Palestinian suffering. What consumers didn't see, however, was the original, un-cropped version of the photo showing a pack of photographers right up in the woman's face.[35]

Was this scene genuine? It's possible. But with such a rare confluence of elements – the woman provocatively positioned in front of the security barrier, alone and weeping, as six photojournalists "just happened" to be strolling by – the chances of it being genuine are about the same odds as a monkey typing out Shakespeare. It's simply too good to be true.

The tip-off in this case was the woman's positioning directly in front of English graffiti, a technique straight out of the Palestinian PR playbook. Graffiti affords the opportunity to make a direct political statement, with the English lettering purely for Western consumption. On one occasion, in an effort by Palestinians "to project a moderate image in advance of the arrival of the UN investigative team," Arabic graffiti declaring "Osama bin Laden is a hero" was painted over with placid slogans in English. Instead of the usual Palestinian graffiti extolling violent "rivers of blood" and "the gates of hell," Western visitors were greeted by images of the olive branch and "give peace a chance."[36]

Then there's the widely-circulated news photo showing dozens of caskets lined up against a wall, with two wailing hijab-clad Lebanese women wedged into the narrow space between the coffins and the wall.[37] The problem with this photo is obvious: Why would the women have forced their way into a crevice, when they could have more easily approached the caskets from the opposite side? The answer, of course, is that the shot was staged for Western audiences, right down to the numbers spray-painted on the wall to signify the enormity of the tragedy. The proof of a set-up? These numbers were written in a Western style, unlike those commonly used in southern Lebanon.[38]

The camera didn't lie – but the cameraman did.

So the next time you see a weeping Palestinian woman astride English graffiti, ask yourself: What's the background of this story? How did this woman get there? How did the photographers happen to be there? Was it candid, or was she playing to the camera? Was she coached to stand near the photographers and cry? Did the photographers ask her to move into a more scenic position? Who wrote the graffiti and when?

An extension of this staging technique is to hire actors and cart them from scene to scene. One Reuters' photo during the Lebanon war, dated July 22, 2006, shows an elderly woman weeping in front of the wreckage of her Beirut apartment.[39] Two weeks later, Associated Press released its own photo of an elderly Lebanese woman weeping in front of her destroyed Beirut apartment.[40] This seemed innocuous enough – except that a closer look confirmed that both photos are of the same woman. Same clothes, same scar on her left cheek, same dark mark under her right eye – and for dramatic effect, the same double-handed heavenward wail. BBC loved the photo so much that it even posted it twice on the same webpage.[41]

These two photos were released weeks apart, yet both captions claimed that the woman's home was destroyed in the *previous night's* bombing. So let's analyze: Either this woman – later identified as Asma Srour – is a professional actor in cahoots with Hezbollah and photojournalists, or she's the most unlucky homeowner in all of Lebanon. Was her home demolished twice, weeks apart? Or perhaps both photos were taken on the same day and then released intermittently – in the hope that nobody would catch this "damage recycling."[42]

The answer became clear two weeks later when – you guessed it – Associated Press released yet another photo of the same Professional Weeping Grandmother, walking through the rubble of her home "destroyed during the Israeli offensive in Southern Lebanon."[43] And just when you thought it couldn't get any worse, a few days later, *the exact same woman* – wailing over a completely different destroyed home – appeared in glorious full color on the cover of London's popular magazine, *The Spectator*.[44]

How did fauxtojournalists have the nerve to feature the same woman again and again? I eventually got to the bottom of the story. "Hezbollah has been tightly controlling the news coverage and is not permitting photographers free access to these areas," a veteran newsman told me. "Instead, photographers were brought in by bus and Hezbollah PR reps took them to various locations where Arab actors were pre-positioned." This same wailing woman, he told me, was used on at least four separate occasions.

Of course, the average media consumer has no idea about any of this behind-the-scenes manipulation. Who has the time and inclination to pour over every photo, looking for manipulation and analyzing the back story? And that's exactly the circumstances that Arab propagandists are counting on. Hassan Ezzieddine, head of the Hezbollah media relations department, explained: "We believe that the media have an important role in the conflict with the Israeli enemy, as important as the military wing."[45] As confirmed by CNN's Nic Robertson: "There's no doubt about it: Hezbollah has a very, very sophisticated and slick media operation."[46]

Call it "Extreme Makeover – Beirut Edition."

Garbage Dumps and Ambulance Attacks

Another trick used to distort events is to take an actual photo and rewrite the context. For example, *U.S. News & World Report* ran a cover photo of a Hezbollah fighter gazing at an out-of-control fire.[47] (The same photo appeared in *Time* magazine.)[48] The photo caption described the scene as "wreckage of a downed Israeli jet billow[ing] smoke near Beirut." A closer look at the photo, however, shows automobile tires burning. Not a war scene, but some sort of garbage dump. Apparently, an accurate caption like, "A Hezbollah media relations expert poses in front of a harmless tire fire," would have spoiled the dramatic effect.[49]

A deeper probe of this photo revealed even further manipulation. Though the blaze was, in fact, caused by a piece of military equipment, it was not an Israeli jet, but rather a Hezbollah missile launcher hidden in a civilian truck on a Lebanese Army base. Is it possible that *Time* and *U.S. News* didn't know about this? Highly doubtful. The original photo caption – submitted by photographer Bruno Stevens two weeks before the photo appeared in *Time* and *U.S. News* – accurately described the scene as depicting "Hezbollah owned trucks" that "contained a medium range ground to ground missile launcher."[50] This time we can't even place the blame on local stringers acting on behalf of Hezbollah. It was editors at these magazines, sitting in comfortable offices, who apparently altered the caption to skew the story.[51]

This tactic of counterfeit captions has a long history. In 1982, at the height of the first Israel-Lebanon war, UPI released a photograph of a

Lebanese baby that appeared to have his limbs blown off. The caption described a seven-month-old who'd been severely burned when Israel bombed an area of Beirut. Legend has it that when President Ronald Reagan opened the *Washington Post* and saw the photo, he put it on his desk and said, "That's it. Now Israel has to be stopped."[52]

It turns out that the caption was a fake. The baby had not lost any limbs, and the burns were actually the result of a *Palestinian* attack on East Beirut.[53] But the media published the fake caption because it fit their template of Israel as the aggressor. The result: the Arabs claimed moral superiority, and Israel was pressured by world opinion to stop its defensive operations.

Then there's the case of the blown-out ambulance. In the midst of the 2006 war, the *New York Times*,[54] MSNBC,[55] *Time* magazine,[56] the *Today Show*[57] and hundreds of other media outlets reported that Israel had deliberately fired missiles at a Lebanese ambulance, causing a huge explosion that wounded six people and knocked the driver 25 feet away. The ambulance was filled with "fire and smoke" and was "entirely destroyed."[58] If true, targeting this ambulance would have been an egregious and indefensible violation of the Geneva Convention, what Britain's ITV News called "tantamount to war crimes."[59]

Upon closer inspection, however, photos of the "destroyed ambulance" revealed glaring inconsistencies that tipped off the *Zombietime* blog and other media monitors to a hoax:[60]

- An exploding missile would typically obliterate the entire vehicle. Yet photos of the ambulance interior show no fire or smoke damage, with the upholstery intact and not even a hole in the floor. If this had been an actual missile strike, it would qualify for the *Guinness Book of Records* as the least amount of missile damage in history.

- Photos reveal that the vehicle's roof is caved inward. As any high school science student knows, when a missile penetrates a closed area and explodes, the concussive force from within blows a hole outward, not inward. Furthermore, the van exhibited none of the massive structural damage typically caused by the pressure wave from such an explosion.[61]

- The hole in the ambulance roof is perfectly circular with clean rounded edges; a missile penetration would be jagged. Further, the hole in these photos is rusted; it normally takes months for a vehicle roof to begin rusting. Finally, the perfectly circular hole is in the exact center of the "red cross" painted on the roof, in the precise spot and exactly the same size as the ambulance's red flashing light or circular roof vent would otherwise be.

So that explains it. Apparently, this ambulance with a rusted-out hole in its roof was dragged out of a junkyard, and – thanks to media carelessness or collusion – used as a prop in the misinformation war against Israel. (It turns out that Western journalists never actually saw the ambulance, and images of the damaged vehicle were taken by "local amateur cameramen.")[62]

Without question, visual images are the most powerful medium, with the greatest potential for abuse. Reading the news requires effort to assimilate the information and create a "mental image." But with images, the processing is immediate – "seeing is believing." When repeated over and over, iconic images penetrate in a deep emotional way and – like a powerful Hollywood film – create the illusion of actually experiencing it.

Beyond this, our age of digital editing provides an even greater potential for images to mislead. We've all seen the bogus photo of a guy standing on the observation deck of the World Trade Center on the morning of 9-11 with an airplane coming straight at him, and we've seen the Dove soap commercial in which a plain-looking woman is "Photoshopped" into a gorgeous picture-perfect billboard model.[63] And as photo-editing technology advances, detection becomes more difficult.[64]

I was reminded of how easily fact and fiction can meld when Reuters issued video footage of a Russian submarine planting a flag at the bottom of the ocean at the North Pole. Everything was fine until a 13-year-old boy in Finland saw the footage and said, "Hey, that looks like a scene from the movie *Titanic!*" He popped in a DVD of the film and sure enough, it was.[65] It's bad enough to pass off stock footage as an actual event, but when that footage is Hollywood-produced fantasy, it says a lot about the power of the media to deceive (and a lot about Reuters' lack of standards).

The old Chinese proverb says, "A picture is worth a thousand words." That applied back in the days before Photoshop. In the Middle East today, with sophisticated multi-media editing tools and the ever-present specter of fraud, a picture is worth a thousand weapons.[66]

Image Recycling

Imagine you're an editor on deadline, but there are no captivating news photos available. So what do you do? Simply recycle the old ones, like *The Times* of London did for its "Image of the Day" feature in March 2008. Alongside feel-good photos of a Thailand-bred white jewel cat, a milkman feeding a parking meter, and elephants decorated for a Hindu festival, the *Times* included a photo with this caption: "A young Palestinian boy defends the rubble of his home in the Jenin refugee camp on the West Bank, razed by the Israeli Army during its assault on the town..."[67]

Putting aside the issue of including such a politicized image in the company of cats, elephants and milkmen, this photo – appearing as an "Image of the Day" in 2008 – was published with no indication of background or context. Readers likely assumed that Israel had just carried out a military assault on Jenin. In truth, however, the photo was from 2002 – but what was it doing there now?

Following a flood of complaints from alert readers (what *The Times* called "one of the dreaded write-ins"), the paper issued this reluctant correction: "It is always bad practice to publish an old photograph and allow readers to think it might be a recent one; against the background of the Middle East it is doubly so, and we were in error. Still, at one point on Monday afternoon the e-mails were landing in the letters inbox at the rate of almost 500 an hour, preventing anything else from getting through, so we had some comeuppance."[68]

How's that for a turnaround: *The Times* slanders Israel and deceives its readers, and when concerned citizens offer genuine feedback to set the record straight, *The Times* places itself in the role of a victim deserving of "comeuppance."

When Canada's CBC News reported on a deadly civil war between Palestinian factions, what video was used to illustrate the story? Not current news footage, nor even file footage of the intra-Palestinian blood feud. Instead, CBC broadcast scenes of Israeli tanks, helicopters and armored personnel carriers – imagery suggesting that Israel, in some way or another, played a role in instigating or perpetuating this intra-Palestinian violence.[69]

At times, the media is so desperate to show Palestinian victimhood that it substitutes Israeli victims instead. When Israel bombed a compound in Gaza, there were no pictures of victims – for the simple reason that Israel struck at empty buildings. So BBC editors compensated by inserting a film clip of *Israeli* victims... of a *Palestinian* terror attack... arriving at an *Israeli* hospital. Then, as the footage rolled, the BBC correspondent in London intoned, "Those are the pictures from Gaza."[70]

When a Palestinian suicide-gunman carried out a massacre at a Jerusalem rabbinic college – killing eight teenagers – BBC television showed a bulldozer demolishing a house, as correspondent Nick Miles declared: "Hours after the attack, Israeli bulldozers destroyed [the gunman's] family home." Imagine BBC's embarrassment the following day, when both Associated Press and Reuters sent out fresh photos showing the terrorist's family sitting at the entrance of their perfectly intact home, joining with well-wishers in "celebrating" the massacre.[71] (BBC later admitted to having falsely used footage of an unrelated house demolition.)[72]

During the 2006 Lebanon war, image recycling came in the form of "multi-use buildings." News agencies released photos of the same destroyed Beirut building – but spaced them a week apart in the hopes that no one would notice.[73] A week later, Adnan "repeating smoke patterns"

Hajj of Reuters cloned up another photo of the same Beirut building – with a caption claiming that the structure was "flattened during an *overnight* Israeli air raid on Beirut's suburbs."⁷⁴

In other words, he really reutered that photograph.

Considering all the fauxtography during the brief 34 days of the 2006 Lebanon war – and extrapolating that over a decade – gives some idea of the barrage of anti-Israel images being foisted on an unsuspecting consumer public. As Reuters CEO Tom Glocer candidly admitted, "It's extremely likely that there are incidents all around us of manipulated images and staged images."⁷⁵

What makes this all the more significant is there is no parallel effort on the Israeli side. Israelis are not producing fake films, planting Mickey Mouse props, or employing set designers to choreograph weeping grandmothers.

To put everything into perspective, I assembled these examples into a short film, *Photo Fraud in Lebanon,* and posted it on Aish.com.⁷⁶ It was my way of harnessing the power of the Internet to counteract the barrage of media trickery. Apparently, consumer outrage was immense. The film, as reported in the *Fort Worth Star-Telegram,* "spread like wildfire throughout cyberspace," and within a few weeks – without even the benefit of YouTube – it had been viewed over 5 million times.⁷⁷

Bustling Stage of Alfresco Cinema

Another twist on Photo Fraud is when journalists take on the role of "film director" – initiating the production of riot scenes and bearing direct responsibility for escalation of the conflict. Hussein Siyam, the Mukhtar (Arab elder) of the Jerusalem neighborhood of Silwan, told how a German news agency – eager for news fodder – recruited Arab youths and paid them to riot against Israelis.⁷⁸ Israel's President Shimon Peres cited the example of a Palestinian leader caught on camera saying, "Don't start the stoning yet. I've just been told that the CNN crew is stuck in traffic near Ramallah."⁷⁹

Back in the days of the first Intifada, NBC's Tel Aviv bureau chief

Martin Fletcher acknowledged that the "whole uprising was media-oriented, and, without a doubt, kept going because of the media." Fletcher admitted to accepting invitations from young Palestinians to film violent attacks in the West Bank. "It's really a matter of manipulation of the media. And the question is: How much do we play that game?" Fletcher's sorry conclusion: "We play along because we need the pictures."[80]

I personally experienced this phenomenon one Friday afternoon down the road from my house at the Arab village of Bilin – the site of a weekly protest against the West Bank security barrier. Suddenly I heard someone shout, "Throw, throw!", and turned to see a Palestinian man instructing rioters to throw large chunks of rocks at Israeli vehicles. "Throw toward the little window!" he shouted. I figured the orders must be coming from some commander of Islamic Jihad. Not so. It was actually Imad Muhammad Intisar Boghnat, a freelance cameraman for Reuters – who was promptly arrested and charged with inciting violence.[81]

Israeli soldiers threw the Reuters' "journalist" into a military jeep, and because he got roughed up a bit, the Foreign Press Association (representing foreign journalists in Israel) had the gall to accuse the IDF of "unprovoked violence against journalists." Though Boghnat's "throw, throw!" incident was captured on videotape, the Foreign Press Association continued to insist "there is no evidence" that he "was doing anything other than pursuing his journalistic duties."[82] Is one to conclude that inciting violence fits the media's definition of "journalistic duties"?

Better than Broadway, Bilin is home of the West Bank's longest continuous run of manufactured grandstanding for the cameras, with protesters trying any gimmick to keep the journalists coming back week after week, year after year.[83] There's the time that activists dressed up as characters from the blockbuster film *Avatar*, hoping to draw resonance between their plight and that of the iconic 10-foot-tall, blue-skinned Na'vi humanoids.[84] And who can forget the news photos from Bilin of a Palestinian demonstrator in a Santa Claus costume (and keffiyeh) throwing stones at Israeli troops?[85] Are we watching the news or a staged production?

Then there's the time that Associated Press issued a photo of a

Palestinian man in Bilin laying dorsal side down and holding aloft a key to symbolize the so-called "loss of his homeland." The photo caption stated that he had "passed out from tear gas."[86] After being reminded that people who pass out from tear gas aren't able to hold keys aloft, AP revised the caption, though still maintained that the man "happened" to be holding an oversized key in his right hand, which happened to be thrust in the air in a dramatic fist, next to a barbed wire fence that happened to be poetically positioned in the background – which all happened to be perfectly positioned for AP photographer Bernat Armangue.[87]

If this "hold the key" scenario sounds outrageous, consider how far Mideast Media Theater can really go. What if Palestinians were to construct an A-to-Z fabrication: bringing in the actors, setting up the props, staging the scenes, hiring the camera crew – and then handing off the post-production package to the media?

Sounds impossible? Not in today's world, where journalists have gone from being casual observers of the conflict, to *causal* observers. Phil Scheffler of CBS News described it like this:

> When I was coming up, reporting meant a reporter and a camera crew going to where the news was happening, asking questions, taking notes, shooting pictures, and then coming back or sending back a "report." Now a lot of coverage is construction. An editor in New York decides what the story is, sends word out to the bureaus that we need a sound bite from this or that type of person saying this and that, gathers up picture coverage supplied by freelancers or agencies, and writes a script that is narrated by a "reporter" who hasn't been within 500 miles of the story.[88]

Which brings us to the events of September 30, 2000, the second day of the Intifada. At the Netzarim junction in Gaza, Israeli soldiers were barricaded in a guard post, while Palestinians – armed with rocks, Molotov cocktails and rifles – were rioting in the streets. Roaming amongst them was a throng of Palestinian cameramen that included Talal Abu Rahma, working for France-2 television.

On that day, Abu Rahma produced some earth-shattering footage: a scared 12-year-old Palestinian boy, Muhammad al-Dura, shown huddling behind a cement barrel, next to his father who is shouting and gesturing. Bullet holes appear in the wall behind them; the last frame shows the boy lying in his father's arms, apparently dead.

France-2 television broke the story, with reporter Charles Enderlin describing how the Israelis had shot and killed the young al-Dura. The video clip was the lead story on evening newscasts worldwide, with the iconic image of the terrified, huddling boy splashed across every front page. The media accepted as "fact" that al-Dura was, in the words of *60 Minutes Australia*, "targeted, murdered, by Israeli soldiers,"[89] and *Time* magazine surmised the chilling scenario that the "pleas for Israeli soldiers to cease fire [were] answered with a fusillade of bullets."[90]

Given the strategic timing at the beginning of the Intifada, this was a PR bonanza for the Palestinians in their campaign to generate world sympathy – in the words of *60 Minutes*, "one of the most disastrous setbacks Israel has suffered in decades."[91]

To add fuel to the fire, the Palestinian Authority produced a doctored photomontage of an Israeli soldier lining up his scope and shooting al-Dura at close range[92] – and act of "artistic expression" that the PA's Ministry of Information said was meant to "convey the truth... and nothing but the truth."[93]

Overnight, al-Dura became the Palestinian poster child, driving the nascent Intifada violence to dizzying heights. Days later, as Palestinians lynched two Israelis in Ramallah, the bloodthirsty crowd shouted: "Revenge for the blood of Muhammad al-Dura!"[94] The boy was immortalized in epic poems,[95] postage stamps were issued,[96] and streets were named in his honor.[97] Over 150 schools in Iran alone were renamed after al-Dura.[98] The boy's crumpled image had crystallized a Palestinian hatred of Israel that would ultimately cost thousands of lives.

There was only one problem. Enderlin, the French correspondent who narrated the al-Dura footage as if he was delivering an eyewitness account, was nowhere near the Netzarim junction that day. The veracity of both the film and the narrative was based solely on the word of the Palestinian cameraman, with no outside verification. It was a 100 percent Palestinian production – stamped with a France-2 voiceover.

Media monitors immediately suspected a fraud. Given the angle of the Israeli position – kitty-corner to the junction – the only way that Israeli bullets could have hit al-Dura was by ricochet. The video, however, clearly shows symmetrical bullet-holes penetrating the wall behind him – indicating a straight hit.

So who fired those bullets? An obvious way to solve the mystery would be to examine the bullets lodged in the wall: are they Israeli M-16, or Palestinian Kalashnikov? Inexplicably, there were no bullets to be found. In a filmed interview, Abu Rahma, the cameraman, admitted to having removed the bullets from the wall. When questioned about what he discovered – and why a cameraman would be involved in ballistics activities in the first place – Abu Rahma flashed a sinister smile and said: "We have some secrets for ourselves."[99]

As this information came to light, intelligent people not prone to conspiracy theories were becoming increasingly convinced that al-Dura was actually shot by Palestinians. Israeli M-16 bullets are smaller (5.56 caliber) than the Palestinian Kalashnikov (7.62 caliber); in a later reenactment, M-16 bullets fired from the Israeli position were unable to replicate the bullet holes that hit the cement barrel in the video; they merely pinged off its surface.[100] When France-2 allowed award-winning producer Daniel Leconte and other senior French journalists to view all 27 minutes of the raw footage, Leconte concluded: "The only ones who could [have] hit the child were the Palestinians from their position. If they had been Israeli bullets, they would be very strange bullets because they would have needed to go around the corner."[101]

And then the levee broke:

Professor Richard Landes of Boston University discovered "outtakes" – hours of additional footage shot that same day at the same Netzarim junction. These tapes – produced by more than a dozen Palestinian cameramen working for Reuters, Associated Press and other networks – depict a variety of unmistakably staged battle scenes. One clip shows a group of Palestinian men running with rifles, then shooting through an archway, Rambo-style. One would assume that the Palestinians were in the heat of battle, firing on Israelis. Yet the unedited footage shows that the archway leads to nothing more than a brick wall. No Israelis, no battle. Just a dramatic, contrived production, what Landes calls "a bustling stage of alfresco cinema."[102]

Incredibly, the following day Enderlin and France-2 broadcast this sequence of the man firing into the brick wall as if it were real news footage.[103]

Other videotape from that day at the junction shows Palestinian actors in multiple roles: Palestinian fighters are carted off to an ambulance, despite showing no signs of injury. Other men fall in apparent agony, then get up, dust themselves off, and re-enter the action. "Emergency evacuation crews" are seen laughing and goofing around – while Palestinian schoolgirls stroll merrily through the scene.

Suspicious of a hoax, Professor Landes tracked down France-2's Enderlin and together they viewed some of the outtakes. During one obviously faked scene of an ambulance evacuation, Enderlin shrugged it off as a matter of course. The Arabs "do that all the time," he said. "It's their cultural style. They exaggerate."[104]

The hoax was now clear. That day at the junction provided the perfect combination of dramatic factors: a terrified young boy, clinging to his frantic father, apparently shot in cold blood – the ultimate image of "Israeli aggressor and Palestinian victim." Best of all, since there was no Western presence at the junction that day, staging this scene required only the cooperation of the Palestinian camera crews. France-2's Enderlin – seduced by the lure of a major international scoop – ignored the obvious deficiencies in the credibility of Palestinian cameraman Abu Rahma, who once declared, "I went into journalism to carry on the fight for my people."[105]

Upon viewing the raw footage, Luc Rosenzweig, former editor-in-chief of France's daily *Le Monde*, called this the "almost perfect media crime."[106]

As the story unfolded, other journalists conducted their own investigations and found the inconsistencies between fact and fiction too great to discount. Esther Schapira, a German television producer, traveled to Israel convinced of IDF guilt – and came away concluding that the boy had been killed by Palestinians.[107] James Fallows, one of America's most respected journalists, documented in *The Atlantic Monthly* how he reached the same conclusion.[108] And Jean-Claude Schlinger, an adviser on ballistic and forensic evidence in French courts for 20 years, recreated the shooting and concluded that al-Dura could not have been shot by Israeli gunfire.[109]

Was France-2 duped? Enderlin, at his meeting with Landes, drew a map of Netzarim junction that placed the Israeli position on the wrong side of the road. Says Landes: "This indicated one of two equally distressing possibilities": Either that Enderlin "understood so little of what had happened that day that he didn't even know the most basic elements of the layout of the scene." Or alternatively, he was outright lying – and must have assumed that Landes "was so little informed that he could get away with it."[110]

French journalist Claude Weill Raynal defended Enderlin with the following bit of logic: "[People are] so shocked that fake images were used and edited in Gaza, but this happens all the time everywhere on television, and no TV journalist in the field or film editor would be shocked."[111] In other words, Palestinian photo fraud is so commonplace, there's no reason to get excited.

For this exceptional piece of propaganda disguised as camera work, Abu Rahma was nominated by MSNBC for "Picture of the Year,"[112] and received various "Journalist of the Year" honors including the coveted Rory Peck award from the Sony Corporation. He achieved legendary status in Arab circles and went on to speaking engagements around the world.[113]

Meanwhile, the boy's father, Jamal al-Dura, was engaging in his own bit of media manipulation. He held a press conference where he lifted his shirt to show journalists the scars on his chest as "proof" that Israeli soldiers had fired on him. In truth, these scars were the result of tendon transplant surgery that Jamal had undergone years earlier at an Israeli hospital, after being severely wounded by an axe-wielding Palestinian thug. Dr. David Yehuda, the surgeon who operated on Jamal, recognized the scars: "His wounds are not bullet wounds, but were produced by two things – first, the knife of the Palestinian who cut him, and second, my knife that fixed him. He faked the case."[114] Jamal had displayed the height of ingratitude: After being saved by an Israeli doctor, he turned that around to foist a libel on the Jews.[115]

As evidence of an al-Dura fraud grew larger, France-2 began to backtrack. Arlette Chabot, the station's deputy general director, later told the *New York Times* that "no one can say for certain who killed him, Palestinians or Israelis."[116] Enderlin himself wrote in the French newspaper *Le Figaro* that his report "may have been hasty," but was justified because "so many children were being killed."[117] In other words, fabricating news coverage is acceptable – when used to support some greater, unproven claim against Israel.

When Philippe Karsenty, a French media watchdog, accused France-2 of fraud, the discredited Enderlin tried to shift the blame by calling this "a campaign designed to harass foreign correspondents,"[118] and – in an amazing show of chutzpah – sued Karsenty for libel. The French court then subpoenaed Enderlin to present the video outtakes from that day at the junction; Enderlin "complied," but edited out whole chunks of the tape, gambling that this obstruction of justice, perjury and tampering with evidence would escape the court's detection. (Rosemary Woods' "18-minute gap," anyone?)[119]

The case, with all the hoopla of a Dreyfus trial, wound its way through the French legal system, and in May 2008, the Paris Court of Appeal ruled there was a "coherent mass of evidence" to support the claims against France-2.[120] Enderlin thus joined Oscar Wilde and Alger Hiss in the pantheon of those who brought libel suits – and ended up destroying their own reputations.[121]

Meanwhile, the shooting of Muhammad al-Dura had become the mother of all fauxtographies.

Pallywood

The PR bonanza sparked by Muhammad al-Dura gave birth to Pallywood, a cottage industry dedicated to producing Palestinian propaganda films. When Palestinian officials alleged that Israel was using radioactive uranium and nerve gas against civilians,[122] official PA television broadcast fake "news footage" of "victims" plagued by vomiting and convulsions.[123] Another clip from state-run Palestinian TV used actors to depict Israeli soldiers "raping and murdering" a Palestinian girl in front of her horrified parents.[124]

When Mohammed Bakri set out to make his documentary film *Jenin, Jenin* – "to tell the Palestinian truth about the Battle of Jenin" – he created the illusion of "atrocities" by intersplicing footage of Israeli tanks with pictures of Palestinian children and "eyewitness testimony" describing "war crimes." When questioned about one manipulative scene that suggested Israeli troops had run over Arab civilians, Bakri admitted to constructing the footage as an "artistic choice."[125] This cinematic farce – rather than being rejected by film critics – was awarded Best Film at the Carthage International Film Festival, and received the International Prize for Mediterranean Documentary Filmmaking and Reporting.

On another occasion, when the Palestinian PR plan called for some footage of dead bodies, Arab actors staged a "funeral" for unsuspecting journalists. This Pallywood production – later exposed in aerial footage shot from an Israeli drone – shows a man walking over to a stretcher, lying down, being wrapped in a shroud, and being carried in the "funeral procession." When the "dead body" falls off the stretcher, he stands up and climbs back on. And when the "corpse" is dropped a second time, he stomps off angrily – apparently regarding his own funeral as too dangerous to his health.[126]

When confronted with this hoax, the Palestinian Human Rights Society quickly invented an alibi: "A Palestinian producer was shooting a film at the same site" where the journalists just happened to be. "What was perceived as a staged 'burial' was actually acting for a film."[127]

That excuse was so laughable that Palestinians had to revert to their old standby: blame Israel. "What the footage actually shows is a group of children playing 'funeral' near the cemetery," the Palestinian Human Rights Society said. "It is not uncommon... to witness Palestinian children playing a game where they pretend they have been killed. It is part of a phenomenon raising fears among child experts that a generation in the Palestinian territories has suffered serious psychological damage from Israeli violence directed against the Palestinian civilian population."[128]

Putting aside the psycho-babble, here's what is really happening: These staged events are part of a precise formula – death, destruction and children – guaranteed to get the most airtime on the evening news. That's why Palestinian PR operatives are quick to exploit an event, sensationalize it, and construct an anti-Israel scenario that caused it all. They're not concerned about getting caught, because by the time Israel is able to gather its wits and unravel the truth, the damage has already been done. And they know that Western journalists – no matter how many times they've been burned before – can always be counted on to rush to judgment against the "Israeli aggressors."

Gaza Beach

Picture the scene:[129] A 10-year-old Palestinian girl, Houda Galiya, is running across an expanse of white sand. We follow her through the jiggling of a shoulder-carried video camera till she comes to what appears to be a clump of discarded clothing in the hollow of a dune. Here, in a scene worthy of Meryl Streep, she flings herself down, throws sand all over herself, and begins to wail.

In June 2006, this scrap of videotape was released across the globe as "evidence of an Israeli atrocity." On CNN International, Finnoula Sweeney intoned with omniscience: "Grief on a Gaza beach: This girl had been having a picnic with family members when artillery shells fired from an Israeli gun boat hit the sand. Her father, among seven people killed. Her despair uncontrollable; she is inconsolable."[130]

Viewers assumed that CNN shot the film. But a closer look shows the logo of a Muslim minaret and Arabic lettering, with the words "Ramattan News Agency." The cameraman: Zakarija Abu Harbed. The agency: headquartered in Gaza.

Foreign desk chiefs were ecstatic about these images which, full of death and drama, were pure gold. Yet attaching the disclaimer that "Israeli guilt is undetermined" would have destroyed the appeal. So the *Washington Post* went ahead and posted a front-page headline, "Israeli Fire Kills 7 Beachgoers in Gaza," while *Newsweek* quoted a seething PA president Mahmoud Abbas declaring the events "a bloody massacre."[131]

For its part, Associated Press proffered the "expert" opinion of Marc Garlasco of Human Rights Watch to "confirm" Israel's guilt.[132] Of course, AP never bothered to mention that Garlasco is an avid collector of Nazi memorabilia, who authored a 430-page book on Nazi war paraphernalia[133] and enthuses over SS leather jackets ("So cool!").[134] No, mentioning any of that would have destroyed Garlasco's credibility and undermined the perception of Israeli guilt as certified fact.

Once again, Israel was left to deconstruct the truth: Where did these explosives come from? After all, this sandy patch of the northern Gaza Strip is a cauldron where nearly every day, dynamite, C-4, gunpowder, you name it, are packed into various delivery systems and then fired, flung, planted and launched – by Palestinians at other Palestinians (clan versus clan, Hamas versus Fatah), by Israelis fighting Palestinians, and by Palestinians who misfire against Israel and hit Palestinian civilians instead. The area is teeming with war materiel; that same month, a Palestinian man and a baby were killed in Gaza while "playing with a grenade."[135]

So in determining responsibility for Gaza Beach, the origin of the shrapnel was the key factor. Israel said it was not possibly theirs, and suggested that the detonation was due to one of the numerous land mines and booby traps planted by Palestinians to prevent the Israeli navy from landing in Gaza.[136] Indeed, film footage from the scene indicates that the crater left on the beach was due to an underground explosion, not a hit from above like an artillery shell.[137]

In the immediate aftermath of the explosion, the wounded were brought to an Israeli hospital in Tel Aviv. (That alone should have lain to rest the canard that Israel was "trying to kill Palestinian civilians.") The shrapnel lodged in the victims' bodies would surely provide key evidence as to the source of the explosion. Yet Israeli doctors discovered something incredibly strange: Before arriving in Tel Aviv, the Palestinian patients had been subjected to multiple knife wounds and all the shrapnel had been removed. According to a hospital spokesman:

> This combination is not routine, and does not correspond to our accumulated medical experience as a result of having treated hundreds of patients who were wounded in terrorist attacks and by bombs, and who usually arrive with fragments in various places throughout their bodies. In such cases, standard medical practice is not to search for or extract the fragments unless they constitute an immediate danger to the patient.[138]

Palestinian doctors – apparently surmising that the explosion was of Palestinian origin – had performed quickie surgeries to remove the shrapnel in an effort to destroy the "incriminating evidence." Yet the Palestinian doctors weren't quite thorough enough. Tests performed on two pieces of shrapnel that they forgot to remove proved beyond all doubt that the wounds did not come from an Israeli shell.

But in this age of information overload, the hoax was racing away and the Western media joined the campaign for little Houda. A headline in *The Australian* proclaimed that the "Shrapnel 'Proves [the] Shell was Israeli,'"[139] and *The Times* of London exulted that the "Girl Who Saw Family Die on Beach Becomes Icon and Media Celebrity."[140]

Meanwhile, Palestinian spin doctors were taking the libel to a new level: After obtaining stock footage of Israeli soldiers aboard a navy vessel – perhaps from a promotional or training film – Palestinian TV producers assembled a "newsreel" showing Israeli sailors scanning the coastline with binoculars, as mechanized cannons swiveled into position. They then intercut selections from Ramattan's tape of the screaming girl on the beach

– all set to a soundtrack of spookily reverberating screams and ambulance sirens.[141]

The spliced-up film was presented as straight news footage on Palestinian television, and generously made available to other media outlets in the hopes of resuscitating the Muhammad al-Dura Libel Corps. The Palestinian Centre for Human Rights, an organization widely relied upon by the United Nations, tried to "mainstream" the fake footage with the false claim that it was broadcast on Israeli television – thus constituting "proof" that "the crime had been perpetrated with a premeditated intent to kill."[142]

Taking the cue, forums like YouTube were flooded with homemade films constructed around the key "scream" footage. One film, entitled "Israel State Terror," was typical of the lurid genre hatched by teenagers equipped with Microsoft Movie Maker working out of their bedrooms. An 18-year-old identifying himself as jasonking10001 posted shots of an Israeli flag, a swastika, Palestinians at checkpoints, and European Jews herded by Nazi soldiers – all intercut with Houda Galiya wailing on Gaza Beach, synchronized to the crashing downbeat of Public Enemy's gangsta rap.[143]

The end of this story is by now familiar: It was confirmed that the Palestinians on the beach were not killed by IDF ammunition, but rather by Hamas, which – in an attempt to defend their arsenal of Qassam rockets – had mined the section of beach where the explosion occurred.[144] Houda's sister Ilham, hospitalized in Tel Aviv, admitted that her father had caused the lethal blast by handling unexploded ordnance.[145] In the end, media outlets quietly retracted their reports, while Pallywood productions continued to fuel more hatred, violence, death and demonization of Israel.[146]

Battle Cry

One would expect by now that the media would treat these Palestinian "news videos" with great suspicion. But incredibly, the level of naiveté seems to only increase with time. In 2009, France-2 television broadcast footage that purported to depict a recent Israeli air strike on Gaza. The video showed bloodied, mangled civilians suffering horrifically, with at least 19 Palestinians killed – children amongst them – and 80 more injured.

There was only one problem. The footage was from 2005.

And one more problem: Those explosions were not due to any *Israeli* attack, but rather caused when a truckload of Palestinian Qassam rockets accidentally exploded at a Hamas rally, killing 15.[147]

Where did France-2 get this footage? And how did they make such a huge error? Simple. The video was posted on a YouTube-style channel called Muslim TV – dated 2009 with the fabricated tag-line, "Israel just bombed a large civilian street market in Gaza." The bait was set and France-2 – the same network that perpetrated the Muhammad al-Dura hoax – gobbled it up. After all, doesn't *every* major news organization get its footage straight from YouTube?[148]

So this is what Israel is fighting against: Palestinians generate video footage of "Israeli atrocities," then obscure the evidence to ensure that Palestinian "eyewitnesses" remain as the only source of information. The media then pronounces Israel guilty until proven innocent. Gaza Beach, Jenin, Tuvia Grossman ("the photo that started it all") all fit the pattern. By the time Israel can gather the facts, the party is over. And with today's news so image-driven – and Palestinian stringers providing the majority of information and images – Palestinians are holding a lot of cards.

These iconic images create a "record of events" that forms the historical narrative for generations to come. Consider the four reels of movie footage from the Warsaw Ghetto discovered after World War II, shot shortly before the mass deportation of Jews to Treblinka. The Nazi-produced film shows scenes of well-fed Jews living a pleasant life in the ghetto – a clear indictment of wealthy Jews cruelly turning a blind eye to their unfortunate brethren who begged on the streets and died there of hunger. (It's an old trick used by oppressive regimes: mitigate their evil by demonizing their victims.) For decades, this footage was granted the historians' seal of authenticity, serving as a primary resource for Holocaust scholars. At least that's what everyone thought until 1998, when a fifth reel turned up – showing outtakes of the ghetto scenes. It turns out that the entire production was filmed using actors (probably Jews forced to cooperate or be killed). In other words, after 60 years, the "historical record" was proven to be a staged fraud.[149]

Once a particular image sears deep into the public consciousness, it is almost impossible to undo. According to Hany Farid, a Dartmouth professor and expert on digital photography, on a neurological level the brain tends to reduce each major historical era into a single emotional image that encapsulates the complex story: raising the Flag on Iwo Jima, the Vietnamese Napalm girl, facing the tank in Tiananmen Square, electrocution wires at Abu Ghraib prison – and Muhammad al-Dura.[150]

This is more than just a convenient memory device. Like the medieval blood libels that launched pogroms across Europe, the legend of al-Dura has become the battle cry of violent Muslim extremists committing the most heinous crimes. In an al-Qaeda recruitment film, Osama bin Laden invoked the memory of al-Dura as a call to arms.[151] In Ramallah, the mob that disemboweled two Israeli reservists declared it as "revenge for the blood of Muhammad al-Dura."[152] And in Daniel Pearl's beheading video, the killers interwove scenes of al-Dura with the gruesome slitting of Pearl's throat.[153]

Hooray for Pallywood.

Notes

1. Greg Myre and Steven Erlanger, "Clashes Spread to Lebanon as Hezbollah Raids Israel," *International Herald Tribune*, July 12, 2006.
2. "Reuters Doctoring Photos from Beirut?", *Little Green Footballs*, August 5, 2006.
3. "Reuters Drops Freelance Lebanese Photographer Over Image," Reuters, August 6, 2006. That same day, Associated Press recalled a photo of an oil pipeline worker in Alaska who appeared to have four hands.
4. Steve Herrmann, "Trusting Photos," BBC News Online, August 8, 2006.
5. Rusty Shackleford, "Another Fake Reuters Photo from Lebanon," *Jawa Report*, August 6, 2006; "Reuters Admits to More Image Manipulation," *Ynetnews* (Israel), August 7, 2006.
6. "Altered Images Prompt Photographer's Firing," Associated Press, August 7, 2006.
7. James Joyner, "Reuters Purges All 920 Adnan Hajj Photos from Database," *Outside the Beltway* blog, August 7, 2006.
8. "Harvard: How the Media Partnered with Hezbollah," *Little Green Footballs*, April 25, 2007.
9. Herrmann, "Trusting Photos."
10. For comprehensive overviews of media irregularities during the 2006 Israel-Lebanon war, see "Fraudulent Photojournalism," *Zombietime*, and Stephen D. Cooper, "A Concise History of the Fauxtography Blogstorm in the 2006 Lebanon War," *American Communication Journal*,

Vol. 9, Issue 2, Summer 2007.
11. "Qana Media Swarm Revealed," *Little Green Footballs*, February 9, 2007.
12. "Green Helmet Acting as Cynical Movie Director in Qana", *Zapp*, NDR – Norddeutscher Rundfunk (Germany); "The Corruption of the Media – Part 7, Act 4: Caught in the Act!", *EU Referendum Blog*, August 15, 2006.
13. Brendan Bernhard, "Reuters' Image Problem," *LA Weekly*, August 10, 2006.
14. David Bauder, "News Agencies Stand by Lebanon Photos," Associated Press, August 1, 2006.
15. Thomas Lifson, "Mr. Green Helmet," *American Thinker*, August 10, 2006.
16. "Who Is This Man?", *EU Referendum Blog*, July 31, 2006.
17. Bryan Denton, posted on "Staged Shots from Lebanon?", *Lightstalkers*, August 11, 2006. Grammar corrected.
18. Martin Asser, "Dangers Await Lebanon Returnees," BBC News Online, August 21, 2006.
19. "Worst Use of Props: The BBC Responds," Mediabackspin.com, January 21, 2007.
20. David D. Perlmutter, "Photojournalism in Crisis," *Editor and Publisher*, August 18, 2006.
21. "The Passion of the Toys," *Slublog*, August 8, 2006.
22. Photo by Ben Curtis, Associated Press, August 7, 2006. Curtis later defended the photo: "A reader might infer from that [photo] that a child had been killed in the attack and that this toy belonged to some child who is dead somewhere... But I didn't say in my caption that children were in that apartment when it was bombed, that children were killed." (Errol Morris, "It Was All Started by a Mouse," *Opinionator* blog / *New York Times*, January 3, 2010.) Curtis claimed he did not reposition the toy even though doing so would have made for better composition. (Errol Morris, *Believing Is Seeing: Observations on the Mysteries of Photography*, Penguin Press, 2011.)
23. Photo by Sharif Karim, Reuters.
24. The full set of "news photos" is online at "The Passion of the Toys," *Slublog*, August 8, 2006.
25. "How the West Wasn't Won," *Yedioth Ahronoth* (Israel), March 17, 2011.
26. Glenn Reynolds, *Instapundit*, September 24, 2006.
27. Photo by Eric Gaillard, Reuters, August 8, 2006.
28. Photo by Lefteris Pitarakis, Associated Press, August 8, 2006. Because Islam does not allow for images of Muhammad, Muslims often use Koranic verses to adorn their homes in the same way that Christians use paintings of Jesus.
29. Ray Robison, "al-AP at it Again with Staged Photos," *Ray Robison Blog*, August 10, 2006; cited in Stephen D. Cooper, "A Concise History of the Fauxtography Blogstorm in the 2006 Lebanon War," *American Communication Journal*, Vol/ 9, Issue 2, Summer 2007.
30. Jules Crittenden, "Photos from Lebanon Can't Be Trusted," *Boston Herald*, August 9, 2006.
31. Frida Ghitis, "How the Media Partnered with Hezbollah: Harvard's Cautionary Report," *World Politics Review*, April 22, 2007.
32. Marvin Kalb, "The Israeli-Hezbollah War of 2006: The Media as a Weapon in Asymmetrical Conflict," John F. Kennedy School of Government, Harvard University, February 2007.
33. "24 Hours Under Attack," *Anderson Cooper's 360 Degrees*, CNN, July 28, 2006. On another occasion, CNN producer Charlie Moore reported: "On cue, a Hezbollah resistance song is now blaring from an apartment. A young man on the porch dressed in black is giving us the victory sign. I look behind me and there's our Hezbollah guide encouraging the young man to lift his hands higher so our camera can see." ("Our Very Strange Day with Hezbollah," *Anderson Cooper's 360 Degrees*, CNN.com, July 23, 2006.)
34. "Guidelines on Our Integrity," *New York Times*, May 7, 1999.
35. The "revealing" photo was taken by Enric Marti of Associated Press, February 7, 2004.
36. Hamza Hendawi, "Jenin Graffiti Artists Adopt English for Benefit of VIP Visitors," Associated Press, April 29, 2002.

37. Photo by Marco Di Lauro, Agence France Press / Getty Images.
38. Kelly Motz, "Media Intimidation," Frontpagemag.com, August 18, 2006; Joel Mowbray, "Presenting False Images," *Washington Times*, August 16, 2006.
39. Photo by Issam Kobeisi, Reuters, July 22, 2006.
40. Photo by Hussein Malla, Associated Press, August 5, 2006; see Steve Herrmann, "Trusting Photos," BBC News Online, August 8, 2006.
41. Hugh Sykes, "Stressed Out and Anxious in Beirut," BBC News Online, August 5, 2006.
42. "Extreme Makeover – Beirut Edition," *Drinking from Home* blog, August 6, 2006.
43. Photo by Lefteris Pitarakis, Associated Press, August 19, 2006; see Jim Hoft, "Hard Luck Beirut Woman Extreme Makeover – Take 3," *Gateway Pundit*, August 20, 2006.
44. *The Spectator* (UK), July 22, 2006. The same photo also appeared on the cover of the periodical *Socialist Worker*.
45. *Daily Star* (Lebanon); cited in Dan Williams and Marc Daugherty, "More Than a War of Words," *Jerusalem Post*, October 12, 2001.
46. "Coverage of Mideast Conflict," *CNN Reliable Sources*, CNN, July 23, 2006. CNN's Nic Robertson confirmed: "(Hezbollah) had control of the situation. They designated the places that we went to, and we certainly didn't have time to go into the houses or lift up the rubble to see what was underneath. (Hezbollah) has very, very good control over its areas in the south of Beirut. They deny journalists access into those areas. You don't get in there without their permission." (Tom Gross, "Media Missiles: Working for the Enemy," *National Post* [Canada], August 2, 2006.)
47. Photo by Bruno Stevens – Cosmos, *U.S. News & World Report*, July 31, 2006.
48. *Time*, July 31, 2006. The caption read: "The wreckage of a downed Israeli jet that was targeting Hizballah trucks billows smoke behind a Hizballah gunman in Kfar Chima, near Beirut. Jet fuel set the surrounding area ablaze."
49. "The Reuters Photo Scandal," *Zombietime*, August 2006.
50. Bruno Stevens, "The Lebanon 'Garbage Dump' Story: Complete Explanation," *Lightstalkers*, November 14, 2006.
51. "The Media are the Enemy," *Little Green Footballs*, November 14, 2006.
52. *Washington Post*, August 2, 1982.
53. Mitchell Bard, "Beware of Disinformation," Aish.com, July 23, 2006.
54. Sabrina Tavernise, "A Night of Death and Terror for Lebanese Villagers," *New York Times*, July 31, 2006.
55. Kerry Sanders, "On a Mission of Mercy with Lebanon Red Cross," MSNBC, July 26, 2006.
56. Nicholas Blanford, "Where No One Is Safe," *Time*, July 25, 2006.
57. Richard Engel, *Today Show*, NBC, August 10, 2006.
58. Suzanne Goldenberg, "Red Cross Ambulances Destroyed in Israeli Air Strike on Rescue Mission," *The Guardian* (UK), July 25, 2006.
59. Julian Manyon, ITV television (UK), July 24, 2006; "The Hoax that Wasn't – Israeli Drone Attack on Ambulances," YouTube.com. Ironically, Wikileaks memos detail Iran's use of Red Crescent ambulances to smuggle missiles and agents to Hezbollah – precisely as the media was condemning Israel for attacking "civilian" ambulances. ("US Embassy Cables: Iran Abuses Iranian Red Crescent to Send Agents and Weapons Overseas," *The Guardian* [UK], November 28, 2010.)
60. For a full treatment of this scandal, see "The Red Cross Ambulance Incident" and "Update to the Red Cross Ambulance Incident: The Human Rights Watch Report," *Zombietime*, August 2006. See also Dan Riehl, "More MSM Propaganda Exposed," *Riehl World View*, August 1, 2006.
61. See Stephen D. Cooper, "A Concise History of the Fauxtography Blogstorm in the 2006 Lebanon War," *American Communication Journal*, Vol. 9, Issue 2, Summer 2007. Australian

blogger Tim Blair found so many inconsistencies in the accounts published by his two local papers, *The Australian* and *The Age*, that he compiled a tongue-in-cheek "composite" story of how victims were "inside the ambulance and outside the ambulance, while it was both moving and parked," at the moment it was simultaneously struck "by rockets, missiles, bombs, small weapons, and a large explosion." ("Missile Story IX," Timblair.net, September 3, 2006.)

62. Manyon, ITV Television. See also, "The Hoax that Wasn't – Israeli Drone Attack on Ambulances," YouTube.com.
63. Tim Piper and Yael Staav, "Evolution," Dove Campaign for Real Beauty, October 2006.
64. The latest version of Photoshop enables users to change the light-source direction, artificially creating an effect where surrounding lights reflect in eyes to form small white dots called specular highlights. (Hany Farid, "Digital Forensics: 5 Ways to Spot a Fake Photo," *Scientific American*, June 2, 2008.)
65. Leigh Holmwood, "Reuters Gets that Sinking Feeling," *The Guardian* (UK), August 10, 2007.
66. Bob Simon, cited in Richard Landes, "Exposing the 'Weapon of the Weak,'" *Jerusalem Post*, September 12, 2009.
67. See "Out of Context: The Times's Image of the Day," HonestReporting.com, April 1, 2008.
68. "Success: Times Acknowledges Photo Gaffe," HonestReporting.com, April 7, 2008.
69. Danielle Bochove, *Newsworld*, Canadian Broadcasting Corporation, June 14, 2009.
70. Lyse Doucet, *Panorama*, BBC News, May 10, 2001; cited in Lenny Ben-David, "BBC's Propaganda War," *Jerusalem Post*, June 22, 2001.
71. Tom Gross, "BBC Again Caught Lying about Israel," Tomgrossmedia.com, March 20, 2008.
72. Jonny Paul, "BBC Admits Inaccuracies in Coverage," *Jerusalem Post*, March 22, 2008.
73. Photo by Ramzi Haidar, Agence France Presse / Getty Images, July 18, 2006; photo by Adnan Hajj, Reuters, July 24, 2006.
74. "Multi-Use Buildings," *Little Green Footballs*, August 9, 2006.
75. *The Situation Room*, CNN, September 22, 2006.
76. www.aish.com/v/is/91361839.html
77. David House, "A Picture is Worth... Ah...", *Fort Worth Star-Telegram*, August 27, 2006.
78. Ezra HaLevi, "German News Agency Pays Arabs to Riot," *Israel National News*, April 6, 2008.
79. Cited in Tom Gross, "New Prejudices for Old," *National Review*, November 1, 2001.
80. Andrew Gold, "NBC Exposed," *Near East Report*, August 5, 1991.
81. See Nissan Ratzlav-Katz, "Reuters Cameraman Remanded for Inciting Rock Attacks," *Israel National News*, November 18, 2006.
82. "IDF Accused of Attacking Journalists," Associated Press, October 12, 2006.
83. See "No Business Like Show Business," Mediabackspin.com, May 18, 2009.
84. Carl Franzen, "The Making of the West Bank's 'Avatar' Protest," Aolnews.com, February 12, 2010; "Palestinians Take a Cue from Avatar," *The Age* (Australia), February 17, 2010.
85. "White Christmas with a Difference," *Sunday Mail* (Australia), December 27, 2009.
86. Photo by Bernat Armangue, Associated Press, May 15, 2009.
87. "Ridiculous Propaganda Photo of the Day," *Little Green Footballs*, May 17, 2009.
88. Columbia University School of Journalism, *Alumni Newsletter*, Winter 2004; cited in Stephanie Gutmann, *The Other War*, Encounter Books, 2005.
89. October 15, 2001; cited in Tzvi Fleischer & Daniel Mandel, "A Bit Rich: Richard Carleton, 60 Minutes and the Middle East," *AIJAC Review*, April 2001.
90. Tony Karon, "Why Now Is Not the Time to Press for Mideast Deal," *Time*, October 2, 2000.
91. Bob Simon, "The Crossroad," *60 Minutes*, CBS News, November 12, 2000.
92. Nidra Poller, "Myth, Fact, and the Al-Dura Affair," *Commentary*, September 2005.
93. Esther Shapira, "Three Bullets and a Dead Child," ARD Television (Germany), March 18, 2002.

94. Melanie Phillips, "Faking a Killing," *Standpoint* (UK), July 2008.
95. Sheikh Mohammed bin Rashid Al Maktoum, Crown Prince of Dubai, "To the Soul of the Child Martyr, Mohammed Al Durra," Sheikhmohammed.co.ae.
96. Stanley Gibbons, *Stamps of the World 2008*.
97. James Fallows, "Who Shot Mohammed al-Dura?", *The Atlantic*, June 2003. For example, one of Baghdad's main streets was renamed Martyr Muhammad al-Dura Street.
98. "Over 150 Iranian Schools Named after Palestinian Boy," Islamic Republic News Agency (Iran), translated by BBC Monitoring, December 24, 2000.
99. Shapira, "Three Bullets and a Dead Child."
100. Stephanie Gutmann, *The Other War*, Encounter Books, 2005.
101. As told to Cybercast News Service; cited in Eva Cahen, "French TV Sticks by Story that Fueled Palestinian Intifada," CNSNews.com, February 15, 2005.
102. Seconddraft.org; Molly Hunt, "Boston U. Professor Claims Media 'Staged' Footage of Middle East Conflict," *Daily Free Press* (Boston University), September 22, 2005.
103. Cited in Richard Landes, "France2 Accused: The Appeals Case Takes Another Turn," *Augean Stables*, March 5, 2008.
104. Richard Landes, "On Seeing the France2 from September 30, 2000," Seconddraft.org.
105. Jonathan Rosenblum, "For Once, the Good Guys Win," *Jerusalem Post*, June 12, 2008.
106. Poller, "Myth, Fact, and the Al-Dura Affair." See also Richard Landes, "Intellectual Probity vs. Cynicism: Where's the Indignation?", *Augean Stables*, September 21, 2007.
107. Shapira, "Three Bullets and a Dead Child."
108. Fallows, "Who Shot Mohammed al-Dura?"
109. Adi Schwartz, "Independent Expert: IDF Bullets Didn't Kill Mohammed al-Dura," *Haaretz* (Israel), March 2, 2008. Rahma, the cameraman, kept the camera focused entirely on al-Dura, mysteriously never taking a moment to swing the camera around to identify the source of the shooting.
110. Richard Landes, "My Statement to the French Court: Maybe Writing Will Work Better," *Augean Stables*, September 18, 2007.
111. Jonathan Rosenblum, "A New Dreyfus Trial," *Jewish Observer*, November 29, 2007.
112. Of the 49 photos up for consideration as MSNBC's "Picture of the Year 2000," the vast majority were nature scenes. The only two politically-related photos both carried an anti-Israel message: the al-Dura photo, and a photo of a young (presumably Arab) boy in a damaged West Bank home. A more obvious and balanced choice, the photo of the Palestinian's bloody hands at the Ramallah lynching, was not nominated by MSNBC. Similarly, of the six pictures from the conflict chosen by Associated Press for its 130-photo retrospective for 2003, all six depicted Palestinian casualties.
113. Abu Rahma was also awarded (partial list): the Festival Scoop Prize (Angers), the Qatar Honoring Prize, the Medal of Bravery (Palestinian Journalists' Association), the Arab Journalism Prize (Dubai), Journalist of the Year from the American-Arab Anti-Discrimination Committee (Washington DC), the Jordanian Syndicates' Complex Prize (Amman), and the Radio & TV Festival Prize (Cairo).
114. Jenny Hazan, "Israeli Defense," Aish.com, October 3, 2010. See also Israeli Channel 10, December 12, 2007; Ricki Hollander and Gilead Ini, "Backgrounder: Mohammed Al Dura," Committee for Accuracy in Middle East Reporting in America, October 13, 2005.
115. Prior to the Netzarim incident, Jamal had worked for 20 years with an Israeli builder, attending his son's bar mitzvah and even sleeping over at their house. It was, Jamal said, "a true relationship between brothers." (Shapira, "Three Bullets and a Dead Child.") It has been suggested that Gazans suspected Jamal of being a "collaborator" – passing intelligence information on to Israel – and in order to redeem himself, Jamal agreed to be filmed with his son in a staged drama. On the film, with horror in his eyes, Jamal looked straight-on toward

the camera (not in the direction of the Israeli outpost), appearing to cry out: "Stop!" It is possible that Jamal al-Dura was set up, never imagining how far this "drama" would go. (Gutmann, *The Other War*.)

116. Doreen Carvajal, "Photo of Palestinian Boy Kindles Debate in France," *International Herald Tribune*, February 7, 2005.
117. David Gelernter, "When Pictures Lie," *Los Angeles Times*, September 9, 2005.
118. Martin Patience, "Dispute Rages Over al-Durrah," BBC News Online, November 8, 2007.
119. Richard Landes, "Gambling with a Lie: Enderlin Pulls a Rosemary Woods," *Augean Stables*, November 14, 2007.
120. "Al-Durra Case Revisited," *Wall Street Journal Europe*, May 27, 2008.
121. Rosenblum, "For Once, the Good Guys Win."
122. Saud Abu Ramadan, "Israel Denies Using Poison Gas," United Press International, February 15, 2001.
123. Fiamma Nirenstein, "How Suicide Bombers Are Made," *Commentary*, September 2001.
124. Itamar Marcus, "Rape, Murder, Violence and War for Allah against the Jews: Summer 2000 on Palestinian Television," Palestinian Media Watch, September 11, 2000.
125. "'Jenin, Jenin' Fabricated Footage, Funded by PA," *Israel National News*, January 19, 2005.
126. Isabel Kershner, "Graveyard Farce," *Jerusalem Report*, June 3, 2002.
127. "Law Refutes Israeli Claims of Staged Jenin 'Burials,'" Palestinian Society for the Protection of Human Rights & the Environment, May 8, 2002.
128. Ibid.
129. The author thanks Stephanie Gutmann for contributing to this section.
130. "After Al-Zarqawi; Seven Dead, 20 Hurt in Shelling of Gaza Beach," *CNN's Live From...*, CNN, June 9, 2006.
131. "Periscope," *Newsweek*, June 19, 2006.
132. Laurie Copans, "U.S.-trained Expert: Explosive that Killed 8 Palestinians on Gaza Beach was Israeli Shell," Associated Press, June 15, 2006.
133. Marc Garlasco, *The Flak Badges of the Luftwaffe and Heer*, B&D Publishing, 2008.
134. John Schwartz, "Rights Group Assailed for Analyst's Nazi Collection," *New York Times*, September 14, 2009. The *Times* injected its own bias, suggesting that the scandal surrounding Garlasco's Nazi fetish was due to the Israeli government's "aggressive approach" to "discredit" groups like Human Rights Watch who are "critical of Israel." One month later, Robert L. Bernstein, the founder of Human Rights Watch, publicly denounced the organization for the fact that "Israel, the repeated victim of aggression, faces the brunt of Human Rights Watch's criticism." (Robert L. Bernstein, "Rights Watchdog, Lost in the Mideast," *New York Times*, October 20, 2009.)
135. "Accidental Grenade Explosion Kills Two Palestinians," Agence France Presse, June 28, 2006.
136. Laurie Copans, "Israel Blames Hamas Mine for Beach Blast," Associated Press, June 13, 2006.
137. Mordechai Plaut, "Palestinians Lied with Deliberate Malice," *Yated Ne'eman*, June 14, 2006.
138. Meital Yasur-Beit Or, "No Shrapnel Found in Gaza Victim's Body," *Ynetnews* (Israel), June 20, 2006.
139. Martin Chulov, "Shrapnel 'Proves Shell was Israeli,'" *The Australian*, June 16, 2006.
140. Stephen Farrell, "Girl Who Saw Family Die on Beach Becomes Icon and Media Celebrity," *The Times* (UK), June 13, 2006.
141. Itamar Marcus and Barbara Crook, "PA TV Falsifies Video of Gaza Deaths," Palestinian Media Watch, June 12, 2006. Zakarija Abu Harbed, the Palestinian cameraman, was later honored with the Sony-sponsored Rory Peck award for Hard News Reporting.
142. "Serious Escalation in Israeli Attacks," Palestinian Centre for Human Rights, June 10, 2006.
143. "Huda Gaza Lebanon Israel State Terror," YouTube.com, July 14, 2006.
144. Noah Pollak, "Show of Force," *Azure*, Autumn 2007.

145. Amir Oren, "Not Really a War," *Haaretz* (Israel), January 5, 2009.
146. After United Nations Secretary-General Kofi Annan implicated Israel in the incident, he later retracted, saying that he had responded to "media speculations." (Yitzhak Benhorin, "Annan Retracts Remarks on IDF's Gaza Blast Probe," *Ynetnews* [Israel], June 15, 2006.) See also "Pallywood IV – Palestine Fake News from Gaza Beach," YouTube.com.
147. The Palestinian Authority confirmed that the blast occurred inside a vehicle carrying Qassam rockets and was not the result of IDF fire. (Ali Waked, "Gaza: Blast During Hamas Rally Kills 19," *Ynetnews* [Israel] September 23, 2005.) See Sarah El Deeb, "At Least 15 Killed in Hamas Truck Blast," Associated Press, September 24, 2005.
148. France-2 later passed off the faux pas as "an internal malfunction in the checking of information." ("French TV Apologises Over Gaza Footage Mix-up," Agence France Presse, January 6, 2009.)
149. Rabbi Benjamin Blech, "A Film Unfinished," Aish.com, August 28, 2010; Yael Hersonski, *A Film Unfinished*, Oscilloscope Pictures, 2010.
150. Errol Morris, "Photography as a Weapon," *Opinionator* blog / *New York Times*, August 11, 2008.
151. Osama Bin Laden, December 26, 2001; cited in James Fallows, "Who Shot Mohammed al-Dura?", *The Atlantic*, June 2003.
152. Melanie Phillips, "Faking a Killing," *Standpoint* (UK), July 2008.
153. Frida Ghitis, "When Bad Journalism Kills: The Mohammed Al-Dura Story," *World Politics Review*, May 30, 2008.

— 8 —

DRIVING THE WEDGE

Two Jewish men are sitting on a park bench. One is reading a newspaper with a headline proclaiming: "Jews Exert World Dominance." The other looks at him disapprovingly and says, "Why are you reading that trash?"

The first man replies: "Most newspapers are filled with depressing reports of problems in Israel, anti-Semitism, and all kinds of troubles facing the Jewish people. This paper, on the other hand, gives me the good feeling that Jews have all the money and power and control the world!"

"Jews control the world" is an ancient canard; its 21st century version is the idea that "agent Israel" and its politically powerful allies influence the U.S. government to engage in policies that contradict America's best interests. Taki Theodoracopulos, a columnist for Britain's *Spectator* for over 30 years, charged that "the way to Uncle Sam's heart runs through Tel Aviv."[1] The *Los Angeles Times* quoted one U.S. politician referring to Capitol Hill as "the little Knesset,"[2] while another described it as "Israel's occupied territory."[3] Meanwhile, *Time* magazine published this alarmist headline: "The Pro-Israel Lobby's Plan to Storm Congress."[4]

The result of this contention – that Israel controls the superpower America – effectively drives a wedge between the U.S. and Israel. And that's no small matter. Healthy American-Israeli relations are crucial to Israel's survival, because in the face of anti-Israel attacks – whether in the form of U.N. condemnations or media outrage – the United States serves as a buffer to blunt that criticism. Thus by undermining the relationship between Israel and the U.S. – its most important and powerful ally – Israel loses a key advocate in support of its security actions, and ultimately weakens its ability to thrive and survive.

The myth that Israel exerts a highly-disproportionate influence has been floating around the diplomatic backwaters for years, but no one could have predicted the wave of publicity that surrounded the 2007 publication of *The Israel Lobby and U.S. Foreign Policy*. This tome by Professors Stephen Walt and John Mearsheimer not only casts Israel as a subversive foreign policy influence, but argues that America's support for Israel is the root cause of global instability and Islamic animosity. Their theory: "Israel gets a free hand with the Palestinians, and the United States does most of the fighting, dying, rebuilding and paying."[5]

With its conspiratorial tone and flavor, *The Israel Lobby* comes across as an updated *Protocols of the Elders of Zion*, the minutes of fictitious "secret meetings" in which Jewish leaders conspire to rule the world. Not surprisingly, *The Israel Lobby* has been applauded by radical Islamic groups and racists like David Duke, who praised the authors for "validating every major point I have been making."[6]

But the biggest boost came from the mainstream media, which elevated *The Israel Lobby* to cover-story status – discussed ad nauseam in newspapers, magazines and talk shows. Which makes one wonder: If the all-powerful "Israel Lobby" controls the media, how does that explain the media's universal coverage of *The Israel Lobby*?[7]

One way *The Israel Lobby* assailed Israel's legitimacy was the contention that the American invasion of Iraq was really "Israel's war." As described in the *New York Times*: "A cadre of pro-Zionist zealots... has long schemed to make the Middle East safer for Israel by uprooting the hostile regime of Saddam Hussein. They have finally succeeded, the theory goes, in pushing their agenda up to the desk of a gullible president."[8]

What, pray tell, might have been Israel's reason for favoring an attack on Iraq? Perhaps it was delayed revenge for the dozens of unprovoked Scud missiles that Saddam launched against Israel during the 1991 Gulf War. Or maybe the Iraq war was a diversion enabling Israel to "implement its long-cherished dream of expelling all Palestinians from the West Bank and Gaza" – a baseless theory that appeared in one of America's largest "mainstream" newspapers, the *Chicago Tribune*.[9]

With popular support for the war wavering, CNN and others reported Congressman Jim Moran's declaration that there would have been no invasion "If it were not for the strong support of the Jewish community for this war with Iraq."[10] And in a *New York Times* op-ed, Tony Judt described how "prominent Israeli leaders and their American supporters pressed very hard for the invasion of Iraq."[11]

All this sounds eerily similar to the 1930s, when Charles Lindbergh publicly blamed the Jews for pushing America into a "pointless war" with Germany.[12]

Walt, Mearsheimer and their media compatriots could not have been more wrong. In the months leading up to the Iraq war, Israeli leaders specifically discouraged the U.S. from attacking, fearing (quite correctly, it turns out) that American troops would get bogged down in Iraq and the U.S. would never move on to dealing with the far more critical threat of Iran. Indeed, the *Washington Post* reported in 2002 how "Israeli officials are redoubling efforts to warn the Bush administration that Iran poses a greater threat than the Iraqi regime of Saddam Hussein."[13] In other words, it wasn't Israel that persuaded the American administration of the war's necessity, but rather the opposite: the U.S. enlisted Israel by arguing that American forces would be better positioned to deal with Iran once it had disposed of Saddam.[14]

Regardless of the reality, mainstream journalists continue to claim that Israel has America in its pocket. Georgie Ann Geyer's syndicated column – printed in the *Chicago Tribune, San Diego Union-Tribune* and other American dailies – quoted the Israeli prime minister as telling his cabinet: "Don't worry about American objections to our actions, I control America."[15] When challenged to back up the quote, Geyer attributed its source to "anonymous individuals." That didn't quite meet journalistic standards, and Geyer was forced to admit that the "quote" originated in a press release from a pro-Hamas group, Islamic Association for Palestine – and was pure fabrication.[16]

It seems that media paranoia sees a sinister pro-Israel lobby lurking in every corner. When Jewish boxer Dmitriy Salita arrived in England to fight for the world welterweight title, London's *Sunday Times* wrote that Salita is "ready for the opportunity of his life, buoyed by the good wishes of the New York fight crowd, the Jewish lobby and all those touched by his struggle and his quiet, serious demeanour."[17]

When the U.S. Congress voted to tighten sanctions against Iran, Anne Flaherty of Associated Press reported that "nervousness about Tehran's intentions in the region" is "a sentiment fueled by the pro-Israeli lobby whose influence reaches across party lines."[18] Even as Congress was voicing legitimate concerns about the Iranian threat to America, AP editorialized it as the narrow worry of the "pro-Israeli lobby."[19]

In 2011, Bibi Netanyahu's address to a joint session of Congress received nearly three dozen standing ovations. Yet the *New York Times* maligned the huge bipartisan support as due – not to American officials sharing Netanyahu's vision – but rather because of a powerful Jewish lobby controlling them: "With elections coming up next year, lawmakers appeared eager to demonstrate their support for Israel as part of an effort to secure backing from one of American politics' most powerful constituencies, American Jews."[20]

This absurd upending of the truth reminds me of the time that Charlie Chaplain entered a Charlie Chaplain look-alike contest – and failed even to make the finals.[21]

Weapons and Aid

Here's a current events question: When American and Israeli leaders got into a spat regarding construction in Jerusalem, who called it an "enjoyable new experience to be able to look on as the Israelis argued with their most important ally"?

1. Khaled Mashal – Chairman of Hamas
2. Hasan Nasrallah – Secretary General of Hezbollah
3. Jeremy Bowen – Mideast Editor of BBC
4. Mahmoud Ahmadinejad – President of Iran
5. Amr Moussa – Secretary General of the Arab League

The answer may (or may not) surprise you. The one who derives such satisfaction from U.S.-Israeli tensions is BBC's Mideast Editor, Jeremy Bowen.[22]

When it comes to driving a wedge between the U.S. and Israel, a perennial media favorite is the incident of the *USS Liberty*, an American surveillance ship that operated off the coast of Gaza during the 1967 Six Day War. In the heat of battle, Israel misidentified the *Liberty* as an Egyptian warship and attacked, leaving 34 crewmen dead. When the tragic error was discovered, Israel immediately informed the Americans, apologized and paid compensation to the victims' families.[23] No diplomatic riff ensued. Indeed, the United States – fearing that a Soviet plane had attacked – was actually relieved to discover that the incident involved its ally Israel.[24]

Yet for over 40 years, Israel's detractors have exploited this episode to portray Israel as an enemy that intentionally kills Americans. Never mind the fact that 10 official U.S. inquiries concluded that the *Liberty* strike was an accident. Conspiratorial rantings that the attack was "deliberate" promise far better ratings, which the media regularly regurgitates[25] every few years with the publication of yet another anti-Israel tome – under titles such as *How the Bombing of the USS Liberty Nearly Caused World War III*.[26] Within one week of the release of *Body of Secrets*, an exposé on U.S. spy activity, author James Bamford was given a forum to slander Israel for the *Liberty* incident on National Public Radio,[27] Salon.com[28] and CNN[29] – propelling his screed to number four on the *New York Times'* Best Sellers list.[30]

Could one imagine the sensationalistic smear of an "Apollo moon landing hoax" being glorified this way in the mainstream American media? Yet slowly but surely, anti-Israel canards are used to chip away at the core of American support for Israel – further isolating Israel in the international community.

Another method the media uses to undermine the U.S.-Israel relationship is to repeatedly emphasize the use of American weaponry in Israeli security measures, the implication being that Israel is abusing American aid. Muslim leader Al-Haaj Ghazi Khankan declared on ABC News that "U.S.-made F-16s and helicopters that shoot rockets are being used by the Israelis to kill more Palestinians."[31] Eric Margolis of the *Toronto Sun* wrote of how "the F-16's, helicopter gunships, and self-propelled heavy artillery raining death on Gaza come from the US courtesy of [the] American taxpayer."[32] A *New York Times* report on a search for terror suspects noted the seemingly unnecessary detail that "Israeli forces [were] brandishing American-made M-16 rifles," and described an air raid where "Israel used an American-made F-16 warplane."[33] And in an obvious attempt to outrage Americans, Reuters snidely reported that the U.S. "gives Israel about $2 billion a year in weaponry used to kill Palestinians."[34]

Another penchant of the media is to overstate the scope of U.S. foreign aid to Israel, in an attempt to portray Israel as a burdensome drain on the American economy. One article in the *Christian Science Monitor* claimed that Uncle Sam has spent twice as much money backing Israel – "in its drawn-out, violent dispute with the Palestinians" – than the hundreds of billions of dollars America spent fighting in Vietnam.[35]

The *Monitor* arrived at these stratospheric figures by including U.S. foreign aid to Egypt (cited as $117 billion) and Jordan ($22 billion) as "part of the total package of support for Israel." The *Monitor* also tagged Israel with the bill for rising oil prices (cost: $450 billion), and a U.S. economic recession (cost: $420 billion). On top of this, claimed the *Monitor*, support for Israel has somehow cost America the loss of 195,000 jobs. Even private charitable donations aren't spared the *Monitor's* poison pen; they too constitute a "net drain" on the American economy.

Just to cover its bases, the *Monitor* "balanced" these overblown claims with one lukewarm sentence: "Many Americans would probably say it is money well spent to support a beleagured [sic] democracy of some strategic interest."

"A beleaguered democracy of some strategic interest"? That line put me over the edge and I fired off an email communiqué to my subscribers.[36] Consider the facts: Israel is America's most trusted and reliable ally in the Middle East, the sole democracy in a region dominated by authoritarian and military regimes. The New York-based organization Freedom House notes that while the trend toward democracy is growing in most regions of the world, these prospects remain bleakest in the Middle East – where Israel is the only country ranked as "free."[37] The U.S. spends untold billions disseminating the ideals of democracy around the world; in Israel, these values come gratis – what has been called "a strategic bonanza for the United States at bargain prices."[38]

These shared values gain expression at the United Nations, where America and Israel vote in concert 88 percent of the time; by contrast, other Mideast "allies" like Egypt and Saudi Arabia vote with the U.S. 7 percent and 8 percent of the time, respectively. In fact, U.S. State Department figures show that Israel votes with the United States not only more than any Arab or Islamic country, but also more than any other country in the world – outpacing major U.S. allies like Great Britain, France and Canada.[39]

Yet despite Israel's loyalty and support, the media continues to push the idea of cutting aid to Israel, as expressed in a readers' poll on the homepage of Toronto's *Globe and Mail* which offered a simple "yes" or "no" vote: "Should all financial and political aid to Israel be cut off until a just peace with the Palestinians is in place?"[40] And in the *New York Times*, the ever-critical Roger Cohen flatly observed: "It does not make sense for America to bankroll Israeli policies that undermine U.S. strategic objectives."[41]

On C-Span, former CIA staffer Michael Scheuer advocated violence against Jews – suggesting that one way to "dissuade" terrorists from attacking the United States is to "persuade them to focus their anger" on Israel instead. On cue, C-Span then broadcast a call from a viewer who rained invective on Israel for having "jewed us into Iraq." C-SPAN host Bill Scanlan made no effort to upbraid the caller, but rather calmly asked Scheuer for "any comments." This was Scheuer's entrée to let it all out:

> One of the big things we have not been able to discuss for the past 30 years is the Israelis. Whether we want to be involved in fighting Israel's wars in the future is something that Americans should be able to talk about... They may want to see their kids killed in Iraq or Yemen or somewhere else to defend Israel. But the question is: We need to talk about it.
>
> Ultimately Israel is a country that is of no particular worth to the United States. Strategically, they have no resources we need. Their manpower is minimal. Their association with us is a negative for the United States. Now that's a fact...[42]

So despite the fact that Israel is America's most stable ally in an otherwise unstable region, Israel as a "strategic negative" remains a popular media notion. The *New York Times* profiled an article by Anthony H. Cordesman entitled, "Israel as a Strategic Liability?,"[43] and a headline on MSNBC.com ominously proposed: "Israel Turning Into a 'Burden' on U.S.?"[44]

America in the Arab World

If journalists are so interested in how much value America gets for its dollars, they might want to explore what "strategic value" is derived from America's $2 billion annual aid to Egypt. The government-sponsored Egyptian media is filled with loathing of America; the editor of *Al-Akhbar* wrote that America "has become a synonym for oppression and for abnegation of justice."[45] Writing in the same Egyptian government daily, columnist Mahmoud Abd Al-Mun'im Murad denounced America as an enemy whose primary goal is to impose "hegemony on the world, primarily on the Middle East and the Arab world,"[46] and suggested that American landmarks like the Statue of Liberty "must be destroyed."[47]

Exactly how much U.S. aid money is *that* worth?

This type of America-bashing is rife throughout the Arab world. The Saudi government daily, *Al-Riyadh*, has called for the establishment of an international court to examine America's "war crimes, plundering, coups, what American intelligence did with the drug barons, the policy of abductions and murder, the Hiroshima and Nagasaki bombings, the claims still pending regarding the black slave trade, and the deliberate annihilation of the Indians."[48] That's quite a mouthful given that the United States, through oil imports, pours about $10 billion annually into Saudi coffers, while supplying the Saudis with some of the world's most advanced weaponry including F-15 combat planes, M1A2 battle tanks and the Patriot air defense system.[49]

Here's what the U.S. gets back in return: Fifteen of the September 11 hijackers were Saudi nationals, and the Council on Foreign Relations reported that "for years, individuals and charities based in Saudi Arabia have been the most important source of funds for al-Qaeda; and for years, Saudi officials have turned a blind eye to this problem."[50]

Meanwhile, as the media exaggerates the gap between American and Israeli interests, it downplays the much larger gulf between American and Palestinian interests. When Palestinian leaders spoke of "the shedding of Palestinian blood, thanks to the blind military machine and international protection,"[51] an Associated Press report deleted the rest of the tirade – an anti-American slur about "influential and hegemonistic powers in the international community" – thus guaranteeing that such Palestinian hate speech never reached U.S. newspapers.[52]

Remember when Palestinians danced in the streets and handed out candies to celebrate the September 11 attacks?[53] That sentiment is reflected in public opinion polls showing that 65 percent of Palestinians support al-Qaeda actions against America and Europe,[54] and a 2009 Pew Research Center survey that showed unwavering Palestinian support for Osama bin Laden and Mahmoud Ahmadinejad.[55]

On the anniversary of 9-11, the Palestinian Authority daily, *Al-Hayat*

Al-Jadida, published a cartoon of a smiling bin Laden, making the "V" for victory sign with two fingers in the shape of the burning Twin Towers.[56] On Palestinian Authority TV, former Palestinian cabinet minister Abu Ali Shahin blessed al-Qaeda with success, saying: "We are fighting the Americans and hate the Americans more than you."[57] PA legislator Nahed Munir Alrayis has threatened "suicide attacks against the United States," while former Hamas chief Abdel Azziz al-Rantissi (mercifully terminated by Israel) proudly declared that "America declared war on God... and God declared war on America."[58]

In 2011, in a direct affront to American honor, Palestinians celebrating the U.N. statehood bid paraded with posters depicting President Obama as an ape.[59] When American officials made a celebratory visit to the West Bank in honor of Palestinians who graduated from American-funded education programs, Palestinian protesters blocked their vehicle, spewed English-language expletives, and hurled shoes – a deeply insulting gesture in Arab culture.[60] Adli Sadeq, Deputy Foreign Minister of the Palestinian Authority, wrote that the U.S. President is "the head of the snake of the American oppression," and opined that "America is sinking deeper and deeper in a putrid swamp, and will extricate itself from it only as a defeated, stinking loser."[61] Imagine the media outcry if an Israeli government official had even made a whiff of such a suggestion.

Yet despite the anti-Americanism that pervades Palestinian society, Western readers still open their newspaper to find headlines like: "Bush Unveils Security Aid for Palestinian Ally."[62] Are these the same "Palestinian allies" who regularly burn the American flag at political rallies? The same "Palestinian allies" who murdered the U.S. ambassador to Sudan?[63] The same "Palestinian allies" who threatened to "mercilessly strike" American targets after the U.S. vetoed a United Nations resolution condemning Israel?[64] The same "Palestinian allies" who sponsor sermons like this from Jerusalem's Al-Aqsa mosque:

> Iraq and Baghdad are being subjected to a savage attack by the most arrogant, cruelest and strongest country in the world today

– the U.S.... The U.S. came [to the Middle East] under the pretext that it is fighting evil and spreading democracy and freedom. But everyone knows that the U.S. heads the list of evildoers in the world. There is no place left against whose citizens the U.S. has not fought, and it has already murdered millions.[65]

Was any of this reported in your local media? Of course not. Doing so would shatter the narrative of Palestinian underdogs deserving of sympathy.

Worse than ignoring this blatant anti-Americanism, the media proactively covers it up. When Palestinians blew up a U.S. diplomatic convoy in Gaza – en route to interview Palestinian students for scholarships at American universities, killing three Americans – the *Washington Post* quoted a Palestinian condemnation of "this ugly crime targeting American observers as they were on a mission for security and peace."[66] Yet while this "remorse and conciliation" was fed to the Western media, the official Palestinian Authority newspaper was singing a different tune: "Perhaps American citizens are so naive to believe the Israeli accusations against us, but... we know that the crime against the American citizens is an Israeli plot masterminded by the minds in the Mossad."[67]

In another cover-up, the *Los Angeles Times* printed the lies of a Palestinian spokesman that "Hamas has never supported attacks on Westerners, as even our harshest critics will concede."[68] The *Times* let this go to print despite the fact that – since "renouncing violence" in the Oslo Accords of 1993 – Palestinians have murdered more than 50 American citizens in terror attacks.[69]

When Hamas leader Khaled Mashal appeared on the *Charlie Rose Show*, he put on a moderate face for the Western audience: "We don't have a problem whatsoever with the United States or with American interests."[70] Rose did not challenge Mashal's supposed love of America, ignoring his previous harsh statements such as: "Our battle is with two sides, one of them is the strongest power in the world, the United States, and the second is the strongest power in the region [Israel]... By God we will defeat both the United States and Israel."[71]

The United States gives hundreds of millions of dollars annually in foreign aid to the Palestinian Authority. So how was this money spent? For starters, there's the $22 million annual allowance to Yasser Arafat's widow, Suha, guaranteed for lifetime.[72] Meanwhile, according to senior Palestinian security officer Abu Yousuf, American-run programs to train Palestinian security forces have been instrumental in the "success" of terror attacks: "I do not think that the operations of the Palestinian resistance would have been so successful, and would have killed more than one thousand Israelis since 2000, and defeated the Israelis in Gaza without these [American] trainings."[73]

If the media wants to criticize how U.S. aid is being spent, it is picking the wrong target.

Terror Risk

Another way the media tries to drive a wedge between the U.S. and Israel is to contend that the relationship places Americans at increased risk for terror. Islamic radicals, the theory goes, are targeting America because their hatred of Israel is so deep that it extends to include Israel's friends. The message: If America wants to be safe, stop supporting Israel.

It's an old trick. Just as Jews were blamed for poisoning water wells during the Black Plague in Medieval Europe, so too when al-Qaeda attacked the United States, several reporters were quick to pin the blame on Israel. At noon on September 11, Peter Jennings of *ABC News* declared that "the hatred of the United States as a patron of Israel, whether you're from Afghanistan, or whether you're from Iran, Iraq, or inside the Palestinian territories is so intense at some levels, and has become more intense in recent months, that nobody will be, very many people will not be surprised at this attack today..."[74]

Jennings ignored the fact that years earlier, Osama bin Laden declared war on the United States when American troops were posted on Saudi soil during the Gulf War. Bin Laden denounced the "occupation" of the Arab Holy Land by "American crusader forces," which he described as "the latest and greatest aggression" against the Islamic world. Israel was barely a footnote in the rambling 11,000-word fatwa.[75] Indeed, more than their hatred of Israel (the Little Satan), Islamists hate America (the Big Satan) for embodying the Western political and cultural "infidel" system that radical Islam so violently opposes.

Instead, Jennings ignored all this and was more interested in pursuing the line that Israel is the source of America's problems. Just hours after 3,000 Americans had been murdered, Jennings welcomed as his guest Palestinian spokesliar Hanan Ashrawi. (Viewers were surely unaware that Ashrawi was Jennings' girlfriend back in the 1970s, when she was a graduate student and he was the head of ABC's bureau in Beirut.)[76] As all of America sat riveted, Jennings gave Ashrawi a platform to claim that the al-Qaeda attack was due to America's "very direct role in the politics and the realities" of the Mideast, particularly its "blind support for Israel." Ashrawi then launched into a tirade about Palestinians being killed "by missiles fired from Apache helicopters, gunships, fired from F-16s. They all have 'made in the USA' on them."

Just to be sure that viewers internalized the message that America's relationship with Israel is the cause of Arab hatred, Jennings echoed back to Ashrawi: "I think – is the point you're making – that Palestinians hold the United States as accountable for that as they do Israel?"[77]

Jennings' report was, in the words of *Washington Post* television critic Tom Shales, "a nauseating display."[78]

If it is true that terrorism against the U.S. stems largely from the American-Israeli alliance, how does that explain the motive for Islamic terror against Spain, Bali, India, Saudi Arabia, Jordan, Beslan, Indonesia, Pakistan and other countries not closely aligned with Israel and even openly hostile to it?

Jennings was not alone in blaming 9-11 on America's relationship with Israel. *Time* magazine's Tony Karon surmised that al-Qaeda's "motivation to launch a spectacular attack would have grown exponentially over the past year as anti-American feeling surged on the Arab streets in response [to] U.S. support for Israel..."[79] As if al-Qaeda would hammer its swords into ploughshares and bin Laden would return to the family construction business if only America would abandon its alliance with Israel.[80]

Some media outlets went a step further and suggested that Israel actually *perpetrated* the 9-11 attacks. Even after bin Laden had claimed responsibility, the *New York Times* quoted Salam Al-Marayati, executive director of the Muslim Public Affairs Council in Los Angeles: "If we're going to look at suspects, we should look to the groups that benefit the most from these kinds of incidents, and I think we should put the state of Israel on the suspect list..."[81] *Newsweek,* meanwhile, quoted Major General Hamid Gul, former head of Pakistan's intelligence service: "I can't say for sure who was behind it, but it's the Israelis who are creating so much misery in the world."[82]

These outrageous smears are eerily reminiscent of those found in the vilest Arabic press. Hezbollah's TV network, al-Manar, reported that on 9-11 more than 4,000 Jews did not show up for work at the World Trade Center – alleging that Israel's intelligence service, the Mossad, had advance warning of the attacks and were likely responsible for carrying them out.[83] And in what can only be called a backhanded compliment, Palestinian diplomat Salim Abu Sultan told the *Gulf News*, a daily in the United Arab Emirates: "I can smell Israeli fingers behind this. The scope of the attack was beyond the capability of Arabs... Only the Israelis have the ability to do such things."[84]

Meanwhile, Sheikh Muhammad Gemeaha of the Islamic Cultural Center in Manhattan cited "proof that Jews were the [9-11] terrorists because only they had the capability to neutralize the automatic pilot, command the control tower, erase the black boxes and infiltrate the White House and Pentagon."[85] In reporting the sheik's inflammatory remarks, the *New York Times* tried to turn Gemeaha into a moderate, citing his sermons "calling for peace, healing and love among people of all religions."[86]

After exhausting the supply of Muslim slander against Israel, the Western media simply made up their own. The *Washington Post* reported that two Israeli employees of the instant-messaging firm Odigo "received text messages warning of an attack on the World Trade Center two hours before terrorists crashed planes into the New York landmarks."[87] This was followed by a Fox News allegation that Israeli intelligence officials failed to share what they knew about September 11 with their American counterparts prior to the attacks.[88]

Pat Buchanan published the claim that the Israeli Mossad blew up the World Trade Center with planted explosives, and used remote control devices to fly the planes into the towers to cover it all up. He also has claimed that Israel stole a nuclear bomb from the U.S. and plans to explode it in an American city to cover up a plot to commit genocide against the Palestinians.[89] The rantings of an extremist wacko? Maybe, yet Buchanan continues to regularly appear as a political commentator on *The McLaughlin Group* and on MSNBC.

Amidst all these stories of Israel causing terror, where are the reports about Israel as the vanguard in the battle *against* Islamic terror? Doesn't Israel regularly provide the U.S. with key intelligence information, bona fide testing of defensive weapons, and frontline defense against radical Muslim regimes bent on causing catastrophic harm – what Joint Chiefs of Staff Chairman Adm. Mike Mullen, America's highest-ranking officer, termed "extraordinary value" that is "absolutely critical" to U.S. national security?[90] Has everyone forgotten how Israel's 1981 strike that destroyed Iraq's Osirak nuclear reactor prevented Saddam Hussein from acquiring nuclear weapons, a move that – despite widespread condemnation at the time – was acknowledged 10 years later as a necessary precondition to the success of Operation Desert Storm? In other words, if Iraq had been a nuclear power in 1991, the U.S. would have been hard pressed to eject Hussein's army from Kuwait and block his regime from monopolizing oil supplies in the Persian Gulf.[91] How much money and how many lives did *that* end up saving America?[92]

Yet the media continues to scare Americans into thinking that support for Israel translates into increased terror. Under the headline, "Israeli Settlements Threaten World Security," Tribune Media Services (a conglomeration of the Los Angeles Times Syndicate and the Chicago Tribune Syndicate) stated: "It is clear that the Israeli/Palestinian conflict stands at the center of what motivates so much terrorism against the United States."[93] *Toronto Sun* columnist Eric Margolis drew a direct correlation between Israeli actions and terror against Americans, suggesting that 9-11 had been "payback" for Israeli security operations – and that "the next attack on the US or its citizens abroad will likely be labeled, 'Gaza'."[94]

Indeed, the Western media has the propensity to blame Israel for every problem in the Arab world. During the Arab Spring, when 60 protesters were killed in Tunisian riots, the *New York Times* suggested a primary cause was "Israeli intransigence." Only 18 paragraphs down did the *Times* mention the true reason for the protests: "rising food prices, corruption, unemployment" and government repression.[95]

To test the theory that Israel threatens world stability, let's imagine for a moment that Israel did not exist. Would that change the basic story line in the Middle East?

During the Arab Spring, would hundreds of thousands of Arabs have refrained from protesting in the streets of Egypt, Tunisia, Algeria, Yemen, Jordan, Morocco, Syria and Libya? Would Iraq have decided not to invade Kuwait in 1990, and not have used chemical weapons against its own Kurdish population? Would Saudi Arabia stop exporting its Wahhabi model of Islam, with its rejectionist view of non-Muslim "infidels" across the globe? Would the danger posed by the Muslim Brotherhood in Egypt magically disappear? Would Shiites and Sunnis, who have been at each other's throats for more than a millennium, spontaneously make peace? Would Iraq and Iran have chosen not to pursue an eight-year war that cost more than a million lives? Would the Sudanese government have stopped its collusion with the Arab Janjaweed militias to end the genocide and displacement in Darfur? Would sectarian groups in Iraq suddenly put aside their internal struggles? Would the Taliban have not blown up ancient Buddha statues? Would radical Islamic movements in the Balkans, Algeria and Chechnya all suddenly become moderate? Would the desperate poverty and widespread illiteracy that afflicts the Arab world quickly disappear? Would women, non-Muslims and other minority groups finally enjoy equal rights in Arab countries, free of government persecution? Would the proportionately miniscule Arab contributions to technology and medicine suddenly be reversed? Would al-Qaeda not have attacked the U.S. on September 11, and would Islamists not have bombed Bali, London and Madrid?[96]

Of course not. Yet the media clings to their mythical "linkage theory." Two days after the 2005 terrorist bombings in London, Tony Blair gave a high-profile interview on BBC Radio mentioning that "some of the critical issues in the Middle East" need to be "dealt with and sorted out."[97] Although Blair never identified any specific issues, Associated Press went ahead and "quoted" Blair as saying that the critical Mideast issue is "easing the conflict between Israel and the Palestinians."[98] Blair never linked Israel with the London attacks; that was purely an AP fabrication revealing its own biased view.[99]

When it comes to linkage, the media's thickest smokescreen is reserved for the illusion that the Israeli-Palestinian conflict would somehow magically make Iran's nuclear and hegemonic ambitions evaporate into thin air. It's a theory termed by Jimmy Carter as a "linkage fact" ("Without doubt, the path to peace in the Middle East goes through Jerusalem")[100] and posited on the pages of the *Washington Post*[101] and the *New York Times*.[102]

The 2011 WikiLeaks totally shattered the false logic of linkage. Diplomatic memos showed that for years, Arab states have regarded the threat from Iran as their highest priority ("obsessed with Iran," says the *New York Times*) and pleaded with the United States to take military action. Saudi King Abdullah "frequently exhorted the US to attack Iran to put an end to its nuclear weapons program" (to "cut off the head of the snake").[103] The King of Bahrain warned that Iran's nuclear program "must be stopped," while the United Arab Emirates defense chief declared: "Ahmadinejad is Hitler."[104] None of the Arab leaders conditioned their opposition to Iran on settling the Israel-Palestinian conflict. Ironically, the memos show Israel keeping its cool, while the Arabs are the ones (justifiably) freaking out.[105]

So in the end, what was all the hullabaloo about "warmongering Israel single-handedly endangering geopolitical stability"? And what was behind the media mantra that solving the Palestinian issue is essential to broad Arab support in confronting Iran? Was it naiveté? An analytical error? Or a malicious attempt to pressure Israel.[106]

And so it goes, with the media claiming that a change in Israeli policy would solve every global challenge from climate change to the common cold. Writing in Australia's *The Age*, Michael Backman declared: "We have paid for Israel's failure with bombs on London public transport, bombs in bars in Bali, and even the loss of the World Trade Centre towers in New York… [Israel] is at the nub of these events."[107]

Christian Wedge

One of the strongest bastions of support for Israel is the evangelical Christian community, which holds strong pro-Israel political views and donates untold millions of dollars toward pro-Israel causes.[108] Fundamentalist Christians act in accord with the prophetic imperative – "For Zion's sake I will not keep silent; for Jerusalem's sake I will not remain quiet" (Isaiah 62:1) – taking seriously the biblical promise that God will make a great nation of Abraham[109] and that the Holy Land belongs to the Jews as an everlasting possession.[110]

And so, for those seeking to weaken support for Israel, a primary tactic is to drive a wedge between the Jewish state and the pro-Israel Christian community. At times, the media creates an impression that Israel is out to destroy the very cradle of Christian civilization. When Israel prepared to build a wall to protect worshippers at Rachel's Tomb on the outskirts of Bethlehem, Reuters published this headline: "Israel to Split Christ's Birthplace with Barrier."[111] Reuters made it sound as though Israel was plowing a bulldozer straight through the Church of the Nativity. To emphasize its (false) point, Reuters repeated the word "Christ" or "Christian" in each of the article's first four sentences – even though Rachel's Tomb has no historical connection to "Christ's birthplace" and is miles from the church.

Far from practicing anti-Christian policies, Israel is the *only* country in the Middle East where the Christian population has increased since

1948 – having risen by more than 400 percent,[112] and continues to rise every year.[113] By contrast, the rest of the Middle East – Lebanon, Egypt, Iraq and Syria – is characterized by widespread "de-Christianization." Turkey, regarded as a moderate Islamic state, has seen its Christian population decline 100-fold in the last century.[114] In Saudi Arabia, the practice of Christianity is plain illegal.[115] Yet this did not stop *Time* magazine reporter Andrew Lee Butters from using Pope Benedict's 2009 visit to Israel to foment the lie that "the creation of Israel has been a disaster for Christians in the Middle East."[116]

If anything has been a disaster for Christians, it is the rise of Muslim fundamentalism. In the West Bank town of Kalkilya, the local YMCA was destroyed,[117] and Palestinian gunmen blew up the YMCA library in the Gaza Strip; two guards were kidnapped, the offices were looted and all 8,000 books were destroyed.[118] When four masked gunmen tried to abduct a church employee in Gaza, a local Christian leader lamented how the incident is "aimed at sending a message to all the Christians here that we must leave. Radical Islamic groups are waging a campaign to get rid of us and no one seems to care."[119]

In 2005, hundreds of Muslims screaming *Allahu Akbar* carried out a pogrom against Christians in the West Bank city of Taibe – setting dozens of homes and businesses on fire, looting valuables, and destroying Christian icons.[120] Palestinian gunmen destroyed a Christian television station based in Bethlehem[121] and the *Boston Globe* reported "a rampage of Palestinian Muslims against Christian shops and churches in Ramallah."[122] In 2009, Muslims desecrated two Christian cemeteries in a West Bank village near Ramallah, desecrating 70 graves and decapitating a statue of the Virgin Mary.[123]

Did any of this get reported in your local newspaper?

In 2007, the manager of Gaza's only Christian bookstore was kidnapped and murdered – shot in the head and stabbed multiple times.[124] The slaying garnered a one-paragraph mention in the *Washington Post*'s "World in Brief" section.[125] Imagine if a Muslim activist had been found shot and stabbed on an Israeli street after receiving death threats for "missionary work." A one-paragraph news brief? Don't bet on it.[126]

It comes as no surprise that following the Hamas takeover in 2006, the Christian population of Gaza fell by 64 percent – from 5,000 to less than 1,800 in 2010.[127] Yet in noting this demographic trend, the *New York Times* made no mention of Palestinian-led violence and intimidation; instead the *Times* cited a Palestinian official expressing his disingenuous hope "to keep the presence of the Christians alive and well."[128]

In the city of Bethlehem, the literal birthplace of Christianity, the Christian population began to drastically decline in 1995, the very year the Palestinian Authority assumed administrative control. The PA unilaterally annexed an additional 30,000 Muslims to Bethlehem and then redistricted the municipal boundaries – ensuring a Muslim majority in any future elections.[129] In order to further freeze Christians out of the Palestinian political process, a 2007 Palestinian summit was intentionally held in Mecca, a city where Christians (and all non-Muslims, for that matter) are barred by law.[130]

Under Palestinian control, the de-Christianization of Bethlehem has been ruthless. A Greek Orthodox monastery next to the Church of the Nativity was confiscated and converted into the PA president's official Bethlehem residence.[131] Bethlehem Christians have been forced to shut down businesses after failing to pay "protection money" to local Muslims.[132] This campaign took another nasty turn in 2006 when Bethlehem City Council member Hassan El-Masalmeh publicly advocated a discriminatory "dhimmi tax" on non-Muslim residents.[133] Not surprisingly, Christians in Bethlehem and neighboring Beit Jala are fleeing in large numbers; after once comprising 60-70 percent of the city's population, they have now dwindled to 15 percent.[134]

Yet the media continues to censure Israel for Bethlehem's woes. A Reuters "news" report squarely placed the "blame [on] Israel for the shrinking community" – an editorialization unsupported by any survey, study or citation.[135] *Scotland on Sunday* newspaper attributed the steep decline of Bethlehem's Christian population to Israel's very existence: "Adding to the gloom is more evidence of a dwindling Christian presence in the town. The exodus of Christians began with the establishment of the State of Israel."[136] And in an article entitled, "Israeli Settlements Squeezing Out Christians and Muslims," the *Irish Times* – Ireland's newspaper of record – claimed that Israel's humanitarian policy of granting travel permits to West Bank Christians is actually an evil scheme "designed to cause animosities" between Muslim and Christian groups.[137]

Not surprisingly, much of this Christian-Israel "wedge" begins in the Palestinian media, where a common – and insidious – theme is to compare the situation of Palestinians today to the persecution of Jesus. The official Palestinian daily, *Al-Hayat Al-Jadida*, described how "the suffering of the first Palestinian – the Messiah – started with the Last Supper."[138] Palestinian TV reported that "Jesus was the first Palestinian martyr... no one denies that."[139] When Israel reduced power to Gaza, a Jordanian cartoon depicted a Palestinian being crucified on an electricity pole.[140] And on the television talk show *Good Morning Jerusalem*, a Palestinian artist displayed a painting of Jesus flanked by two Israeli soldiers, explaining that "our struggle today against [Israel] is an eternal one. It can be said that it started 2,000 years ago and continues until today..."[141]

Palestinians cleverly present themselves as the heirs to the legacy of Christ, playing off the millennia-old hatred of Jews for rejecting Jesus. The Palestinian newspaper *Al-Hayat Al-Jadida* described Nazareth as "the city in which the Jews murdered the first of its Palestinian sons,"[142] and called Jesus "the first Palestinian martyr for Allah."[143] This ignores the basic facts of history: Given that the region under discussion was not called "Palestine" until years after Jesus' lifetime, and Islam itself only came into existence centuries later, Jesus could never have been a "Palestinian martyr for Allah."

And though this imagery begins in the Palestinian press, before long Western journalists are latching on as well. *Aftonbladet*, the most widely circulated newspaper in Sweden, headlined an editorial: "The Crucifixion of Arafat."[144] The Italian daily *La Stampa* ran a front-page cartoon showing an Israeli tank emblazoned with a Jewish star, pointing a large gun at baby Jesus in a manger, as the infant pleads, "Surely they don't want to kill me again, do they?"[145]

The media presents this as part of the same ongoing struggle: just as the Jews opposed Jesus, so too Israel is hostile toward the Palestinians. For Christians, this imagery is as negative and as visceral as it gets.

At Christmas time, the media makes a special effort to strain Christian-Israel relations. Portraying Israel as the grinch, BBC's Orla Guerlin delivered a bleak report from Nazareth entitled, "How the Israelis Stole Christmas."[146] The London *Independent*, meanwhile, wrote about an Arab woman who claims she was stopped at a checkpoint on her way to deliver a baby; the article compares her plight to "the birth pains" of Mary Magdalene, a "Palestinian refugee in Bethlehem."[147] Savor the irony of Mary – a Jew who lived years before the term "Palestine" ever came to describe the region – being revised as a "Palestinian refugee."

In the run-up to Easter, Reuters described "hardships" experienced by Christians wanting to celebrate at holy sites in Jerusalem. Under the headline, "In Holy Land, Easter Not What it Was," Reuters reported that Israel had issued 10,000 entry permits to Palestinian Christians, and then noted that "as a result, there has been a big drop in local participation in Easter week ceremonies."[148]

Readers got the distinct impression that Israel is hindering the celebration of Christian holidays. Yet media monitors dug into microfilm archives to reveal the truth of whether Easter participation has dropped under Israeli rule. News reports from the era when Jerusalem was under Jordanian control (1948-1967) show a total of 5,000 pilgrims in Jerusalem for Easter festivities[149] – half the number of permits that Israel allotted to Palestinians alone. Similarly, when Jerusalem was under British control (1917-1948), only a few thousand pilgrims would come every year.[150] Things were even worse during the pre-1917 Ottoman era, when Easter services in Jerusalem would often turn violent. So despite the fact that Easter participation has increased significantly under Israeli rule, Reuters could not resist ascribing anti-Christian motives to Israel.[151]

The media loves to go this route, no matter how remote and ludicrous. In 2002, when a group of 128 armed Palestinians invaded Bethlehem's

Church of the Nativity – stealing gold objects from the monks and urinating on the church floor[152] – the media still found a way to blame the Jews. Writing in the *PostGlobal* blog produced jointly by *Newsweek* and the *Washington Post*, journalist Lamis Andoni fallaciously claimed that the Church of the Nativity was "bombed by the Israeli army" during the siege in Bethlehem.[153] And in describing the event on ABC's *Nightline*, reporter Jim Wooten spoke of Israel's prime minister as "the hated architect of Israeli expansion" and "the devil incarnate."[154] Within a few years, the Palestinian takeover of the church had been all but erased from history; in 2007, *National Geographic's* 6,000-word exploration of events in Bethlehem made zero mention of that appalling episode.[155]

Adding their own brand of libel, McClatchy Newspapers – publisher of 32 dailies in the U.S. – squarely blamed Israel for all of Bethlehem's woes: "Gone is the olivewood stable shielding the baby Jesus, Mary and Joseph. In its place, looming over the angelic family, are an Israeli watchtower and three towering sections of an adjoining wall… [Bethlehem] remains largely isolated from the outside world by Israel's 25-foot-tall concrete walls, part of Israel's separation barrier."[156]

Is Bethlehem really surrounded by a wall? Israel built a wire fence in the area where northern Bethlehem interfaces with Jerusalem and added only a small segment of concrete wall – facing a major Israeli roadway – to prevent gunmen from shooting at Israeli motorists.[157] Yet the media makes this out to be a direct attack on the heart of Christianity.

All this "news" about Israel being "anti-Christian" is more than just harmless chatter. In 2004, the Presbyterian Church (U.S.A.) approved a resolution calling for "phased selective divestment in multinational corporations operating in Israel," such as Motorola and Citigroup.[158] And in 2008, the United Methodist Church debated whether to pull its holdings in Caterpillar, which provides the Israel Defense Forces with bulldozers.[159] (The United Church of Christ and the Church of England have held similar discussions.)[160] Meanwhile, the *Christian Science Monitor* added fuel to the fire with an online poll asking: "Should US-based churches boycott certain companies doing business with Israel?"[161]

Israel is a vanguard of religious freedom in a region where Christians are widely persecuted and treated as second class. As Monsignor Robert Stern, secretary general of the Catholic Near East Welfare Association, acknowledged: Christians "feel a lot of social pressure living in an Islamic world. A lot of them are in politically very uncertain circumstances – where they're at risk."[162]

Yet reading your local newspaper, you'd be forgiven for thinking that Israel is the Mideast's worst offender. It's all part of the media's efforts to drive a wedge between Israel and the Christian community, further demonizing Israel and eroding its support in the West.

The Deep Bond

Despite the media's audacious efforts to influence the American public otherwise, opinion polls consistently exhibit overwhelming support for Israel. A 2011 CNN poll showed that 82 percent of Americans view Israel as an ally and/or friend of the United States; only Great Britain received higher marks.[163]

What is at the root of this longstanding and durable support? It surely isn't grounded in energy policy or a quest for diplomatic popularity. Nor, as the conspiracy-minded critics have claimed, is it because a "Zionist lobby" has hijacked U.S. foreign policy to manipulate Washington into serving Israel's ends.[164]

Back in the 1980s when I had the privilege of working for Congressman Jack Kemp, I wrote position papers on the American-Israeli relationship, identifying core reasons for this deep bond. Israel stands as a beacon of Western-style democracy amidst a sea of totalitarian Arab states. Diplomatic disasters – such as the 1979 Islamic revolution in Iran (until then America's most important ally in the Persian Gulf) and more recently, the chaos of the Arab Spring with U.S. allies like Mubarak in Egypt being supplanted in part by the radical Muslim Brotherhood – have highlighted America's need for reliable Mideast allies. Indeed, Israel has proven an island of stability, giving America the security of knowing that a change in leadership will not cause a shift in allegiance.

Further, Israel's location at the strategic crossroads of North Africa and Southwest Asia – a junction of paramount American interests – means that the U.S. can minimize its military deployments in this vital area. U.S. Navy ships routinely dock in Haifa; Air Force planes refuel at Israeli bases; $800 million of U.S. arms and medical equipment are pre-positioned in Israel. (In the Persian Gulf, by contrast, the absence of a dependable and sturdy ally like Israel has impelled the United States to commit hundreds of thousands of troops and trillions of dollars.) Secretary of State Alexander M. Haig's observation 30 years ago still resonates today: "Israel is the largest American aircraft carrier in the world that cannot be sunk, does not carry even one American soldier, and is located in a critical region for American national security."[165]

Beyond this, Israel stands on the frontline of the war against terror, providing America with advanced intelligence and security know-how.[166] In the assessment of Maj. Gen. George J. Keegan Jr., former head of U.S. Air Force intelligence, America's military defense capability "owes more to the Israeli intelligence input than it does to any single source of intelligence," the worth of which, he estimates, exceeds "five CIAs."[167] It is for this reason that many have urged that U.S. assistance to Israel be classified not as foreign aid, but as an American "defense expenditure."

Americans also identify with Israel's immigrant- and refugee-based culture, and a pioneering spirit that is mindful of what America must have been like in its earliest days. Israel's War of Independence was won by a motley crew of Holocaust survivors and kibbutz farmers who used even broomsticks for weapons; America's War of Independence was won by frontier farmers who grabbed the muskets off their walls, using weapons better suited to hunting rabbits than to fighting the mighty British Army.

These scrappy beginnings bred an entrepreneurial ideal that has today made the U.S. and Israel the two countries with the largest number of startup companies in the world. Incredibly, the tiny nation of Israel – population 7 million – is at the forefront of cutting-edge technologies in the fields of medicine, agriculture, communications, software and sustainable energies, boasting the largest number of NASDAQ-listed companies outside of North America.[168]

Yet in the final analysis, these reasons do not fully account for the depth of the U.S.-Israel connection. At its root, I believe that Americans identify so closely with Israel because Jewish history and the Hebrew Bible resonate with the American experience. The pilgrims who sailed on the Mayflower in 1620 – Puritan refugees escaping religious persecution in Europe – viewed their emigration as a virtual re-enactment of the Jewish exodus from Egypt. The Pilgrims considered Britain as modern-day Egypt, with King Charles in the role of Pharaoh. The tumultuous Atlantic Ocean was the Red Sea, America was the Promised Land, and the goal was to build a new Jerusalem.[169] As expressed by John Winthrop, the first Governor of Massachusetts: "God has entered into a Covenant with those who are on their way to wilderness in America, just as he had entered into Covenant with the Israelites in the wilderness of Sinai."[170]

Thus the story of Moses became the story of America.

America's first institutions of higher learning, including Harvard and Princeton, made Bible study and Hebrew part of the required curriculum.[171] The Founding Fathers would later suggest that Hebrew be designated as America's official language.[172] When designing the Great Seal of the United States, Benjamin Franklin proposed an image of the Israelites fleeing the tyranny of Egypt across the Red Sea. Thomas Jefferson suggested the Jews in the wilderness, guided by a pillar of cloud by day and pillar of fire by night.[173]

As America expanded westward, the popular code-word became "Manifest Destiny," expressing the belief that the United States was destined, even divinely ordained, to expand across the North American continent.[174]

Beyond this, the teachings of the Jewish Bible have formed America's ideological foundation. The Liberty Bell in Philadelphia – America's premier symbol of freedom – carries an inscription from Leviticus 25:10: "Proclaim liberty throughout all the land and unto all the inhabitants thereof." John Locke, the author the first draft of the constitution of the Carolinas, considered the 613 Laws of Moses to be the ideal legal foundation for America.[175] The opening lines of the Declaration of Independence – "We hold these truths to be self evident that all men are created equal, that they are endowed by their Creator with certain unalienable rights" – marks the first time in history that Jewish ethics were legally enshrined into the laws of a non-Jewish nation.[176]

These biblical values have taken deep root. In the words of historian Paul Johnson, to the Jews "we owe the idea of equality before the law, both divine and human; of the sanctity of life and the dignity of human person; of the individual conscience and so a personal redemption; of collective conscience and so of social responsibility; of peace as an abstract ideal and love as the foundation of justice, and many other items which constitute the basic moral furniture of the human mind."[177] President Calvin Coolidge affirmed that "the Hebraic mortars cemented the foundations of American democracy,"[178] and President Franklin D. Roosevelt articulated in a 1935 radio address: "We cannot read the history of our rise and development as a nation, without reckoning the place the Bible has occupied."[179]

No wonder that there are towns across America named Zion, Jerusalem, Jericho, Mount Sinai and more than a dozen "Bethlehems." By the same token, Washington and Lincoln streets are a feature of modern Israel. Alone in the Middle East, Israel hosts memorials for John F. Kennedy, Martin Luther King Jr, September 11, and two exact replicas of the Liberty Bell.

Nor should it be a surprise that U.S. Presidents as far back as John Adams and Abraham Lincoln backed the "noble dream" of a re-created independent Jewish state in the Holy Land.[180]

In this sense, the American-Israel relationship transcends any ephemeral political, military or economic considerations. It is rooted in a shared belief that "freedom with responsibility" is the cornerstone of human exceptionalism. Americans recognize that Israel is an eternal guardian of these divine values, which the Jewish prophets brought to the world and which the United States fights valiantly to uphold. Thus, on the deepest level, pro-Israel sentiment stems from the belief that Israel is an American value, part of the American soul.

This has forged a relationship so profound and enduring that even media manipulations have been unable to drive a wedge.

Not that they don't try. In July 2010, just hours prior to an important White House meeting between President Obama and Israeli Prime Minister Netanyahu, the *New York Times* published a major 4,800-word story, highlighting how U.S. tax laws have helped Israelis receive funding from American donors.[181] The article contained no "new information" and had no "timely" news aspect, yet the *Times* – in a cleverly-timed effort to create a new bone of contention between Obama and Netanyahu – gave it prominent page-one coverage above the fold.

A year later, when Netanyahu flew to Washington for talks with U.S. leaders, the media was positioned to sway public opinion either for or against his policies. The *New York Times* made its position clear: "Israelis See Netanyahu Trip as Diplomatic Failure."[182] Yet when real Israelis were asked their opinion, the headline in *Haaretz* (ironically the *Times'* Israel partner) declared: "Netanyahu's Popularity Soaring Following Washington Trip."[183] *Globes,* Israel's leading business periodical, confirmed that "according to all opinion polls," support for Netanyahu "is soaring to heights it hasn't known for years."[184] The *New York Times'* declaration of "diplomatic failure" flew in the face of reality – yet reflected what the *Times* apparently hoped to be true.

Journalists have tried other low-handed tactics to undermine the U.S.-Israel bond. During the first months of Obama's presidency, he enjoyed a 60 percent favorable rating among Israelis. Then, after an intense dispute over Israeli construction in Jerusalem, Obama's popularity in Israel took a huge drop. The reason? According to Ethan Bronner of the *New York Times*, it had nothing to do with politics. Appearing on MSNBC's *Hardball,* Bronner explained that Obama's low popularity among Israelis was due to "racism." For viewers who may have missed it, host Chris Matthews helpfully added: "Because they see it as a black man."[185]

What a horrific distortion of the truth. Obviously, Obama was just as much "a black man" during his period of huge popularity in Israel; the drop in support was a purely political, not racial, issue.

The "Israel is racist" fantasy was echoed by *New York Times'* columnist Roger Cohen, who wrote that an Israeli cartoon which depicted "Obama cooking Netanyahu in a pot" was not a symbol of an Israeli politician in hot water, but rather the image of "a black man cooking a white man over an open fire."[186] Genuine policy differences may exist, but why is the media shamefacedly interjecting racist hatred where none exists?

Of course nobody bothered to consider the fact that "racist" Israel has granted asylum to black Muslims fleeing the war in Sudan.[187] Or that "racist" Israel airlifted tens of thousands of Ethiopian Jews – marking the only time in history that blacks have been systematically moved to another country in freedom rather than in chains.[188]

And yet, Peter Jennings told viewers of *World News Tonight* about Palestinian "artists" who'd created a model of the Statue of Liberty with the torch pointed downward – in order to "symbolize," Jennings helpfully explained, "how the U.S. was inverting its own values by supporting Israel."[189]

Ironically, this media bias against Israel may actually strengthen support from Americans who, deep down, recognize that Israel – surrounded by Arab enemies, vilified in international forums, and badgered by the Media Goliath – is an underdog in the truest sense of the word.

Notes

1. Taki, "Rich Rewards," *The Spectator* (UK), February 24, 2001.
2. David Lauter, "Baker's Reported Slam at Jews is Denied," *Los Angeles Times*, March 7, 1992.
3. Julie Wiener, "Presidential Aspirant Buchanan Attacked for 'Aura of Anti-Semitism,'" Jewish Telegraphic Agency, September 22, 1999.
4. Michael Scherer, "The Pro-Israel Lobby's Plan to Storm Congress," *Time*, March 22, 2010.
5. Stephen Walt and John Mearsheimer, *The Israel Lobby and U.S. Foreign Policy*, Farrar Straus Giroux, 2007.
6. Eli Lake, "David Duke Claims to be Vindicated by a Harvard Dean," *The Sun* (New York), March 20, 2006. It is noteworthy that the European Union's definition of anti-Semitism refers in part to "stereotypical allegations about Jews" including "the myth about a world Jewish conspiracy or of Jews controlling the media, economy, government or other societal institutions." ("Working Definition of Antisemitism," European Forum on Antisemitism.)
7. When mogul Mortimer Zuckerman was singled out by Walt and Mearsheimer as a member of the "Israeli lobby," Zuckerman responded: "The allegations of this disproportionate influence of the Jewish community remind me of the 92-year-old man sued in a paternity

suit. He said he was so proud; he pleaded guilty." (Meghan Clyne, "Kalb Upbraids Harvard Dean Over Israel," *New York Sun*, March 21, 2006.)
8. Bill Keller, "Is It Good for the Jews?", *New York Times*, March 8, 2003. The *Washington Post* likewise invoked U.S. policymakers as "presumably too weak and gullible to evade the manipulations of these Jews." (Editorial, "Blaming the Jews," *Washington Post*, March 12, 2003.)
9. Fred Donner, *Chicago Tribune*, March 10, 2003.
10. Ted Barrett, "Lawmaker Under Fire for Saying Jews Support Iraq War," CNN.com, March 12, 2003.
11. Tony Judt, "A Lobby, Not a Conspiracy," *New York Times*, April 19, 2006. This is a replay of 1991 when Pat Buchanan said that the only forces in favor of U.S. involvement in the Persian Gulf War were "the Israeli Defense Ministry and its amen corner in the United States." (Julie Wiener, "Presidential Aspirant Buchanan Attacked for 'Aura of Anti-Semitism,'" Jewish Telegraphic Agency, September 22, 1999.)
12. "Blaming the War on Israel," *The Economist*, March 13, 2003.
13. Alan Sipress, "Israel Emphasizes Iranian Threat," *Washington Post*, February 7, 2002. Similarly, the *New York Times* quoted Lt. Gen. Moshe Yaalon, Israel's chief of staff: "I'm not losing any sleep over the Iraqi threat." (James Bennet, "Sharon Tells Cabinet to Keep Quiet on U.S. Plans," *New York Times*, October 6, 2002.)
14. Martin Kramer, "Israel and the Iraq War," *Sandstorm* blog, April 12, 2006.
15. Georgie Ann Geyer, "Now Isn't the Time for Bush League Moves," Universal Press Syndicate, May 10, 2002.
16. Israel H. Asper, "Dishonest Reporting: Media Bias Against Israel," Aish.com, November 10, 2002.
17. Nick Pitt, "Confident Dmitriy Salita Plots Black Sabbath for Amir Khan," *Sunday Times* (UK), November 29, 2009.
18. Anne Flaherty, "Congress Denounces Iran's Ahmadinejad," Associated Press, September 25, 2007.
19. James Taranto, "Best of the Web Today," *Wall Street Journal Online*, September 26, 2007.
20. Helene Cooper and Ethan Bronner, "Netanyahu Gives No Ground in Congress Speech," *New York Times*, May 24, 2011; cited in "Bibi's Speech to Congress and Media Reaction," *Snapshots* blog, May 24, 2011. In contrast to the Israeli lobby with its hundreds of thousands of grass root members, the powerful Arab lobby has virtually no popular support among Americans, and yet its petro-dollars are used to influence American policy-makers. Prince Bandar, former Saudi ambassador to the United States, explained: "If the reputation then builds that the Saudis take care of friends when they leave office, you'd be surprised how much better friends you have when they are just coming into office." (Mitchell Bard, *The Arab Lobby*, Harper, 2010; Alan M. Dershowitz, "The Arab Lobby Rules America," *The Daily Beast*, August 24, 2010.)
21. *Chicago Herald*, July 15, 1915; cited in Joyce Milton, *Tramp: The Life of Charlie Chaplin*, HarperCollins, 1996.
22. Jeremy Bowen, "Analysis: Bleak Climate for Mid-East Talks," BBC News Online, May 9, 2010.
23. For a comprehensive refutation of the accusations against Israel, see Michael B. Oren, "USS Liberty: Case Closed," *Azure*, Spring 2000; A. Jay Cristol, *The Liberty Incident: The 1967 Attack on the U.S. Navy Spy Ship*, Potomac Books, 2002.
24. Berel Wein, *Faith and Fate*, Shaar Press, 2001.
25. For example, Bruce Ramsey, "Story of Assault on U.S. Ship Offers Much But Not the Reason," *Seattle Times*, June 21, 2009; Ron Martz, "Was it Fog of War, Or an Act of War, in '67 Attack?", *Atlanta Journal-Constitution*, June 8, 2007; John Crewdson, "New Revelations in Attack on

American Spy Ship," *Chicago Tribune*, October 2, 2007.
26. Peter Hounam, *Operation Cyanide: How the Bombing of the USS Liberty Nearly Caused World War III*, Vision, 2003. See also: James Scott, *The Attack on the Liberty: The Untold Story of Israel's Deadly 1967 Assault on a U.S. Spy Ship*, Simon & Schuster, 2009; John E. Borne, *The USS Liberty: Dissenting History vs. Official History*, 1993; Andrew and Leslie Cockburn, *Dangerous Liaison: The Inside Story of the U.S.-Israel Covert Relationship*, Bodley Head Ltd, 1991; John Ranelagh, *The Agency: The Rise and Decline of the CIA*, Simon & Schuster, 1986; Stephen Green, *Taking Sides: America's Secret Relations with a Militant Israel*, William Morrow & Co, 1984; Donald Neff, *Warriors for Jerusalem: The Six Days that Changed the Middle East*, Amana Books, 1984; James M. Ennes Jr., *Assault on the Liberty*, Random House, 1979; Richard Deacon, *The Israeli Secret Service*, 1977.
27. Neal Conan, "Interview with James Bamford," *Fresh Air from WHYY*, National Public Radio, April 24, 2001.
28. Suzy Hansen, "The Assault on the USS Liberty," Salon.com, April 25, 2001. ("Bamford's research adds weight to long-held insider beliefs that the attack was deliberate.")
29. David Ensor, "Israel's 1967 Attack on U.S. Ship Deliberate, Book Says," CNN.com, April 23, 2001.
30. "Best Sellers: Nonfiction," *New York Times*, May 27, 2001. The hype was generated by praise-laden book reviews including: Joseph Finder, "Bugging the World," *New York Times*, April 29, 2001; Malcolm Jones, "What to Read Now," Newsweek.com, September 29, 2001; Debbie Lincoln, "Book Review: Anatomy of the NSA," United Press International, September 12, 2001; Lee Milazzo, "Book Briefs," *Dallas Morning News*, July 29, 2001. ("Only a very brave person would attempt to investigate the investigators...")
31. "How Could This Happen?", ABCNews.com, September 15, 2001.
32. Eric Margolis, "Eradicating Hamas," Ericmargolis.com, January 12, 2009.
33. James Bennet, "U.S.-Mideast Connection: The News Becomes Less Foreign," *New York Times*, August 4, 2002.
34. Reuters, January 10, 2002; cited in Brit Hume, "Political Headlines," *Fox Special Report with Brit Hume*, Fox News, January 14, 2002.
35. David R. Francis, "Economist Tallies Swelling Cost of Israel to US," *Christian Science Monitor*, December 9, 2002.
36. "U.S. Aid to Israel," HonestReporting.com, December 10, 2002.
37. "Map of Freedom 2008," Freedomhouse.org.
38. Robert Satloff, "Israel: Not Just a Strategic Asset, But a Strategic Bonanza," Washington Institute for Near East Policy, July 20, 2010.
39. "Voting Practices in the United Nations," U.S. State Department, 2008; Michael Rubin, "Israel Votes with U.S. in UN More Than Any Other Country," *The Enterprise Blog*, June 3, 2009.
40. Theglobeandmail.com, February 12, 2004.
41. Roger Cohen, "Hard Mideast Truths," *New York Times*, February 11, 2010.
42. Bill Scanlan, *Washington Journal*, C-SPAN, January 4, 2010; cited in "Michael Scheuer: Terrorists Should Focus on Israel, Not the U.S.", *Adam Holland* blog, January 5, 2010. Scheuer also declared that "Obama is completely owned by the Israelis." (Michael Scheuer, "America First? – Never for U.S. Media or Politicians?", Non-intervention.com, May 18, 2010.)
43. Helene Cooper, "Washington Asks: What to Do About Israel?", *New York Times*, June 4, 2010, citing Anthony H. Cordesman, "Israel as a Strategic Liability?", Center for Strategic and International Studies, June 2, 2010.
44. MSNBC.com's headline on Scott Wilson, "Obama's Agenda, Israel's Ambitions Often at Odds," *Washington Post*, June 5, 2010.
45. *Al-Akhbar* (Egypt), August 23, 2001; cited in "Anti-American Statements in the Egyptian Media," Middle East Media Research Institute, September 17, 2001.

46. *Al-Akhbar* (Egypt), August 26, 2001; cited in Middle East Media Research Institute.
47. *Al-Akhbar* (Egypt), August 28, 2001; cited in Middle East Media Research Institute.
48. *Al-Riyadh* (Saudi Arabia), August 18, 2002; cited in "Saudi Reactions to the Lawsuit by September 11 Families," Middle East Media Research Institute, August 30, 2002.
49. "Background Note: Saudi Arabia," U.S. Department of State, Bureau of Near Eastern Affairs, January 2009.
50. *Terrorist Financing*, Council on Foreign Relations, October 2002.
51. "Arafat Urges Palestinians to Remain Steadfast in Al-Nakbah Day Speech," Palestinian Satellite Channel TV, May 15, 2001; translated by BBC Worldwide Monitoring.
52. "Excerpts from Arafat's Al-Naqba Speech," Associated Press, May 15, 2001; cited in Jeff Helmreich, "Journalistic License: Professional Standards in the Print Media's Coverage of Israel," Jerusalem Center for Public Affairs, August 15, 2001.
53. "Attacks Celebrated in West Bank," *The Times* (UK), September 11, 2001.
54. Fafo – Institute for Applied International Studies (Norway), December 22, 2005.
55. Roee Nahmias, "Palestinians Favor bin Laden, Ahmadinejad over Hamas," *Ynetnews* (Israel), February 8, 2010.
56. *Al-Hayat Al-Jadida* (Palestinian Authority), September 12, 2007; cited in Itamar Marcus and Barbara Crook, "Palestinian Authority Celebrates 9-11 Terror Attacks," Palestinian Media Watch, September 18, 2007.
57. Palestinian Authority Television, January 1, 2007; cited in Itamar Marcus and Barbara Crook, "Palestinian Authority Celebrates 9-11 Terror Attacks," Palestinian Media Watch, September 18, 2007.
58. Ben Lynfield, "Hamas Leader Turns His Focus on Bush, the 'Enemy of Islam,'" *The Scotsman*, March 29, 2004.
59. Photos at "Palestinians Abuse Donkey and Depict Obama as an Ape in Statehood Demonstrations," *Challah Hu Akbar* blog, September 25, 2011.
60. Mohammed Daraghmeh, "Palestinians Accost US Delegation in West Bank," Associated Press, October 4, 2011.
61. Adli Sadeq, *Al-Hayat Al-Jadida* (Palestinian Authority), June 3, 2003; cited in "President Bush is the Head of the Snake," Middle East Media Research Institute, June 5, 2003. A few weeks later, the official PA daily referred to Condoleezza Rice as "the black spinster." (Hassan Al-Batal, *Al-Ayyam* [Palestinian Authority], June 22, 2003; cited in Itamar Marcus, "PA Daily: Condoleezza Rice is the 'Black Spinster,'" Palestinian Media Watch, June 23, 2003.)
62. "Bush Unveils Security Aid for Palestinian Ally," Agence France Presse, January 30, 2007.
63. "The Seizure of the Saudi Arabian Embassy in Khartoum," U.S. Department of State, Intelligence Memorandum: Foreign Relations, 1969-1976, Volume E-6, Documents on Africa, 1973-1976.
64. Ali Waked, "Palestinian Groups Call on Muslims to Strike American Targets," *Ynetnews* (Israel), November 13, 2006.
65. Hayyan al-Adrisi, December 10, 2004, posted on Alminbar.net; cited in "Recent Anti-American Sermons by Palestinian Authority Preachers," Middle East Media Research Institute, January 11, 2005.
66. Molly Moore and John Ward Anderson, "Bomb Kills 3 Americans in Gaza Strip," *Washington Post*, October 16, 2003.
67. Khaled Abu Toameh, "PA Blames Israel for Gaza Bombing," *Jerusalem Post*, October 16, 2003.
68. "Mousa Abu Marzook, "Hamas' Stand," *Los Angeles Times*, July 10, 2007.
69. "American Citizens Killed or Injured by Palestinian Terrorists," Republican Study Committee, U.S. House of Representatives, December 10, 2003.
70. "Hamas Leader Khaled Meshaal," *Charlie Rose*, PBS, May 28, 2010; "Hamas Leader Says Group Has No Problem with US," Agence France Presse, May 29, 2010.

71. "Hamas Leader Seeks Arab-Muslim Pact vs. Israel-U.S.," Reuters, April 20, 2004; cited in "The Western Media Eats Up Khaled Meshal's Lies to Them," *Elder of Ziyon* blog, May 30, 2010.
72. Howard M. Berlin, "Palestinians' Woes Started with Arafat," *The News Journal* (Delaware), May 31, 2006.
73. Aaron Klein, "Fatah Militant: U.S. Training Was Key to Intifada's Success," *The Sun* (New York), August 21, 2007.
74. Peter Jennings, "ABC News Special Report: America Under Attack," ABC, September 11, 2001.
75. Osama bin Laden, "Declaration of War against the Americans Occupying the Land of the Two Holy Places," 1996. Bin Laden's 1998 fatwa spelled out three reasons to kill Americans, with support for Israel a distant third: "First, for over seven years the United States has been occupying the lands of Islam in the holiest of places, the Arabian Peninsula, plundering its riches, dictating to its rulers, humiliating its people, terrorizing its neighbors, and turning its bases in the Peninsula into a spearhead through which to fight the neighboring Muslim peoples." (Osama bin Laden, "Jihad against Jews and Crusaders," World Islamic Front, February 23, 1998.) See also Michael Dobbs, "Bin Laden: a 'Master Impresario,'" *Washington Post*, September 13, 2001.
76. Charles Fenyvesi, "Washington Whispers," *US News & World Report*, December 30, 1991 / January 6, 1992.
77. Peter Jennings, "ABC News Special Report: America Under Attack," September 13, 2001.
78. Tom Shales, "The Broadcast Networks, Putting Telling Above Selling," *Washington Post*, September 17, 2001. (Jennings "hosted what looked like a little intercontinental tea party for alleged experts on the Middle East, one of whom was Hanan Ashrawi, whom Jennings hailed as 'widely known in the United States.' Also widely disliked. Jennings and Ashrawi greeted each other like old pals, with broad smiles and warm greetings... Jennings deferred to Ashrawi, as usual, and let her filibuster.")
79. Tony Karon, "Why Didn't We Know?", *Time*, September 14, 2001.
80. See Tim Rutten, "Israel's Lobby as Scapegoat," *Los Angeles Times*, September 12, 2007.
81. David Firestone, "For Some Jewish Leaders, Partnership with Muslims Is a Casualty of Sept. 11 Attacks," *New York Times*, October 22, 2001.
82. Rob Nordland, "Prejudice in Pakistan," Newsweek.com, September 14, 2001.
83. Michael Slackman, "Response to Terror; Lebanon; One Country's Terrorists Are Another's Liberators," *Los Angeles Times*, October 4, 2001.
84. James Cox, "Conspiracy Theories Say Israel Did It," *USA Today*, September 27, 2001. Allegations of an Israeli role in such terror attacks were, ironically, rejected by Abu Jandal, Osama bin Laden's former bodyguard: "The allegations that the Mossad was responsible are nonsense and are an attempt to cast doubt on the ability of the Muslims to do something of this sort." (*Al-Quds Al-Arabi* [London], August 3, 2004; translated in "Interview with Osama bin Laden's Former Bodyguard," Middle East Media Research Institute, August 20, 2004.)
85. Gemeaha also stated: "Muslims do not feel safe even going to the hospitals, because some Jewish doctors in one of the hospitals poisoned sick Muslim children, who then died.... You see these people (i.e. the Jews) all the time, everywhere, disseminating corruption, heresy, homosexuality, alcoholism, and drugs... They do this to impose their hegemony and colonialism on the world..." (Cited in Seth Lipsky, "A Fair Sheik?", *Wall Street Journal*, October 24, 2001.)
86. Laurie Goodstein, "New York Cleric's Departure from Mosque Leaves Mystery," *New York Times*, October 23, 2001.
87. Brian McWilliams, "Instant Messages to Israel Warned of WTC Attack," Newsbytes, *Washington Post*, September 28, 2001.

88. Cited in Melissa Radler, "Israel Dismisses TV Report it Failed to Share Data on WTC Attack," *Jerusalem Post*, December 20, 2001. Fox later deleted the report from its website. Similarly, in the aftermath of the London Tube bombing in 2005, Associated Press claimed that minutes before the explosions, "the Israeli Embassy received warnings of possible terror attacks in the city," and that Israeli officials changed travel plans to avoid a location where one of the blasts occurred. (Amy Teibel, "Netanyahu Changed Plans Due to Warning," Associated Press, July 7, 2005.) Associated Press later retracted the story. See Tom Gross, "As Bombs Rock London, bin Laden's Brother Says He Will Pay for His Defense," Tomgrossmedia.com, July 7, 2005.
89. Paul Joseph Watson, "Top Construction Firm: WTC Destroyed by Controlled Demolition," Buchanan.org, May 27, 2010; cited in "The Pat Buchanan-Alex Jones Convergence: Israel Destroyed the World Trade Center," *Little Green Footballs*, May 29, 2010.
90. Hearing of the House Appropriations Defense Subcommittee, U.S. Congress, March 2, 2010.
91. Caroline Glick, "The Plain Truth about Israel," *Jerusalem Post*, June 7, 2010.
92. James Taranto, "Best of the Web Today," *Wall Street Journal Online*, December 9, 2002.
93. Nathan Gardels, "Israeli Settlements Threaten World Security," Tribune Media Services, March 18, 2010.
94. Eric Margolis, "Eradicating Hamas," Ericmargolis.com, January 12, 2009.
95. Anthony Shadid, "Joy as Tunisian President Flees, Offers Lesson to Arab Leaders," *New York Times*, January 14, 2011; cited in "My New York Times Prophecy," *Elder of Ziyon* blog, January 16, 2011.
96. See David Harris, "It's Not About Israel," *Huffington Post*, January 10, 2010. Since Israel's birth in 1948, there have been dozens of conflicts in the Middle East completely unrelated to the Arab-Israeli conflict: the Iraqi coup of 1958, the Lebanon crisis of 1958, the Yemeni civil war of 1962-68 (including subsequent civil wars in the 1980s and 1990s), the Iraqi Kurdish revolt of 1974, the Egyptian-Libyan Border War of 1977, the Persian Gulf War of 1990-91 (including Iraqi Kurdish and Iraqi Shiite revolts the same year), the Yemeni-Eritrean and Saudi-Yemeni border conflicts of the mid-1990s, and the U.S.-Iraq War, begun in 2003. (Dennis Ross and David Makovsky, *Myths, Illusions, and Peace*, Viking, 2009.)
97. "Blair Pays Tribute to Resilience," *Today*, BBC Radio 4, July 9, 2005.
98. Matt Moore, "Investigators Search for Clues, While Families Search for Loved Ones in London Bomb Blasts," Associated Press, July 9, 2005.
99. After reader complaints, Associated Press issued a correction. See "Bad News From London," HonestReporting.com, July 11, 2005.
100. Nathan Gardels, "Jimmy Carter Takes on Israel's Apartheid Policies and the Pro-Israeli Lobby in the US," Los Angeles Times Syndicate / *Huffington Post*, December 12, 2006.
101. Daniel Brumberg, "Engagement and Peacemaking," *Washington Post*, April 27, 2010.
102. Martin Indyk, "When Your Best Friend Gets Angry," *New York Times*, April 19, 2010.
103. Arshad Mohammed and Ross Colvin, "Saudi King Urged U.S. to Attack Iran: WikiLeaks," Reuters, November 28, 2010.
104. David E. Sanger, James Glanz and Jo Becker, "Around the World, Distress Over Iran," *New York Times*, November 28, 2010.
105. Josh Block, Progressive Policy Institute, Politico.com, November 24, 2010.
106. Martin Kramer of Harvard University suggests that the concept of linkage stems from the mistaken belief that the Middle East is an interlocking system, like Europe, where events in one corner can set off a chain reaction – e.g. resolving the conflict between Germany and France was a post-war condition for bringing peace to the entire continent. (Martin Kramer, "The Myth of Linkage," National Security Studies Program, Harvard University, June 12, 2008.)
107. Michael Backman, "Israelis are Living High on US Expense Account," *The Age* (Australia),

January 17, 2009.
108. In 2008, the International Fellowship of Christians and Jews announced plans to donate $45 million over three years. (Anshel Pfeffer, "U.S. Jews' Opposition Holds Up Jewish Agency Deal with Christian Group," *Haaretz* [Israel], February 28, 2008.) At his 2009 "Night to Honor Israel," Pastor John Hagee of San Antonio handed out checks for $9 million. (Colin McDonald, "Cornerstone Honors Israel with $9 Million Gift," *San Antonio Express-News*, October 26, 2009.)
109. Genesis 12:2.
110. See, for example: "He remembers His covenant forever, the word He commanded, for a thousand generations, the covenant He made with Abraham, the oath He swore to Isaac. He confirmed it to Jacob as a decree, to Israel as an everlasting covenant: 'To you I will give the land of Canaan as the portion you will inherit.'" (Psalms 105:8-11, 1-Chronicles 16:15-18) See also Genesis 13:15, 15:18, 17:8, 48:4; Exodus 6:4, 6:8, 12:25, 13:5, 13:11, 32:13, 33:1; Leviticus 14:34, 20:24; Numbers 11:12, 14:16, 14:23, 27:12, 32:7, 32:11, 33:53, 34:2; Deuteronomy 1:8, 1:21, 1:39, 2:29, 3:28, 4:1, 4:21, 4:37-38, 6:10, 6:18, 6:23, 7:13, 8:1, 9:5, 10:11, 11:9, 11:21, 11:31, 12:1, 12:10, 15:4, 17:14, 19:8, 19:10, 19:14, 25:19, 26:1, 26:15, 27:3, 28:11, 30:20, 31:7, 31:20, 34:4. See also the biblical books of Joshua, Judges, Kings, Isaiah, Jeremiah, Ezekiel, Psalms, Nehemiah and Chronicles.
111. "Israel to Split Christ's Birthplace with Barrier," Reuters, February 8, 2003.
112. The Christian population in Israel was 34,000 in 1949, 73,000 in 1972, and 153,000 in 2008. ("Statistical Abstract of Israel: Population by Religion," Israeli Central Bureau of Statistics, 2009.)
113. Ibid.
114. Turkey's Christian population dropped from 20 percent in the early 20th century to 0.2 percent today. (Daniel Greenfield, "The Vanishing Christians of the Middle East," *Sultan Knish* blog, October 13, 2010.)
115. "International Religious Freedom Report 2010," U.S. Department of State, November 17, 2010.
116. Andrew Lee Butters, "Why the Pope Can't Help Middle Eastern Christians," *The Middle East Blog*, Time.com, May 8, 2009.
117. Isabel Kershner, "Palestinian Christians Look Back on a Year of Troubles," *New York Times*, March 11, 2007.
118. Father Raymond J. De Souza, "Palestinian Christians Live in Constant Fear," *National Post* (Canada), February 19, 2008; "Militants Bomb Gaza YMCA Library," BBC News Online, February 15, 2008.
119. Khaled Abu Toameh, "Muslim Gunmen Target Christian in Gaza," *Jerusalem Post*, December 8, 2007. In the words of Reverend Tomey Dahoud, head of a West Bank church that was firebombed in 2006: "The Islamic people want to kill us. That's their principle and belief. They don't want Christians in this country... That's the reality." (Justus Reid Weiner, "Palestinian Crimes against Christian Arabs and Their Manipulation Against Israel," Jerusalem Center for Public Affairs, September 2008.) See also Edmund Sanders, "West Bank Oktoberfest Raises a Glass to Palestinian Culture," *Los Angeles Times*, October 5, 2010.
120. Lucy Williamson, "A Frightening Family Feud," BBC News Online, September 10, 2005; Harry de Quetteville, "'Islamic Mafia' Accused of Persecuting Holy Land Christians," *The Telegraph* (UK), September 9, 2005.
121. Khaled Abu Toameh, "Gunmen Destroy Bethlehem TV Studio, Suspending Broadcasts," *Jerusalem Post*, March 24, 2006.
122. *Boston Globe*, February 6, 2002.
123. "Vandals Strike in Two Christian Cemeteries in Palestine Desecrating 70 Graves," *Daily Mail* (UK), May 25, 2009.

124. "Murder in a Bookshop," *Haaretz* (Israel), November 5, 2007.
125. "Christian Activist Slain in Gaza," *Washington Post*, October 8, 2007.
126. "Murder in Gaza, One Paragraph in the Post," *Snapshots* blog, October 8, 2007. When Palestinian assailants threw a grenade into the playground of Gaza's YMCA, no mainstream media picked up the story – aside from a single, buried mention in AP. (Ashraf Sweilam, "Libyan Ship with Aid for Gaza Reaches Egypt Port," Associated Press, July 14, 2010.)
127. "Christmas in Bethlehem: The Cross Banished From Souvenirs," *Asia News* (Italy), December 22, 2010.
128. Ethan Bronner, "Mideast's Christians Losing Numbers and Sway," *New York Times*, May 12, 2009. In 1914, Christians represented 26.4 percent of the population of the Near East (what today is known as Israel, the PA, Jordan, Lebanon and Syria); by 1998 they were estimated at no more than 9.2 percent. (Justus Reid Weiner, "Human Rights of Christians in Palestinian Society," Jerusalem Center for Public Affairs, 2005.)
129. Justus Reid Weiner, "Palestinian Crimes against Christian Arabs and Their Manipulation against Israel," Jerusalem Center for Public Affairs, September 2008. Since the establishment of the Palestinian Authority in 1993, not a single Christian has been appointed to a senior security post. (Khaled Abu Toameh, "The Beleaguered Christians in Bethlehem," Hudson New York, May 12, 2009.)
130. Father Raymond J. De Souza, "The Islamification of Palestine," *National Post* (Canada), February 20, 2007.
131. Aaron Klein, "Media's Two-faced Christmas Coverage," *Ynetnews* (Israel), December 24, 2007. Christians in Bethlehem and nearby towns of Bet Sahour and Bet Jalla frequently complain that Muslims seize their lands either by force or through forged documents. (Abu Toameh, "The Beleaguered Christians in Bethlehem.")
132. Abu Toameh, "The Beleaguered Christians in Bethlehem."
133. Weiner, "Palestinian Crimes Against Christian Arabs and Their Manipulation Against Israel."
134. Weiner, "Palestinian Crimes Against Christian Arabs and Their Manipulation Against Israel"; Abu Toameh, "The Beleaguered Christians in Bethlehem."
135. Tom Perry, "In Holy Land, Christians a Community in Decline," Reuters, October 7, 2010; cited in "Christmas Comes Early This Year," Reuters Middle East Watch, October 9, 2010.
136. *Scotland on Sunday*, December 22, 2003.
137. Michael Jansen, "Israeli Settlements Squeezing Out Christians and Muslims," *Irish Times*, October 7, 2010; cited in Alex Margolin, "'Squeezing Out Christians and Muslims' – Irish Times Blames Israel," HonestReporting.com, November 30, 2010.
138. *Al-Hayat Al-Jadida* (Palestinian Authority), April 30, 2008.
139. Palestinian Authority Television, December 3, 2010; cited in Itamar Marcus and Nan Jacques Zilberdik, "Jesus Was A Palestinian – No One Denies That, Says PA TV," Palestinian Media Watch, December 24, 2010.
140. Emad Hajjaj, "Israel Cuts Gaza Electricity," Mahjoob.com, January 21, 2008.
141. Palestinian Authority Television, July 21, 2000; cited in Itamar Marcus and Barbara Crook, "Jesus the Palestinian in Palestinian Authority Ideology," Palestinian Media Watch, July 6, 2006.
142. *Al-Hayat Al-Jadida* (Palestinian Authority), January 24, 2000; cited in "Jesus Misrepresented as 'Muslim Palestinian,'" Palestinian Media Watch.
143. *Al-Hayat Al-Jadida* (Palestinian Authority), January 17, 2005; cited in "Jesus Misrepresented as 'Muslim Palestinian,'" Palestinian Media Watch.
144. Cited in Amiram Barkat, "Jews in Sweden are Afraid to be Known as Jews," *Haaretz* (Israel), February 10, 2004.
145. *La Stampa* (Italy), April 2002.

146. Cited in Barbara Amiel, "How Can the BBC be Impartial Between Tyranny and Democracy?", *Daily Telegraph* (UK), March 26, 2003.
147. Johann Hari, "What Would Happen if the Virgin Mary Came to Bethlehem Today?", *The Independent* (UK), December 23, 2006.
148. Tom Perry, "In Holy Land, Easter Not What it Was," Reuters, April 1, 2010.
149. "Easter Procession in Jerusalem," *Glasgow Herald*, April 9, 1955.
150. "Holy Fire Ceremony at Holy Sepulchre," *Palestine Post*, April 28, 1940 (citing a total of 1,500 pilgrims).
151. "Incredible Reuters Bias in Article on Easter in Jerusalem," *Elder of Ziyon* blog, April 2, 2010.
152. Matt Rees, "The Saga of the Siege," *Time*, May 20, 2002.
153. Lamis Andoni, "Christmas in a Strangled Bethlehem," *PostGlobal*, December 24, 2007.
154. *Nightline*, ABC News, June 12, 2003.
155. Michael Finkel, "Bethlehem 2007 A.D.", *National Geographic*, December 2007.
156. Dion Nissenbaum and Cliff Churgin, "Reality in Bethlehem Mars Christmas Tradition," McClatchy Newspapers, December 22, 2007.
157. Klein, "Media's Two-faced Christmas Coverage."
158. "RNS Daily Digest," Religion News Service, June 30, 2008.
159. Rachel Pomerance, "Methodists to Weigh Divestment as Tool to Shift Israel," *Washington Post* / Religion News Service, February 16, 2008.
160. Mark D. Tooley, "A Feast with the Beast; Ahmadinejad Dines with Church Officials in New York," October 2, 2008; Neela Banerjee, "Anglicans Vote to Divest from Concerns in Israel-Occupied Areas," *New York Times*, February 9, 2006. The idea also gained the support of the Archbishop of Canterbury, leader of 77 million Anglicans.
161. Jane Lampman, "From Churches, a Challenge to Israeli Policies," *Christian Science Monitor*, December 6, 2004.
162. "Middle East Synod Participant Explains Factors Behind Its Controversial Conclusion," Catholic News Agency, October 31, 2010. Tellingly, a declaration adopted at the 2010 gathering of Catholic bishops in the Middle East criticized Israel in detail, but omitted most criticism against Islamic governments.
163. CNN Opinion Research Poll, May 31, 2011.
164. Jeff Jacoby, "Why Are Americans So Pro-Israel?", *MetroWest Jewish Reporter* (Massachusetts), December 2009.
165. Michael Oren, "The Ultimate Ally," *Foreign Policy*, May/June 2011.
166. Israel's destruction of Syria's Soviet-made weaponry in 1982 was the first clear demonstration of the absolute superiority of U.S. military technology – a decisive factor in convincing Ronald Reagan that it was possible to win the Cold War. In this regard, even Walt and Mearsheimer acknowledge Israel as a U.S. strategic asset: "By serving as America's proxy after the Six Day War, Israel helped contain Soviet expansion in the region and inflicted humiliating defeats on Soviet clients like Egypt and Syria. Israel occasionally helped protect other U.S. allies (like Jordan's King Hussein), and its military prowess forced Moscow to spend more backing its losing clients. Israel also gave the United States useful intelligence about Soviet capabilities." (John Mearsheimer and Stephen Walt, "The Israel Lobby," *London Review of Books*, March 23, 2006.)
167. Oren, "The Ultimate Ally."
168. "NASDAQ Appoints Asaf Homossany as New Director for Israel," NASDAQ, February 6, 2005. As of 2008, Israel had 3,850 start-up companies – one for every 1,844 Israelis. (Dan Senor and Saul Singer, *Start-Up Nation*, Twelve, 2009.) Intel and Microsoft built their first overseas research and development centers in Israel, and Warren Buffett's first non-U.S. acquisition was the Israeli company Iscar in 2007.
169. Aboard the Mayflower, leader William Bradford compared the journey to "Moses and the

Israelites when they went out of Egypt." Upon arriving in Cape Cod, the pilgrims thanked God for letting them pass through the fiery Red Sea. (Bruce Feiler, *America's Prophet: How the Story of Moses Shaped America*, Harper Perennial, 2010.)

170. Sermon aboard the *Arbella* en route from England to Massachusetts, 1630; cited in Yoram Ettinger, "Passover Guide for the Perplexed 2011," April 3, 2011. Yale University President Ezra Stiles articulated in 1783: "Moses, the man of God, assembled 3 million people – the number of people in America in 1776."
171. The Yale seal depicts the Hebrew words *"Urim V'Tumim,"* an item worn by the High Priest in the days of the Holy Temple. The seals of both Columbia University and Dartmouth feature the Hebrew name of God. So popular was the Hebrew language in the 18th century that several students at Yale delivered their commencement orations in Hebrew. (Rabbi Ken Spiro, *Crash Course in Jewish History*, Targum Press, 2010.)
172. Abraham I. Katsh, *The Biblical Heritage of American Democracy*, Ktav Publishing, 1977, p. 70.
173. Exodus 13:21. John D. MacArthur, "First Great Seal Committee 1776," GreatSeal.com.
174. Spiro, *Crash Course in Jewish History*.
175. Ettinger, "Passover Guide for the Perplexed 2011."
176. In 1655, New Haven legislators adopted a legal code of 79 statutes, half of which contained biblical references, virtually all from the Hebrew Bible. The Plymouth Colony had a similar code, as did the Massachusetts Assembly, whose 1641 "Capital Laws of New England" was based almost entirely on Mosaic law. (Spiro, *Crash Course in Jewish History*.)
177. Paul Johnson, *A History of the Jews*, Harper & Row, 1987, p. 585.
178. May 3, 1925.
179. Gabriel Sivan, *The Bible and Civilization*, Keter Publishing, 1973, p. 178.
180. Theodore Roosevelt and Woodrow Wilson likewise urged that a Zionist state be created. Cited in Oren, "The Ultimate Ally."
181. Jim Rutenberg, Mike McIntire and Ethan Bronner, "Tax-Exempt Funds Aid Settlements in West Bank," *New York Times*, July 5, 2010.
182. Ethan Bronner, "Israelis See Netanyahu Trip as Diplomatic Failure," *New York Times*, May 25, 2011.
183. Yossi Verter, "Haaretz Poll: Netanyahu's Popularity Soaring Following Washington Trip," *Haaretz* (Israel), May 26, 2011. (Opinion polls showed that only 10 percent of the Israeli public viewed Netanyahu's U.S. trip as "a failure.")
184. Lilach Weissman, "Netanyahu Rides High," *Globes* (Israel), May 26, 2011.
185. Chris Mathews, *Hardball*, MSNBC, March 8, 2010.
186. Roger Cohen, "The Biden Effect," *New York Times*, March 15, 2010.
187. Yonit Farago and Stephen Farrell, "Muslims Seek a Haven in Israel After Their Exodus from Darfur," *The Times* (UK), June 6, 2006.
188. William Safire, *New York Times*, January 7, 1985; Editorial, "Anti-Zionist Racism," *National Post* (Canada), March 16, 2001.
189. Peter Jennings, *World News Tonight*, ABC, November 1, 2002; cited in "Jennings Highlights Desecration of Statue of Liberty," *CyberAlert*, Media Research Center, November 4, 2002.

– 9 –

GAZA WAR & "EXCESSIVE FORCE"

In December 2008, on the wall of the Israeli government press office in Jerusalem, a huge stack of yellow Post-it notes was pasted one atop the next. The number 10,048 was scrawled on top, marking the total number of Palestinian rockets fired from Gaza into Israel since 2001.[1] Mortars, Qassams, Katyushas, and medium-range Grad missiles – supplied by the mad mullahs of Iran – had placed 20 percent of Israel within striking range.[2]

Sound terrifying? Associated Press brushed it all off as insignificant: "Palestinians have been firing primitive, homemade Qassam rockets... Most of them miss their target, and those that land cause little damage with their small explosive warheads."[3]

"Small explosive warheads"? The Qassam's payload is packed with more than 7,000 metal ball bearings, each capable of ripping apart internal organs or punching a hole in the head – guaranteeing that the victim is dead before emergency help arrives.[4] And regardless of how "primitive" AP claims these rockets are, they're lethal enough to have killed dozens of Israeli civilians since 2001, wounded hundreds more, and – with just 15 seconds to run into a shelter before impact – sown panic in streets and schools.[5]

I've spent time in the southern Israel town of Sderot, and am certain that no one who has dismissed these rockets as harmless homemade toys has ever had the guts to stay there a few weeks, scurrying from shelter to shelter. Sderot is perhaps the only place on Earth where seat belts are forbidden, lest someone be unable to get out of their vehicle quickly;[6] a place where up to 94 percent of children exhibit signs of post-traumatic stress.[7]

Yet the media continues to downplay the threat. *The Economist* made the strange claim that "rudimentary" Qassam rockets "have maimed more Gazans than Israelis."[8] Major networks like CNN and Fox News gave airtime to Palestinian spokeswoman Diana Buttu asserting that Palestinian rockets fired at Israeli civilians contain no explosive warhead.[9] Apparently the Qassam's standard 20 pounds of TNT simply slipped her mind.[10]

Even as thousands of rockets rained on Israeli towns, the *New York Times* published the ludicrous claim of Hamas spokesman Ahmed Yousef that "We did not intentionally target civilians. We were targeting military bases, but the primitive weapons make mistakes."[11] Meanwhile, a *Washington Post* op-ed referred to Israel's "efforts to stop amateur rockets from nagging the residents of some of its southern cities."[12] According to the *Post*, the Israeli civilians killed in "amateur rocket" attacks were merely "nagged" to death.

The Hudna Trap

Back in June 2008, in a diplomatic effort to quell the rocket-fire, Israel signed a six-month truce with Hamas. What the Western world calls a "truce," however, Palestinians call "tahadiya" or "hudna" – Arabic terms that go back to the days when Muhammad struck a hudna with the Quraysh tribe that controlled Mecca. Muhammad then re-armed and took advantage of a minor infraction to break the hudna and launch a full conquest of Mecca.

And so the hudna has been ever since: not a step toward peace as the English term "truce" implies, but rather a temporary cessation of hostilities[13] – a tactical time-out to replenish strength during the quiet periods, and then return to the next stage of attack with increased deadliness.[14] Indeed, over the years Hamas has agreed to no less than 10 ceasefires, and each time reverted to the path of terror.[15] As Hamas leader Nizar Rayan explained, "The only reason to have a hudna is to prepare yourself for the final battle."[16]

Yet the media treated the hudna as if it were a sincere commitment to peace, with Associated Press asserting that "the success of peacemaking" depends on the hudna,[17] and another AP article calling such a truce "crucial for implementing" the peace plan.[18]

Would a Palestinian hudna really mark a major peacemaking breakthrough? Thomas Friedman, a 25-year veteran of Middle East reporting, offered this advice to reporters: "Never lead your story out of Lebanon, Gaza, or Iraq with a cease-fire; it will always be over by the time the next morning's paper is out."[19]

During the so-called "truce" of 2008, Hamas fired hundreds of rockets and mortars into Israel, conducted sniper attacks against Israeli civilians, and attempted to kidnap Israeli soldiers.[20] "Nobody among our sons and grandsons will accept Israel as a legal state..." Hamas foreign minister Mahmoud Zahar declared. "Israel is a foreign body. Not in this generation, not in the next generation, will we accept it here."[21]

Yet these facts did not stop newsrooms from casting Israel as the villain for treating the hudna with due skepticism, as evident from the Reuters' headline: "Israel Pours Scorn on Truce with Militants."[22] And when Israel demanded that Hamas release kidnapped Israeli soldier Gilad Shalit, Reuters blamed Israel, rather than Hamas, for pushing the situation to the brink of disaster, with this headline: "Israeli Brinkmanship Puts Gaza Truce in Peril."[23]

Even Israel's basic counter-terrorist measures are blamed for causing hostilities. In December 2008, when Israel stopped Hamas from building tunnels designed to ferry lethal weapons and kidnap more IDF soldiers, Ethan Bronner of the *New York Times* cited that as evidence of Israel breaking the truce and driving "the cycle of violence to a much higher level."[24]

And writing in the *Washington Post,* former peanut farmer Jimmy Carter denounced Israel for attacking what he insanely called *"defensive* tunnel[s] being dug by Hamas."[25]

Human Shields

Shortly before the onset of the 2008/9 war (dubbed Operation Cast Lead), I got a call from a tipster down in Gaza: "Hamas has broken the ceasefire in order to set a media trap," he said. "Hamas is losing street cred and needs a PR victory. The goal is to draw Israeli fire toward Palestinian civilians, to produce a high body count and dramatic TV images. The more carnage, the better."

The Hamas strategy was two-fold: First, turn the entire population of Gaza into "human shields" by rigging Gaza with "a deadly maze of tunnels, booby traps and sophisticated roadside bombs."[26] Second, goad Israel into battle by firing thousands of rockets from densely-populated residential areas. This combination would force Israel to strike back – invariably causing civilian casualties, drawing international condemnation, and pushing the conflict to a far more radical situation.[27]

During all those years of rocket fire, Israel displayed enormous restraint – fully aware that Hamas was provoking conflict. But at a certain point, the danger to Israelis had reached ludicrous proportions: hundreds of rockets a day hit major Israeli cities like Beer Sheva, Ashdod and Ashkelon, with 7,500 rockets battering the town of Sderot alone[28] in what one reporter called "the most heavily bombed place in the world."[29] After eight years of incessant attacks, it was time to stop playing Islamic Roulette. Enough was enough.

Barack Obama acknowledged that – like any democracy under attack – Israel had no choice but to respond. "I can assure you," he said in Israel against a backdrop of Palestinian missile fragments, "if someone was sending rockets into my house where my two daughters sleep at night, I'm going to do everything in my power to stop that. And I would expect Israelis to do the same thing."[30]

Yet as the rockets rained from Gaza and tens of thousands of Israelis fled into their bomb shelters, journalists continued to call the missiles "primitive" (*Washington Post*),[31] "crude" (Associated Press),[32] "falling harmlessly" (*Seattle Post-Intelligencer*),[33] "symbolic" (BBC)[34] and "ineffective" (*Washington Post*).[35]

The media makes it sound as if these attacks were perpetrated by 10-year-old kids playing with a chemistry set. Would they be so cavalier if Mexicans were lobbing "primitive rockets" onto Houston?

In a perversion of the age-old adage, "Women and Children First," Hamas integrated Palestinian women and children into the active military effort, turning residential areas and the battlefield into one fluid frontline. Weapons were hidden in mosques, schoolyards and civilian homes;[36] rockets were launched from apartment buildings[37] and elementary schools;[38] mosque minarets served as sniper posts; and Hamas forces took refuge in and around international aid facilities like the Red Cross and United Nations.[39]

In many cases, Palestinian civilians were forced to stand on rooftops so that Israeli pilots would not bomb,[40] and those attempting to flee were forced back at gunpoint by Hamas men. In videotaped scenes, Hamas fighters are seen pulling children by the ears from place to place, fearing that without a human shield they'd be fair game to the IDF.[41] Such tactics cynically exploit the special protection afforded to civilian areas – what one newspaper called "waging war amid suburbia."[42]

This use of human shields provided a win-win for the terrorists: If Israel didn't attack, Hamas would succeed in creating a safe haven where they could operate freely. And if Israel *did* attack, then Hamas covered its bets with the knowledge that should civilians be harmed, Israel would be censured by Western journalists who can forever be relied on to report the standard line that "Palestinian casualties are Israel's fault." In the words of Bassam Eid of the Palestinian Human Rights Monitoring Group: Palestinian casualties are ultimately "in the interest of Hamas."[43]

It's a ruse we'd seen before. During the battle of Jenin, an entire lexicon of terms was invented to describe Israel's attempts to stop the terror: "disproportionate," "wanton," "indiscriminate," "catastrophic." And in

Gaza 2008/9, the media made no secret about its passion for sensationalizing the intensity and scope of Israeli actions. On the very first day of the war – Israel's first serious response to thousands of Hamas missiles – the London *Daily Telegraph* already concluded that "the attack on the Gaza strip is proof that Israel is addicted to violence."[44]

I headed down to the journalists' favorite hangout, the American Colony Hotel in Jerusalem, to try to stave off this "Israel aggression" line. I approached one group of reporters discussing the war and asked in exasperation: "What choice does Israel have but to engage Hamas in civilian areas? That's where all the Hamas fighters are located, and international law clearly states that any civilian target used for military purposes loses its immunity and becomes a legitimate target. Any other rule would grant these fighters an illogical advantage!"[45]

One of them shot back: "But you can't deny that Israel is killing Palestinian civilians."

"Actually," I said, "it is those militants hiding among civilians who are morally and legally responsible for civilian deaths." And then I pulled out a *New York Times'* clipping which reported how, after one bloody fight in which 100 civilians were killed, army officers asserted that the

> "gunmen who have opposed us have frequently used women and children and, at times, have worn women's clothing, to cover their movements and to protect them from attack. These gunmen do not wear uniforms or distinctive insignia... and they do not comply with international law. It is they who initiated the firefight and who bear ultimate responsibility for this tragic loss of life."[46]

One of the reporters gave a sarcastic grin and said, "Well, that's the kind of rhetoric I would expect from Israeli officials down in Gaza." At which point I revealed the source of this quote: the U.S. Army Central Command following a battle in Somalia.

In downplaying Palestinian culpability, the media often ignored

Hamas' use of civilian shields. When Israel bombed a mosque in the Gaza town of Jabaliya, the *Los Angeles Times* reported flatly that "Israeli jets Friday targeted a prominent mosque."[47] The *Times* mysteriously omitted the essential point that the mosque was being used as an operations center for Hamas, a staging ground for terror attacks, and a warehouse to stockpile ammunition and rockets.[48] In another instance, the *Washington Post* questioned whether Hamas facilities were indeed "military targets" – while helpfully noting that Hamas "runs an extensive social services network."[49]

Exactly which "social services" was the *Post* referring to? Hamas terrorists masquerading as doctors and nurses while soldiering out of hospitals and maternity wards?[50] The fact that one-third of Gaza homes were booby-trapped?[51] The Gaza zoo wired up with Hamas explosives, ready and waiting for Israeli soldiers to fall into the booby trap and set off a barnyard massacre?[52] Hamas placing a mannequin near a building's entrance, then rigging the mannequin to explode and bring down the building?[53] Hamas fighters shooting at Palestinian homes – then instructing residents to blame Israel for the damage?[54] A hand-drawn map showing Hamas' plans for a gasoline station rigged to explode?[55] Hamas turning Gaza's largest medical facility, Shifa Hospital, into a military command center based on the theory that it offered a safe haven from Israeli fire?[56]

Apparently, Hamas is an acronym for "Hiding Among Mosques And Schools."[57]

Gruesome Responsibility

From the first days of the Gaza war, it was clear that the media was trying to resurrect a Jenin-style "massacre" myth. Reuters placed the death count at 287 Palestinians – including 15 civilians – and then quoted Hamas leader Ismail Haniyeh that "Palestine has never seen an uglier massacre."[58] The 15 civilian deaths are regrettable, but given that 94.8 percent of the casualties were combatants, by what means does that constitute a "massacre"?

The media showed its short-sightedness by focusing solely on

Palestinian casualties, without taking a half-step back to consider who circumstances of the carnage. Take the case of Hamas chief Nizar Rayan, whose Gaza apartment-cum-weapons warehouse was cynically "protected" by the human shields of his entire family. Before hitting the target, Israel gave a humane, 30-minute evacuation warning. Yet in the same way that Rayan sent his son on a suicide bombing in 2001, he ordered his four wives and nine children to ignore the warning and be sacrificed in a vain attempt to protect the weapons cache beneath their home.[59]

Any rational person would conclude that responsibility for these deaths lies solely with Rayan himself. Yet while the *Los Angeles Times* made sure to include all the basic bloody facts – "13 members of Rayan's family, including all four of his wives, were also killed in the strike"[60] – the report completely omitted the crucial evacuation warning and the fact that the home doubled as an ammunition depot. Readers of the *Times* came away with the impression that the Israeli strike was simply an indiscriminate killing of civilians.

I got on the phone with a *Times* editor. "Imagine you're walking in downtown LA and you come across a bank robbery. The thief takes a hostage and fires from behind his human shield. A policeman then tries to stop the shooting, accidentally killing the hostage. Who do you think is responsible for that civilian casualty?"[61]

He mumbled something about "LA not being the Middle East," but he knew the right answer. The law of every country – the "felony murder" rule – would hold the bank robber guilty of murder even though the policeman fired the fatal shot. So too, in attacking legitimate military targets lodged among civilians, international law places full responsibility for any civilian deaths on the fighters who've embedded themselves.[62]

That's what I told the *LA Times* editor: With Hamas holding the Palestinians hostage, although civilians may have died via Israeli bombs, Israel didn't kill them. Hamas did.[63] For Hamas, this amounts to no less than a triple war crime: indiscriminately attacking Israeli civilians; using Palestinian civilians as human shields; and bearing ultimate responsibility for those casualties.

In an effort to reduce collateral damage, whenever Israel was compelled to bomb a Gaza target, warnings were issued to evacuate the area. One Israeli innovation is what the *New York Times* called a "knock on the roof" – a tiny projectile sent onto the corner of a roof, making a loud noise and harming no one, in order to frighten residents into leaving before the real bomb destroys the weapons cache.[64] Palestinian residents were also warned to evacuate target areas via an innovative computer system that sent hundreds of thousands of telephone calls and Arabic-language SMS cell-phone messages – a type of "reverse-911 system" whose direct personalized warnings went far beyond the traditional paper leaflets (though Israel also distributed 2 million of those).[65] Israel did all this even though it sacrificed the crucial element of surprise – not to mention offering considerably more warning than Hamas gives when blowing up Israeli buses and cafes.

So imagine my shock to click on the *Miami Herald* and find this front-page headline: "Israel Tells Gaza to Brace for a Bloodbath."[66] Had Israel really said such a thing? No. Yet the fact that it was Palestinian President Mahmoud Abbas – not an Israeli source – who referred to a "bloodbath" did not seem to faze the *Herald's* editors.[67]

In response to this blatant bias, I sent the *Herald* editor a video showing an Israeli fighter pilot honing in on a Hamas mobile rocket-launcher positioned on the flatbed of a truck. As the Israeli pilot launches a missile to take out the Hamas weaponry, the truck travels toward a group of Palestinian civilians. The video shows how – right on the spot, as the missile is flying through the air – the Israeli pilot re-directs the missile, causing it to land harmlessly in an empty field.[68]

Is this what the *New York Times* meant when it accused Israel of "excessive force and wanton killing"[69] and what Associated Press termed "disproportionate force and failing to protect civilians"?[70]

On an earlier occasion, the IDF had pinpointed the entire leadership of Hamas – 16 of the worst terrorists – together in a three-story house. A one-ton bomb would have eliminated them, yet due to the ethical factor of innocent Palestinians being killed (and the anticipated criticism in the media), the IDF hit the building instead with a much smaller bomb. Amos Yadlin, head of Israeli Military Intelligence, told the outcome: "There was a lot of dust, a lot of noise, but they all got up and ran away – and we missed the opportunity."[71]

Is this the type of activity that Bill Moyers referred to on PBS as Israel "killing indiscriminately" and "doing exactly what terrorists do"?[72]

As the media decries "excessive Palestinian casualties," it is noteworthy that during the early years of the Intifada – when Palestinians instigated a total of 17,000 attacks against Israeli targets – Palestinian injuries averaged less than one per incident. Does the media ever stop to consider how many thousands of Palestinians would be dead if Israeli forces actually did what they are accused of – what *Time* magazine called "indiscriminate machine-gun fire into crowded neighborhoods"?[73]

In Gaza, logic and facts fell by the wayside as the media repeatedly pressed the canard of Israel's use of "disproportionate force." *Today's Zaman*, the leading English-language newspaper in Turkey, sounded an apocalyptic tone with this front-page headline: "Reckless Israel Endangering Roots of Our Civilization."[74] Ethan Bronner of the *New York Times* harnessed all his creative writing skills to pack the most disdain into one description: calling Israeli actions in Gaza "a wildly disproportionate response to the rockets of Hamas, causing untold human suffering and bombing an already isolated and impoverished population into the Stone Age."[75]

With such "wildly disproportionate" descriptions, I got on the phone and asked one correspondent point-blank: "Please tell me what exactly would constitute a 'proportionate' response to eight years of Palestinian rocket fire against Israeli towns?"

He stammered for a moment, so I figured I'd help him out. "When Hamas sends 100 missiles into Israel, would it be proportionate for Israel to send 100 missiles randomly into Gaza? How about employing an anti-missile device that actually turns the Hamas projectiles right back to where they came? Or since Hamas' stated objective is to annihilate Israel, should an appropriate response be to obliterate Gaza?"[76]

Given that Israel is up against enemies who boast of their intention to commit genocide – and given that in the past, enemies of the Jews have unfortunately succeeded – this ought to grant Israel a degree of latitude in judging what is a proportionate action.[77] Israel can show tolerance, but as Mortimer B. Zuckerman observed, only to a certain point: "If Israel proves to be 10 percent ethically superior to the rest of the world, it will be a 'light unto the nations'... But if it is 50 percent better, it will be dead."[78]

The truth is that Israel's response *was* disproportionate – disproportionately *low*. According to international law expert Dr. Robbie Sabel, Israel's operation in Gaza – compared to other cases of crowded urban warfare – produced the lowest number of civilian casualties on record.[79] And speaking on BBC, military analyst Colonel Richard Kemp – surely more informed on these matters than most of us – concluded: "I don't think there has ever been a time in the history of warfare when any army has made more efforts to reduce civilian casualties and deaths of innocent people, than the IDF is doing today in Gaza."[80]

Israel was acting with moral restraint unheard of in the history of warfare. Yet the media condemnations struck with full fury: the *New Zealand Herald* called Israel's actions in Gaza "slaughter" and "butchery,"[81] while the *New York Times* described it as a "gruesome"[82] "massacre."[83]

It is said that only two things are infinite: the universe and the human capacity to err. Einstein proved the former; media coverage in Gaza confirmed the latter.

The U.N. School

As Hamas continued to operate from civilian areas, it was inevitable that – despite Israel's best efforts to avoid it – Palestinian casualties would occur. And so, on December 31, 2008, Boston University Professor Richard Landes predicted an impending "Hamas Media Massacre":

> Whether by Israeli accident or Hamas engineering, expect a spectacular civilian massacre in the coming days, followed by an orgy of Pallywood photography, amplified by a compliant Western media, and even greater fury in the streets of the Muslim and

Western world. It's in the Hamas playbook...[84]

Journalists should have been on guard for this kind of massacre myth, especially given the lessons of the battle of Jenin where reporters had jumped to invoke false comparisons to Manhattan's "Ground Zero"[85] and the horrific destruction of a "nuclear wasteland."[86]

Regrettably, the lessons were not learned. Within days of Professor Landes' premonition – and right on schedule for the Palestinian PR machine – a firefight occurred in the vicinity of a United Nations elementary school in Jabalya, Gaza.

According to U.N. official Christopher Gunness, Israeli shells hit the school where Palestinians had taken refuge, killing 43. Israel disputed the number and maintained that Hamas fighters had been using the area as a rocket-launching pad; video footage from 2007 showed Palestinians firing from the same U.N. school and carrying a rocket launcher as they fled the scene.[87] It was clear that by firing directly adjacent to the school, Hamas tried to play both sides of the coin: relying on the neutrality of a U.N. installation for protection, and then crying "foul" when Israel treated it as a legitimate military target.

As predicted, the media bought into this Palestinian ruse, labeling it "exceedingly disproportionate" and demonizing Israel in banner headlines like "Gaza's Day of Carnage"[88] and "Hell in Gaza."[89]

I quickly phoned one leading British correspondent. "Calling this a 'disproportionate response' – especially by the British media – is the height of hypocrisy," I said, reminding him of World War II when London was rocketed by the German blitz. Churchill's response was to completely flatten the German city of Dresden, dropping one bomb for every two people and causing 25,000 civilian casualties. Dresden contained no military objectives of any consequence, but was packed with civilians – and that's precisely why it was chosen.[90]

"You can't compare today's situation to the Nazis," the correspondent told me. "The British would never treat Palestinians that way."

I reminded him: "When your British government was faced with Arab riots in Palestine in the 1930s, entire villages were razed and thousands of Palestinians were killed, including hundreds hanged.[91] When Arabs assassinated a British district commissioner in Jenin in 1938, British authorities decided that 'a large portion of the town should be blown up' as punishment, and a British convoy brought 4,200 kilos of explosives to Jenin for that very purpose.[92]

"On another occasion," I continued, "British forces responded to Palestinian Arab terrorists in the village of Miar by blowing up hundreds of houses in a matter of days. The *New York Times* reported that when the British troops left, 'there was little else remaining of the once-busy village except a pile of mangled masonry.'[93] If anything, Israel's response has been tame by comparison."

He became flustered and blurted out: "You Jews have a lot of nerve preaching to us decorous and cultured British."

"You probably don't want to use that argument," I said, reminding him of the response of Benjamin Disraeli, on the receiving end of an anti-Semitic slur in British Parliament: "When my ancestors were priests in the Temple of Solomon, yours were brutal savages on an unknown island."[94]

He got the point, but the dam had burst, and other media outlets were blowing the U.N. school far out of proportion. Though the bombing of Dresden in WWII caused 500 times more casualties than the number being reported at the U.N. school in Gaza, Reuters' correspondent Douglas Hamilton equated the two incidents – and for good measure compared Gaza to the American bombing of Japan that killed 310,000 people, injured 412,000 more, and rendered over 9 million homeless.[95]

These media condemnations against Israel continued for an entire month, until finally the United Nations retracted its original accusations, concluding that no IDF shells had hit the school, and that a total of 12 Palestinians died in the incident – nine Hamas operatives and three noncombatants.[96]

The media's irresponsible spreading of battlefield rumors reminds me of the time Associated Press reported that Iraqi militants had taken an American soldier hostage and were threatening to behead him. According to AP, militants posted online the photo of "an American soldier, wearing desert fatigues and seated on a concrete floor with his hands tied behind his back."[97] AP noted that "the photo's authenticity could not be confirmed." That's probably because the whole thing was a sham, and the "American soldier" in the photo – obvious to anyone paying attention – was actually a tiny plastic action figure of the type sold at Toys 'R Us.[98]

These incidents make one yearn for the days of Woodward and Bernstein. When hot on the trail of Watergate and being fed scandalous tips, they would meet with *Washington Post* executive editor Benjamin Bradlee who would tell them, "You have to go back and check this again. In the meantime, we'll sit on it." That was a hallmark of accountable journalism.

But it doesn't work that way anymore. With the 24/7 news cycle, journalists are under intense competitive pressure, and the time-consuming process of fact-checking often takes a back seat to "getting the scoop." As Pulitzer Prize-winning columnist Ellen Goodman said, "In journalism, there is always a tension between getting it first and getting it right."[99]

I was taught a bit differently in journalism school: "It's good to be first, but it's better to be right." The media's priorities, it seems, have changed.

So with the U.N. school in Gaza – even though Israel's good name was cleared once again – it was too little, too late. As predicted, Hamas had scored its big "massacre" story. The specter of Israel intentionally targeting civilians, the imagery of wounded children, and the violation of U.N. sanctity, had all penetrated deep into the public consciousness. Within 72 hours of the alleged shelling of the school, Australian Broadcasting Corporation had already reported the event 22 times and even continued to do so months after the U.N. retraction.[100] As Patrick Martin of Canada's *Globe and Mail* somberly noted: "Most people [only] remember the headlines: 'Massacre of Innocents as... Israeli Strike Kills Dozens at UN School.'"[101]

Gigantic Photo Op

If Hezbollah's PR strategy in Lebanon 2006 was to produce images of wailing women in front of destroyed homes, Hamas took the Pallywood concept to a new level in 2009 by turning the war into one gigantic photo op – orchestrated and funded by Tehran.

About halfway through the war, I got a phone call from a graphic artist. He was designing a webpage and was having trouble finding images of missiles being launched by Hamas. "I don't understand," he said. "We're in the midst of a major international conflict being covered by thousands of media personnel. Hamas is launching 100 missiles a day, and there are 15,000 Hamas fighters roaming the Gaza Strip. Yet I can't find one single photo of Palestinian rocket crews or missiles being fired. How can that be?"

"Simple," I told him. "Gaza is a closed military zone, and Palestinians are the only ones recording the images. Hamas tightly controls the flow of information out of Gaza, and they won't allow any photos that make Palestinians look bad."[102] Or as NBC's Martin Fletcher bluntly put it: Hamas "simply threatens to kill anybody who films them" firing missiles.[103]

There was, however, no shortage of images depicting Palestinian victimhood, in what *Time* magazine termed a PR effort to "stack civilian bodies like cordwood for the cameras."[104] Associated Press fauxtographer Khalil Hamra, for example, distributed photos of a wounded Gaza man alongside three forlorn toddlers in a hospital. At first glance, the children also seem to be wounded, as the AP caption alludes: "Palestinian children and a man wounded in Israeli missile strikes are seen in the emergency area at Shifa hospital in Gaza City."[105] A closer look at the photo, however, shows the children appearing quite healthy, with no signs of injury. Perhaps they are the man's children who accompanied him to the hospital, or perhaps they were positioned for propaganda purposes. Either way, the impression from AP is of wounded Palestinian children.[106]

A lone case of deception? Far from it. A Google search turns up hundreds of Khalil Hamra's carefully crafted images of "grieving and wounded" Palestinians – work which earned him the Gold Medal Award by the Overseas Press Club.

When there weren't enough Palestinian casualties to be photographed, they merely recycled old ones. Jeffrey Goldberg of *The Atlantic* wrote how

Hamas "prevents the burial, or even preparation of the bodies for burial, until the bodies are used as props in the Palestinian Passion Play. Once, in Khan Younis [Gaza], I actually saw gunmen unwrap a shrouded body, carry it a hundred yards and position it atop a pile of rubble – and then wait a half-hour until photographers showed. It was one of the more horrible things I've seen in my life. And it's typical of Hamas."[107]

A leading character in this "Palestinian Passion Play" was Mads Gilbert, a Norwegian doctor based in Gaza who was portrayed in news reports as a respected physician, impartial to politics. Reporters never revealed, however, that Gilbert is actually a radical Marxist who – days after September 11, 2001 – declared that Muslim terrorists have "a moral right to attack the United States."[108] So readers thought nothing was amiss when the London *Times* blasted this headline quoting Dr. Gilbert from Gaza: "We're Wading in Death, Blood and Amputees. Pass it On, Shout it Out."[109] And viewers of CNN would never have suspected fraud when Gilbert appeared in a video showing a Palestinian boy undergoing "emergency medical treatment" – a dubious scene that *Time* magazine cited as an example of "suspicious-looking videos showing civilian suffering"[110] and what others called "the sort of thing you see in bad TV dramas."[111]

All this got me wondering: Who allowed news cameras there in the first place? In Western hospitals, photographers are not permitted inside emergency rooms, let alone hovering over wounded bodies. One can only imagine what an American nurse would do to a photographer who tried to pull a stunt like this. Apart from interfering with the treatment itself, videotaping medical emergencies is a gross invasion of privacy. But in Gaza, even the exigencies of medical care yield in service of Gaza's most successful export industry: images of death and disaster that demonize Israel.[112]

Supply Shortage

Another component of the campaign to discredit Israel was the concoction of a "full-blown humanitarian crisis,"[113] whereby – as described in a *New York Times* op-ed – "Fuel, electricity, imports, exports and the movement of people in and out of the [Gaza] Strip have been slowly choked off, leading to life-threatening problems of sanitation, health, water supply and transportation."[114]

While many Gazans were indeed suffering from a supply shortage, the media could not fathom the possibility that Hamas was intentionally exacerbating the crisis as a propaganda weapon against Israel – while creating a flourishing black market that filled the pockets of Hamas thugs.

Yet this is exactly what happened. During the war, Hamas repeatedly intercepted humanitarian convoys and then sold the goods to Palestinians on the black market.[115] In one incident, Palestinian gunmen attacked and seized a convoy of trucks ferrying Western aid supplies through the Kerem Shalom crossing.[116] A few weeks later, Hamas seized control of United Nations' warehouses and stole 200 *tons* of food and supplies, including thousands of blankets and 10 truckloads of flour and rice earmarked for needy Palestinians.[117] How's that for biting the hand that feeds you?

On another occasion, Hamas ordered bakery owners in Gaza to keep their businesses closed in order to create the impression of a humanitarian crisis. "Hamas is preventing people from buying bread," a Palestinian Authority official said. "They want to deepen the crisis so as to serve their own interests."[118]

When Palestinians themselves weren't doing enough to stoke the crisis, the media simply distorted statistics to overstate the problem. An op-ed in the *Boston Globe* claimed that "although Gaza daily requires 680,000 tons of flour to feed its population, Israel had cut this to 90 tons per day… a reduction of 99 percent."[119] *Globe* editors never bothered to check the stats, but you don't need to be a math genius to figure out that if Gaza has a population of 1.5 million people, the quoted figure – 680,000 tons of flour a day – comes out to nearly half a ton of flour per Gazan, per day.[120] Even NFL linebackers don't eat that much.

What was the source of these wildly inflated numbers? It turns out that the *Boston Globe* writers copied this information directly from the propaganda arm of the Egyptian government, *Al-Ahram*.[121] This absurd "statistic" then made its way up the media food chain: beginning in an Egyptian newspaper, recycled through a Palestinian activist and a Harvard "research scholar," and then published in the "respectable" *Boston Globe*. Finally, in a viral contagion, it spread across the Internet, where Israel's malevolent "reduction of 99 percent" became a well-attested fact.[122]

Another aspect of the so-called "humanitarian crisis" promoted by the media was that of an "electricity shortage." Back in 2008, when Israel reduced – *by one percent* – the supply of electricity to Gaza,[123] Palestinian Prime Minister Ismail Haniyeh convened a candlelight meeting to dramatize the "suffering and humiliation" of Gazans. Reuters' fauxtographer Mohammed Salem dutifully sent photos of this "electricity blackout" around the world. A closer look at the photos, however, reveals that the sun is blazing through the drawn curtains. In other words, the "candlelight" meeting was held in broad daylight to foist a fraud. A few days later, journalists covering a Palestinian legislative session were asked to wait a few minutes before entering the council chamber – in order to give legislators time to light their candles.[124]

Editors would have to be blind not to see the scam, but sure enough, these photos appeared throughout the mainstream media. CNN's Ben Wedeman reported on the "blackout" in Gaza City and – as images of Gazans holding candles appeared on the screen – intoned how the electric shortage has made life difficult for Palestinians. Only when CNN anchor Adrian Finnigan gave a not-so-subtle prod, did Wedeman finally admit: "I think it does appear that there is a fair amount of manipulation of the power cuts by Hamas for publicity purposes."[125]

The creative minds at Pallywood followed up with a more evocative stunt: thousands of children parading with candles through the streets of Gaza City. Though the surrounding buildings were fully illuminated, this didn't stop Associated Press from parroting the Palestinian propaganda with the headline, "Israeli Fuel Cuts Force Gaza Blackouts."[126]

Media consumers, meanwhile, were left in the dark.[127]

As part of its unusual energy policies, Hamas also created a "fuel fraud" by leaving huge supplies of gasoline and diesel lying untapped in tanks in Gaza[128] and by seizing more than 220,000 liters of fuel intended for generators.[129] When Gaza's sole power plant was shut down due to a shortage of industrial diesel needed to operate the plant, Agence France Presse cited "an Israeli blockade of Gaza";[130] Associated Press, however, told the real story: The plant "stopped operating because of a lack of fuel caused by the ongoing dispute between Palestinian political rivals."[131]

For Palestinians, dysfunction has been deliberately implemented as a media relations tools. In the eyes of the Western world, only successful states take the blame, because only they are judged as being responsible. Failed states, on the other hand, are always someone else's victim. In Gaza, there is dust and dirt; militia gangs prowling the streets; donkeys used as primitive transportation; electrical power is unreliable. Naturally these people must be the victims. So at the end of the day, Israel is demonized because Fatah and Hamas can't provide basic services – even with billions of dollars in foreign aid.

For Israel, perhaps the solution is a race to the bottom, to appear just as dysfunctional. During a crisis, major cities in Israel could repeatedly lose power. The Knesset can hold raucous debates by candlelight. Raw sewage will spill out in the street, donkeys will replace taxis, and politicians will do nothing but conduct press conferences denouncing Arab countries for making Israel live this way. An entire branch of the U.N. can be dedicated to feeding and clothing Israelis. With this, the public relations battle will finally be won. Because Israel will truly be a failed state – and thus paradoxically, in the eyes of the media, a successful state.[132]

Body Count

In January 2009, as the Gaza war dragged on, one journalist told me: "Israel is clearly using excessive force. Just look at the stats. The Palestinians are dying at a rate of 10 to 1."

I nearly choked on my coffee. "The only reason Israel has such low casualties is because it spends millions of dollars on civil defense like missile detection systems and neighborhood bomb shelters," I told him. "For Pete's sake, even playgrounds in southern Israel have been 'missile-proofed' with millions of dollars of reinforced steel.[133] Palestinians could have used their billions of foreign aid dollars for civilian construction projects, but instead they're building weapons factories and smuggling tunnels to ratchet up the violence. It's almost as if Israel is blamed for properly protecting its citizens. If a bunch of Israelis arranged to kill themselves to match the number of Palestinian casualties, would that make you happy?"

I knew I was fighting an uphill battle, especially with reporters constantly citing the infamous "body count" – that media predilection for reporting casualties as if it were a football scorecard.

During the Gaza war, when Associated Press reported 1,000 Palestinians killed versus 13 Israelis,[134] I called AP's Jerusalem bureau to complain: "By what absurd logic is justice and legitimacy measured by which side suffers the most casualties? Using this yardstick, the U.S. should be regarded as 'immoral' for its role in the 1990 Gulf War when 100,000 Iraqis died compared to American losses of 225. And during World War II, should we have seen headlines painting the Germans – who suffered 7 million casualties – as 'victims of the American aggressors' who lost 6 percent of that number?"

The AP desk editor was apparently trained not to respond to rational and reasoned complaints. "These are the numbers and we're just reporting them as fact."

I went straight to the issue: "Your body count numbers aren't even correct," I told her. "Even the doctors in Gaza are saying that Hamas has intentionally inflated these figures three-fold."[135]

Indeed, the body count has long been a propaganda tool to increase the perception of Palestinian victimhood. During the first Lebanon war, the Palestine Red Crescent (headed by Yasser Arafat's brother, Dr. Fathi Arafat) declared that 600,000 Palestinians had "become homeless in the first few days of the war." That claim was unquestioningly swallowed by journalists like NBC's Jessica Savitch, who looked into the eyes of millions of Americans and breathlessly reported, "It is now estimated that 600,000 refugees in south Lebanon are without sufficient food or medical supplies."[136] Had Savitch bothered to do a simple fact-check she'd have realized the ludicrousness of that claim, given that the *total* population of southern Lebanon was fewer than 300,000.[137]

When I pointed out to the AP desk editor that their 2009 body count was similarly overblown, she deftly shifted the focus of discussion: "Whatever the raw numbers, the significant fact is that 65 percent of these casualties are innocent civilians," she said.[138]

"Where are you getting those figures from?" I asked. "Are you really taking seriously the ridiculous Hamas claim that only a handful of its members are among those killed?"[139]

She agreed to raise my concerns at the next editorial meeting, but as I hung up, I realized that any body count that distinguishes between Palestinian fighters and civilians is inherently flawed – for the simple reason that Palestinian guerillas often do not wear uniforms or distinguish themselves in any way from the civilian population.[140] During the 2009 war, Hamas fighters would frequently hide in a tunnel, pop out to launch an attack, and then reemerge in a house or backyard[141] – disguised as an unarmed farmer, schoolteacher or even "pregnant woman."

Take the case of Anas Naim, the nephew of Hamas Health Minister Bassem Naim, who was killed during clashes in Gaza City. Following his death, media outlets reported that Naim was a medic with the Palestinian Red Crescent, "a life-saving humanitarian worker nobly killed in the line of duty." That fable lasted for a few days until I did some digging around and located photographs – posted on a Hamas Web site – showing the "medic" Naim wielding a Kalashnikov assault rifle and a rocket-propelled grenade launcher.[142]

Yet the damage was done. *The Australian*, the continent's biggest-selling newspaper, reported how "medical rescue workers, including doctors, paramedics and ambulance drivers, have repeatedly come under fire from Israeli forces" – and then for "proof" cited the selfsame Anas Naim who, as urban legend goes, was killed "on the way to rescue two wounded men in a nearby orchard."[143]

Score one for the Palestinian PR department, playing off the emotional knee-jerk reaction of Western journalists obsessed with exaggerating Palestinian casualties. During the war, Reuters reported that 280

Palestinians killed were under age 18[144] – never mentioning, however, the legions of 16- and 17-year-old Palestinians being trained in military camps and equipped with firearms;[145] nor mentioning the doctor at Gaza's Shifa Hospital who noted the majority of Palestinian casualties were young men drafted by Hamas and sent to their deaths.[146]

Just the mere fact that Palestinian children are positioned in fight zones – what one pundit calls "living camouflage"[147] – increases the danger of casualties. The *Washington Post* reported on the death of 14-year-old Jawad Harb: "He was standing on his balcony, watching the bombs. Then a big fragment penetrated his head... He died on the spot."[148] The boy's death is tragic. But why he was standing on a balcony in the middle of a war zone "watching the bombs"?

"Palestinian authorities have done nothing to stop children playing with their lives," Sam Kiley once wrote in the London *Times*. It's the Palestinian PR strategy, and they welcome the casualties. "Let's face it," said Kiley, "dead kids make great telly."[149]

Indeed, Hamas leader Abdel Azzis Rantissi explained how Palestinian casualties are the best thing that could happen to Hamas. Under the headline, "How Hamas Wins by Losing," *Time* magazine quoted Rantissi that "it didn't matter if a few dozen – or a few hundred – Hamas fighters were killed"; what the Israelis don't realize is that "when they win, we don't lose – we win, too."[150]

As the *Washington Post's* media critic Howard Kurtz observed: Palestinians "put children out there on the front lines, and therefore reap a lot of sympathy when these horrible casualties take place."[151]

Worst of all, Palestinians think it's a big joke. One video clip, widely viewed on YouTube, shows Al Arabiya reporter Hannan al-Masri live on the air in Gaza, reacting to the news that Hamas had just fired rockets from *inside the television studio building*. Was she frightened? Appalled? No, she simply gave a smirky laugh.[152]

Who can forget Palestinian leader Yasser Arafat standing before a crowd of admirers and declaring: "This child who is grasping the stone, facing the tank – is it not the greatest message to the world when that hero becomes a martyr?"[153] As Arafat adviser Bassam Abu Sharif told *Time* magazine:

> "If [Arafat] knows he will achieve a political point that will get him closer to independence and if that will cost him 10,000 killed, he wouldn't mind."[154]

Read it again. Palestinian leaders are willing to sacrifice thousands of innocent Palestinians in order to "achieve a political point."

As if to prove this, the Palestinian Authority produced a TV spot with an actor depicting Muhammad al-Dura shown romping in a child's paradise – at an amusement park, flying a kite, and frolicking on the beach. A stirring song plays, "How pleasant is the smell of martyrs, how pleasant the smell of land, the land enriched by the blood, the blood pouring out of a fresh body." The young al-Dura then exhorts viewers to "Follow me." The message: Martyrdom is the path to paradise, and Palestinian children are encouraged to be next.[155]

Yet because none of this gets reported in the mainstream media, Palestinians continue to cultivate the mantle of victimhood. When Palestinian spokesliar Hanan Ashrawi was asked on *60 Minutes* why Palestinians intentionally put their children in dangerous settings, she turned to her interviewer with angry, smug, self-righteous hypocrisy and said:

> "They're telling us we are – we have no feelings for our children? We're not human beings? We're not parents? We're not mothers or fathers? This is just incredible... I mean, even animals have feelings for their children."[156]

Instead of responding to the allegations based on solid evidence, Ashrawi spun it back as absurd beyond imagination. Palestinians boast of recruiting women and children into the war effort (as one Palestinian leader explained, "Our ability to die is greater than the Israelis' ability to go on killing us")[157] and then cry "victimhood" when taken at their word. What a neat trick.

Given that casualty numbers "favor" the Palestinians, the media jumps on this to denounce Israel. *Teen Newsweek* published a chart illustrating the number of Palestinian and Israeli children killed. The Palestinian numbers, represented in bright red, many times exceed Israeli losses, shown in a less visible yellow. But with no explanation of the circumstances – Palestinian children involved in battlefield pursuits (having been brainwashed by the 10th grade Palestinian textbook which declares: "Martyred jihad fighters are the most honored people after the prophets,")[158] versus the Israeli children killed in innocent activities like riding a public bus or eating a slice of pizza – the chart implies equivalence.[159]

At times, the media simply ignores Israeli casualties altogether. In 2009, the *New York Times' Opinionator* blog quoted journalist Jano Charbel that "the last Palestinian suicide bombing took place in November 2004."[160] Was the *Times* somehow unaware of the deadly Palestinian suicide bombings during this time at the nightclub in Tel Aviv,[161] the shopping mall in Netanya (twice),[162] the open-air market in Hadera,[163] the road near Kedumim,[164] the shwarma restaurant in Tel Aviv,[165] the shopping center in Dimona,[166] and the bakery in Eilat?[167] Doesn't anyone at the *Times* bother to fact-check?[168]

This skewed "body count" reminds me of the globetrotting Nadwa Sarandah, a one-woman Palestinian propaganda machine who went on a six-month speaking tour, telling the story of her sister who was "stabbed to death by a Jewish settler" on the streets of Jerusalem. New York's *Newsday*,[169] the *Chicago Tribune*,[170] the *Kansas City Star*,[171] and countless other newspapers reported Sarandah's tale of the allegedly "cold-blooded Israeli murderers." The media, however, had been duped: Sarandah's sister was not killed by a Jew, but rather by a Palestinian Arab named Mohammed Shalan who was arrested, convicted and sentenced to life imprisonment for the murder of Sarandah's sister – whom he had mistaken for a Jew.[172]

Then there's the time that a crowded Hamas rally in Gaza was rocked by an explosion, killing 16 people. Media outlets like the *Los Angeles Times* echoed the Hamas claim that an Israeli fighter jet had bombed the crowd.[173] (Hamas bolstered its contention by launching what it called a "retaliatory" barrage of rockets into Israel.)[174] Later investigations showed there was never any Israeli air strike; the blast was caused by Hamas mishandling their own rockets which had been recklessly paraded through a crowd of Palestinian civilians.[175] Chalk up 16 more to the bogus body count.

A 2010 report from the Ma'an News Agency claimed that a Palestinian teen had been killed by the IDF. Though Israel denied the charge, the story was picked up by the media, producing headlines like this from Agence France-Presse: "Palestinian Teen Killed as Israelis Fire on Gaza Protests."[176] The truth later emerged that not only did the teen return home alive, but his absence was due to having been detained by Egyptian forces after passing through one of Gaza's underground smuggling tunnels. (AFP issued a follow-up story that half-repeated the lie: "Gaza Teenager 'Shot Dead' by Israelis Returns Home.")[177]

This body count soars even further when factoring in the huge number of Palestinians killed at the hands of other Palestinians – colloquially called the "Intra-fada." Consider the time that Palestinians tried to assassinate Prime Minister Ismail Haniyeh by firing a rocket-propelled grenade at his home, while other Palestinians fired mortars at the Gaza compound of President Mahmoud Abbas. Or the time that three Palestinians were shot dead in Beit Hanoun Hospital in northern Gaza. Or the time that Hamas gunmen attacked the home of a Fatah security official with mortars and grenades; not finding him at home, they executed his 14-year-old son and three women instead.[178] And all these incidents happened in a *single day*.

You'd never know any of this from the Associated Press report which referred simply to "a year of violence that has killed more than 400 Palestinians and seven Israelis"[179] – a clear implication of Israeli culpability, with no reference to the high numbers of Palestinians killed in fierce intra-Palestinian fighting.[180]

Astoundingly, even suicide bombers are included in the body count.[181] Terror attacks that backfire are included, too. When one Palestinian teenager hurled rocks at Israeli-owned vehicles along a highway and was later found dead from a serious head injury, media reports presumed that Israelis had delivered a lethal gunshot wound. Incorrect. Forensic experts later determined that the Palestinian boy had been throwing rocks at Israeli vehicles when one stone hit a car tire and bounced back at high speed, striking him in the head with a fatal injury.[182]

In the cynicism that comprises Palestinian war strategy, even animals are not exempt. When Palestinians suffered a temporary shortage of suicide bombers (after all, they can only be used once), terrorists instead strapped explosives to a donkey and – as an Israeli bus passed by – detonated the bomb by cell phone. (The animal rights group PETA issued a protest, pleading with Palestinian leaders to stop the reckless killing of donkeys. As for the hundreds of Israeli civilians blown up in suicide attacks, PETA remained silent. "It's not my business to inject myself into human wars," PETA President Ingrid Newkirk told the *Washington Post*.)[183]

Israel is even held accountable for Palestinians killed in accidents. Several media outlets amplified Palestinian claims that Issam Judeh Mustafa Hamed was beaten and burned to death by Israelis near Ramallah.[184] An official PA website included Hamed's name on the list of "martyrs"; another PA website showed photos of Hamed's wounds with the claim he'd been "severely tortured, both arms and legs broken, and his skull smashed."[185] This morbid charade continued for weeks until Palestinian pathologists concluded unequivocally that Hamed had died in an auto accident.[186]

Then there's the Associated Press news photo that showed a mangled girl being carried by a screaming man, with the caption: "An Israel air strike against Islamic militants in Gaza City on Wednesday killed three people, including 5-year-old Rajaa Abu Shaban."[187] Not quite. Thanks to the work of alert media monitors, AP was forced to issue a correction that the girl "apparently died after sustaining head injuries during a fall from a swing."[188]

The day before the Gaza war outbreak, when a Hamas rocket fell short of its intended target and landed in Gaza itself, killing two Palestinian girls, ages 5 and 12,[189] the headline in the *Vancouver Sun* – "Israeli Militants

Fire Rockets and Mortars" – blamed Israel for the killing.[190] The *Sun* might have explained away the headline as a careless mistake, except that the accompanying article omitted the central point that *Palestinians* had fired the rocket. Media monitors later obtained a correction; the two girls, however, remain in the Palestinian "body count."[191]

And the list goes on and on. Traffic accidents, intra-Palestinian fighting, women and children on the front lines, Hamas missiles gone astray – in the eyes of the Media Goliath, it's all Israel's fault. When the *New York Times* published an illustrated graph comparing Israeli and Palestinian casualties, I objected that no distinction was made between Palestinian attacks which intentionally target civilians, and Israeli actions which are designed to minimize civilian casualties.[192]

This distinction is crucial. A two-year study by the International Policy Institute for Counter-Terrorism showed that 13.6 percent of Palestinian casualties were "non-combatants," compared to 69 percent of Israeli casualties.[193] One cartoon depicted this dichotomy by showing an Israeli soldier standing in front of a baby carriage to defend it against a Palestinian attacker; the Palestinian is positioned *behind* another baby carriage being used as a human shield.

When questioned about the *New York Times'* horribly misleading chart, Bill Borders of the *Times* responded with curt insensitivity: "The graphs are correct because everyone that they count as dead is in fact dead. All of them."[194]

I shook my head in exasperation. In order to paint a picture of Israeli brutality, the *Times* was using statistics as a drunken man uses lampposts – for support, rather than illumination.[195]

Notes

1. Stephen Farrell, "For Hamas, Logic Led to Cease-Fire's End," *New York Times*, December 29, 2008.
2. "IDF Map of Rocket Ranges," Israel Defense Forces Spokesperson, January 9, 2009.
3. Ibrahim Barzak, "Israeli Tanks Move Into Gaza Again; Arafat Names Premier," Associated Press, March 6, 2003.
4. Linda Halderman, "Qassam Rockets Fired on Selma... What If?", *Fresno Bee* (California), December 23, 2006.

5. "Q&A: Gaza Conflict," BBC News Online, January 18, 2009.
6. Philip Jacobson, "Code Red in Sderot: Living in the Most Heavily Bombed Place in the World," *Daily Mail* (UK), February 15, 2008.
7. Eli Ashkenazi and Mijal Grinberg, "Study: Most Sderot Kids Exhibit Post-traumatic Stress Symptoms," *Haaretz* (Israel), January 17, 2008.
8. "An Alternative to Violence?", *The Economist*, April 15, 2010.
9. Interviewed by Rick Sanchez, CNN, December 29, 2008: "It's important to add that none of these rockets actually have an explosive head on them"; interviewed by Greg Jarrett, Fox News, December 30, 2008: "It's important to note that these rockets do not have explosive heads"; interviewed by Octavia Nasr, CNN International, January 1, 2009: "It's important to recognize that these rockets do not have any explosives"; cited in Ricki Hollander and Alex Safian, PhD, "Diana Buttu: Palestinian Rockets Don't Explode!", Committee for Accuracy in Middle East Reporting in America, January 21, 2009.
10. Tony Karon, "The Homemade Rocket that Could Change the Mideast," *Time*, February 11, 2002.
11. Neil MacFarquhar, "Inquiry Finds Gaza War Crimes from Both Sides," *New York Times*, September 16, 2009.
12. Daoud Kuttab, "Has Israel Revived Hamas?", *Washington Post*, December 30, 2008.
13. Ethan Bronner, "Israel in the Season of Dread," *New York Times*, June 22, 2008.
14. Yasser Arafat invoked Muhammad's hudna in a speech at Al-Azhar University in Cairo, August 1995: "If some of you are opposed to the [Oslo] agreement or at least to some of its terms, I have a thousand objections to that document. But I must remind you, my brothers and sisters, of just one thing: The Prophet Muhammad signed the Hudaybiyah Agreement (with the Quraysh tribe)... I am not introducing anything new; all I am doing is providing you with a reminder."
15. Shoshanah Haberman, "Between Hudna and Crackdown: Assessing the Record of Hamas Ceasefires," *Peace Watch* #424, Washington Institute, June 2, 2003.
16. Jeffrey Goldberg, "Nizar Rayyan of Hamas on God's Hatred of Jews," *The Atlantic*, January 2, 2009. Mkhaimer Abusada, political scientist at Egypt's Al-Azhar University, explained: The Hamas hudna is "not of peace or reconciliation with Israel. They believe over time they will be strong enough to liberate all historic Palestine." (Steven Erlanger, "In Gaza, Hamas's Fiery Insults to Jews Complicate Peace Effort," *New York Times*, April 1, 2008.)
17. Karin Laub, "Hard-liners Edge Toward Truce with Israel," Associated Press, June 21, 2003.
18. Ibrahim Barzak, "Palestinian Officials Say They Expect Hamas Agreement on Truce Soon," Associated Press, June 23, 2003.
19. Thomas L. Friedman, "Ballots and Boycotts," *New York Times*, January 13, 2005.
20. "The Six Months of the Lull Arrangement," Intelligence and Terrorism Information Center at the Israel Intelligence Heritage & Commemoration Center, December 2008.
21. Chris McGreal, "Hamas Swaps Bullets for Ballots in Attempt to Sweep Away Old Guard," *The Guardian* (UK), January 18, 2006.
22. Jeffrey Heller, "Israel Pours Scorn on Truce with Militants," Reuters, June 24, 2003.
23. Adam Entous, "Israeli Brinkmanship Puts Gaza Truce in Peril," Reuters, February 15, 2009.
24. Ethan Bronner, "A Gaza Truce Undone by Flaws May be Revived by Necessity," *New York Times*, December 18, 2008.
25. Jimmy Carter, "An Unnecessary War," *Washington Post*, January 8, 2009. Emphasis added.
26. Steven Erlanger, "A Gaza War Full of Traps and Trickery," *New York Times*, January 11, 2009.
27. Matt Rees, "Fields of Fire," *Time*, December 10, 2000. This same tactic was used in the 1950s by Egypt: Arab terrorists would infiltrate Israeli territory, followed by Israelis military reprisals against the terrorist infrastructure – then culminating with a U.N. resolution condemning Israel for the violence. (Berel Wein, *Faith and Fate*, Shaar Press, 2001, p. 238.)

28. Haviv Rettig Gur, "Sderot Residents Welcome Ground Op After Years of Rocket-Fire," *Jerusalem Post*, January 4, 2009.
29. Philip Jacobson, "Code Red in Sderot: Living in the Most Heavily Bombed Place in the World," *Daily Mail* (UK), February 15, 2008.
30. "CNN Student News Transcript," CNN.com, January 22, 2009.
31. Editorial, "Escalation in Gaza," *Washington Post*, January 4, 2009.
32. Ibrahim Barzak, "Hamas and Israel Trade Rocket Fire Over Gaza as Violence Pushes Peace Efforts to the Side," Associated Press, January 17, 2008.
33. Sandy Tolan, "'Never Again' Gone Mad in Israel," *Seattle Post-Intelligencer*, July 12, 2006.
34. "Funerals for Gaza Beach Victims," BBC News Online, June 10, 2006.
35. Sudarsan Raghavan and Griff Witte, "Invasion Offers Benefits But Also Risks to Both Sides," *Washington Post*, January 4, 2009.
36. Erlanger, "A Gaza War Full of Traps and Trickery."
37. Rod Nordland, "Hamas and Its Discontents," Newsweek.com, January 20, 2009.
38. Ethan Bronner and Sabrina Tavernise, "In Shattered Gaza Town, Roots of Seething Split," *New York Times*, February 4, 2009.
39. Avi Issacharoff, "Hamas Puts Gazans in Danger by Drawing IDF into Urban Warfare," *Haaretz* (Israel), January 6, 2009. See "Hamas Exploitation of Civilians as Human Shields," Intelligence and Terrorism Information Center at the Israel Intelligence Heritage & Commemoration Center, January 2009.
40. Erlanger, "A Gaza War Full of Traps and Trickery."
41. "Hamas Using Boy as Human Shield," YouTube.com, July 4, 2007. A surveillance video from January 6, 2009 shows a Hamas member shooting at troops from the roof of a building. After spotting an Israeli aircraft, he goes to the building's entrance and calls to nearby civilians; a few moments later, a group of children arrive and accompany the terrorist. Another video shows a senior Hamas official walking down a street; after spotting an Israeli aircraft, he quickly accompanies an "elderly woman" – really a Hamas operative in disguise. (Yaakov Katz, "Hamas Used Kids as Human Shields," *Jerusalem Post*, March 15, 2010.)
42. Chris Link, "Photos that Damn Hezbollah," *Herald Sun* (Australia), July 20, 2006.
43. Griff Witte, "Gaza War Sparks Debate on Civilians," *Washington Post*, January 15, 2009.
44. Sean Rayment, "Israel is Addicted to Violence," *Daily Telegraph* (UK), December 27, 2008.
45. See Robbie Sabel, "Operation Cast Lead and International Law," *Strategic Assessment*, Institute for National Security Studies, Tel Aviv University, February 2009. The Geneva Convention regards it as illegal for combatants to implant themselves among civilians, and the presence of "civilians shall not be used to render... areas immune from military operations... in attempts to shield military objectives from attack." (Protocol Additional to the Geneva Conventions, Part IV: Civilian Population; Section 1: General Protection Against Effects of Hostilities; Chapter II: Civilians and Civilian Population; Article 51: Protection of the Civilian Population, June 8, 1977.)
46. John H. Cushman Jr., "Death Toll About 300 in Oct. 3 U.S.-Somali Battle," *New York Times*, October 14, 1993.
47. Ashraf Khalil and Rushdi abu Alouf, "Israeli Invasion of Gaza Anticipated," *Los Angeles Times*, January 3, 2009.
48. Isabel Kershner and Taghreed El-Khodary, "Escalation Feared as Israel, Continuing Bombing, Lets Foreigners Leave Gaza," *New York Times*, January 3, 2009.
49. Griff Witte, "Gaza War Generates Debate on Civilians," *Washington Post*, January 15, 2009.
50. Jonathan Mark, "Israel is Winning in Media, Too," *Jewish Week* (New York), January 7, 2009.
51. Ethan Bronner, "Israel Lets Reporters See Devastated Gaza Site and Image of a Confident Military," *New York Times*, January 16, 2009.
52. For good measure, these Hamas explosives were wired up to a nearby school. See "Hamas

Booby Trapped School and Zoo," YouTube.com, January 11, 2009; "IDF Uncovers Booby-Trapped School Next To Gaza Zoo," *Haaretz*, (Israel), January 11, 2009.
53. Erlanger, "A Gaza War Full of Traps and Trickery."
54. "Cosi i Ragazzini di Hamas ci Hanno Utilizzato Come Bersagli," *Corriere della Sera* (Italy), January 21, 2009; "Gazan Doctor Says Death Toll Inflated," *Ynetnews* (Israel), January 22, 2009; Ulrike Putz, "Gaza in Ruins: Who Has Won Here?", *Der Spiegel* (Germany), January 23, 2009.
55. Erlanger, "A Gaza War Full of Traps and Trickery."
56. The official Hamas "war room" was located in a bomb-proof bunker beneath Shifa Hospital in Gaza City – ironically fortified by Israel during a refurbishing project in the 1980s. See Matthew Kalman and Helen Kennedy, "Israel Threatens Gaza with 'Iron Fist' as Hamas Rejects Truce," *Daily News* (New York), January 13, 2009.
57. Steve Breen, Editorial Cartoon, *San Diego Union-Tribune*, January 10, 2009.
58. Nidal al-Mughrabi, "Israel Pounds Gaza for Second Day, Nearly 290 Killed," Reuters, December 28, 2008.
59. Rayan's son-in-law, Mahmoud Albaik, said the family refused to leave, and that moments before the attack, Rayan announced: "I want to be a martyr." (Donald Macintyre, "Israeli Bomb Strike Kills Senior Hamas Leader," *Independent* [UK], January 2, 2009.) See also Matthew Kalman and Helen Kennedy, "Israel Fells Key Hamas Strongman, Escalating Conflict; Says it's Ready for Ground Invasion," *Daily News* (New York), January 1, 2009; Jonathan Fighel, "The Mujaheed Sheikh – Dr. Nizar Rayyan: the Spiritual Mentor of Iz A-Din Al Qassam Brigades," International Institute for Counter-Terrorism, January 2, 2009; "Gaza Humanitarian Situation Report," United Nations' Office for the Coordination of Humanitarian Affairs (OCHA), January 2, 2009.
60. Ashraf Khalil and Ahmed Burai, "Key Hamas Leader Killed in Gaza Strikes," *Los Angeles Times*, January 2, 2009.
61. See Alan M. Dershowitz, "The Hamas CNN Strategy," *National Post* (Canada), January 7, 2009.
62. Yoram Dinstein, *The Conduct of Hostilities Under the Law of International Armed Conflict*, Cambridge University Press, 2004.
63. See Ralph Peters, "The Demons of Gaza," *New York Post*, January 10, 2009.
64. Erlanger, "A Gaza War Full of Traps and Trickery."
65. Ibrahim Barzak and Amy Teibel, "Israeli Assault on Hamas Kills More than 200," Associated Press, December 28, 2008; Isabel Kershner, "In a Broadening Offensive, Israel Steps Up Diplomacy," *New York Times*, January 1, 2009; Erlanger, "A Gaza War Full of Traps and Trickery"; Hanan Greenberg, "IDF to Give Better Warnings Before Attacks," *Ynetnews* (Israel), July 29, 2009; Sean Hannity and Alan Colmes, "Is Media Fair in Portrayal of Israeli-Hamas Conflict?", *Hannity & Colmes*, Fox News Network, January 7, 2009; Colonel Richard Kemp, UN Human Rights Council: 12th Special Session, October 16, 2009.
66. Ibrahim Barzak and Christopher Torchia, "Israel Tells Gaza to Brace for a Bloodbath," *Miami Herald* / Associated Press, January 11, 2009.
67. Max Socol, "World Media: Israel 'Endangers Roots of Our Civilization,'" *Jerusalem Post*, January 13, 2009.
68. Lt. Barak Raz, "IDF Vlog: Strikes Aborted to Protect Civilians," YouTube.com, January 11, 2009.
69. Ethan Bronner, "Accounts of Gaza Killings Raise Furor in Israel," *New York Times*, March 20, 2009.
70. Amy Teibel, "Israel to Probe Reported Abuse by Soldiers in Gaza," Associated Press, March 20, 2009.
71. Amos Yadlin, "Updating the Concept of War: The Ethics of Fighting Terrorism," *The Review*,

January 2005. As described by an Israeli Air Force pilot: "Sometimes, even in the air, you look at the bomb that was designated for the operation and discover that it's smaller than you thought. So I pick up a phone and ask, 'Guys, doesn't the target require a bit more?' Then they say, 'Yes, but there's a lean-to there and we don't know how many people are inside.'" (Eitan Beckerman, "IAF Pilot to Haaretz: Hamas is Using the Civilian Population in Gaza," *Haaretz* [Israel], January 18, 2009.)

72. Bill Moyers, "Bill Moyers Reflects on Middle East Violence," *Bill Moyers Journal*, PBS, January 9, 2009.
73. Rees, "Fields of Fire."
74. Kerim Balci, "Reckless Israel Endangering Roots of Our Civilization," *Today's Zaman* (Turkey), January 11, 2009.
75. Ethan Bronner, "Israelis United on War as Censure Rises Abroad," *New York Times*, January 13, 2009.
76. See Mitchell G. Bard, "The Gaza War," *Jewish Virtual Library*, January 2009.
77. Michelle Sieff, "Gaza and After: An Interview with Paul Berman," *Z Word*, March 2009.
78. Mortimer B. Zuckerman, "The PLO as Image Maker," *U.S. News & World Report*, January 22, 1990.
79. Sabel, "Operation Cast Lead and International Law."
80. Cited in Alan M. Dershowitz, "Put Hamas, Not Israel, on Trial," *Sun-Sentinel* (Florida), February 26, 2009.
81. Matt McCarten, "Palestinians Fight is a Struggle Against Apartheid," *New Zealand Herald*, January 4, 2009.
82. Kershner and El-Khodary, "Escalation Feared as Israel, Continuing Bombing, Lets Foreigners Leave Gaza."
83. Bronner and Tavernise, "In Shattered Gaza Town, Roots of Seething Split."
84. Richard Landes, "Get Me a Massacre: Up Next – the Kfar Qana of Operation Cast Lead," *Augean Stables*, December 31, 2008.
85. Mitch Potter, "'Ground Zero' of Jenin Still Site of Spin Battles," *Toronto Star*, August 2, 2002.
86. "The Silence of the Dead: Jenin Refugee Camp Like a Nuclear Wasteland after Ferocious Israeli Onslaught," *The Star* (South Africa), April 16, 2002.
87. "UN Rejects IDF Claim Gaza Militants Operated from Bombed-out School," *Haaretz* (Israel) / Associated Press, January 7, 2009. Slowly but surely, information surfaced confirming that the school had been used by Hamas as a staging ground for rocket attacks. One Palestinian witness identified Hamas mortar operator Abu Asker in the area of the school right before the attack, when Palestinian volunteers were asked to pile sandbags "to help protect the resistance fighters." (Taghreed El-Khodary and Isabel Kershner, "Israeli Shells Kill 40 at Gaza U.N. School," *New York Times*, January 7, 2009.) Two local residents confirmed that a Hamas mortar crew fired from a street near the school, then fled into a nearby crowd of people. (Ibrahim Barzak and Steve Weizman, "Israel Shells Near UN School, Killing at Least 30," Associated Press, January 7, 2009.)
88. Chris McGreal and Hazem Balousha, "Gaza's Day of Carnage – 40 Dead as Israelis Bomb Two UN Schools," *The Guardian* (UK), January 7, 2009.
89. "Hell in Gaza as Israeli Shells Kill 40 People Sheltering in a UN School," *Daily Mail* (UK), January 7, 2009.
90. Frederick Taylor, "How Many Died in the Bombing of Dresden?", *Der Spiegel* (Germany), October 2, 2008. Sir Arthur Travers Harris, head of the British Royal Air Force, explained in 1943: "The destruction of houses, public utilities, transport and lives, the creation of a refugee problem on an unprecedented scale, and the breakdown of morale, are accepted and intended aims of our bombing policy." (Cited in Randall Hansen, "An Air Raid Like Any Other," *National Post* [Canada], February 17, 2009.)

91. Charles Krauthammer, "Judging Israel," *Time*, February 26, 1990. The British put down the revolt "without mercy, without qualms." (Fouad Ajami, "Intifada: the Future as History," *U.S. News & World Report*, May 27, 2001.)
92. Raphael Medoff, "How the British Fought Terror in Jenin," *Jerusalem Post*, April 19, 2002.
93. "Palestine Rebels Declared 'On Run,'" *New York Times*, October 27, 1938.
94. See Josef Joffe, "The Lost Art of the Insult," *Time*, July 6, 2003.
95. Douglas Hamilton, "Death, Destruction and Moral Relativity," *Reuters Blogs*, July 16, 2009.
96. Amos Harel, "UN Backtracks on Claim that Deadly IDF Strike Hit Gaza School," *Haaretz* (Israel), February 3, 2009; Yaakov Katz, "World Duped by Hamas Death Count," *Jerusalem Post*, February 15, 2009.
97. "Web Site Claims GI Captured in Iraq," Associated Press, February 1, 2005.
98. "G.I. Don't Know...", Snopes.com, February 5, 2005.
99. Ellen Goodman, "Media Tolls Clinton's Political Death," *Boston Globe*, February 7, 1993.
100. Commonwealth of Australia, "Minutes of the Senate Environment, Communications and the Arts Legislation Committee," February 8, 2010.
101. Patrick Martin, "Account of Israeli Attack Just Doesn't Hold Up to Scrutiny," *Globe and Mail* (Canada), January 29, 2009.
102. See Anderson Cooper, "U.N. vs. Israel; Limited Access," *CNN Newsroom*, CNN, January 7, 2009. Similarly, throughout the entire 2006 Lebanon war, searches of the major wire services showed not one photo of Hezbollah fighters – except at funerals. ("Where Have All the Fighters Gone?", *Snapshots* blog, January 6, 2009.)
103. Martin Fletcher, "Israel and Hamas: Controlling the Message," MSNBC.com, January 5, 2009.
104. Andrew Lee Butters, "Fighting the Media War in Gaza," *Time*, January 14, 2009.
105. Photo by Khalil Hamra, Associated Press, December 27, 2008.
106. Lenny Ben-David, "Israel Attacks Hamas – Here Comes the Hamas Propaganda Attack," Lennybendavid.com, December 27, 2008.
107. Jeffrey Goldberg, "The World's Pornographic Interest in Jewish Moral Failure," *The Atlantic Online*, January 6, 2009.
108. Kristian Sarastuen, "Forsvarer Angrepet pa USA," *Dagbladet* (Norway), September 30, 2001.
109. Azmi Keshawi and James Hider, "We're Wading in Death, Blood and Amputees. Pass it On, Shout it Out," *The Times* (UK), January 6, 2009.
110. Butters, "Fighting the Media War in Gaza."
111. "A Staged Scene in a Gaza Hospital?", *Little Green Footballs*, January 8, 2009. The video depicts doctors performing "chest compressions" in the form of gentle finger-taps on the child's sternum. The video's veracity is further suspect given that it was shot by Ashraf Mashharawi, an operator of various Hamas websites, and that the supplier of the video – Paul Martin of World News & Features – admitted to distributing the tape to Western media sources before ever having viewed it. ("Gaza Video Supplier Responds," *Little Green Footballs*, January 11, 2009.)
112. "Manufacturing Disaster," *Powerline* blog, January 11, 2009.
113. "Gaza Clashes Spark 'Major Crisis,'" BBC News Online, January 6, 2009.
114. Rashid Khalidi, "What You Don't Know About Gaza," *New York Times*, January 8, 2009.
115. Rebecca Anna Stoil, "Israel Hits Back at War Crimes Charges," *Jerusalem Post*, January 26, 2009.
116. Roee Nahmias, "Report: Hamas Stealing Aid Supplies to Sell to Residents," *Ynetnews* (Israel), January 6, 2009.
117. "UNRWA Suspends Gaza Aid after Hamas Steals Food and Supplies," *Haaretz* (Israel) / Associated Press, February 6, 2009.
118. Khaled Abu Toameh, "Arab Editor Blames Hamas for Gaza Crisis," *Jerusalem Post*, January

21, 2008.
119. Eyad al-Sarraj and Sara Roy, "Ending the Stranglehold on Gaza," *Boston Globe*, January 26, 2008.
120. Martin Kramer, "Gaza Buried in Flour," *Sandbox Blog*, January 28, 2008.
121. Saleh Al-Naami, "As the World Forgets Gaza," *Al-Ahram* (Egypt), November 1-7, 2007.
122. Kramer, "Gaza Buried in Flour."
123. Isabel Kershner, "Israel Reduces Gaza's Electricity as Rocket Attacks Continue," *New York Times*, February 9, 2008.
124. Khaled Abu Toameh, "Hamas Staged Some of the Blackouts," *Jerusalem Post*, January 22, 2008.
125. "Gaza City in the Dark," CNN.com, January 21, 2008.
126. Ibrahim Barzak, "Israeli Fuel Cuts Force Gaza Blackouts," Associated Press, January 6, 2008.
127. With untold cynicism, Palestinian mortar shells damaged the power cables that transfer electricity from Israel to Gaza (Amos Harel and Avi Issacharoff, "Three Qassams Hit West Negev, Further Unraveling Gaza Truce," *Haaretz* [Israel], December 3, 2008), and rockets were fired at the Ashkelon Power Station that provides the Gaza Strip with 70 percent of its electricity. (Amir Mizroch, "Sderot's Facebook Status: Angry," *Forecast Highs*, February 10, 2008.)
128. Adam Entous, "Abbas Meets Olmert Before Seeking Foreign Support," Reuters, April 13, 2008.
129. Khaled Abu Toameh, "PA: 'Hamas is Staging Gaza Blackouts,'" *Jerusalem Post*, November 19, 2008. ("There's no shortage of fuel and as such there is no reason for a crisis.")
130. "Fuel-hit Gaza Power Plant Resumes Limited Operations," Agence France Presse, April 12, 2010.
131. "Gaza Power Plant Shuts Down Over Political Dispute," Associated Press, April 9, 2010.
132. Daniel Greenfield, "A Terrorist's Guide to Improving Israel's Media Coverage," *Sultan Knish* blog, June 23, 2010.
133. Ethan Bronner, "For Israeli Children, a Playground Shielded from Rockets," *International Herald Tribune*, March 12, 2009.
134. Ibrahim Barzak and Christopher Torchia, "Israel Shells UN Headquarters in Gaza," Associated Press, January 15, 2009.
135. Damien McElroy, "Gaza Death Toll 'Was Exaggerated by Palestinians,'" *Daily Telegraph* (UK), January 23, 2009.
136. Cited in John Corry, "TV: View of NBC Coverage of Lebanon Invasion," *New York Times*, February 18, 1984.
137. The problem seems to repeat in every generation. In reference to the 2006 Lebanon War – when less than 1,000 people died – the *Toronto Sun* reported that "5,000 people died" from Israeli air strikes. (Amy Chung, "Tempers Flare Over Palestinian Deaths," *Toronto Sun*, December 29, 2008.) CBC News reported that the 2009 "Israeli offensive killed thousands." (Harry Forestall, *Around the World*, CBC News [Canada], June 23, 2009.)
138. See Karin Laub, "Rights Group Names 1,417 Gaza War Dead," Associated Press, March 19, 2009.
139. "Hamas Plays Down Death Toll," Agence France-Presse, January 19, 2009.
140. Erlanger, "A Gaza War Full of Traps and Trickery."
141. Nordland, "Hamas and Its Discontents."
142. Dale Gavlak, "Clinton to Press Israel on Gaza as Children Suffer," *Washington Times*, February 26, 2009.
143. "Green Ideologists Taking Potshots from Their Armchairs," *The Australian*, February 18, 2009.
144. "Israel Hit at U.N. Over Palestinian Child Rights," Reuters, March 11, 2009.

145. Bronner, "Soldiers' Accounts of Gaza Killings Raise Furor in Israel."
146. Damien McElroy, "Gaza Death Toll 'Was Exaggerated by Palestinians,'" *Daily Telegraph* (UK), January 23, 2009. After the war, Gaza's Palestinian Centre for Human Rights reported that the majority of Palestinians killed were civilians. A cross-check of these names with lists of "military martyrs" published by Hamas showed that at least 342 of those classified by PCHR as "civilians" were in fact Hamas fighters. ("Preliminary Results of PCHR Gaza Casualty Analysis [Updated]," *Elder of Ziyon* blog, May 5, 2009.)
147. John Podhoretz, "Hamas Kills Its Own," *New York Post*, July 24, 2002.
148. Witte, "Gaza War Sparks Debate on Civilians."
149. Sam Kiley, "A Deadly Game," *The Times* (UK), October 19, 2000.
150. Bobby Ghosh, "How Hamas Wins by Losing," Time.com, January 6, 2009.
151. Howard Kurtz, "Is the Media Doing a Good Job Covering Violence in the Middle East?", *Reliable Sources*, CNN, October 14, 2000.
152. "Al Arabiya Studio Used as Rocket Launching Site," YouTube.com, January 2009.
153. Palestinian Authority Television, January 15, 2002; cited in "Arafat: Dead Children are the Greatest Message to the World," Palestinian Media Watch.
154. Scott Macleod, "Waiting for History to Happen," *Time*, February 26, 2001.
155. Video by Palestinian Ministry of Information and Culture; cited in Ellis Shuman, "What Do alestinians Teach Their Children?", *Israel Insider*, May 16, 2001.
156. Bob Simon, "To Be Continued...", *60 Minutes*, CBS, October 24, 2000.
157. Cited in Thomas L. Friedman, "Foreign Affairs; Diplomacy by Other Means," *New York Times*, November 3, 2000.
158. Cited in Itamar Marcus and Barbara Crook, "Palestinian Children in Combat Support Roles: Behavior Mirrors Teachings in PA Schoolbooks and Popular Culture," Palestinian Media Watch, October 17, 2004.
159. "Days of Rage," *Teen Newsweek*, October 23, 2000; cited in Tamar Sternthal, "Teen Newsweek Readers Beware!", Committee for Accuracy in Middle East Reporting in America, November 15, 2000.
160. Eric Etheridge, "Hearing What Obama Said in Cairo," *Opinionator* blog / *New York Times*, June 4, 2009.
161. Five people were killed and 50 wounded in a Palestinian suicide bombing outside the Stage club on the Tel Aviv promenade, February 25, 2005.
162. Three Israelis were killed and 90 wounded in a Palestinian suicide bombing outside Hasharon Mall in Netanya, July 12, 2005. Five were killed and 50 wounded in a Palestinian suicide bombing outside Hasharon Mall in Netanya, December 5, 2005.
163. Six people were killed and 55 wounded in an Islamic Jihad suicide bombing at Hadera's open-air market, October 26, 2005.
164. Four Israelis were killed in a Palestinian suicide bombing near the entrance to Kedumim, March 30, 2006.
165. Eleven people were killed and 60 wounded in a Palestinian suicide bombing at a shwarma restaurant near the old central bus station in Tel Aviv, April 17, 2006.
166. One woman was killed and 38 wounded in a Palestinian suicide bombing at a shopping center in Dimona, February 4, 2008. A second terrorist was killed before he could detonate his explosive belt.
167. Three people were killed in a Palestinian suicide bombing at a bakery in the southern city of Eilat, January 29, 2007.
168. "NYT Repeats an Egyptian Journalist's Lie," *Elder of Ziyon* blog, June 4, 2009.
169. Martin C. Evans, "Linked by Their Loss," *Newsday* (New York), November 1, 2004.
170. Pamela Sherrod, "Light of Hope, Light of Peace," *Chicago Tribune*, November 28, 2004.
171. "Two to Speak on Peace in the Middle East," *Kansas City Star*, May 18, 2005.

172. Becky Johnson and Lee Kaplan, "Tour Promotes Blood Libel," *Santa Cruz Sentinel* (California), June 19, 2005.
173. Laura King, "Blast at Hamas Rally Kills 15," *Los Angeles Times*, September 24, 2005.
174. Jamie Doward, "Gaza Erupts as Israel Strikes Back at Hamas," *The Observer* (UK), September 25, 2005.
175. Sarah El Deeb, "At Least 15 Killed in Hamas Truck Blast," Associated Press, September 24, 2005.
176. Sakher Abu El Oun, "Palestinian Teen Killed as Israelis Fire on Gaza Protests," Agence France-Presse, March 30, 2010.
177. Adel Zaanoun, "Gaza Teenager 'Shot Dead' by Israelis Returns Home," Agence France-Presse, March 31, 2010.
178. "President Warns of Hamas 'Coup,'" BBC News Online, June 12, 2007.
179. Matti Friedman, "Israel-Hamas Gaza Truce Goes into Effect," Associated Press, June 19, 2008.
180. Palestinian Human Rights Monitoring Group reported 888 Palestinians killed by Palestinians since the start of the Intifada. During the first Intifada as well, approximately 1,000 Palestinians were killed by other Palestinians – one-half of the total death toll. ("One Year Al-Aqsa Intifada: Fact Sheets and Figures: Collaborators," Palestinian Human Rights Monitoring Group, October 2001.) Incredibly, some even blame Israel for Palestinians killing other Palestinians: "Subject, oppressed, or embattled peoples throughout history have commonly turned on themselves. The occupation and war conditions under which Palestinians currently live readily foster internal hostility..." (Erika Waak, "Violence Among the Palestinians," *Humanist*, January-February 2003.)
181. Jean-Luc Renaudie, "Israel Readies Diplomatic Offensive as Suicide Bomber Explodes in Gaza," Agence France Presse, February 27, 2004.
182. Maayana Miskin, "Eye for an Eye: Arab Attacker Killed by His Own Rock," *Israel National News*, January 17, 2009. On another occasion, when a Palestinian boy threw rocks in the streets of Silwan (Jerusalem) and was subsequently hit by the Israeli car he was targeting, the child, Amran Mansur, recalled the incident in a way completely at odds with the explicit video evidence: "I saw a car speeding towards me... It was clear he did it on purpose. I was on the sidewalk, so there's no chance it wasn't deliberate." (Ali Waked, "Boy Run Over By Settler Says Attacked 'On Purpose,'" Ynetnews [Israel], October 9, 2010.)
183. Kerry Dougherty, "Arafat Gets Asinine Plea from PETA on Intefadeh," *The Virginian-Pilot*, February 6, 2003.
184. Jamie Tarabay, "Israel Said to Use Excessive Force," Associated Press, November 4, 2000.
185. Margot Dudkevitch, "Physicians' Group Finds Palestinian Killed in Accident, Not by Settlers," *Jerusalem Post*, November 28, 2000.
186. "Investigative Report Pertaining to the Death of Issam Judeh Mustafa Hamed," Physicians for Human Rights, November 2, 2000.
187. Photo by Adel Hana, Associated Press, August 9, 2006.
188. Associated Press, August 10, 2006.
189. "Gaza Rocket Kills Palestinian Girls," Al Jazeera, December 27, 2008.
190. "Israeli Militants Fire Rockets and Mortars," *Vancouver Sun*, December 27, 2008.
191. Mike Fegelman, "Israel at War – Canadian Media Coverage Deconstructed," HonestReporting Canada, January 4, 2009.
192. *New York Times*, March 2002.
193. Don Radlauer, "An Engineered Tragedy – Statistical Analysis of Casualties in the Palestinian-Israeli Conflict, September 2000 – September 2002," International Policy Institute for Counter-Terrorism (ICT), November 29, 2002. Similarly, while only 5 percent of Palestinian casualties are women, the Israeli numbers are six times greater.

194. See "Hammer Misses the Point," HonestReporting.com, March 15, 2002.
195. Attributed to Andrew Lang (1844–1912); cited in Susan Ratcliffe, *Concise Oxford Dictionary of Quotations*, Oxford University Press.

—10—

THE RIGHT TO SECURITY

One day at the zoo, a little girl was standing next to the lion's cage. Suddenly, the lion reached out and pulled her into the cage right in front of her screaming parents. The lion was about to devour the girl when a bystander jumped into the cage and punched the lion squarely on the nose. Whimpering from the pain, the lion let go of the girl. The man then returned the girl to her terrified parents, who thanked him profusely.

A reporter happened to witness the entire scene. "That was the bravest act of kindness I've ever seen!" he said.

"Oh, it was nothing," said the man. "I just saw this little kid in danger, and acted as I felt right."

"I notice you have an accent," the reporter said.

"Yes, I'm Israeli," the man replied.

"Well, I'll make sure this gets covered in tomorrow's newspaper," promised the reporter.

And sure enough, the next morning the local paper had this headline plastered across the front page:

"Israeli Assaults African Immigrant and Steals His Lunch"

A joke can be funny only if it contains some element of truth. The most basic function of any sovereign nation is to defend its citizens. Yet time and again, it seems that every security measure taken by Israel – no matter how reasonable and within international norms – is flipped around and used to denounce Israel.

A classic case is the 2008/9 Gaza war. Hamas drew Israel into confrontation, knowing that the eventual number of casualties – whether 10 or 10,000 – could be used to generate malicious headlines such as "Arab Leaders Accuse Israel of 'Crimes of War and Genocide'" (Agence France Presse)[1] and "Israel to Defend Troops Accused of War Crimes" (Associated Press).[2]

Even if these contemptuous labels don't stick, a seed is planted every time readers open up the *New York Times* to find that "human rights groups are crisscrossing Gaza, documenting what they believe will form the basis for war crimes proceedings,"[3] or the *Washington Post's* reference to Israel's "blatant violation of the laws of warfare" and "the commission of war crimes."[4] Irrespective of the eventual outcome, Palestinians achieve victory by raising these ideas in public discourse – shifting the demonization of Israel from an extremist view to the realm of acceptable opinion.

The Guardian crossed the line into outright activism with a memo to bloggers and website owners asking them to promote the *Guardian's* documentary films highlighting Israel's alleged war crimes in Gaza – hoping to "add weight to calls this week for a full inquiry into the events."[5]

What is shocking is how easily the media echoes these calls, with nary a thought to their validity. I posed to one magazine correspondent the idea that any discussion of war crimes must be comparative and contextual: If Russia did not commit war crimes when its soldiers massacred tens of thousands of Chechnyans in an aggressive war, on what basis can Israel be accused of *accidentally* killing a far fewer number of human shields in a defensive effort to stop rocket attacks from Gaza?[6]

He mumbled something about Chechnya being an exception due to the complex political, military and social realities, while the Israeli-Palestinian conflict is somehow more "black and white."

"Nice try," I said, "But how do you explain that no war crimes trials have convened in Pakistan, Afghanistan, Rwanda, Darfur, Sri Lanka, Zimbabwe, Congo or the other places where civilians are systematically targeted in military and terrorist campaigns? So why does the media take seriously the calls for an "international war crimes trial against Israel"?

He heard my point, but this didn't stop Irish Public Broadcasting from posing precisely this question in an online poll: "Should Israel be investigated for war crimes over Gaza?"[7] Note the wording of the question: Not an angst-ridden discussion of what truly occurred in Gaza, but rather the presumption that Israel committed war crimes – the only question being whether an investigation would be prudent, as indicated by one of the response choices: "Only if it doesn't hurt the peace process."

Of course, this campaign to delegitimize Israel does not arise in a vacuum. Much of it derives from international bodies like the United Nations that are so virulently anti-Israel. Consider: 126-0. No, that's not the score of the Knicks' latest loss. Here's what 126-0 really means: Since 1947, there have been 126 U.N. resolutions dealing specifically with Palestinian refugees. Not one of these resolutions makes reference to the plight of the comparable number of Jews (856,000) displaced from Arab countries during the same period.[8]

In 1975, in what Kofi Anan called the "low point" in U.N. history, the General Assembly passed Resolution 3379 equating Zionism with racism. Israeli Ambassador Chaim Herzog said that "Hitler would have felt at home listening to the UN debate."[9] The canard persists till today; a 2009 front-page article in the *New York Times* opened with the line: "Israel, whose founding idea was branded as racism by the United Nations General Assembly in 1975..." The *Times* made no mention that the U.N. vote had been pushed through by despots and was rescinded 25 years later.[10]

Whenever I visit U.N. headquarters and see the engraved words of the Jewish prophet Isaiah – "They shall beat their swords into plowshares"[11] – I am reminded of the U.N.'s original, noble concept to promote world peace and justice. Yet the entire apparatus has been hijacked by a bloc of Arab, Muslim and dictatorial Third World forces who abuse the mechanism of democracy to undermine the trust and goodwill upon which an effective international body depends. These nations constitute an automatic voting majority, the result being that Israel is condemned by more U.N. resolutions than any other nation in the world.[12] The only countries that regularly support Israel at the U.N. are that troika of world powers: the United States, Micronesia and the Marshall Islands.[13] In the words of Abba Eban, former Israeli Ambassador to the U.N.: If the U.N. "introduced a resolution declaring that the earth was flat and that Israel had flattened it, it would pass by a vote of 164 to 13 with 26 abstentions."[14]

Here's how this translates into slanted media coverage: Palestinians are able to push their agenda aided by the "halo effect" – the phenomenon whereby the U.N., due to its humanitarian focus, is insulated from scrutiny and regarded above reproach. No matter how biased the U.N. may be, the media refuses to call its bluff. Every U.N. condemnation of Israel treated as major "news," producing an ad nauseum wave of headlines:

"U.N. Condemns Israel's Actions on Palestinian Territories"[15]

"U.N. Economic Panel Censures Israel"[16]

"U.N. Condemns Israel's Incursion into West Bank"[17]

"U.N. Denounces Israel's Use of Force"[18]

"U.N. Condemns Israel's Deadly Raid on Qana"[19]

"U.N. Demands Probe into Israel's Strikes on Gaza Schools"[20]

"U.N. Condemns Israel's Deportation of Palestinians"[21]

"U.N. Head Slams Israel"[22]

Beyond the mere vilification of Israel, this phenomenon has a more sinister side. U.N. resolutions – bolstered by a supportive media – have the effect of granting Palestinians a license for terror. One U.N. resolution endorsing Palestinian resistance by "all available means, including armed struggle"[23] was cited by Palestinians as justification for setting off bombs in Jerusalem.[24] On another occasion when the U.N. denounced Israel, Yasser Arafat quipped, "This resolution comprises the liquidation of the Zionist existence."[25]

Before you know it, this warped perspective is channeled through the despot-dominated U.N. and flowing right back into the Western mainstream.

Goldstone Report

The potency of this halo effect was in full force in September 2009 with the Goldstone report – the U.N. Human Rights Council's "fact-finding mission" on the war in Gaza – where accusations of "excessive force" became a prelude to more ruthless charges.[26] The report, named after its principal author, South African jurist Richard Goldstone, devoted the bulk of its 575 pages to charging that Israel had intentionally targeted Palestinian civilians, with the suggestion that Israeli soldiers be prosecuted in international courts for "war crimes."[27]

Incredibly, nowhere does the report hold Hamas responsible for the "war crimes" of relentless suicide bombings and rocket attacks against Israeli civilians; instead, nebulous "Palestinian armed groups" are named.[28]

When the Goldstone report hit cyberspace, I quickly compiled a list of its key failings:

- All four of the commission members had denounced Israel's Gaza operation even before beginning their "investigation." Three members – Goldstone, Hina Jilani and Desmond Travers – had signed a letter stating that "events in Gaza have shocked us to the core,"[29] while the fourth, Christine Chinkin, had already gone on public record labeling Israeli actions in Gaza a "war crime."[30] Chinkin's preordained conclusion did not bother Goldstone; he was "satisfied that she's got a completely open mind."[31]

- Despite the preponderance of proof that Hamas used Palestinian civilians on the front lines (Hamas legislator Fathi Hamad spoke proudly of how Hamas "creates a human shield of women, children, the elderly"),[32] the Goldstone report "found no evidence" of this.[33] Incredibly, the report also found no evidence that Palestinian hospitals, schools and mosques were used for military purposes, nor that "Palestinian armed groups engaged in combat in civilian dress" – despite widely available aerial photographs and videos to the contrary. Later, when Goldstone was confronted with this mass of evidence, he played dumb, feigning regret that this information was not "shown to us during the investigation."[34] Meanwhile, commission member Desmond Travers declared, "I do not believe the photographs" and rejected them as "spurious in the extreme";[35] he took umbrage that these "charges reflect Western perceptions in some quarters that Islam is a violent religion."[36]

- The Goldstone commission accused Israel of "shooting children in front of their parents,"[37] yet failed to explain why – if the IDF was so intent on killing Palestinians – it took the extraordinary precautions of sending millions of warning leaflets and Arabic-language phone calls,[38] aborting missile strikes to prevent civilian casualties,[39] opening a medical clinic for Palestinians on the Gaza border,[40] and transferring tons of humanitarian aid during the conflict.[41]

- The report whitewashed the years of Hamas rocket-fire against Israeli towns. The first time the word "Hamas" appears regarding rocket attacks (outside the footnotes) is all the way down on page 453. Incredibly, Hamas is credited – not with inflicting 10,000 rocket attacks – but rather with allegedly calling on other armed groups to *stop* firing rockets "in the interests of the Palestinian people." With no sense of irony, the report glowingly describes Hamas as employing "cultural resistance" and eschewing rocket attacks in favor of "cultural initiatives and public relations."[42] As Hamas leader Musa Abu Marzuq rejoiced, "The report acquits Hamas almost entirely."[43]

- The Goldstone report relies heavily on the "credible testimony" of Hamas operatives like Gaza policeman Islam Shahwan, who previously foisted the wild accusation that Israel "destroys the Palestinians' social infrastructure" by handing out aphrodisiac chewing gum to Arab youth.[44] And when Hamas official Muhammad Abu Askar told the Goldstone panel that his house had been "unjustly" blown up by Israel, nobody bothered to check that Abu Askar's house had been used to stockpile weapons including Iranian-supplied Grad rockets, and that Abu Askar's son was working for the military supply unit of Hamas. Instead, Goldstone naively concluded that Abu Askar's home was of an "unmistakably civilian nature."[45]

- The report draws a fictitious distinction between Hamas and "Palestinian armed groups" – as if Hamas was somehow on the side of preventing attacks on Israel. With a straight face, Goldstone asserted that the Gaza police force is a "civilian" agency, and quoted Hamas spokesmen that they "had nothing to do, directly or indirectly, with al-Qassam Brigades or other armed groups, and had no knowledge of their tactics."[46] This absurd conclusion was directly contradicted by the disclosure of Palestinian cabinet minister Fathi Hamad that Hamas "coordinates with all the resistance factions" (i.e. terror organizations) and directly assists them "to carry out every aspect of their jihadist missions."[47]

Having so fully exonerated Hamas, Goldstone, not surprisingly, became a folk hero in Gaza, where gift shops began marketing souvenir keffiyeh headscarves embroidered with the name "Goldstone."[48]

One rationale why the report was so terribly one-sided is that Hamas security men often accompanied Goldstone's team in Gaza, hampering the ability of Palestinian witnesses to freely describe the Hamas reign of terror.[49] Initially, Goldstone "categorically denied" being guided by Hamas officials,[50] but when photos emerged of him accompanied by Hamas spokesman Ghazi Hamad, Goldstone confessed to having worked under intimidation: "I was afraid to enter Gaza. I had nightmares that Hamas would kidnap me."[51]

Exactly how lopsided was the Goldstone report? Using special software, the report's top 250 words can be displayed in a graphic format; the size of each word indicates how often it is used. Even with a magnifying glass, it is nearly impossible to spot the word "Hamas."[52]

If moral ineptitude were a competitive sport, the Goldstone committee would win the gold medal. Yet despite these fundamental flaws – obvious to anyone who bothered to read the report – the media accepted it, no questions asked:

- "U.N. Inquiry Sees Gaza War Crimes; Israel Chastised" – *New York Times* (front page)[53]
- "Israel Committed 'War Crimes' in Gaza: UN Probe Chief" – Agence France Presse[54]
- "UN Report Claims Israel Committed War Crimes" – *Belfast Telegraph*[55]
- "Israel Looks to Fend Off Prosecution of War Crimes" – Associated Press[56]
- "UN Says Israel Should Face War-Crimes Trial Over Gaza" – *The Independent* (London)[57]

The report was so packed with bias that I couldn't conceive how journalists so unthinkingly played along.[58] So I phoned one Jerusalem correspondent and invited him to dinner to discuss the report. Over a plate of Middle Eastern kebab (spicy grilled meat brings out the fighter in me), I asked him: "Let's take a step back and examine the source of these charges. Imagine that a group like the U.S. Congress was accusing Israel of war crimes. Do you think that should be taken seriously?"

"Of course," he said. "Congress is a credible, democratically-elected body, with a longstanding reputation for balance and fairness."

"Okay," I said. "What if Islamic Jihad would make these same accusations – should the media report that at face value?"

"Of course not," he said. "They're a radical, violent group sworn to Israel's destruction, and reporters would need to qualify any such statements accordingly."

Which brought me to my point about the sponsor of the Goldstone report, the U.N. Human Rights Council (HRC).[59] The average reader assumes this to be an impartial and credible organization – but the truth is far different. The HRC has condemned Israel more often than it has condemned the U.N.'s other 191 member states *combined*. At annual meetings of the HRC, Israel is the only country in the world whose human rights record is examined as a permanent feature of every council session.[60] As of 2011, 44 percent of HRC resolutions have targeted democratic Israel; by contrast, resolutions against Iran totaled one percent.[61]

For eight years, the sole task of John Dugard, a human rights official at the United Nations, was to condemn Israel: "I shall not consider the violation of human rights caused by Palestinian suicide bombers. Nor shall I consider the violation of human rights caused by the political conflict between Fatah and Hamas... My mandate precludes me from examining them."[62]

The poor folks at the (mistakenly-named) Human Rights Council are so overworked dealing with Israel's "crimes against humanity" that they haven't a spare moment to condemn truly abhorrent human rights violators like Nigeria, Saudi Arabia, China or Cuba. Undoubtedly the reason for this is because – unbelievably – Nigeria, Saudi Arabia, China and Cuba themselves sit on the Human Rights Council.[63] What's next: Jack the Ripper on the Commission for the Protection of Women?[64]

It's even worse. Richard Falk, the current HRC investigator for the Palestinian territories, is the same "human rights" expert who

- supported the Ayatollah's revolution in Iran, writing in the *New York Times* that Khomeini "may yet provide us with a desperately-needed model of humane governance for a third-world country."[65]
- advocates Palestinian suicide bombings as the "only means still available by which to inflict sufficient harm on Israel so that the struggle could go on."[66]
- contends "there is a lot of grounds for suspicion" that 9-11 was an "inside job" most probably by neocons (read: Jews).[67]
- has "no reluctance" comparing Israel's treatment of Palestinians with the genocide in Darfur, and sees no "irresponsible overstatement to associate the treatment of Palestinians with the criminalised Nazi record of collective atrocity."[68]

Sometimes it's hard to distinguish between the HRC and the HPR – Hamas Public Relations department. That's precisely the problem with the Goldstone report, I told this journalist over dinner. Given that the "halo effect" means the U.N. is perceived as impartial, any objective news story must provide one or two background sentences to put HRC's credibility (or lack thereof) into perspective. The failure to do so is a serious omission.

But it goes deeper than this. The HRC only maintains its veneer of credibility due to the media's perpetual blind spot: Where the U.N. is involved, Israel's guilt is always taken for granted. Thus the media, by presenting the Goldstone report and other U.N. positions as "objective," actually produces the double-barreled bias of intensifying public misperceptions even more.

My dinner guest peered over his kebab-filled pita and said, "I think you're taking all this too seriously. It could be that Goldstone affects some public opinions polls, but at the end of the day this conflict comes down to the negotiating table."

"Actually, media coverage of Goldstone has a direct, adverse affect on the possibility of peace," I said. "In 2005, Israel took the tangible risk of evacuating Gaza with the assurance that if Palestinians turned violent, the world would understand Israel's need to defend itself. Yet when Gaza turned into a lawless enclave of Hamas-led, Iranian-backed rocket barrages, the world did not react to Israel's response with support and understanding, but rather with accusations of 'war crimes.' This sows mistrust between Israel and the international community, discouraging Israel from future withdrawals – especially West Bank lands that lie adjacent to Israel's major population centers. In other words, Goldstone leaves Israelis asking themselves: If we're damned when we do and damned when we don't, why are such sacrifices worth it?"[69]

The correspondent began to look anxiously at his watch and said, "I need to get going. Anything else?"

"Actually, yes," I said. "Goldstone also creates an obstacle in the global battle against terror. By condemning Israel's response to these rockets, the U.N. essentially grants immunity to Hamas, setting a dangerous precedent for any democracy trying to defend itself. This year, it may be Israel as the target of international kangaroo courts designed to strip its right to self-defense. Next year, it may be Washington that is forced to defend its actions in Afghanistan – not behind closed White House doors – but at an arraignment at The Hague of U.S. generals and political leaders charged with 'war crimes' so serious that even a Nobel Peace Prize couldn't secure President Obama a get-out-of-jail-free card. What goes around comes around."[70]

He got up to leave, but I offered one parting shot: "It's a good thing the United Nations wasn't around during World War II. Just imagine how Goldstone and the media might have condemned the Allies for the bombing of German cities – while glossing over the actions of 'unidentified German groups' responsible for abuses such as incinerating Jews. The recommendation, I'm afraid, would have been that FDR and Churchill be tried for war crimes, with Adolf Hitler invited to testify against them."[71]

The inescapable conclusion is that condemning Israel for the "crime" of self-defense is not only a Palestinian PR weapon, but also part of its military effort. Indeed, one journalist suggested to Richard Goldstone that the report wipes out Israel's ability to ever again say, "We were under attack... we have the right to self-defense."[72] In other words, the HRC promotes the perverse notion that for Israel, international law is akin to signing a suicide pact.[73]

The end of this story is that 18 months later, Goldstone delivered a belated exoneration of Israel on the pages of the *Washington Post*, stating clearly that Palestinian "civilians were not intentionally targeted as a matter of policy." Goldstone termed his work a "mistaken enterprise" and acknowledged that his employer in this fiasco – the U.N. Human Rights Council – has a "history of bias against Israel [that] cannot be doubted."[74]

The retraction brought relief, but one couldn't help wonder at the choice of venue. Goldstone had written previous op-eds in the *New York Times* defending his report,[75] and none in the *Washington Post*. So why not publish the retraction in the same forum used for its defense?

The answer to this mystery is that Goldstone had indeed approached the *Times* with an op-ed, but – due to the *Times'* apparent unwillingness to participate in the exoneration of Israel – it was rejected.[76] To wit: The *Times* relegated news of Goldstone's retraction to page 10, and tried to discredit the retraction by emphasizing that other human rights groups plan "to take further action on the Goldstone report's findings to ensure justice for the war's victims."[77]

For its part, the London *Guardian* simply denied there was any retraction, claiming that Goldstone's original report "did not in fact claim that Israel set out deliberately to murder civilians." Anyone with an Internet connection was able to ferret this out as a bold-faced lie: Paragraph 46 of the Goldstone report clearly censures Israel for "the direct targeting and arbitrary killing of Palestinian civilians."[78]

In the poisoning of Israel's name, Goldstone gave succor to terrorists, encouraging them to believe they could kill Israelis not with mere impunity, but with active international support. Yet after causing such irreversible damage and putting innocent lives at risk, even Goldstone's retraction fell short of his moral and legal obligation: to directly apologize to Israel and actively work to undo the damage he caused.[79]

Checkpoints

Every time I travel from my home in central Israel to Jerusalem, I have to pass through two Israeli army checkpoints. There is frequently a long line of cars waiting for inspection, and it slows down my commute considerably. Especially at the end of a long day when I'm tired and hungry, it's a big inconvenience – but one that I understand is necessary. Given that Israel has been the target of over 1,000 attempted suicide bombings in the past decade, these checkpoints have proven highly effective in keeping the terrorists at bay.

Beyond this are the metal detectors I have to pass through every time I enter a bank, post office, or pick up a carton of milk at the supermarket. No aspect of Israeli life is immune: armed guards accompany every school trip, restaurant bills come with an added "guard surcharge," and even wedding invitations assure guests that the event will be secured by armed guards.[80] These measures to stop Palestinian terror are time-consuming and expensive – costing Israel an estimated $30 billion annually, or 15 percent of total GDP.[81]

In a perfect world, one would expect dozens of media reports detailing how Palestinian terror has caused Israel this inconvenience and cost. Yet in a classic case of double standard, the media turns the tables by focusing exclusively on the "time-consuming and often dangerous" hardships that Palestinians have to endure at checkpoints (*Time* magazine),[82] which the media says exemplify Israel's "use of force in the struggle" (*New York Times*)[83] and are "manned by young and sadistically aggressive Israeli soldiers" (*New Zealand Herald*)[84] who "routinely humiliate and harass Palestinians" (*The Guardian*).[85]

Are the checkpoints really as despicable as the media makes them out to be? When journalist Tom Gross escorted the editors of London's *Guardian* newspaper across a checkpoint near Bethlehem, they witnessed "with their own eyes that the Israeli soldiers were courteous and polite to Palestinians. They saw that Palestinians were allowed to cross the checkpoint, both by car and on foot, in a matter of seconds."[86]

So how did these same journalists later describe the experience? "Endless humiliating queues waiting to pass through Israeli army checkpoints."[87]

Typical of the exaggerated reporting was a front-page *Washington Post* article claiming that "at least 83 Palestinians seeking medical care have died during delays at checkpoints."[88] The *Post* cited the Palestinian Human Rights Monitoring Group (itself a dubious source) which listed 83 deaths anecdotally associated in any imaginable way with checkpoints, not necessarily due to delays in medical care. For example, the list includes Yusef Mohammed Abu-al-Tabeekh, a 78-year-old man who "died at al-Hamra military checkpoint in the Jordan valley," apparently of natural causes. Yet the *Post* misleadingly presented this and other deaths as due to "Israeli checkpoint delays."[89]

It seems that whenever an incident occurs anywhere near a checkpoint, the media pins the blame on Israel. Associated Press, under the headline "Palestinian Newborn Dies, Woman Shot," described how "a Palestinian woman in labor was barred from passing an Israeli military checkpoint for two hours, giving birth in her car to a baby boy who died before reaching a medical clinic."[90] The way AP reported it, Israel maliciously caused the death of the Palestinian newborn.

The next day, however, Palestinians confirmed that Israeli soldiers had not prevented the woman from passing the checkpoint, and AP had to sheepishly admit they'd been taken in by a scam: "A doctor said the boy suffocated because the family members assisting in the birth did not know how to keep his airway open."[91] AP's misreporting proved once again the adage of "never confuse newspapers with the news."

And then there's the classic case of Violin Man. The *Washington Post* described how Israeli soldiers at a checkpoint "ordered a Palestinian to open his violin case and play for them"[92] – giving readers the impression that soldiers abused the man for their own amusement. BBC, for its part, cited the incident as proof that "border controls impose dangerous and humiliating restrictions on their freedom of movement."[93] Reporters apparently never bothered to view the video of the event, which shows soldiers casually going about the business of inspections while the man calmly plays.[94]

Further, media outlets mysteriously chose to omit the crucial reason why soldiers so carefully checked this violin in the first place. When a Palestinian terrorist perpetrated the heinous suicide bombing of Jerusalem's Sbarros pizzeria in 2001 – using a guitar case to transport his bomb – it became standard security procedure to check musical instruments for explosives. Frimet Roth, whose teenage daughter was murdered at Sbarros, explains the necessity of such vigilance: "One day, an IDF soldier on checkpoint duty, distracted and intimidated by those camera-clicking, note-scribbling activists, is going to cut short a routine security check to appease them. The results might be very far from routine."[95]

And while the media decries checkpoint inconveniences, rarely do they highlight the hundreds of cases where checkpoints have succeeded in preventing Palestinian terrorists from trying to smuggle bombs and suicide belts hidden in the most creative of places: in truckloads of food, children's backpacks, baby strollers, computers, and even explosive underwear.[96] At one West Bank checkpoint, a Palestinian truck was caught carrying 6.5 tons of potassium nitrate – disguised in sugar bags marked as "humanitarian aid provided by the European Union." The chemicals were headed for terrorists in Gaza to be used in producing the rocket fuel that forms the core of Qassam missiles.[97]

In many cases where Israel has eased checkpoint restrictions for humanitarian reasons, Palestinians have turned these gestures around for terror. One Palestinian woman, nine months pregnant with her tenth child, obtained a permit to enter Israel for medical treatment; her plan was to carry out a suicide bombing at a restaurant in Tel Aviv.[98] Another Palestinian woman bypassed the metal detector at a Gaza checkpoint by claiming she had surgical plates in her legs; she then blew herself up at the crossing, killing four Israelis.[99] Wafa al-Bis, a burn patient from Gaza who had been treated several times by the Israeli National Skin Bank, was caught at a checkpoint wearing a suicide belt of high-explosives; she intended to blow herself up at the outpatient clinic of the same hospital that had saved her life.[100] Yet despite these and other abuses, Israel continues to provide thousands of Palestinians with "humanitarian permits" for medical care in Israeli hospitals.[101]

Is this what Bob Simon of *60 Minutes* was referring to when he bemoaned that Palestinians feel "corralled" due to "humiliating delays at checkpoints and roadblocks"?[102]

Even ambulances – that international hallmark of neutrality and non-violence – are abused by infiltrators. Wafa Idris, the first Palestinian female suicide bomber, worked for the Palestinian Red Crescent and was assisted in her terror attack by ambulance driver Mohammed Hababa. Red Crescent credentials – and perhaps even a Red Crescent vehicle itself – provided them with easy passage through IDF roadblocks en route to her bloody bombing in downtown Jerusalem.[103]

In another instance, a Palestinian Red Crescent ambulance driver was caught transporting an explosive belt, hidden under the stretcher upon which a Palestinian boy was lying.[104] Reuters Television filmed an Israeli police robot removing the bomb belt from the stretcher and carrying out a controlled explosion;[105] predictably, the PA later claimed that Israel planted it there to make them look bad.

After one journalist ran a series of one-sided articles lambasting the checkpoints, I presented him with the following scenario:

> A 19-year-old soldier is commanding a checkpoint. An ambulance arrives, transporting a woman who is seemingly pregnant. The woman appears to be in pain and her husband is highly anxious. But suicide bombs have been previously disguised as "pregnancies," and the IDF has a specific warning that a Palestinian ambulance is en route carrying a terrorist and explosive belt for a

suicide attack. It is a hot day and there is a long line of cars. The soldier's commanders are instructing him on a two-way radio to "examine each ambulance thoroughly until we find the terrorist." To complicate matters, a news video crew is present.

The soldier has to make an incredible number of decisions in a very short time. He knows that if he lets the ambulance through and it contains a terrorist, innocent people will die and he will have failed in his mission. On the other hand, if there is not a terrorist in this particular ambulance, and he delays a pregnant woman from reaching a hospital, the mother and baby could be endangered.[106]

So I asked this journalist the pointed question: What would you do?
"It's not my job to speculate about theoretical cases," he said.
In fact, these are real cases happening all the time – and the media does a horrendous job of providing proper context. When two Palestinians were shot by Israeli troops at a checkpoint, Associated Press gave precise details of the Palestinians' ages, names, background, medical condition, and a graphic description of the bloody wounds. Yet readers had to wade 250 words deep into the article to discover that the Palestinian vehicle had run a barricade, ignored warning calls, and then attempted a reverse detour around the checkpoint. Only at the very end of the article did AP reporter Mohammed Daraghmeh provide the most salient point of context – that six Israeli soldiers had been killed in a similar checkpoint incident just days before.[107]

This type of reporting, when compared to coverage of U.S. checkpoints in Iraq, reveals a gross double standard. When five American soldiers were killed by an Iraqi suicide bomber at a checkpoint outside Najaf,[108] the U.S military was instructed to shoot and kill anyone disobeying orders at a checkpoint. Within two days, this policy was implemented when a van failed to stop at a checkpoint near Najaf; U.S. soldiers opened fire, killing seven Iraqi women and children. The civilian deaths were regrettable, but given the volatile circumstances, the American policy was justified.

Indeed, there was nary a peep from the media questioning the ethics of that incident. The *New York Times* headline read: "Failing to Heed G.I.'s, 7 Iraqis Die at Checkpoint."[109] Note how the *Times* placed blame on the victims (for "failing to heed" the warning), and rather than ascribe the killings to U.S. soldiers, stated the casualties in passive terms ("Iraqis Die"). In its report, the *Times* made no moral judgments against the soldiers, and actually praised them for "following established procedure" and doing "the right thing."[110]

Could we ever imagine the *New York Times* reporting an Israeli checkpoint incident in such an approving way?

The *Los Angeles Times* went one step further, effusing sympathy and understanding for "the bewildering predicament American troops find themselves in as Iraqi forces disguise themselves as civilians, women are used as human shields, and any vehicle driving down the road could be a suicide bomb."[111]

Another *LA Times* report even blamed Iraqi leaders for the checkpoint deaths: "The blood is on the hands of the regime for their decisions and their willingness to use their population this way," said U.S. Brig. Gen. Vincent Brooks. "If there's a question of morality, it really should go back to the [Iraqi] regime. While we regret the loss of any civilian lives, at this point they remain unavoidable."[112]

Has the media ever entertained the idea that Palestinian leaders are to blame for difficulties endured by Palestinians at checkpoints? Indeed, in the years when Israel was in full control of the territories – before suicide bombers were terrorizing Israel – there were no roadblocks, and Palestinians could move freely throughout the country. The checkpoints are not gratuitous acts of unkindness by Israel, nor are they artifacts of occupation. Only because of the Palestinian terror war was Israel forced to implement such security measures. In other words, Palestinians have brought this on themselves.[113]

It is also instructive to note how Palestinian security guards handle similar situations. In 2007, when a Palestinian man refused to stop at a

Palestinian roadblock in the West Bank city of Qalqilyah, Palestinian Authority security forces showed no mercy, shooting the man dead along with a 5-year-old boy. Predictably, there were no *New York Times'* editorials or United Nations' resolutions condemning the action. In fact, the incident was ignored by the media; a LexisNexis search produced only one brief mention – in the Qatar News Agency.[114]

The evidence of a double standard is unmistakable. The media, it seems, doesn't really object to these checkpoint tactics – unless it is Israel manning the station.

When I caught one journalist doing just that, I challenged him: "It's okay to hold Israel to a higher standard. Do you know why? Because the Jewish people have always held ourselves to a higher standard. But it is not okay to condemn Israel for actions that everyone else in the world – whether the U.S. or NATO – is doing, has done, and would do in the same situation. If you want to hold Israel to a higher standard, then state clearly: 'We oppose these actions by the Jewish state because – as the torch-bearers of the monotheistic moral message – the world expects more.' If that's your thinking, I'm fine with that. But be upfront about it. Otherwise it's a libel against Israel, an unfair double standard."

Security Fence

When it comes to delegitimizing Israel's right to self-defense, another favorite target is the West Bank security barrier that separates some Israeli and Palestinian population centers. Terms like "land grab" (*The Guardian*)[115] and "apartheid wall" (*The Australian*)[116] cast the issue from a purely Palestinian perspective, without noting the barrier's primary purpose of saving Israeli lives. Indeed, terror chieftains Moussa Abu Marzouq of Hamas and Ramadan Shalah of Islamic Jihad have confirmed how the barrier presents a significant obstacle to carrying out suicide attacks.[117] In areas where the barrier has been completed, Palestinian attacks have declined by as much as 90 percent.[118] An Israeli official from the northern Gilboa region described: "Instead of 600 terrorist incidents per year around here, in the last five months we've had zero."[119] As construction of the barrier neared completion, 2009 marked the first time in 10 years without a single suicide attack in Israel.[120]

One might hope that journalists would celebrate the security barrier's effectiveness in keeping terrorists out of Israel. Yet appearing on MSNBC, *Time* magazine editor Richard Stengel lamented: "They [Israel] haven't had a car bombing in two and a half years and the sad truth, really, is that the wall with the West Bank has actually worked... the wall is functioning."[121] For Stengel, stopping Palestinian terror is a "sad truth."

Does the barrier impose hardships? Of course it does – for both Palestinians and Israelis. When I'm driving and see the fence, I recoil at how it scars the rolling hills and valleys of the holy land. It limits my freedom of movement; many roads are closed off and require circuitous routes. But this temporary inconvenience must be balanced against deadly terror attacks – which are far more permanent and "inconvenient."

Yet the media – driven by sensationalistic images of "Israeli aggression" – are far less interested in dry statistics of how the fence stops terror. Douglas Hamilton of Reuters played up this theme in an article commemorating the 20th anniversary of the fall of the Berlin Wall: "Now I work in Jerusalem, in another place scarred by fences and fortifications, by deep mistrust and by a forbidding wall, which is even taller than Berlin's."[122] Of course, Hamilton omitted the salient point that whereas the Berlin Wall was built to prevent people from *escaping* the ravages of their own fascist system employing oppression and terror, the Israeli security barrier is to *protect* people from the ravages of an outside fascist system employing oppression and terror.[123]

This media exaggeration gains a foothold in the public consciousness and ultimately affects government policy: When Belgian Prime Minister Guy Verhofstadt referred to the West Bank barrier using the Palestinian term "wall," he was reminded that 94 percent of the barrier is chain-link fence, with concrete walls in only the most high terror-risk locations.[124] Verhofstadt's response? "I know, I know, but this is what the national media is making of it – that's always like that, the simplification of the situation."[125]

In its rush to sensationalize, the media also overstates the degree to which the security barrier cuts into the West Bank. Bob Simon of *60 Minutes* charged that the barrier appropriates "large chunks of Palestinian land";[126] an op-ed in the *Detroit News* said it "would leave less than half the West Bank in Palestinian hands";[127] BBC called it a "structure which will hem [Palestinians] into discontiguous 'bantustans' on 42% of the West Bank";[128] and a *Seattle Post-Intelligencer* op-ed claimed that the majority of West Bank land falls on Israel's side of the wall.[129]

These figures are simply not true; even the most liberal estimates place less than 10 percent of the West Bank on the "Israeli side" of the barrier.[130] Yet an op-ed in the *Boston Globe* claimed that "according to current maps, the wall will confiscate 55 percent of the Palestinian West Bank."[131] (Following reader complaints, the *Globe* later downgraded the number to a still-exaggerated 20 percent.)[132]

In a clear double standard, the media obsesses over Israel's fence at the same time that other nations have erected similar barriers: the British "peace line" in Ireland; the iron partition on the Kuwait-Iraq border; the massive U.S. border fence with Mexico; the 300-mile-long electric fence between Botswana and Zimbabwe; 500 miles of mined fence separating Syria and Turkey; fences between India and Bangladesh; the miles of blast walls and 1,600 checkpoints built by American soldiers throughout Baghdad.[133]

Yet only the Israeli barrier is criticized, a hypocrisy noted by London's *Independent*: "Saudi Arabia, one of the most vocal critics in the Arab world of Israel's 'security fence' in the West Bank, is quietly emulating the Israeli example by erecting a barrier along its porous border with Yemen"[134] to – guess what – "prevent terrorist infiltration."[135]

Ironically, the security barrier has in many cases proven a boon to Palestinian life itself. With reduced terror activity, Jenin – the infamous "suicide bombers' capital" – has experienced a newfound vitality. Ziad Mifleh, director-general of the Jenin Chamber of Commerce, said that the fence has brought about "positive business indicators, as people are starting to think of capital and investment and commerce again." Palestinian official Hader Abu Sheikh adds: "We are talking about the resumption of traditional Palestinian nightlife. Weddings, men sitting in cafes late at night, women visiting each other..."[136]

The West Bank town of Nablus recently opened its first-ever cinema multiplex; Ramallah's real estate prices are skyrocketing;[137] and the Palestinian economy in the West Bank is growing at an annual rate of 7 percent[138] – none of which would have been possible had Israel not shut down the terror activity. Yet the media continues to focus almost exclusively on Israeli security actions and – by omitting important follow-up reports of how these actions yield positive results – creates a "barrier" for a proper understanding of Israel's security concerns.

Hit in Dubai

Not long ago, I was riding in a taxi as some rock music wafted through the speakers.

The neighborhood bully just lives to survive,
He's criticized and condemned for being alive...
He's always on trial for just being born.

It sounded so familiar, but I just couldn't place the tune. I listened to a few more lines:

He's not supposed to fight back, he's supposed to have thick skin.
He's supposed to lay down and die when his door is kicked in.

And then it hit me. It was Bob Dylan singing about Israel – the "Neighborhood Bully."[139]

This got me thinking: If Israel is denounced for protecting its citizens with the use of checkpoints, the security barrier, and engaging Hamas on the ground in Gaza, then exactly what option remains in Israel's fight against terror?

Over the years, Israel has conducted a policy of "targeted killings"

– pinpoint missile strikes – to eliminate terror leaders like Abdel Aziz al-Rantissi, Thabet Thabet and Salah Shehadeh. The killings are clean, precise, and go a long way in shaking up the operational structure of terror groups. So why is this practice roundly condemned by the media as a "controversial tactic"[140] that itself constitutes "unspeakable terror,"[141] which is "morally and legally no better than a suicide bomb on a bus"?[142]

When Israel took out Sheikh Ahmed Yassin – the Hamas chieftain responsible for planning and launching terror attacks – the editorial staff of the *Washington Post* called it "reckless"[143] and the *Los Angeles Times* called it "ominous."[144] Beyond this, media outlets across the board – *New York Times*,[145] *Washington Post*,[146] CNN,[147] BBC[148] – described Yassin not as a terrorist, but as a "spiritual leader." This suggests that Yassin operated in a peaceful, contemplative realm and was therefore unfairly targeted by the IDF. Actually, Yassin's brand of "spirituality" is the very ideological and emotional fuel that drives Palestinian (and worldwide Islamic) terrorism. Yassin repeatedly called for suicide bombings as a religious obligation, and said about himself that "the day in which I will die as a *shahid* [martyr] will be the happiest day of my life."[149] Yet readers of Associated Press had to wade through 44 paragraphs before any reference to Yassin's connection to terrorism – in the final sentence of the report.[150]

Despite the clear strategic effectiveness of targeted killings, an Associated Press analysis of the issue quoted six pro-Palestinian spokespersons (and only one pro-Israeli) to drive home its point: the IDF anti-terrorist strikes are "counterproductive," "extremely dangerous," "provoke more attacks," "add to resentment among Palestinians," "escalate [terrorist] responses," and are a mere "aspirin to cancer."[151]

On the contrary, I've often argued to reporters that if Israel is expected to protect itself by using "proportionate" measures, there could be no better method than the targeted killing of terrorists. If only Israel could fight all its battles this way, it would be the cleanest and least-deadly method in the history of warfare.[152]

So imagine how pleased journalists must have been in February 2010, when intelligence agents trailed top Hamas terrorist Mahmoud al-Mabhouh to his hotel room in Dubai and killed him. Mabhouh, on a mission to acquire and smuggle Iranian weapons to be used against Israeli civilians, was taken out quietly without harming (or even disturbing the sleep of) any civilians.[153]

Journalists *should* have been pleased – but they weren't. The assumption that Israel's Mossad was behind the operation[154] led to an orgy of Israel-bashing, with the London *Observer* calling the incident a "self-defeating cycle of using extreme force,"[155] and Ireland's newspaper of record, the *Irish Times*, censuring Israel for "this act of international terrorism."[156]

Other media outlets such as the *New York Times* played a game of selective omission, obscuring the key information of what Mabhouh did to merit his end. Readers would have had to reach the final paragraph of the *Times'* report to learn that he was an unrepentant terrorist who participated in the "abduction and killing of two Israeli soldiers, and was also involved in smuggling weapons into Gaza."[157]

Taking a cue from the media (or vise-versa), Israel's policy is roundly denounced by world leaders. The Italian foreign minister said that "the European Union has always condemned the practice of targeted assassinations," the Russian government "repeatedly stressed the unacceptability of extrajudicial settling of scores and targeted killings," and Kofi Annan declared that "extrajudicial killings are violations of international law."[158]

These condemnations are unfortunately nothing new. In 1960, when Adolf Eichmann – the Nazi officer in charge of deporting millions of Jews to ghettos and extermination camps – was captured by Israeli agents near Buenos Aires, the Argentine government and Arab states called for a U.N. Security Council meeting to condemn Israel's "nefarious and brazen criminal behavior." Similarly, in the aftermath of Israel's daring 1976 raid to free hostages in Entebbe, the U.N. Security Council cynically debated Israel's "violation of Ugandan sovereignty."[159]

Yet nobody seemed to mind in 2003 when – acting upon intelligence indicating Saddam Hussein's whereabouts – an American B-1B aircraft dropped four 2,000-pound bombs on a Baghdad building, killing at least 10 civilians under four collapsed structures. The Western media almost uniformly highlighted the remarkable intelligence gathered by the CIA, the swiftness of the B-1B's call to duty, and a U.S. spokesman's proud declaration that "a leadership target was hit very hard"[160] – even though Saddam was not even there. And in 2006, when a U.S. Air Force F-16C jet dropped nearly a ton of bombs on the building where Iraqi terror mastermind Abu Musab al-Zarqawi was hiding – killing six others, including women and children – nobody uttered a peep.[161]

Perhaps those who oppose the very concept of targeted killings should have protested the killing of Osama bin Laden who, after all, held no governmental position and wore no military uniform. Perhaps they should have decried the collateral killing of four others in the raid. But of course, no media outlet or world leader would have any reason to criticize the killing of bin Laden.[162] (Meanwhile, Palestinians rallied in the streets of Gaza City *in support of* bin Laden,[163] while Hamas officials called the attack "state terrorism that America carries out against Muslims.")[164]

When covering military strikes against terror leaders, why does Israel suddenly form a black hole, warping the media's moral compass? All this huffing and puffing makes one wonder if those decrying Israel's policy care less about the lives of real human beings and more about finding another excuse to bash Israel.[165]

Gaza Flotilla

The issue of Israel's right to self-defense came to a head in the early hours of May 31, 2010, in the murky waters off the coast of Gaza. It was there that Israeli soldiers encountered the *Mavi Marmara*, a Turkish ship from the Free Gaza movement ostensibly trying to deliver humanitarian supplies to Gaza. Israel – suspicious that the boat may contain weapons, and determined to prevent Hamas from its incessant efforts to acquire war materiel – offered to unload the ship at the Ashdod port, inspect the cargo, and then deliver it overland to Gaza. Spokesmen for the Free Gaza movement refused – preferring instead a confrontation that would make headlines.

In enforcing its blockade of Gaza, Israel had stopped six other ships in this flotilla, all without violent incident. Again this time, the soldiers expected minimal resistance, coming "armed" with only paintball guns designed for crowd control, and pistols in case of emergency.

What Israel didn't know was that 40 operatives from IHH – a Turkish group with close ties to Hamas, Hezbollah and al-Qaeda[166] – were recruited especially for this mission and had taken control of the ship.[167] Nor did Israel know that these "peace activists" had been preparing weapons, chanting jihadist battle cries, and invoking the seventh century battle of Khaybar where Muslims carried out a massacre of Jews.[168]

As the Israeli soldiers rappelled down from a helicopter onto the ship's deck, they were immediately attacked with lethal weapons – steel pipes, wooden clubs, knives and (of course) slingshots designed to invoke the imagery of the tiny stone-throwing David against the mighty gunships of the Israeli Goliath. The so-called "activists" stabbed, beat and shot the soldiers,[169] throwing three off a 30-foot deck and taking them hostage in the ship's cabin.[170] In the ensuing melee, nine activists were killed, and 10 Israeli soldiers were wounded – two in critical condition with gunshot wounds, and others with broken bones and a fractured skull.

Within 10 hours, the IDF released video footage showing the activists beating and stabbing the soldiers the moment their feet hit the deck. But 10 hours was simply too late. With today's instantaneous news cycle, where every split-second determines who will get the "scoop," reporters are compelled to leap to conclusions based on pre-conceived notions. As one photojournalist explained: "The media has no time, everything has to be immediate, and stereotypes do the job... Due to the lack of time, we have to rely on a superficial understanding of the event and its dynamics."[171]

In some ways, news agencies can convey information better than ever – there is nary a reporter in America who does not know how to tweet, blog, and use a flip video camera. But in other ways things have regressed. Stories are gathered faster and under greater pressure by a smaller, less experienced staff of reporters, then are passed more quickly through fewer, less experienced, editing hands on their way to publication. Newsrooms have shrunk by 25 percent in the past three years, and old-fashioned "shoe-leather reporting" – the kind where a journalist hits the street, conducts interviews, probes and unearths key information – is too often replaced by a superficial Google search.[172]

Where newsrooms once rewarded more deeply reported stories, the push is now toward work that can be turned around quickly and generate a bump in Web traffic.[173] As Robert Thomson, managing editor of the *Wall Street Journal,* said: "The scoop has never had more significance... a few minutes, or even seconds, are a crucial advantage."[174] Call it "keeping up with the Huffingtons."

That's the only way to explain the frenzied misreporting of events at the Gaza flotilla. A *Washington Post* headline quoted Turkey's foreign minister that Israel's raid "is like 9-11 for his country,"[175] and the United Nations – which predictably called an emergency session – censured Israel for "lawless and murderous behavior."[176] Even after the video evidence was out, the *New York Times* described it as merely "supporting an Israeli claim," and then quoted Greta Berlin of the Free Gaza movement calling the Israeli version "a lie."[177]

Calling the Israelis "liars" is a favorite technique of pro-Palestinian groups. It deflects even the most clear-cut evidence and shifts the burden of proof back onto Israel. BBC played into this ruse, lending credence to the idea of activists possessing weapons as merely "cheap [Israeli] propaganda."[178] By presenting the two sides with equal credibility, media outlets in pursuit of a "level playing field" failed in the basic journalistic duty to distinguish between irrefutable evidence and lame, defensive denials.

In a classic case of "hide the facts," the *International Herald Tribune* – the global edition of the *New York Times* – described the video of soldiers aggressively "sliding down ropes from helicopters" in the presence of "Israeli high-speed naval vessels" – yet ignored how this same video clearly showed the soldiers under attack. Similarly, Associated Press – in a report sent to 15,000 media outlets worldwide – forced readers to go 560 words deep into the article before any mention of the attack on Israeli soldiers.[179] Weeks later, the London *Times* was still referring to the "activists *allegedly* armed with metal clubs and knives."[180]

Like so many times before, the media seemed unable to shake the narrative of Israeli aggression. Who could be surprised at the Reuters news photo showing an injured Israeli soldier – misidentified as a pro-Palestinian activist?[181]

Even with all the evidence of terror ties – and video footage of activists chanting "jihad" and sawing off the deck's railings to use as metal weapons – CNN still described the IHH as a "Turkish humanitarian group,"[182] while the *New York Times* quoted a flotilla spokesman saying the activists "were not military personnel," but rather a group of "artists, intellectuals and journalists."[183]

Paul McGeough of the *Sydney Morning Herald* "reported" that the IDF "hunted like hyenas," that the Israeli operation was "timed for dawn prayers," and claimed that when activists beat commandos and took them into the ship's hold, it was not to kidnap them, but rather "for treatment by the flotilla doctors."[184] For this fine work of fiction, McGeough won the prize for "best print news report" at the annual Australian journalism awards.[185]

Meanwhile, *Toronto Star* columnist Linda McQuaig charged Israel with the "killing of nine *peace* activists" and dismissed all the weapons found on board "as mythical as Saddam Hussein's weapons of mass destruction." Then, in a gross moral equivalence, she called the *Mavi Marmara* "as horrific as the killing on the *Achille Lauro*," the ship hijacked by Palestinian terrorists who then shot wheelchair-bound American Jewish passenger Leon Klinghoffer in cold blood and dumped his body overboard.[186]

For Reuters – the same folks who pioneered the field of fauxtography during the 2006 Lebanon war – the flotilla incident provided ripe fare. One photo from the flotilla incident shows an Israeli soldier being taken hostage and an Islamic "activist" wielding a knife. Yet when Reuters released the photo, the knife was slickly cropped out, erasing a clear indictment of this so-called "peace flotilla."[187]

A single cleverly-cropped photo might be explained as an honest mistake. But within a few hours, Reuters had released a second photo that again carefully cropped out an activist's knife – and for good measure, also removed a pool of blood and a badly injured Israeli soldier lying on the floor.[188]

The impact of Reuters' creative cropping was to make the event look more like an Israeli attack on innocent civilians, and less like an act of Islamist thugs masquerading as humanitarian aid workers. When challenged, the folks at Reuters insisted that nothing was amiss, that the photos were subjected to "normal editorial practice."[189] Normal for Reuters, perhaps.

Piracy on the High Seas

When it became undeniably clear that the flotilla passengers had initiated the violence, reporters went to Plan B: portraying Israel's stopping the ship in international waters as a violation of maritime law. CNN broadcast the idea that "no country has the right to touch ships traveling in international waters,"[190] and the *New York Times* reported that Israel's "operation in international waters... is unacceptable under any clause of the international law."[191] A *Chicago Tribune* headline called it "Piracy on the High Seas,"[192] and the French daily *Liberation* ran the decisive headline, "Israel, Pirate State."[193]

This was all a media smokescreen. According to the *San Remo Manual*, the definitive guide to international law as applicable to armed conflicts at sea, it is permissible to attack a vessel on the high seas when that vessel is "believed on reasonable grounds to be carrying contraband or breaching a blockade, and after prior warning they intentionally and clearly refuse to stop."[194] Similarly, the U.S. Defense Department's *Handbook on the Law of Naval Operations*[195] and the United Nations' *Charter on the Law of the Sea* explicitly permit enforcing a blockade even in international waters.[196]

For any journalist seeking the facts, five minutes of research on Google would have proffered this information.

When the "violation of international law" charade was quickly disproved, the media shifted to Plan-C: denouncing the very policy of an Israeli blockade. The editorial staff of the *Los Angeles Times* called for "an end to the blockade,"[197] while the *New York Times* declared it "clear that the blockade is unjust" and urged Israel to "permanently lift the blockade."[198]

Media reports, however, failed to supply the crucial context: the long history of naval blockades going back to the Spartan blockade of Athens in 404 BCE. In modern times, the Royal Navy's blockade of Napoleon protected England from invasion and laid the groundwork for the liberation of Europe. Lincoln's blockade of the South helped win the Civil War, preserve the Union and end slavery. Kennedy's blockade of Cuba forced Khrushchev to withdraw Soviet nuclear weapons and contributed to the eventual American victory in the Cold War.[199]

Israel's blockade – restricting supplies that could be used to construct Hamas rockets, smuggling tunnels and weapons factories – is based on a very real threat. Palestinian terror groups had already fired tens of thousands of rockets onto Israeli cities, while smuggling weapons through a massive state-sponsored network of tunnels. Seaport smuggling is another favored supply route: Remember when Israeli troops intercepted the *Karine-A*, a freight ship bound for Gaza with 50 tons of Iranian rifles, ammunition and missiles?[200] And the *Santorini*, caught ferrying 40 tons of rockets, anti-tank weaponry, mortars and automatic weapons for armed groups in Gaza.[201] And the 50 tons of Iranian weapons destined for terrorists in Gaza seized aboard the *Victoria* cargo ship.[202]

With the *Mavi Marmara*, why was Israel placed in the preposterous position of having to defend itself for defending itself? Does the media really expect Israel to permit the free flow of weapons to these terrorists from the sea?

The end of the story: Sixteen months later, a U.N. investigative committee issued the Palmer Report, concluding that the Israeli naval blockade on Gaza is a reasonable military necessity in accordance with international law. The inquiry also found that Israeli commandos who boarded the flotilla ship encountered "organized and violent resistance" and required the use of force to protect themselves. Israel was criticized on one point only: for what the U.N. inquiry called "excessive force."[203]

So what were the headlines? You guessed it:

- "U.N. Calls Israel Force on Flotilla 'Excessive'" – *Wall Street Journal*[204]
- "Israel Used Excessive Force on Flotilla: UN Inquiry" – MSN News India[205]
- "U.N. Calls Israeli Raid 'Unreasonable'" – *Washington Post*[206]
- "UN Censures Israel for Raid on Flotilla that Killed Nine Turks" – *The Independent* (UK)[207]

Even this wasn't enough for Reuters, which trotted out several UN "experts" who disagreed with the conclusions of the Palmer Report.[208] Unfortunately, Reuters didn't mention that one "expert" cited, Richard Falk, is a radical anti-Israel activist and 9/11 conspiracy theorist. Reuters' own *Handbook of Journalism* mandates the ethical duty to "take no side; tell all sides."[209] Yet to Reuters, Richard Falk is just an "expert."[210]

Humanitarian Crisis?

Underlying this incident is the question of why the Gaza flotilla set sail in the first place. Ostensibly the goal was to deliver badly-needed supplies and alleviate what the media defined as an "ongoing humanitarian crisis" in Gaza.

One purveyor of this "humanitarian crisis" theme was Lauren Booth – sister-in-law of former British Prime Minister Tony Blair, columnist for several British newspapers, guest commentator on BBC, convert to Islam,[211] and on the Iranian payroll as correspondent for Iran's satellite news channel, Press TV. Booth's earlier reports from Gaza alarmingly described it as "the largest concentration camp in the world" and a "humanitarian crisis on the scale of Darfur."[212] So imagine Booth's embarrassment when photographs were circulated of her shopping carefree at a well-stocked Gaza grocery store, buying candy bars and soft drinks. Concentration camp? Darfur?

In fact, at the time of the flotilla, 15,000 tons of humanitarian supplies – food, medicine and other goods – were being transferred into Gaza each week. In the 18 months prior, Israel delivered more than *one million tons* of humanitarian aid to the people of Gaza – nearly one ton for every man, woman and child. By contrast, the cargo on the seven-ship flotilla amounted to a mere three-day supply.

Yes, Gaza has poverty. But is there starvation? The way the media presents it, one would expect that Gaza is filled with Third World scenes of hungry children with food bowls waiting in long lines at U.N. food stations. But some astute bloggers revealed a luxury side of Gaza – five-star hotels, Olympic-size swimming pools, water parks and gourmet restaurants where you can "dine on steak *au poivre* and chicken *cordon bleu*."[213] When a new American-style shopping mall opened in Gaza City, the worst case of humanitarian suffering was when thousands of Palestinians were sent in desperate search of sales and specials, then forced to stand for hours at crammed checkout lines.[214]

Once this information was out there on the blogosphere, the mainstream media finally decided to stop relying on Palestinian propaganda and check things out for themselves. One candid report from Gaza observed that "grocery stores are stocked wall-to-wall with everything from fresh Israeli yogurts and hummus to Cocoa Puffs. Pharmacies look as well-supplied as a typical Rite Aid in the United States."[215] Another report noted that in addition to Israeli aid convoys, smuggling tunnels have "flooded Gaza with Korean refrigerators, German food mixers and Chinese air-conditioning units," while products like Coca-Cola, Snickers and Heinz ketchup are both cheap and widely available.[216]

So imagine my surprise to see the UK's best-selling broadsheet, the *Daily Telegraph*, publishing a large photo of a squalid, rubble-filled alleyway in Gaza filled with destitute people.[217] Was this really the situation in Gaza? Some detective work revealed that the photo had been taken 18 months earlier; in order to falsely portray Israel as crippling everyday life in Gaza, the *Telegraph* had simply recycled an old image.[218] Alas, even having been called out on this breach of ethics, the same tact continued: Months later, in another report on life in Gaza, the *Telegraph* published a two-year-old photo of a girl sleeping on the rubble of her "now-destroyed" house.[219]

Steffen Jensen, Mideast correspondent for Denmark's TV2, visited a market in Gaza where one woman – well-trained in the art of Palestinian PR – tried to espouse the idea of starvation in Gaza: "We have nothing. We need everything. Food, drinks... everything!" Jensen, however, called her bluff: "It disturbed her not the least that she stood between the mountains of vegetables, fruit, eggs, poultry and fish, while she spun this doomsday scenario."[220] Even Hamas admitted that the blockade had not caused a humanitarian crisis in its classic sense. "There is no starvation in Gaza," said senior Hamas official Khalil Hamada.[221]

Yet the media had done its damage. When pollsters presented Americans with the suggestion that "there is no humanitarian crisis in Gaza," only 8 percent agreed.[222]

If anyone still harbored illusions, flotilla organizer Greta Berlin made it clear: "This mission is not about delivering humanitarian supplies."[223] Indeed, after the *Mavi Marmara* cargo was checked by Israeli inspectors and loaded onto trucks for delivery to Gaza, Hamas refused to accept the goods.[224] Hamas leader Mahmoud Zahar then promised that more flotillas would be arriving – but only after completion of the 2010 World Cup soccer event.[225] How obliging of the allegedly starving Gazans to hold out till the end of the tournament, in deference to the news cycle.

In the end, Israel bowed to pressure and announced an easing of the Gaza blockade. With illegal smuggling activity no longer necessary, the media found a new way to criticize Israel: The caption on a Getty Images news photo of a (now-inactive) smuggling tunnel impugned Israeli policy for "dealing a potentially fatal blow to the tunnel trade that has largely sustained" the Gaza Strip.[226]

The misrepresentation doesn't stop there. Over the years, the media has bolstered an image of Palestinian suffering by referring to Gaza as "the most overpopulated few square miles in the whole world"[227] and "the most densely populated place on earth."[228] This may have a nice ring to it, but it's simply not true. While Gaza does have a relatively high population density, reports from the United Nations and other world bodies rank it lower on the list.[229]

Ironically, the media never considers that Gaza's high population density is due primarily to improved health care introduced by Israel. During Israeli control of the Gaza Strip from 1967–2005, life expectancy rose from 48 years to over 72 years – a rate higher than even Russia and the Philippines.[230] In other words, Israeli policies – described by *Harper's Magazine* as "barbarism," "fierce prejudice," "systematic violence" and "ethnic cleansing"[231] – succeeded in raising Gaza's health-care system from Third World status to that comparable to Western societies.

In exasperation, I contacted one Mideast correspondent. "These claims of Israel generating a humanitarian crisis simply contradict the historical record," I told him. "It's common knowledge that prior to 1967, under Arab rule, living conditions in Gaza were atrocious. Medical and social services were almost nonexistent; residents were subjected to a permanent 9 p.m. curfew; three-quarters of the able-bodied were unemployed; and only 18 percent of homes in Gaza had electricity."[232]

"The fact that the Arabs may have mistreated the Palestinians doesn't give Israel any right to do the same," he said.

"Have you researched the topic?" I asked him. "Under Israeli control, the standard of living in Gaza surged. By 1987, 88 percent of homes in Gaza had electricity and the use of basic appliances had increased 25-fold."[233]

"That probably reflects an isolated phenomenon," he snickered.

"Actually, not," I said. "Under Israeli rule, childhood diseases like polio, whooping cough, tetanus and measles were eradicated.[234] The number of Palestinian universities shot from zero to seven.[235] And Palestinian illiteracy rates dropped to 14 percent – far better than the 69 percent in Morocco and 61 percent in neighboring Egypt."[236]

I managed to influence the thinking of one journalist, but there were hundreds more distorting the facts to portray Israel as crushing Palestinian life. Associated Press reporter Maria Cheng suggested that Israeli policy is to blame for "major health problems, including malnutrition, stunted growth in children and high infant mortality rates."[237] In fact, however, Gaza's infant mortality rate in 1967 was 85 per 1,000 live births; under Israeli control that number dropped to 15.[238] It was only after the Oslo Accords of 1993, when Palestinians assumed responsibility for their own civil administration, that the infant mortality rate again began to rise – as Palestinian corruption drained international aid dollars away from the people, and instead into the production of weapons and lining politicians' pockets.[239]

Yet the canard persists. Canadian Broadcasting Corporation reported that the Gaza Strip "has one of the world's highest infant mortality rates"[240] – though the infant mortality rate in the Gaza Strip is better than Brazil and Romania, and half the rate in Iran.[241] Indeed, with life expectancy, literacy rates and infant mortality rates all better in Gaza than in neighboring Arab lands, perhaps it is time for Palestinians to be sending humanitarian aid in the other direction.[242]

In the economic sphere as well, the media is bent on blaming Israel for all the Palestinian woes. Following Israel's disengagement from Gaza in 2005, the *New York Times* lamented that abandoned Jewish settlements "came with greenhouses that offered the prospect of thousands of agricultural jobs. Yet the greenhouses sit idle."[243] The *Times* suggests Israeli blame for the loss of Palestinian agricultural jobs, but here's the real story: Prior to withdrawing from Gaza, Israel arranged for a cadre of American investors – including Bill Gates, former World Bank president James Wolfensohn, and publisher Mortimer B. Zuckerman – to purchase 3,000 Jewish greenhouses in Gaza; they then transferred ownership to the Palestinian Authority so that the thousands of Palestinians employed there could keep their jobs. But Palestinians – in yet another act of self-destructive anarchy – looted and destroyed the farms, rendering them useless.[244] In its report, however, the *New York Times* eliminated this crucial context, implying Israeli culpability as "the greenhouses sit idle."[245]

This Palestinian propensity – in the words of Israeli statesman Abba Eban, "to never miss an opportunity to miss an opportunity" – reminds me of the story about a scorpion that asked a fox to carry him across the river. The fox refused: "You might sting me!" The scorpion scoffed: "Don't be ridiculous. Why would I sting you? If I did, we'd both drown." The fox thought this made sense and told the scorpion to climb on his back.

Halfway across the river, the scorpion stung the fox. "Why did you do that? We're both going to drown!" cried the fox. "I know," said the scorpion. "Welcome to the Middle East."[246]

The *New York Times* seemingly cannot blame the scorpion. A report on the Palestinian export of 25,000 carnations spoke of how an Israeli "blockade has crushed Gaza's economy," and noted that "Gaza used to export about 60 million flowers a year."[247] The *Times* clearly implies that Israel is to blame for the massive reduction in flower exports from Gaza. In truth, however, the figure of "60 million flowers" refers to exports from former *Jewish* farms in Gaza, which once comprised 15 percent of Israel's overall agricultural exports. The only reason that flower exports dropped to a fraction of their prior output is because Jewish farmers were evacuated from Gaza and Palestinians demolished the greenhouses left behind.

I fired off an email to the *Times'* editor, reminding him that under Israeli rule, the Palestinian economy experienced astounding growth, and during the 1970s constituted the fourth fastest-growing economy in the world – ahead of such "wonders" as Singapore, Hong Kong, Korea, and substantially ahead of Israel itself.[248] It was only since 1994, when 96 percent of Palestinians came under the autonomous rule of the Palestinian Authority, that their economy fizzled; by 2003, GDP in the West Bank had shrunk to about one-tenth of its 1992 level.[249]

So who exactly is crushing the Palestinian economy? The media has flipped myth and reality upside down. It's like Chico Marx used to say: "Who you gonna believe – me or your own eyes?"[250]

Suicide Activists

When taking a step back from it all, the Gaza flotilla incident raises the most basic question: Why would the ship's passengers initiate a violent confrontation with the powerful Israeli military in the first place? They could have unloaded the cargo peacefully in Ashdod. What positive outcome could they have anticipated? It almost sounds suicidal.

The answer is that goading Israel into violent conflict is a primary tactic of Hamas and its cohorts. That's what prompted Hamas to fire 10,000 rockets into Israel, until finally drawing Israel into battle which produced Palestinian casualties and ultimately a PR victory in the form of exorbitant media coverage.[251]

The ensuing violence – particularly the death of a U.S. citizen – was exactly what pro-Palestinian activists had been so cynically waiting for. On cue, the *Christian Science Monitor* played up the American angle with the headline, "Israeli Raid on Gaza Freedom Flotilla Killed US Citizen Furkan Dogan."[252] ABC News noted that Dogan was "a high school student studying social sciences,"[253] and the *New York Times* characterized him as "clean-hearted with a happy face"[254] who "was proud of his American passport."[255]

In fact, Dogan's Americanism was by accident of birth. Though born in upstate New York, his parents were Turkish, he grew up in Turkey, and he was far from the all-American boy the media made him out to be.[256] Writing in his personal diary prior to the attack, Dogan declared: "Only a short time left before martyrdom. This is the most important stage of my life. Nothing is more beautiful than martyrdom..."[257]

Many of the flotilla passengers echoed this wish for martyrdom.[258] One of the activists killed, Ali Khaider Benginin, vowed before setting sail: "I am going to be a martyr; I dreamed I will become a martyr."[259] Another passenger told Iran's Press TV: "When I went on the first convoy, I wanted to be a martyr. I wasn't that lucky. Second time, I wanted to be a martyr. Didn't work. Third time lucky – with the help of God – I will be a martyr." And en route to Gaza, a middle-aged woman in head covering beamed as she described the win-win: "Right now we face one of two happy endings: either achieve martyrdom, or reach Gaza."[260]

For Western journalists, this idea of glory through martyrdom is nearly impossible to fathom. The Western world defines "success" as returning from battle victorious and alive. But for these activists, a martyr's death allows them to claim the mantle of victimhood and declare a moral victory.[261] Indeed, the activists' motive was clear: "A violent response from Israel will breathe new life into the Palestine solidarity movement."[262]

Despite the facts, media outlets still clung to the illusion that those aboard the flotilla were on a "humanitarian mission." CNN called the Free Gaza movement a "human rights organization,"[263] and on Voice of America – funded by the U.S. Government and reaching 125 million people worldwide – former U.S. diplomat Phil Wilcox deplored Israel's "use of armed force against unarmed civilians who were engaging in a nonviolent peaceful resistance."[264] Other newspapers bluntly charged that "the IDF *murdered* nine passengers on board."[265]

The media still wasn't getting it, and I decided to take my message directly to the people. I went down to the port of Ashdod where the ship was docked, and filed a video report entitled, "Suicide Activists on the Gaza Flotilla." The video struck a chord and received hundreds of thousands of views.[266] I asserted that the activists' willingness to be killed is really an extension of the Hamas tactic of suicide bombings. A suicide bomber says: I'm willing to sacrifice my life in order to inflict damage on the Israeli enemy. Similarly, the activists on the ship initiated a violent confrontation, knowing full well they could be "martyred." But they were undeterred in their quest to damage the Israeli enemy.

Unlike a suicide bomber, however, whose "success" is measured by the number of Israelis killed, the goal of these activists is to damage Israel in the world's eyes, using the media.

I call them "suicide activists."[267] Their ultimate weapon is not a bomb belt. Rather, the media is their weapon. These activists were willing to be killed in order to delegitimize and demonize Israel. And incredibly, media outlets worldwide fell for it – hook, line and sinker.[268]

Notes

1. "Arab Leaders Accuse Israel of 'Crimes of War and Genocide,'" Agence France Presse, January 17, 2009.
2. "Israel to Defend Troops Accused of War Crimes," Associated Press, January 26, 2009.
3. Ethan Bronner and Sabrina Tavernise, "In Shattered Gaza Town, Roots of Seething Split," *New York Times*, February 4, 2009.
4. Griff Witte, "Gaza War Sparks Debate on Civilians," *Washington Post*, January 15, 2009.
5. Mustafa Khalili of *The Guardian*; cited in Ami Isseroff, "Unbelievable: Guardian Marketing Pallywood Gaza Propaganda," Zionism-israel.com, March 23, 2009.
6. See Alan Dershowitz, "The Phony War Crimes Accusation Against Israel," *Huffington Post*,

January 22, 2009.
7. RTE – Irish Public Broadcasting (www.rte.ie/news), January 20, 2009.
8. Irwin Cotler, "The Forgotten Exodus," *National Post* (Canada), November 29, 2007; see "126-0," Mediabackspin.com, December 2, 2007.
9. Chaim Herzog, *Who Stands Accused?*, Random House, 1978, p. 4-5.
10. Ethan Bronner, "Israel Confronts Deeper Isolation in Gaza's Wake," *New York Times*, March 18, 2009.
11. Isaiah 2:4.
12. There are 193 member states of the United Nations; approximately 30 percent of the resolutions passed each year by the General Assembly target the State of Israel. Prior to 1990, of the 175 U.N. Security Council resolutions passed, 97 were directed against Israel (55 percent of the total), and 429 of the 690 General Assembly resolutions (62 percent) were directed against Israel.
13. Even this is no longer secure; the U.S. has sought to link its diplomatic support to Israeli peace concessions. (Allyn Fisher-Ilan, "Israel's Netanyahu Unveils U.S. Plan for New Talks," Reuters, November 13, 2010.) Meanwhile, the Marshall Islands is in danger of disappearing completely. (Charles J. Hanley, "If an Island State Vanishes, is it Still a Nation?", Associated Press, December 6, 2010.)
14. Cited in Silvan Shalom, "A Fence Built for Peace," *The Guardian* (UK), February 3, 2004.
15. "U.N. Condemns Israel's Actions on Palestinian Territories," Itar-Tass News Agency (Russia), April 15, 2002.
16. "U.N. Economic Panel Censures Israel," Associated Press, July 27, 2006.
17. "U.N. Condemns Israel's Incursion into West Bank," Associated Press, August 6, 2002.
18. Edith M. Lederer, "U.N. Denounces Israel's Use of Force," *Contra Costa Times* (California), October 8, 2000.
19. "U.N. Condemns Israel's Deadly Raid on Qana," Agence France Presse, July 30, 2006.
20. Patrick Moser, "U.N. Demands Probe into Israel's Strikes on Gaza Schools," Agence France Presse, January 6, 2009.
21. Victoria Graham, "U.N. Condemns Israel's Deportation of Palestinians," Associated Press, December 19, 1992.
22. "U.N. Head Slams Israel," *Vancouver Province* (Canada) / Reuters, December 7, 2007.
23. United Nations General Assembly Resolution A/RES/3246 (XXIX), November 29, 1974.
24. Chaim Herzog, *Who Stands Accused?*, Random House, 1978, p. 4-5; Arnold Beichman, "U.N. Lynching Prelude," *Washington Times*, May 2, 2002.
25. Cited in *al-Balagh* (Lebanon), January 5, 1975.
26. "Human Rights in Palestine and Other Occupied Arab Territories: Report of the United Nations Fact Finding Mission on the Gaza Conflict," United Nations Human Rights Council, Twelfth Session, Agenda Item 7, September 15, 2009.
27. Goldstone Report, paragraphs 50, 55, 60, 928, 934, 1101, 1102, 1169, 1170, 1171, 1172, 1173, 1402, 1732, 1756.
28. Goldstone Report, paragraph 1784, which contrasts "war crimes committed by both the Israeli forces and Palestinian armed groups." See also paragraphs 108, 1724, 1747. The failure to directly indict Hamas was so astonishing that *Time* magazine mistakenly claimed that the report "accused both Israel and Hamas of war crimes." (Abigail Hauslohner, "Abbas' Move on War-Crimes Report: A Boost for Hamas," *Time*, October 6, 2009.) Dozens of newspapers made the same mistake; see for example, Colum Lynch, "U.N. Panel Accuses Israel, Hamas of War Crimes," *Washington Post*, September 16, 2009; Cliff Churgin, "U.N. Commission Accuses Israel, Hamas of Gaza War Crimes," McClatchy Newspapers, September 15, 2009; Patrick Martin, "UN Finds Evidence of Israel, Hamas War Crimes in Gaza," *Globe and Mail* (Canada), September 16, 2009.

29. "Gaza: World's Leading Investigators Call for War Crimes Inquiry," Amnesty International UK, March 16, 2009. Some point out the hypocrisy of Goldstone preaching human rights, when – as a South African judge in the Apartheid regime – he approved the whipping of blacks and sent dozens of blacks to the gallows. (Tehiya Barak, "Judge Goldstone's Dark Past," *Ynetnews* [Israel], May 6, 2010.)
30. "Israel's Bombardment of Gaza is Not Self-Defense – It's a War Crime," *Sunday Times* (UK), January 11, 2009,
31. Speaking on Israel Television; cited in Daniel Friedmann, "Goldstone Report – The Terrorists' Magna Carta," *Jerusalem Post*, October 29, 2009. Further, German law professor Christian Tomuschat, who headed the U.N. committee to enforce the Goldstone Report, has frequently accused Israel of "state terrorism" and compared Israeli actions to "barbarism which was the particular hallmark of World War II." ("Goldstone II: Questions on the Impartiality of the U.N. Tomuschat Committee," UN Watch, October 21, 2010.) Tomuschat previously performed legal work for Yasser Arafat.
32. Al-Aqsa Television (Hamas), February 29, 2008; cited in Itamar Marcus, Barbara Crook and Nan Jacques Zilberdik, "Eye-witnesses: Hamas Used Human Shields in Gaza War," Palestinian Media Watch, September 16, 2009.
33. Richard Boudreaux, "War Crimes in Gaza Reported," *Los Angeles Times*, September 16, 2009. Commission member Desmond Travers averred: "We found no evidence that Hamas used civilians as hostages." (Ken Silverstein, "Six Questions for Desmond Travers on the Goldstone Report," *Harper's Magazine*, October 29, 2009.)
34. Jeff Jacoby, "At Brandeis, Israel's Guilt and Innocence on Display," *Boston Globe*, November 7, 2009. An Israeli Air Force video shows Gaza residents, after being warned of an imminent Israeli strike against the munitions being stored in their building, running to the roof instead of evacuating; Israel consequently aborted the air strike. Other videos show Hamas operatives deliberately moving toward groups of children or using them in the fighting in order to escape any possible Israeli attack. Detained Hamas combatants confirmed this was part of their military tactics. (Dore Gold, "The Dangerous Bias of the United Nations Goldstone Report," *U.S. News & World Report*, March 24, 2010.)
35. Dr. Hanan Chehata, "Exclusive MEMO interview with Colonel Desmond Travers – Co-author of the UN's Goldstone Report," *Middle East Monitor*, February 2, 2010.
36. Ken Silverstein, "Six Questions for Desmond Travers on the Goldstone Report," *Harper's Magazine*, October 29, 2009.
37. United Nations Fact Finding Mission on the Gaza Conflict: Public Hearings (Morning Session), Gaza City, June 29, 2009.
38. Isabel Kershner, "In a Broadening Offensive, Israel Steps Up Diplomacy," *New York Times*, January 1, 2009.
39. Lt. Barak Raz, "IDF Vlog: Strikes Aborted to Protect Civilians," YouTube.com, January 11, 2009.
40. Judy Siegel-Itzkovich, "Israeli Clinic for Gaza Civilians Closes for Lack of Patients," *Jerusalem Post*, February 1, 2009.
41. Tovah Lazaroff, "IDF to Step Up Flow of Humanitarian Aid," *Jerusalem Post*, January 13, 2009.
42. Ethan Bronner, "Hamas Shifts from Rockets to Culture War," *New York Times*, July 23, 2009.
43. Speaking on Al Jazeera; cited in Dore Gold, "The Dangerous Bias of the United Nations Goldstone Report," *U.S. News & World Report*, March 24, 2010.
44. Ali Waked, "Hamas: Israel Distributes Libido-increasing Gum in Gaza," *Ynetnews* (Israel), July 13, 2009.
45. Cited in Dore Gold, "The Dangerous Bias of the United Nations Goldstone Report," *U.S. News & World Report*, March 24, 2010.

46. Goldstone Report, page 134, paragraph 439; see also page 459, paragraph 1668.
47. Safa News Agency (Hamas), October 28, 2009; cited in "The Interior Minister of the de Facto Hamas Administration Describes the Support His Office Gives the Terrorist Organizations...", Intelligence and Terrorism Information Center, October 29, 2009.
48. "Gaza Gift Shop Markets 'Goldstone' Headscarves," Agence France Presse, November 4, 2009.
49. Ben Hubbard, "UN's Gaza War Crimes Investigation Faces Obstacles," Associated Press, June 9, 2009.
50. Letter from Richard Goldstone to Ambassador Leshno Yaar, July 17, 2009, included in appendix to the Goldstone Report.
51. Yitzhak Benhorin, "Goldstone: I Was Afraid of Being Abducted in Gaza," *Ynetnews* (Israel), November 6, 2009.
52. "Goldstone Wordle," *Elder of Ziyon* blog, October 27, 2009.
53. Neil MacFarquhar, "U.N. Inquiry Sees Gaza War Crimes; Israel Chastised," *New York Times*, September 16, 2009.
54. "Israel Committed 'War Crimes' in Gaza: UN Probe Chief," Agence France Presse, September 16, 2009.
55. Donald MacIntyre, "UN Report Claims Israel Committed War Crimes," *Belfast Telegraph* (Ireland), September 16, 2009.
56. Amy Teibel and Paisley Dodds, "Israel Looks to Fend Off Prosecution of War Crimes," Associated Press / *Newsday* (New York), October 2, 2009.
57. MacIntyre, "UN Says Israel Should Face War-Crimes Trial Over Gaza."
58. Goldstone himself later questioned the authenticity of his report, musing that "If this was a court of law, there would have been nothing proven." (Gal Beckerman, "Goldstone: 'If This Was a Court of Law, There Would Have Been Nothing Proven,'" *Jewish Daily Forward*, October 16, 2009.)
59. In 2006, the Human Rights Council replaced the previous U.N. Commission on Human Rights, which was disbanded due to its reputation as biased and ineffective.
60. "U.N.: Mixed Start for New Human Rights Council," Human Rights Watch, June 30, 2006.
61. "Resolutions by the Human Rights Council," Human Rights Watch. By comparison, the HRC voted to affirm Sri Lanka's right to self-defense against the Tamil Tigers – even at the cost of an estimated 20,000 civilian Tamil lives in one month alone. (Editorial, "The UN's Double Standard on Israel and Sri Lanka," *National Post* [Canada], May 30, 2009.)
62. John Dugard, "Report of the Special Rapporteur on the Situation of Human Rights in the Palestinian Territories Occupied Since 1967," United Nations Human Rights Council, Fourth Session, January 29, 2007.
63. At the time of Goldstone report, the Human Rights Council Advisory Committee was chaired by Halima Warzazi of Morocco, whose history-making contribution to human rights came when Saddam Hussein used poison gas against Iraq's Kurds in 1988; Warzazi proudly blocked the U.N.'s move to condemn the massacre. The vice-chair of the committee was Swiss diplomat Jean Ziegler, who helped Libya's despot create the "al-Qaddafi International Prize for Human Rights," and became its first winner – subsequently awarded to luminaries of freedom including Fidel Castro, Louis Farrakhan and Hugo Chávez. (Frida Ghitis, "The Human Rights Council is a Tragic Joke," *Miami Herald*, June 25, 2010.)
64. During the Arab Spring of 2011, as the Libyan revolution raged, the U.N. Human Rights Council was hailing Libya's "commitment to upholding human rights." ("Report of the Working Group on the Universal Periodic Review: Libyan Arab Jamahiriya," U.N. Human Rights Council, Sixteenth Session, Agenda Item 6, January 4, 2011. Gadhafi's Libya had previously been elected to chair the Human Rights Council with 155 votes.) Meanwhile, amidst the widespread shooting of civilians in Syria, the Assad regime – smugly pledging

"to uphold the highest standards in promotion and protection of human rights" – remained a frontrunner for a seat on the Human Rights Council. (Edith M. Lederer, "Campaign to Bar Syria from UN Human Rights Body," Associated Press, April 26, 2011.)

65. Richard Falk, "Trusting Khomeini," *New York Times*, February 16, 1979.
66. Richard Falk, "Ending the Death Dance," *The Nation*, April 29, 2002.
67. Eli Lake, "U.N. Official Calls for Study of Neocons' Role in 9/11," *The Sun* (New York), April 10, 2008; interview with Kevin Barrett, *Truth Jihad Radio*, Republic Broadcasting Network, March 24, 2008; see also Falk's foreword to *The New Pearl Harbor* by David Ray Griffin, Interlink Books, 2004.
68. Richard Falk, "Slouching Towards a Palestinian Holocaust," Transnational Foundation for Peace and Future Research, June 29, 2007; Tim Franks, "UN Expert Stands by Nazi Comments," BBC News Online, April 8, 2008.
69. See Danny Ayalon, "The Goldstone Mission vs. the Peace Process," *Jerusalem Post*, October 19, 2009.
70. See Rabbi Abraham Cooper, "Fatally Flawed UN Goldstone Report Could Come Back to Bite America for Fighting Terrorists," *Huffington Post*, October 13, 2009.
71. See Max Boot, "The Goldstone Report," *Contentions* blog / *Commentary*, September 16, 2009.
72. Shihab Rattansi, *Talk to Jazeera*, Al Jazeera, October 22, 2009.
73. Cooper, "Fatally Flawed UN Goldstone Report Could Come Back to Bite America for Fighting Terrorists."
74. Richard Goldstone, "Reconsidering the Goldstone Report on Israel and War Crimes," *Washington Post*, April 1, 2011.
75. Richard Goldstone, "Justice in Gaza," *New York Times*, September 17, 2009.
76. Eldad Beck, "NYT Refused to Publish Goldstone Retraction," *Ynetnews* (Israel), April 4, 2011. The *Times* later claimed that the op-ed it received from Goldstone just days earlier was somehow fundamentally different from that which appeared in the *Washington Post*. ("NYT: Goldstone's Never Submitted Retraction Op-ed," *Yediot Ahronot* [Israel], April 5, 2011.)
77. Ethan Bronner and Isabel Kershner, "Head of U.N. Panel Regrets Saying Israel Intentionally Killed Gazans," *New York Times*, April 2, 2011; Jeff Dunetz, "The NY Times Never Lets the Facts Get in the Way of a Good Blood Libel," *News Real* blog, April 4, 2011.
78. Melanie Phillips, "For Israel-Bashers, Recantation is Heresy," *The Spectator* (UK), April 6, 2011.
79. See David Horovitz, "Goldstone the Belated Penitent," *Jerusalem Post*, April 2, 2011. Goldstone has made some efforts to amend, with a *New York Times'* op-ed defending Israel against the Apartheid slander: "In Israel, there is no apartheid… [Those who compare Israel] to the old South Africa do a disservice to all who hope for justice and peace." (Richard J. Goldstone, "Israel and the Apartheid Slander," *New York Times*, October 31, 2011.)
80. Eli E. Hertz, "A Letter to 60 Minutes," Aish.com, February 1, 2009.
81. "Terror Costs Israel 15% of GDP," BBC News Online, June 8, 2004. Israel's current GDP is $200 billion. (*World Economic Outlook Database*, International Monetary Fund, April 2009).
82. Matt Rees, "Inside the Hurricane," *Time*, February 25, 2002.
83. Ethan Bronner, "The Painful Truth in Mideast Talks: Force Has Trumped Diplomacy," *New York Times*, October 19, 2009.
84. Graham Reid, "Jewish Champion of Palestinians," *New Zealand Herald*, August 11, 2004.
85. Chris McGreal, "Brothers in Arms," *The Guardian* (UK), February 7, 2006.
86. Tom Gross, "New Prejudices for Old," *National Review*, November 1, 2001.
87. Alan Rusbridger, "Separate and Unequal," *The Spectator* (UK), June 2, 2001.
88. Molly Moore, "Checkpoints Take Toll on Palestinians, Israeli Army," *Washington Post*, November 29, 2004.
89. "Checkpoints Take Toll on Post Reporting," *Eye on the Post*, November 29, 2004.

THE RIGHT TO SECURITY

90. Greg Myre, "Palestinian Newborn Dies, Woman Shot," Associated Press, July 11, 2001.
91. Mohammed Daraghmeh, "Questions Over West Bank Newborn Death," Associated Press, July 12, 2001.
92. Moore, "Checkpoints Take Toll on Palestinians, Israeli Army."
93. "Israel Army Forces Violin Recital," BBC News Online, November 25, 2004.
94. Horit Herman-Peled, posted at www.horit.com/violin.htm.
95. Frimet Roth, "The Violin and the Guitar," *Israel Insider*, December 2, 2004.
96. David Ratner, "Checkpoints Really Do Save Lives," *Haaretz* (Israel), November 28, 2002; "Checkpoint Arrests," *Maariv* (Israel), October 14, 2003; Hillel Halkin, "Off-Key Comparison," *The Sun* (New York), November 30, 2004.
97. Matti Friedman, "EU Condemns Use of Phony Sugar Bags by Palestinians to Conceal Banned Chemicals," Associated Press, December 30, 2007. Iraqi resistors have adopted similar techniques: When U.S. soldiers manning a checkpoint near Baghdad stopped a suspicious wedding convoy, it was discovered that not only was the "groom" a wanted terrorist, but another terror suspect – a stubbly-faced man, Haider al-Bahadli – was decked out in a white bride's dress and veil. (Mohammed Tawfeeq, "Official: Bride, Groom Stopped in Iraq Actually Terror Suspects," CNN.com, November 26, 2007.)
98. Andy Soltis, "9-Months Pregnant Bomber Nabbed," *New York Post*, June 14, 2007. She was joined by her niece, a mother of four, in a planned double-suicide bombing.
99. Ibrahim Barzak, "Israel Closes Gaza Crossing in Response to Suicide Bombing," Associated Press, January 15, 2004.
100. Uri Dromi, "When Will the Palestinians Engage in Real Nation-building?", *Miami Herald*, July 1, 2005.
101. Raffi Berg, "Israel's Dilemma Over Sick Gazans," BBC News Online, April 30, 2008.
102. Bob Simon, "Time Running Out for a Two-State Solution?", *60 Minutes*, CBS, January 25, 2009.
103. Amos Harel, "Red Crescent Ambulance Believed to Have Brought Woman Bomber to Jerusalem," *Haaretz* (Israel), February 6, 2002.
104. Daniel Gordis, "Needing Israel," *New York Times*, April 13, 2002; "Roth's Supersessionism," *The Sun* (New York), July 31, 2006.
105. See "Ambulances are Used by Terrorists to Smuggle Explosives," YouTube.com, March 27, 2002.
106. See Mitchell G. Bard, "The Palestinian Uprisings," *Myths & Facts Online*.
107. Mohammed Daraghmeh, "Second Pregnant Woman Shot by Israeli Checkpoint Troops," Associated Press, February 25, 2002.
108. Gretchen Carlson, "Latest Headlines from War in Iraq," *Saturday Early Show*, CBS, March 29, 2003.
109. Bernard Weinraub, "Failing to Heed G.I.'s, 7 Iraqis Die at Checkpoint," *New York Times*, April 1, 2003.
110. Anthony DePalma, "Battles in Central Iraq, Defiance in Baghdad and Quarrels in Washington," *New York Times*, April 1, 2003.
111. David Zucchino and Geoffrey Mohan, "The Civilian Factor; 'It's Hard to Know Who Is Who' in War," *Los Angeles Times*, April 2, 2003.
112. Richard T. Cooper, "As Combat Escalates, Sparing Civilians Gets Harder Too," *Los Angeles Times*, April 2, 2003.
113. Bret Stephens, "A History of Violence," *Wall Street Journal*, October 22, 2005.
114. "PA Forces Shoot Dead Two Palestinians, Including 5-year-old Boy," Qatar News Agency, October 14, 2007.
115. Geraldine Bedell, "Set in Stone," *The Guardian* (UK), June 15, 2003. BBC even managed to include the "land grab" reference in an entertainment article about Paul McCartney. ("Israelis

Flock to McCartney Show," BBC News Online, September 26, 2008.)
116. Ian MacKinnon, "Israel to Cut 100km Off 'Apartheid Wall,'" *The Australian*, February 10, 2004.
117. Al-Manar Television (Hezbollah), November 11, 2006.
118. "After Sharon," *Wall Street Journal*, January 6, 2006; Abigail Cutler, "Security Fences," *Atlantic Monthly*, March 2005. Due to a security fence on the Gaza-Israel border, not a single suicide bomber has entered Israel directly from the Gaza Strip.
119. Matthew Gutman, "Security Fence Yields Results in Northern Israel," *Jerusalem Post*, June 2, 2004.
120. "Data and Trends in Palestinian Terrorism – 2009 Summary," Israel Security Agency, January 15, 2010.
121. *Morning Joe*, MSNBC, September 2, 2010; cited in Jim Hoft, "Time Mag Editor: It's Too Bad that Israeli Wall Worked," *Gateway Pundit*, September 2, 2010.
122. Douglas Hamilton, "Witness: Strangers United in a Euphoric Moment," Reuters, November 4, 2009. Likewise, the *New York Times Magazine* featured a dramatic photo of a snaking, towering concrete wall – referring to Israel's barrier as another "Berlin wall." (Roger Cohen, "Her Jewish State," *New York Times Magazine*, July 8, 2007.)
123. "Why is This Thing Unlike the Other?", *Reuters Middle East Watch*, November 14, 2009. Canadian Broadcasting Corporation similarly blanketed its television, radio and Internet platforms equating Israel's security barrier with the Berlin Wall. (Margaret Evans, *The National*, Canadian Broadcasting Corporation, November 6, 2009; *The World This Hour*, CBC Radio, November 6, 2009; Stephanie Jenzer, "The Other Wall: Israel's Barrier – A Dangerous Game of Guns and Ladders," CBC News Online, November 6, 2009. Cited in Mike Fegelman, "CBC Promotes False Barrier Analogy," HonestReporting Canada, November 10, 2009.)
124. "Israel's Security Fence: Operational Concept," Israeli Ministry of Defense, January 31, 2007.
125. Cited in Sharon Sadeh, "Banal Messages in Bad English," *Haaretz* (Israel), August 13, 2004.
126. Bob Simon, "The Fence," *60 Minutes*, CBS, December 21, 2003.
127. Hasan Newash and David Finkel, "Pulling Investments in Israel Will Promote Mideast Peace," *Detroit News*, April 6, 2005.
128. "Q&A: What is the West Bank Barrier?", BBC News Online, September 15, 2005.
129. Ghada Karmighada Karmi, "Sharon is Not a Man of Peace," *Seattle Post-Intelligencer*, January 13, 2006.
130. "The United Nations estimates that 10 percent of the West Bank will fall on the Israeli side of the barrier." ("Guide to the West Bank Barrier," BBC News Online.) Others place the figure at 8 percent. (Daniel Klaidman, "A Plan of Attack for Peace," *Newsweek*, January 12, 2009.)
131. Tom Wallace, "Israel's Unholy Wall," *Boston Globe*, December 3, 2003.
132. "CAMERA Obtains Clarification from Boston Globe," Committee for Accuracy in Middle East Reporting in America, December 11, 2003.
133. Muhanad Mohammed, "As U.S. Withdraws, Baghdad Eyes Checkpoints," Reuters, October 19, 2011. See also Edward Wong and David S. Cloud, "U.S. Erects Baghdad Wall to Keep Sects Apart," *New York Times*, April 21, 2007; Oliver August, "Baghdad to Enclose City with 15ft Wall to Keep Suicide Bombers Out," *The Times* (UK), May 18, 2010.
134. John Bradley, "Saudi Arabia Enrages Yemen with Fence," *The Independent* (UK), February 11, 2004.
135. Abigail Cutler, "Security Fences," *Atlantic Monthly*, March 2005.
136. Matthew Gutman, "Nightlife, in Jenin?", *Jerusalem Post*, June 4, 2004.
137. Thomas L. Friedman, "Green Shoots in Palestine II," *New York Times*, August 9, 2009; Mohammed Assadi, "Ramallah Building Boom Symbolizes West Bank Growth," Reuters, August 2, 2010.
138. "Macroeconomic and Fiscal Framework for the West Bank and Gaza: Fourth Review of

Progress," International Monetary Fund, September 22, 2009.
139. Bob Dylan, "Neighborhood Bully," Special Rider Music, 1983.
140. "Israel Court Backs Targeted Kills," BBC News Online, December 14, 2006.
141. "Attack by Israel Shows Disregard for Civilian Lives," San Jose Mercury News, July 24, 2002.
142. Jonathan Steele, "The Palestinians' Democratic Choice Must Be Respected," *The Guardian* (UK), January 27, 2006.
143. Editorial, "Death in Gaza," *Washington Post*, March 23, 2004.
144. Editorial, "An Unwise Assassination," *Los Angeles Times*, March 23, 2004.
145. James Bennet, "Leader of Hamas Killed by Missile in Israeli Strike," *New York Times*, March 22, 2004.
146. Molly Moore and John Ward Anderson, "Emotional Protests in Slaying of Sheik; Israel Defends Attack on Hamas Founder," *Washington Post*, March 23, 2004.
147. "Hamas Names Interim Leader in Gaza," CNN.com, March 23, 2004.
148. "Sheikh Yassin: Spiritual Figurehead," BBC News Online, March 22, 2004.
149. *Al-Quds*, July 26, 1998; cited in "Interview with the Hamas Leader," Middle East Media Research Institute, July 30, 1998. Further, the media tried to spin Israel's strike as unjust by presenting Yassin as "a frail man who could barely see. His voice was thin and quavering." ("Sheikh Yassin: Spiritual Figurehead," BBC News Online, March 22, 2004.) Although Yassin had been in a wheelchair since a sporting accident at age 12, but this did not hamper his ability to orchestrate unprecedented terror.
150. Ibrahim Barzak, "Israel Kills Hamas Founder in Airstrike," Associated Press, March 22, 2004.
151. Ian James, "Critics: Israeli Strikes Doing More Harm," Associated Press, September 2, 2003.
152. Michael J. Totten, "More Like This Please," *Middle East Journal*, February 23, 2010.
153. "Hamas Aide: Assassinated Leader Smuggled Weapons," Associated Press, March 3, 2010.
154. Though Israel never acknowledged involvement, the *Vancouver Sun* and other newspapers stated the Israeli connection as fact. See Jonathan Manthorpe, "Assassins Caught on Video Reveals Possible Mossad-Fatah Link," *Vancouver Sun*, February 24, 2010.
155. "Israel Can Accelerate Peace by Exercising Restraint," *The Observer* (UK), February 21, 2010.
156. "Forged Passports and Terrorism," *Irish Times*, February 20, 2010.
157. Robert F. Worth, "Inquiry Grows in Dubai Assassination," *New York Times*, February 24, 2010. See Barry Rubin, "When It's Necessary and Desirable to Assassinate Terrorists," Global Research in International Affairs Center, March 5, 2010.
158. Alan Dershowitz, "There's that Double Standard Again," *Jerusalem Post*, May 6, 2011.
159. Berel Wein, *Faith and Fate*, Shaar Press, 2001.
160. Chris Tomlinson and Hamza Hendawi, "U.S. Forces Bomb Neighborhood Where Saddam and Top Leadership Believed to be Meeting," Associated Press, April 7, 2003.
161. "Iraq Terror Chief Killed In Airstrike," CBS News, June 8, 2006.
162. Dershowitz, "There's that Double Standard Again."
163. Palestinian Prime Minister Ismail Haniyeh told reporters: "We regard this as a continuation of the American policy based on oppression and the shedding of Muslim and Arab blood. We condemn the assassination and the killing of an Arab holy warrior. We ask God to offer him mercy with the true believers and the martyrs." (Dan Williams and Nidal al-Mughrabi, "Hamas Condemns Killing of 'Holy Warrior' Bin Laden," Reuters, May 2, 2011.)
164. Fares Akram, "Hamas Condemns the Killing of bin Laden," *New York Times*, May 2, 2011.
165. Totten, "More Like This Please."
166. Evan F. Kohlmann, "The Role of Islamic Charities in International Terrorist Recruitment and Financing," Danish Institute for International Studies, 2006. IHH is also an unindicted co-conspirator to groups found guilty of helping plan terror attacks in the U.S. Holland-based *Teltarif* newspaper reported that one of the dead activists, Amin Abou Rashed, was the local Hamas leader. IHH is outlawed in Germany and Israel for its terror-related activities, and

was shunned by Turkey's former secular regime. (Daniel Schäfer, "Germany Bans Charity Over Hamas Claims," *Financial Times* [UK], July 13, 2010; "The War on Financing Terrorism," Intelligence and Terrorism Information Center, July 8, 2008.)
167. Passengers later testified that the IHH squad ordered all noncombatants below deck before the Israeli forces approached. (Anshel Pfeffer, "Report: 40 IHH Activists on Mavi Marmara Planned Violent Resistance," *Haaretz* [Israel], June 10, 2010.)
168. Al Jazeera, May 28, 2010; cited in "MEMRI TV Clips on the Gaza Flotilla: Activists on Board Chant Songs of Martyrdom at Departure," Middle East Media Research Institute, May 31, 2010.
169. Activists snatched soldiers' pistols and began firing. Further, spent bullet cartridges were discovered on the *Mavi Marmara* that are not of the caliber used by Israeli soldiers. (Michael B. Oren, "An Assault, Cloaked in Peace," *New York Times,* June 2, 2010.)
170. "Cameraman: 4 Commandos Were Captured During Flotilla Raid," Reuters, June 4, 2010.
171. "Exposed: Photographer Reveals Market, Not Truth, Behind Conflict Images," HonestReporting.com, October 10, 2011.
172. Steven Waldman, "The Information Needs of Communities," United States Federal Communications Commission, July 2011; "State of the News Media 2010," Project for Excellence in Journalism.
173. Dean Starkman, "The Hamster Wheel," *Columbia Journalism Review,* September/October 2010.
174. Robert Thomson, "A Matter of Urgency," memo to *Wall Street Journal,* May 19, 2010.
175. Glenn Kessler, "Turkish Foreign Minister: Israeli Raid on Gaza Aid Flotilla 'Like 9/11' For His Country," *Washington Post,* June 1, 2010.
176. "Secretary-General 'Shocked' by Deadly Raid on Gaza Aid Flotilla," UN News Centre, May 31, 2010.
177. Isabel Kershner, "At Least 10 Are Killed as Israel Halts Flotilla with Gaza Aid," *New York Times,* May 31, 2010.
178. "Deaths as Israeli Forces Storm Gaza Aid Ship," BBC News Online, May 31, 2010.
179. Steven Gutkin, "Bloody Israeli Raid on Flotilla Sparks Crisis," Associated Press, June 1, 2010.
180. James Hider, "Gaddafi Aid Ship Heads for Showdown as Israel Vows to Defend Gaza Blockade," *The Times* (London), July 11, 2010. Emphasis added.
181. Photo by Alex Rozkovsky, Reuters, May 31, 2010 ("Israeli soldiers evacuate a pro-Palestinian activist to a hospital near Tel Aviv"); cited in "Reuters Corrects: The Wounded Was Israeli," *Snapshots* blog, May 31, 2010.
182. Rosemary Church, *iDesk,* CNN, May 28, 2010.
183. Isabel Kershner, "Deadly Israeli Raid Draws Condemnation," *New York Times,* May 31, 2010. Months later, the *Times* was still sticking to the line that it "remains a matter of controversy... how aggressive the passengers were." (Ethan Bronner, "Israeli Military Finds Flotilla Killings Justified," *New York Times,* July 12, 2010.)
184. Paul McGeough, "Prayers, Tear Gas and Terror," *Sydney Morning Herald,* June 4, 2010.
185. Aaron Cook, "Herald Journalists Dominate Walkley Awards," *Sydney Morning Herald,* December 10, 2010; cited in "How Do You Treat a Lying, Biased Reporter?", *Elder of Ziyon* blog, December 9, 2010.
186. Linda McQuaig, "Partner in Flotilla 'Farce,'" *Toronto Star,* June 15, 2010. Emphasis added.
187. "Did Reuters Crop a Photo to Remove a Peace Activist's Weapon?", *Little Green Footballs,* June 6, 2010.
188. "Another Cropped Reuters Photo Deletes Another Knife – and a Pool of Blood," *Little Green Footballs,* June 6, 2010.
189. Editorial, "Lying with Photos," *New York Post,* June 9, 2010.
190. "Interview with Turkish Foreign Minister," *Fareed Zakaria GPS,* CNN, June 6, 2010.

191. Isabel Kershner, "Deadly Israeli Raid Draws Condemnation," *New York Times*, May 31, 2010.
192. Bill Press, "Piracy on the High Seas," *Chicago Tribune*, June 4, 2010.
193. Cited in Bernard Henri-Levy, "It's Time to Stop Demonizing Israel," *Haaretz* (Israel), June 9, 2010.
194. *San Remo Manual on International Law Applicable to Armed Conflicts at Sea*, Rule 67(a), June 12, 1994. International law expert Dr. Robbie Sabel cited the legality of IDF action in international waters: A state, in a time of conflict, can impose an embargo and – in international waters – legally detain a civilian vessel trying to break an embargo. If, in the course of detaining the vessel, force is used against the soldiers carrying out the detention, then the soldiers have every right to act in self-defense. (Dr. Aaron Lerner, "Int'l Law Expert Dr. Robbie Sabel: IDF Action in International Waters Legal," IMRA, May 31, 2010.) Before boarding the ship, the IDF issued three separate warnings. Flotilla spokeswoman Huwaida Arraf replied that the convoy was carrying only humanitarian aid: "We do not carry anything that constitutes a threat to your armed forces." ("Gaza Convoy Tapes Edited, Israel Acknowledges," CNN.com, June 6, 2010.)
195. *The Commander's Handbook on the Law of Naval Operations*, Section 7.7.4., U.S. Department of Defense, July 1, 2007. ("Attempted breach of blockade occurs from the time a vessel or aircraft leaves a port or airfield with the intention of evading the blockade, and for vessels exiting the blockaded area, continues until the voyage is completed.")
196. See also *Helsinki Principles on the Law of Maritime Neutrality* (5.1.2/3) and Article 23 of the Geneva Convention. Further, the U.N. Convention on the Law of the Sea (Article 101) defines piracy as an act "committed for private ends"; there is no concept of state-perpetrated piracy.
197. Editorial, "Easing the Gaza Blockade is a Step Forward," *Los Angeles Times*, June 22, 2010.
198. Editorial, "Israel and the Blockade," *New York Times*, June 1, 2010.
199. "Obama Should Support Israel's Legal and Necessary Blockade of Gaza, Says FPI Director William Kristol," *Weekly Standard*, June 4, 2010.
200. James Bennet, "Seized Arms Would Have Vastly Extended Arafat Arsenal," *New York Times*, January 12, 2002.
201. "Boat Containing Weapons Found Off Israel," CNN.com, May 7, 2001.
202. Yaakov Katz, "Navy Intercepts Ship with Iranian Arms Bound for Hamas," *Jerusalem Post*, March 15, 2011.
203. Geoffrey Palmer, "Report of the Secretary-General's Panel of Inquiry on the 31 May 2010 Flotilla Incident," United Nations, September 2, 2011.
204. Joe Lauria, Marc Champion and Joshua Mitnick, "U.N. Calls Israel Force on Flotilla 'Excessive,'" *Wall Street Journal*, September 2, 2011.
205. Yoshita Singh, "Israel Used Excessive Force on Flotilla: UN Inquiry," MSN News India, September 2, 2011.
206. Colum Lynch, "U.N. Calls Israeli Raid 'Unreasonable,'" *Washington Post*, September 2, 2011.
207. Donald Macintyre, "UN Censures Israel for Raid on Flotilla that Killed Nine Turks," *The Independent* (UK), September 2, 2011.
208. Stephanie Nebehay, "U.N. Experts Say Israel's Blockade of Gaza Illegal," Reuters, September 13, 2011.
209. "Freedom from Bias," *Reuters' Handbook of Journalism*, Reuters.com.
210. "Reuters Conceals Questions About Credibility of 'Expert' Falk," *Snapshots* blog, September 13, 2011.
211. Booth prays five times a day and wears a hijab head covering whenever leaving home. She described her conversion to Islam as a "shot of spiritual morphine." ("Tony Blair's Sister-in-law Lauren Booth Converts to Islam After a 'Holy Experience' in Iran," *Mail on Sunday* [UK], October 24, 2010.)
212. Noa Raz, "Blair Sister-in-law: Gaza World's Largest Concentration Camp," *Ynetnews* (Israel),

September 11, 2008; "George Galloway & Lauren Booth: Concentration Camp Gaza," YouTube.com, September 6, 2008.
213. "Fancy Restaurants and Olympic-size Swim Pools: What the Media Won't Report About Gaza," Tomgrossmedia.com, May 25, 2010.
214. "The Humanitarian Crisis of the Gaza Mall," *Elder of Ziyon* blog, July 20, 2010.
215. Janine Zacharia, "Living, Not Thriving, in Gaza," *Washington Post*, June 3, 2010.
216. Tobias Buck, "Gaza Looks Beyond Tunnel Economy," *Financial Times* (UK), May 24, 2010.
217. Adrian Blomfield, "Israel Vows to Lift Gaza Blockade But Offers Little Detail," *Daily Telegraph* (UK), June 17, 2010.
218. "Telegraph Caught Recycling Gaza War Photo to Distort Today's Reality," HonestReporting.com, June 29, 2010.
219. Mary Riddell, "The Wretched Scandal of Gaza," *Daily Telegraph*, October 20, 2011.
220. Steffen Jensen, "The Problem: More Than a Lack of Work and Food," www.steffen-jensen.dk, June 2, 2010.
221. Adrian Blomfield, "Dispatch: Just How Hungry is Gaza?", *Daily Telegraph* (UK), June 5, 2010.
222. David Horovitz, "The Word According to Frank," *Jerusalem Post*, July 16, 2010.
223. "Gaza Aid Fleet Undeterred as Israel Steps Up Warnings," Agence France Presse, May 27, 2010. See also "FG Update and Call to Action," Free Gaza Movement, January 4, 2009; "Help Us Raise Money for Boats," Free Gaza Movement, November 26, 2009. ("We firmly believe that activists and people who care about Palestine should not be raising money for humanitarian aid.")
224. "IDF: Hamas Stops Flotilla Aid Delivered by Israel," CNN.com, June 2, 2010.
225. Donald MacIntyre, "Iranian Ships Could Join Wave of Flotillas to Gaza, Says Hamas Chief," *The Independent* (UK), June 28, 2010.
226. Getty Images, June 21, 2010.
227. Robert Fisk, "Why Bombing Ashkelon is the Most Tragic Irony," *The Independent* (UK), December 30, 2008.
228. Suzanne Goldenberg, "Cradle for Martyrs," *The Guardian* (UK), June 16, 2001.
229. The world's most densely populated cities are, in order: Mumbai (India), Kolkata (India), Karachi (Pakistan), Lagos (Nigeria), Shenzhen (China); cited in "The Largest Cities in the World by Land Area, Population and Density," Citymayors.com, January 6, 2007. The most densely populated countries are, in order: Macau, Monaco, Singapore, Hong Kong, Gibraltar; data estimates current as of 2010, based on the *United Nations World Prospects Report*.
230. *CIA World Factbook* (2008 estimates).
231. Stephen R. Shalom, "The Palestinian Question," *Harper's Magazine*, January 2001.
232. Eliezer Whartman, "When Egypt Was in Gaza," *Jerusalem Post*, June 3, 2009. During the 19 years of Egyptian rule in Gaza, no elections were held; the military governor acted as judiciary, and there was no appeal; secret police probed everywhere; no one was immune from sudden arrest and unlimited imprisonment without trial or, at best, a secret trial; jails were always full and torture was common; there was official censorship of the press and mail, and telephone lines were regularly tapped. So harsh was the Egyptian rule in Gaza that Saudi radio decried it as "the very methods used by the dictator Hitler." (Jeddah Radio, March 10, 1962.)
233. Yitzhak Zaccai, *Judea, Samaria and the Gaza District, 1967-1987*, Carta, 1987. In 1967, a miniscule percentage of Gazans owned a stove (3 percent), refrigerator (3 percent) and television (3 percent). After 1967, Israel replaced Gaza's old generators with a high-tension electricity network, giving rise to an exponential increase in appliance usage: stove (87 percent), refrigerator (77 percent) and television (78 percent). Similarly, the number of Palestinians with running water rose from 16 percent in 1967, to 85 percent in 1986. ("Forty Years of Israeli Administration of the Disputed Territories," Media Central, Jerusalem, 2008.)

234. Efraim Karsh, "History of the Territories," *Commentary*, July-August 2002. See also Yitzhak Zaccai, *Judea, Samaria and the Gaza District, 1967-1987*, Carta, 1987.
235. David Meir-Levi, "Occupation and Settlement: The Myth and Reality," Frontpagemag.com, June 24, 2005.
236. Karsh, "History of the Territories."
237. Maria Cheng, "Violence Cited in Palestinian Health Woes," Associated Press, March 5, 2009.
238. Karsh, "History of the Territories." See also Zaccai, *Judea, Samaria and the Gaza District, 1967-1987*. Similarly, the average life expectancy for Palestinians rose from age 42 in 1967, to 72 in 2000. ("Forty Years of Israeli Administration of the Disputed Territories," Media Central, 2008.)
239. Cheng, "Violence Cited in Palestinian Health Woes"; Jimmy Carter, "Peace and Health in the Occupied Palestinian Territory," *The Lancet*, Vol. 373, March 7, 2009.
240. Peter Mansbridge, *National*, Canadian Broadcasting Corporation (CBC), June 1, 2010.
241. Barry Rubin, "Is Canadian TV Falsely Implying Israel is Responsible for the Death of Gaza Babies?", *The Rubin Report*, June 6, 2010.
242. "A Nice New Shopping Mall Opened Today in Gaza: Will the Media Report on It?", Tomgrossmedia.com, July 17, 2010.
243. Greg Myre, "Israelis are Gone, But Gaza Rebuilding is Slow," *New York Times*, February 18, 2007.
244. Lara Sukhtian, "Palestinians Loot Gaza Strip Greenhouses," Associated Press, September 13, 2005.
245. Writing in *The New Yorker*, Lawrence Wright similarly lamented the fate of those Gaza greenhouses which "were meant to become an important part of the agricultural economy... Now the greenhouses are nothing more than bare frames, their tattered plastic roofing fluttering in the sea breeze." Wright made no mention of the Palestinian vandalism that created those bare frames and tattered roofing – leaving the neglected greenhouses as just one more example of "Israeli cruelty and collective punishment." (Lawrence Wright, "Captives: What Really Happened During the Israeli Attacks?", *The New Yorker*, November 9, 2009.)
246. At a meeting in Zavidovo, Russia in May 1973, versions of this story were exchanged by Soviet Premier Leonid Brezhnev and U.S. Secretary of State Henry Kissinger. *(Foreign Relations of the United States 1969–1976, Volume XXV Arab-Israeli Crisis and War, 1973*, U.S. Department of State, 2011.)
247. Isabel Kershner, "Israel Opens the Gaza Border for 25,000 Carnations, Bound for Europe," *New York Times*, February 12, 2009.
248. Karsh, "History of the Territories." Nearly 2,000 industrial plants, employing close to half the work force, were established in the territories under Israeli rule. Per-capita GNP expanded tenfold between 1968 and 1991, bringing Palestinians to a level of economic prosperity higher than their Muslim neighbors in Jordan, Egypt, Syria and Turkey; only the oil-rich Gulf states and Lebanon were more affluent.
249. "Palestinian Authority (PA)," Discoverthenetworks.org.
250. *Duck Soup*, Paramount Pictures, 1933.
251. In the *British Medical Journal*, deaths of Palestinians receive hundreds of times more coverage than other major conflicts. ("BMJ's Bad Medicine," HonestReporting.com, March 3, 2009.)
252. Scott Peterson, "Israeli Raid on Gaza Freedom Flotilla Killed US Citizen Furkan Dogan," *Christian Science Monitor*, June 3, 2010.
253. Zoe Magee, "American, 19, Among Gaza Flotilla Dead," *ABC News*, June 3, 2010.
254. Sabrina Tavernise, "Thousands in Turkey Mourn Victims of Israeli Raid," *New York Times*, June 3, 2010.
255. Roger Cohen, "The Forgotten American," *New York Times*, July 26, 2010.

256. James Taranto, "Best of the Web Today," *Wall Street Journal Online*, June 8, 2010.
257. Al Jazeera, June 5, 2010; cited in "Eyewitness Reports about the Flotilla Clash," Middle East Media Research Institute, June 6, 2010.
258. Speaking on Al Jazeera, IHH official Hussein Orush declared: "All the passengers on board the ship were... ready to become a martyr... Our goal was to reach Gaza or to die trying. All the ship's passengers were ready for this." (Cited in "Eyewitness Reports about the Flotilla Clash," Middle East Media Research Institute, June 6, 2010.)
259. *Haber* (Turkey); cited in Aviel Magnezi, "3 Flotilla Fatalities 'Dreamt of Martyrdom,'" *Ynetnews* (Israel), June 2, 2010.
260. Al Jazeera, May 28, 2010; cited in Itamar Marcus and Nan Jacques Zilberdik, "Gaza Flotilla Participants Created War Atmosphere Before Confronting Israel," Palestinian Media Watch, May 31, 2010.
261. "Losing Is the New Winning," *Zombietime / Pajamas Media,* June 4, 2010.
262. Cited in Editorial, "Israel and the Blockade," *New York Times,* June 1, 2010.
263. Rosemary Church, *iDesk,* CNN, May 28, 2010.
264. Jerome Socolovsky, "Israel Finds Little International Sympathy for Its Justification to Stage Raid," Voice of America, June 2, 2010.
265. Jennifer Bray, "People See Me as a Terrorist," *Sunday Tribune* (Ireland), August 8, 2010. Emphasis added.
266. Lee Chottiner, "U.S. Jews Play 'Historic Role' in Campaigning for Israel," *Jewish Chronicle* (Pittsburgh), June 18, 2010.
267. Professor Richard Landes calls them "demopaths": those who invoke democratic language and pose as humanitarian peace activists, even while spouting genocidal jihadi rhetoric. (Richard Landes, "The Consequences of Media Failure: Demopaths Setting the Global Agenda," *Pajamas Media,* June 8, 2010.)
268. Subsequent flotilla projects have fizzled out. A much-ballyhooed 2011 ship (audaciously named the *Audacity of Hope)* was stopped by the Greek Coast Guard a few minutes after leaving port. No matter; organizers declared victory anyway (Christopher Torchia, "Gaza Flotilla Activists Dispersing After Troubled Weeks in Greece," *Huffington Post,* July 7, 2011), and the media glibly concurred: A newspaper in Massachusetts "termed the venture a success" (Fred Contrada, "Northampton Activist Paki Wieland Talks of Her Role in Trying to Break Israel's Blockade of Gaza," *Springfield Republican,* July 8, 2011), while one in California publicized the failed flotilla as "surprisingly effective, beyond our wildest dreams." (Kristin J. Bender, "Activist Talks about Failed Mission to Reach the Gaza Strip," *San Jose Mercury News,* July 8, 2011.)

—11—

THE RIGHT TO EXIST

Not long ago I was having lunch with an American broadcast journalist. It was Israeli Independence Day, and we were reflecting on the fact that from day one, Israel has been engaged in a struggle to exist. Within hours of Israel's declaration of statehood on May 14, 1948, five Arab armies invaded with the goal of aborting the Jewish state at birth,[1] with Azzam Pasha, the Arab League Secretary, declaring on Cairo radio: "This will be a war of extermination and a momentous massacre which will be spoken of like the Mongolian massacres and the Crusades."[2] Although Arabs outnumbered the Jews 100-to-1, Israel rebuffed that threat, as well as subsequent attempted annihilations in 1967 and 1973.[3] Ironically for the Arab aggressors, these wars produced the opposite of their intended effect: Israel became the most powerful army in the Middle East.

Unable to overpower Israel using military force, Israel's enemies tried another tack: seeking to stifle it with an economic boycott that targeted not only Israeli products, but also blacklisted any company conducting business with Israel.[4] McDonald's arches and the Pepsi challenge were conspicuously absent from the Israeli landscape until the boycott began waning in the late 1980s;[5] even today, the Mideast conflict has saddled Israel with an "opportunity cost" estimated at a trillion dollars over the last two decades alone.[6] Yet despite all this, Israel's economy today is among the healthiest in the world, registering positive GDP growth even in the face of the 2009 global downturn, and posting an unemployment rate lower than most Western countries.[7]

And so, in search of yet another method to destroy the Jewish state, Israel's enemies shifted their focus in recent years to the terror track: blowing up buses and raining rockets on Israeli towns, hoping to scare Israelis into leaving the country, or cowering them into submission. Yet Israel has proved resilient once again, stopping the terrorism with intelligence, technology and real-time deterrence like checkpoints and the security barrier.

Sitting over lunch, this journalist and I wondered what might be the next decisive tactic in the campaign to destroy Israel. I told him that I'd been thinking a lot about apartheid South Africa. Global activists – employing a combination of U.N. condemnations, diplomatic isolation, an arms embargo, economic sanctions and divestment, and a cultural boycott that shunned South African academics, artists and athletes – created the perception of a regime that was illegitimate and immoral, to the point where the world demanded that it be dismantled.

The pressure worked and apartheid collapsed.

And so today, the State of Israel has become the target of a new warfare, designed to portray it as an outcast nation – the 21st century version of apartheid South Africa. Ted Koppel may have been the first mainstream journalist to make this association; after producing a series of programs on South African apartheid, he went searching for "the next South Africa." In 1987, Koppel discovered that "it was Israel. The equivalent of Bishop Tutu versus Foreign Minister Botha would be the Palestinians versus the Israelis... a replay of the biblical tale of David and Goliath."[8] In targeting Israel, Koppel first painted a bullseye, then shot his arrow.

With an extraordinary degree of irony that only the U.N. is capable of, this movement was formally launched in 2001 when Israel bashers convened for the U.N.'s Durban Conference Against Racism. Meeting in

South Africa (note the symbolism), the conference called for "the imposition of mandatory and comprehensive sanctions and embargoes, the full cessation of all links (diplomatic, economic, social, aid, military cooperation, and training) between all states and Israel" – adopting "a policy of complete and total isolation of Israel as an apartheid state."[9]

Predictably, there has been no shortage of media outlets willing to jump on the bandwagon. Writing on the op-ed pages of the *Atlanta Journal-Constitution*, under the headline "Israelis Adopt What South Africa Dropped," U.N. official John Dugard attacked Israel for displaying "many of the worst characteristics of apartheid."[10] Matt McCarten penned a column for the *New Zealand Herald* entitled, "Palestinians' Fight is a Struggle Against Apartheid,"[11] and Jimmy Carter not-so-subtly named his book, *Palestine: Peace Not Apartheid*[12] (and earned the praise of Osama bin Laden).[13]

Logically, this comparison just doesn't add up. In apartheid South Africa, hospitals were segregated and interracial marriage was illegal. Blacks could not vote, could not attend white universities, and could not eat in white restaurants. In this regard, any comparison to Israel is ludicrous: Jewish and Arab babies are born in the same delivery room, attended by the same doctors and nurses. Jews and Arabs share meals in restaurants and travel on the same buses and trains. Could any of this possibly have happened under apartheid? Of course not.[14]

Yet the *Hartford Courant* granted op-ed space to an academic "calling for an end to U.S. aid to the Israeli apartheid system,"[15] and at least five American newspapers, including the *Washington Post*, published Robert D. Novak's column, "Worse than Apartheid?" (His answer: yes.)[16]

Ironically, Arabs living in Israel enjoy more freedom and rights than Arabs elsewhere in the Middle East, where autocratic regimes regularly suppress freedom of the press, freedom of speech, freedom of association and freedom of religion. Israel permits Muslims to freely build minarets, wear burqas and pray in the streets – activities that are variously illegal in the "progressive" nations of Switzerland,[17] Holland,[18] Belgium[19] and France.[20]

So as I sat there over lunch with the Mideast correspondent, I asked rather nonchalantly, "Which was the first country in the Middle East to grant Arab women the right to vote?" He wasn't sure, but surmised that it was either Egypt, Jordan or Kuwait. "No," I told him, "it wasn't any of the 23 Arab states. It was Israel."

In Israel today, Arabs are represented in all strata of society. Salim Joubran is a justice on the Israeli Supreme Court,[21] and another Arab judge, George Karra, was entrusted with sending former Israeli President Moshe Katsav to prison on misconduct charges.[22] Hisham Abu Rayya is an officer in the IDF[23] and Israeli-Arab women serve in elite paratrooper units.[24] Ali Yahya was Israel's ambassador to Finland and to Greece,[25] and Reda Mosnsieur is the youngest ambassador in Israel's history. Arab-Israeli writer Emile Habibi was awarded the Israel Prize, the country's highest civilian honor.[26] Walid Badir is a soccer star on the Israeli national team, and Rana Raslan was crowned "Miss Israel."[27] Currently, 10 percent of Israeli parliament (Knesset) members are Arab. Majalli Wahabi, an Arab, has served as both Deputy Speaker of the Knesset and – you heard right – acting President of Israel.[28]

Israel's sincere effort to bring minorities to parity in socio-economic spheres – whether Russians, Ethiopians or Arabs – shatters the myth of an "oppressive apartheid state." Yet this didn't stop Salon.com, under the headline "Israel's Apartheid," from declaring that "Arabs are still waiting for Israel to uphold their basic human rights."[29] Nor did it deter BBC from publishing the headline: "Israeli Arabs: 'Unequal Citizens.'"[30]

One-third of the staff at Israel's Hadassah Hospital – arguably the leading hospital in the Middle East – are Arabs. At Haifa University, 20 percent of the student population is Arab,[31] and at Hebrew University in Jerusalem, 30 percent of students are Arab.[32] Hundreds of Arabs are enrolled at Ariel University in the West Bank.[33] Yet Britain's largest college teachers' union (the same group that supports the Cuba Solidarity Campaign, defending a country not widely noted for upholding academic freedoms) voted to boycott Israeli academics over what it termed "apartheid" policies toward Palestinians.[34]

The media goes in search of any "data" to bolster the apartheid perception. When an Arab resident of Jerusalem was convicted of rape for having lured an Israeli woman after lying about his identity, the media wildly denounced Israel for employing a racist, anti-Arab policy. ABC News asserted that the case "has raised some very difficult questions about discrimination" in Israel,[35] while CNN joined the frenzy with an online video report, "Rape by Deception, Or Racist?"[36]

The media was creating a "racist" charge that was simply false. Israel's "rape-by-deception" law is based on a 2008 Israeli Supreme Court ruling that convicted a Jewish man who impersonated a government official. Since then, other Jews have been convicted under the same law. But in the rush to cast judgment against Israel, media outlets spun the Arab case as "racist."[37]

One voice of reason is Muslim author Irshad Manji, who rhetorically asks: "Would an apartheid state award its top literary prize to an Arab?... Would an apartheid state encourage Hebrew-speaking schoolchildren to learn Arabic? Would road signs throughout the land appear in both languages [with Arabic an official language of Israel]?... Would the vast majority of Arab-Israeli citizens turn out to vote in national elections?... Would an apartheid state ensure conditions for the freest Arabic press in the Middle East?"[38] Even Richard Goldstone declared: "In Israel, there is no apartheid. Nothing there comes close to the definition of apartheid."[39]

Yet incredibly, *Time* magazine parallels the Palestinian plight to the iconic human rights stories of "Birmingham, Soweto and Gandhi's Salt March."[40]

If Israel is such an oppressive, racist state, then why did a survey by the Arab Center for Applied Social Research find that 90 percent of Israeli Arabs would rather live in the Jewish state than anywhere else – a position so fiercely held that 73 percent of Israeli Arabs say they would violently oppose any diplomatic agreement to include them in a future Palestinian state.[41]

If the media is looking for discrimination against Palestinians today, it ought to focus instead on Arab states – the apartheid laws in Lebanon, where Palestinians are legally banned from owning property and working in most professions;[42] Jordan revoking the citizenship of thousands of Palestinians in 2010;[43] and Kuwait's eviction of a quarter-million Palestinians,[44] acknowledged by even Yasser Arafat that "what Kuwait did to the Palestinian people is worse than what has been done by Israel."[45]

Yet on all this, the media is virtually silent.

Nor does the media utter a word about gender apartheid in Saudi Arabia, where Saudi men control virtually every aspect of women's lives: women have been arrested for driving a car,[46] have no independent right to leave the country,[47] and make up just 5 percent of the workforce – the lowest proportion in the world.[48] A recent Saudi fatwa pronounced execution for anyone who dares to compromise on absolute gender apartheid.[49]

By contrast, in 2008, four of the top positions in Israeli society were filled by women: Tzipi Livni was Foreign Minister, Dorit Beinisch was President of the Supreme Court, Dalia Itzik was Speaker of the Knesset, and Gabriela Shalev was Israeli Ambassador to the U.N. In a perfect world, one would expect the media to embrace this example of Israel's dedication to equal rights. So imagine my surprise when a full-page paid advertisement honoring these women – under the slogan, "This is Israel" – was rejected by the editors at *Ms.* magazine. For a publication that fancies itself at the forefront of women's rights, the rules significantly differ when the women are Israeli.[50]

In the realm of religious freedom, too, Israel stands as a beacon of light. Since 1948, Israel is the only country in the Middle East where the Christian population has increased – rising by more than 400 percent.[51] The headquarters of the Bahai faith is in Haifa, for the simple reason that Israel is the only country in the Middle East where a Bahai Temple is allowed.[52] And in what can only be described as an unprecedented show of religious tolerance, after recapturing the Temple Mount in 1967 – the center of the Jewish world for over 3,000 years – Israel shocked the world by handing Muslim religious leaders autonomy over the site.[53] Then, to further protect Muslim rights, the Israeli government – incredibly – passed a law forbidding *Jews* from praying at their holiest site.[54]

By contrast, much of the Arab Middle East remains rife with religious intolerance. Saudi Arabia openly practices religious apartheid, with special roads and even entire cities for "Muslims only."[55] In Saudi Arabia, the public practice of any religion other than Islam is illegal, and non-Muslim religious activities carry the risk of arrest, imprisonment, lashing and deportation.[56] A notice on the Saudi Airlines website prohibited the possession of any non-Islamic religious symbols – Bibles, crucifixes and the Star of David – mentioning them in the same breath as narcotics, firearms and pornography.[57]

When it comes to Jews, the restrictions are even more severe: Most Arab countries refuse entry to Jews and Israelis, or even to anyone whose passport shows evidence of having visited Israel.[58] The Palestinian Authority regards selling land to Jews as punishable by death and has issued the verdict dozens of times.[59] Even in Egypt and Jordan – countries with longstanding peace agreements with Israel – it is illegal to sell or rent land to Israelis.[60]

At times, the media itself shows little more respect for the Jewish faith. Here's how *Time* magazine described weekend life in Israel: "Jerusalem turns into a mausoleum in observance of the Jewish Sabbath."[61] A mausoleum? Would *Time* dare to describe the quiet that descends over Arab villages on Ramadan as a "mausoleum"? Can one imagine *Time* describing an American town on Christmas Eve as a "mausoleum"? It's unthinkable. But it's not unthinkable to describe the capital city of the Jewish state, in observance of a 4,000-year-old tradition whose influence is felt throughout the entire civilized world, as a "mausoleum."[62]

Imagine the chutzpah of *New York Times* columnist Maureen Dowd quoting Saudi Prince Saud al-Faisal's attack on religious practice in Israel: "The religious institutions in Israel are stymieing every effort at peace."[63] Underscoring the sad irony of Dowd's column was a *Saudi Gazette* story that very same day about a Saudi woman who was gang-raped by five men near Jeddah – and then convicted of "adultery" for which she was sentenced to one year in jail and lashed 100 times.[64]

Where are the media protests against this Arab-sponsored apartheid?

There are none. A Google search for "Israeli apartheid" turns up 2.6 million results; a search for "Saudi apartheid" lists 1,800 results – less than one-tenth of one percent.[65] The numbers are equally disparate on a LexisNexis news search: "Israeli apartheid" produces 2,136 results; "Saudi apartheid" a mere seven.[66]

All these references are designed to portray Israel as an illegitimate enterprise that, for the sake of humanity, needs to be terminated. And slowly but surely, the canard is taking hold; Israel Apartheid Week is now observed in 100 cities around the world.[67]

Here's one small example of how this deligitimization works: In 2009, when the Toronto Film Festival announced plans to showcase films from Tel Aviv, "Hanoi" Jane Fonda boycotted the festival in protest. This petty maneuvering might have otherwise gone unnoticed were it not for a scandal-obsessed media intent on fanning the flames. A *New York Times* headline blared: "Protests Grow Louder Over Israeli Presence at Toronto Film Festival,"[68] while Associated Press distributed the story to its 15,000 subscribing publications.[69]

Journalists get directly into the act as well. In 2007, in protest against Israeli policies, Britain's National Union of Journalists voted to boycott all Israeli goods.[70] Political arguments aside, is there any greater declaration of media bias than a journalists' organization taking on the role of political activists?

Kevin Blackistone, a panelist on the sports network ESPN, added his two cents: "Maybe a sports boycott of Israel, where sports are beloved the same as in South Africa… could exercise the same leverage on Israel that it did for nearly 30 years with South Africa."[71]

In 2011 at Britain's Edinburgh University, a speech by an official from the Israeli Foreign Ministry was boycotted by the school's International Relations Society, on the grounds of being "unjust to the Palestinian people who live under an apartheid regime." Protesters disrupted the speech with chants and taunts, forcing the speaker to abandon the stage. The incredible irony is that the speaker was Ismail Khaldi, an Israeli Arab-Muslim who holds a senior position in the Israeli government – living proof there is no "apartheid" in Israel – and yet was the target of protesters screaming "apartheid!"[72]

In the meantime, while one million Arabs enjoy full citizenship rights in the State of Israel, journalists never consider the moral irony of Palestinians calling for a future state that is *Judenrein*, the Nazi-era word that means "cleansed of Jews."[73] Has the media ever campaigned against this policy of blatant racism, reiterated in 2010 by Palestinian leader Mahmoud Abbas: "I would not agree... that there will live among us even a single Israeli on Palestinian land."[74] On the contrary, when Israel's Prime Minister raised this very issue, Reuters twisted it around and accused *Israel* of employing Nazi methodologies, with this wild tabloid-style headline: "Judenrein! Israel Adopts Nazi Term to Back Settlers."[75]

Israel's human rights record may not be perfect, but it is doing its best in a difficult situation. If restrictions such as checkpoints and the security barrier are placed on Palestinians, there is genuine justification – unlike in South Africa, where black communities were not producing terrorists nor threatening to annihilate the white population. Apartheid-era South Africa was a repugnant regime intent on preserving white supremacy; Israel is a democracy intent on preserving itself from destruction. In other words, Hamas is not Mandela.

Kenneth Meshoe, a black South African Member of Parliament, set the record straight: "If anyone says to you there is apartheid in Israel, tell them the man who was oppressed by apartheid in South Africa says it's a big lie. Coming from South Africa, it is laughable to draw a parallel. If the government of Israel is accused of being heavy-handed for wanting to wipe out terrorism, we are here from South Africa to say: 'You are not alone.'"[76]

Holocaust: Justification for the Jewish State

In May 2008 an email popped into my inbox. It was a confidential link to an advance copy of the BBC documentary, *The Birth of Israel*, promoting the idea that the Holocaust created the moral argument for a Jewish state.[77] European Jews were persecuted and needed a place to go, the theory goes, so European imperialists – wracked with guilt – looked around and plunked the Jews down on a piece of "Muslim land" in the colonized Middle East.

This was an incredible perversion of history, and I immediately called my contact at BBC. "While it is true that the Nazi genocide intensified the urgent need for a Jewish state," I told her, "placing the Holocaust as the start of Israeli history disconnects it from the 4,000 years of Jewish national, religious and historic connection to the land. Did BBC forget that Abraham, Isaac and Jacob, King David and Solomon, the Jewish prophets and the Holy Temple are all rooted in Israel? Is BBC unaware that the Jewish yearning for the land, having spanned millennium, is known as 'the longest, deepest love affair in history'?"[78]

"Are you suggesting that the tragedy of the Holocaust played no role in the United Nations decision to partition Palestine in 1947?" she asked.

"Of course it had an influence," I said. "But the facts on the ground had a far more profound effect. Prior to the outbreak of World War II, the Jewish community had already established the institutions of an independent state: schools, newspapers, agriculture, industry, health care and a quasi-government. Prior to the war, the Jewish population of Palestine already numbered 450,000,[79] with Jewish workers constituting 79 percent of the total work force."[80]

Surely the Jewish state did not arise from a vacuum in the mid-20th century – yet *Time* magazine wiped out 4,000 years of Jewish history in stating that the idea of Israel as "the national home of the Jewish people... emerged in the late 19th century."[81] Likewise when media outlets like CNN,[82] *Newsweek*,[83] the *Washington Post*[84] and *Chicago Tribune*[85] describe Israel as rising "out of the ashes of the Holocaust," it promotes the myth that despite millennium of history, Jews are outsiders in the region.

It is this type of thinking that led Helen Thomas – the Washington-based correspondent for 57 years who held the honored "front and center" chair at presidential press conferences – to declare that Israel "should get the hell out of Palestine" and that Jews should go back to "Poland, Germany and America and everywhere else."[86]

Was this outrage reported on the front page of every newspaper in

America? Nope. Did the White House Correspondents Association immediately expel her? Nope. In fact, when former White House Press Secretary Ari Fleischer called for Thomas to resign, Ann Compton – White House correspondent for ABC News and past president of the White House Correspondents Association – flippantly dismissed Fleischer's remarks as being that of "a private citizen [who is] certainly free to express his opinion."[87] Would Compton have been as cavalier if Helen Thomas was advocating that blacks "get the hell out of America and go back to Africa"?

A few days later, when Thomas was forced to retire (read: resign), the *New York Times* reported that this followed "an uproar over her recent remarks that Jews should 'get the hell out of Palestine.'"[88] In a classic case of selective omission, the *Times* never mentioned the most shocking and offensive part of Thomas' statement – advocating that Jews go back to Poland and Germany, the places of the Final Solution.

Note the thrust of Thomas' argument: She didn't rail against Israeli policies like the security barrier or settlements. This was not an issue of "get out of the territories and go back to Tel Aviv." No, this was get out of the Middle East altogether.[89] With this, Thomas revealed her ignorance of basic Israeli demography: In the years immediately following Israel's creation, 860,000 Jews fled from Arab lands amidst threats and violence, and today they and their descendants – Jews indigenous to the region – form the core of Israel's population.[90]

As for Thomas' argument that the Jews have no connection with the land of Israel, Jay Leno, in his *Tonight Show* monologue, got to the heart of the matter:

> "Helen Thomas said that Jews should leave the Middle East and go back to where they came from. The problem is, that's where they came from: the Middle East. It's in a book. It's called the Bible."[91]

Holy Sites

All this got me thinking about what really lies behind the myth – most commonly found in the British media – that Jews are so-called "European colonialists" who allegedly "stole the land."

The answer lies in the British historical experience. While the American media sees the Israeli-Palestinian conflict as an underdog story, the British have latched onto a very different narrative: They see it through the lens of colonialism, the idea of expanding an empire through conquering and subjugating other lands. The British Empire practiced this policy for centuries, holding sway over one-quarter of the world – India, the Caribbean, Gibraltar, Falklands, Singapore, Australia, Canada, New Zealand, parts of Africa – to the point where "the sun never set on the British Empire." And now, the British media views Israel's presence in the Middle East as yet another "colonial sin."

There are fatal flaws with this comparison. Israel is the ancient Jewish homeland; control of the disputed territories resulted from a defensive war; and Israel has never sought to subjugate or exploit the Arabs. So what is driving this narrative?

Support for the Palestinian "liberation struggle" is – perhaps subconsciously – a way for the British to alleviate their own colonial guilt. As political analyst Robin Shepherd observed: Europe is "awash in post-imperial guilt, and I frequently get the sense that Israel's claim to a piece of land in the Middle East revives guilt-inducing memories, among my English countrymen and others, of white Europeans carving up the Third World and subjugating 'lesser peoples' in the 19th century." This, Shepherd discerns, "can make for an intoxicating cocktail of anti-Israeli sentiment."[92]

Once this "colonial" narrative is out there, Palestinians exploit it as a way to deny any Jewish connection to the land. "The claims of historic and religious ties between Jews and Palestine are incompatible with the facts of history," reads the Palestinian National Charter.[93] When archeologists in Jerusalem discovered a small golden bell, possibly from a tunic worn by a high priest during the Second Temple period, Palestinian officials angrily said this "underlines the efforts of the occupation and the extremist Jewish groups to falsify history and plant Jewish history forged in the region."[94] And following the release of an iPhone app that sends prayers to the

Western Wall, Palestinians immediately went into protest mode, insisted that "the Wailing Wall is an integral part of the Al Aqsa Mosque, and it is exclusively Islamic... and non-Muslims have no right to it, even to the dust of the Wailing Wall."[95]

The deceit goes straight to the top: In the words of Palestinian leader Mahmoud Abbas, the Jewish people "claim that 2,000 years ago they had a Temple. I challenge the claim that this is so."[96] The Palestinian ambassador to Washington, Maen Rashid Areikat, claimed that historically the Jewish presence in Israel "never was in Jerusalem, it never was on the coast, it never was in Hebron."[97] A music video with the verse "O Zion, no matter how much you dig... your imaginary Temple will not come into being," is broadcast regularly on Palestinian TV.[98] *Le Monde*, the French newspaper of record, quoted PA cabinet minister Yasser Abed Rabbo: "Looking at the situation from an archaeological standpoint, I am sure there is no temple."[99]

In 2010, when Israel held dedication ceremonies for the rebuilt Hurva synagogue – a centerpiece of the Jerusalem's Old City which had been destroyed (along with every other Old City synagogue) by the Jordanian army in 1948[100] – Palestinian cabinet member Khatem Abd el-Kader called it an "Israeli attempt to destroy the mosque and replace it with the [Jewish] temple."[101]

Leaving aside the basic right of Israel to rebuild a synagogue that Arabs had destroyed, was this really the provocation it was made out to be? In order for the Hurva synagogue to undermine the Al Aqsa mosque, you'd have to dig a tunnel across the Jewish Quarter, descend the steep Tyropoeon Valley to the Western Wall plaza, and ascend another steep hill before ever reaching the Temple Mount. Even Gaza's best tunnel diggers aren't that good.[102]

Yet this didn't deter media outlets like CNN from sensationalizing the synagogue as being located "just 300 meters or so from the Al Aqsa mosque,"[103] and Reuters from presenting the idea that the Hurva synagogue "endangered al-Aqsa."[104]

It's all part of an ongoing campaign – aided by a willing media – to minimize Jewish connection to the land. When archaeologists unearthed a biblical ruin in the ancient city of Shechem (Nablus), Associated Press cited this as "evidence" that all local history, "including that of the biblical Israelites, are part of Palestinian history." AP then showed where its sympathies lie, quoting Palestinian official Hamdan Taha that such findings "give Palestinians the opportunity to participate in writing or rewriting the history of Palestine."[105]

Even canonized Jewish writings, accepted for millennia by billions of people worldwide, are targeted for revision. Speaking on Palestinian TV, researcher Dr. Hayel Sanduqa claimed that the well-known verse from Psalm 137, "If I forget thee, oh Jerusalem," is not a Jewish source at all, but rather words uttered by a Christian Crusader, now "falsified in the name of Zionism."[106] And when the iconic 1970s disco group Boney M played a concert in Ramallah, Palestinian organizers demanded that the band not perform one of its biggest hits, "Rivers of Babylon." Why? Because the song's chorus quotes from the Book of Psalms which – in a brazen act of Zionist propaganda! – refers to the Jewish yearning for the land of Israel.[107]

Follow the steps: First, Palestinians claim that Jews never lived in Israel, nor was there a Holy Temple. And while clear historical facts engrained over millennia cannot be erased in one fell swoop, these claims have an incremental effect by planting seeds of doubt, courtesy of the media. Then before you know it, standard media references to the Jewish Temple – accepted as historical fact by every legitimate archeologist and scholar – is deemed debatable. London's *Daily Telegraph* referred to "the Temple Mount, where the two Jewish temples of antiquity are *believed* to have been built,"[108] and *Time* magazine identified the "Dome of the Rock, where Jews *believe* Solomon and Herod built the First and Second Temples."[109] Not an indisputable fact of history; just something that "Jews believe."

Another way the media downplays the Jewish connection is to promote the Arabic names of holy sites. In referring to the Temple Mount, the Associated Press,[110] *New York Times*,[111] *Los Angeles Times*,[112] *USA Today*,[113] et al, typically cite the Muslim-Arabic name – "Haram al Sharif, the Noble Sanctuary." But did you ever see the Temple Mount referred to by its

Hebrew name, "Har Habayit"? A Lexis-Nexis search of tens of thousands of mainstream news articles relating to Jerusalem revealed – aside from direct quotes – just one single reference to "Har Habayit."[114]

Four thousand years of uncontested history is now being brazenly erased on news sites everywhere. Is this what qualifies today as responsible journalism?

One popular and nefarious media devise is to describe the Temple Mount as Islam's "third-holiest site" – while omitting its more germane and long-standing identity as Judaism's "first-holiest site." This "third-holiest" reference starts with the *New York Times*,[115] *Washington Post*,[116] Associated Press[117] and Reuters[118] – and then filters down to nearly every other mainstream media outlet.

When it comes to Judaism's "first-holiest site," journalists can't even get that right. Across the board, the media routinely refers to the Western Wall as "Judaism's holiest site,"[119] while in fact the Western Wall is but a retaining wall of Judaism's true holiest site – the Temple Mount.

As for Islam's "first-holiest site" – the Kaaba in Mecca – journalists misrepresent that, too, referring instead to Jerusalem's Dome of the Rock as "Islam's holiest shrine."[120] And while there is significance to the Temple Mount as Islam's "third-holiest site," as one pundit notes, "When the topic is love, third place suggests a certain lack of ardor."[121]

At the very least, shouldn't balanced reporting refer likewise to the Cave of the Patriarchs in Hebron as "Judaism's second-holiest site," and to Rachel's Tomb in Bethlehem as "Judaism's third-holiest site"? Yet a Lexis-Nexis search of thousands of articles over the past decade reveals no such reference in any mainstream Western news report.[122]

These distinctions are not merely semantic; they directly impact international policy. In 2010, when the Israeli government announced a seemingly innocuous plan to include the Cave of the Patriarchs and Rachel's Tomb on its list of "national heritage sites," Palestinians went ballistic – calling it a "provocative" plan "meant to provoke a violent response"[123] and a new Intifada.[124] The Western media followed the Palestinians' lead, blaring bombastic headlines like "Heritage Plan 'Could Lead to Religious

War.'"¹²⁵ The fact that Israel would be investing its own money in routine infrastructure improvements, such as new bathrooms and roofing at sites that it already controls, was deemed sufficient provocation for United Press International to call it an Israeli "takeover of West Bank shrines."¹²⁶

Of course, the media never bothered to mention that the Cave of the Patriarchs is the oldest Jewish shrine, revered for nearly 4,000 years as the burial site of the patriarchs Abraham, Isaac, Jacob and their wives. Voice of America – broadcasting to 1,200 affiliates worldwide – erased this profound Jewish connection, describing Hebron as "the front line of the conflict between Palestinians who have lived here for hundreds of years, and Jewish settlers who have made this their home here over the past few decades."¹²⁷ Meanwhile a photo in the *Philadelphia Inquirer* of two Jewish men praying at the Cave the Patriarchs carried a caption describing the location as "the Mosque of Ibrahim" – ignoring its status as the second holiest site in Judaism and framing it instead as an exclusively Islamic site.¹²⁸

Rachel's Tomb in Bethlehem, Judaism's third-holiest site with a tradition uninterrupted for nearly four millennia,¹²⁹ is assailed by Palestinians as a "fake" that was "originally a Muslim mosque" – allegedly named after Bilal ibn Rabah, known in history as one of Muhammad's black African slaves.¹³⁰ Right on cue, Reuters mimicked this outrageous claim, reporting that "Muslims say the real Rachel's Tomb is elsewhere and the compound in question contains a revered old mosque, Bilal al-Rabah."¹³¹

The media somehow forgets the fact that Rachel's Tomb – with its famed dome-and-olive-tree design – has appeared in thousands of Jewish religious books, paintings, photographs, stamps and works of art.¹³² The media forgets that centuries before Islam was even founded, Christian pilgrims wrote of Rachel's Tomb as a solely Jewish site.¹³³ The media also forgets that Islamic historians – Muhammad al-Idrisi, the great 12th century geographer,¹³⁴ 16th century Arab historian Mujir al-Din,¹³⁵ and even decades of modern Palestinian publications¹³⁶ – refer to the site exclusively as "Rachel's Tomb."

Yet a combination of recent Palestinian propaganda¹³⁷ and a complicit media has managed to expunge 4,000 years of Jewish history, and in 2010, the United Nations' cultural arm, UNESCO, voted 44 to one to officially declare Rachel's Tomb as the Bilal ibn Rabah Mosque, adding that any action by Israel to preserve the site for Jewish purposes would be considered a violation of international law.[138] The international community willingly accepted the ruling, effectively trampling on the 1995 Oslo II Accords (Article V, Annex I) that clearly acknowledge Israeli control and use of these sites.[139]

Similarly, Joseph's Tomb in Nablus is presented not as the 3,300-year-old resting place of the biblical patriarch Joseph, but rather – as dutifully reported by BBC – the tomb of a Muslim cleric named Sheikh Yussif Dawiqat who was supposedly buried there two centuries ago.[140] As for the millennia of Jewish tradition which says otherwise,[141] the *Daily Telegraph* passed that off as the machinations of some fringe element: "The site is believed by extreme nationalist Jews to be the burial site of the biblical patriarch Joseph."[142] Associated Press likewise suggested that the site is a Jewish sham, explaining that "Most Jews do not believe that Joseph, the biblical patriarch, has anything to do with the site," given that "tradition holds that Joseph was buried in Egypt."[143] That may be AP's version of "tradition," but not for the two-thirds of humanity who own a copy of the standard Bible stating that Joseph's body was taken from Egypt and reinterred in Shechem, the Hebrew name for Nablus. (Joshua 24:32, if you want to look it up.)

The degree of ignorance on these points is astounding. During the Intifada, one of the most recognized names in broadcast journalism planned to do a report from atop the Aish HaTorah building overlooking the Temple Mount. An hour before the shoot, his producer turned to my friend Elliot Mathias, director of the Hasbara Fellowships program, and – while gesturing toward the Temple Mount – said in a somewhat apologetic tone, "You'll have to excuse my ignorance, but what exactly are we looking at?"

Elliot inquired if perhaps she was unsure of a specific building: Al-Aqsa Mosque, Dome of the Rock, the Southern Wall excavations, Warren's Gate,

Robinson's Arch?

"No," she said, "what is this entire area we are looking at?"

Elliot could barely contain his shock. "It's the Temple Mount – the focal point of this entire conflict!"

A few minutes later, the veteran anchorman arrived. He climbed the stairs to join his team on the roof. As he reached the top stair, he looked at the Temple Mount spread out before him. "Oh, I've been here before," he said with an air of vague familiarity. Then, looking at his producer, he asked quietly, "What is this we're looking at?"

If this is the quality of reporting on major news networks, then – as Dan Rather would say – things are shakier than cafeteria Jell-O.[144]

Palestinians and the Holocaust

The idea that Israel "arose from the ashes of the Holocaust on land stolen from the Palestinians" is but stage one of the media's historic mythology. BBC's documentary, *The Birth of Israel*, took it further and used the Holocaust as a weapon against Israel, quoting one interviewee: "Why should the Palestinians who had not heard of it pay the price of the Holocaust?... Why displace the Palestinian people to pay a price for a crime which they had not committed?"[145]

I watched this video and shook my head in dismay. How ironic that BBC was trying to turn the Palestinians into "Holocaust victims," given the fact that Palestinian leaders during the 1940s were avowed and active partners in that very same Holocaust. Palestinian founding father Mufti Haj Amin al-Husseini organized 42,000 Muslim troops to form Nazi SS divisions – carrying out police actions in fascist Hungary, fighting against Yugoslav partisans, and participating in the genocide of Yugoslav Jews.[146] Husseini enjoyed a close relationship with Hitler (upon whom he conferred the Islamicized name, Abu Ali),[147] and engaged in frequent correspondence with Nazi leaders like SS Chief Heinrich Himmler and German Foreign Minister Joachim von Ribbentrop.

Husseini spent the war years in Berlin where, at the behest of Nazi propaganda minister Joseph Goebbels, he delivered a daily pro-Nazi radio broadcast to the Muslim world.[148] He organized a Palestinian youth group – called the "Nazi Scouts" – modeled after the Hitler Youth. He issued fatwas calling for the destruction of the United States and Great Britain,[149] and exhorted Arabs living in the U.S. not to support the Allied war effort. "If those Allies win this war..." he said, "then the world will become hell, God forbid."[150]

Husseini was an early architect of the genocidal Final Solution, one of the few non-Germans made privy to the mass exterminations while they were taking place. High-ranking SS officer Dieter Wisliceny would later testify at the Nuremberg trials: "The Mufti was one of the initiators of the systematic extermination of European Jewry, and had been a collaborator and advisor of Eichmann and Himmler in the execution of this plan... He was one of Eichmann's best friends and had constantly incited him to accelerate the extermination measures."[151] Husseini was even plotting to construct his own Nazi-style death camp in the West Bank.[152]

Whenever I present this information to journalists, the response I invariably get is: "You can't blame the Palestinian people for the actions of one man."

This may have the ring of a good argument, but it doesn't square with the historical facts. As the premier political and religious leader of the Palestinians, Husseini enjoyed near-total support of the Palestinian Arab population. On a wartime visit to Palestine, Adolf Eichmann swelled with pride at how "Nazi flags fly in Palestine and they adorn their houses with Swastikas and portraits of Hitler."[153] In the words of Edward Said, the well-known advocate for Palestinian rights, Husseini "represented the Palestinian Arab national consensus, had the backing of the Palestinian political parties that functioned in Palestine, and was recognized in some form by Arab governments as the voice of the Palestinian people."[154]

After the war, Husseini was convicted as a war criminal by the Yugoslav Supreme Military Court. He escaped and was welcomed as a hero in Egypt – where he promptly won election as president of the National Palestinian Council.[155]

Was it intentional obfuscation when BBC falsely reported that

Husseini was "discredited" amongst Palestinians for being "associated with defeat"?[156]

The great irony of this attempt to disassociate Palestinians from the Holocaust is that the goal of today's Palestinian terror groups is to foment genocide – read Holocaust – of the Jewish state. It's no wonder that various Palestinian militants use the moniker "Hitler,"[157] and *Mein Kampf* regularly appears on the Palestinian best-seller list.[158] Meanwhile, the Nazi salute has been resurrected for contemporary use by Hamas, Fatah, Hezbollah and Iranian troops.

Given this Palestinian link to the Holocaust, it is a bizarre paradox that today's Arab leaders are some of the worst purveyors of Holocaust denial. We all know about Mahmoud Ahmadinejad's 2006 "International Conference to Review the Global Vision of the Holocaust," and the regular Holocaust denial in the Syrian and Egyptian media.[159] But how about the president of the Palestinian Authority, Mahmoud Abbas? While studying at Moscow's Oriental College in the 1950s, Abbas wrote as his doctoral thesis a tome of classic Holocaust denial that refers to the "Zionist fantasy, the fantastic lie that six million Jews were killed."[160] Later published in book form as *The Other Side: The Secret Relationship Between Nazism and Zionism,* Abbas writes that the small number of Jewish victims was actually part of a Zionist-Nazi plot; Hitler did not decide to kill the Jews until David Ben-Gurion provoked him into doing so.[161]

The strategy of such Holocaust denial is clear: If the State of Israel was founded on the basis of Holocaust guilt – and the Holocaust itself was a scam – then Israel's very existence is deemed "illegitimate."

Meanwhile, the official PA newspaper, *Al-Hayat Al-Jadida,* declared that "the figure of six million Jews" murdered by the Nazis "is a lie for propaganda,"[162] and on Palestinian TV, Dr. Issam Sissalem of Gaza's Islamic University explained "there was no Dachau, no Auschwitz – [they] were cleansing sites."[163] The Palestinian Authority has officially banned teaching about the Holocaust in schools;[164] after a West Bank youth orchestra played for a group of Holocaust survivors in Israel, Palestinian authorities disbanded the orchestra and arrested its conductor.[165]

Never heard any of this before? That's because the media does a good job of covering it up. Following President Barack Obama's 2009 speech in Cairo in which he chastised the Muslim world for Holocaust denial, news outlets including Associated Press,[166] *Washington Post*[167] and Agence France Presse[168] reported the reaction of Mahmoud Abbas to the speech – but failed to connect the dots in flagging him as a prominent source of that selfsame Holocaust denial. And in its biographical sketch of Abbas, the *New York Times* made no mention of his Holocaust denial, referring to him dryly as "a lawyer and historian," and describing the topic of his doctoral thesis simply as "Zionism."[169]

Here's what makes this Holocaust denial so subversive: With genocide against the Jews a historical reality, the trauma of the Holocaust drives much of Israel's intensity for self-defense. The slogan "Never Again" is embedded in Israel's psyche, informing its decision-making, both politically and militarily.[170] That's why whenever journalists visit my office, I always point out the piece of brick from the Auschwitz crematoria that sits on my desk. The constant memory of the Holocaust is a key aspect of Israel's heightened vigilance – and Holocaust denial is designed to remove that.[171]

So Palestinian Holocaust revisionism vacillates between two main themes: Either the Holocaust didn't happen, in which case Israel's *raison d'etre* as a refuge from persecution is fraudulent; or it did happen, in which case Europeans should atone for their crimes by granting Jews a state in Europe rather than confiscate land from "innocent" Palestinians.[172] In the meantime, the media bolsters the whole sham by ignoring Israel's ancient right to its homeland and glossing over the Palestinian role in the Holocaust and their disingenuous denial of it.

Downplaying the Existential Threat

I'll never forget the time I flicked on National Public Radio, the "impartial" network whose executives – when told that NPR stands for "National *Palestinian* Radio" – were caught on camera laughing and commenting, "That's good. I like that."[173] Hamas had just set off a deadly bus bomb in Israel, and NPR was taking the opportunity to praise Hamas as "terrific community organizers" who sponsor "business projects like honey, cheese making and home-based clothing manufacture."[174]

Honey and cheese?! Isn't this the same Hamas that makes clear its goal of the total destruction of Israel? "There is no solution for the Palestinian question except by jihad," reads the Hamas charter in the cynically-named section, "Peaceful Solutions."[175] Even after Israel withdrew from Gaza in 2005, senior Hamas leader Nizar Rayan declared: "We do not distinguish between what was occupied in the 1940s and what was occupied in the 1960s. Our jihad continues... until the very last usurper is driven out of our land."[176]

Yet the media repeatedly downplays this existential threat to Israel. When Hamas won the 2006 Palestinian elections, Jonathan Steele of London's *Guardian* called Hamas the "best news from the Middle East in a long time,"[177] and a *Guardian* editorial hailed Hamas as bringing "new opportunities to the immense task of building peace."[178] Writing in the *Chicago Sun-Times* under the headline "Hamas Talks Peace," Robert Novak declared – in total contradiction of reality – that Hamas "recognizes Israel's right to exist and forgoes violence."[179]

Even outright calls for "genocide of the Jews" are obscured by the media. Here's how one case of Palestinian incitement was reported in the *New York Times*:

> Israelis cite as one egregious example a televised sermon that defended the killing of the two [Israeli] soldiers. "Whether Likud or Labor, Jews are Jews," proclaimed Sheik Ahmad Abu Halabaya in a live broadcast from a Gaza city mosque...[180]

In a classic case of selective omission, the *Times* went out of its way to choose a one-sentence quotation that – when taken out of context – could be seen as innocuous political posturing ("whether Likud or Labor"). But here's the salient point delivered in that same Gaza sermon:

> "Even if an agreement for Gaza is signed, we shall not forget

Haifa, and Acre, and the Galilee, and Jaffa, and the Triangle and the Negev, and the rest of our cities and villages [in pre-1967 Israel]. It is only a matter of time... Have no mercy on the Jews, no matter where they are, in any country. Fight them, wherever you are. Wherever you meet them, kill them."[181]

For readers of the *New York Times*, the key points of "conquer the entire land" and "kill all the Jews" were watered to down to a mere dislike for "Labor and Likud."[182]

Time and again, the media spins the most violent Palestinian groups as passive and calm. The *Globe and Mail*, Canada's newspaper of record, bought into the false notion that Hamas – best known for perfecting the art of bus bombings, rocket fire and restaurant explosions – has evolved into "ethical," "truthful," "pragmatic"[183] peaceniks who advocate "non-violent resistance."[184] *Newsweek* characterized Hamas as "admired for their ethos of resistance and their network of social services,"[185] and Steven Erlanger of the *New York Times* referred to Hamas as "the Islamic group that combines philanthropy and militancy..."[186]

Raw acts of Palestinian violence are similarly understated. In the West Bank town of Bilin, where Palestinian rioters regularly hurl rocks, Molotov cocktails and burning tires, 170 Israeli soldiers were injured in an 18-month period.[187] So how did the *Christian Science Monitor* describe this violence? "Peaceful Palestinian Resistance is Paying Off."[188] The *Los Angeles Times* – under the front-page headline, "Palestinians Who See Nonviolence as Their Weapon" – described how Palestinian weapons consist of an innocuous "bullhorn, banners, and a fierce belief" in "peaceful protest."[189] Incredibly, the *Times* suggests that 170 Israelis were injured after being overwhelmed by bullhorns and banners.

The upshot of it all? The more the media presents Palestinian radicals as peaceniks, the more Israel is stripped of its license to fight against them – endangering the very foundation of Israeli's security.

In May 2011, the *New York Times* stated as fact that Hamas is "fully committed" to a two-state solution, implicitly accepting Israel's right to exist.[190] Hamas, meanwhile, must not be reading the *Times*, because the Hamas representative to Iran, Khaled al-Qoddoumi, refuted any compromise, declaring that "the Zionist regime is a cancer and cancer must be uprooted." But who are you going to believe – the *New York Times'* wishful thinking, or what Hamas actually says in Arabic?[191]

So while the *raison d'etre* of Hamas is to destroy Israel entirely, journalists would have you believe otherwise. Hamas leader Khaled Meshal, interviewed on the *Charlie Rose Show*, said he did not support violence against civilians, and that attacks on Israel would stop once it withdrew to the 1967 borders.[192] Rose failed to challenge Meshal on the obvious contradiction between those words and Hamas' history of suicide bombings and its determination that "Palestine means Palestine in its entirety – from the [Mediterranean] Sea to the [Jordan] River... We cannot give up a single inch of it. Therefore, we will not recognize the Israeli enemy's [right] to a single inch..."[193]

For its part, BBC wrote that Hamas is "accused of carrying out suicide bombings as part of its campaign for a Palestinian state"[194] – a description that not only obscures Hamas' true goal of Israel's destruction, but also preposterously suggests that Hamas is merely "accused" of violence. When readers complained, BBC issued this unintelligible excuse: "We feel the article was correct to state that the Hamas' ultimate aim is the creation of a Palestinian state, as we did not comment on the proposed borders of that state."[195] That makes as such sense as saying that Hitler's "ultimate aim" was to strengthen Germany, without mentioning his quest for world domination and his genocidal methods of getting there.

In downplaying Hamas extremism, the worst offender is the "news agency" Reuters, for consistently repeating the falsehood that Hamas is engaging in an "uprising for independence,"[196] an "uprising for statehood,"[197] and a "Palestinian militant uprising against Israel for a state in Gaza and the West Bank."[198] According to Reuters, it apparently matters little if Hamas is blowing up Israeli buses and pizza shops – it's all a noble "pursuit of independence." It also apparently matters little that Hamas openly declares again and again its ultimate goal to free the entire

Palestinian land and destroy the Zionist regime; according to Reuters they seek only "Gaza and the West Bank."

This point was crucial and I decided to pour all my energies into fighting it. I produced a powerful online film, *Uprising for Reuters*, which went viral, generating a mass of publicity and helping to nudge Reuters toward this more balanced description:

> Hamas, sworn to Israel's destruction, has led a suicide bombing campaign during the three-year-old Palestinian uprising for independence.[199]

That was a bit better. But media monitors[200] kept up the pressure with swarms of emails and grassroots protests, and within days of my presenting Reuters with a "Dishonest Reporting Award,"[201] they began describing Hamas in more accurate terms:

> Hamas has led a suicide bombing campaign that has killed hundreds of Israelis during more than three years of violence. It has rejected peace talks and demanded that a Palestinian state be formed on all the land that was Palestine under the British mandate preceding the creation of Israel...[202]

Of course, Reuters stopped short of calling Hamas the "terrorists" they really are. But what can you expect from the same "news agency" that refused to call 9-11 "terror."

Mad Mullahs of Iran

When it comes to turning a blind eye to Israel's mortal enemies, the media reserves especially soft treatment for the Islamic Republic of Iran.

Iran directly reaches its tentacles into the Arab-Israeli conflict by supplying weapons and training to their Palestinian proxies: Hezbollah in the north and Hamas in the south.[203] In 2009, Israel's navy apprehended the MV *Francop* carrying no less than 320 tons of weapons including half a million rounds of ammunition – courtesy of Iran and destined for Hezbollah terror forces in Lebanon.[204] And remember the *Karine-A* shipment of 50 tons of Iranian weapons seized by Israeli naval commandos en route to Hamas terrorists in Gaza?

But not to worry. According to the *New York Times,* these huge stockpiles pose no threat to Israel: "Israel is a nuclear power and has jet fighters and tanks supplied by the United States. Had the arms shipment gotten through, Israel would have retained overwhelming firepower."[205]

In the meantime, Iranian president Mahmoud Ahmadinejad assails Israel with the most vicious genocidal threats:

- Israel "must be wiped off the map."[206]
- "The Zionist regime is a dried up and rotten tree which will be annihilated with one storm."[207]
- "The elimination of the Zionist regime will be smooth and simple."[208]

This is not mere rhetoric. Iran is moving quickly to build nuclear weapons, giving Tehran the means to make good on those threats. The mad mullahs have 3,000 centrifuges spinning in Natanz,[209] and Iran's Shahab-3 missile (already successfully tested) can carry nuclear warheads to a range of 2,000 kilometers – capable of reaching Israel, Europe and American forces in the Middle East.[210]

Sixty years after the Holocaust, the Jews are again the only nation in the world threatened with annihilation. Holocaust survivor and Nobel Peace Prize laureate Elie Wiesel had this to say about Ahmadinejad: "It would be wrong to question his determination... I belong to a generation that learned to take the enemy's words of hate seriously."[211]

Yet the media passes it all off as bluster. In 2009, Walt Rodgers, a former senior international correspondent for CNN and now columnist for the *Christian Science Monitor,* waved off Ahmadinejad's atomic ambitions as "bombast."[212] Jonathan Power, a foreign affairs columnist syndicated in dozens of papers worldwide, asserted "there is no evidence" that

Arab states are interested or able to "fight the kind of war that would be catastrophic for Israel."[213] And Reuters offered its own sanitization: "Ahmadinejad has repeatedly forecast the imminent disappearance of the Jewish state" – making nuclear apocalypse sound as innocuous as a weather report.[214]

In reporting on Ahmadinejad's horrific threat that Israel "must be wiped off the map," the *New York Times* and Associated Press cleverly re-translated the original Farsi into the far milder wish that Israel should "vanish from the pages of time"[215] – ignoring the fact that the Iranian government has erected billboards with the phrase "Israel should be wiped out of the face of the world" in plain English[216] and the slogan is painted on Iranian ballistic missiles.[217]

Some journalists even accuse Israel of fabricating these genocidal threats in order to perpetrate its own injustices. *Time* magazine's Joe Klein claimed that Israel's "wild overstatement of the Iranian threat" is a "subterfuge" to allow for settlement building,[218] while *The Economist* suggested that Israel's "Iran first" approach is a diversion tactic to avoid negotiating with the Palestinians.[219]

Despite the very real threat to Israel and democracies worldwide, some journalists have nothing but praise for Iran. Agence France-Presse – the world's third-largest news agency – warmly embraced the "human side" of madman Ahmadinejad, fawning over his "image as a simple peace-loving man who offers friendship to everyone." AFP described Ahmadinejad as a "handy cook who prepares 'delicious' food and regrets not spending more time at home," and quoted the delightfully "hardworking husband" Ahmadinejad: "I help in the kitchen and I know how to make all the Iranian food... I can make all the different kinds of soups and Iranian stews."[220] Martha Stewart, look out.

As for the Jewish community of Iran – dating back 2,600 years to biblical times – ongoing persecution has reduced their number to only a few thousand. Yet according to *New York Times* columnist Roger Cohen, there is nothing to fear: "I'm a Jew and have seldom been treated with such consistent warmth as in Iran."[221] Perhaps Cohen should read the U.S.

State Department's 2008 Report on International Religious Freedom that describes a "threatening atmosphere" and "official discrimination" of the Jewish community in Iran, where "officially sanctioned anti-Semitic propaganda involving official statements, media outlets, publications and books" continues to "create a hostile atmosphere for Jews."[222]

Cohen is the kind of guy who would have been fooled by the Nazi sham at Theresienstadt, the concentration camp that was "dressed up" to accommodate a visit by the Red Cross – with fake shops and cafés, freshly painted rooms, and a children's opera performance. Tellingly, Cohen is not the first *New York Times* columnist to be duped by a dictatorial maniac. In the 1930s, Walter Duranty raved about Stalin's wonderful Soviet Union, and in the 1950s *Times* columnist Herbert Matthews glorified Fidel Castro, helping lead the dictator to victory by giving readers a false impression of his good intentions.[223] In the same way, Cohen's naive portrait of the Jews in Iran plays into the Ayatollah's hands and ultimately endangers the lives of all Jews in the region.[224]

Cohen repeatedly uses the pages of the *Times* to belittle Israel's concerns, claiming that the "'existential threat' to Israel is overplayed."[225] In yet another column, Cohen ensured that "Iran's Islamic Republic is no Third Reich redux. Nor is it a totalitarian state." And to allay fears of another Auschwitz, he noted that the Iranian regime does not operate with "trains-on-time Fascist efficiency."[226] As if "trains-on-time efficiency" is a prerequisite to dropping the Bomb.

Writing under the headline, "Israel Cries Wolf," Cohen trivialized fears of a genocidal Iran, decrying "Israel's attempt to frame Iran as some Nazi-like incarnation of evil."[227] Let's deconstruct the "Boy Cries Wolf" analogy. When the mischievous boy in the fable first cried wolf, not only was there no wolf, there was no evidence of a wolf. Whenever he cried wolf and the villagers came running, he revealed immediately that he had played a joke at their expense. By contrast, three successive U.S. presidents have been sounding the alarm about a nuclear Iran, as have the European Union and the International Atomic Energy Agency. The Iranians, meanwhile, have bolstered their eliminationist rhetoric and open pursuit of nuclear capability. As for the boy who cried wolf, Cohen seems to have forgotten the rest of the story. In the end, there really is a wolf.[228]

These columns generated an intense groundswell of criticism which eventually had its affect: In 2009, following election protests which the Iranian government put down with tear gas grenades and shootings, Cohen confessed: "I erred in underestimating the brutality and cynicism of a regime that understands the uses of ruthlessness."[229]

Cohen's conclusion is a testament to the power of consumer activism – yet is so stunningly obvious that it reminds one of Abba Eban's quip: "His ignorance is encyclopedic."

These media trends – whitewashing terror, obscuring the calls for genocide, and downplaying the existential threat to Israel – all contribute to the effort to dismantle the Jewish state. If Israel is not genuinely being threatened, the theory goes, then Israel has no justification for security actions such as checkpoints and the separation barrier – or more crucial measures like targeted strikes and nuclear deterrence.

During one visit to the journalists' favorite hangout, the American Colony Hotel in Jerusalem, I caught wind of a correspondent pooh-poohing the nuclear threat to Israel. "How can you deny the obvious?" I asked him. "Even if Iran decides *not* to push the button, the mere possession of nuclear weapons could be enough to cause a wave of Israeli emigration and scare off millions of tourists that form the heart of Israel's economy."

He waved his hand dismissively. "Oh, you're being an alarmist. Everyone knows that nuclear weapons are kept in check by Mutually Assured Deterrence" – the idea that no country would dare to launch a nuclear strike, given that the other side would retaliate in kind and bring about the assured destruction of both parties.

"Actually," I said, "in the case of an Iranian regime driven by religious messianism, the exact opposite may be true. With Iran's apocalyptic mindset, mutually assured destruction is not a deterrent, but rather an inducement.[230] Just as Muslim extremists have perpetrated hundreds of suicide bombings, Iran advocates the ultimate suicide bomb: While a nuclear exchange with Israel could cost Iran 15 million people, Iranian leaders have already said they regard that as a small 'sacrifice' for wiping out Israel's 6 million Jews."[231]

He thought for a moment and said, "I guess you're right about that. But I'm writing for an American audience that is less concerned with distant regional confrontations."

He was invoking the old "Iran is not a threat to America" line. "Besides the fact that Iran supplies tons of weapons and training to Iraqi insurgents,[232] did you read the report from the U.S. Department of Defense outlining the threats that a nuclear Iran poses to the United States?" I asked. "Not only would a nuclear Iran destabilize world petroleum markets and threaten American influence in the Middle East, but Iran could develop and test an intercontinental ballistic missile capable of reaching the U.S. mainland by 2015."[233]

"Perhaps," he said, "but with today's technology, 2015 is still generations away."

So I reminded him of the little matter of an electromagnetic pulse (EMP) attack, a nuclear bomb that Iranian proxies could launch from a ship off the U.S. coast and detonate a few hundred miles in the air. Such an explosion would destroy the chips that are at the heart of every electronic device – knocking out America's electrical power grid, along with the computer systems that operate telecommunications, hospitals, financial institutions, fuel production, water treatment and food storage facilities.[234] Additionally, unsecured fuel and munitions could detonate. In the scramble for basic necessities, coupled with the paralysis of law enforcement and emergency services, chaos would likely prevail. It is estimated that within one year, millions of Americans could be dead as a result of exposure, starvation and disease.

His response: "That sounds like the apocalyptic conjectures of the extremist right."

"Hardly," I said, "I'm quoting from the Commission to Assess the Threat to the United States from Electromagnetic Pulse (EMP) Attack – an elite group of scientists and technologists authorized by U.S. Congress to prepare national security reports.[235] And Iran already has announced plans to deploy naval vessels in the Atlantic Ocean near the U.S. maritime borders."[236]

"Whatever the case," he said, "these Iranian doomsday scenarios are of little concern to middle America."

"I think you may be losing touch with your audience," I said. "The latest Pew Research Center survey found that Americans cite Iran as the country posing the single greatest danger to the U.S."[237]

He agreed to think more about it, but in the meantime the media seems determined to frame Iran as a purely Israeli problem. In 2009, when Congress passed a resolution "to condemn Tehran's crackdown on demonstrators," Anne Flaherty of Associated Press – the same reporter who previously wrote that U.S. sanctions against Iran are "fueled by the pro-Israeli lobby"[238] – was at it again, declaring that "Democrats, who are quick to voice their support for Israel anytime the Jewish state is seen as under siege, easily agreed to push through" the resolution. Actually, the text of the resolution made no mention of Israel; the only one who saw some exclusively pro-Israel agenda lurking there was Associated Press.[239]

Zionazis

In the campaign to delegitimize Israel, accusations like "war criminals" and "apartheid state" are small-time slander compared to the big prize: casting Israel as the 21st century Nazis.

Remember the theory that the State of Israel was born out of the ashes of the Holocaust? Although in one respect that works *against* Israel – by casting it as a colonial usurper and eliminating Israel's 4,000-year-old connection to the land – in another respect it works in Israel's favor. Given the world's collective guilt over the 6 million murdered, the Holocaust provides Israel with a degree of moral capital that Palestinians can never match. So in today's media war, if the Jews can somehow be portrayed as "the new Nazis," then Israel's "Holocaust advantage" is effectively cancelled out.

Predictably, the Arabic media takes the lead in inventing the worst Nazi atrocities and ascribing them to the Jews. In a *Gulf News* essay entitled "Zionists are the New Nazis," sociology professor Mohammad Abdullah al-Mutawa described how "The charred and bloodied bodies of innocent [Palestinian] children, women and civilians in houses and streets, are testimonies to the Nazi character of the Zionists."[240] Egypt's *Al-Ahram* declared that "the atrocities committed by the Israeli army show... how those [Jews] who complain about Nazi practices use the same methods against the Palestinians."

On Palestinian television, viewers were treated to a dramatized scene of mass executions straight out of the Holocaust: "Israelis" lined up Palestinian men "in rows of seven or eight. They told them to dig a deep ditch in the cemetery... The first row of men stood in front of the hole and were shot to death. Then they asked the second row to bury them and in this manner [killed them] all, row after row."[241] The Palestinian Authority newspaper *Al-Hayat Al-Jadida* accused Israel of sadistic Nazi-style medical experiments such as poisoning Palestinians' food in order to study the toxic effects.[242] And on Palestinian TV, a children's program promoted the allegation that Israel burns Palestinians in ovens.[243]

This Zionazi approach appears to be working. Code-words like "genocide" (London's *Evening Standard*)[244] and "ethnic cleansing" (CBS's *60 Minutes*)[245] are getting plenty of play in the mainstream media. Speaking on CNN, Turkish leader Tayyip Erdogan accused Israel of "genocide" and claimed that "hundreds of thousands of Palestinians were killed" by Israel. (CNN's Fareed Zakaria did not challenge the lie.)[246] Radio-Canada presented Israel as a "rogue state" comparable to the Iranian madmen and the genocidal regime of Sudan.[247] And *Der Spiegel*, Germany's leading news magazine, likened Israeli policies to those pursued by Hitler.[248]

When one Western journalist claimed that Israel is perpetrating genocide, I confronted him with a logical difficulty: "Why hasn't Israel acted worse? Where are the slave labor camps and the nightly massacres? It is difficult to reconcile the idea of 'genocidal Israelis' with a few thousand Palestinians, mostly combatants, killed in decades of fighting," I said. "Two-thirds of European Jewry exterminated by the Nazis? That's genocide. Half the population of Darfur – 3 million people – either dead or displaced?[249] That's genocide. But the Arab population of the territories soaring from under one million in 1967 to four million today?[250] Is this what *The Times* of London meant in referring to 'the Israeli genocide against the Palestinian people'?[251] If Israel is committing genocide, then it's the least efficient genocide in history – so much so that it's moving backwards!"

Despite all logic, this slander continues to gain currency in the "civilized" world. Portuguese Nobel Prize-winning writer Jose Saramago declared, "What is happening in Palestine is a crime which we can put on the same plane as what happened at Auschwitz."[252] Richard Falk, the U.N. Human Rights Council official assigned to monitor Israel, compared Israel to the Nazis in his article, "Slouching Toward a Palestinian Holocaust."[253] And Mairead Corrigan Maguire, the Irish winner of the 1976 Nobel Peace Prize, likened Israeli weapons to Auschwitz, calling them "gas chambers perfected."[254]

These canards seep in and, slowly but surely, mainstream news reports begin to adopt them as well. "UK Jewish Lawmaker: Israeli Forces Acting Like Nazis,"[255] proclaimed a CNN headline. "Saudi Likens Gaza Assault to Nazi War Crimes," blared one from Agence France Presse.[256] And who can forget the charges of Israeli-perpetrated "genocide" in Jenin,[257] which the *Irish Times* claimed "looked uncannily like the attack on the Warsaw Jewish ghetto in 1944."[258]

It's a simple equation: The same techniques that the Nazis practiced against the Jews, Israelis are now using against Palestinians. The result is an absolute inversion of reality, the "great mutation of anti-Semitism."[259] The Jews – who taught the world the ideals of "love your neighbor as yourself," "might does not make right" and "all people are created equal" – are now cast as the planet's worst barbarians.

Thomas Friedman explained why the world loves to see Jews as immoral:

> It was the Israelites who introduced the world to the concept of a divine moral code, the Ten Commandments. And since Jews were victims throughout history, they were always in a position to

criticize the morality of other nations. Today people enjoy seeing the Jews failing to live up to their own code of ethics... Indeed for some people, there is something almost satisfying about catching the Jewish state behaving improperly. It is a bit like catching one's Sunday school teacher in an indiscretion.[260]

Case in point: In 2009, Sweden's largest newspaper, *Aftonbladet*, published a baseless, loosely-woven conspiracy theory charging that Israeli soldiers were abducting Palestinians in order to steal their organs for sale on the black market.[261] Outraged readers immediately called on *Aftonbladet* editors and the Swedish government to clean up this libelous mess. But they wouldn't budge; Swedish Foreign Minister Carl Bildt stood by the article on the grounds of preserving freedom of the press.[262] I wrote him back, pointing out that unfortunately the idea of a "free-expression paradise" – where every whim is published without consequence – is patently false. Just as it is immoral to yell "fire" in a crowded movie theater, so too is it immoral to spread baseless blood libels guaranteed to stoke tensions in the already-volatile Middle East.[263]

I did some legwork and discovered that when dealing with the Muslim community, Sweden's "free speech" policy operates on a – surprise! – hypocritical double standard. A few years earlier, the same Swedish government had shut down websites which published the controversial Muhammad cartoons.[264] And one month after the organ-harvesting story, another *Aftonbladet* article – about the threat of radical Islam – was loudly denounced by Swedish Prime Minister Fredrik Reinfeldt.[265]

Israel can't win either way. When pushed for a retraction of the organ-harvesting story, the media used this to castigate Israel as an enemy of human rights: "Sweden's Free Speech Tradition Runs into Israeli Ire," declared the Agence France Presse headline.[266] Meanwhile, Jan Helin, editor of *Aftonbladet*, passed off criticism of the organ-harvesting story as the work of some sinister Jewish "propaganda machine."[267]

What began as a false and malicious report in a Swedish newspaper soon snowballed into a full-fledged global campaign. Within weeks, news outlets publicized the claim that 25,000 Ukrainian children had been taken to Israeli medical centers to be used for "spare parts."[268] Other newspapers "reported" of Jewish-led gangs roaming the streets of Algerian cities, kidnapping young children and transporting them across the border into Morocco, where their organs would be harvested and sold to Israelis and American Jews.[269]

With predictable cynicism, the Council of Arab Foreign Ministers demanded the establishment of a United Nations committee to "investigate Israel's crimes of stealing Palestinian organs."[270] To complete the aura of credibility, a statement entitled "Israeli Illegal Trafficking in Organs of Dead and Kidnapped Palestinian Victims" became publicly available on the United Nations website.[271]

From here it was a small step to raising the "Jews as Nazis" canard: In Scotland's best-selling newspaper, under the headline, "Dark Echoes of Holocaust," columnist George Galloway invoked Dr. Josef Mengele – history's infamous "Angel of Death" who performed tortuous "medical" experiments on Jews in Auschwitz – by describing Israel as "playing mini-Mengele" on Palestinians.[272]

This is not just a matter of "setting the record straight" or the theoretical demonization of Israel as an "illegitimate entity." Throughout history, these same type of blood libels have incited violent mobs to torture and murder untold thousands of Jews. The Nazis harnessed the media weapon *Der Stuermer* to perpetrate the greatest mass murder in history. A hundred years from now, Arab schoolchildren will probably be learning about Israel's "institutionalized campaign of organ harvesting." Given that the most inconceivable accusations involving Jews are readily believed by millions in the Muslim world, *Aftonbladet's* reckless blood libel is nothing less than an incitement to terror.[273]

No matter how preposterous, these lies creep into the public consciousness and simmer to the surface at the most inauspicious times. In 2010, in the wake of the devastating earthquake in Haiti, the State of Israel (well-trained in treating human carnage after years of suicide bombings) quickly dispatched rescue workers to establish the first cutting-edge, fully-equipped field hospital in Haiti, what CBS called the "Rolls Royce of emergency medical care."[274]

The Israeli effort received widespread news coverage[275] and – given that tiny Israel sent hundreds of relief workers, compared to China which sent 60 – it was a classic case of an "Israeli disproportionate response."[276]

But not everyone embraced Israel's rescue-and-relief mission. The *Washington Post* cynically called the Israeli efforts in Haiti an attempt to deploy "soft power" diplomacy.[277] Others concocted the claim that the Israeli field hospital was just a ploy to steal more organs from unsuspecting victims[278] – "information" that was then posted in a Wikipedia entry, "Haiti Organ Harvesting." When it comes to Israel, even the most virtuous deeds can be twisted into evil intent.

And the list goes on. In 2009, Holland's largest daily, *De Telegraf*, published a proposal that the bird flu pandemic, caused by the virus H5N1, was part of an international Jewish conspiracy.[279]

This isn't traditional, religious anti-Semitism based on the claim that "Jews killed Jesus." Nor is it the classic medieval libel of "the Jews bake matzah with children's blood." It isn't even modern anti-Semitism of "the Jews are rich and control the world." No, this is post-modern anti-Semitism – all about selling newspapers, publicity and turning a profit. Reporters don't necessarily care about the truth because most editors – and certainly most readers – don't have time for proper research and corroboration. The writer gets his 15 minutes of fame; the paper makes millions; Israel is spun as the planet's worst purveyor of evil – and damn the consequences.[280]

How could consumers be expected to believe otherwise, given the barrage of images demonizing Israel? Bruce Beattie, one of America's leading editorial cartoonists, published a cartoon entitled "Which Nukes are You Most Afraid Of?" that depicts a short list of despotic terror regimes: North Korea, Iran, al-Qaeda, and – you guessed it – Israel.[281] *Time* magazine reprinted the cartoon – not to condemn it as a perverse distortion – but to honor it as "Cartoon of the Week."[282]

Then there's editorial cartoonist Tony Auth of the *Philadelphia Inquirer*, portraying the Israeli separation barrier as enclosing Palestinians with a chain-link fence shaped like the Star of David.[283] I did some digging around and discovered that this drawing was nearly identical to a 1930s Nazi poster. It is unclear whether Auth realized he was replicating Nazi propaganda; assuming he did *not* realize, it is far more unsettling that a Pulitzer Prize-winning cartoonist would independently revive what is historically considered the worst anti-Semitic imagery.

When Iran's leading newspaper, *Hamshahri*, ran a contest of "Holocaust cartoons" (in retaliation for the Muhammad cartoons that enraged Muslims worldwide), one featured entry – comparing Gaza to Auschwitz – was drawn by Michael Leunig, staff cartoonist for Australia's leading newspaper, *The Age*.[284] Then there's the cover of *Time* magazine depicting a Jewish star peering over barbed wire, evoking Nazi concentration camps. Only this time, it is Israel "committing genocide" against the Palestinians.[285]

This Zionazi canard seems to be cropping up everywhere. Writing in the London *Observer*, Tom Paulin of Oxford University referred to "the Zionist SS,"[286] while the *New Zealand Herald* declared that "Israelis are getting the same results the Nazis got."[287] Yasmin Alibhai-Brown, a leading columnist for London's *Independent*, wrote that Israeli leaders "should be tried for crimes against humanity... for so debasing the profoundly important legacy of the Holocaust, which was meant to stop forever nations turning themselves into ethnic killing machines."[288] Even television star Roseanne Barr got into the act, declaring flatly that "Israel is a Nazi state."[289]

Toronto Sun columnist Eric Margolis wrote of Israel's "final solution" against Hamas – an unmistakable reference to Nazi Germany's systematic plan to annihilate European Jewry. He wondered aloud whether "comparisons with the Warsaw ghetto uprising will inevitably be made," and quoted a "high-ranking Vatican official" who described Gaza as "a concentration camp."[290]

Bashing Israel as the "new Nazis" even extends to local papers that don't usually cover foreign affairs, such as the double-page spread entitled "Jews in Jackboots" in the normally tame British *Luton on Sunday*.[291]

And when some Israel protesters engaged in the relatively mild acts of flattening tires and putting dishwashing soap on automobile windshields, the *Washington Post* referred to them as "shock troops" – as in the German word *stosstruppen*.[292]

Not to be outdone, Pat Oliphant, the most influential political cartoonist in the world, syndicated a cartoon that depicts a goose-stepping uniformed figure wheeling a fanged Star of David, menacing a small female figure labeled "Gaza."[293] How's that for a throwback to 1940 Germany?

Clean Conscience

Why does the media so eagerly promote this Zionazi narrative?

My theory is that given the deep human need to be good, people constantly seek to vindicate themselves by justifying their actions in a positive way. For those who have committed a terrible misdeed, one way of rationalizing is to show that if others are doing the same, then by comparison "I'm not so bad after all." Even better – if it can be shown that the *very one* who was victimized is now turning around and victimizing others, that completely erases one's sense of accountability and guilt for the original sin. Therefore, if Israelis are behaving like Nazis, that effectively wipes away humanity's collective guilt over the Crusades, Spanish Inquisition, countless expulsions, blood libels, pogroms and the systematic murder of 6 million. No more bad memories, no more Jews having the right to complain. We're all even now. It's what one writer called "a sick mixture of Holocaust envy and Holocaust denial."[294]

This explains why some of the worst Zionazi imagery appears in the European press. Greece's largest newspaper, *Eleftherotypia*, ran a front-page cartoon entitled "Holocaust II," depicting an Israeli "Nazi officer" and a Palestinian "concentration camp inmate."[295] A cartoon in the Spanish daily *Cambio 16* showed Israel's prime minister with a combination swastika-Star of David symbol, proclaiming: "At least Hitler taught me how to invade a country and destroy every living insect."[296] A cartoon in the Greek daily *Ethnos* showed two Israeli soldiers – dressed as Nazis and stabbing knives into Arabs – proclaiming: "Do not feel guilty, my brother.

We were in Auschwitz and Dachau not to suffer, but to learn."²⁹⁷

Here's how Georges-Elia Sarfati, a professor of linguistics in France, describes this phenomenon: "Europe created Nazism, totalitarianism, racism and colonialism... All these traumatizing elements in Europe's history are [now] redirected toward Israel."²⁹⁸ Pilar Rahola, the well-known Spanish-Catalan journalist, explained: Europe's "deviant way of dealing with" centuries of anti-Semitism and the Holocaust "is to attack Israel, of all countries. Because the worse Israel is, the less guilty we are. The attacks against Israel are our way of clearing our conscience."²⁹⁹

It looks like a lot of people are seeking to clear their conscience these days. Protestors in New York City carry signs that read: "Israel: The Fourth Reich" and "Holocaust by Holocaust Survivors,"³⁰⁰ while those in Paris wave placards with the Star of David redrawn to resemble a swastika.³⁰¹ When demonstrators held aloft the image of Muhammad al-Dura, juxtaposed with the iconic photo of a Jewish boy held at Nazi gunpoint, Europe 1 anchorwoman Catherine Nay explained the symbolism: "This death annuls, erases that of the little boy in the Warsaw ghetto."³⁰²

In Italy, the website of the respected newspaper *La Repubblica* published the notorious anti-Semitic forgery, *Protocols of the Elders of Zion*, in its entirety, without providing any disclaimer or historical explanation.³⁰³ Meanwhile, a cartoon in the Catalan daily *La Vanguardia* showed one building with a sign reading "Museum of the Jewish Holocaust" next to another building with a sign, "Future Museum of the Palestinian Holocaust."³⁰⁴

NBC's Tom Brokaw attempted to draw this comparison in an interview with President Obama conducted at the Buchenwald concentration camp. Brokaw asked:

"What can the Israelis learn from your visit to Buchenwald? And what should they be thinking about their treatment of Palestinians?"³⁰⁵

Obama rightly replied that "there's no equivalency here." But one can only assume by virtue of the question that Brokaw thinks otherwise.[306]

This warped view is precisely why Natan Sharansky, the former Soviet dissident, developed a "3-D test" to measure bias against Israel:

- Demonization – comparing Israeli actions to the worst of evil, e.g. Nazis
- Double standard – singling out Israel for criticism while ignoring comparable actions of other countries
- Delegitimization – denying Israel's fundamental right to exist[307]

Given this objective measure, it is nearly impossible to deny widespread media bias against Israel. And this 3-D perversion is producing real results: A recent poll in Germany showed that 68 percent believe Israel is waging a "war of extermination" against the Palestinian people, and a majority of respondents agreed with the following statement: "What the state of Israel does today to the Palestinians, is in principle not different from what the Nazis did in the Third Reich to the Jews."[308]

By continually portraying Israel as brutal Nazi-like occupiers, the media may be encouraging not only hatred of Israel, but also violence against Jews worldwide. In 2009, following Israel's operation in Gaza, a Jewish cultural center in Sweden was attacked by arsonists – twice in one week. On Yom Kippur, automatic rifle fire shattered the quiet outside the Great Synagogue of Paris, sending worshipers diving for cover. A Danish school principal declared that Jewish students were no longer welcome in his school, advising Jewish parents to send their children elsewhere. In Chicago, an unprecedented chain of anti-Semitic attacks left synagogues and schools with their windows smashed, walls covered in graffiti, and charred by a Molotov cocktail. In London, attempts were made to burn down synagogues and loot Jewish businesses; one Jewish motorist was pulled out of his car and beaten. Similar events took place in Belgium, Australia and Brazil.[309] Jewish cemeteries in Germany are being defaced, vandalized or destroyed on average once every 10 days.[310] All told, there were more anti-Semitic incidents in 2009 than in any period since World

War II.[311]

In France, an op-ed published in *Le Monde* entitled, "Israel-Palestine: The Cancer," whipped up such anti-Semitic fervor that a civil court found both the writers and the newspaper guilty of "racist defamation" against Israel and the Jewish people. Tellingly, this landmark decision was not mentioned anywhere in the English news services of Associated Press, Reuters and Agence France Presse – the world's three largest agencies.[312]

I'll never forget that summer evening when I received a call from my rabbinical colleague in London describing how his synagogue had been torched by arsonists and Torah scrolls desecrated.[313] Whether the media's demonization of Israel is intentional or not, such is the cumulative effect. As the London *Evening Standard* declared: "What starts in the lazy moral confusion of the television studio, ends with the swastika on the wall."[314]

Encounter on the 443

In the fall of 2010, I was driving along route 443, a main highway connecting Jerusalem and Tel Aviv. Since the early days of the Intifada, access to this road for Palestinians had been limited due to frequent fire-bomb attacks and fatal shootings. But then the Israeli high court – overriding security concerns – ruled to reopen Palestinian access to the road [315] (another of the many proofs against the canard of Israeli apartheid).

The landscape along the road is quite barren, but on the approach to Jerusalem, in a spot called the Ascent of Beit Horon, lies an anomaly: a fresh spring of water that gushes nonstop from a piece of bedrock. This has become a popular rest spot for travelers, a sort of oasis where people fill their plastic bottles and pause to shmooze.

I pulled over to the side of the road, thinking this would be a good place to do some research and observe traffic on the 443.

It was there that I met Achmad. Middle-aged and slightly built, Achmad noticed my reporter's notebook and video camera, and asked what I was doing. I said I was writing a book about media bias in the Mideast conflict, and asked if he thought the media was indeed biased one way or the other.

"I don't know if there's bias," he said. "But I do know that Palestinians are pouring a lot of energy and resources into getting their message across in the media."

Then he paused, as if wondering whether he really wanted to continue talking. I kept quiet, and took a drink from the cool, crisp spring water.

After a minute, Achmad pointed in the direction of Ramallah, a mile or two to the east.

"Just over that hill," he said, "is a research center where Palestinians study the media. My younger brother works there and I've seen it. It's fascinating – Skype lines, video banks, WIFI. There's a group of young Palestinians – mostly with MBAs from American universities – who scour the Internet, tabulate data from Google News, write algorithms, and crunch the numbers. They conduct market research to see which sound bites are most effective in swaying Western views. They have a full library of Nazi propaganda films which they study for techniques. All this information is then fed to Palestinian spokesmen to formulate media strategies. And it's funded by Iran."[316]

I stood there, stunned, not knowing what to say.

Then it hit me.

The Arabs had failed in every attempt to destroy the State of Israel – through military attack, economic boycott and relentless terror. And now came the final effort: using the media to position Israel as the dregs of humanity; isolated, demonized, and the source of all the world's problems; a nation that not only commits evil, but is the essence of evil.

A few years ago when this propaganda war first got underway, there was no government, organization or individual that stood as the prime propagator. Though there were pockets of intense activity – college campuses, European capitals – there was no global coordination. But now Achmad was describing a calculated, centralized strategy for manipulating public opinion in order to finally defeat Israel. And the glue binding it all together is the Mass Media.

Is the media's participation conscious or not? There is no way to measure that. Some reporters and editors may be naively following the trend and are susceptible to manipulation. For others, a pro-Palestinian spin may evolve from business considerations: "David and Goliath" is a way to keep Western consumers tuned in and emotionally engaged, day after day. Just as manufacturers of traditional weapons make money during traditional wars, the media is cashing in on this media war. Cable ratings are rising, and news websites are registering billions of views.[317]

Other journalists, it seems, identify with the Palestinians out of sympathy. I once asked a prominent correspondent point blank: "Why are you so biased against Israel?"

"What are you talking about?" he said. "I live in Israel, eat at Israeli restaurants, and read the Israeli newspapers. If anything, I have an affinity for the comfortable Western values that I find in Israel."

That seemed to make sense, and he almost had me convinced – until I read Steve McNally's description of how he, as a Western broadcast journalist, has an "unconscious bias" in favor of Palestinians. "I live on the Israeli side of Jerusalem... a lot of the Jewish reality has become my reality..." McNally explained in the *Columbia Journalism Review*. And then the kicker: "I try to compensate by mentally changing one hat for the other, but it's only a partial solution."[318]

In other words, plagued by the guilt of having a comfortable lifestyle, journalists bend over backwards to identify with the so-called Palestinian underdog.

Echoing this idea, Joe Klein of *The New Yorker* pinpointed "underdog ethics" as a primary source of media bias against Israel: "From my own experience... the press corps – especially the foreign press corps – tend to lean a little bit toward the Palestinians because their situation is a bit more desperate." Klein noted that even the reporters' nicknames for the two combatants reveals a pro-Arab slant: The Palestinians are endearingly called "the Pals," while the Israelis are disparagingly called "the Issies."[319]

Other reporters undoubtedly harbor a genuine desire to see Israel fail. Orly Halpern of Toronto's *Globe and Mail* wrote on her personal Twitter page how Israeli actions in Gaza "makes me sick to my stomach."[320] The *St. Louis Post-Dispatch* featured a front-page blurb hailing Palestinian suicide bombings as "a success."³²¹ And when British journalist Chas Newkey Burden met with fellow reporters for some drinks in the West End of London, one of them gushed: "Boy, those [Palestinian] suicide bombers have got guts. I wish more people in the world had their courage."³²²

Is there any hope for objective and balanced reporting when – rather than facts – an emotional attachment to one side of the conflict is driving the coverage?

Thus it is no great surprise that the media is now taking the logical, final step: If the State of Israel was founded on post-Holocaust sympathy, and the Palestinians are now suffering the next Holocaust, then Israel's very existence can be called into question.

Remember the story of the Palestinian man at a checkpoint being asked to play his violin in order to verify it didn't contain explosives? Some media outlets compared this with Jewish musicians who were sadistically forced to provide background music as the Nazis shoveled Jews into the Auschwitz crematoria.³²³ As Agence France Presse reported, since Israel's "entire existence" is "justified by suffering," this Nazi-like activity "throws the justification of the state's very existence into doubt."³²⁴

The mainstream media seems obsessed with Israeli fatalism. *Time* magazine published the cover story: "Why Israel Can't Win,"³²⁵ while *Newsweek* posed the question: "Is Israel Over?"³²⁶

This is not merely some PR contest. It is a fight for survival. Israel is the only country in the world whose very right to exist is challenged, and the only one threatened in a serious way with extinction. Historians note that the Nazi strategy consisted of three partly-overlapping phases. The first focused on the extreme defamation of the Jews. The second aimed at their isolation from mainstream society. The third sought to eliminate them completely through physical destruction. That final act was possible only after the first two stages had laid the foundation.³²⁷

As such, the media's twisting of the Mideast conflict is a verbal weapon of mass destruction, opening the door for a perverse "moral obligation" to wage a war of extermination against Israel. Writing in London's *Independent*, columnist Yasmin Alibhai-Brown hinted to a Muslim-led 21ˢᵗ century Holocaust, connecting the idea of a nuclear Iran to the injustice of Palestinian "children turned to ash, blistered mothers weeping... the hungry and dying in Gaza."[328] This explains Mahmoud Ahmadinejad's ferocious denial of the Holocaust on one hand and his threats to commit a second (nuclear) Holocaust on the other; as Iranian foreign minister Manouchehr Mottaki declared: "If the official version of the Holocaust is thrown into doubt, then the identity and nature of Israel will be thrown into doubt."[329]

And so, Israel's enemies and their media cohorts have arrived at the ultimate conclusion: For the sake of humanity, Israel must be destroyed. This idea was articulated by Pulitzer Prize-winning playwright Tony Kushner whose view regarding the State of Israel is that "It would have been better if it never happened."[330] Meanwhile, BBC host Tom Paulin declared: "I never believed that Israel had the right to exist at all."[331] (BBC News considered it all a joke, declaring that Paulin's "knockabout style has ruffled feathers in the US, where the Jewish question is notoriously sensitive.")[332]

The London *Guardian*, the newspaper of choice for Britain's academics and media elites, suggested on its front page that Israel's license to exist has expired: "The establishment of [the State of Israel] has been bought at a very high cost in human rights and human lives. It must be apparent that the international community cannot support this cost indefinitely."[333] Another *Guardian* article gave voice to the idea that Israel has "no moral right... as a state that rose from the Holocaust," and that its Zionazi behavior "negates the very possibility of the existence of Israel as a Jewish state."[334]

And so, anti-Israel propagandists are foisting the ultimate libel: Other countries commit relative crimes, which can be measured and compared. But Israel, by its very existence, commits the absolute crime.[335]

Tragically, these sentiments easily transition from newsprint to "reality." A 2007 BBC poll showed that fully two-thirds of respondents viewed Israel as a "mainly negative" influence on the world.[336] An opinion poll conducted by the European Union named Israel as the number one "threat to world peace" – beating out axis-of-evil states North Korea and Iran.[337] Thanks to the media, a caricature that once flourished on the ideological fringe is now mainstreamed: Israel as the sadistic oppressor, the wanton slaughterer of civilians, the relentless Middle East warmonger, and a grave strategic liability for the United States and the Western world.[338]

Standing there on the 443, Achmad finished filling up his water bottle. Before we parted, he begged me not to use his real name, for fear that Palestinian thugs would take retribution on him or his family. (Achmad is not his real name.)

Achmad had revealed an epiphany, yet I had no way of knowing whether this grand Palestinian media research center really exists. I can't simply drive into Ramallah and start snooping around; that's too dangerous. And anyone who knows about it will deny it anyway.

"How can I verify everything you've told me?" I asked him.

"You want evidence?" he replied with a cynical laugh. "Just open the *New York Times*."

I shuddered at this ultimate irony. The Jewish people, whom U.S. President John Adams praised for having "done more to civilize men than any other nation,"[339] are now falsely portrayed as the paradigm of evil – accused of practicing apartheid without racism; of perpetrating a Holocaust without gas chambers; of engaging in genocide without mass murder; of committing war crimes without targeting civilians; and of being a horrific human rights violator while having one of the most responsible legal systems in the world.[340]

What it all comes down to is casting Israel as the pariah state deserving of destruction. If there was any doubt, the *Guardian* spelled it out in a clear and unequivocal headline: "Israel Simply Has No Right to Exist."[341]

And so, with the preeminent influence of the news media, things have come full circle. Back in 1948 and 1967, it was the Arab Goliath intent on Israel's destruction. In the ensuing years, the powerful Israeli army became cast as the mighty Goliath against the Palestinians. And at the outset of the Intifada a decade ago, I had perceived that role being assumed by the Media Goliath.

Yet perhaps that understanding was too shallow. For now I see the truth behind the veil. This is not anti-Israel bias driven by mere journalistic ideology or pursuit of profit. Worse, it is a catastrophic case of manipulation. The Arab Goliath is waging a media jihad to defeat Israel in the court of public opinion, and their most powerful weapon – the media – is being wielded as the very sword in Goliath's hand.

Notes

1. Five of the seven members of the Arab League – Egypt, Iraq, Jordan, Lebanon and Syria – invaded Palestine on the night of May 14, 1948. The other two states – Saudi Arabia and Yemen – aided with corps of volunteers. In a cablegram from the Arab League to the U.N. Secretary-General on May 15, 1948, the Arab states proclaimed their aim of eliminating the Jewish state and creating a united state of Palestine in its stead. ("The Origins and Evolution of the Palestine Problem: 1917-1988," United Nations, Division for Palestinian Rights, June 20, 1979.)
2. Cited in Benny Morris, *Righteous Victims,* Sachar, 1979.
3. On the eve of the 1967 war, Egyptian President Gamal Abdel Nasser declared: "Our basic objective will be the destruction of Israel." ("On This Day: June 5," BBC News Online.)
4. Gil Feiler, "Arab Boycott," *The Continuum Political Encyclopedia of the Middle East*, Continuum, 2002.
5. Though U.S. Congress had passed a law mandating fines against any American company cooperating with the boycott, McDonald's and others chose to pay the fine rather than endanger the loss of business in the Arab world.
6. Researchers compared current GDP to the potential GDP in times of peace. ("Cost of Conflict in the Middle East," Strategic Foresight Group, 2010.)
7. Moti Bassok, "GDP, Jobs Figures End 2009 on a High," *Haaretz* (Israel), January 3, 2010.
8. Ted Koppel and Kyle Gibson, *Nightline: History in the Making and the Making of Television,* Times Books, 1996.
9. "NGO Forum: Declaration and Programme of Action" (paragraph 424), World Conference Against Racism, Racial Discrimination, Xenophobia and Related Intolerance, Durban, South Africa, September 1, 2001.
10. John Dugard, "Israelis Adopt What South Africa Dropped," *Atlanta Journal-Constitution,* November 29, 2006.
11. Matt McCarten, "Palestinians' Fight is a Struggle Against Apartheid," *New Zealand Herald,* January 4, 2009.
12. Jimmy Carter, *Palestine: Peace Not Apartheid,* Simon & Schuster, 2007. Carter's foundation, the Carter Center, has received million-dollar donations from the Kingdom of Saudi Arabia, the Sultanate of Oman, the United Arab Emirates, and Osama bin Laden's brothers. Additionally, Carter pocketed more than $10 million from Saudi King Fahd and another $5 million from Al-Walid bin Talal, the Saudi prince who offered cash to New York Mayor Rudolph Giuliani in the smoldering ruins of the World Trade Center. ("Donations to the Carter Center," Discoverthenetworks.org; "Jimmy Carter's Li'l Ol' Stink Tank," *Investor's Business Daily,* January 2, 2007.)
13. Elisabeth Bumiller, Carlotta Gall and Salman Masood, "Bin Laden's Secret Life in a Diminished, Dark World," *New York Times,* May 7, 2011.
14. Benjamin Pogrund, "Apartheid? Israel Is a Democracy in which Arabs Vote," *Focus 40,*

December 2005.
15. Mazin Qumsiyeh, "News Media Ignore Israeli Terrorism," *Hartford Courant*, February 2, 2004.
16. Robert D. Novak, "Worse than Apartheid?", *Washington Post*, April 9, 2007; see also *Augusta Chronicle* (Georgia), *Chicago Sun-Times*, *Pittsburgh Tribune Review*, *San Diego Union-Tribune*.
17. "Swiss Voters Back Ban on Minarets," BBC News Online, November 29, 2009.
18. "Dutch to Ban Full-Face Veils," Reuters, September 16, 2011.
19. "France Burqa Ban Comes into Force," Agence France Presse, April 11, 2011.
20. Henry Samuel, "Praying in Paris Streets Outlawed," *The Telegraph* (UK), September 15, 2011.
21. Greg Myre, "Israel: Supreme Court Gains First Arab," *New York Times*, May 7, 2004.
22. Ron Friedman, "Moshe Katsav Convicted of Rape, Faces Long Jail Term," *Jerusalem Post*, December 12, 2010.
23. "I Am Breaking Cycle of Arab Distrust, Says 'Traitor' Army Officer," *The Times* (UK), November 3, 2010.
24. "Faces of the IDF: Israel's First Female Arab-Israeli Paratrooper," Israelpolitik.org, July 23, 2010.
25. "Israeli Arab Appointed New Israeli Ambassador to Greece," *European Jewish Press*, November 26, 2006.
26. Joel Greenberg, "To a Novelist of Nazareth, Laurels and Loud Boos," *New York Times*, May 7, 1992.
27. "Arab Crowned Miss Israel," BBC News Online, March 10, 1999.
28. "MK Wahabi First Druze to Act as Knesset Speaker, President," *Haaretz* (Israel), February 26, 2007.
29. Flore de Préneuf, "Israel's Apartheid," Salon.com, November 3, 2000.
30. Jonathan Marcus, "Israeli Arabs: 'Unequal Citizens,'" BBC News Online, May 2, 2005.
31. "The Apartheid Analogy: Wrong for Israel," ADL.org, August 29, 2005.
32. "Do Arab Students Face Police Discrimination?", *NGO Monitor Analysis*, January 17, 2003.
33. Yair Altman, "500 Arabs Begin Studies in Ariel: 'There's No Racism Here'," *Ynetnews* (Israel), October 17, 2010.
34. "British Academics' Union Votes to Boycott Israeli Academics Over 'Apartheid' Policies," Associated Press, May 29, 2006.
35. Simon Mcgregor-Wood, "Palestinian Who Claimed to Be a Jew Jailed for Rape by Deception," ABCNews.go.com, July 21, 2010.
36. "Israeli Palestinian Man to Appeal Rape-by-Deception Conviction," CNN.com, July 21, 2010.
37. Kendrick MacDowell, "Another Round of Misdirected Israel-bashing," *Daily Caller*, July 23, 2010.
38. Irshad Manji, "Modern Israel is a Far Cry from Old South Africa," *The Australian*, February 9, 2007.
39. Richard J. Goldstone, "Israel and the Apartheid Slander," *New York Times*, October 31, 2011.
40. Karl Vick, "The Trouble with Nonviolence: A Tale of Two Palestinian Marches," *Time*, June 5, 2011.
41. Cited in Daniel Pipes, "The Hell of Israel is Better than the Paradise of Arafat," *Middle East Quarterly*, Spring 2005.
42. Alaa Shahine, "Poverty Trap for Palestinian Refugees," Aljazeera.net, March 29, 2004.
43. "Jordan Strips Palestinians' Citizenship," Associated Press, February 1, 2010.
44. Judith Miller and David Samuels, "No Way Home: The Tragedy of the Palestinian Diaspora," *The Independent* (UK), October 22, 2009.
45. Efraim Karsh, "The Palestinians, Alone," *New York Times*, August 1, 2010.
46. Neil MacFarquhar, "Saudis Arrest Woman Leading Right-to-Drive Campaign," *New York*

Times, May 23, 2011.
47. "Saudi Women Given Right to Vote, Stand for Election," Reuters, September 25, 2011.
48. *Al-Sharq Al-Awsat* (UK), July 23, 2006; cited in L. Azuri, "Public Debate in Saudi Arabia on Employment Opportunities for Women," Middle East Media Research Institute, November 17, 2006.
49. Alan M. Dershowitz, "Let's Have a Real Apartheid Education Week," *Double Standard Watch*, March 7, 2010.
50. See "Ms. Magazine Blocks Ad on Israeli Women," American Jewish Congress, January 10, 2008.
51. Justus Reid Weiner, "Palestinian Crimes against Christian Arabs and Their Manipulation against Israel," Jerusalem Center for Public Affairs, September 2008.
52. Bahailocations.com.
53. Israel Harel, "Share the Temple Mount," *Haaretz* (Israel), October 15, 2009.
54. Nadav Shragai, "Three Jews Expelled from Temple Mount for Praying," *Haaretz* (Israel), September 1, 2003.
55. Francis E. Peters, *The Hajj: The Muslim Pilgrimage to Mecca and the Holy Places*, Princeton University Press, 1994, p. 206.
56. "Saudi Arabia: International Religious Freedom Report," U.S. Department of State, Bureau of Democracy, Human Rights and Labor, 2002. In 2008, Saudi police arrested 40 Christians for the "crime" of praying in a private house. (Alan Baker, "The Poisonous Myth of 'Israeli Apartheid,'" *National Post* [Canada], February 14, 2008.) When President George H.W. Bush went to celebrate Thanksgiving with American troops, Saudi authorities protested his intention to say grace; the celebration had to be moved to international waters aboard the U.S.S. Durham. (Daniel Pipes, "The Scandal of U.S.-Saudi Relations," *National Interest*, Winter 2002/2003.)
57. "Visa & Customs," Saudiairlines.com (subsequently removed from the website). See also Michael Freund, "Saudis Might Take Bibles from Tourists," *Jerusalem Post*, August 8, 2007.
58. Currently, Algeria, Iran, Kuwait, Lebanon, Libya, Pakistan, Saudi Arabia, Sudan, Syria and Yemen do not allow entry to anyone with evidence of travel to Israel. During the 1991 Gulf War, American-Jewish soldiers stationed in Saudi Arabia were advised to wear non-denominational dog tags. (Andrea Stone, "Jewish Leaders, Cheney Discuss Religious Concerns Today," *USA Today*, August 24, 1990.) In order to avoid the "prohibition" of practicing Judaism on Saudi soil, they were flown to religious services on nearby American ships (*USA Today*, March 21, 1991). In 2009, Israeli tennis star Shahar Pe'er was prevented from playing in the Dubai Tennis Championships – having been denied a visa by the United Arab Emirates. (Richard Sandomir, "Tennis Channel Won't Televise Dubai Event in Protest," *New York Times*, February 16, 2009.) The next year, Pe'er was allowed to play after Venus Williams threatened not to compete if Pe'er were denied entry.) Similarly, when Washington-based Israeli journalist Orly Azoulay traveled with U.N. Secretary General Ban Ki-moon, she was denied entry to Saudi Arabia. (Warren Hoge, "Saudi Arabia Bars Israeli Journalist Traveling with U.N. Chief," *New York Times*, March 24, 2007.) As Saudi Ambassador Rashad Nowilaty once stated: "No Jewish journalist will be allowed into Saudi Arabia... Official policy has always been to refuse entry to Jews because they support Israel as a state" (March 6, 1975).
59. "PA Court: Sale of Palestinian Land to Israelis is Punishable by Death," *Haaretz* (Israel), September 20, 2010; "Palestinian Handed Death Sentence," BBC News Online, April 29, 2009. In 1997, PA Attorney General Khaled Al-Qidreh said that 172 people had been sentenced to death under this law *(Palestine Report*, June 6, 1997), and PA Justice Minister Meddein stated that 10 violators had been executed *(Los Angeles Times*, June 1, 1997); cited in Alex Safian, PhD, "Land, the Palestinian Authority, and Israel," Committee for Accuracy in Middle East

Reporting in America, June 25, 1997.
60. "Egyptian Security Report Warns of Israeli Jews in Sinai," Palestine Press Agency, October 18, 2010. Following the 1995 Israel-Jordan peace treaty, the sale of land to Israelis was downgraded from a capital crime but remains illegal.
61. Karl Vick, "Why Israel Doesn't Care About Peace," *Time*, September 2, 2010.
62. Daniel Gordis, "Acceptable in Polite Society," Contentions blog / *Commentary* Magazine, September 7, 2010.
63. Maureen Dowd, "Loosey, Goosey Saudi," *New York Times*, March 3, 2010.
64. Adnan Shabrawi, "Girl Gets a Year in Jail, 100 Lashes for Adultery," *Saudi Gazette*, March 3, 2010.
65. Search conducted on November 8, 2011.
66. Search conducted on July 21, 2010.
67. Ethan Bronner, "After Gaza, Israel Grapples with Crisis of Isolation," *New York Times*, March 19, 2009.
68. Michael Cieply, "Protests Grow Louder Over Israeli Presence at Toronto Film Festival," *New York Times*, September 5, 2009.
69. "Palestinian Artists Boycott Toronto Film Festival," Associated Press, September 10, 2009. Though the damage had already been done, Fonda later apologized for having signed the petition "without reading it carefully enough." (Ben Child, "Jane Fonda Apologises Over Toronto Petition," *The Guardian* [UK], September 15, 2009.)
70. "NUJ Votes to Boycott Israeli Goods in War Protest," *The Guardian* (UK), April 13, 2007.
71. Kevin Blackistone, "Of Sports Boycotts, South Africa and Israel," Fanhouse.com, June 9, 2010.
72. Marcus Dysch, "Anti-Israel Protesters Clash with Israel's Top Muslim Politician," *Jewish Chronicle* (UK), February 4, 2011; "Apartheid Irony," Elder of Ziyon blog, February 4, 2011.
73. Oren Dorell, "PLO Ambassador Says Palestinian State Should be Free of Jews," *USA Today*, September 18, 2011; David Samuels, "Q&A: Maen Rashid Areikat", *Tablet*, October 29, 2010.
74. *Al-Hayat Al-Jadida* (Palestinian Authority), July 30, 2010; cited in Jonathan Dahoah Halevi, "Beware Palestinian Apartheid," *Ynetnews* (Israel), August 4, 2010.
75. Dan Williams, "Judenrein! Israel Adopts Nazi Term to Back Settlers," Reuters, July 9, 2009. See also Peter Beaumont, "Netanyahu Turns to Nazi Language," *The Guardian* (UK), July 10, 2009.
76. Kenneth Meshoe, speaking in Jerusalem, October 2003.
77. Jeremy Bowen, *The Birth of Israel*, BBC, May 4, 2008.
78. Leon and Jill Uris, *Jerusalem*, Doubleday and Company, 1981, p. 13. This explains why, in 1903, when the British government offered the Jews a homeland in Uganda, the proposal was rejected. Even the Jews suffering from horrific Russian pogroms declared: "We don't want just any country. We want to return to our ancient, ancestral homeland." (Yigal Lossin, *Pillar of Fire: The Rebirth of Israel – a Visual History*, Shikmona Pub., 1983.)
79. Bob Feferman, "The Myth That Fuels Mideast Conflict," Realclearworld.com, September 19, 2009.
80. Professor Kenneth Stein of Emory University, "A Zionist State in 1939," *Chai* (Atlanta), Winter 2002. ("The United Nations decided to partition Palestine into an Arab and Jewish state because of the realities on the ground, not because of collective emotions of guilt.") In November 1947, after the U.N. General Assembly voted to accept the partition of Palestine, a *London Times* editorial declared: "It is hard to see how the Arab world, still less the Arabs of Palestine, will suffer from what is mere recognition of an accomplished fact – the presence in Palestine of a compact, well-organized, and virtually autonomous Jewish community." In the words of Ramzi Khoury, executive director of the Palestine Network: "What they did is create all the programs on the ground to bring in Jews into Palestine, and create the

infrastructure that is still needed for the state of Israel today." (Arieh O'Sullivan and Felice Friedson, "Palestinian's New Network," *The Media Line*, March 2, 2010.)
81. Tony Karon, "Is Israel the 'National Home of the Jewish People'?", *Global Spin* blog / *Time*, July 7, 2011.
82. Atika Shubert, "United Nations Urges Myanmar to Accept Help for Storm Victims," *CNN Newsroom*, CNN, May 7, 2008.
83. Daniel Klaidman, "A Plan of Attack for Peace," *Newsweek*, January 12, 2009.
84. Glenn Frankel, "A Beautiful Friendship?", *Washington Post*, July 16, 2006.
85. Ron Grossman, "A Timely Look at the '67 Mideast War," *Chicago Tribune*, July 21, 2002.
86. "Helen Thomas Apologizes for Saying Jews Should 'Get the Hell Out of Palestine,'" FoxNews.com, June 4, 2010. Months later, Thomas exceeded the tolerance level again with the assertion that "Congress, the White House, and Hollywood, Wall Street, are owned by the Zionists." (Glynnis MacNicol, "Helen Thomas Outdoes Herself," *Business Insider*, December 3, 2010.) For these remarks, the Arab-American Anti-Discrimination Committee conferred upon Thomas a lifetime achievement award. ("Helen Thomas Recipient of the 2010 Mehdi Courage in Journalism Award," adc.org, November 1, 2010.) However, the Society of Professional Journalists' lifetime achievement prize – named the Helen Thomas Award – was subsequently retired from service. (Joe Skeel, "Explaining the Process Behind Retirement of Helen Thomas Award," *SPJ Works* blog, January 25, 2011.)
87. Patrick Gavin, "Thomas Under Fire for Israel Remarks," Politico.com, June 5, 2010. A few months later, the American-Arab Anti-Discrimination Committee gave Thomas a lifetime achievement award – an odd choice for an "anti-discrimination committee."
88. Jeremy W. Peters, "An End for Helen Thomas and the Helen Thomas Rules," *Media Decoder* / *New York Times*, June 7, 2010. Other newspapers similarly quoted "get the hell out of Palestine," while omitting the part about Poland and Germany. (See Ed Pilkington, "Scramble to Fill White House Press Chair Vacated by Helen Thomas," *The Guardian* [UK], June 9, 2010.)
89. David F. Nesenoff, "I Asked Helen Thomas About Israel. Her Answer Revealed More Than You Think," *Washington Post*, June 20, 2010.
90. Jeff Jacoby, "Musings, Random and Otherwise," *Boston Globe*, June 13, 2010.
91. Jay Leno, *The Tonight Show*, NBC, June 7, 2010.
92. Robin Shepherd, "In Europe, an Unhealthy Fixation on Israel," *Washington Post*, January 30, 2005.
93. Palestinian National Charter, Article 18, 1964.
94. "Disclosure of a New Tunnel in Silwan," Palpress.co.uk, July 26, 2011; cited in "Palestinian Arabs Not Happy with Biblical Archaeological Discoveries," *Elder of Ziyon* blog, July 26, 2011.
95. Mustafa Sabri, "Judaizing Electronic Wailing Wall to Falsify Historical Facts," *Palestine News Network*, January 4, 2011; cited in "Muslims Freak Out Over Kotel iPhone App," *Elder of Ziyon* blog, January 4, 2011. Consider the irony of Jerusalem – mentioned hundreds of times in the Jewish Bible and not once in the Koran – being denied as a Jewish holy site. The Muslim connection to Jerusalem is found in Sura 17, which recounts a dream where Muhammad takes a midnight ride on his flying horse to an unidentified "further mosque." Some early Muslims understood this metaphorically, or as a place in heaven; later theologians placed it at the Jewish Temple Mount in Jerusalem. (Ken Spiro, "Jerusalem: Jewish and Muslim Claims to the Holy City," Aish.com, November 11, 2000.) As for where Muhammad tethered his winged horse during the celestial ride, Muslim scholars identified the location as either the southern or eastern wall of the Temple Mount; only much later was any claim made to the western wall, sacred to Judaism – a claim that overtly intensified in the 20th century. (Shmuel Berkowitz, *The Wars of the Holy Places*, Jerusalem Institute for Israeli Studies and

Hed Artzi, 2000; cited in Nadav Shragai, "Rachel's Tomb, a Jewish Holy Place, Was Never a Mosque," Jerusalem Center for Public Affairs, November-December 2010.)
96. *Kul Al-Arab* (Israel), August 25, 2000.
97. David Samuels, "Q&A: Maen Rashid Areikat," Tabletmag.com, October 29, 2010.
98. Palestinian Authority Television, September 23, 2008; cited in Itamar Marcus and Barbara Crook, "PA TV: Jewish Temple did Not Exist," Palestinian Media Watch, September 25, 2008.
99. *Le Monde* (France), September 25, 2000.
100. Benjamin Balint, "In the Holy Land, a Rebuilding for the Generations," *Wall Street Journal*, March 10, 2010.
101. Khaled Abu Toameh, "PA Calls Arabs to 'Defend Al Aksa,'" *Jerusalem Post*, March 14, 2010.
102. "400 Meters and a Day of Rage," Mediabackspin.com, March 16, 2010.
103. Paula Hancocks, *CNN Newsroom* (10 a.m.), March 16, 2010.
104. Jeffrey Heller, "Palestinians, Israeli Police Clash in Jerusalem," Reuters, March 16, 2010.
105. "In Palestinian City, Diggers Uncover Biblical Ruin," Associated Press, July 22, 2011; cited in "Palestinian Arabs Using Archaeology 'to Rewrite History,'" *Elder of Ziyon* blog, July 22, 2011.
106. Palestinian Authority Television, June 2, 2011; cited in Itamar Marcus and Barbara Crook, "Palestinian Distortion: 'If I Forget Thee, Oh Jerusalem' was Crusader Expression Usurped by Zionists," Palestinian Media Watch, June 9, 2011.
107. "Boney M Asked to Skip Hit in West Bank Gig," Associated Press, July 22, 2010.
108. Adrian Blomfield, "Middle East Peace Process 'in Danger of Collapse,'" *Daily Telegraph* (UK), October 25, 2009. Emphasis added. See also Adrian Blomfield, "Israel Imposes Security Clampdown on Jerusalem," *Daily Telegraph* (UK), October 9, 2009.
109. Romesh Ratnesar, "The Peacemaker," *Time*, October 13, 2003. Emphasis added.
110. "Religion News in Brief," Associated Press, January 5, 2006.
111. Isabel Kershner, "Western Wall Feud Heightens Israeli-Palestinian Tensions," *New York Times*, November 25, 2010.
112. Ken Ellingwood, "Israeli Police Head Off Small Rally by Jewish Group at Temple Mount," *Los Angeles Times*, April 11, 2005.
113. Matthew Kalman, "Israeli Military Poised for War," *USA Today*, October 9, 2000.
114. The lone reference: Nomi Morris, "Clashes Erupt after Israeli Pays Visit to Disrupted Shrine," *Philadelphia Inquirer* / Knight Ridder News Service, September 29, 2000.
115. Isabel Kershner, "Western Wall Feud Heightens Israeli-Palestinian Tensions," *New York Times*, November 25, 2010.
116. Slide show, "Palin Makes Trip to Holy Site in Jerusalem," *Washington Post*, March 20, 2011.
117. Photo caption, "Critical Moment Approaching as Palestinians Appear Determined to Seek UN Nod for Statehood," Associated Press, September 3, 2011.
118. Allyn Fisher-Ilan, "Israel Plans Work at Contested Jerusalem Holy Site," Reuters, March 6, 2011.
119. See, for example: Harriet Sherwood, "Jerusalem Western Wall Development Plan Opposed by Palestinians as 'Illegal,'" *The Guardian* (UK), November 22, 2010; "Israeli Newspaper Publishes Obama's Western Wall Prayer," *CNN Newsroom*, CNN, July 28, 2008; Aron Heller, "Israeli Newspaper Publishes Obama's Private Prayer," Associated Press, July 25, 2008.
120. Kim Murphy, "Obituaries: George Habash, 1925-2008," *Los Angeles Times*, January 27, 2008. Later corrected.
121. David Gelernter, "A New Synagogue in the Old City," *Weekly Standard*, October 7, 2002. For Shi'ite Muslims, Jerusalem is the *fourth*-holiest site after Nejef, the birthplace of Muhammad's son-in-law.
122. Reuters, however, has mistakenly referred to Rachel's Tomb as "Judaism's holiest site." (Cynthia Johnston, "Israel Explodes Bomb Hidden in Tomb, Muslims Angry," Reuters,

September 9, 2004.)
123. Sheera Frenkel, "Fight Over Holy Sites Clouds New Mideast Peace Bid," *All Things Considered*, National Public Radio, March 5, 2010.
124. Josh Mitnick, "Israel Names Two Biblical Tombs in West Bank Heritage Sites," *Christian Science Monitor*, February 23, 2010.
125. Linda Gradstein, "Netanyahu's Heritage Plan 'Could Lead to Religious War'; Decision Over Disputed Jewish, Muslim Site Fuels Palestinians' Anger," *Toronto Star*, March 4, 2010.
126. "Uprising Fears Grow as Bibi Digs in Heels," United Press International, March 4, 2010.
127. Luis Ramirez, "Palestinian Residents Say Peace Only Possible Without Jewish Settlers," Voice of America, September 15, 2010.
128. Cited in "Model Activism in Philly," HonestReporting.com, August 28, 2003.
129. See Genesis, chapter 35. For millennia, the site has served as a sort of Wailing Wall, attracting thousands of Jews who come to pray and find solace.
130. "Slavery in Islam," BBC Online, September 7, 2009; Nadav Shragai, "The Palestinian Authority and the Jewish Holy Sites in the West Bank: Rachel's Tomb as a Test Case," *Jerusalem Viewpoints*, Jerusalem Center for Public Affairs, December 2, 2007.
131. Cynthia Johnston, "Israel Explodes Bomb Hidden in Tomb, Muslims Angry," Reuters, September 9, 2004.
132. In 1998, due to repeated Palestinian shooting attacks on Jewish worshippers at Rachel's Tomb, Israel encased the small, domed structure behind huge walls of defensive concrete.
133. In 333 CE, a Christian known as the "Bordeaux Pilgrim" recorded having seen Rachel's Tomb on the outskirts of Bethlehem. Jerome, the early Church figure who moved to Bethlehem from Rome in the year 386 CE, also mentions the tomb. The fourth century historian and bishop Eusebius, writing in *Onomasticon*, recorded the presence of Rachel's Tomb, as did Epiphanius the Monk in his seventh century volume, *The Holy City and the Holy Places*. (Michael Freund, "Hands Off Mother Rachel," *Jerusalem Post*, November 4, 2010.)
134. Al-Idrisi wrote: "On the road between Bethlehem and Jerusalem is the tomb of Rachel, the mother of Joseph and Benjamin." (Cited in Michael Freund, "Hands off Mother Rachel," *Jerusalem Post*, November 4, 2010.)
135. Shmuel Berkowitz, *The Wars of the Holy Places*, Jerusalem Institute for Israeli Studies and Hed Artzi, 2000, p. 301.
136. See *Palestinian Lexicon*, issued by the Arab League and the PLO in 1984; *Al-mawsu'ah al-Filastiniyah* published by the Palestinian Encyclopedia organization in 1996; *Palestine: the Holy Land*, published by the Palestinian Council for Development and Rehabilitation, with an introduction by Yasser Arafat.
137. On October 8, 2000, six days after the Palestinian takeover of Joseph's Tomb in Nablus, the official PLO newspaper *Al-Hayat al-Jadida* published an article indicating Rachel's Tomb as the next Palestinian target. Thus launched a Palestinian PR effort to "recast" the site as Bilal Bin Rabah Mosque.
138. Jonathan Mark, "Media Watch: Rachel's Tomb is Now a Mosque – Who Cares?", *Jewish Week* (New York), November 23, 2010. In classic U.N. form, the protests of Israel's Ambassador to UNESCO, Nimrod Barkan, was expunged from the record. (Gideon Kutz, Israel Radio, October 29, 2010; cited in Nadav Shragai, "Rachel's Tomb, a Jewish Holy Place, Was Never a Mosque," Jerusalem Center for Public Affairs, November-December 2010.)
139. In October 1995, one month before his assassination, Israeli Prime Minister Yitzhak Rabin asked the Knesset to ratify the Oslo II Accords. Referring specifically to the Tomb of the Patriarchs, Rachel's Tomb and Joseph's Tomb, Rabin declared: "As a Jewish nation, we must, first and foremost, pay attention to the holy places, to our religion, tradition, and culture. We were strict about this in the Interim Agreement." (Yitzhak Rabin, "Ratification of the Israel-Palestinian Interim Agreement," Speech at the Knesset, October 5, 1995.)

140. "Israeli Army Returns to Arafat Compound," BBC News Online, October 1, 2002.
141. Throughout the centuries, Jewish and non-Jewish sources have described Joseph's Tomb and its current location. See Dr. Joel Elitzur, "The Authenticity of Chelkat HaSadeh – Joseph's Tomb."
142. Alan Philps, "Protesters Wreck Jewish Shrine as Troops Withdraw," *Daily Telegraph* (UK), June 19, 2001.
143. Jamie Tarabay, "West Bank Tomb Site of Many Clashes," Associated Press, October 2, 2000.
144. Cited in Bernard Goldberg, *Bias: A CBS Insider Exposes How the Media Distort the News*, Regnery Publishing, 2001.
145. Jeremy Bowen, *The Birth of Israel*, BBC, May 4, 2008. This strangely echoes the words of Iranian President Mahmoud Ahmadinejad who questioned why "the Palestinian people should be paying" for the Holocaust: "After all, it happened in Europe. The Palestinian people had no role to play in it. So why is it that the Palestinian people are paying the price of an event they had nothing to do with? The Palestinian people didn't commit any crime. They had no role to play in World War II." ("President Ahmadinejad Delivers Remarks at Columbia University," CQ Transcripts Wire, September 24, 2007.) Associated Press extended the concept, reporting that even Israel's 1.2 million Arabs "resentfully view the Holocaust as the catalyst of their own suffering." (Diaa Hadid, "Yad Vashem Struggles to Teach Holocaust to Arabs," Associated Press, December 13, 2010.)
146. Seán Mac Mathúna, "The Role of the SS Handschar Division in Yugoslavia's Holocaust." Husseini's Muslim troops served in the Albanian Skanderbeg 21st Waffen SS division, and the Bosnian 13th Waffen Hanjar (Sword) SS division that decimated Bosnian Jewry.
147. Julian Schvindlerman, "When Hitler became Abu Ali," *Miami Herald*, June 7, 2002. ("A Mideast song popular in the late 1930s crooned: 'In Heaven Allah, on Earth Hitler.'")
148. Alan M. Dershowitz, *The Case Against Israel's Enemies*, Wiley, 2008, p. 198.
149. David Dalin and John Rothmann, *Icon of Evil*, Transaction Publishers, 2009, p. 140.
150. Haj Amin al-Husseini, radio speech in Rome, March 19, 1943; cited in *The Arab War Effort: A Documented Account*, American Christian Palestine Committee, New York, 1947.
151. Cited in Joseph B. Schechtman, *The Mufti and the Fuehrer*, Thomas Yoseloff Pub., 1965. Incredibly, Husseini himself may have originated the idea of gas chambers and crematoria. The Nazis originally confined the Jews to ghettos and used them as slave laborers, with plans to expel them to Palestine. But at a meeting with Hitler in Berlin in November 1941, Husseini objected that such a plan would result in a powerful Jewish state; he argued that a better "Final Solution" would be to kill all the Jews. (Jack Kelly, "Jews Under Siege," *Pittsburgh Post-Gazette*, March 17, 2002.)
152. Chuck Morse, *The Nazi Connection to Islamic Terrorism*, iUniverse, 2003. Husseini regularly toured Auschwitz, and in 1944 arranged for a Nazi-Arab commando unit to enter Palestine with the goal of poisoning the water wells of Tel Aviv. (Morse, *The Nazi Connection to Islamic Terrorism*.) Husseini wrote in his memoirs: "Our fundamental condition for cooperating with Germany was a free hand to eradicate every last Jew from Palestine and the Arab world. I asked Hitler for an explicit undertaking to allow us to solve the Jewish problem in a manner befitting our national and racial aspirations, and according to the scientific methods innovated by Germany in the handling of its Jews. The answer I got was: 'The Jews are yours.'" (Cited in Ami Isseroff and Peter FitzGerald-Morris, "The Iraq Coup Attempt of 1941, the Mufti, and the Farhud," Mideastweb.org.)
153. Morse, *The Nazi Connection to Islamic Terrorism*.
154. Edward W. Said and Christopher Hitchens, editors, *Blaming the Victims*, Verso, 2001.
155. Similarly, Johannes von Leers, a Goebbels collaborator, was brought to Egypt by Husseini where he converted to Islam, changed his name to Omar Amin, and became an adviser to the Egyptian government. Alois Brunner, an Austrian Nazi war criminal and assistant to

Adolf Eichmann, fled to Syria in the mid-1950s where he became a government adviser. (Dr. Manfred Gerstenfeld, "Holocaust Inversion: The Portraying of Israel and Jews as Nazis," Jerusalem Center for Public Affairs, April 2007.)
156. "Hitler's Muslim Legions," BBC Radio 4, July 26, 2010.
157. Greg Myre, "A Man Called Hitler Runs for a Seat He May Not Fill," *New York Times*, January 22, 2006; see also *New York Times*, April 6, 1989.
158. Katie Engelhart, "The Return of Hitler," *Maclean's* (Canada), April 26, 2010; "Mein Kampf Makes it to Palestinian Bestseller List," Agence France Presse, September 8, 1999.
159. "Gas chambers only existed for purification... clothes and personal tools were put in to sterilize them." (See Mohammad Daoud, "Holocaust Again?!", *Syria Times*, September 6, 2000.) "There are no findings to indicate the existence of mass graves, because the size of the ovens makes it impossible for many Jews to have been killed there... no more than 70,000 Jews were registered as having been at Auschwitz." ("The New Hitler," *Al-Akhbar* [Egypt], December 21, 1997.)
160. Cited in Arie Stav, *Nativ* (Israel), 1995; see Charles A. Morse, "The Nazism of Abu Mazen," April 14, 2003.
161. Cited in Tom Gross, "Abu Mazen and the Holocaust," Tomgrossmedia.com, June 8, 2003. Abbas wrote: "It seems that the interest of the Zionist movement... is to inflate this figure so that their gains will be greater. This led them to emphasize this figure in order to gain the solidarity of international public opinion with Zionism. Many scholars have debated the figure of six million and reached stunning conclusions – fixing the number of Jewish victims at only a few hundred thousand." (Mahmoud Abbas, *The Other Side: The Secret Relationship Between Nazism and Zionism*, 1983; translation by Wiesenthal Center.)
162. *Al-Hayat Al-Jadida* (Palestinian Authority), April 13, 2001; cited in "Holocaust Denial and Distortion," Palestinian Media Watch.
163. *Pages from Our History*, Palestinian Authority Television, November 29, 2000.
164. Alan M. Dershowitz, "Building a State on Lies," Frontpagemag.com, September 2, 2009. (Younis Al-Astal of Hamas declared that the United Nations' proposal to include Holocaust education in a course on human rights would constitute the "war crime" of "marketing a lie and spreading it.")
165. Khaled Abu Toameh and Associated Press, "PA Dismantles W. Bank Youth Orchestra," *Jerusalem Post*, March 29, 2009; Yoav Stern, "PA Expels Founder of Jenin Youth Orchestra Over Concert for Survivors," *Haaretz* (Israel), April 2, 2009.
166. Steven Gutkin, "Israel Hopes Obama Speech will Lead to Peace," Associated Press, June 4, 2009.
167. Howard Schneider, "Netanyahu's Speech to Inject Zionist Perspective," *Washington Post*, June 14, 2009.
168. Ron Bousso, "Israel Hopes for Arab Reconciliation After Obama," Agence France Presse, June 4, 2009.
169. James Bennet and John Kifner, "Mideast Turmoil: Succession; 6 Men Who Could Be Contenders to Lead the Palestinians if Arafat Goes," *New York Times*, June 14, 2002.
170. Asked about the lessons of Jewish history, Israeli president Shimon Peres explained, "If we have to make a mistake of overreaction or underreaction, I think I prefer the overreaction." (Jeffrey Goldberg, "Israel's Fears, Amalek's Arsenal," *New York Times*, May 17, 2009.)
171. Some take the attitude that Israel should just "get over it." Stefan De Clerck, Belgium's justice minister, called for blanket amnesty for 56,000 Belgians convicted of collaborating with the Nazis: "Perhaps we should be willing to forget, because it is the past." (Bruno Waterfield, "Nazi Hunters Call on Belgium's Justice Minister to be Sacked," *Telegraph* [UK], May 17, 2011.) Archbishop Desmond Tutu has also urged that Israelis "pray for and forgive" those responsible for the Nazi genocide. (Alan Cowell, "Tutu Urges Israelis to Pray for and

Forgive Nazis," *New York Times,* December 27, 1989.)
172. "Freaky Deaky: Iranian Holocaust Miniseries Sympathetic to Jews?", *Allahpundit* / Hotair.com, September 16, 2007. According to Mahmoud Ahmadinejad: "Although we don't accept" the historicity of the Holocaust, "our question for the Europeans is: Is the killing of innocent Jewish people by Hitler the reason for their support of the occupiers of Jerusalem? If the Europeans are honest, they should give some of their provinces" so that "Zionists can establish their state in Europe." (Benny Avni, "Iranian President's Latest Rage Against Jews is Part of Pattern," *The Sun* [New York], December 9, 2005.)
173. Eric Rozenman, "NPR Execs Dine with Fake Islamists," Committee for Accuracy in Middle East Reporting in America, March 8, 2011.
174. Daniel Zwerdling, *All Things Considered,* National Public Radio, October 22, 1994.
175. "The Charter of Allah: The Platform of the Islamic Resistance Movement (Hamas), Article Thirteen: Peaceful Solutions, [Peace] Initiatives and International Conferences," 1988.
176. Sheik Nizar Rayan, Al Jazeera, September 16, 2005; translation by Middle East Media Research Institute.
177. Jonathan Steele, "The Palestinians' Democratic Choice Must Be Respected," *The Guardian* (UK), January 27, 2006.
178. "Palestinian Elections: After the Hamas Earthquake," *The Guardian* (UK), January 27, 2006.
179. Robert Novak, "Hamas Talks Peace, but U.S. Not Listening," *Chicago Sun-Times,* April 17, 2007.
180. William A. Orme Jr., "A Parallel Mideast Battle: Is It News or Incitement?", *New York Times,* October 24, 2000.
181. Palestinian Authority Television, October 13, 2000.
182. "7 Principles of Media Objectivity," Aish.com, March 20, 2001.
183. Patrick Martin, "Trying to Find a New Road to His Lost Home," *Globe and Mail* (Canada), July 7, 2009.
184. Orly Halpern, "Hamas Tries New Strategy: A Peaceful Human Chain," *Globe and Mail* (Canada), February 26, 2008.
185. Kevin Peraino, "Palestine's New Perspective," *Newsweek,* September 14, 2009.
186. Steven Erlanger, "Hamas will Take Part in Vote for a Palestinian Legislature," *New York Times,* March 13, 2005.
187. Ethan Bronner, "In Village, Palestinians See Model for Their Cause," *New York Times,* August 27, 2009.
188. Ben White, "Peaceful Palestinian Resistance is Paying Off," *Christian Science Monitor,* February 11, 2010
189. Richard Boudreaux, "Palestinians Who See Nonviolence as Their Weapon," *Los Angeles Times,* November 4, 2009. Another *Times* article referred to these same "nonviolent Palestinian protesters." (Edmund Sanders, "Israel Begins Rerouting West Bank Barrier," *Los Angeles Times,* February 12, 2010.)
190. Ethan Bronner, "Hamas Leader Calls for Two-State Solution, but Refuses to Renounce Violence," *New York Times,* May 5, 2011; Editorial, "A Fatah-Hamas Deal," *New York Times,* May 8, 2011.
191. "I Guess Hamas Doesn't Read the New York Times," *Elder of Ziyon* blog, June 10, 2011.
192. "Hamas Leader Khaled Meshaal," *Charlie Rose,* PBS, May 28, 2010; cited in "The Western Media Eats Up Khaled Meshal's Lies to Them," *Elder of Ziyon* blog, May 30, 2010.
193. Hamas foreign minister Mahmoud Zahar, Al-Manar TV (Hezbollah), January 25, 2006.
194. "Israeli Arabs 'Funding Hamas,'" BBC News Online, May 13, 2003.
195. Email correspondence with Dr. Rony Doeuk; cited in "The Stubborn Scottish Script," HonestReporting.com, May 22, 2003.
196. For example, Nidal Al-Mughrabi, "Targeted Attack," Reuters, September 27, 2002.

197. For example, "Israel Agrees to Withdraw from Gaza," Reuters, June 28, 2003.
198. Shahdi al-Kashif, "Israeli Tank in Flames after Hitting Bomb in Gaza," Reuters, February 15, 2003.
199. Rami Amichai, "Israel Remands Arab-Canadian in Alleged Bomb Plot," Reuters, December 15, 2003.
200. See Ricki Hollander, "The Power of Words: Reuters' and Camera's," Committee for Accuracy in Middle East Reporting in America, December 24, 2003.
201. "The Dishonest Reporter 'Award' 2003," HonestReporting.com, December 15, 2003.
202. Wafa Amr, "Hamas Hints at Truce with Israel in Return for Pullout," Reuters, January 26, 2004.
203. Mark Mazzetti, "Striking Deep Into Israel, Hamas Employs an Upgraded Rocket Arsenal," *New York Times*, January 1, 2009.
204. Amy Teibel, "Hezbollah Denies Link to Arms Ship," Associated Press, November 5, 2009; Steven Gutkin, "Israel: Weapons Would Let Hezbollah Fight a Month," Associated Press, November 6, 2009.
205. James Bennet, "Seized Arms Would Have Vastly Extended Arafat Arsenal," *New York Times*, January 12, 2002.
206. Speech in Tehran at the Islamic Student Association's Conference on "The World Without Zionism," Iranian Student News Agency, October 30, 2005; translation by Nazila Fathi, "Text of Mahmoud Ahmadinejad's Speech," *New York Times*, October 30, 2005.
207. Speech in Tehran at the "International Conference of Holy Qods and Support for the Rights of the Palestinian Nation," April 14, 2006; cited in "Iran's Ahmadinejad Says Israel Close to 'Annihilation,'" *Iran Focus*, April 15, 2006, and "Is Iran Preparing for War?", *Washington Times*, April 17, 2006.
208. Speech in Tehran at the Islamic Student Association's Conference on "The World Without Zionism," Iranian Student News Agency, October 30, 2005; cited in "Iranian President at Tehran Conference: 'Very Soon, This Stain of Disgrace [i.e. Israel] Will Be Purged From the Center of the Islamic World – and This Is Attainable,'" Middle East Media Research Institute, October 28, 2005.
209. Nazila Fathi, "Iran Says It Can Enrich Uranium on a Large Scale," *New York Times*, April 10, 2007.
210. Kim Sengupta, "Iranians Test-fire Missile Capable of Hitting Israel," *The Independent* (UK), July 10, 2008. See "Stand Up to Ahmadinejad," Aish.com, February 14, 2007.
211. Elie Wiesel, "Kick Him Out," November 27, 2006.
212. Walt Rodgers, "The Danger of an Israeli Strike on Iran," *Christian Science Monitor*, April 24, 2009.
213. Jonathan Power, "Israel's Nukes Serve to Justify Iran's; Deterring the Deterrents," *International Herald Tribune*, September 22, 2004.
214. "Iran's Ahmadinejad Urges Egypt to Rebuild Ties," Reuters, June 1, 2011; cited in "Ahmadinejad has Repeatedly Forecast the Imminent Disappearance of the Jewish State," Reuters Middle East Watch, June 1, 2011.
215. "Iran President Tones Down Israel Attack," Associated Press, February 14, 2007; Ethan Bronner, "Just How Far Did They Go, Those Words Against Israel?", *New York Times*, June 11, 2006.
216. Glenn Kessler, "Did Ahmadinejad Really Say Israel Should be 'Wiped Off the Map'?", *Washington Post*, October 5, 2011. Dariush Rezaiinejad, chief commander of Iran's Basij militia, has stated clearly: "We have no option but to have the Zionist regime wiped off the map." ("IRGC Basij: No Choice But to Wipe Out Israel," *Home Daily News* (Iran), July 27, 2011. The English section of Ahmadinejad's own website quotes him as saying that Israel "will be wiped off the map." ("President Says Zionist Regime of Israel Faces Deadend,"

www.president.ir/en/, June 3, 2008. See Ethan Bronner, "Just How Far Did They Go, Those Words Against Israel?", *New York Times*, June 11, 2006.)
217. Dan De Luce, "Iran Parades New Missiles Daubed with Threats to Wipe Israel Off Map," *The Guardian* (UK), September 23, 2003.
218. Joe Klein, "Israel's Iran Game," Time.com, April 22, 2009.
219. "A Grand Bargain?", *The Economist*, April 23, 2009.
220. "Iran's Ahmadinejad Defiant... Over His Culinary Skills," Agence France Presse, August 28, 2007; cited in James Taranto, "Best of the Web Today," *Wall Street Journal Online*, August 28, 2007.
221. Roger Cohen, "What Iran's Jews Say," *New York Times*, February 22, 2009.
222. "International Religious Freedom Report 2008," U.S. Department of State, Bureau of Democracy, Human Rights and Labor.
223. Ed Lasky, "*New York Times* Columnist Roger Cohen a Useful Idiot for Iran," *American Thinker*, February 23, 2009.
224. This calls to mind CBS' Mike Wallace, who visited Syria in 1975 and reported that "life for Syria's Jews is better than it was in years past," and that assertions of mistreatment are mere "Zionist propaganda." (Mike Wallace, "Israel's Toughest Enemy," *60 Minutes*, CBS, February 1975.) Shortly thereafter, nearly every Syrian Jew fled the country in fear. A decade later, Wallace repeated his naiveté by reporting that Soviet Jews "live more or less satisfying lives." More than a million Soviet Jews disagreed and emigrated the first chance they had. (Lenny Ben-David, "NYT's Roger Cohen Betrays Iranian Jews and the Truth," Lennybendavid.com, March 15, 2009.)
225. Roger Cohen, "Hard Mideast Truths," *New York Times*, February 11, 2010.
226. Roger Cohen, "Iran, the Jews and Germany," *New York Times*, March 1, 2009.
227. Roger Cohen, "Israel Cries Wolf," *New York Times*, April 9, 2009.
228. James Taranto, "Best of the Web Today," *Wall Street Journal Online*, April 9, 2009.
229. Roger Cohen, "Iran's Day of Anguish," *New York Times*, June 14, 2009.
230. Bernard Lewis, quoted in the film, *Iranium*, Clarion Fund, 2011.
231. Hashemi Rafsanjani, former President of Iran, cited in Suzanne Fields, "Confronting the New Anti-Semitism," *Washington Times*, July 24, 2004. Similarly, King Ibn Saud of Saudi Arabia purportedly said before the Arab invasion of Israel in 1948: "There are 50 million Arabs. What does it matter if we lose 10 million people to kill all the Jews? The price is worth it."
232. "Captured Video Shows Iraqi Insurgents Firing Sophisticated Iranian-Made Rockets at U.S. Positions," Fox News, August 9, 2007; "Iraqi Insurgents Being Trained in Iran, U.S. Says," CNN.com, April 11, 2007.
233. "Report of the Commission to Assess the Threat to the United States from Electromagnetic Pulse (EMP) Attack," presented to U.S. Congress, June 2004; Mike Emanuel, "Iranian Missile May Be Able to Hit U.S. by 2015," Fox News, April 20, 2010.
234. EMP was first detected in 1962 when a nuclear explosion in the Pacific Ocean blew out street lamps, television sets and telephone communications in Hawaii nearly 1,000 miles away. (See "Nuclear Weapon EMP Effects," Federation of American Scientists, 1998.)
235. "Report of the Commission to Assess the Threat to the United States from Electromagnetic Pulse (EMP) Attack," presented to U.S. Congress, April 2008.
236. "Iranian Naval Vessels to be Deployed Near U.S. Sea Borders: Commander," *Tehran Times*, September 27, 2011.
237. "U.S. Seen as Less Important, China as More Powerful" (Section 2: Global Threats and Use of Military Force), Pew Research Center, December 3, 2009.
238. Anne Flaherty, "Congress Denounces Iran's Ahmadinejad," Associated Press, September 25, 2007; cited in James Taranto, "Best of the Web Today," *Wall Street Journal Online*, September

26, 2007.
239. Anne Flaherty, "House Condemns Tehran Crackdown on Protesters," Associated Press, June 19, 2009; cited in James Taranto, "Best of the Web Today," *Wall Street Journal Online*, June 19, 2009.
240. Mohammad Abdullah Al Mutawa, "Zionists are the New Nazis," *Gulf News* (UAE), January 8, 2009.
241. Palestinian Authority Television, April 10, 2008; cited in Itamar Marcus and Barbara Crook, "Palestinian Authority Libels and Lies, Part 3: 2006-2008," Palestinian Media Watch.
242. *Al-Hayat Al-Jadida* (Palestinian Authority), September 1, 2007; cited in Itamar Marcus and Barbara Crook, "Palestinian Authority Libels and Lies, Part 3: 2006-2008," Palestinian Media Watch.
243. Palestinian Authority Television, March 25, 2004; cited in Itamar Marcus and Barbara Crook, "When Hatemongering is Common Currency," *Ottawa Citizen* (Canada), April 27, 2009.
244. A.N. Wilson, "A Demo We Can't Afford to Ignore," *Evening Standard* (UK), April 15, 2002.
245. Bob Simon, *60 Minutes*, CBS, December 23, 2003.
246. Fareed Zakaria, "Interview with Turkish Prime Minister Erdogan," *Fareed Zakaria GPS*, CNN, September 25, 2011.
247. "Is it not a bit dangerous to align ourselves to this point to a country whose policies are controversial and even condemned by the UN? I would ask the same question if Canada decided to represent Iran or Sudan somewhere in the world." Simon Durivage, *Le Match des élus*, Radio-Canada, Canadian Broadcasting Corporation, October 15, 2010; cited in "Radio-Canada Equates Israel with Iran and Sudan," HonestReporting Canada, November 8, 2010.
248. "Israel Envoy Protests German Magazine's Hitler-Sharon Comparison," Associated Press, December 17, 2001.
249. Alfred de Montesquiou, "African Union Force Ineffective, Complain Refugees in Darfur," Associated Press, October 16, 2006.
250. According to the Palestinian Central Bureau of Statistics, the population in the territories was 3,935,249 in 2009. In the first half of 2011, an average of 140 babies were born in Gaza every day. That same period averaged only 12 deaths per day. ("More than 25,000 Births in the Gaza Strip During the First Half of this Year," Palestinian Ma'an News Agency, July 11, 2011.)
251. Azmi Keshawi and Martin Fletcher, "Tears and Anger Among Wreckage of Gaza as Families Return Home," *The Times* (UK), January 20, 2009.
252. Jack Katzenell, "Author Saramago Sets Off Storm by Comparing Blockaded Palestinian Town to Nazi Death Camp," Associated Press, March 26, 2002.
253. Richard Falk, Slouching Toward a Palestinian Holocaust," Transnational Foundation for Peace and Future Research, June 29, 2007. (Compared to "genocidal conduct in Darfur" and Rwanda, Israel's action in Gaza are "morally far worse.")
254. Robin Shepherd, "In Europe, an Unhealthy Fixation on Israel," *Washington Post*, January 30, 2005.
255. "UK Jewish Lawmaker: Israeli Forces Acting Like Nazis," CNN.com, January 16, 2009.
256. "Saudi Likens Gaza Assault to Nazi War Crimes," Agence France Presse, March 2, 2008.
257. A.N. Wilson, "A Demo We Can't Afford to Ignore," *Evening Standard* (UK), April 15, 2002.
258. Cited in Bret Stephens, "Eye on the Media: The Inversion Syndrome," *Jerusalem Post*, April 25, 2002.
259. Rabbi Jonathan Sacks, "The New Antisemitism," *Jewish Chronicle* (UK), November 2007.
260. Thomas Friedman, *From Beirut to Jerusalem*, Anchor Books, 1990.
261. Donald Bostrom, "They Plunder the Organs of Our Sons," *Aftonbladet* (Sweden), August 17, 2009. The *Aftonbladet* account never held up to basic scrutiny: If the goal was to harvest organs worth hundreds of thousands of dollars, why would Israeli soldiers shoot in the

chest and abdomen, causing the organs to become damaged and unusable for transplant? (Andrea Meyerhoff MD, "Israel Organ Harvesting Scandal 'Medically Impossible,'" *The Local* [Sweden], August 31, 2009.) The *Aftonbladet* story also ignored the fact that "black market organs must mostly be from live donors. Live donors can take blood tests well in advance and travel to where the patient is. Deceased organs have to be put on ice, and the clock starts ticking immediately and fast." (Harvard professor Al Roth, cited in Stephen J. Dubner, "Why the Israeli Organ-Harvesting Story is Probably False," *Freakonomics* blog / *New York Times*, August 25, 2009.) Bostrom later back-tracked when speaking to the Western media: On CNN, he stressed there is no proof that Israeli soldiers were stealing organs (Tricia Escobedo, "Swedish Paper's Organ Harvesting Article Draws Israeli Outrage," CNN.com, August 19, 2009), and Associated Press quoted him as saying: "Whether it's true or not – I have no idea, I have no clue." ("Israel Furious Over Swedish Newspaper Article," Associated Press, August 19, 2009.) Even Bostrom's "sources" denied having ever said that organs were stolen; Jalal Ghanem, brother of the supposed Palestinian victim, admitted that "we don't have any evidence to support this." (Khaled Abu Toameh, "Palestinian Family Denies Telling Foreign Media that Organs were Stolen," *Jerusalem Post*, August 24, 2009; see also "Swedish Daily Admits No Proof for Organ Smuggling Claim," Agence France Presse, August 23, 2009.) Months later, it was revealed that Israeli pathologist Dr. Yehuda Hiss had harvested organs from corpses of Israeli soldiers, civilians, Jews and non-Jews during the 1990s. ("Israel Admits Harvesting Organs in '90s," Associated Press, December 20, 2009.) Though there was no linkage to Bostrom's false allegations, the London *Guardian* posted the headline, "Israel Admits Harvesting Palestinian Organs." The *Guardian* later changed the headline, citing "a serious editing error." ("Corrections and Clarifications," *The Guardian*, December 22, 2009.)

262. Isabel Kershner, "Accusation of Organ Theft Stokes Ire in Israel," *New York Times*, August 24, 2009. When Sweden's ambassador to Israel, Elisabet Borsiin Bonnier, called the organ accusations "shocking and appalling," she was denounced in her home country for interfering with freedom of speech. ("Swedish Envoy to Israel Slammed for Media Comment," Associated Press, August 20, 2009.)

263. Palestinians were the first to invent the libelous idea of Israelis stealing Palestinian organs: "The occupying authorities steal body parts of Palestinian martyrs, in order to use them in Israeli hospitals for Israeli patients in need of transplants." *(Al-Hayat Al-Jadida* [Palestinian Authority], December 24, 2001.)

264. "Sweden Shuts Website Over Cartoon," BBC News Online, February 10, 2006.

265. "Sweden Democrats Attack on Islam Criticised," *Stockholm News*, October 19, 2009.

266. Igor Gedilaghine, "Sweden's Free Speech Tradition Runs into Israeli Ire," Agence France Presse, August 27, 2009.

267. Alastair Macdonald, "Israel Slams Swedish Tabloid's Organ Theft Story," Reuters, August 19, 2009.

268. Lily Galili, "Ukraine Academic: Israel Imported 25,000 Kids for Their Organs," *Haaretz* (Israel), December 3, 2009. The Canadian Muslim newspaper, *Al-Ameen Post*, "reported" the Ukrainian conspiracy under the headline, "Ukrainian Kids: New Victims of Israeli Organ Theft."

269. *Al-Khabar* (Algeria), September 6, 2009. The Algerian story quickly spread, appearing in American news outlets such as the California-based weekly *Watan*. The official Iranian news agency cited the Algerian report as evidence of "an international Jewish conspiracy to kidnap children and harvest their organs." ("Algerian Kids Falling Prey to Jewish 'Organ Harvest,'" Press TV [Iran], September 17, 2009; see Haviv Rettig Gur, "Jews Harvesting Algerian Kids' Organs," *Jerusalem Post*, September 14, 2009.)

270. "The Arab League Council Publishes Resolutions Supporting the Palestinian Issue and

Demands an Investigation into the Theft of the Organs of our Shahids (Martyrs)," WAFA News Agency, September 10, 2009; cited in "Arab Foreign Ministers Demand Investigation of Israel's Organ Theft," Palestinian Media Watch.
271. "Israeli Illegal Trafficking in Organs of Dead and Kidnapped Palestinian Victims," Statement by International Organization for the Elimination of all Forms of Racial Discrimination (EAFORD), United Nations Human Rights Council, 13th Session, Agenda Item 7, February 24, 2010.
272. George Galloway, "Dark Echoes of Holocaust," *Daily Record* (Scotland), December 28, 2009.
273. Yossi Klein Halevi, "Take Them to Court," Shalem Center, August 13, 2009. Media outlets in Jordan, Qatar, Oman, Syria and the United Arab Emirates all presented Israeli soldiers as vicious butchers, gleefully cutting off Arab body parts. ("Anti-Semitic Canard About 'Organ Harvesting' Spreads Globally," Anti-Defamation League, September 16, 2009.) A blockbuster film in Turkey, *Valley of the Wolves*, depicted the Iraq War as a conspiracy by Israelis and Americans to harvest organs of Iraqi women and children. (Rabbi Abraham Cooper, "Confronting 'History's Longest Hatred,'" *Washington Post*, July 14, 2010.)
274. Dr. Jennifer Ashton, "Life-Saving Efforts Continue," *CBS Evening News*, January 17, 2010. The Israeli medical team set up X-ray machines, respirators, blood transfusions, ultrasound, and incubators for premature babies – while elsewhere in Port-au-Prince, doctors were reduced to cutting off infected legs with razor blades and no anesthetic. (Catherine Porter, "Israeli Field Hospital Carries on Inspiring Work in Japan," *Toronto Star*, April 4, 2011.)
275. Craig Rivera, "Haiti: Mission of Hope," Fox News, January 17, 2010; Elizabeth Cohen, CNN.com, January 18, 2010; Dominic Waghorn, "Sky Man Spends Day With Haiti Search Team," Sky News, January 18, 2010; Paula Hancocks, "Israel Aids Haiti," CNN.com, January 19, 2010; Nancy Snyderman, *Nightly News*, NBC, January 19, 2010 ("the best field medicine available... a model for medical disaster response"). A baby boy delivered at the Israeli field hospital was given the name "Israel" by his grateful mother. See another amazing story at "Dr. Besser Assists in Haitian Baby's Birth," *Good Morning America*, ABC News, January 18, 2010.
276. Stephanie Gutmann, "Israel Builds a Field Hospital in Haiti, Anti-Zionists Not Fooled!", *Daily Telegraph* (UK), January 19, 2010; see "International Aid to Haiti: Who's Giving," Associated Press / CBSNews.com, January 14, 2010.
277. Howard Schneider, "Israel and Pacific Republics, United by an Island Mentality," *Washington Post*, February 1, 2010; cited in Leo Rennert, "WaPo Hits Trifecta of Biased Journalism Today," Americanthinker.com, February 1, 2010.
278. See Stephen Lendman, "Focus on Israel: Harvesting Haitian Organs by an American Researcher," *Palestine Telegraph*; Uri Dromi, "A Lib Dem and a Blood Libel," *The Guardian* (UK), February 12, 2010; Simon Rocker and Martin Bright, "Tonge: Investigate IDF Stealing Organs in Haiti," *Jewish Chronicle* (UK), February 11, 2010; Yitzhak Benhorin, "Anti-Semitic Video Against Israel Team in Haiti," *Ynetnews* (Israel), January 20, 2010; T West, "Israeli Defense Force in Haiti, and Demonizing Jean Wyclef," YouTube.com, January 18, 2010.
279. Cnaan Liphshiz, "Dutch Journalist: Flu Pandemics are Jewish Conspiracy," *Haaretz* (Israel), August 10, 2009.
280. David Stavrou, "Cyncism Prevails for Vote-hungry Officials in Sweden and Israel," *The Local* (Sweden), August 28, 2009. Bostrom capitalized on the publicity by appearing on Iranian television to peddle his organ transplant theory ("Bostrom Tells Press TV of Israel Organ Scenario," Press TV [Iran], August 22, 2009), and proudly accepting the National Federation of Algerian Journalists' award for excellence, along with a cash prize.
281. Bruce Beattie, *News Journal* (Florida) / Copely News Service, October 30, 2002.
282. "Cartoons of the Week," *Time*, October 26 – November 1, 2002; see "Scorning the Island of Democracy," HonestReporting.com, November 7, 2002.

283. Tony Auth, *Philadelphia Inquirer* / Universal Press Syndicate, July 31, 2003.
284. Someone apparently submitted the cartoon on Leunig's behalf. ("The Age May Sue Over Leunig Cartoon Hoax," *The Age* [Australia], February 14, 2006.)
285. "Why Israel Can't Win," *Time*, January 19, 2009.
286. Tom Paulin, "Killed in Crossfire," *The Observer* (UK), February 18, 2001.
287. Matt McCarten, "Palestinians' Fight is a Struggle Against Apartheid," *New Zealand Herald*, January 4, 2009.
288. Yasmin Alibhai-brown, "Why I'm Boycotting Anything 'Made in Israel,'" *The Independent* (UK), April 15, 2002.
289. Roseanne Barr, "I Told My Friend: Don't Go!", Roseanneworld.com/blog, December 30, 2008.
290. Eric Margolis, "Eradicating Hamas," Ericmargolis.com, January 12, 2009.
291. Cited in Tom Gross, "J'Accuse," *Wall Street Journal Europe*, June 2, 2005.
292. Scott Wilson, "Eviction Notices are Served in Gaza, as Pullout Begins, Israeli Army Blocked from Entering Some Settlements," *Washington Post*, August 16, 2005; cited in "Post Refuses to Call Palestinian Terrorists 'Terrorists,' Yet Calls Israeli Settlers 'Shock Troops,'" *Eye on the Post*, August 16, 2005.
293. Pat Oliphant, Universal Press Syndicate, March 25, 2009. Oliphant later spelled out the rationale behind his cartoon: "My complaint was that Israel, the Israeli state, was behaving very much like their former tormentors were behaving back in the '30s and '40s... a somewhat Nazi side to the way they were behaving." (Pat Oliphant, Australian Cartoonists Association's Stanley Awards Conference, Sydney, Australia, November 14, 2009.)
294. Jonah Goldberg, "Who are the Real Nazis?", *Jewish World Review*, January 7, 2009.
295. *Eleftherotypia* (Greece), April 2002; cited in Gross, "J'Accuse."
296. *Cambio 16* (Spain), June 4, 2001; cited in Gross, "J'Accuse."
297. *Ethnos* (Greece), April 7, 2002.
298. Manfred Gerstenfeld, "Language as a Tool against Jews and Israel: Interview with Georges-Elia Sarfati," Jerusalem Center for Public Affairs. February 1, 2004.
299. Roi Bet Levi, "Look Left in Anger," *Haaretz* (Israel), October 20, 2008.
300. Jonah Goldberg, "Who are the Real Nazis?", *Jewish World Review*, January 7, 2009.
301. Gerard Rabinovitch, "Petit lexique du prêt à penser," *Observatoire du Monde Juif* (France), March 2, 2002.
302. Cited in Richard Landes, "Camera Obscura: How French TV Fudged the Death of Mohammed Al Durah," *Augean Stables*, October 18, 2006.
303. *La Repubblica* (Italy), October 2001; cited in Gross, "J'Accuse." The newspaper also suggested that *Protocols* would help readers understand why the U.S. had taken military action in Afghanistan.
304. *La Vanguardia* (Italy), May 25, 2001; cited in Gross, "J'Accuse."
305. "Obama: 'No Patience' for Holocaust Denial," MSNBC.com, June 5, 2009.
306. "NBC, Obama & the Lessons of Buchenwald," HonestReporting.com, June 8, 2009.
307. Natan Sharansky, "3D Test of Anti-Semitism: Demonization, Double Standards, Delegitimization," *Jewish Political Studies Review*, Spring 2005.
308. Robin Shepherd, "In Europe, an Unhealthy Fixation on Israel," *Washington Post*, January 30, 2005.
309. Yuli Edelstein, "Verbatim: Anti-Semites Have Warped Tiny Israel into Goliath," *Jerusalem Post*, December 16, 2009.
310. Sven Röbel, "Anti-Semitic Alliance: The Shared Extremism of Neo-Nazis and Migrant Youth," *Der Spiegel* (Germany), July 14, 2010.
311. Nir Hasson, "More Global Anti-Semitic Incidents Reported in 2009 than Any Year Since WWII," *Haaretz* (Israel), February 7, 2010. When the Stephen Roth Institute at Tel-Aviv

University began monitoring anti-Semitism in 1989, it found 78 anti-Semitic incidents worldwide; in 2009 a record 1,129 violent anti-Semitic attacks were recorded. (Cnaan Liphshiz, "Study: Anti-Semitism in Europe Hit New High in 2009," *Haaretz* [Israel], April 11, 2010.)

312. Tom Gross, "J'Accuse."
313. Rabbi Naftali Schiff, "A Fire that Destroys, a Fire that Builds," Aish.com, June 24, 2004.
314. Editorial, "Swastikas on the Wall," *Evening Standard* (UK), April 30, 2002.
315. Amy Teibel, "Court Lets Palestinians Use Major Israeli Highway," Associated Press, December 30, 2009.
316. In 2002, ministers and senior officials from 12 Arab countries met in Cairo to discuss a multi-million-dollar public relations campaign against Israel. The campaign would "target the international community with the goal of refuting Israeli and American attempts to portray the Palestinians' national struggle as an unjust terror campaign." ("Why is There So Much Anti-Israel Bias in the Press and the American Educational System?", AFSI.org.) One pro-Palestinian website offers a guidebook of dysphemisms to apply negative connotations to all things Israel: "The object is to make the word 'Israelis' become synonymous with 'occupier,' and 'Palestinians' with the 'occupied.' Israeli 'settlements' are to be called 'colonies,' and Israeli 'settlers' should be called 'colonizers.' 'Israeli Defense Forces' should be referred to as 'Israeli Occupation Forces.' 'Security measures' in this lexicon becomes 'collective punishment measures.' Israel's 'security fence' should be called an 'Apartheid Wall.' Editors and opinion leaders should be told that Israeli 'military operations' were really 'Israeli assaults against Palestinian civilians.' Israel's 'crack down on militants' should be described as 'political assassinations.' 'Physical pressure' by the 'Israeli military' should be called 'torture' by 'the U.S.-financed Israeli military.' 'Palestinian violence' by 'militants' should instead read 'the resistance of Palestinian fighters.' Israel's claim to legitimacy should be challenged linguistically. 'Jerusalem,' Israel's capital, should be called 'occupied Arab Jerusalem.'" (Bruce J. Evensen, "Reporting the Israeli-Palestinian Conflict: A Personal View," in *Media Bias: Finding It, Fixing It*, McFarland & Company, 2007.)
317. See Lisa Katz, "Newsflash: Goliath is Jewish," About.com, October 2000.
318. Steve McNally, "Letter from Jerusalem, Caught in the Middle," *Columbia Journalism Review*, January/February, 2002.
319. Howard Kurtz, "Is the Media Doing a Good Job Covering Violence in the Middle East?", *Reliable Sources*, CNN, October 14, 2000.
320. Orly Halpern, JerusalemBureau, Twitter.com, July 14, 2009.
321. *St. Louis Post-Dispatch*, April 8, 2002; cited in David Limbaugh, "Are the Media Pro-Israel?", Townhall.com, April 10, 2002.
322. Chas Newkey Burden, "Not in My Name," *Ynetnews* (Israel), April 19, 2007.
323. Chris McGreal, "Israel Shocked by Image of Soldiers Forcing Violinist to Play at Roadblock," *The Guardian* (UK), November 29, 2004.
324. "Scandal-shocked Israelis Ask If the Army Has Lost Its Way," Agence France Presse, November 28, 2004.
325. "Why Israel Can't Win," *Time*, January 19, 2009. Commenting in his blog for *The Atlantic*, Jeffrey Goldberg said the cover got him thinking: Which one will last longer – Israel, or *Time* magazine? Eighty-give years or 3,300 years? Concludes Goldberg: "I'm betting on Israel."
326. Benny Morris, "Is Israel Over?", *Newsweek*, September 11, 2011.
327. Dr. Manfred Gerstenfeld, "The Twenty-first Century Total War Against Israel and the Jews," Jerusalem Center for Public Affairs, November 2005.
328. Yasmin Alibhai-Brown, "Don't Israel's Nuclear Weapons Count?", *Independent* (UK), September 28, 2009.
329. Anne Barnard, "Conference in Iran on Holocaust Begins," *Boston Globe*, December 12, 2006.

330. Daphna Berman, "Speaker Accuses Israel of Committing Genocide," *The Sun* (New York), October 14, 2002.
331. Omayma Abdel-Latif, "That Weasel Word," *Al-Ahram* (Egypt), April 4-10, 2002.
332. Andrew Walker, "Tom Paulin: Poetic Polemicist," BBC News Online, November 15, 2002.
333. "Between Heaven and Hell," *The Guardian* (UK), May 21, 2001.
334. Chris McGreal, "Israel Shocked by Image of Soldiers Forcing Violinist to Play at Roadblock," *The Guardian* (UK), November 29, 2004.
335. See Michelle Sieff, "Gaza and After: An Interview with Paul Berman," Z-word.com, March 2009.
336. Noah Pollak, "Show of Force," *Azure*, Autumn 2007; Nick Childs, "Israel, Iran Top 'Negative List,'" BBC News Online, March 6, 2007.
337. Peter Beaumont, "Israel Outraged as EU Poll Names it a Threat to Peace," *The Observer* (UK), November 2, 2003. Overall, 59 percent of Europeans put Israel in the top spot; in the Netherlands, that figure was 74 percent.
338. Pollak, "Show of Force."
339. John Adams wrote in 1809: "I will insist that the Hebrews have done more to civilize men than any other nation. If I were an atheist and believed in blind eternal fate, I should still believe that fate had ordained the Jews to be the most essential instrument for civilizing the nations... The Romans and their Empire were but a bauble in comparison to the Jews. They have given religion to three quarters of the globe and have influenced the affairs of mankind more, and more happily than any other nation, ancient or modern." (Letter to F.A. Van Der Kemp, February 16, 1809; cited in Allan Gould, *What Did They Think of the Jews*, Stewart House, 1991, p. 71-72.)
340. Alan M. Dershowitz, *The Case Against Israel's Enemies*, Wiley, 2008.
341. Faisal Bodi, "Israel Simply Has No Right to Exist," *The Guardian* (UK), January 3, 2001.

EPILOGUE

THE PEACE PROCESS

In September 2011, I was sitting with a friend at a café in Jerusalem. That week, Palestinian leaders were bypassing direct negotiations in favor of a unilateral declaration of statehood at the U.N. and, as usual, I was bemoaning how the media was blaming Israel for the negotiating impasse.[1] I was outraged, and expected my friend to react with a similar sense of ire and urgency.

Instead, he looked at me and said, "So what. Why should I even care about this?"

It dawned on me that the idealistic pursuit of truth and accuracy – which has been driving my passion all along – was too abstract to resonate with my friend. He needed to understand in a practical sense how media bias affects him personally and the world at large.

Beyond the problem of factual inaccuracy, media foibles can impede the peace process. Invariably, the starting point in any negotiation is whatever is defined in common terms as "normative." With pro-Palestinian views consistently reinforced in the media, Palestinians feel the momentum of issues predisposed in their favor, and gain the false illusion that they can bring these demands to the negotiating table. Inevitably, Palestinians get a rude awakening every time that Israel – having waited 2,000 years for a return to their land – refuses to allow these skewed perceptions to dictate terms of an agreement.

Consider the issue of Palestinians displaced during the 1948 war. Palestinians demand that these refugees and their descendents be given the "right of return" to settle in the State of Israel. Israel counters that such an influx is incompatible with a two-state solution: A flood of 4 million refugees, when combined with Israel's one million existing Arab citizens, would turn Israel into a second Palestinian-majority state, thereby eliminating the world's only Jewish one. In other words, Arabs could use the tool of democracy to demographically annihilate Israel.[2] As Palestinian leader Sakher Habash said: "The refugee issue is the winning card which means the end" of Israel.[3]

The *Los Angeles Times* promoted this untenable position with an op-ed declaring that "All refugees have the right to return… that cannot be negotiated away,"[4] while David Hearst of the *Guardian* wrote that he looks forward to "a one-state solution in which Jewish citizens lose an in-built majority" – which he hailed as "the end of Zionism, no less."[5] And when the 2011 WikiLeaks diplomatic cables showed that direct negotiations had actually achieved progress in bridging the sticky refugee issue,[6] the media reacted not with joy, but rather with dozens of articles castigating Palestinian negotiators for not adopting a sufficiently hard-line stance.[7]

With this media backing, the Palestinian public gets entrenched in unsupportable positions. A survey of Palestinian refugees showed a whopping 97 percent would refuse to accept any peace agreement that does not include the right to resettle in Israel proper.[8] Thus the media, by presenting radical Palestinian positions as if they were mainstream, creates unrealistic expectations, perpetuates a state of intransigence, and obstructs the hope for a peaceful accord.[9]

Incitement and Indoctrination

Peace is more than just a piece of paper signed by two opposing leaders. Genuine peace requires an environment where moderation, coexistence and tolerance are taught and practiced as core values. On the Israeli side, decades of "peace education" has prepared the public to accept compromise for the sake of peace. The two-state solution – once a marginalized position of the Israeli left – is now accepted by the vast majority of Israelis.[10]

Meanwhile, Palestinian society remains rife with rhetoric that vilifies Jews, encourages violence and denies Israel's right to exist. Suicide bombers are elevated to the pinnacle of Palestinian society, lionized with poems and immortalized with dozens of schools, roads – even sporting events – named in the bombers' honor.[11]

This glorification of terror is a message delivered directly to children. An eighth-grade Palestinian textbook explains: "The Muslim sacrifices himself for his belief... his death as a martyr on the field of battle is preferable to death in his bed."[12] In a fifth-grade textbook, "The Poem of the Shahid" extols a yearning for martyrdom: "I see my death, but I hasten my steps toward it."[13] On Palestinian television, an articulate 11-year-old girl named Yussra thoughtfully explained: "Death by martyrdom is very good. Every Palestinian child... would like to become a martyr."[14]

Though this anti-Israel incitement and fiery rhetoric runs rampant in Palestinian society,[15] the Western media denies it all. In the *International Herald Tribune*, Roger Avenstrup ignored reality and declared there is "no incitement to hatred in the Palestinian textbooks" and that "teachers are trying to promote peace in the classroom."[16] Writing in the *New York Times*, Daoud Kuttab falsely claimed that Palestine television has been "totally revamped and cleaned of anti-Israeli incitement."[17]

Meanwhile, a Palestinian Sesame Street-style program features a Bugs Bunny character telling kids: "I will eat the Jews, G-d willing."[18] On Hamas TV, Nassur the Teddy Bear exclaims: "Dear children, when we grow up, we will become martyrs, God willing."[19] Another popular children's program starred Farfur, a Mickey Mouse look-alike who called on Palestinian children to "annihilate the Jews" and "commit martyrdom."[20]

It's a far cry from Big Bird and the Cookie Monster. Yet the *New York Times* downplayed it all, characterizing these genocidal calls as merely an "insult to Jews."[21]

This indoctrination campaign – mixed with a lethal dose of nationalistic fervor – has proved compelling enough to counteract even the basic human instinct for survival: Palestinians have launched 700 suicide missions since 2000, with over 150 reaching their target.[22] As for the next generation, a shocking survey in the Palestinian newspaper *Al-Hayat Al-Jadida* showed that 80 percent of Palestinian children desire to become suicide bombers,[23] and a 2009 poll found that the majority of Palestinian adults continue to support suicide bombings against Israeli civilians.[24]

There are literally thousands of examples, and this information is easily accessible to anyone with an Internet connection. So why is the topic of Palestinian incitement – with its profound implications for the peace process – universally ignored by Western journalists?

The uncomfortable answer is that since this contradicts the David and Goliath narrative, the media's most expedient option is to whitewash it away. The *Christian Science Monitor* made it sound as if Palestinians are teaching their youth to emulate Gandhi, quoting a Palestinian TV director that encouraging kids to jihad "isn't for teaching hate. It's for teaching children to think in the right way, to socialize them in our culture's way of life."[25]

And so it goes. Tom Gross told me that when he was Jerusalem correspondent for the New York *Daily News*, he wanted to report on how Palestinian society was promoting violent jihad in mosques, school textbooks and even music videos. So Tom called his editor and suggested an article exploring the topic of Palestinian incitement in the media.

"Sure," the editor replied. "As long as half of your article deals with incitement in the Israeli media."

"But there is no similar incitement of this kind and magnitude in the Israeli media," Tom said.

"Then we can't run the story," the editor said. "We have to present everything in this conflict 50-50, and this doesn't fit."

Unfortunately, there's a lot about the Mideast reality that "doesn't fit" the mainstream media narrative. Western culture favors quick solutions, a "get the deal done" mentality. But the Middle East conflict goes back millennia, and is not something that can be glossed over with photo ops of smiling diplomats. The reality of today – as evidenced by a 2011 survey

– is that 92 percent of Palestinians oppose any form of sharing Jerusalem with the Jews; 73 percent agree with the Hamas Charter urging Muslims to "kill Jews wherever they can find them"; and two-thirds see the "two-state solution as an interim stage to the ultimate goal of a single Palestinian state in all the territory between the Jordan River and the Mediterranean Sea."[26]

Yet *Time* magazine, in its perennial effort to prop up the Palestinian side, employed a "pick 'n choose" methodology – ignoring these alarming statistics and instead promoting the notion that the poll's "most striking finding... was Palestinians' focus on daily life."[27]

For peace to exist, all parties need to sincerely condemn violence, embrace compromise, and accept the idea of permanent, peaceful coexistence. If the Western world truly desires an end to the conflict, the media needs to begin presenting a clear picture of reality. In the words of John F. Kennedy, "Peace does not rest in charters and covenants alone. It lies in the hearts and minds of people."[28]

In the meantime, Palestinian incitement remains the elephant in the room.

Web 2.0

While the consequences of media bias are clear, the question remains: What can we do about it?

The key for consumers is to be aware and not take things at face value. We need to be on the lookout for the subtle techniques, because if the media won't give it straight, we need to be armed with the knowledge of how to identify bias and filter it out. From day one on my involvement with Tuvia Grossman and "the photo that started it all," I learned the importance of stepping back to ask the question: Who is the victim and who is the aggressor? Things are not always as they appear.

I also learned not to rely solely on the "experts." The emergence of Web 2.0 – with collaborative tools like blogs, Facebook, Wikis and Twitter – represents a seismic shift in the way that news is reported. The real shock of Rathergate – Dan Rather's attempt to sway the U.S. presidential election with forged memos – was the way an average citizen, armed with only a

PC and an Internet connection, exposed the scandal. The initial reaction of one CBS executive was to dismiss the blogger as "a guy sitting in his living room in his pajamas."[29] But in the end, it was the guy in his pajamas who brought down a pillar of mainstream media, forcing Dan Rather to resign.

This parallels the experience I've had in 11 years of monitoring the media. When the Intifada first broke out, the conflict was essentially media-driven: Major news outlets set the tone for public opinion, selectively choosing details and background information. With the news controlled by a handful of media conglomerates, it was becoming an increasingly narrow, biased view of events. If editors ran a story, it became news; if they ignored an event, it might as well have never happened. This widespread idea of "crafting" the news rather than reporting it is what one media mogul described as the work of "editorial demigods."[30]

In recent years, however, the conflict has shifted toward being more consumer-driven. Bloggers are not constricted by corporate earnings reports or by some unofficial "Editors' Club." They can dig up and publicize facts that have been overlooked, ignored or hidden – often providing that one photo, quote or statistic that irrevocably alters the way a story is perceived by the public. By allowing everyone to become a content publisher, the Internet promotes the idea of multiple views rather than the drift toward a single narrative. And with that, the mainstream media has lost its monopoly on information. Call it Gutenberg's digital revolution.

As such, many blogs have built up a reputation for fairness and accuracy to the point of becoming an alternative news source. When kidnapped soldier Gilad Shalit was exchanged for 1,000 Hamas prisoners – among them bombers and mass murders whom the mainstream media blithely referred to as "members of Hamas"[31] – bloggers were flooded with people looking for the real scoop. This was a new breed of educated consumers, exercising their options for a more reliable and accurate source of news.

With stiffer competition, the mainstream media now seems to be making fewer blunders. In the early days of the Intifada, the disinformation was blatant and pervasive: The *Washington Post* placed Jerusalem's

Hebrew University – inaugurated in 1925 – in the West Bank,[32] and following a Palestinian shooting rampage in Jerusalem, CNN's homepage headline proclaimed: "Israel Shooting Wounds Dozens," giving the false impression that Israelis had perpetrated the shooting spree.[33] These days, however, with thousands of "living room watchdogs" monitoring them carefully, the mainstream media can no longer afford to be sloppy.[34]

And so, slowly and incrementally, traditional newsrooms now have to compete for an audience they once took for granted."[35] When one journalist was challenged for his double standard of calling an Israeli strike "terror" – but not the Palestinian missile barrage that precipitated it – he responded uncomfortably by saying, "I had no idea I was being watched so closely. Now I'm on notice."

Of course, the tide flows both ways. Pro-Palestinian groups have taken their fight to the Internet, spawning a genre known as "e-Jihad." One group calling itself "Digital Intifada" offered rewards of $2,000 for hacking Israeli websites.[36] Another organized effort – through online groups "Wikipedians for Palestine" and "Wiki Project Palestine" – aims at promoting the Palestinian agenda through the altering of Wikipedia articles.[37] This gave rise to a phenomenon called "edit war," whereby mobs of like-minded people aggressively inject their views into online entries.[38] When the article "Palestinian Territories" became closely monitored by Wikipedia's own editors, Palestinian activists turned to creating a new entry, "Occupied Palestinian Territory," that came up in similar searches alongside the original.[39]

Even family-friendly Facebook is rife with anti-Israel content. In 2010, I produced an online film, *Hating Israel on Facebook,* that exposed dozens of Facebook pages – with names like "Destroy Israel," "Kill the Zionists" and "I Hate Israel" (153,385 members) – that explicitly violate Facebook's terms of use which prohibit "incitement to violence."[40] But the hatred continues. After Israel secured the release of Gilad Shalit, Saudi Sheikh Awad al Qarni launched a Facebook page offering a $100,000 reward to anyone who kidnaps another Israeli soldier.[41] (Saudi Prince Khaled bin Talal promptly upped the ante to a cool one million dollars.)[42]

Yes, the days are over when terrorists disseminate their hatred via a spooky video cassette sent to Al Jazeera. Today, you can simply "follow" Hamas missile squads at www.twitter.com/AlqassamBrigade, or surf www.qassam.ps where you even have the option to select your favorite color scheme.[43] More nefariously, Palestinian rocket-launching teams now use Google Earth to select their civilian targets.[44]

For better and for worse, that's the nature of the Internet: Anyone can do it. If you aren't satisfied with the thousands of news sources available today, you can start your own blog and cover the news yourself. In June 2009, when protests broke out in Iran over the presidential election, the shooting death of Neda Soltan – captured on video by bystanders – spread virally on Twitter with the hashtag #neda. Only later did the mainstream media catch up in presenting information that the public already knew. The Iranians who filmed her death were later awarded the coveted George Polk Award for videography – the first time the award was given to an anonymously-produced work.

Today, the discussion of media bias is increasingly "a water-cooler topic," with consumers becoming ever-more educated and aware. "Passivity is giving way to more aggressive public scrutiny," notes the *Boston Globe*, "and more readers are turning into whistle-blowers."[45] It all comes down to staying alert and if you see something important, share it. For after all, freedom of the "press" is guaranteed only to those who own one.[46]

Guidelines for Monitoring

Whether your issue is anti-Israel bias, poverty in Mumbai, or Occupy Wall Street, by following these basic guidelines, you can become an analyst and genuinely affect media coverage.[47]

1) **Put yourself in the journalist's shoes.** The media, like anyone else, is more receptive to constructive criticism than to pressure. Don't simply demand that journalists adopt your particular viewpoint. Rather, insist that they be accurate and

impartial. Praise good reporting when it occurs. Keep your remarks respectful. Stick to the facts and avoid name-calling. Otherwise, even if you have a valid point to make, the media will immediately dismiss your criticism as outrageous. Point out not only what's wrong with the story, but suggest how it could have been reported in a more balanced way. Give journalists the benefit of the doubt by stating it in terms of, "Perhaps you weren't aware, but..." This is the difference between complaining and constructive criticism.

2) **Mobilize a monitoring group.** Build an email list of friends and colleagues, so that whenever bias is spotted, you can alert others to also file a complaint. This increases your impact exponentially. Make your voice heard as well in Internet forums and talk radio. Start a blog. Hand out informational flyers at your local community center, school, and house of worship. Formulate a name for your group – e.g. the Concerned Citizens Coalition; this indicates a serious broad-based effort. One person acting alone may not be able to make a huge difference, but hundreds or thousands working together can.

3) **Identify patterns of bias.** While particular examples may intuitively indicate bias, it is far more effective to discover a pattern. The way to achieve this is by conducting an accurate, extensive study. Construct a series of *a priori* questions, then analyze every article or broadcast from a particular media outlet for 30-to-90 days. Systematically tabulate the headlines, photos, spokespeople quoted, etc., and draw conclusions based on any irregular patterns. Keep a log-book and note the specific article (with URL), or the precise date and time of broadcast.

4) **Pick your battle.** You will never be able to convince the media to do things 100 percent your way. Refrain from nitpicking

little points. Instead, select one key idea that underlies many others. For example, demanding that suicide bombers be labeled "terrorists" frames the conflict in completely different terms. Choose your main battle and hammer away until your point is heard.

5) **Meet face-to-face.** Request a meeting with reporters and editors to explain your position, express your concerns, and hold them accountable for what they publish. At the meeting, make your case persuasively and with as much documentation as possible. The media's ability to stay in business is based on a perception of being fair and objective. Rather than attack anyone's character, appeal to their sense of professional integrity. If you have evidence of bias, they will usually listen. A face-to-face meeting is also important in creating an ongoing dialogue, whereby journalists can feel comfortable turning to you as a resource. Remember: The goal is to build a relationship.

6) **Take the protest public.** If the media agency ignores your reasoned criticism and continues to be biased and belligerent, then consider a public protest. This may take the form of a rally in front of their building (this must be coordinated with local police), a refusal to patronize their advertisers, or a campaign to cancel subscriptions (even for one day). Beware, however, that these methods can have a negative backlash, as they strike some people as an attempt to limit freedom of the press. Further, these tactics – since they undermine the hope of a relationship and leave you with little recourse – should be used only as a last resort, when other methods have failed to produce results.

So whether your issue is fighting radical Islam, climate change, or municipal garbage collection, you can take responsibility and make a difference. As Izzy Asper, founder of the CanWest media group, explained: The solution to media bias begins "in the journalism schools, then goes to the boardrooms of the media owners, and finally, and most importantly, with you, the public."[48]

If things seem hopeless, don't get discouraged. In the Mideast conflict – with a worldwide Muslim community 100 times larger than the Jewish community – I know I have to work that much harder to make my voice heard. But I keep my eye on the ball, believe in the justness of the cause, and am encouraged when it pays off in better coverage.

Today, with global terror networks and unconventional weapons, the stakes are even greater. As al-Qaeda spokesman Ayman al-Zawahiri has made clear: "We are in a battle, and more than half of this battle is taking place in the battlefield of the media."[49] When al-Qaeda places the media battle at the top of its priorities, there is no question that we have to engage in this fight.

At times, the enemies of freedom may seem to be holding sway, but at the end of the day, might does not make right. Looking back at world history, it is words and ideas that have ultimately moved people to action. The great tyrants are gone, but civilized values and ethics remain. "Words," said Churchill, "are the only things that last forever… It is for us to see that this great lever of a common language is rightly used."[50]

Thus is the purpose of this book. As Franklin D. Roosevelt said: "A war of ideas can no more be won without books than a naval war can be won without ships. Books, like ships, have the toughest armor, the longest cruising range, and mount the most powerful guns."[51]

This media war is a decisive struggle, and if truth is to prevail, we can't just "read" the newspaper. We need to be discerning and become part of the process, not allowing the mainstream media to operate unchecked and unrestrained. Each one of us is obligated to understand the media's subtle techniques of distortion, consume the news with a critical eye, and make our voice heard. Otherwise, we'll end up intimidated and manipulated, just another victim of the media war.

Notes

1. See, for example, Editorial, "Face-off at the U.N.," *Los Angeles Times*, September 20, 2011.
2. Egyptian leader Gamal Abdel Nasser once declared: "If Arabs return to Israel, Israel will cease to exist." (Interview in *Zibicher Woche* [Switzerland], September 1, 1961.)
3. Lecture at An-Najah University, Nablus, 1998.
4. Ghada Ageel, "Locked Out by Peace?", *Los Angles Times*, December 1, 2007.
5. David Hearst, "Could Arab Staying Power Ultimately Defeat Zionism?", *The Guardian* (UK), August 5, 2011.
6. Wikileaks documents quote Palestinian leader Mahmoud Abbas: "On refugees, we said some but not all would return to what is now Israel... It is illogical to ask Israel to take 5 million, or indeed one million. [That] would mean the end of Israel." (Ethan Bronner, "Documents Open a Door on Mideast Peace Talks," *New York Times*, January 25, 2011.)
7. Editorial, "The Palestinian Papers: Pleading for a Fig Leaf," *The Guardian* (UK), January 23, 2011; Editorial, "The Palestinian Papers: Despair. But We Still Need a Deal," *The Guardian* (UK), January 25, 2011. See Carmel Gould, "The Palestine Papers: Implications of the Guardian's Coverage," *Just Journalism*, February 11, 2011; Robin Shepherd, "British Foreign Office, BBC, European Liberal-Left Devastated by Leaked Revelations on Israeli Settlements...", *Think Tank* blog, January 24, 2011.
8. "Survey of 1,830 Palestinian Refugees Throughout the West Bank and Gaza," Israel-Palestine Center for Research and Information, August 2001. A 2011 survey of all Palestinians in Gaza and the West Bank found that 66 percent deem the "right of return" to be one of the top two "most vital Palestinian goals." (Evelyn Gordon, "How the Media Fosters the Myth Palestinians Want Peace," *Jerusalem Post*, July 6, 2011.)
9. Palestinian Legislative Council member Hussam Khader stated categorically: "Any Palestinian leader who will forego the right of return will be considered a traitor, and will be shot to death. And we, in the refugee camps, have 100,000 people who are willing to do this." (Roni Shaked, "The Palestinian Refugees," *Yediot Achronot* [Israel], July 21, 2000.)
10. Seventy-one percent of Israelis favor a two-state solution, according to a joint poll by the Palestinian Center for Policy and Survey Research, and the Harry S. Truman Institute at Hebrew University; cited in Dan Murphy, "Palestinian Support for 'Two-State' Solution Drops with Israel Defiant on Settlement Freeze," *Christian Science Monitor*, March 23, 2010.
11. See Carolynne Wheeler, "Our Son is a Martyr: Families Make Rival Claims to Bombers," *Sunday Telegraph* (UK), February 10, 2008; David Brooks, "The Culture of Martyrdom," *Atlantic Monthly*, June 2002.
12. Itamar Marcus and Barbara Crook, "Palestinian Children in Combat Support Roles: Behavior Mirrors Teachings in PA Schoolbooks and Popular Culture," Palestinian Media Watch, October 17, 2004.
13. Barbara Demick, "'Martyrdom' Dreams Take Root Early in the West Bank," *Los Angeles Times*, July 20, 2002.
14. Palestinian Authority Television, June 9, 2002; cited in Itamar Marcus, "Ask for Death," Palestinian Media Watch, 2003.
15. Khaled Abu Toameh, "How to Solve the Arab-Israeli Conflict," Hudson New York, August 11, 2009.
16. Roger Avenstrup, "Where Is All that 'Incitement'?", *International Herald Tribune*, December 18, 2004.
17. Daoud Kuttab, "Counterpoint: Palestinians and the U.N.," *New York Times*, January 24, 2011.
18. Matthew Kalman, "Hamas Launches TV Bugs Bunny-Lookalike Who Declares 'I Will Eat the Jews,'" *Daily Mail* (UK), February 12, 2008.
19. *The Pioneers of Tomorrow*, Al-Aqsa TV, April 2, 2010; cited in "Martyrdom Indoctrination on Hamas TV Children's Show: Children all Over the World Will Become Martyrs," Middle

East Media Research Institute, May 14, 2010.
20. Anderson Cooper, *360 Degrees*, CNN, May 7, 2007. After a few months on the air, Farfur was depicted as beaten to death by Israelis; he was replaced by another character, Nahool the Bee, who encourages kids to become holy warriors and take back Jerusalem from the "criminal Jews": "I want to continue the... path of heroism, the path of martyrdom, the path of the jihad warriors. My friends and I will continue the path of Farfur. And in his name we shall take revenge upon [the Jews] – the enemies of Allah, the murderers of the prophets, the murderers of innocent children – until Al-Aqsa (Jerusalem) will be liberated from their filth." (David Horovitz, "Hamas's New Buzz," *Jerusalem Post*, July 20, 2007.)
21. Steven Erlanger, "Hamas's Insults to Jews Complicate Peace Effort," *New York Times*, April 1, 2008.
22. "The Nature and Extent of Palestinian Terrorism, 2006," Israel Intelligence Heritage and Commemoration Center (IICC), March 1, 2007.
23. John Perazzo, "The Palestinian Culture of Hate," Frontpagemag.com, January 12, 2004. Another survey, conducted by Dr. Fatsil Abu Hin, found that 90 percent of Palestinians aged 9-17 desire to participate in violent activities, and 73 percent aspire to become martyrs. ("Children Who Love Their Motherland and Die Martyrs," Palestinian Authority Television, June 27, 2002; cited in Margot Dudkevitch, "PA Intensifies Campaign of Incitement Against Israel," *Jerusalem Post*, September 4, 2002.)
24. "Public Opinion Poll no. 67," Jerusalem Media & Communication Centre (jmcc.org), January 2009.
25. Dan Murphy, "Hamas's Approach to Jihad: Start 'em Young," *Christian Science Monitor*, August 20, 2007.
26. Gil Hoffman, "6 in 10 Palestinians Reject 2-State Solution, Survey Finds," *Jerusalem Post*, July 15, 2011. A 2010 poll of Palestinians showed that 85.2% reject a peace deal resulting in a Palestinian state if it requires compromise, and 64.8% consider it "essential" that a Palestinian state replace Israel – "from the Jordan River to the sea." (Opinion Poll of Palestinians in the West Bank & Gaza, Arab World for Research & Development [awrad.org], November 9, 2010.) See also Evelyn Gordon, "How the Media Fosters the Myth Palestinians Want Peace," *Jerusalem Post*, July 6, 2011; Avi Issacharoff, "Poll: Most Palestinians See Two-State Solution as Precursor to Single State," *Haaretz* (Israel), November 21, 2010; "More than Half of Palestinians Do Not Follow News of Negotiations," Firas Press, September 19, 2010; Joshua Mitnick, "Why Most Palestinians Don't Support Israeli-Palestinian Talks – Or Another Intifada," *Christian Science Monitor*, September 2, 2010.
27. Karl Vick, "Poll Finds Palestinians Disenchanted with Hamas, Iran and the Peace Process," *Global Spin* blog / *Time*, July 14, 2011. See also Harriet Sherwood, "Palestine: The Flags are Already Waving but will a Declaration of Statehood Help?", *The Guardian* (UK), July 16, 2011.
28. John F. Kennedy, Speech to the 18th General Assembly of the United Nations, New York, September 20, 1963.
29. Jonathan Klein, quoted in "How the Blogosphere Took on CBS' Docs," *Special Report with Brit Hume*, Fox News, September 17, 2004.
30. Charles Cooper, "Murdoch to Media: You Dug Yourself a Huge Hole," CNET News, November 16, 2008. When France's premier daily, *Le Monde*, announced – after posting its seventh straight year without a profit – that it was laying off 25 percent of its employees, assistant managing editor Laurent Greilsamer observed: "To understand what's happening to *Le Monde*, it's necessary to talk about the arrogance of newspapers." (Doreen Carvajal, "Finances Frail, Le Monde Contemplates the Unthinkable," *New York Times*, April 21, 2008.)
31. BBC reporter Jon Donnison – interviewing to freed terrorist Ahmed Abu Taha, responsible for car bombings and suicide bombings – explained that he is "serving a life sentence for being a member of Hamas." (Jon Donnison, "Gilad Shalit Freed in Israeli-Palestinian

Prisoner Swap," BBC News Online, October 8, 2011.) See also Tara Todras-Whitehill, "Freed Palestinian Prisoners Hope to Rebuild Lives," Associated Press, October 23, 2011.
32. John Ward Anderson, "3 Americans Killed in Jerusalem; Bombing at University Leaves 4 Others Dead, More than 60 Hurt," *Washington Post*, August 1, 2002.
33. "Israel Shooting Wounds Dozens," CNN.com, January 22, 2002.
34. In the words of Juan Vasquez, world editor of the *Miami Herald*: "We can't afford to be sloppy on the most minute detail. For example, if we do a story in which a suicide bomber kills 10 people and himself or herself, we can't say he killed 11. Our readers will catch that." (Dan Fost, "Jewish Groups Battle Media Over Perceived Bias," *San Francisco Chronicle*, May 2, 2002.)
35. For many newspapers, dwindling ad revenues and increased production costs have put the nail in the coffin. The *Christian Science Monitor* and *Seattle Post-Intelligencer* closed up their print shop and now publish exclusively online. Next on the docket for shut-down are mainstays like the *San Francisco Chronicle, Philadelphia Daily News, Minneapolis Star Tribune, Miami Herald, Detroit News, Boston Globe, Chicago Sun-Times, Fort Worth Star-Telegram* and *Cleveland Plain Dealer*. (Douglas A. McIntyre, "The Ten Major Newspapers that Will Fold or Go Digital Next," www.247wallst.com, March 9, 2009.)
36. Malkah Fleisher, "'The Digital Intifada Promises to Fight Zionism Online," *Israel National News*, November 25, 2008.
37. See Andre Oboler, "Back Story on Wiki Project Palestine" and "Electronic Intifada's Manipulation," *Zionism on the Web*, May 2008; "Exposed – Anti-Israeli Subversion on Wikipedia," HonestReporting.com, May 14, 2008.
38. It was this type of "mob rule" that prompted Wiki co-founder Larry Sanger to leave the project in protest. (Paul Jay, "The Wikipedia Experiment," CBC News [Canada], April 19, 2007.)
39. Haviv Rettig Gur, "Israeli-Palestinian Conflict Rages on Wikipedia," *Jerusalem Post*, May 16, 2010. Since deleted.
40. *Hating Israel on Facebook*, Aish.com, May 13, 2010. Mark Zuckerberg, CEO of Facebook, emphasized that "We are really careful in not allowing hate speech." (Simon Garfield, "So How Many Friends Do You Have, Mark?", *The Observer* [UK], November 16, 2008.)
41. "100,000 Dollars for Each Israeli Captured," *Palestine Today*, October 25, 2011.
42. "Saudi Prince, Cleric Offer $1m to Kidnap Israeli Soldier," *The Peninsula* (Qatar), October 30, 2011.
43. Jacob Shrybman, "Tweeting Terror," *Winnipeg Jewish Review*, May 11, 2010.
44. Clancy Chassay and Bobbie Johnson, "Google Earth Used to Target Israel," *The Guardian* (UK), October 25, 2007. ("We obtain the details from Google Earth and check them against our maps of the city centre and sensitive areas," said Khaled Jaabari, the group's commander in Gaza.) Hamas also uses Google Earth to map the routes of weapons smuggling tunnels. ("Surviving in the Gaza Strip," *The Economist*, November 15, 2007.)
45. Mark Jurkowitz, "The Purloined Letters: Since the Jayson Blair Scandal, More Readers are Becoming Watchdogs," *Boston Globe*, June 11, 2003.
46. Credited to A. J. Liebling, *The New Yorker*, May 14, 1960.
47. See "How to Monitor the Media," HonestReporting.com.
48. Israel H. Asper, "Dishonest Reporting: Media Bias Against Israel," Aish.com, November 9, 2002.
49. Cited in Sally Neighbour, "Propagandists of Terror Prevailing," *The Australian*, April 22, 2009.
50. Winston Churchill, "Our Friendship with America," *Liberty Magazine*, May 31, 1941.
51. Franklin D. Roosevelt, letter to W. W. Norton, chairman of the Council on Books in Wartime, 1942.

PHOTOS

An Israeli policeman and a Palestinian on the Temple Mount.

Tuvia Grossman misidentified as a Palestinian victim – *New York Times* / *Associated Press*, September 29, 2000. **(page 12)**

"In the West Bank city of Ramallah, bloodied Palestinian protestors express their rage – *Teen Newsweek*, October 23, 2000; photo by Ilkka Uimonen / Corbis Sygma. **(page 16)**

Posted on Facebook: "A reminder of snapshots taken at Abu Ghraib of Iraqi detainees naked, humiliated and terrified" – *Associated Press*, August 16, 2010. **(page 37)**

Equating bomber and victim: the article is headlined, "How Two Lives Met in Death" – *Newsweek, April 15, 2002*. **(page 50)**

Rachel Corrie: brandishing an automatic weapon in Gaza, and with Palestinian children burning a replica of the American flag. **(page 50)**

"Palestinian children learn at a young age about the struggle for freedom" – *BBC News, November 18, 2005.* **(page 54)**

Selective omission: "An Israeli bomb squad robot dragged a wounded Palestinian man on a road in northern Israel " – *Reuters, May 9, 2002.* **(page 59)**

Suicide bomber Wafa Idris: "chestnut hair curling past her shoulders" – *New York Times, January 31, 2002.* **(page 92)**

"Tension has been high around the Jewish settlements" – *BBC News, November 27, 2000.* **(page 59)**

Terrorist as the victim: "Palestinian bus driver Khalil abu Olbeh, 35, sits wounded after leading police on a 19-mile chase. Family members said he was distraught over financial problems and upset by current unrest." *Los Angeles Times, February 15, 2001.* **(page 92)**

Glamour shot: Ahlam Tamimi, sentenced to 320 years in Israeli prison for the Sbarro Pizzeria bombing – *New York Times, June 27, 2007.* **(page 93)**

NBC's Martin Fletcher, with terrorist Ahmed Sanakreh and his brother – *NBC News World Blog, January 23, 2008.* **(page 94)**

Palestinian terrorist Leila Khaled with bullet ring: "Fragile hands, the shiny hair wrapped in a keffiah, the delicate Audrey Hepburn face" – *The Guardian, January 26, 2001.* **(page 93)**

"Kickin' it with Samir Kuntar": Dion Nissenbaum (L) of McClatchy Newspapers, with Palestinian terrorist Samir Kuntar – *July 20, 2008.* **(page 95)**

Palestinian Authority payments for terror activities: "a fraud by the Israeli intelligence... some kind of James Bond activities" – *CNN*, April 3, 2002. **(page 121)**

Palestinian baby bomber photo: "cheap Israeli propaganda" – *BBC News*, June 28, 2002. **(page 121)**

Rachel Corrie: CNN distorts the "before and after" chronology – *March 25, 2003.* **(page 143)**

PHOTOS

Palestinian children in Jerusalem celebrate news of the World Trade Center attack – *Lefteris Pitarakis, Associated Press, September 11, 2001.* **(page 155)**

Beirut skyline: Repeating patterns of smoke (circled) and duplicate buildings – *Adnan Hajj, Reuters, August 5, 2006.* **(page 195)**

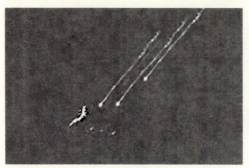

Israeli jet dropping a single flare, "cloned" to appear like a missile attack – *Adnan Hajj, Reuters, August 6, 2006.* **(page 196)**

Green Helmet Guy posing with a "dead baby trophy" in Qana, Lebanon – *Adnan Hajj, Reuters, July 20, 2006.* **(page 197)**

Photojournalists line up to shoot the dead baby – *Jeroen Oerlemans, Panos Pictures, July 20, 2006.* **(page 197)**

Unexploded bomb in southern Lebanon: the boy was "pushed forward to stand reluctantly next to it while we get our cameras out and record the scene" – *BBC News, August 21, 2006.* **(page 198)**

PHOTOS

Mannequin in a wedding dress posed in front of the wreckage at Qana, Lebanon – *Sharif Karim, Reuters, August 2006.* **(page 199)**

Mickey Mouse in the rubble of Tyre, Lebanon – *Ben Curtis, Associated Press.* **(page 199)**

Minnie Mouse in the rubble of Tyre, Lebanon – *Sharif Karim, Reuters.* **(page 199)**

"Prop man" distributing stuffed animals in the rubble of Beirut. **(page 199)**

Top photo: Bombed-out car in Beirut – *Eric Gaillard, Reuters*. Bottom photo: Same car, now with wall-hanging of Koran verses – *Lefteris Pitarakis, Associated Press.* **(page 200)**

PHOTOS

Palestinian woman weeping in front of security barrier with English graffiti – *Enric Marti, Associated Press.* **(page 201)**

Lebanese women wedged into narrow space between coffins and wall; spray-painted numbers are specifically a Western style – *Marco Di Lauro, Agence France Press / Getty Images.* **(page 202)**

Weeping Palestinian grandmother: home destroyed on July 22, 2006 – *Issam Kobeisi, Reuters*. **(page 203)**

The same woman: home destroyed on August 5, 2006 – *Hussein Malla, Associated Press*. **(page 203)**

Same woman, same heavenward wail, different clothes – *London's Spectator, July 22, 2006*. **(page 203)**

U.S. News & World Report: "Wreckage of a downed Israeli jet," or a harmless tire fire? – Bruno Stevens, Cosmos. **(page 204)**

Lebanese ambulance "destroyed by Israeli missiles." The hole is in the precise spot where the ambulance's flashing light or circular roof vent would be. **(page 205)**

Bilin in the West Bank: Palestinian activists as blue-skinned characters from the film Avatar — *Oren Ziv, AFP/Getty Images, February 12, 2010.* **(page 210)**

"Slingshot Santa": Palestinian demonstrator in Bilin – *Muhammed Muheisen, Associated Press, December 26, 2008.* **(page 210)**

Bilin: A Palestinian man "passed out from tear gas" – *Bernat Armangue, Associated Press, May 15, 2009.* **(page 211)**

Muhammad al-Dura and father huddling behind a cement barrel: "targeted, murdered, by Israeli soldiers" – *Abu Rahma, France-2 television.* **(page 212)**

Muhammad al-Dura commemorative stamp from Tunisia. **(page 212)**

Marc Garlasco of Human Rights Watch: sweatshirt with German writing depicts the Iron Cross. **(page 219)**

On the anniversary of 9-11, cartoon in Palestinian Authority daily: Bin Laden flashes "V" for victory. *courtesy Palestinian Media Watch* **(page 240)**

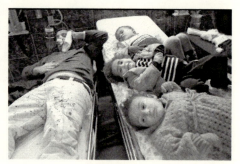

American soldier held hostage in Iraq, or a plastic toy action figure? *Associated Press, February 1, 2005.* **(page 282)**

"Palestinian children and a man wounded in Israeli missile strikes" – *Khalil Hamra, Associated Press.* **(page 283)**

"Electricity blackout" in Gaza City: daytime candlelight meeting, with sunlight streaming through the drawn curtains – *Mohammed Salem, Reuters.* **(page 286)**

"Medical rescue worker"? Anas Naim with rocket-propelled grenade launcher. **(page 289)**

"Israel air strike": Palestinian girl injured in fall from a swing – *Rajaa Abu Shaban, Reuters.* **(page 294)**

Richard Goldstone accompanied by Hamas official Ghazi Hamad: "I had nightmares that Hamas would kidnap me." **(page 312)**

Wordle web tool shows the Goldstone report's top 250 words, according to frequency of use. The word "Hamas" is microscopic. **(page 312)**

Violin Man at "dangerous and humiliating" roadblock, as soldiers casually go about their business. **(page 319)**

Palestinian terrorist caught at a checkpoint, disguised as a woman. **(page 320)**

PHOTOS

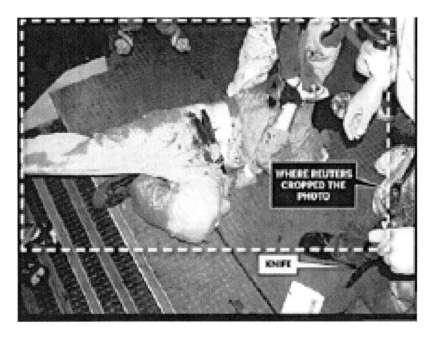

Gaza Flotilla: Dotted line shows where Reuters cropped the incriminating knives from the photos. **(page 332)**

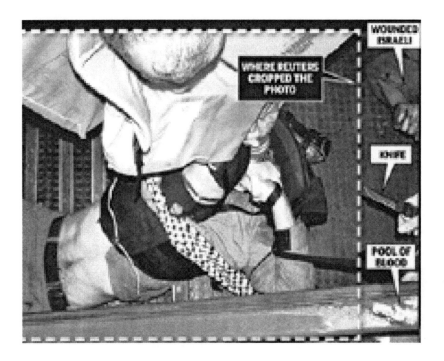

Lauren Booth buying candy bars and soft drinks at a well-stocked Gaza grocery store: "concentration camp on the scale of Darfur." **(page 335)**

Apartheid road in Saudi Arabia, banning any non-Muslim from entering the cities of Mecca and Medina. **(page 361)**

Palestinian founding father Mufti Haj Amin al-Husseini reviews Muslim troops which he organized into Nazi SS divisions. *credit: Topham Picturepoint* **(page 372)**

From one of America's leading editorial cartoonists: "Which Nukes are You Most Afraid Of?" – Bruce Beattie, News Journal (Florida) / Copely News Service, October 30, 2002. **(page 390)**

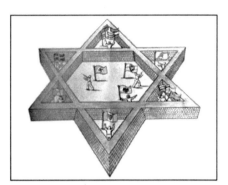 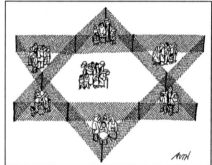

Left: Nazi propa ganda poster, 1930s. Right: Pulitzer Prize-winner Tony Auth – *Philadelphia Inquirer / Universal Press Syndicate*, July 31, 2003. **(page 391)**

Goose-stepping Star of David menacing Gaza – Pat Oliphant, *Universal Press Syndicate*, March 25, 2009. **(page 392)**

Jewish star peering over barbed wire – *Time*, January 19, 2009. **(page 391)**

MAPS OF ISRAEL
Credit: "Israel 101" by StandWithUs.com

Biblical Era

Israel's biblical borders included the entire West Bank, Gaza Strip, most of modern-day Lebanon, and the western half of modern-day Jordan.

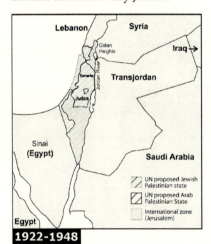

1922-1948

In 1922, Britain cut off 77% of Palestine to create (Trans-) Jordan. U.N. Resolution 181 recommended partitioning the remaining Mandate. Jewish leaders accepted the plan; Arab leaders launched a war to annihilate the Jewish state.

1917-1922

The British Balfour Declaration of 1917 promised to help reestablish the Jewish homeland in Palestine. During the British Mandate, the term "Palestinian" described both Jewish and Arab residents.

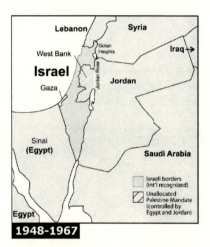

1948-1967

When the 1948 war ended, Jordan annexed the West Bank, while Egypt occupied the Gaza Strip. With these 1949 Armistice Lines, Israel was only 9 miles wide at its center. In the ensuing years, Arab terrorists used the West Bank and Gaza to launch deadly raids against Israeli population centers.

1967-1979

In 1967, Israel's neighbors mobilized for a full-scale invasion. Israel launched a preemptive strike, and in the ensuing Six Day War captured the important security zones of the Golan Heights, Sinai Peninsula, Gaza Strip and West Bank. Israel offered "land for peace," but was rebuffed with a resounding "No."

1979-present

As part of the 1979 Camp David Accords, Israel relinquished the entire Sinai Peninsula to Egypt, a land mass three times the size of Israel proper. In 1994, Israel and Jordan signed a peace treaty. In 2005, with no Palestinian partner for peace, Israel unilaterally withdrew from the Gaza Strip, evicting 9,000 Jewish residents.

The Arab World

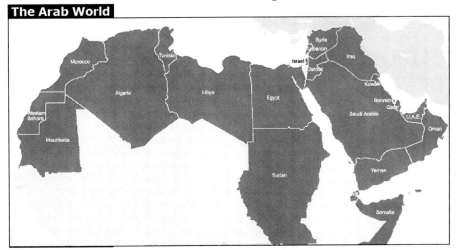

Israel is the only Jewish state amidst 22 members of the Arab League. These states, most of whom have no diplomatic relations with Israel, comprise 640 times the land mass as Israel, and have 300 million more people than Israel. Additionally, major Muslim states such as Turkey and Iran are in close proximity to Israel.

ACKNOWLEDGMENTS

My unending gratitude to:

Shaul Rosenblatt and Yaacov Bash for planting the seed.

Irwin Katsof for perceiving early on the potential of this work.

Yitz Greenman for insisting that I get involved.

Lenny Ben-David for establishing such a high editorial standard.

Mick Weinstein for being a great partner during the good years.

Pesach Benson for his top-notch blogging.

Tom Gross for groundbreaking research and insights, and for being gracious in every way.

Elder of Ziyon, James Taranto, Charles Johnson, Mike Fegelman, Kevin

Unger, Stephanie Gutmann, Sara Yoheved Rigler and Shmuel Veffer for helping to formulate many of these ideas.

Dr. Shmuel & Evelyn Katz for their generous support.

Dick Horowitz and Greg Yaris for coming through in a pinch.

Leslie Rubin, David Lieberman and Amos Fried for sharing so generously of their knowledge.

Uriela Sagiv and Sorelle Weinstein for reviewing the manuscript and making spot-on comments.

Seth Aronstam for his top-notch cover design.

Rafi Shachar for a crackerjack job in laying out the photo section.

Tim Berners-Lee, Bill Gates, Sergey & Larry, Jimmy Wales and LexisNexis for creating the amazing tools that made this project possible.

Eric Coopersmith, Ephraim Shore and Nechemia Coopersmith for their brotherhood.

Jack Kaminker, for true friendship.

Rich Brownstein, for always being there.

Nathan D. Wirtschafter, Esq., for holding down his corner of the battle.

My sister, Minna Feather, for careful reading, perpetual patient listening, and keeping me on deadline.

My in-laws, Shaul and Ora Shefi, for their constant support.

My mother, Barbara G. Simmons, for eagle-eye editing, and for putting up with me longer than anyone else.

Rabbi Noah Weinberg, o.b.m., who strongly encouraged me to write this book, and whose flawless sense of objectivity and clarity pervades throughout.

My wife, Keren, for allowing me the freedom to pursue my dreams, while she raises the most incredible children on the planet.

The Guardian of Israel for making it all possible.

DISCLAIMERS

Photos appearing in this volume are for the sole purpose of commentary, criticism, teaching, research and scholarship, as permitted under the fair use doctrine of United States copyright law: Copyright Act of 1976, 17 U.S.C. § 107.

David & Goliath is the sole work product of Shraga Simmons. Honest Reporting.com, Inc. has no responsibility for its contents, other than material and information accurately identified as having been prepared or furnished by Honest Reporting.com, Inc.

INDEX

1948 War, 39, 355, 367, 420
443 Highway, 33, 395
60 Minutes, examples of bias, 34, 320, 325, 386
Abbas, Mahmoud, 293
   denial of Jewish rights, 363, 367, 374
   libel against Israel, 119, 219, 277
   portrayed as moderate, 23–24,
Abu Ghraib, 37, 223
Abu Rahma, Talal, 211–215
Abu Shamala, Fayad, 185–86
Abu Toameh, Khaled, 158, 179
access, sacrificing objectivity for, 162–64
Achille Lauro, 332
Adams, John, 257, 400, 418
Aftonbladet, 251, 388–90
Agence France Presse, examples of bias, 2, 23, 55, 59, 77, 92, 118, 175, 287, 293, 306, 375, 381, 387, 395, 398
Ahmadinejad, Mahmoud,
   Holocaust denial, 374, 399
   Palestinian support for, 239
   portrayed as moderate, 381
   threat to Arab countries, 247
   threat to Israel, 380-81, 399
Aish.com, 209
Aish HaTorah, 371

Al-Aqsa mosque, 11, 15, 240, 367
al-Dura, Jamal, 215–16
al-Dura, Muhammad, 212–16, 223, 291, 393
al-Qaeda, 24, 80-83, 89, 95, 243, 223, 330
   Fort Hood connection, 177
   in Gaza, 120
   media battle, 429
   Palestinian support for, 239–40
   Saudi backing, 239
   see also bin Laden, Osama
   see also Islam
   see also September 11
Alibhai-Brown, Yasmin, 391, 399
Amanpour, Christiane, 144
ambulance
   use in photo fraud, 197–98, 201, 205–6, 214
   use in terror, 320–1
American Colony Hotel, 38, 41, 274, 383
Amnesty International, 155, 162
Amr, Wafa, 179–80
Annan, Kofi, 112, 307, 328
anti-Semitism, 231, 387, 390, 393–95
apartheid, 21, 323, 356–63, 395
Arab Spring, 7, 246, 254
Arafat, Suha, 117, 242

Arafat, Yasser, 87, 360
  corruption, 53
  duplicity, 81, 120, 156
  media daring, 42–43
  promoter of violence, 19, 20, 108, 290–291, 309
Ashrawi, Hanan, 27, 36, 82, 243, 291
Asper, Izzy, 99, 429
Assad, Bashar, 24
Asser, Martin, 198
Associated Press, examples of bias, 12, 37, 40–41, 45–47, 49, 55–57, 60, 77, 82, 87, 93, 95–96, 168, 170, 176, 181, 197–200, 203, 210–11, 219, 234, 239, 247, 269, 271, 273, 277, 283, 286, 288, 293–94, 318, 321, 327, 331, 338, 362, 368–69, 371, 375, 381, 385, 395
Auschwitz, 375, 382, 387, 389, 391, 393, 398
Australian media, examples of bias, 55–56, 74, 123, 132, 177, 212, 220, 248, 282, 289, 323, 391,
Auth, Tony, 391
Avatar, 210
Ayalon, Danny, 145
Bahai, 360
Balen Report, 184
Barak, Ehud, 19, 25, 26,
Barghouti, Marwan, 20, 119
Bari Atwan, Abdul, 182
Barzak, Ibrahim, 46, 180–81
BBC, examples of bias, 16, 20, 23–24, 42–43, 47, 54–55, 58–59, 63, 86, 96–97, 112, 120–21, 136, 160, 173–74, 176, 182–86, 196, 198–99, 201, 203, 208, 235, 252, 273, 319, 325, 327, 331, 358, 363–64, 371, 373, 378, 399
Beattie, Bruce, 390
Bennet, James, 87, 165

Benson, Tim, 166–67
Berlin Wall, 324
Bernstein, Carl, 164
  see also Watergate
Bethlehem, 248–53, 318
  see also Rachel's Tomb
Bible, 12, 34, 248, 256–57, 356, 365, 368, 371, 388
Bilal ibn Rabah, 370–71
Bilin, 210–211, 377
bin Laden, Osama, 182, 223, 242, 244
  as freedom fighter, 81
  killing of, 329
  Palestinian support for, 202, 239-40
  praise for Jimmy Carter, 357
  wealthy background, 83
  see also al-Qaeda
  see also September 11
bin Mahfouz, Khalid 172
bin Talal, Alwaleed, 134
bin Talal, Khaled, 425
Blackistone, Kevin, 362
Blair, David, 124
Blair, Jayson, 35
Blair, Tony, 247, 335
Blitzer, Wolf, 115, 140
blood libel, 114, 125, 143, 223, 388–89, 392
body count; see casualty count
Bolderson, Clair, 183
Borders, Bill, 295
Borders bookstore, 170
Booth, Lauren, 335
Boston Globe, examples of bias, 56, 285, 325
Bowen, Jeremy, 235
British Empire, 366
British military, 109, 280–81
British Political Cartoon Society, 166–67

INDEX

Bronner, Ethan, 116, 258, 271, 278
Brown, Dave, 166
Buchanan, Pat, 245, 260
Buttu, Diana, 4, 270
CanWest, 99, 429
Carleton, Richard, 74–75
Carter, Jimmy, 247, 272, 357
casualty count, 112, 281, 287–95
   distinction between fighters and civilians, 289, 292, 311
   Palestinians killed by Palestinians, 293
Cave of the Patriarchs, 369–70
Chaplain, Charlie, 234
Charlie Rose Show, 241, 378
checkpoints, 40, 317–22
Christians
   holiday pilgrims, 252
   mistreatment in Palestinian areas, 249, 250
   population in Middle East, 249, 360
   support for Israel, 248–254
Christian Science Monitor, examples of bias, 236–37, 253, 377, 380, 422
Church of the Nativity, 248, 250, 253
Churchill, Winston, 51, 113, 280, 429
Clinton, Bill, 19
Clinton, Hillary, 117
CNN
   examples of bias, 1, 15–18, 79, 85, 96, 110, 113, 118, 120, 132–134, 141–46, 176, 182, 218, 286, 332, 342, 359, 367, 425
   influence on journalists, 17, 132, 140
   loss of market share, 139
   public pressure against, 136
   sacrificing objectivity for access, 163–64
   statistical study of, 25–27

Cohen, Richard, 125
Cohen, Roger, 237, 259, 381–83
Collins, Peter, 164
colonialism, 364, 366
Comedy Central, 173
Compton, Ann, 365
Cooper, Anderson, 201
corrections, 124
Corrie, Rachel, 50, 142–43
Couric, Katie, 177
Crittenden, Jules, 200
Cronkite, Walter, 4–5
cycle of violence, 44–49, 56, 140, 271
Daraghmeh, Muhammad, 49, 181, 321
David and Goliath narrative, 3, 34, 36, 39, 42, 64, 356, 397
Denton, Bryan, 198
di Giovanni, Janine, 123–24
digital photography, 178, 195–96, 206, 223
Disraeli, Benjamin, 281
divestment, 253, 356
double standard, 16, 38, 57, 61, 87, 95–98, 173, 317, 321–23, 325, 388, 394, 425
Dowd, Maureen, 361
Dubai, 328
Dubno Maggid, 114
duplicity, 119–20, 241
   see also spokesmen, unreliability of Palestinian
Dylan, Bob, 326
Eban, Abba, 308, 339, 383
Egypt, 3, 38–39, 118, 236, 246, 254, 256, 285, 338, 361, 373–74, 286
   denouncing America, 237–38
Ehrenfeld, Rachel, 172
Eichmann, Adolf, 328, 373
Eid, Bassem, 183, 273

electromagnetic pulse attack (EMP), 384
Enderlin, Charles, 212–16
Entebbe, 329
Erekat, Saeb, 111, 122
European Union, 328, 382,
Facebook, 37, 423, 425
Fadlallah, Ayatollah Mohammed Hussein, 146
Falk, Richard, 314, 335, 387
fatwa, see Islam
Fayyad, Salam, 120
Fisk, Robert, 88
Fitna, 171
Flaherty, Anne, 234, 385
flat earth, 124–25
Fletcher, Martin, 52, 64, 94, 210, 283
Fort Hood shooting, 177
Fox News, 139, 161, 178, 245, 270
France-2 Television, 212–16, 221–22
Frankel, Max, 135–36
freedom of religion, 89, 357, 360, 382
freedom of the press, 4, 18, 89, 152, 156, 172, 357, 388
Free Gaza movement; see Gaza flotilla
Friedman, Thomas, 157, 167, 271, 387
Garlasco, Marc, 219
Gaza 2008/9 war
   civilian casualties, 277, 306, 310
   "disproportionate" force, 278–79
   elementary school, 280
   human shields, 272, 275, 310
   weapons stored in civilian areas, 276, 280, 301
   see also Goldstone Report
   see also humanitarian crisis
Gaza Beach incident, 218–221
Gaza flotilla, 329–335, 341
Gaza Strip, 18, 37, 40, 50, 82, 91, 120, 142–43, 182, 186, 211, 218, 222, 241, 249–51, 391
   economy, 339–40
   health measurements, 338–39
   intimidation of journalists, 151–61, 165–66, 169, 179
   Israeli blockade of, 334
   Israeli evacuation of, 1, 315
   population density, 338
   standard of living, 336, 338
   see also Gaza 2008/9 war
   see also Gaza Beach incident
   see also Gaza flotilla
genocide, accusation of Israeli-perpetrated, 3, 110, 245, 306, 314, 386–87, 391
Geyer, Georgie Ann, 233–34
Gilbert, Mads, 284
Globe and Mail, examples of bias, 3, 60, 237, 377, 397
God's Warriors (CNN), 144–45
Goldberg, Bernard, 34
Goldberg, Jeffrey, 84, 283
Goldstone Report, 309–317
Goldstone Richard, 359
   see also Goldstone Report
graffiti, 202, 394
Green Helmet Guy, 197–98
Griffin, Jennifer, 145, 161
Gross, Tom, 184, 318, 422
Grossman, Tuvia, 11–14, 36
Guardian, examples of bias, 43–44, 79, 93, 110, 123, 306, 316, 318, 376, 399–400, 420
Guerlin, Orla, 252
Hadid, Diaa, 180
Haiti earthquake, 389–90
Hajj, Adnan, 195–98, 209
Hamas, 50, 61, 118, 222, 240–41, 250,

330, 337, 374
 goal to destroy Israel, 40–41, 75, 91, 378–79, 421, 423
 intimidation of journalists, 152–58, 166
 media's sympathetic description of, 2, 24, 41, 94, 133, 376–77
 see also Gaza 2008/9 war
 see also Goldstone Report
 see also rockets, Palestinian
Hamilton, Douglas, 324
Hammer, Joshua, 151
Hamra, Khalil, 181, 283
Haram al Sharif, 368
headlines, 47, 54–58, 61–62, 282, 308, 335
Hebrew, 256
Hebrew University, 50, 93, 141, 358, 425
Hebron; see Cave of the Patriarchs
Herrmann, Steve, 199
Hezbollah, 98, 244, 330, 374
 intimidation of journalists, 159
 manipulation of media, 200–201, 203–4
 rockets at Israel, 47–48, 56, 195, 200, 204
 support from Iran, 379-380
 support from journalists, 146, 196
 support from Palestinians, 23
Hitler, 91, 136, 176, 247, 307
 Palestinian support of, 372–74
Holocaust, 108, 125, 222, 373, 380, 285
 denial of, 23, 41, 374–75, 392, 399
 justification for the Jewish state, 363–64
 media coverage of, 135–36
 Palestinian support for, 372–73
 see also Nazis, Israel compared to
HonestReporting, 140

hudna, 270–271
human rights, 36–37, 112, 158, 306, 313, 358
human shields; see Gaza 2008/9 war
Human Rights Watch, 112, 122, 219
humanitarian crisis, 284–86, 336
Hurva synagogue, 367
Hussein, Saddam, 163–64, 185, 233, 245, 328–29
Husseini, Mufti Haj Amin, 372–73
International Herald Tribune, examples of bias, 54, 58, 331, 421
intimidation of journalists, 99, 154–55, 174
 kidnappings, 151, 159–62, 165
 Palestinian journalists, 179
 self-censorship, 156–59
 TV and film, 173
Iraq, 3, 37, 153, 245–46, 249, 281, 325
 government officials, 121, 163–65
 Gulf War, 233, 245, 288
 nuclear reactor, 245
 terrorism in, 86, 96, 321–322
 U.S. invasion of, 232–33, 238
 see also Hussein, Saddam
Iran, 313, 374, 391, 399
 election protests, 383, 426
 nuclear ambitions, 7, 380, 383
 support for Palestinians, 108, 119, 212, 269, 311, 328, 334, 379, 396
 support from journalists, 182, 184, 335, 381–82
 threat to America, 384
 threat to Arab states, 247–48
 threat to Israel, 233–34, 379–85
 see also Ahmadinejad, Mahmoud
Islam, 77, 162, 172, 174, 200, 246, 310, 335, 361
 fatwa, 146, 167, 173–75, 243, 360, 373

history of, 39, 251
holy sites, 369–70
jihad, 20, 120, 144, 170, 176, 330, 376, 422
Koran, 119, 405
martyrdom, glorification of, 22, 43, 180, 291–92, 327, 341–42, 421
Muhammad, 170–74, 270, 370, 388
not identifying in news stories, 175–178
radical Islam, 80, 82–84, 90, 144, 166, 169–70, 173, 176, 232, 243, 246, 249, 388
see also mosques
Israel, Jewish presence prior to World War II, 364
Israel, State of
   American ally and asset, 237, 245, 254
   Arab representation in society, 358–59
   economy, 53, 255, 317, 356
   endangering soldiers to reduce civilian casualties, 109, 112
   military power, 39, 356
   small size, 2, 52
Israel Apartheid Week, 362
Israel Defense Force; see Israel
Israel Lobby, The, 232
Jacoby, Jeff, 81
Jaffa Gate, 132
Jenin, battle of, 207, 273
   burial of bodies, 115–116
   false testimony, 113–114
   Israeli strategy, 108–109
   massacre claims, 110–112, 116, 122–25
Jenin, Jenin, 217
Jennings, Peter, 15, 242–43, 259
Jerusalem, 235, 256–257

construction in, 235
in peace negotiations, 19–20, 423
religious portrayal of, 22, 132, 252, 361
terror attacks in, 11–14, 17, 45–46, 49, 50, 58, 79, 86, 91, 98, 107, 138, 146, 292, 309, 319, 425
see also, Temple Mount
Jesus, 390
   portrayed as Palestinian martyr, 251–53
Jewish influence
   in media, 134–36
   in politics, 231
   see also *Israel Lobby*
jihad; see Islam
Johnson, Paul, 257
Johnson, Tom, 164
Johnston, Alan, 159–60
Jordan, 3, 39–40, 236, 252, 360, 367
Jordan, Eason, 139–40, 163
Joseph's Tomb, 371
journalistic ethics, 35, 113, 164, 181, 185, 201
Judenrein, 363
Jukes, Stephen, 46, 80, 86, 100
Kalb, Marvin, 21, 201
Karim, Sharif, 199
Karine-A; see weapons ships
Karsenty, Philippe, 216
Kemp, Colonel Richard, 279
Kemp, Jack, 254
Kennedy, John F., 257, 334, 423
Khaldi, Ismail, 362
Khaled, Leila, 93
kidnapping of journalists; see intimidation of journalists
King Jr, Martin Luther, 81, 257
Koppel, Ted, 356

Koran; see Islam
Kuwait, 245, 325, 360
Landes, Professor Richard, 213–15, 279
lawfare, 172
Lebanon, 3, 60, 180, 249, 288, 359
   PLO reign of terror, 167–69
   photo fraud during 2006 war, 195–209
   see also Hezbollah
Leconte, Daniel, 213
Le Monde, 367, 395
Leno, Jay, 365
LexisNexis, 23, 323, 362
Liberty Bell, 256–57
Lincoln, Abraham, 81, 257, 334
Lindbergh, Charles, 233
linkage theory, 247
Livni, Tzipi, 25, 360
Los Angeles Times, examples of bias, 43, 46, 48, 85, 91–92, 170, 180, 241, 275–76, 292, 377
Margolis, Eric, 1, 236, 246, 391
Martyrdom; see Islam
Mashal, Khaled, 241, 278
Mathias, Elliot, 371
Mavi Marmara, see Gaza flotilla
McCartney, Paul, 172
McClatchy newspapers, 94–95, 253
McGeough, Paul, 332
Mecca, 77, 173, 250, 270, 369
media monitoring guidelines, 426–28
Mein Kampf, 176, 374
Miami Herald, 277
militant, as descriptive term, 3, 61, 73, 77, 86, 96, 98
Miller, Wiley, 174
Minneapolis *Star Tribune*, examples of bias, 97–99, 123
Minnesotans Against Terrorism, 98

moral equivalence, 49, 140–41, 144, 332
Moran, Michael, 75–76
Moyers, Bill, 278
MSNBC, 75–76, 146, 177, 215, 238, 245, 258
mosques, 19
   fiery sermons, 240, 376
   used to store weapons, 273, 275
   see also Al-Aqsa mosque
Mossad, 118–21, 154, 241, 244–45, 328
Ms. Magazine, 360
Muhammad; see Islam
Murrow, Edward R., 5, 22, 34
Mutually Assured Deterrence, 383
Nablus, 15, 155, 326, 368, 371
Nasr, Octavia, 146
National Geographic, 253
Nazis, Israel compared to, 1, 111, 314, 336, 385–87, 391–94
Netanyahu, Bibi, 23, 234, 258–259
Newsweek, examples of bias, 16, 50, 151, 168, 292, 377
Nissenbaum, Dion, 94–95, 159
New York Times
   coverage of Holocaust, 135–36
   deification of, 6
   examples of bias, 13–14, 16, 24, 41, 49, 55, 58, 87, 92–95, 168, 170, 175–77, 201, 233–34, 246, 250, 258, 270–71, 277–78, 292, 295, 308, 328, 331–33, 339–40, 361, 375–78, 380–81, 421
news cycle, 4, 22, 44, 282, 330
Nightline, 84, 253
Norris, Molly, 174
Novak, Robert, 357, 376
NPR (National Public radio), 38, 175, 375
nuclear weapons, 173, 245, 247, 380–84
Obama, Barack, 34, 240, 258–259, 272,

375, 393
Okrent, Daniel, 90
Oliphant, Pat, 392
Operation Cast Lead; see Gaza 2008/9 war
Operation Defensive Shield; see Jenin, battle of
organ theft, Israel accused of, 388–90, 414
Orwell, George, 27, 80
Oslo Accords, 120, 241, 339, 371
over-reporting of Israel, 1, 51–52
pack journalism, 21–22, 114
Palestine Red Crescent, 288, 320
Palestinian Human Rights Society, 217–18
Palestinian
  children on battlefield, 290–92
  corruption, 53, 339
  declaration of statehood, 419
  denouncing America, 238, 329, 241, 373
  denying Jewish connection to land, 366–371
  economy, 326, 340
  fake videos, 220, 222
  incitement to violence, 157, 210, 376, 421–25
  media strategies, 396
  stringers and translators, 145, 159, 178–79, 181, 196, 222
  television, 217, 221, 251, 386, 421
  violence, influenced by the media, 63–64, 210
  see also Gaza Strip
  see also refugees, Palestinian
  see also rockets, Palestinian
  see also spokesmen
Pallywood, 217, 282

Palmer Report, 334–35
Paulin, Tom, 391, 299
peace negotiations, 19, 419
Pearl, Daniel, 83, 171, 223
PETA, 294
Philadelphia Inquirer, examples of bias, 78–79, 92, 97, 131, 370, 390
Pillai, Nisha, 183
Pitarakis, Lefteris, 200
photo captions, biased, 12–13, 16, 59–60, 92–93, 143, 204–5, 209, 211, 283, 294, 337, 370
photo fraud
  actors portrayed in news photos, 201–3
  cropping, 333
  recycled images, 208, 283, 336
  see also digital photography
Photoshop; see digital photography
Pilgrims, 256
Plett, Barbara, 42–43
polls, public opinion, 2, 6, 27, 170, 201, 239, 237, 239, 254, 337, 359, 385, 394, 399, 420, 422–23
Protocols of the Elders of Zion, 232, 393
Qassam; see rockets, Palestinian
Rachel's Tomb
racism, accusation of Israeli, 258–59
Raddatz, Martha, 177
radical Islam; see Islam
  see also al-Qaeda
Rafa, Nidal, 145
Rahola, Pilar, 393
Ramallah, 22, 158, 249, 326, 396
  lynching, 15–16, 92, 153, 212, 223
Ramattan News Agency, 219
Rather, Dan, 5–6, 372, 423–24
Rayan, Nizar, 41, 44, 271, 276, 376
Reeves, Phil, 112, 122–23

refugees, Jews from Arab lands, 307, 365
refugees, Palestinian, 19, 39, 288, 307, 420
Reporters Without Borders, 153
Reuters, examples of bias, 37–38, 45–47, 59, 61–62, 80–81, 86, 180, 184, 195–96, 199, 207, 209, 210, 236, 248, 250, 252, 271, 275, 281, 286, 324, 332–33, 335, 363, 367, 370, 378–79, 381
right of return; see refugees, Palestinian
rockets, Palestinian, 46, 76, 88, 200, 221–22, 269–73, 294, 309–11, 319, 341, 356, 426
Roosevelt, Franklin D., 257, 429
Sabel, Dr. Robbie, 279
Said, Edward, 87, 373
Safire, William, 20, 100
Salita, Dmitriy, 234
San Diego Union-Tribune, 50
San Jose Mercury News, 95–96
San Remo Manual, 333
Sarandah, Nadwa, 292
Saudi Arabia, 52, 119, 425
 denouncing America, 237, 239
 intolerance in, 246, 249, 360–61
Savitch, Jessica, 288
Sbarro terror attack, 79, 93, 319
Scheuer, Michael, 237–38
Schlesinger, David, 99
Sderot, 17, 76, 270, 272
security barrier
 in other countries, 325
 West Bank, 201, 210, 323–25
selective omission, 54–57
September 11 attacks, 134
 blaming Israel for, 242–245
 comparing Israeli actions to, 110, 116, 133, 280, 331

Palestinian support for, 155, 239–40
 see also al-Qaeda
 see also bin Laden, Osama
Sharansky, Natan, 112, 394
shark attack, Egyptian, 118–119
Shalit, Gilad, 271, 424–25
Shehadeh, Salah, 141, 327
Shepherd, Robin, 366
Simon, Bob, 320, 325
Six Day War, 39, 235
Slackman, Michael, 88
South Park, 173
spokesmen
 outlandish accusations by Arab, 117–19
 unreliability of Palestinian, 111, 117, 120–22, 241, 294, 311, 320
 see also duplicity
Stockholm Syndrome, 162
suicide bombings; see terrorism
Sulzberger, Arthur Hays, 135–36
supply shortage; see humanitarian crisis
survey; see polls, public opinion
targeted killings, 141, 326–29
Temple Mount, 11–15, 19–20, 77, 360, 368–69, 371–72
terrorism / terrorist
 blamed on poverty and despair, 82–85
 definition of, 74, 76, 96
 euphemisms for, 77–78, 87–88, 96
 prior to 1967, 40
 suicide bombings, 18, 37, 43, 50, 57–58, 60, 74–87, 94–95, 107–8, 138, 146, 154, 276, 292–94, 314, 319–21, 324, 327, 342, 378–79, 383, 397, 421–22
 sympathetic description of, 43–44,

91–95
  to describe Israeli actions, 79, 86–87, 133, 138
  see also militant, as descriptive term
Thomas, Helen, 364–365
Time magazine, examples of bias, 1, 15, 24, 49, 205, 212, 231, 243, 249, 278, 324, 359, 361, 364, 368, 381, 390–91, 423
tit-for-tat; see cycle of violence
Tomb of the Patriarchs; see Cave of the Patriarchs
Toronto Star, 20, 332
Turner, Ted, 138
Twain, Mark, 18, 116, 125
Twitter, 146, 397, 423, 426
two-state solution, 420
underdog, 33–34, 36, 39, 52–54, 63, 85, 259, 397
United Nations, 39, 74, 81, 122, 237, 280, 285, 328, 334, 356, 389
  condemnations of Israel, 2, 112, 307–8, 313, 331
  halo effect, 308–9
  Human Rights Council, 309, 313–17
  UNESCO, 371
United States, 16, 38
  aid to Israel, 232, 236
  see Egypt, denouncing America
  see Israel, American ally and asset
  see Palestinian, denouncing America
  see Saudi Arabia, denouncing America
USS Liberty, 235
van Gogh, Theo, 171
Vogue, 24
vulture spy, 119
war crimes, charges of Israeli, 1, 26, 205, 306, 309, 312, 387

Warsaw Ghetto, 135, 222, 391, 393
Washington Post, examples of bias, 16, 43–44, 49, 52, 92, 168, 174, 201, 219, 244, 249, 253, 270, 272–73, 275, 318, 327, 357, 375, 390, 392, 424
Watergate, 4, 134, 282
weapons ships, 108, 334, 380
Wedeman, Ben, 17–18, 113, 286
Weinberg, Rabbi Noah, 7
West Bank, 179, 240, 340, 358, 370, 373
  territorial issues, 19, 46, 315, 378-79
  violence in, 11, 16, 40, 45, 55, 57, 58, 210, 249, 377
  see also security barrier
Western Wall, 19, 367, 369
Wiesel, Elie, 380
WikiLeaks, 247, 420
Wikipedia, 390, 425
Williams, Pete, 177
World War I, 3, 20
World War II, 89, 135, 222, 280, 288
Xinhua, 3, 118
Yassin, Sheikh Ahmed, 43, 327
YouTube, 209, 221, 222
Zionazi; see Nazis, Israel compared to
Zionism, 307, 375, 420
Zuckerman, Mortimer B., 279, 339

MORE THAN A BOOK

Shraga Simmons' widely-acclaimed seminar, "Bias in the Media," has been presented to a variety of community, youth and university groups. A half-day workshop is also available for students and community activists, providing practical guidelines for fighting media bias and promoting an accurate view of the crucial peace issues – security, borders, Jerusalem and refugees.

For information on bringing him to your community, write to: info@emesphere.com

CPSIA information can be obtained at www.ICGtesting.com
Printed in the USA
BVOW010651191111

276478BV00001B/1/P